Frommer's®

South Florida

with the Best of Miami & the Keys

8th Edition

by Lesley Abravanel

WILEY

John Wiley & Sons, Inc.

Published by:
JOHN WILEY & SONS, INC.
111 River St.
Hoboken, NJ 07030-5774

ISBN 978-1-118-35946-4 (paper); ISBN 978-1-118-47646-8 (ebk); ISBN 978-1-118-47647-5 (ebk)

Editors: Jennifer Polland & Andrea Kahn
Production Editor: Jana M. Stefanciosa
Cartographer: Roberta Stockwell
Photo Editor: Richard Fox
Production by Wiley Indianapolis Composition Services
Front Cover Photo: A car parked in front of the Avalon Hotel in Miami Beach. ©John Norman / Alamy Images.
Back Cover Photo: Dawn at Smathers Beach on Key West. ©Rod McLean / Alamy Images.

For information on our other products and services or to obtain technical support, please contact our Customer Care Department within the U.S. at 877/762-2974, outside the U.S. at 317/572-3993 or fax 317/572-4002.

Wiley also publishes its books in a variety of electronic formats. Some content that appears in print may not be available in electronic formats.

Manufactured in the United States of America

5   4   3   2   1

CONTENTS

LIST OF MAPS

ABOUT THE AUTHOR

Born and raised in New York, **Lesley Abravanel** now resides in Florida, where she writes three weekly celebrity gossip and nightlife columns (and a blog) for the Miami Herald; dishes restaurant gossip for Herald website Miami.com; pens Florida guidebooks for Frommer's; and, in her spare time, collects hot sauces, raises twin toddlers, and attempts to learn Swedish from her Stockholm-born husband. You can always find her on Twitter, where she has no qualms speaking—er, tweeting—her mind on everything, from reality television to politics.

HOW TO CONTACT US

In researching this book, we discovered many wonderful places—hotels, restaurants, shops, and more. We're sure you'll find others. Please tell us about them, so we can share the information with your fellow travelers in upcoming editions. If you were disappointed with a recommendation, we'd love to know that, too. Please write to:

Frommer's South Florida, 8th Edition
John Wiley & Sons, Inc. • 111 River St. • Hoboken, NJ 07030-5774
frommersfeedback@wiley.com

ADVISORY & DISCLAIMER

FROMMER'S STAR RATINGS, ICONS & ABBREVIATIONS

Every hotel, restaurant, and attraction listing in this guide has been ranked for quality, value, service, amenities, and special features using a **star-rating system.** In country, state, and regional guides, we also rate towns and regions to help you narrow down your choices and budget your time accordingly. Hotels and restaurants are rated on a scale of zero (recommended) to three stars (exceptional). Attractions, shopping, nightlife, towns, and regions are rated according to the following scale: zero stars (recommended), one star (highly recommended), two stars (very highly recommended), and three stars (must-see).

In addition to the star-rating system, we also use **seven feature icons** that point you to the great deals, in-the-know advice, and unique experiences that separate travelers from tourists. Throughout the book, look for:

special finds—those places only insiders know about

fun facts—details that make travelers more informed and their trips more fun

kids—best bets for kids and advice for the whole family

special moments—those experiences that memories are made of

overrated—places or experiences not worth your time or money

insider tips—great ways to save time and money

great values—where to get the best deals

The following **abbreviations** are used for credit cards:

AE American Express	**DISC** Discover	**V** Visa
DC Diners Club	**MC** MasterCard	

TRAVEL RESOURCES AT FROMMERS.COM

Frommer's travel resources don't end with this guide. Frommer's website, **www.frommers. com**, has travel information on more than 4,000 destinations. We update features regularly, giving you access to the most current trip-planning information and the best airfare, lodging, and car-rental bargains. You can also listen to podcasts, connect with other Frommers.com members through our active-reader forums, share your travel photos, read blogs from guidebook editors and fellow travelers, and much more.

THE BEST OF SOUTH FLORIDA

From the bright lights and thumping clubs of Miami Beach to the vast, unspoiled expanse of Everglades National Park, South Florida offers a little something for everyone. Don't be fooled by the hipper-than-thou celebrity playground known as South Beach. While the chic elite do, indeed, flock to Miami's coolest enclave, it is surprisingly accessible to the average Joe, Jane, or José. For every Philippe Starck–designed, bank account–busting boutique hotel on South Beach, there's a kitschy, candy-coated Art Deco hotel that's much less taxing on the pockets. For each Pan-Mediterranean-Asian haute cuisine restaurant, there's a down-home, no-nonsense Cuban bodega offering hearty food at ridiculously cheap prices.

Beyond all the glitzy, *Us Weekly*–meets–beach blanket bacchanalia, Miami offers an endless number of sporting, cultural, and recreational activities to keep you entertained. Its sparkling beaches are beyond comparison. Plus, it has an array of shopping and nightlife activities, including ballet, theater, and opera (as well as all the celebrity-saturated hotels, restaurants, bars, and clubs that have helped make Miami so famous).

Leave Miami, be it for the Keys, the Gold Coast, or southwest Florida, and you'll expose yourself not only to more UV rays, but to a world of cultural, historical, and sybaritic surprises. You can take in a spring baseball game, walk in the footsteps of Hemingway, get up-close and personal with the area's sea life, soak up the serenity of unspoiled landscapes, catch the filming of *Burn Notice* or a big-budget Hollywood flick, and much more.

THE best SOUTH FLORIDA EXPERIENCES

- **Driving along Florida A1A:** This oceanfront route, which runs north up Miami Beach and into Fort Lauderdale (and changes names several times along the way), embodies the essence of South Florida. From time-warped hotels steeped in Art Deco kitsch to multimillion-dollar modern high-rises, A1A is one of the most scenic, albeit heavily trafficked, roads in all of Florida.
- **Relishing the View from Bill Baggs Cape Florida State Park:** You haven't truly seen South Florida until you've checked out the view from the southern point of Key Biscayne. Whether it's the turquoise water or the sight of Stiltsville—seven still-inhabited aquatic cabins dating back

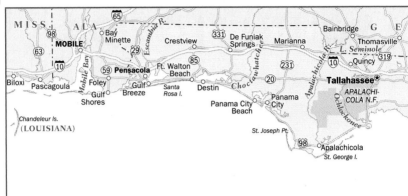

MISS. ALA.

Biloxi Pascagoula MOBILE Bay Minette Crestview De Funiak Springs Marianna Bainbridge G E Thomasville L. Seminole Quincy Tallahassee Foley Pensacola Ft. Walton Beach APALACHI-COLA N.F. Gulf Shores Gulf Breeze Santa Rosa I. Destin Choctawhatchee Panama City Beach Panama City St. Joseph Pt. Apalachicola St. George I.

Chandeleur Is.
(LOUISIANA)

G U L F   O F

M E X I C O

to the 1930s, perched smack in the middle of the Biscayne Channel—it may take a little coercing to get you to leave. See p. 72.

o **Channeling Andy Warhol in Miami's Wynwood Arts District:** After waiting patiently for this arty, funky area to come into its own, Miami's hipsters and artists have finally been rewarded with this still raw neighborhood of galleries, studios, and even a few cool bars, lounges, and restaurants that exude that New York City's SoHo–meets–Meatpacking District vibe. See chapters 4 and 8.

o **Discovering Your Inner Flipper at the Dolphin Research Center:** Learn to communicate with and touch, swim, or play with the mammals at the nonprofit Dolphin Research Center in Marathon Key, home to a school of approximately 15 dolphins. See p. 239.

o **Canoeing the Everglades:** The Everglades are Florida's outback, resplendent in their swampy nature. The Everglades are best explored by slow-moving canoes, which offer an up-close and personal view of the area's inhabitants, from alligators and manatees to raccoons and Florida panthers. See chapter 10.

o **Ogling the Estates on Palm Beach:** The winter playground for the *Lifestyles of the Rich and Famous* set, Palm Beach is lined with jaw-dropping palatial estates. Though many of them are hidden behind towering shrubbery, head south on South County Road, from Brazilian Avenue, where you will see some of the most opulent homes ever built. See chapter 12.

o **Water Taxiing Through the Intracoastal Waterway:** The waterway that connects the natural bays, lagoons, and rivers along Florida's east coast snakes around from the Florida-Georgia border all the way to the port of Miami. A ride through the Fort Lauderdale Intracoastal provides a sublime view of million-dollar waterfront houses. See p. 303.

THE best FOOD & DRINK EXPERIENCES

o **Unleashing Your Inner Gourmand in Miami's Design District:** The home of high-end furniture showrooms and interior design firms is also home to some of Florida's most lauded eateries—**Michael's Genuine Food & Drink** (p. 119) and Sra. Martinez. Michael's Genuine is one of the hottest reservations in town, thanks to its locally sourced, organic seasonal cuisine, out-of-control desserts, buzzy bar scene, and colorful crowd. Some tapas with your tapestries, perhaps?

o **Slowing Down on the Miami River:** Some consider dining on the Miami River to be industrial chic; others consider it seedy in a *Miami Vice* sort of way. Either way, dining here will offer a soothing escape from the city's hectic pace. **Garcia's Seafood Grille & Fish** (p. 114) is an urban oasis of fresh seafood with lots of local flavor.

o **Snacking in Miami's Little Havana:** For the true, frenetic Miami Cuban experience, head to **El Palacio de los Jugos** (p. 125) for greasy fare and sort-of-healthy fresh-squeezed juices. Then stop in at **Versailles** (p. 125), an iconoclastic, garish Cuban diner filled with mirrors in which you can view the colorful—and audible—clientele that congregates here for down-home Cuban cuisine and hearty conversation.

o **Experiencing Joe's Stone Crab Restaurant:** You *will* wait in line at Miami Beach's landmark spot for crab, but it's never dull, and the cacophony of mostly Northeastern U.S. accents and the occasional celebrity sighting will keep you entertained until you are seated for your feast of crustacean. Dip medium, large, or jumbo crab into a tasty mustard-mayo sauce or just mustard, and save room for Key lime pie. It's open October through May only. See p. 90.

o **Spending a Sunday at Alabama Jack's:** There is nothing like hanging out, chugging a cheap beer, chowing down on amazing conch fritters, and watching a bunch of sauced octogenarians dressed like extras from *Hee Haw* line-dancing to incredible live country music, all in a Sunday afternoon. Even better is the spectacular waterfront setting that makes you truly appreciate why you're in Florida in the first place. See p. 236.

o **Invoking the Bootleggers at Cap's Place Island Restaurant:** The only way to get to this rustic Lighthouse Point seafood restaurant—the former bootlegging and gambling hangout of Al Capone—is by boat. Churchill, Roosevelt, Marilyn Monroe, and Sylvester Stallone have all indulged in this delicious taste of Old Florida. See p. 307.

THE best WAYS TO SEE SOUTH FLORIDA LIKE A LOCAL

o **Rummaging Through Other Peoples' Treasures:** A collector's dream come true, Miami's **Wolfsonian** is a treasure trove of miscellany (e.g., a matchbook that once belonged to the King of Egypt) and artifacts hailing from the propaganda age of World War II. See p. 61.

o **Strolling Through Little Havana:** A walk through **Little Havana** is a fascinating study in the juxtaposition and fusion of two very vibrant cultures in which pre-Castro Cuba is as alive and well as the McDonald's right next door. See p. 123.

o **Snorkeling in Looe Key National Marine Sanctuary, Bahia Honda State Park:** With 5.3 square miles of gorgeous coral reef, rock ledges up to 35 feet tall, and a colorful and motley marine community, you may never want to come up for air. See p. 259.

o **Foreplay at Miami's Biltmore Golf Course, Biltmore Hotel:** If it's good enough for former President Clinton, it's good enough for those of you who don't travel with a bevy of Secret Service agents. But the real question is: Are *you* good enough for the course? The 6th hole is notoriously difficult, with distracting water hazards among other difficulties. Nonetheless, it's an excellent course with a picture-postcard setting. See p. 207.

o **Getting on the "List" at a Hot Miami Club:** I despise velvet ropes and "lists," but it's what makes Miami's nightlife what it is. And to experience it like a local, you need to be on a list. Ask your concierge, ask a friend, ask a stranger, but whatever you do, do not pay to get on these lists. It's not worth it. For more on Miami nightlife, see chapter 8.

o **Hitting the Water:** What freeways are to Los Angeles, the water is to Florida. Getting out on the water—by boat, jet ski, kayak, or canoe—will offer a unique perspective on the Florida landscape—and a tan.

o **Schmoozing with the Locals on Islamorada:** Located right on the water right before a bridge, **Island Grill** (p. 248) is *the* place locals go to for fresh fish, views, and live music on any given day or night. Locals also gather at the **Islamorada Fish Company** (p. 249) for politics and gossip while enjoying the stellar seafood and views.

o **Wearing Sunscreen:** You can see Florida however you choose, but whatever you do, don't forget the sunscreen. Bad sunburns are a dead giveaway that you're a tourist. Even in nasty weather, the sun's rays are still there.

THE best FAMILY EXPERIENCES

- **Airboating Through the Everglades:** Kids who can't slow down may do just that after they speed through the saw grass on an Everglades airboat. But it's more than just speed, it's an educational thrill ride, to say the least. See p. 224.
- **Flitting Around in Butterfly World:** Kids will be enchanted by this magical place where live, exotic, rainbow-hued butterflies dwell in acres of waterfalls, orchids, roses, tropical gardens, and more. See p. 299.
- **Riding the Carousel at Crandon Park's Family Amusement Center:** Catch a ride on the restored carousel, the centerpiece of the park's new **Family Amusement Center** that includes an old-fashioned outdoor roller rink, dolphin-shaped splash fountain, and a host of marine play sculptures at the beachfront playground. See p. 64.
- **Exploring Jungle Island:** You'll need to watch your head here because hundreds of parrots, macaws, peacocks, cockatoos, and flamingos are flying above. Tortoises, iguanas, and a rare albino alligator are also on exhibit. A bit cheesy, but the kids love it. See p. 59.
- **Discovering Miami's Museums:** Aspiring rock stars can lay down tracks and play instruments at the working music studio, while future news anchors will love the re-creation of the NBC 6 television studio at the **Miami Children's Museum** (p. 60). The **Miami Science Museum** (p. 68) explores the mysteries of the universe with hands-on exhibits and engaging live demonstrations.
- **Learning about Nature at Sea Grass Adventures:** With **Sea Grass Adventures,** you will be able to wade in the water on Key Biscayne with your guide and catch an assortment of sea life in the provided nets. At the end of the program, participants gather on the beach while the guide explains what everyone has just caught, passing the creatures around in miniature viewing tanks. See p. 65.

> ### Impressions
> *What could be better than to sit on the beach playing cards in my shirt sleeves in January?*
> —Anonymous Miami Beach resident

- **Learn to Fly in the Florida Keys:** Check out Hawks Cay's high-tech, superhero-caliber JetLev flying experience, allowing guests to strap on a water-propelled jetpack and soar up to 30 feet into the air. If the kids are too young or too scared, a Segway tour of the resort's lush property is an excellent alternative. See p. 251.
- **Seeing Lions and Tigers and Bears, Oh My!:** Almost as good as flying to Africa and possibly better than Disney's Animal Kingdom is **Lion Country Safari,** a 500-acre preserve where over 1,300 animals roam free while you drive through in the comfort of your own (or rented) air-conditioned car. See p. 331.
- **Playing Marco Polo in 820,000 Gallons of Water:** The massive **Venetian Pool** is unlike any other pool out there, with its 820,000 gallons of water that's replaced every single night. For particularly obsessive parents, that's enough said. See p. 67.

THE best OFFBEAT TRAVEL EXPERIENCES

- **Eating Burgers at Le Tub:** This former 1959 Sunoco gas station was transformed into a kitschy waterfront oasis whose resplendent scenery is almost secondary to the decor: old toilet bowls, bathtubs, and sinks—seriously. Not the least bit as gross as it sounds, Le Tub also has the best hamburgers, excellent chili, a 4am closing time, and a strict "no children" policy. See p. 309.

o **Plunging down to a "Dive" Bar:** In May 2000, the legendary tequila company Cuervo celebrated Cinco de Mayo by submerging an actual, $45,000 full-size bar and six stools about 600 feet off South Beach's First Street beach. For expert divers, **Jose Cuervo Underwater Bar** is more than your average watering hole. See p. 79.

o **Satisfying Your Morbid Curiosity on the Ghostly, Ghastly Vice & Crime Coach Tour.** Not that I'm implying anything here, but Miami is a haven for people like O. J. Simpson and, at one time, Al Capone. It's a place where shady characters come to reinvent themselves. However, at times, they also tend to reincriminate themselves. See the spots where some of these criminals fell off the wagon—it's morbidly delicious. See p. 80.

o **Admiring the Coral Castle:** A 26-year-old crazed Latvian, suffering from the unrequited love of a 16-year-old who left him at the altar, immigrated to South Miami and spent the next 25 years of his life carving huge boulders into a prehistoric-looking roofless "castle." See p. 69.

o **Experiencing Miami Duck Tours:** Sure it's touristy, but there's something to be said about cruising through town in a Hydra Terra Amphibious Vehicle—especially when you're driving down Ocean Drive and your guide asks everyone to quack. See p. 82.

o **Exploring the Key West Cemetery:** This funky cemetery is the epitome of quirky Key West: irreverent and humorous. Many tombs are stacked several high, condominium-style, because the rocky soil made digging 6 feet under nearly impossible for early settlers. Epitaphs reflect residents' lighthearted attitudes toward life and death. "I told you I was sick" is one of the more famous, as is the tongue-in-cheek widow's inscription "At least I know where he's sleeping tonight." See p. 267.

o **Sleeping under the Sea at Jules' Undersea Lodge:** Originally built as a research lab, this small underwater compartment, which rests on pillars on the ocean floor, now operates as a two-room hotel. To get inside, guests swim 21 feet under the structure and pop up into the unit through a 4×6-foot "moon pool" that gurgles soothingly all night long. The 30-foot-deep underwater suite consists of two separate bedrooms that share a common living area. See p. 252.

THE best HISTORIC EXPERIENCES

o **Remembering the Civil Rights Era: Virginia Key Beach Park** is the former "colored only" beach that opened in 1945 and closed in 1982 because of high maintenance costs. After an $11-million renovation, the 83-acre historic site features picnic tables and grills, a new playground for children with special needs, and a miniature railroad. The beach eventually plans to open a civil rights museum as well. See p. 55.

o **Exploring the Art Deco District:** A lot more than just pastel-colored buildings and neon, the Art Deco District is a Miami Beach landmark, and its preservation has been the passion of many. While a historic building may today house a Fat Tuesday, it's what's on the outside that really counts. See chapter 5.

o **Barnacle State Historic Site:** Long before the condos invaded, Cracker-style houses were all the rage—well, the only choice in town. At the Barnacle sits

Miami's oldest house, complete with period furnishings that some would say are back in again. See p. 68.

o **Nike Hercules Missile Base HM-69:** A product of collective thinking by President John F. Kennedy and his advisors that arose out of very real Cold War fears, this base was turned back over to Everglades National Park in 1979 but wasn't open to the public until 2009. From January to March, free ranger-led tours take visitors on a 90-minute driving and walking tour of the missile assembly building, three barns where 12 missiles were stored, the guardhouse, and the underground control room. See p. 221.

o **Crane Point Hammock:** This privately owned, 64-acre nature area is considered one of the most important historic sites in the Keys. It contains what is probably the last virgin thatch-palm hammock in North America, as well as a rainforest exhibit and an archaeological site with prehistoric Indian and Bahamian artifacts. See p. 238.

o **Ernest Hemingway Home & Museum:** Hemingway's handsome stone Spanish colonial house, built in 1851 and designated a literary landmark by the American Library Association in 2010, was one of the first on the island to be fitted with indoor plumbing and a built-in fireplace. It also has the first swimming pool built on Key West (look for the penny that Hemingway pressed into the cement). The author owned the home from 1931 until his death in 1961, and lived here with about 50 cats, whose descendants, including the famed six-toed felines, still roam the premises. See p. 266.

o **Harry S. Truman Little White House:** On temporary leave from the Big House, Truman discovered the serenity of Key West and made his escape to what became known as the Little White House, which is open to the public for touring. The house is fully restored; the exhibits document Truman's time in the Keys. See p. 267.

o **Hillsboro Inlet Lighthouse:** Not just any lighthouse, this one contains a 5,500,000-candlepower light—the most powerful on the East Coast of the United States. See p. 299.

o **Flagler Museum:** The Gilded Age is preserved in this luxurious mansion commissioned by Standard Oil tycoon Henry Flagler as a wedding present to his third wife. Whitehall, also known as the Taj Mahal of North America, is a classic Edwardian-style mansion containing 55 rooms, including a Louis XIV music room and art gallery, a Louis XV ballroom, and 14 guest suites outfitted with original antique European furnishings. See p. 330.

THE best FREE EXPERIENCES

o **Seeing a Concert at the New World Center:** This stunning, sonically stellar, $154-million Frank Gehry–designed training facility, performance space, and outdoor park is said by the *New York Times* to have "the potential to be a game changer in classical music." About 15% of the music events at New World Center are free to the public. See p. 156.

o **Exploring Artists' Studios: CANDO Arts Co-Op** is a 5,000-square-foot gallery at 309 23rd St. on Miami Beach that's free and open to the public, featuring over a dozen resident artists doing their arty thing. See p. 62.

o **Taking In the Holocaust Memorial:** This heart-wrenching memorial is hard to miss and would be a shame to overlook. The powerful centerpiece, Kenneth Treister's *A Sculpture of Love and Anguish*, depicts victims of the concentration camps crawling up a giant yearning hand stretching up to the sky, marked with an Auschwitz number tattoo. Along the reflecting pool is the story of the Holocaust, told in cut marble slabs. Inside the center of the memorial is a tableau that is one of the most solemn and moving tributes to the millions of Jews who lost their lives in the Holocaust I've seen. See p. 59.

○ **Discovering the Patricia and Phillip Frost Art Museum:** Among the permanent collections is the General Collection, which holds a strong representation of American printmaking from the 1960s and 1970s, photography, pre-Columbian objects dating from A.D. 200 to 500, and a growing number of works by contemporary Caribbean and Latin-American artists. The museum is a Smithsonian affiliate and the only museum in South Florida to offer free admission daily. See p. 64.

○ **Learning at the Florida Keys Eco-Discovery Center:** With 6,000 square feet of interactive exhibits, the Discovery Center depicts Florida Keys underwater and upland habitats—with emphasis on the ecosystem of North America's only living contiguous barrier coral reef, which parallels the Keys. Kids dig the interactive yellow submarine, while adults seem to get into the cinematic depiction of an underwater abyss. See p. 263.

○ **Being a Ranger for a Day with the Everglades Ranger Programs:** More than 50 ranger programs, free with entry, are offered each month during high season and give visitors an opportunity to gain an expert's perspective. They range from canoe and walking tours to birding and biking. See p. 220.

○ **Walking Through the Gumbo Limbo Environmental Complex:** Named for an indigenous hardwood tree, the 20-acre complex protects one of the few surviving coastal hammocks, or forest islands, in South Florida. Walk through the hammock on a half-mile-long boardwalk that ends at a 40-foot observation tower, from which you can see the Atlantic Ocean, the Intracoastal Waterway, and much of Boca Raton. From mid-April to September, sea turtles come ashore here to lay eggs. See p. 320.

THE best BEACHES

○ **For Tranquillity:** Matheson Hammock Park Beach (© 305/665-5475) in South Miami features an enclosed man-made lagoon that is flushed naturally by the tidal action of the adjacent Biscayne Bay. The serene beach is surrounded by the bay's warm, calm waters and a backdrop of tropical hardwood forest. The beach at **Bahia Honda State Park** (© 305/872-2353; p. 261) in Bahia Honda Key is one of the nicest and most peaceful in Florida, located amid 635 acres of nature trails and even a portion of Henry Flagler's railroad.

○ **For Watersports:** Hobie Beach (© 305/361-2833), located on the south side of Key Biscayne's Rickenbacker Causeway, is one of South Florida's most popular beaches for watersport enthusiasts, featuring jet ski, sailboat, windsurfing, and sailboard rentals; shade, if necessary, from the Australian pine; and a sublime view of the downtown Miami skyline.

○ **For People-Watching:** Lummus Park Beach (© 305/673-7714; p. 54) is world renowned, not necessarily for its pristine sands, but for its location in Miami Beach's **South Beach** neighborhood. Here, seeing, being seen, and, at times, the obscene go hand in hand with sunscreen and beach towels. Not nearly as scenic, but still heavily populated, **Fort Lauderdale Beach** (© 954/468-1597; p. 298) was the site of many a bacchanalian, Frankie and Annette–style Spring Break back in the day and is now an eclectic—albeit calmer—mix of young, buff beach bums.

○ **For Nature Lovers: MacArthur Beach** (www.macarthurbeach.org; © 561/624-6950), in West Palm Beach, is considered by many nature enthusiasts to be the most beautiful nature park in South Florida, with a nice stretch of sand set against a lush and diverse background of foliage, plus a state-of-the-art nature center and a renowned sea turtle awareness program.

○ **For Nude Sunbathing:** For that all-over tan, head to the north end of **Haulover Beach** (© 305/944-3040), north of Miami Beach between Bal Harbour and Sunny Isles, nestled between the Intracoastal Waterway and the ocean. A gay nude beach is also there, as is an area for nude volleyball.

○ **For Seclusion:** The producers of *Survivor* could feasibly shoot their show on the ultrasecluded, picturesque, and deserted **Virginia Key** (© 305/361-2749), on Miami's Key Biscayne, where people go purposely not to be found. **John U. Lloyd Beach State Park** (© 954/923-6711; p. 298) in Dania Beach is unfettered by high-rise condos, T-shirt shops, and hotels, and remains intact with an untouched shoreline surrounded by a canopy of Australian pine to ensure that your seclusion is, indeed, highly guarded.

○ **For Gay Beachgoers:** In Miami, South Beach's **12th Street Beach** (© 305/673-7714) is the beach of choice for gay residents and travelers who come to show off just how much time they've spent in the gym and share news of upcoming parties and events. Oftentimes, this beach is the venue for some of the liveliest parties South Beach has ever seen. See p. 54.

○ **For Kids:** Miami's **Crandon Park Beach** (© 305/361-5421) is extremely popular among families with kids because of the shallow water created by a neighboring sandbar. The beach features convenient parking; picnic areas; a winding boardwalk; eco-adventure tours; and a multiethnic mix of families grilling, dancing, and relaxing.

SOUTH FLORIDA IN DEPTH

S ince the roaring '20s, South Florida has been a playground for the rich, famous, and freezing. It took a handful of wealthy folk to begin South Florida's transition from swamp to vacation destination. Tycoons Carl Fisher, Henry Flagler, and George Merrick get the credit for that, kickstarting the region's fondness for development back in the '20s. The land boom eventually busted, a hurricane destroyed what was started, then came the Great Depression, and they were back at square one. But not for long. As the economy rebounded, roadways improved, and frosty weather pervaded, South Florida was once again on the radar of everyone from entrepreneurs and vacationers to those looking for a permanent vacation in warmer climes. Enter the age of the condo canyons. But condos and development aren't the area's *only* history. South Florida has been inhabited for at least 10 centuries, making its stereotypical blue hairs seem downright young. Par for the course, South Florida's history is an illustrious and rich one.

SOUTH FLORIDA TODAY

Like the calm after the storm, South Florida is carefully coming out of its economic slumber, repressing its desires to break out with the reckless abandon of years past. Signs of that recklessness still hover over the skyline in empty high-rise condominiums, built for another economic era. That said, some of that emptiness is being filled with optimism and paying customers. This is the case for the hotel industry, which, despite its own downturns, is experiencing promising upturns for a change.

While the überluxury condo/hotel craze has thankfully died down—with even a formerly rabid Donald Trump wiping the foam of avarice off his face and backing off from his original aim to conquer every remaining sliver of South Florida beachfront—there's still a big market for luxury, especially in these parts where the Bentleys and Rolls-Royces that weren't repo-ed still fill the valet slots of some of the region's highest-grossing restaurants.

Unwilling and unable to alienate tourists who actually do adhere to a budget, a bipartisan law, the Travel Promotions Act, was signed in order to attract tourists and, ultimately, create the jobs that the region so sorely needed. "The tourism industry has faced challenges because of the difficult economy, which is part of the reason why we need the Travel Promotions Act now more than ever," said Congressman Ron Klein. "This new law will pump up the advertising dollars we invest around the world in order to attract tourists from all corners of the globe and strengthen South Florida's economy and create jobs locally."

Apparently the law is working. In April 2010, Broward County tourism director Nicki Grossman told the *Miami Herald,* "We feel like we're seeing recovery. We've stopped hemorrhaging." That bleeding also stopped, albeit temporarily, back in February 2010 thanks to a Super Bowl that helped boost lodging taxes 33% up from the year before. To put that into perspective, hotel taxes *plummeted* 24% the year before. Not so super, however, were the cancellations in trips—pleasure *and* business. "It was devastating, not only financially, but you start to lose your confidence that you've got what people are looking for," Grossman said. "And that confidence is back."

As a result of the regaining of confidence, some projects that weren't outright canceled and just put on hold have resumed; others weren't as fortunate.

In Fort Lauderdale, the credit crunch stunted plans for resort development, especially for the 298-unit Trump International Hotel & Tower, which may—gasp!—just be called International Hotel & Tower after a mortgage holder filed to take back the property. Yep, Trump, you could be fired.

In an interview with the *Palm Beach Post,* Peter Henn, a developer with LXR Luxury Resorts (which, as of April 2010, was in the throes of a $500-million Waldorf-Astoria revamp at the Bahia Mar), said, "The small-hotel families that built Fort Lauderdale couldn't develop the kind of hotels we're developing now on the beach."

Unfortunately, several plans were nixed and/or still looking for deep pockets; among them are a Howard Johnson on Fort Lauderdale Beach that was to be transformed into a high-end resort, a $15-million expansion at Lago Mar Resort & Club, and several other run-down hotels and motels that were, prior to the recession, promising champagne wishes and caviar dreams.

New projects aside, those hotels, restaurants, and attractions that have managed to stay afloat may have suffered some nicks and scratches to their bottom lines, but they are doing whatever they can to chug along and back into black, even if it means reducing rates—something that was unthinkable during boom times.

The antithesis of years past, the 2010s saw a major slowdown in building, condos, hotels and otherwise. That said, the downtown Miami revitalization continued in full throttle, with a spate of mostly restaurant openings offering locals and visitors alike an excellent alternative to the tried-and-true, beaten path of South Beach. Like the Energizer Bunny, South Beach managed to keep chugging along despite a bit of a slowdown, the white elephant on the beach which everyone tried to ignore. In fact, that slowdown did nothing to stop über-high-end restaurants like Mr Chow and STK Miami from opening to throngs of people who think nothing of dropping hundreds of dollars on dinners that could easily have be had at places like PF Chang's and Applebee's.

And while downtown and Midtown Miami saw a boost in activity with the openings of area hot spots like Zuma at the EPIC and Sugarcane Raw Bar Grill, sadly, Coconut Grove, the once thriving, buzzing nucleus of bohemian activity in Miami, saw more for RENT, FOR SALE, and GOING OUT OF BUSINESS signs than peace signs.

Fort Lauderdale and the Palm Beaches saw similar contradictions, with openings (walk into the $205-million W Fort Lauderdale and ask yourself, "What recession?"), closings and drops in hotel rates allowing for a spate of frugal, budget-conscious tourists who normally wouldn't have had the opportunities they did after hotels admitted to defeat and got into recession-friendly mode. But jitters are still out there.

"Consumers are starting to feel more confident and are starting to spend more, but now we're all wondering what will happen as the stock market dips below 10,000 again," said consumer psychologist Kit Yarrow to the *Palm Beach Post*. Also contributing to those nerves is the fact that the state still ranks high in foreclosures and joblessness. Add to that the growing fears of the oil spill reaching South Florida (as of this writing, it was a no show, thank goodness), and you've got some pretty anxious folks.

Down in the pre–oil spill Keys, where tar balls may or may not have been a side effect of the BP disaster (one charter boat company in the Keys even sued the oil company for creating the "perception" of oil from the spill when it, in fact, didn't even yet exist in the Keys), a bounce back came from the fact that the recession made things more affordable, be it hotel rates or even real estate.

At some point in 2011, it was almost like the halcyon days of boomtown South Florida, which saw the Miami openings of a few swank, luxe hotels and *Top Chef*-caliber restaurants—for example, the JW Marriott Marquis in downtown Miami and its anchor restaurant db Bistro Moderne by the celebrated French chef Daniel Boulud, and the Dream South Beach and its anchor restaurant Tudor House by star chef Geoffrey Zakarian. En route to South Beach, luxury-boutique hotel brand James dropped $130 million for the historic Royal Palm to bring its third hotel to Miami in 2012. "It's a market that really welcomes more independent and artistically minded brands," said Brad Wilson, COO of Denihan Hospitality Group. "We think it's a perfect match for the James." For those who considered the words *culture* and *Miami* in the same sentence to be oxymoronic, January silenced many of them with the opening of the magnificent, multi-multi-million-dollar Frank Gehry-designed New World Center. And while new hotel openings have slowed down considerably in the region as compared to the past few years, that hasn't stopped Hollywood Beach from approving the $130-plus-million Margaritaville Resort that's expected sometime in this century.

As 2012 progressed, things looked up for South Florida, to which cash-carrying Russians and Brazilians began flocking and buying up much of that real estate left vacant over the past few years. While $5 million for an oceanfront penthouse may be no bargain for the rest of us, for those who can afford not to ask how much, it is a downright deal. Bolstering South Florida's reputation as a sunny place for shady people, according to a *Sun Sentinel* article in January 2012, personal income there jumped 4.2% despite the fact that no one down there seems to actually work. In Fort Lauderdale, things weren't too shabby either, with Broward County setting a major tourism record with 11 million overnight visitors in 2011 who spent—wait, sit down—$9 billion. Said the *Sun Sentinel*, "Hotel and restaurant jobs hit an all-time high. Credit Brazilians and other international guests, who tend to stay longer and spend more than U.S. tourists." In 2012, Fort Lauderdale was expecting 4% *more* visitors and even more spending. Speaking of money, Asian gaming giant Genting set its sights on downtown Miami, where it plunked down $236 million in cash for the *Miami Herald*'s waterfront headquarters and announced plans for a $3.8 billion casino-and-hotel complex on the site, which ignited fury and dollar signs in the eyes of locals and nonlocals alike. As for whether or not this will even happen has yet to be decided, but a state Senate committee voted in January of 2012 to allow the proposal to be debated by the state's lawmakers, which will definitely be a heated debate, to say the least.

THE MAKING OF SOUTH FLORIDA

South Florida's Swampy Beginnings

Fourteen thousand years ago, Florida would have made an ideal location for the show *Land of the Lost*—that is, if there were actually dinosaurs down here. Not so much. During the age of dinosaurs, the Florida peninsula was underwater and did not exist as a land mass. Therefore, no dinosaur remains were ever deposited in Florida. However, in 1998, archaeologists discovered a slew of artifacts in downtown Miami in an area now known as the Miami Circle. With origins dating back at least 2,000 years, it was discovered that the artifacts belonged to the Calusa or Tequesta tribes.

The post-Archaic cultures of eastern and southern Florida developed in relative isolation, and it is likely that the peoples living in those areas at the time of first European contact were direct descendants of the inhabitants of the areas in late Archaic times.

Spanish Rule & Native-American Culture

Spanish explorers of the early 16th century were likely the first Europeans to interact with the native population of Florida. The first documented encounter of Europeans with Native Americans of the United States came with the first expedition of Juan Ponce de León to Florida in 1513, although he encountered at least one native that spoke Spanish. In 1521, he encountered the Calusa Indians, who established 30 villages in the Everglades and successfully resisted European colonization.

The Spanish recorded nearly 100 names of groups they encountered. Tribes in South Florida at the time of first contact included the Tequesta, who lived on the southeast coast of the Everglades. Unfortunately, all tribes diminished in numbers during the period of Spanish control of Florida.

The Seminole, originally an offshoot of the Creek people who absorbed other groups, developed as a distinct tribe in Florida during the 18th century, and are now represented in the Seminole Nation of Oklahoma, the Seminole Tribe of Florida, and the Miccosukee Tribe of Indians of Florida, whose presences are alive and well today.

And Then There Was Miami

It wasn't long after Florida became the 27th state in the union (in 1845) that Miami began to emerge as a city—or somewhat one. During the war, the U.S. created Fort Dallas on the north bank of a river that flowed through southern Florida. When the soldiers left, the fort became the base for a small village established by William H. English, who dubbed it Miami, from the Indian word *Mayami*, meaning "big water."

In 1822, the Homestead Act offered 160 acres of free land to anyone who would stay on it for at least 5 years. Edmund Beasley bit and in 1868 moved into what is now Coconut Grove. Two years later, William Brickell bought land on the south bank of the Miami River and Ephraim Sturtevant took over the area called Biscayne. In 1875, his daughter Julia Tuttle visited him and fell in love with the area, although not returning for another 16 years, when she would further transform the city.

In the meantime, Henry Flagler, who made a $50-million fortune working with John Rockefeller in the Standard Oil Company, came to Florida in the late 1800s because he thought the warm weather would help his wife's frail health. After moving to the area, he built a railroad all the way down the east coast of Florida, stopping in each major town to build a hotel. Another railway honcho, Henry Plant, laid his tracks from Jacksonville to Tampa.

When her husband died in 1886, Julia Tuttle decided to leave Cleveland for Florida and asked Plant to extend his railroad to Miami. Plant declined, so Tuttle went to Flagler, whose own railroad stopped 66 miles away in what is now known as Palm Beach. Flagler laughed at Tuttle's request, saying he didn't see what Miami had to offer in terms of tourism.

After a devastating winter that killed all crops north of the state, Tuttle sent Flagler a bounty of orange blossoms to prove that Miami did, indeed, have something to offer. After Tuttle agreed to give Flagler some of her land along with William Brickell's, Flagler agreed to extend the railway. When the first train arrived in Miami on April 15, 1896, all 300 (!) of the city's residents showed up to see it. Miami had arrived, and the tourist bureau began touting the city as "the sun porch of America, where winter is turned to summer."

Unlocking the Keys

No one knows exactly when the first European set foot on one of the Florida Keys, but as exploration and shipping increased, the islands became prominent on nautical maps. The nearby treacherous coral reefs claimed many lives. The chain was eventually called "keys," also attributed to the Spanish, from *cayos,* meaning "small islands." In 1763, when the Spanish ceded Florida to the British in a trade for the port of Havana, an agent of the king of Spain claimed that the islands, rich in fish, turtles, and mahogany for shipbuilding, were part of Cuba, fearing that the English might build fortresses and dominate the shipping lanes.

The British realized the treaty was ambiguous, but declared that the Keys should be occupied and defended as part of Florida. The British claim was never officially contested. Ironically, the British gave the islands back to Spain in 1783, to keep them out of the hands of the United States, but in 1821 all of Florida, including the necklace of islands, officially became American territory.

Many of the residents of Key West were immigrants from the Bahamas, known as Conchs (pronounced "Conks"), who arrived in increasing numbers after 1830. Many were sons and daughters of Loyalists who fled to the nearest crown soil during the American Revolution.

In the 20th century, many residents of Key West started referring to themselves as "Conchs," and the term is now generally applied to all residents of Key West. In 1982, Key West and the rest of the Florida Keys briefly declared its "independence" as the Conch Republic in a protest over a United States Border Patrol blockade. This blockade, set up on U.S. 1 where the northern end of the Overseas Highway meets the mainland at Florida City, was in response to the Mariel Boatlift, a mass emigration of Cubans to Miami during a 6 month period in 1980. A 17-mile traffic jam ensued while the Border Patrol stopped every car leaving the Keys, supposedly searching for illegal aliens attempting to enter the mainland United States. This paralyzed the Florida Keys. The Conch Republic Independence Celebration—including parades and parties—is celebrated every April 23.

Recognizing the River of Grass

Thanks to the work of the Everglades' foremost supporter, Ernest F. Coe, Congress passed a park bill in 1934. Dubbed by opponents as the "alligator and snake swamp bill," the legislation stalled during the Great Depression and World War II. Finally, on December 6, 1947, President Harry Truman dedicated the Everglades National Park. In that same year, Marjory Stoneman Douglas first published *The Everglades: River of Grass.* She understood its importance as the major watershed for South Florida and as a unique ecosystem.

Holding Down the Fort . . . Lauderdale

Fort Lauderdale is named after a series of forts built by the United States during the Second Seminole War. However, development of the city did not begin until 50 years after the forts were abandoned at the end of the conflict. Three forts named "Fort Lauderdale" were constructed; the first was at the fork of the New River, the second at Tarpon Bend, and the third near the site of the Bahia Mar Marina. The forts took their name from Major William Lauderdale, who was the commander of the detachment of soldiers who built the first fort.

The area in which the city of Fort Lauderdale would later be founded was inhabited for more than 1,000 years by the Tequesta Indians. Contact with Spanish explorers in the 16th century proved disastrous for the Tequesta, as the Europeans unwittingly brought with them diseases to which the native populations possessed no resistance, such as smallpox. For the Tequesta, disease, coupled with continuing conflict with their Calusa neighbors, contributed greatly to their decline over the next 2 centuries. By 1763, there were only a few Tequesta left in Florida, and most of them were evacuated to Cuba when the Spanish ceded Florida to the British in 1763, under the terms of the Treaty of Paris, which ended the Seven Years' War. Although control of the area changed between Spain, England, the United States, and the Confederate States of America, it remained largely undeveloped until the 20th century.

It was not until Frank Stranahan arrived in the area in 1893 to operate a ferry across the New River, and the Florida East Coast Railroad's completion of a route through the area in 1896, that any organized development began. The city was incorporated in 1911, and in 1915 was designated the county seat of newly formed Broward County.

Fort Lauderdale's first major development began in the 1920s, during the Florida land boom. The 1926 Miami Hurricane and the Great Depression of the 1930s caused a great deal of economic dislocation. When World War II began, Fort Lauderdale became a major U.S. Navy base, with a naval air station to train pilots, radar and fire-control operator training schools, and a Coast Guard base at Port Everglades.

After the war ended, service members returned to the area, spurring an enormous population explosion which dwarfed the 1920s boom. Today, Fort Lauderdale is a

DATELINE

1980 Race riots tear apart Miami. The Mariel Boatlift brings 140,000 Cubans to Florida. The Miami Seaquarium celebrates its 25th anniversary.

1983 Thirty-eight overseas highway bridges from Key Largo to Key West are completed under the Florida Keys Bridge Replacement Program.

1984 The Miami Metro Rail, the only inner-city, elevated rail system in Florida, begins service in May.

1986 Treasure hunter Mel Fisher continues to salvage vast amounts of gold and silver from his discovery of the Spanish galleon *Nuestra Senora de Atocha*, which sank in 1622 during a hurricane off Key West. The television series *Miami Vice* continues to capture the nation's imagination, revitalizing interest and tourism for South Florida.

1987 U.S. Census Bureau estimates indicate that Florida has surpassed Pennsylvania to become the fourth most populous

major yachting center, one of the nation's largest tourist destinations, and the center of a metropolitan division with 1.8 million people.

Positioning Posh Palm Beach

Palm Beach County was created in 1909. It was named for its first settled community, Palm Beach, in turn named for the palm trees and beaches in the area. The county was carved out of what was then the northern half of Dade County. The southern half of Palm Beach County was subsequently carved out to create the northern portion of Broward County in 1915. Henry Flagler was instrumental in the county's development in the early 1900s, with the extension of the Florida East Coast Railway through the county from Jacksonville to Key West. After Flagler came Addison Mizner, an architect with a flair for Mediterranean styles. You can blame or thank Mizner for all those pink houses. As Palm Beach became a haven for the über-rich, it also became a political focal point and was one of the counties at the center of the 2000 U.S. presidential election recount controversy, and ended up turning the state in favor of George W. Bush by 537 votes.

THE LAY OF THE LAND

Because the population of South Florida is largely confined to a strip of land between the Atlantic Ocean and the Everglades, the Miami Urbanized Area (that is, the area of contiguous urban development) is about 110 miles long (north to south), but never more than 20 miles wide, and in some areas only 5 miles wide. South Florida is longer than any other urbanized area in the United States except for the New York metropolitan area. It was the eighth most densely populated urbanized area in the United States in the 2000 census. As of the 2000 census, the urbanized area had a land area of 1,116 square miles, with a population of 4,919,036, for a population density of 4,407.4 per square mile. Miami and Hialeah (the second largest city in the metropolitan area) had population densities of more than 10,000 per square mile. The Miami Urbanized Area was the fifth largest urbanized area in the United States in the 2000 census, ahead of the Dallas–Fort Worth–Arlington, Texas, Urbanized Area.

state in the nation. The ranking will not become official until the bureau publishes its report in early 1988. It is predicted that Florida will be the third most populous state by the year 2000.

1990 Panama's governor Manuel Noriega is brought to Miami in January for trial on drug charges. Joe Robbie, Miami Dolphins founder, dies in January.

1991 Queen Elizabeth II visits Miami. Five Navy bombers found by treasure salvagers are determined not to be the "Lost Squadron" of Bermuda Triangle fame that went down in 1945 off the coast of Florida. Miami and Denver are awarded new national Major League Baseball franchises. The 1990 federal census puts Florida's population at 12,937,926, a 34% increase from 1980.

1992 Homestead and adjacent South Florida are devastated on August 24 by the (then) costliest natural disaster in American history, Hurricane Andrew, requiring billions in aid. There were 58 deaths directly or indirectly related to Andrew. The hurricane destroyed 25,000 homes and damaged 10,000 others.

continues

In 2010, the area, including Fort Lauderdale and Palm Beach, had an estimated 5,564,635 persons; this after, for the first time in over 60 years, the state experienced a net loss of approximately 58,000 people in 2009. According to Mark Wilson, president of the Florida Chamber of Commerce, the state, once the fifth cheapest state to live in, had become the 14th most *expensive*. Some optimists predict a positive trend for long-term growth in the state. The job forecast, however, is expected, according to economists, to remain dismal until 2012.

As we wait for the economy to rebound, we realize there are other pressing issues to be dealt with. Scientists have observed changes in Florida consistent with the early effects of global warming: retreating and eroding shorelines, dying coral reefs, saltwater intrusion into inland freshwater aquifers, an upswing in forest fires, and warmer air and sea-surface temperatures. As glaciers melt and warming waters expand, sea levels will rise anywhere from 8 inches to 2½ feet over the next century. In Florida, seawater will advance inland as much as 400 feet in low-lying areas, flooding shoreline homes and hotels, limiting future development, and eroding the state's beloved beaches. People aren't kidding when they say that one day, Florida will be underwater.

On a more positive note, some say this perceived global warming threat has been greatly exaggerated. Though preliminary research raised concerns that warmer ocean temperatures would lead to more frequent hurricanes, scientists now discount this theory. Nevertheless, global warming may increase hurricanes' maximum intensity, which will serve to exacerbate a natural cyclical trend toward more severe storms—a trend likely to persist for the next 25 to 40 years.

SOUTH FLORIDA IN POP CULTURE

South Florida—and Florida in general—is an author's dream come true. In this state of much diversity, inspiration is practically hanging from the palm trees. The area is so rife with material, you can't not be inspired. In this setting, Key West's well-deserved, ongoing status as a literary enclave is no surprise.

Twenty-two thousand federal troops were deployed. Shelters housed 80,000 persons.

Among African Americans elected to Congress was Carrie Meek of Miami. Sixty-six in 1993, her political career saw her elected first to the Florida House of Representatives, next the Florida Senate, and then the U.S. House of Representatives.

1993 Janet Reno, state attorney for Dade County (Miami) for 15 years, is named attorney general of the U.S. by President Bill Clinton; Reno is the first woman to so serve in U.S. history. Although a pro-choice Democrat, she managed to win reelection four times in a conservative stronghold, the last time without opposition.

1996 Miami turns 100.

2000 Florida became the battleground of the controversial 2000 U.S. presidential election between Al Gore and George W. Bush (whose brother, Jeb Bush, was Florida's governor). A count of the popular votes held on Election Day was extremely close (in favor of Bush), and mired in accusations of fraud and manipulation. Subsequent recount efforts degenerated into arguments over mispunched ballots,

Fiction

- ***The Perez Family*** (W. W. Norton & Co. Inc.) by Christine Bell—Cuban immigrants from the Mariel Boatlift exchange their talents for an immigration deal in Miami (also a 1995 movie by Mira Nair).

- ***Miami, It's Murder*** (Avon) by Edna Buchannan—Miami's Agatha Christie keeps you in suspense with her reporter protagonist and her life as an investigative crime solver in Miami.

- ***To Have and Have Not*** (Scribner) by Ernest Hemingway—One of the many must-reads by Key West's most famous resident.

- ***In Cuba I Was a German Shepherd*** (Grove Press) by Ana Menendez—Stories of people who gather in Little Havana to lament the loss of the good old days.

- ***Naked Came the Manatee*** (Ballantine Books) by Carl Hiassen—Thirteen *Miami Herald* writers contributed to this hilarious story about the discovery of Castro's head.

- ***Killing Mister Watson*** (Vintage Books USA) by Peter Matthiessen—A fascinating story about the settlement of the Everglades and the problems that ensued.

- ***The Yearling*** (Collier MacMillan Publishers) by Marjorie Kinnan Rawlings—A classic about life in the Florida backwoods.

- ***Seraph on the Suwanee*** (Harper Perennial) by Zora Neale Hurston—A novel about turn-of-the-century Florida "white crackers."

- ***Nine Florida Stories*** (University Press of Florida) by Marjory Stoneman Douglas—The beloved Florida naturalist's fictional take on Florida, set in a scattering of settings—Miami, Fort Lauderdale, the Tamiami Trail, the Keys, the Everglades—and revealing the drama of hurricanes and plane crashes, kidnappers, escaped convicts, and smugglers.

- ***Rum Punch*** (Harper Torch) by Elmore Leonard—The story of a stewardess, bail bondsman, and gun runner in Palm Beach County.

- ***Swim to Me*** (Algonquin Books) by Betsy Carter—A wacky novel set in Weeki Wachee about a shy teenager who finds her purpose at the mermaid-happy theme park.

"hanging chads," and controversial decisions by Florida Secretary of State Katherine Harris and the Florida Supreme Court. Ultimately, the United States Supreme Court ended all recounts and let stand the official count by Harris, which was accepted by Congress.

2003 The Florida Marlins win the World Series.

2004 George W. Bush wins the presidential election again. His brother, Florida Gov. Jeb Bush, celebrates in the state capitol.

2006 The Miami Heat win the NBA championships.

2007 Jeb Bush vacates the governor's office, which is taken over by Charlie Crist.

2008 Florida continues to be one of the fastest-growing states in the country. The economy still depends greatly on tourism, but expanding industries in business and manufacturing are strengthening its growth potential. State leaders are working on problems created due to huge population increases and environmental concerns.

2009 In October 2009, Florida, along with California and Nevada,

continues

- *Tourist Season* (Warner Books) by Carl Hiaasen—Hiaasen is at his darkest, funniest, and finest in this book about a newspaper columnist who kills off tourists on a quest to return Florida to its long gone, unfettered, pristine state.

Nonfiction

- *Fool's Paradise: Players, Poseurs and the Culture of Excess in South Beach* (Crown) by Steven Gaines—A New Yorker's love/hate take on America's alleged Riviera.
- *Miami Babylon: Crime, Wealth and Power—A Dispatch from the Beach* (Simon & Schuster) by Gerald Posner—The name says it all about this investigative look at the sybaritic paradise that is Miami.
- *Miami* (Vintage) by Joan Didion—An intriguing compilation of impressions of the Magic City.
- *Miami, the Magic City* (Centennial Press) by Arva Moore Parks—An authoritative history of the city.
- *The Everglades: River of Grass* (Pineapple Press) by Marjory Stoneman Douglas—Eco-maniacs will love this personal account of the treasures of Florida's most famous natural resource.
- *Celebration USA: Living in Disney's Brave New Town* (Holt Paperbacks) by Douglas Frantz and Catherine Collins—An eye-opening true story about living in Disney's "model town."

Movies Filmed in Florida

- Clarence Brown's *The Yearling* (1946), based on novel by M.K. Rawlings
- John Huston's *Key Largo* (1948), based on novel by Hemingway (gangsters, hurricanes, and Bogey and Bacall)
- Harry Levin's *Where the Boys Are* (1960; Spring Break in Fort Lauderdale)
- John Schlesinger's *Midnight Cowboy* (1969), based on novel by James Leo Herlihy
- Ernest Lehman's *Portnoy's Complaint* (1972), based on novel by Philip Roth (Jewish culture)

posted the highest foreclosure rates in the country. To make matters worse, unemployment rates in the state skyrocketed to over 11%. For the first time in over 60 years, Florida experienced a population decline.

2010 Like the calm after the storm, South Florida ekes carefully out of its economic slumber. If funds from the Travel Promotions Act aren't enough to drive tourism, LeBron James's move to the Miami Heat is seen in some circles as the panacea to all economic problems. A massive spill of oil from a BP oil rig in the Gulf raises fears of sullied coastlines (one charter boat company in the Keys sued the oil company for even creating the "perception" of oil from the spill), though no such effects are evident.

2011 Cautiously optimistic and on the rebound from that so-called burst bubble, South Florida shows serious signs of stability thanks to an influx of cash-heavy foreigners hailing from all parts of the globe, namely South America, Russia and, in the case of a monstrous multi-billion dollar downtown Miami casino project, China.

- Lawrence Kasdan's **Body Heat** (1981; crime)
- Ron Howard's **Cocoon** (1985), based on novel by David Saperstein (retirees)
- Tim Burton's **Edward Scissorhands** (1990; modern fairy tale filmed in Dade City and Lakeland)
- Mike Nichols's **Birdcage** (1996; South Beach comedy)
- Andrew Bergman's **Striptease** (1996), based on novel by Carl Hiassen
- John Singleton's **Rosewood** (1997), based on historic Rosewood massacre (African-American culture)
- Victor Nunez's **Ulee's Gold** (1997; Panhandle family drama)
- Peter Weir's **The Truman Show** (1998; sci-fi in Seaside)
- Spike Jonze's **Adaptation** (2002), loosely based on Susan Orleans's *The Orchid Thief*
- Patty Jenkins's **Monster** (2003), biopic of serial killer Aileen Wournos
- Taylor Hackford's **Ray** (2004), biopic of musician Ray Charles, born in Florida
- David Frankel's **Marley & Me** (2008), based on the best-selling novel of the same name by a former Fort Lauderdale *Sun Sentinel* reporter
- Jason Reitman's **Up in the Air** (2009; starring George Clooney as a frequent flyer who comes through MIA and the Miami Airport Hilton)
- **Rock of Ages** (2012; starring Tom Cruise, Catherine Zeta-Jones, Alec Baldwin, and some '80s rock and pop relics in the celluloid version of the Broadway hit musical. Parts of downtown Miami's sketchier streets were magically transformed into LA's landmark Sunset Strip)

Miami Sound

The Miami recording industry did not begin with Gloria Estefan's Miami Sound Machine, contrary to popular belief. In fact, some major rock albums were recorded in Miami's Criteria Studios, among them *Rumours* by Fleetwood Mac and *Hotel California* by the Eagles. Long-time local music entrepreneur Henry Stone and his label, TK Records, created the local indie scene in the 1970s. TK Records produced the R&B group KC and the Sunshine Band along with soul singers Betty Wright, George McCrae, and Jimmy "Bo" Horne, as well as a number of minor soul and disco hits, many influenced by Caribbean music. In the 2000s, Miami has seen an enormous rap boom in the form of Daddy Yankee, Pitbull, Rick Ross, and more.

South Florida's Fab Fare

Before Florida started evolving into a bona fide gastronomic destination, one respected by eaters and chefs alike, two things about Floridian fare may have come to mind—oranges and early bird. And while both still play a very important role in the state's reputation, pop culturally or otherwise, there's a lot more to Florida food than just citrus and $3.99 prime rib; as the locavore craze continues in which people prefer to eat or cook with only local ingredients, the following list of foods indigenous to the state can be considered the holy grail for Florida gourmands. Today, expect to savor fresh and flavorful ingredients such as avocado, hearts of palm, star fruit, spiny lobster, and stone crabs, whether in some fancy, five-star fusion restaurant or a hands-on sea shanty with ice-cold beer, paper napkins, and plastic cutlery.

As for the unofficial term *Florida cuisine,* it can mean many things, but we suppose Floribbean, the fusion of Caribbean and Latin flavors with the aforementioned local Florida flavors, says it best; this is especially true down in South Florida and in Tampa, where the Latin influences are so enormous. Some food snobs shudder at the term and prefer the phrase *New World cuisine,* the product of Miami-based chef

Norman Van Aken. But it's all semantics. Think crack conch chowder with orange, saffron, and coconut. Or spiny lobster salad with mango.

But Florida cuisine really does vary by region. The farther north you go, the closer to the Deep South you are, and instead of Latin influences, you'll see more of a Southern comfort twist on Florida cuisine—a locally caught fish with, say, hush puppies and collard greens, or gator tail with grits and butter. Over on the Gulf Coast, you tend to see a lot of smoked fish, most commonly mullet, in many incarnations but most ubiquitously as a dip or spread eaten with crackers and, if you dare, hot sauce. Near Lake Okeechobee, the fish is usually catfish, and it's almost always fried.

The following is a good, but by no means comprehensive, list of typical (or atypical, rather) South Florida cuisine:

o **Cuban Sandwiches** (also known as *medianoche,* translation: "at midnight"): some say they originated in Miami, others say Tampa; but wherever it was, it's a delicious combo of ham, roasted pork, Swiss, pickles, mustard, and, depending on where you are, sometimes salami on crispy, crusty, toasted "Cuban bread," whose origin is still questionable.

o **Grouper Sandwiches:** Or pretty much any fish (snapper, mahimahi, pompano, and so on) sandwich, though grouper is the Ryan Seacrest of Florida fish, appearing on many menus in many incarnations, from grilled and fried to blackened or jerked.

o **Mango Salsa:** A widely used condiment. The Floribbean version of ketchup.

o **Conch Fritters:** Fried balls of chewy conch, usually found in the Keys or anywhere where there's water views.

o **Key Lime Pie:** Made from those luscious limes found, yes, in the Keys, these pies are everywhere throughout the region, and everywhere claims to have the best. You be the judge.

o **Hearts of Palm Salad:** Often found in old school $6.99 prime rib, steak, and lobster houses, though often found in chichi eateries as well.

WHEN TO GO

To a large extent, the timing of your visit will determine how much you'll spend—and how much company you'll have—once you get to South Florida. That's because room rates can more than double during so-called high seasons, when countless visitors flock to Florida.

The weather determines the high seasons (see "Climate," below). In subtropical South Florida, high season is in the winter, from mid-December to mid-April, although if you ask tourism execs, the high season is now creeping longer into spring and even, in some parts, summer. On the other hand, you'll be rewarded with incredible bargains if you can stand the heat, humidity, and daily rain storms of a South Florida summer between June and early September.

Hurricane Season runs from June to November, and, as seen in 2005, the most active hurricane season on record, and 2009, the quietest, you never know what can happen. Pay close attention to weather forecasts during this season and always be prepared. See "Climate," below.

Presidents' Day weekend in February, Easter week, Memorial Day weekend, the Fourth of July, Labor Day weekend, Thanksgiving, Christmas, and New Year's are busy throughout the state.

South Florida's so-called shoulder season is April through May, and September through November, when the weather is pleasant throughout Florida and the hotel rates are considerably lower than during the high season. If price is a consideration, these months of moderate temperatures and fewer tourists are the best times to visit.

See the accommodations sections in the chapters that follow for specifics on the local high, shoulder, and off seasons.

CLIMATE Contrary to popular belief, South Florida's climate is subtropical, not tropical. Accordingly, Florida sees more extremes of temperatures than, say, the Caribbean islands.

Spring, which runs from late March to May, sees warm temperatures throughout Florida, but it also brings tropical showers.

Summer in Florida extends from May to September, when it's hot and very humid throughout the state. If you're in an inland city during these months, you may not want to do anything too taxing when the sun is at its peak. Coastal areas, however, reap the benefits of sea breezes. Severe afternoon thunderstorms are prevalent during the summer heat (there aren't professional sports teams here named Lightning and Thunder for nothing), so schedule your activities for earlier in the day, and take precautions to avoid being hit by lightning during the storms. Those storms, by the way, often start out fierce and end with a rainbow and sunshine, so don't worry; just don't stand under a tree or on a golf course during the main act.

Autumn—about September through November—is a great time to visit, as the hottest days are gone and the crowds have thinned out. Unless a hurricane blows through, November is usually Florida's driest month. These days, however, one can never predict 100% sunshine. June through November is hurricane season here, but even if one threatens, the National Weather Service closely tracks the storms and gives ample warning if there's need to evacuate coastal areas.

Winter can get a bit nippy throughout the state, and in recent years even downright freezing. Although snow is rare, the end of 2009 saw flakes falling as north as Pensacola and as south as Kendall in South Miami. Speaking of cold in Miami, locals have been known to whip out the coats, hats, and boots when the temperature drops below 80. The "cold snaps" usually last only a few days in the southern half of the state, however, and daytime temperatures should quickly return to the 70s (20s Celsius). Again, that was before all the El Niño, La Niña, and global warming took effect, so whenever you travel to Florida, bring a jacket. Even in summertime you may need it indoors when air-conditioning reaches freezing temperatures.

For up-to-the-minute weather info, tune into cable TV's Weather Channel or check out its website at www.weather.com.

Miami's Average Monthly High/Low Temperatures & Rainfall

	JAN	FEB	MAR	APR	MAY	JUNE	JULY	AUG	SEPT	OCT	NOV	DEC
HIGH (°F)	76	77	80	83	86	88	89	90	88	85	80	77
HIGH (°C)	24	25	27	28	30	31	32	32	31	29	27	25
LOW (°F)	60	61	64	68	72	75	76	76	76	72	66	61
LOW (°C)	16	16	18	20	22	24	24	24	24	22	19	16
RAIN (IN.)	2.0	2.1	2.4	3.0	5.9	8.8	6.0	7.8	8.5	7.0	3.1	1.8

Calendar of Events

For an exhaustive list of events beyond those listed here, check http://events.frommers.com, where you'll find a searchable, up-to-the-minute roster of what's happening in cities all over the world.

JANUARY

Orange Bowl (www.orangebowl.org; ℂ **305/341-4700**), Miami. Football fanatics flock to the big Orange Bowl game (now held at Sun Life Stadium) on New Year's Day, featuring what seems to be a different corporate sponsor every year and two of the year's best college football teams. Call early if you want tickets; they sell out quickly. First week of January.

Key West Literary Seminar (www.kwls.org; ℂ **888/293-9291**), Key West. Literary types have a good reason to put down their books and head to Key West. This 3-day event features a different theme every year, along with a roster of incredible authors, writers, and other literary types. The event is so popular it sells out well in advance, so call early for tickets. Second week of January.

FEBRUARY

Everglades City Seafood Festival (www.evergladesseafoodfestival.com; ℂ **239/695-2561**), Everglades City. What seems like schools of fish-loving people flock down to Everglades City for a 2-day feeding frenzy, in which Florida delicacies from stone crab to gator tails are served from shacks and booths on the outskirts of this quaint Old Florida town. Admission is free, but you pay for the food you eat, booth by booth. First full weekend in February.

Miami International Boat Show (www.miamiboatshow.com; ℂ **954/441-3231**), Miami Beach. If you don't like crowds, beware, as this show draws a quarter of a million boat enthusiasts to the Miami Beach Convention Center. Some of the world's priciest megayachts, speedboats, sailboats, and schooners are displayed for purchase or for gawking. Mid-February.

South Beach Wine & Food Festival (www.sobewineandfoodfest.com; ℂ **877/762-3933**), South Beach. A 3-day celebration featuring some of the Food Network's best chefs, who do their thing in the kitchens of various restaurants and at events around town. In addition, there are tastings, lectures, seminars, and parties that are all open to the public—for a price, of course. Last weekend in February.

MARCH

Winter Party (www.winterparty.com; ℂ **305/538-5908**), Miami Beach. Gays and lesbians from around the world book trips to Miami far in advance to attend this weekend-long series of parties and events benefiting the Dade Human Rights Foundation. Travel arrangements can be made through Different Roads Travel, the event's official travel company, by calling ℂ **888/ROADS-55** (762-3755), ext. 510. Early March.

Spring Break, Miami Beach, Key West, and other beaches. College students from all over the United States and Canada flock to Florida for endless partying, wet-T-shirt and bikini contests, free concerts, volleyball tournaments, and more. Three weeks in March.

Calle Ocho Festival (www.carnavalmiami.com; ℂ **305/644-8888**), Little Havana. What Carnaval is to Rio, the Calle Ocho Festival is to Miami. This 10-day extravaganza, also called Carnival Miami, features a lengthy block party spanning 23 blocks, with live salsa music, parades, and, of course, tons of savory Cuban delicacies. Those afraid of mob scenes should avoid this party at all costs. Mid-March.

APRIL

Conch Republic Independence Celebration (www.conchrepublic.com; ℂ **305/296-0213**), Key West. A 10-day party celebrating the day the Conch Republic seceded from the union. Events include a kooky bed race and drag queen race to minigolf tournaments, cruiser car shows, and booze, lots of it. Mid-April.

JULY

Lower Keys Underwater Music Fest (www.lowerkeyschamber.com/underwatermusicfest.htm; ℂ **800/872-3722**), Looe Key. When you hear the phrase "the music and the madness," you may think of this amusing aural aquatic event in which boaters head out to the underwater reef at the Looe Key Marine Sanctuary, drop speakers into the water, and pipe in all sorts of music, creating a disco-diving spectacular. Considering the heat at this time of year, underwater is probably the coolest place for a concert. Early July.

Fantasy Fest (www.fantasyfest.net; $\mathcal{C}$ **305/ 296-1817**), Key West. Mardi Gras takes a Floridian holiday as the streets of Key West are overtaken by costumed revelers who have no shame and no parental guidance. This weeklong, hedonistic, X-rated Halloween party is not for children 17 and under. Make reservations in Key West early, as hotels tend to book up quickly during this event. Last week of October.

Miami Book Fair International (www.miami bookfair.com; $\mathcal{C}$ **305/237-3258**), Miami. Bibliophiles, literati, and some of the world's most prestigious and prolific authors descend upon Miami for a weeklong homage to the written word, which also happens to be the largest book fair in the United States. The weekend street fair is the best attended of the entire event, in which regular folk mix with wordsmiths such as Tom Wolfe, Nora Ephron, Salman Rushdie, and Jane Smiley while indulging in snacks, antiquarian books, and literary gossip. All lectures are free but fill up quickly, so get there early. Mid-November.

Art Basel Miami Beach (www.artbaselmiami beach.com), Miami Beach/Design District. Switzerland's most exclusive art fair and the world's most prominent collectors fly south for the winter and set up shop on South Beach and in the Design District with thousands of exhibitions, not to mention cocktail parties, concerts, and containers—as in shipping—that are set up on the beach and transformed into makeshift galleries. First or second weekend in December.

Seminole Hard Rock Winterfest Boat Parade (www.winterfestparade.com; $\mathcal{C}$ **954/ 767-0686**), Fort Lauderdale. People who complain that the holiday season just isn't as festive in South Florida as it is in colder parts of the world haven't been to this spectacular boat parade along the Intracoastal Waterway. Forget decking the halls. At this parade, the decks are decked out in magnificent holiday regalia as they gracefully—and boastfully—glide up and down the water. If you're not on a boat, the best views are from waterfront restaurants or anywhere you can squeeze in along the water. Mid-December.

RESPONSIBLE TRAVEL

Florida's biggest attraction isn't a theme park, but rather its natural resources. Thanks to some of the state's initiatives, keeping Florida green is becoming second nature. The **Florida Green Lodging** program, for instance, is a voluntary initiative of the Florida Department of Environmental Protection that designates and recognizes lodging facilities making a commitment to conserving and protecting Florida's natural resources. As of April 2012, there were 621 designated Florida Green Lodging properties. In order to be considered for membership in this very exclusive, green group, motels, hotels, and resorts must educate customers, employees, and the public on conservation; participate in waste reduction, reuse, recycling, water conservation, and energy efficiency; and provide eco-friendly transportation. The designation is valid for 3 years from the date of issue, and all properties are required to submit environmental performance data every year as well as implement at least two new environmental practices from any of the six areas of sustainable operations. For a list of these properties, go to **www.dep.state.fl.us/greenlodging/lodges.htm**.

Eco-tourism isn't just a trendy catchphrase when it comes to tourism in Florida. The Florida Fish and Wildlife Conservation Commission estimates that outdoor activities have almost a $10-billion impact on the state's economy. The Everglades is an eco-tourism hot spot where responsible tourism isn't an option but a requirement for anyone visiting or working there. In fact, in 2010, the **Comprehensive Everglades**

Restoration Plan began a process that will return some lands previously squandered for development to their formerly pristine, natural conditions. It's a multi-tiered $13.5 billion restoration plan covering 16 counties over an 18,000 square-mile area that will take over 30 years to complete.

Similar efforts can be seen throughout the state, such as in North Florida, where the new Northwest Florida Beaches International Airport in Panama Beach is the nation's first certified Leadership in Energy and Design (LEED) passenger terminal. This "green" airport encompasses 4,000 acres donated by the St. Joe Company that will be part of a landmark conservation effort to include a National Audubon Nature Center. See www.frommers.com/planning for more tips on responsible travel.

OUTDOOR ACTIVITIES

Diving, boating and sailing, camping, canoeing and kayaking, fishing, golfing, tennis—you name it, South Florida has it. These and other activities are described in the outdoor-activities sections of the following chapters, but here's a brief overview of some of the best places to move your muscles, with tips on how to get more detailed information.

The **Florida Sports Foundation,** 2390 Kerry Forest Pkwy., Ste. 101, Tallahassee, FL 32309 (www.flasports.com; ✆ **850/488-8347;** fax 850/922-0482), publishes free brochures, calendars, schedules, and guides to outdoor pursuits and spectator sports throughout Florida. I've noted some of its specific publications in the sections below.

For excellent color maps of state parks, campgrounds, canoe trails, aquatic preserves, caverns, and more, contact the **Florida Department of Environmental Protection,** Office of Communications, 3900 Commonwealth Blvd., Tallahassee, FL 32399 (www.dep.state.fl.us; ✆ **850/245-2118**). Some of the department's publications are mentioned below.

BIKING & IN-LINE SKATING   Florida's relatively flat terrain makes it ideal for bicycling and in-line skating. You can bike right into **Everglades National Park** along the 38-mile-long Main Park Road. Many towns and cities have designated routes for cyclists, skaters, joggers, and walkers, such as the paved pathways along Fort Lauderdale Beach and **Ocean Drive** on South Beach.

BOATING & SAILING   With some 1,350 miles of shoreline, it's not surprising that Florida is a boating and sailing mecca. In fact, you won't be anyplace near the water very long before you see flyers and other advertisements for rental boats and sailboat cruises. Many of them are mentioned in the chapters that follow.

Key West keeps gaining prominence as a world sailing capital. *Yachting* magazine sponsors the largest winter regatta in America here each January, and smaller events take place regularly.

The prestigious **Annapolis Sailing** (www.annapolissailing.com) has a base in Marathon in the Keys.

Florida Boating & Fishing, available for free from the Florida Sports Foundation (see the introduction to this section, above), is a treasure trove of tips on safe boating; state regulations; locations of marinas, hotels, and resorts; marine products and services; and more.

CAMPING   Florida is literally dotted with RV parks (if you own such a vehicle, it's the least expensive way to spend your winters here). But for the best tent camping, look to Florida's national preserves and 110 state parks and recreation areas. Options range from luxury sites with hot-water showers and cable TV hookups, to primitive island and beach camping with no facilities whatsoever.

Top spots include **Bill Baggs Cape Florida State Park,** on Key Biscayne in Miami. Down in the Keys; the oceanside sites in **Long Key State Park** are about as nice as they get.

In each of these popular campgrounds, reservations are essential, especially during the high season. Each of Florida's state parks takes bookings up to 11 months in advance.

The **Florida Department of Environmental Protection,** Division of Recreation and Parks, Mail Station 535, 3900 Commonwealth Blvd., Tallahassee, FL 32399-3000 (www.dep.state.fl.us; ✆ **850/245-2118**), publishes an annual guide of tent and RV sites in Florida's state parks and recreation areas.

Pet owners, note: Pets are permitted at some—but not all—state park beaches, campgrounds, and food service areas. Before bringing your animal, check with the department or the individual park to see if your pet will be allowed. And bring your pet's rabies certificate, which is required.

For private campgrounds, the **Florida Association of RV Parks & Campgrounds,** 1340 Vickers Dr., Tallahassee, FL 32303 (www.campflorida.com; ✆ **850/562-7151;** fax 850/562-7179), issues an annual *Camp Florida* directory with locator maps and details about its member establishments in the state.

CANOEING & KAYAKING Canoers and kayakers have almost limitless options for discovery here: picturesque rivers, sandy coastlines, marshes, mangroves, and gigantic Lake Okeechobee. Exceptional trails run through several parks and wildlife preserves, including **Everglades National Park** and **Briggs Nature Center,** on the edge of the Everglades near Marco Island.

Based during the winter at Everglades City, on the park's western border, **North American Canoe Tours, Inc.** (www.evergladesadventures.com; ✆ **239/695-3299**), offers weeklong guided canoe expeditions through the Everglades.

Thirty-six creek and river trails, covering 950 miles altogether, are itemized in the excellent free *Canoe Trails* booklet published by the Florida Department of Environmental Protection, Office of Communications, 3900 Commonwealth Blvd., Tallahassee, FL 32399 (www.dep.state.fl.us; ✆ **850/245-2118**).

Specialized guidebooks include *A Canoeing and Kayaking Guide to the Streams of Florida: Volume 1, North Central Florida and Panhandle,* by Elizabeth F. Carter and John L. Pearce; and *Volume 2, Central and Southern Peninsula,* by Lou Glaros and Doug Sphar. Both are published by Menasha Ridge Press (www.menasharidge.com).

ECO-ADVENTURES If you don't want to do it yourself, you can observe Florida's flora and fauna on guided field expeditions—and contribute to conservation efforts while you're at it.

The **Sierra Club,** the oldest and largest grass-roots environmental organization in the U.S., offers eco-adventures through its Florida chapters. Recent outings have included canoeing or kayaking through the Everglades, hiking the Florida Trail in America's southernmost national forest, camping on a barrier island, and exploring the sinkhole phenomenon in North-Central Florida. You do have to be a Sierra Club member, but you can join at the time of the trip. Contact the club's national outings office at 85 Second St., 2nd Floor, San Francisco, CA 94105-3441 (www.sierraclub.org; ✆ **415/977-5500**).

The Florida chapter of the **Nature Conservancy** has protected 578,000 acres of natural lands in Florida and presently owns and manages 36 preserves. For a small fee, you can join one of its field trips or work parties that take place periodically throughout the year; fees vary from year to year and event to event, so call for more information. Participants get a chance to learn about and even participate in the preservation of the ecosystem. For details on all the preserves and adventures, contact the Nature Conservancy, Florida Chapter, 222 S. Westmonte Dr., Ste. 300, Altamonte Springs, FL 32714 (www.nature.org; ✆ **407/682-3664;** fax 407/682-3077).

A nonprofit organization dedicated to environmental research, the **Earthwatch Institute,** 3 Clocktower Place, Ste. 100 (P.O. Box 75), Maynard, MA 01754 (www. earthwatch.org; ✆ **800/776-0188** or 978/461-0081), has excursions to survey dolphins and manatees around Sarasota and to monitor the well-being of the whooping cranes raised in captivity and released in the wilds of Central Florida.

Another research group, the **Oceanic Society,** Fort Mason Center, Building E, San Francisco, CA 94123 (www.oceanic-society.org; ✆ **800/326-7491** or 415/441-1106; fax 415/474-3395), also has Florida trips among its expeditions, including manatee monitoring in the Crystal River area, north of Tampa.

FISHING   In addition to the amberjack, bonito, grouper, mackerel, mahimahi, marlin, pompano, redfish, sailfish, snapper, snook, tarpon, tuna, and wahoo running offshore and in inlets, Florida has countless miles of rivers and streams, plus about 30,000 lakes and springs stocked with more than 100 species of freshwater fish. Indeed, Floridians seem to fish everywhere: off canal banks and old bridges, from fishing piers and fishing fleets. You'll even see them standing alongside the Tamiami Trail (U.S. 41) that cuts across the Everglades—one eye on their line, the other watching for alligators.

Anglers 16 and older need a license for any kind of saltwater or freshwater fishing, including lobstering and spearfishing. Licenses are sold at bait-and-tackle shops around the state and online at www.fl.wildlifelicense.com/start.php.

The **Florida Department of Environmental Protection,** 3900 Commonwealth Blvd., Tallahassee, FL 32399-3000 (www.dep.state.fl.us; ✆ **850/245-2118**), publishes the annual *Fishing Lines,* a free magazine with a wealth of information about fishing in Florida, including regulations and licensing requirements. It also distributes free brochures with annual freshwater and saltwater limits. And the Florida Sports Foundation (see the introduction to this section, above) publishes *Florida Fishing & Boating,* another treasure trove of information.

GOLF   Florida is the unofficial golf capital of the United States. One thing is for certain: Florida has more golf courses than any other state—more than 1,150 at last count, and growing. I picked the best for chapter 1, but suffice it to say that you can tee off almost anywhere, anytime there's daylight. It's a rare town in Florida that doesn't have a municipal golf course—even Key West has 18 great holes.

Greens fees are usually much lower at the municipal courses than at privately owned clubs. Whether public or private, greens fees tend to vary greatly, depending on the time of year. You could pay $150 or more at a private course during the high season, but less than half that when the tourists are gone. The fee structures vary so much that it's best to call ahead and ask, and always reserve a tee time as far in advance as possible.

You can learn the game or hone your strokes at one of several excellent golf schools in South Florida, including **Jimmy Ballard's** school at the Ocean Reef Club on Key Largo or at the **PGA National Resort & Spa** in Palm Beach Gardens, where they live, breathe, and eat golf.

You can get information about most Florida courses, including current greens fees, and reserve tee times through **Tee Times USA,** P.O. Box 641, Flagler Beach, FL

32136 (www.teetimesusa.com; ✆ **888/GOLF-FLO** [465-3356] or 386/439-0001), which publishes a vacation guide with many stay-and-play golf packages.

Florida Golf, published by the Florida Sports Foundation (see the introduction to this section, above), lists every course in Florida. It's the state's official golf guide and is available from Visit Florida (www.visitflorida.com).

Golfer's Guide magazine publishes monthly editions covering most of Florida. It is available free at local visitor centers and hotel lobbies, or you can contact the magazine at 2 Park Lane, Ste. E, Hilton Head Island, SC 29928 (www.golfersguide.com; ✆ **800/864-6101** or 843/842-7878; fax 843/842-5743).

You can also get more information from the **Professional Golfers' Association (PGA),** 400 Ave. of the Champions, Palm Beach Gardens, FL 33418 (www.pga.com; ✆ **800/633-9150**); or from the **Ladies Professional Golf Association (LPGA),** 100 International Golf Dr., Daytona Beach, FL 32124 (www.lpga.com; ✆ **904/254-6200**).

More than 700 courses are profiled in *Florida Golf Guide,* by Jimmy Shacky (Open Roads Publishing), available at bookstores for $20.

SCUBA DIVING & SNORKELING   Divers love the Keys, where you can see magnificent formations of tree-size elk-horn coral and giant brain coral, as well as colorful sea fans and dozens of other varieties, sharing space with 300 or more species of rainbow-hued fish. Reef diving is good all the way from Key Largo to Key West, with plenty of tour operators, outfitters, and dive shops along the way. Particularly worthy are **John Pennekamp Coral Reef State Park** in Key Largo, and **Looe Key National Marine Sanctuary** off Big Pine Key. *Skin Diver* magazine picked Looe Key as the number-one dive spot in North America. Also, the clearest waters in which to view some of the 4,000 sunken ships along Florida's coast are in the Middle Keys and the waters between Key West and the Dry Tortugas. Snorkeling in the Keys is particularly fine between Islamorada and Marathon. If you want to keep up with what's going on statewide, you can subscribe to the monthly magazine *Florida Scuba News* (www.scubanews.com; ✆ **904/783-1610**). You might also want to pick up a specialized guidebook. Some good ones include *Coral Reefs of Florida,* by Gilbert L. Voss (Pineapple Press; www.pineapplepress.com); and *The Diver's Guide to Florida and the Florida Keys,* by Jim Stachowicz (Windward Publishing).

TENNIS   Year-round sunshine makes Florida great for tennis. There are some 7,700 places to play throughout the state, from municipal courts to exclusive resorts. Some municipal facilities are equal in quality to expensive resorts—except they're free, or close to it. Some retired professionals even have their own tennis centers, including Chris Evert in Boca Raton.

The three hard courts and seven clay courts at the **Crandon Tennis Association,** 6702 Crandon Blvd. (✆ **305/365-2300**), get crowded on weekends because they're some of Miami's most beautiful. You'll play on the same courts as Lendl, Graf, Evert, McEnroe, Roddick, Nadal, Federer, and other greats; this is the venue for one of the world's biggest annual tennis events, the Sony Ericsson Open. There's a pleasant, if limited, pro shop, plus many good pros. Only four courts are lighted at night, but if you reserve at least 48 hours in advance, you can usually take your pick. Hard-court fees are $4 per person per hour during the day, or $6 per person per hour at night. Clay court fees are $7 per person per hour during daytime only. Grass courts are $11 per person per hour during daytime only. The courts are open daily from 8am to 9pm.

Famous as the spot where Chris Evert got in her early serves, the **Jimmy Evert Tennis Center,** 701 NE 12th Ave. (off Sunrise Blvd.), Fort Lauderdale

(📞 **954/828-5378**), has 18 clay and 3 hard courts (15 lighted). Her coach and father, James Evert, still teaches young players here, though he is very picky about whom he'll accept. Nonresidents of Fort Lauderdale pay $9 an hour per person before 5pm and $11 an hour per person after 5pm.

2 SOUTH FLORIDA WILDLIFE

In addition to the usual suspects—the alligator and the crocodile—the Sunshine State is home to a growing list of **endangered species,** including wild panthers, bobcats, and black bears. In fact, a total of 98 species of mammals call Florida home, among them armadillos, hogs, shrews, rabbits, possums, coyote, fox, lemurs, monkeys, deer, apes, and bats. Yes, bats. In fact, the Mexican free-tailed bat, the evening bat, and the big brown bat are common sightings everywhere in the state except the Keys and major metropolitan areas. Much cuter than bats are deer, the only native in the state being the **white-tailed deer,** which happens to be the major prey of the Florida panther. A smaller subspecies of these are **Key deer,** which live only in the Keys and are few and far between—only around 800 or so are in existence.

And contrary to popular belief, the "snowbird" is not the official fowl of Florida, a state with hundreds of species of land birds and water birds from vultures, eagles, and ospreys to owls, woodpeckers, pelicans, herons, ducks, loons, and anhingas.

Marine mammals, however, are the true stars of the state, with the **manatee** at the top of the endangered list. According to experts, the highest count of manatee in the state at one time was in 2001 with 3,276. As for Flipper, the most common dolphin in the state is the bottlenose dolphin, while the most frequent orca known to the state is the Atlantic northern white whale. Bottlenose dolphins are not endangered and have a stable future thanks to their adaptability. Climate change, however, is an inevitable factor many species are facing rapidly with little time to adapt. And while some animal activists protest that keeping dolphins in captivity for tourism is cruel, in some cases, the dolphin swims are performed in the ocean with wild dolphins, while other programs are conducted in aquarium environments. Those programs which are neither are what come under fire from the activists.

But back to that alligator. No thanks to global warming, the American alligators are most affected by damage to their habitats. But global warming isn't the only reason the alligator is endangered: Increased levels of dioxins found in the bodies of water are also a key ingredient. Some would also say the alligator is also newly threatened by the recent Burmese python invasion that's straight out of a horror flick. While the python situation is out of control due to irresponsible pet owners who discard them in the Everglades when they become unmanageable, it's not a major factor in the alligator's status as an endangered species.

In December 2009, Congress allotted an additional $15 million to the federal State and Tribal Wildlife Grant program to help bring wildlife action plans into alignment with climate change. For a list of opportunities, sites, and outfitters and guides for wildlife viewing throughout the state, visit http://myfwc.com/viewing.

SUGGESTED SOUTH FLORIDA ITINERARIES

3

South Florida isn't just Miami. The Keys, the Everglades, the Gold Coast, and Southwest Florida offer beautiful beaches, natural wonders, and a respite from the bustle and crowds of Miami. Set your sights on what you want to do and see the most, and then simply unwind.

The range of possible itineraries is endless; what I've suggested below is a very full program covering South Florida over a **2-week period.** If possible, you should extend your time—2 weeks is not really enough time if you plan to actually explore the Sunshine State, but if you plan to veg out on a beach, then it's plenty of time—or cut out some of the destinations suggested. You can always tack on one itinerary to the next. We've done our best to keep it geographically viable and logical. We highly recommend that you at least include a stop at one of Florida's natural wonders, be it the beaches, the Everglades, or the Keys.

Important: Should limited time force you to include only the most obvious stops in your itinerary, you will invariably make contact with only those who depend on you to make a living, which regrettably could leave you with a frustrated sense that Florida is one big, long tourist trap. This is why it is so important to *get off the beaten tourist track*—to experience the wacky, the kitschy, the stunning, the baffling, and the fascinating people, places, and things that make Florida an incredible destination.

SOUTH FLORIDA HIGHLIGHTS

Whether you're a beach bum, a club hopper, a nature lover, or a people-watcher—there's something for everyone in South Florida. This tour provides you with a local's-eye view of some of the best diversions So Flo is known for. Feel free to mix and match stops from this itinerary to create your own perfect So Flo experience.

Days 1 & 2: Arrive in Key West ★★★

After arriving in the so-called Conch Republic, or Margaritaville if you will, plan to spend at most a day or two here. A full day on the 4×2-mile island is plenty for exploring, but if you're into doing the

Duval Bar Crawl, you may want to leave yourself with a day to recover from that inevitable hangover. Focus most of your sightseeing energy on Old Town, where you'll see stunning, restored Victorian-style homes; lush, tropical greenery; and the old Bahama Village. Make sure not to miss the sunset celebration at Mallory Square and, if possible, do dinner at **Blue Heaven** (p. 275) in the Bahama Village. Then hit the Duval Street bars if you're so inclined. The next day, either spend the day relaxing at your hotel pool or explore the historic seaport and all its shops and Key West kitsch.

Day 3: Miami: Coral Gables, Little Havana & South Beach ★★★

Take the 3-hour drive on the Overseas Highway to **Miami**—one of the most scenic drives you'll ever take, albeit sometimes a boring one. If you've seen it before, just fly. Make a pit stop in Coral Gables, where you can either get a bite to eat on **Miracle Mile** or cool off in the **Venetian Pool** (p. 67). If you like what you see, check into the historic **Biltmore Hotel** (p. 207). If not, make sure to at least see the hotel and then continue on to SW Eighth Street, otherwise known as **Calle Ocho,** the heart of Little Havana. Either take an organized walking tour or go it on your own. A tour is recommended for those who are interested in the history of the neighborhood. If not, peruse the cigar stores, the old men playing dominoes in Domino Park, and buy an old Cuban phone book at Little Havana to Go. Grab a Cuban coffee at **Versailles** (p. 125) and then head north to South Beach and watch the cruise ships leave from **Smith & Wollensky** (p. 92). Spend the night in Miami.

Day 4: South Beach ★★★

Wake up early and catch the sunrise on the beach. Have breakfast at the **Front Porch Cafe** (p. 101). Stake your claim on the sand and spend the morning on the beach, or check out the original Miami supermodel, the Art Deco District, via a walking tour. Hit **Lincoln Road** for lunch. Try **David's Cafe II** (p. 100) for a delicious, inexpensive Cuban feast. Shop along Lincoln and Collins avenues before having a cocktail at the **Rose Bar at the Delano Hotel** (p. 160) or, if they're not letting regular folk in, head to **The Living Room** at the **W South Beach** (p. 186) for a gourmet cocktail. Walk that drink off out back on the paved path along the beach and stop at the delightfully deco **Raleigh Hotel** (p. 183) for an old-fashioned cocktail or freshly muddled mojito. Return to your own hotel for a disco nap; wake up around 9pm. Have dinner at **Prime One Twelve** (p. 92) if you can score a reservation; if not, try the equally sublime yet lower-key **Red, the Steakhouse** (p. 92) around the corner. Then hit the clubs: **Wall** (p. 165), **Mansion** (p. 164), **Cameo** (p. 164), and **SET** (p. 165). If you're still up for the boogie, hop in a cab and head to **LIV** (p. 164) at the **Fontainebleau.** Grab a late night snack at **La Sandwicherie** (p. 101) or the **11th St. Diner** (p. 100) and then crash at your hotel.

Day 5: From South Beach to Fort Lauderdale ★★

Have breakfast and watch the club kids coming home from the night before at the **Big Pink** (p. 96). Get in the car and take A1A north—the scenic route. Hit the Hollywood Beach Broadwalk, our version of Atlantic City without the casinos. If you're hungry for lunch, have the world's best burger at **Le Tub** (p. 309). Continue along A1A until you reach the famous Fort Lauderdale strip. Take a

South Florida Highlights

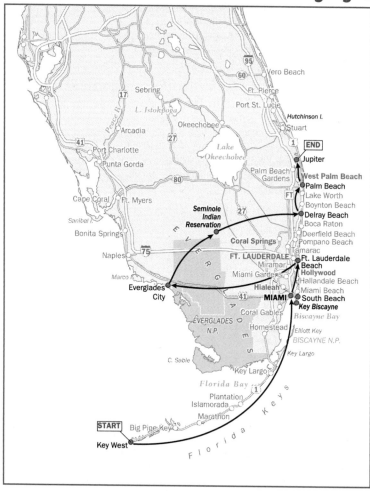

break at the world-famous **Elbo Room** and watch the action on the beach, or consider cocktails at **Beach Place** where spectacular views of the ocean make it okay to go to a chain restaurant on vacation. Spend the night at the **Riverside Hotel** (p. 313) on Las Olas Boulevard or, for a trendier stay and scene, the **W Fort Lauderdale** (p. 312).

Day 6: Sand, Seminoles & Santana ★★

Hit the famous Fort Lauderdale Beach, where Frankie and Annette used to play beach blanket bingo. Then take a bit of a diversion and head west to the **Seminole Hard Rock Hotel & Casino** (p. 315), where you may catch a concert by a Billboard-charting artist or even Jerry Seinfeld; hit the jackpot on one of the hundreds of slot machines (the hotel claims it pays out $12.9 million daily!); try your hand at blackjack and poker; or relax by the pool which is almost as nice, if not nicer, than the one at the Hard Rock Hotel in Vegas. Also check out the **Seminole Okalee Indian Village and Museum,** at the Seminole Hard Rock Hotel & Casino, 5716 Seminole Way, Hollywood (www.semtribe.com; ✆ **954/797-5551**), before heading over and out to spot signs of real wildlife in the Everglades.

Days 7 & 8: Seminole Indian Reservation & Everglades National Park ★★★

Travel 45 minutes west on I-75 to the Seminole Indian Reservation, which encompasses over 69,000 acres of the Everglades' Big Cypress Swamp. Hop on a swamp buggy at the **Billie Swamp Safari** (p. 299) to see hogs, bison, 'gators, and deer. Continue west to Everglades City, check into the **Ivey House B&B** (p. 227), and ask owners Sandee and David if they can hook you up with a special insiders' tour of the 'Glades.

Days 9 & 10: The Palm Beaches ★★

Skip Boca Raton unless you feel like hitting the Town Center mall and head directly to Delray Beach, where its Atlantic Avenue is full of stores, restaurants, bars, and clubs. Check into the **Sundy House** (p. 327) and peruse the hotel's **Taru Gardens.** The next day, do not miss the **Morikami Museum** (p. 320) and Japanese Gardens before moving on to West Palm Beach, where you should check into the **Hotel Biba** (p. 343) and do a little antique shopping in downtown West Palm. At night, check out the clubs and restaurants in downtown West Palm, on Clematis Street. Make sure to have a beer and enjoy the view at **E.R. Bradley's Saloon** (p. 337).

Day 11: From Mar-A-Lago to the Moon— Well, Jupiter, at Least ★★

Spend the morning driving around Palm Beach proper, making sure to stop and catch a glimpse of Donald Trump's palatial **Mar-A-Lago** (p. 331). Stop by **Worth Avenue** to see the ladies with little dogs who lunch and shop. It's the Rodeo Drive of South Florida, truly, and you can't miss the people-watching there. For an actual glimpse inside a Palm Beach manse, go to the **Flagler Museum** (p. 330), where you can explore Whitehall, Standard Oil tycoon Henry Flagler's wedding present to his third wife. Go back to reality and head toward Jupiter, the home of Burt Reynolds. Check into the **Ritz-Carlton Palm Beach** (p. 341).

BEACHY KEEN SOUTH FLORIDA

South Florida's beaches have been more photographed—we think—than Paris Hilton. In addition to the sand and sparkling waters of the Atlantic, the beaches have various personalities, from laid-back and remote to year-round partying. It may be fun to get a taste of all of these, if not for an hour or two at a time.

Day 1: Arrive in Islamorada ★★★

Check into the **Cheeca Lodge and Spa** (p. 251) and take in the panoramic ocean views. Park yourself on a chair and enjoy one of the Florida Keys'

best—and only—private beaches. Waste no time making a dinner reservation for an outside table on the upstairs verandah at **Pierre's** (p. 246), where you must, *must* try the Florida Keys Hogfish Meuniere. After dinner, park yourself on the beach at the **Morada Bay Café** and listen to some live music while sipping a piña colada.

Day 2: Bahia Honda State Park ★★★

Just an hour south of Islamorada is one of South Florida's most resplendent beaches. Spend the day on the 524-acre park and lose yourself in the mangroves, beach dunes, and tropical hammocks. Not in the mood to spend all day in the park? Go be one with nature and check out the **National Key Deer Refuge**

(p. 257), where you'll catch a glimpse of the most famous residents of the Lower Keys, or go snorkeling at the **Looe Key National Marine Sanctuary** (p. 259), where you'll see over 150 varieties of coral and magnificent tropical fish. Head back to Cheeca and have dinner at the **Atlantic's Edge** (p. 246) for serious seafood and locally grown, organic produce, or the **Green Turtle Inn** (p. 247), where authentic, gourmet Florida Keys cooking comes with a serious sense of humor.

Day 3: To Key Biscayne ★★

Take the scenic, sleepy, and often slow-moving Overseas Highway north to Key Biscayne, make a fish-dip stop at rustic **Alabama Jack's** (p. 236), and check into the **Ritz-Carlton Key Biscayne, Miami** (p. 202). On this, the southern-most barrier island on the Atlantic coast, you will be able to beach hop until the sun goes down. For the party people, **Crandon Park Beach** is the place to be, with 2 miles of beach and lots of salsa emanating from various sunbath-ers' boom boxes. To counter that bass, check out the park's new Family Amuse-ment Center, where a 1940s carousel spins to the tune of old-school organ music. Grab some much-needed peace and quiet at **Bill Baggs Cape Florida State Park** (p. 72), where you will forget you're in Miami, thanks to the miles of nature trails and completely unfettered beach. Do lunch at the park's charm-ing **Lighthouse Cafe** (p. 72) before heading over to Virginia Key, the place where *Flipper* was filmed and Old Florida cracker-style houses serve as a back-drop to a beachfront bacchanal.

Days 4 & 5: South Beach/Miami Beach ★★★

Going to "the beach" takes on a totally different meaning when you're in South Beach. Not only does it mean sunbathing on **Lummus Park Beach** (p. 54), also known as South Beach, with a cornucopia of half-naked beautiful people, but it also means enjoying the surrounding sights, sounds, and tastes of the area's bars, restaurants, shops, hotels, and Art Deco relics. There's a plethora of places to stay, whether you're on a budget or are willing to splurge; and best of all, the beach is free and a great place to crash and watch the sun set after spending the night out in the clubs!

Days 6 & 7: Swanky & Annette—also known as Fort Lauderdale Beach ★★★

Your dad may have spent Spring Break here with his frat buddies when the Beatles were just a random group of country bumpkins from Liverpool, but if he saw it now, he'd be completely surprised. Sure, the beach is beautiful, clean, and visible from A1A, but the surrounding area—the infamous Fort Lauderdale Strip—has matured into a sophisticated cafe society with outdoor eateries, bars, and more. If you must enter a beer-drinking contest, however, we're sure you'll find one nearby. Don't miss a cruise through the Venice of America, a scenic, informative, and convenient way to make your way from one end of the strip to another. See chapter 12.

SOUTH FLORIDA, FAMILY STYLE

Despite a thriving nightlife and sometimes R-rated (or worse) sensibility—and dress code (or lack thereof)—South Florida is definitely a kid-friendly destination. While we don't recommend you taking the little ones to South Beach, there are tons of other places that are family-friendly and won't have the kids screaming that they wish they were at Disney World.

Days 1 & 2: Key Biscayne ★★★

The **Ritz-Carlton Key Biscayne, Miami** (p. 202) has fabulous children's programs, not to mention pretty cool diversions for adults, too. Head to the **Miami Seaquarium** (p. 64), where the kids can swim with the dolphins, and then spend the rest of the day at the **Marjory Stoneman Douglas Biscayne Nature Center** (p. 65), where the entire family can explore an ancient fossil

HOLLYWOOD SOUTH—celebrities'
SOUTH BEACH (& BEYOND)

It's not that ironic that the French Riviera is now billing itself as a European South Beach. Between all the jet-setters, celebrities, rock stars, and magazine stories on the place, it's about time! Some people come to South Florida just for a taste of this fabulous life. This is not an itinerary per se, but the following tips will help you plan a busy social schedule so you don't miss out on a Paris or Diddy sighting.

Haute Hotels If you're looking for celebrities on South Beach, you'll end up spying most of them by the end of your trip. We suggest you do breakfast at Bianca at the Delano, where you may catch a glimpse of a Jonas brother sunbathing by the wading pool. Linger as long as you are able to before heading next door to the Raleigh, where you may find *Vogue* editor Anna Wintour hiding behind her sunglasses and sipping an iced tea at the pool. Grab some lunch if you're hungry or wait until you go next door to the Shore Club, where Nobu acts as the hotel's resident star magnet, a place where Britney Spears always stops when in town. Hit Lincoln Road and see if you can spot J-Lo. If you

don't, she's probably at the Bal Harbour Shops, so you may want to go there. For early evening cocktails, head to the Setai, where Jay Z, Beyoncé, Bono, and Lenny Kravitz have all partied, eaten, and slept. Next door at the W South Beach, young Hollywood rules, and you may be downing a beer next to the 'tween star from the *Twilight* series. For a mature caliber of celebrity, head to Mr Chow, where the A-listers dine on exorbitant Chinese food. For a little *Gossip Girl* with your sunset cocktail, the Mondrian on South Beach's bayside is command central for celebrity-studded cocktail chatter. For reality-star sightings, the Perry South Beach and its STK Miami and rooftop pool are the places to check. Hit the Ritz-Carlton South Beach for a nightcap, where some of the *Desperate Housewives* have stayed. Off of South Beach, you'll probably spot the likes of Miley Cyrus, Lady Gaga, Tom Cruise, J-Lo, and Janet Jackson, either at the Fontainebleau, the Viceroy on Brickell, the Mandarin Oriental on Brickell Key, the Four Seasons Miami, and, on Key Biscayne, the Ritz-Carlton Key

tidal pool. If there's time left, check out the **Bill Baggs Cape Florida State Park** (p. 72) and rent a hydrobike, or check out the brand-new **Crandon Park Family Amusement Center** (p. 64).

Days 3 & 4: Coral Gables ★★★ & South Miami ★★

Get an early start and head south to Homestead's legendary **Coral Castle** (p. 69). After the kids tire of seeing this wacky attraction, grab lunch at the family-friendly, family-run barbecue mainstay, **Shiver's BBQ** (p. 132). On your way to Coral Gables, make a stop at **Zoo Miami** (p. 70) or **Monkey Jungle** (p. 70), depending on your preference in animals, and then clean off that stinky animal scent with a splash in Coral Gables's resplendent, refreshing **Venetian Pool** (p. 67). If you're up for it, check out **Vizcaya Museum and Gardens** (p. 69) and/or the **Miami Science Museum** (p. 68). After working up an appetite, take the kids for a rockin' dinner at Burger & Beer Joint, where everyone will marvel at the 10-pound Motherburger!

Biscayne. For complete coverage of Miami hotels, see chapter 9.

Stars & Bars On Monday night, clubs are usually at rest, so hit the hotel bars at the W South Beach, the Mondrian, Delano, Shore Club, and Setai. Tuesday night, head to the Shelborne Hotel, where aging rockers try to blend in (or buy drinks for) the pretty young things. On Wednesdays, head to Mokai for the cheekily titled Relapse Wednesdays, featuring the hottest hump-day dance music and almost guaranteed appearances by the likes of Lil Wayne, Michael Jordan, and more. Thursday night, check out Skybar and Set, where you're likely to run into everyone from Mary J. Blige and her famous friends to Simon Cowell, Randy Jackson, and Ryan Seacrest. On Friday, head to Cameo, where Matt Damon actually met his wife, Luciana, who was a cocktail waitress there. On Saturday it's all about LIV, where any celeb who's in town will stop by—if not for the evening, at least for one drink. Mansion is also hot on Saturday, but even hotter is WALL, the club at the W South Beach, where a keen eye may spot an A-lister lounging in or dancing on a banquette. Sunday afternoon is the day of pool parties—Shore Club, Viceroy, Shelborne, Dream Hotel, and Mondrian all have one (call and check that they're still on before you go)—where you can lounge by the pool along with the likes of chart-topping rappers to starlets. On any given night you may run into Bono or Lou Reed at Ted's Hideaway or Mac's Club Deuce, two of Miami's beloved dive bars. For details on Miami's nightlife, see chapter 8.

Eating It Up (Stars Eat, Too) Among the places you'll find celebs stuffing their faces: Asia de Cuba; Casa Tua; Mr Chow; Philippe; Macaluso's; Nobu; The Restaurant at the Setai; The Dutch; Yardbird Southern Table & Bar; Bianca; Sugarcane Raw Bar Grill; Meat Market; Barton G. The Restaurant; Prime One Twelve; Prime Italian; Azul; Michael's Genuine Food & Drink; db Bistro Moderne; Shake Shack; Altamare; Scarpetta; Hakkasan; Burger & Beer Joint; News Cafe; China Grill; and, we kid you not, La Sandwicherie, the late-night sandwich bar across the street from Club Deuce. For more on Miami's dining scene, see chapter 6.

Days 5 & 6: Miami–Port St. Lucie ★★★

Before leaving Miami, make sure to stop at the **Miami Children's Museum** (p. 60), where the kids can spend a few hours channeling their inner grown-up in a bona fide TV and recording studio. If they'd rather see animal antics, head across the causeway to **Jungle Island** (p. 59). Grab a TV dinner at the G-rated **Big Pink** (p. 96) on South Beach or a burger and a frozen custard at **Shake Shack** (p. 102), and then hit the road to Vero Beach and check into the **Club-Med Sandpiper** on the St. Lucie River, where there are four different children's clubs for ages 4 months all the way up to 13 years. En route to Vero, you may want to take the kids to West Palm Beach's whimsical **Playmobil Fun-Park** (p. 332) or on a ride through **Lion Country Safari** (p. 331), then grab lunch at **Tom's Place for Ribs** (p. 324).

Day 7: Vero Beach ★★★

As if Club Med doesn't have enough for the family to do—or not do—you may want to take the kids out to **Disney's Vero Beach Resort,** which is situated on 71 acres of beach and features that Disney vibe the kids may be in the mood for at this point!

GETTING TO KNOW MIAMI

A week in Miami is not unlike watching an unbelievable reality show, only it's *actually* real. Miami: the city where, despite the abysmal economy, Jay-Z tipped a Miami Beach nightclub waitress $50,000; where Justin Bieber cruised down bustling Ocean Drive at the wheel of a Rolls-Royce; where basketball superstar LeBron James's mother was arrested after an altercation with a Fontainbleau valet parking attendant; and where the paparazzi camps out for days, hoping to catch a glimpse of something or someone fabulous. But that's just a small sample of the surreal, Fellini-esque world that exists way down here at the bottom of the U.S. map. Nothing in Miami is ever what it seems.

4

Things to Do   Miami has an endless number of sporting, cultural, and recreational activities to keep you entertained. From watersports and sunbathing on **Miami Beach** to alligators in the **Everglades,** Miami lives outdoors. Play golf at **Crandon Park,** watch manatees on **Coconut Grove**'s waterfront, or simply soak up the sun. On rainy days, you can school yourself in Dutch and Italian tapestries at the upstanding **Bass Museum of Art** or learn about the city's humble beginnings with a walking tour led by historian **Paul George.**

Shopping   Miami provides an eclectic shopping experience, from designer boutiques at **Bal Harbour** and the **Village of Merrick Park** to mainstream chains at **Bayside Marketplace.** Miami likes its megamalls, and one of the best is **Aventura Mall.** Look for new art and furniture in the **Design District,** or take home a little bit of Cuba with a hand-stitched *guayabera* shirt from **Little Havana.** Pick up incense and Indian imports from **Española Way**'s Mediterranean storefronts, which close to traffic on Sunday afternoons.

Restaurants & Dining   Despite the economic slowdown, throngs of people still flock to über-high-end restaurants like **Mr Chow** and **STK Miami.** Downtown and Midtown Miami host some new dining hot spots, like **Zuma** and **Sugarcane Raw Bar Grill.** Also try Cuban along **Calle Ocho,** locally sourced foodie fare in the **Design District,** and casual comfort food at the Grove. Dine at an open-air cafe in **Coral Gables** while enjoying stone crab claws and a mojito, the city's unofficial yet signature drink.

Nightlife & Entertainment   South Beach is Miami's uncontested nocturnal nucleus, but **Midtown/Wynwood, Brickell, South Miami,** and **Little Havana** are increasingly providing fun alternatives without the ludicrous cover charges and "fashionably late" hours (the action in South Beach starts after 11pm). Follow Latin grooves to tiny **Española Way.** Try some creative cocktails on **Lincoln Road** and sip martinis in the swanky bars in the **Design District.** Watch live jazz and flamenco at the **Fillmore Miami Beach at the Jackie Gleason Theater** or listen to a star DJ spin at the **New World Center's Soundscape.**

THE best MIAMI EXPERIENCES

○ **Picking Strawberries in Homestead:** Long before Miami became all about local, sustainable and organic, Homestead was rocking all three categories, and still is thanks to its roadside farm stands and fields aplenty of strawberries, tomatoes, and all sorts of exotic fruit. There's nothing like going down there and picking your own.

○ **Picnicking at the New World Center:** There's something singularly sensational about picnicking at Miami Beach's sonically stunning, visually arresting, culturally unparalleled **New World Center** (p. 156)—especially when, like most of the time, the entertainment is free.

○ **Jet-Skiing Among the Rich and Famous:** Yachts are a dime a dozen in Miami and they sure are pretty, but when it comes to being one with the water, the preferred transportation of choice for the biggest players in town—such as Enrique Iglesias, Rosie O'Donnell, or Justin Bieber—is the jet ski. It's easy, it's zippy, and you never know who you may be cruising past.

○ **Drinking Cuban Coffee in Little Havana:** Little Havana is Miami's most culturally rich neighborhood, where pre-Castro Cubans mix with everyone else in a frenzied fusion set to a Latin beat. You needn't speak the language to appreciate the energy.

○ **Learning to Salsa:** If the only salsa you're familiar with is the kind you put on your tacos, get over to **Bongos Cuban Café** (p. 146), the hottest salsa club north of Havana, where Miami's most talented salsa dancers will teach you how to move your two left feet in the right direction.

ORIENTATION

Miami is a fascinating city to explore, be it by foot, bike, scooter, boat, or car. Because of its larger-than-life persona, Miami may seem a lot bigger than it really is, and although the city comprises many different neighborhoods, it's really not that difficult to learn the lay of the land. Much like the bodies beautiful on Ocean Drive, the Magic City is a tidy package that's a little less than 2,000 square miles.

Arriving

Originally carved out of scrubland in 1928 by Pan American Airlines, **Miami International Airport (MIA)** has become 2nd in the United States for international passenger traffic and 10th in the world for total passengers. Despite the heavy traffic, the airport is quite user-friendly and not as much of a hassle as you'd think. You can change money or use your ATM card at Bank of America, located near the exit. Visitor information is available 24 hours a day at the

Words to Live By

I figure marriage is kind of like Miami; it's hot and stormy, and occasionally a little dangerous . . . but if it's really so awful, why is there still so much traffic?
—Sarah Jessica Parker's character, Gwen Marcus, in *Miami Rhapsody*

Miami International Airport Main Visitor Counter, Concourse E, second level (© **305/876-7000**). Information is also available at **www.miami-airport.com**. Because MIA is the busiest airport in South Florida, travelers may want to consider flying into the less crowded **Fort Lauderdale Hollywood International Airport (FLL;** © **954/359-1200**), which is closer to north Miami than MIA, or the **Palm Beach International Airport (PBI;** © **561/471-7420**), which is about 1½ hours from Miami.

GETTING INTO TOWN

Miami International Airport is about 6 miles west of downtown and about 10 miles from the beaches, so it's likely you can get from the plane to your hotel room in less than half an hour. Of course, if you're arriving from an international destination, it will take more time to go through Customs and Immigration.

BY CAR   All the major car-rental firms operate off-site branches reached via shuttles from the airline terminals. See the "Rentals" section, under "Getting Around," on p. 49, for a list of major rental companies in Miami. Signs at the airport's exit clearly point the way to various parts of the city, but the car-rental firm should also give you directions to your destination. If you're arriving late at night, you might want to take a taxi to your hotel and have the car delivered to you the next day.

BY TAXI   Taxis line up in front of a dispatcher's desk outside the airport's arrivals terminals. Most cabs are metered, though some have flat rates to popular destinations. The fare should be about $20 to Coral Gables, $25 to downtown, and $35 to South Beach, plus tip, which should be about 15% (add more for each bag the driver handles). Depending on traffic, the ride to Coral Gables or downtown takes about 15 to 20 minutes, and to South Beach, 20 to 25 minutes.

BY VAN OR LIMO   Group limousines (multipassenger vans) circle the arrivals area looking for fares. Destinations are posted on the front of each van, and a flat rate is charged for door-to-door service to the area marked.

   SuperShuttle (www.supershuttle.com; © **305/871-2000**) is one of the largest airport operators, charging between $10 and $50 per person for a ride within the county. Its vans operate 24 hours a day and accept American Express, MasterCard, and Visa. This is a cheaper alternative to a cab (if you are traveling alone or with one other person), but be prepared to be in the van for quite some time, as you may have to make several stops to drop passengers off before you reach your own destination. SuperShuttle also has begun service from Palm Beach International Airport to the surrounding communities. The door-to-door, shared-ride service operates from the airport to Stuart, Fort Pierce, Palm Beach, and Broward counties.

   Private limousine arrangements can be made in advance through your local travel agent. A one-way meet-and-greet service should cost about $50. Limo services include **Aventura Limousine** (© **800/944-9886**) and **Limo Miami** (© **305/742-5900**).

BY PUBLIC TRANSPORTATION   Public transportation in South Florida is a major hassle bordering on a nightmare. Painfully slow and unreliable, buses heading downtown leave the airport only once per hour (from the arrivals level), and connections are spotty, at best. It could take about 1½ hours to get to South Beach via public transportation. Journeys to downtown and Coral Gables, however, are more direct. The fare is $2, plus an additional 50¢ for a transfer. For those heading to South Beach from the airport, a new bus route, the Airport-Beach Flyer Route, provides direct express service from MIA to Miami Beach and costs $2.35. With only one minor stop en route, the trip to the beach takes about a half-hour. Not bad.

Visitor Information

The most up-to-date information is provided by the **Greater Miami Convention and Visitor's Bureau,** 701 Brickell Ave., Ste. 700, Miami, FL 33131 (© **800/933-8448** or 305/539-3000; fax 305/530-3113). Several chambers of commerce in Greater Miami will send out information on their particular neighborhoods.

If you arrive at the Miami International Airport, you can pick up visitor information at the airport's main visitor counter on the second floor of Concourse E. It's open 24 hours a day.

Always check local newspapers for special events during your visit. The city's only daily, the *Miami Herald,* is a good source for current-events listings, particularly the "Weekend" section in Friday's edition. Even better is the free weekly alternative paper *Miami New Times,* available in bright red boxes throughout the city.

Information on everything from dining to entertainment in Miami is available on the Internet at www.miami.citysearch.com, www.citysbest.aol.com/south-florida, www.miaminewtimes.com, www.miami.com, and www.miamiherald.com.

City Layout

Miami seems confusing at first, but quickly becomes easy to navigate. The small cluster of buildings that make up the downtown area is at the geographical heart of the city. In relation to downtown, the airport is northwest, the beaches are east, Coconut Grove is south, Coral Gables is west, and the rest of the city is north.

FINDING AN ADDRESS   Miami is divided into dozens of areas with official and unofficial boundaries. Street numbering in the city of Miami is fairly straightforward, but you must first be familiar with the numbering system. The mainland is divided into four sections (NE, NW, SE, and SW) by the intersection of Flagler Street and Miami Avenue. Flagler divides Miami from north to south, and Miami Avenue divides the city from east to west. It's helpful to remember that avenues generally run north-south, while streets go east-west. Street numbers (1st St., 2nd St., and so forth) start from here and increase as you go farther out from this intersection, as do numbers of avenues, places, courts, terraces, and lanes. Streets in Hialeah are the exceptions to this pattern; they are listed separately in map indexes.

Getting around the barrier islands that make up Miami Beach is easier than moving around the mainland. Street numbering starts with First Street, near Miami Beach's southern tip, and goes up to 192nd Street, in the northern part of Sunny Isles. As in the city of Miami, some streets in Miami Beach have numbers as well as names. When listed in this book, both name and number are given.

The numbered streets in Miami Beach are not the geographical equivalents of those on the mainland, but they are close. For example, the 79th Street Causeway runs into 71st Street on Miami Beach.

STREET MAPS   It's easy to get lost in sprawling Miami, so a reliable map is essential. The **Trakker Map of Miami,** available at most bookstores, is a four-color accordion map that encompasses all of Dade County. Some maps of Miami list streets according to area, so you'll have to know which part of the city you are looking for before the street can be found.

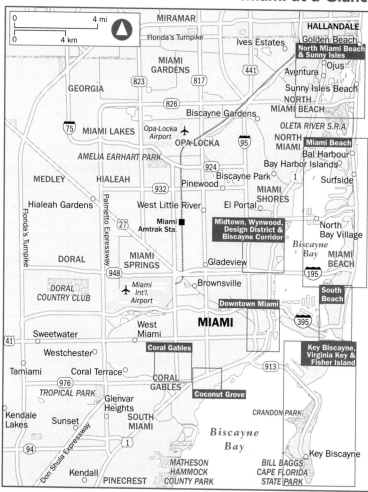

The Neighborhoods in Brief

South Beach—The Art Deco District
South Beach's 10 miles of beach are alive with a frenetic, circuslike atmosphere and are center stage for a motley crew of characters, from eccentric locals, seniors, snowbirds, and college students to gender-benders, celebrities, club kids, and curiosity seekers.

Bolstered by a Caribbean-chic cafe society and a sexually charged, tragically hip nightlife, people-watching on South Beach

(1st St.–23rd St.) is almost as good as a front-row seat at a Milan fashion show. But although the beautiful people do flock to South Beach, the models aren't the only sights worth drooling over. The thriving Art Deco District within South Beach has the largest concentration of Art Deco architecture in the world (in 1979, much of South Beach was listed in the National Register of Historic Places). The pastel-hued structures are supermodels in their own right—except *these* models improve with age.

Miami Beach   In the fabulous '50s, Miami Beach was America's true Riviera. The stomping ground of choice for the Rat Pack and notorious mobsters such as Al Capone, its huge self-contained resort hotels were vacations unto themselves, providing a full day's worth of meals, activities, and entertainment. Then in the 1960s and 1970s, people who fell in love with Miami began to buy apartments rather than rent hotel rooms. Tourism declined, and many area hotels fell into disrepair.

However, since the late 1980s and South Beach's renaissance, Miami Beach has experienced a tide of revitalization. Huge beach hotels, such as the renovated and Vegas-esque Fontainebleau and Eden Roc, are finding their niche with new international tourist markets and are attracting large convention crowds. New generations of Americans are quickly rediscovering the qualities that originally made Miami Beach so popular, and they are finding out that the sand and surf now come with a thriving international city—a technologically savvy city complete with free Wi-Fi with 95% coverage outside, which means on the sand, and 70% indoors up to the second floor of any building.

Before Miami Beach turns into Surfside, there's North Beach, where there are uncrowded beaches, some restaurants, and examples of Miami modernism architecture. For information on North Beach and its slow renaissance, go to www.gonorthbeach.com.

Surfside, Bal Harbour, and **Sunny Isles** make up the north part of the beach (island). Hotels, motels, restaurants, and beaches line Collins Avenue and, with some outstanding exceptions, the farther north one goes, the cheaper lodging becomes. Excellent prices, location, and facilities make Surfside and Sunny Isles attractive places to stay, although, despite a slow-going renaissance, they are still a little rough around the edges. Revitalization is in the works for these areas, and, while it's highly unlikely they will ever become as chic as South Beach, there is potential for this, especially as South Beach falls prey to the inevitable spoiler: commercialism. Keep in mind that beachfront properties are at a premium, so many of the area's moderately priced hotels have been converted to condominiums, leaving fewer and fewer affordable places to stay.

In exclusive and ritzy Bal Harbour, few hotels besides the swanky Regent and St. Regis remain amid the many beachfront condominium towers. Instead, fancy homes, tucked away on the bay, hide behind gated communities, and the Rodeo Drive of Miami (known as the Bal Harbour Shops) attracts shoppers who don't flinch at four-, five-, and six-figure price tags.

Note that **North Miami Beach,** a residential area near the Dade-Broward County line (north of 163rd St.; part of North Dade County), is a misnomer. It is actually northwest of Miami Beach, on the mainland, and has no beaches, though it does have some of Miami's better restaurants and shops. Located within North Miami Beach is the posh residential community of **Aventura,** best known for its high-priced condos, the Turnberry Isle Resort, and the Aventura Mall.

Note: South Beach, the historic Art Deco District, is treated as a separate neighborhood from Miami Beach.

Key Biscayne   Miami's forested and secluded Key Biscayne is technically a barrier island and is not part of the Florida Keys. This island is nothing like its southern neighbors. Located south of Miami Beach, off the shores of Coconut Grove, Key Biscayne is protected from the troubles of the mainland by the long Rickenbacker Causeway and its $1.50 toll.

Largely an exclusive residential community with million-dollar homes and sweeping water views, Key Biscayne also offers visitors great public beaches, a top (read: pricey) resort hotel, world-class tennis facilities, and a few decent restaurants. Hobie Beach, adjacent to the causeway, is the city's premier spot for windsurfing, sailboarding, and jet-skiing (see "Outdoor Activities," p. 74). On the island's southern tip, **Bill Baggs State Park** has great beaches, bike paths, and dense forests for picnicking and partying.

Downtown   Miami's downtown boasts one of the world's most beautiful cityscapes. Unfortunately, that's about all it offers—for now. During the day, a vibrant community of students, businesspeople, and merchants make their way through the bustling streets, where vendors sell fresh-cut pineapples and mangoes while young consumers on shopping sprees lug bags and boxes. However, at night, downtown is mostly desolate (except for NE 11th St., where there is a burgeoning nightlife scene) and not a place where you'd want to get lost. The downtown area does have a mall (Bayside Marketplace, where many cruise passengers come to browse), some culture (Metro-Dade Cultural Center), and a few decent restaurants, as well as the sprawling American Airlines Arena (home to the Miami Heat). A slow-going downtown revitalization project in the works promises a cultural arts center, urban-chic dwellings and lofts, and an assortment of hip boutiques, eateries, and bars, all to bring downtown back to a life it never really had. The city has even rebranded the downtown area with a new ad campaign, intentionally misspelling it as DWNTN to inexplicably appeal to hipsters. We don't get it either. The **Downtown Miami Partnership** offers guided historic walking tours daily at 10:30am (© **305/379-7070**). For more information on downtown, go to **www.downtownmiami.com**.

Midtown/Wynwood What used to be called El Barrio is now one of Miami's hippest, still burgeoning areas. Just north of downtown and roughly divided by I-395 to the south, I-195 to the north, I-95 to the west, and Biscayne Boulevard to the east, Wynwood actually includes the Miami Design District, but has developed an identity of its own thanks to an exploding, albeit still very rough and gritty, arts scene made popular by cheap rents and major exposure during Art Basel Miami Beach. While there are still only a very small handful of bars and restaurants, Wynwood is an edgy area for creative types with loft and gallery spaces affordable and aplenty—for now. Also within Wynwood is Midtown Miami, a mall-like town-center complex of apartment buildings surrounded by shops—namely Target—and restaurants. Like its Wynwood neighbor, it's gritty and a work in progress favored by

young hipster types who aren't averse to living in transitional neighborhoods.

Design District With restaurants springing up between galleries and furniture stores galore, the Design District is, as locals say, the new South Beach, adding a touch of New York's SoHo to an area formerly known as downtown Miami's "Don't Go." The district, which is a hotbed for furniture-import companies, interior designers, architects, and more, has also become a player in Miami's ever-changing nightlife. Its bars, lounges, clubs, and restaurants—including one of Miami's best, Michael's Genuine Food & Drink (p. 119)—ranging from überchic and retro to progressive and indie, have helped the area become hipster central for South Beach expatriates and artsy bohemian types. In anticipation of its growing popularity, the district has also banded together to create an up-to-date website, **www.designmiami.com**, which includes a calendar of events, such as the internationally lauded Art Basel, which attracts the who's who of the art world. The district is loosely defined as the area bounded by NE 2nd Avenue, NE 5th Avenue East and West, and NW 36th Street to the south.

Biscayne Corridor From downtown, near Bayside, to the 70s (affectionately known as the Upper East Side), where trendy curio shops and upscale restaurants are slowly opening, Biscayne Boulevard is aspiring to reclaim itself as a safe thoroughfare where tourists can wine, dine, and shop. Once known for sketchy, dilapidated 1950s- and 1960s-era hotels that had fallen on hard times, this boulevard is getting a boost from residents fleeing the high prices of the beaches in search of affordable housing. They're renovating Biscayne block by block, trying to make this famous boulevard worthy of a Sunday drive.

Little Havana If you've never been to Cuba, just visit this small section of Miami and you'll come pretty close. The sounds, tastes, and rhythms are highly reminiscent of Cuba's capital city, and you don't have to speak a word of English to live an independent life here—even street signs are in Spanish and English.

Cuban coffee shops, tailor and furniture stores, and inexpensive restaurants line Calle Ocho (pronounced *Ka-yey O-choh*), SW 8th Street, the region's main thoroughfare. In Little Havana, salsa and merengue beats ring loudly from old record stores while old men in *guayaberas* (loose-fitting cotton short-sleeved shirts) smoke cigars over their daily game of dominoes.

Coral Gables "The City Beautiful," created by George Merrick in the early 1920s, is one of Miami's first planned developments. Houses here were built in a Mediterranean style along lush, tree-lined streets that open onto beautifully carved plazas, many with centerpiece fountains. The best architectural examples of the era have Spanish-style tiled roofs and are built from Miami oolite, native limestone commonly called "coral rock." The Gables's European-flaired shopping and commerce center is home to many thriving corporations. Coral Gables also has landmark hotels, great golfing, upscale shopping to rival Bal Harbour, and some of the city's best restaurants, headed by renowned chefs.

Coconut Grove An arty, hippie hangout in the psychedelic '60s, Coconut Grove once had residents who dressed in swirling tie-dyed garb. Nowadays, they prefer the uniform color schemes of Gap. Chain stores, theme restaurants, a megaplex, and bars galore make Coconut Grove a commercial success, but this gentrification has pushed most alternative types out. Ritzier types have now resurfaced here, thanks in part to the anti-boho Ritz-Carlton Coconut Grove (p. 209) and the Mayfair (p. 209), which is in its umpteenth resurgence as a boutique hotel. The intersection of Grand Avenue, Main Highway, and McFarlane Road pierces the area's heart. Right in the center of it all is CocoWalk, filled with boutiques, eateries, and bars. Sidewalks here are often crowded, especially at night, when University of Miami students come out to play.

Southern Miami–Dade County To locals, South Miami is both a specific area, southwest of Coral Gables, and a general region that encompasses all of southern Dade County, including Kendall, Perrine, Cutler Ridge, and Homestead. For the purposes of clarity, this book has grouped all these southern suburbs under the rubric "Southern Miami–Dade County." The area is heavily residential and packed with strip malls amid a few remaining plots of farmland. Tourists don't usually stay in these parts, unless they are on their way to the Everglades or the Keys. However, Southern Miami–Dade County contains many of the city's top attractions, meaning that you're likely to spend at least some of your time in Miami here.

GETTING AROUND

Officially, Miami–Dade County has opted for a "unified, multimodal transportation network," which basically means you can get around the city by train, bus, and taxi. However, in practice, the network doesn't work very well. Things have improved somewhat thanks to the $17-billion Peoples' Transportation Plan, which has offered a full range of transportation services at several community-based centers throughout the county, but unless you are going from downtown Miami to a not-too-distant spot, you are better off in a rental car or taxi.

With the exception of downtown Coconut Grove and South Beach, Miami is not a walker's city. Because it is so spread out, most attractions are too far apart to make walking between them feasible. In fact, most Miamians are so used to driving that they do so even when going just a few blocks.

By Public Transportation

BY RAIL Two rail lines, operated by the **Metro-Dade Transit Agency** (www.co.miami-dade.fl.us/transit; ☎ **305/770-3131** for information), run in concert with each other.

Metrorail, the city's modern high-speed commuter train, is a 21-mile elevated line that travels north-south, between downtown Miami and the southern suburbs. Locals like to refer to this semiuseless rail system as Metro*fail*. If you are staying in Coral Gables or Coconut Grove, you can park your car at a nearby station and ride the rails downtown. However, that's about it. There are plans to extend the system to service Miami International Airport, but until those tracks are built, these trains don't go most places tourists go, with the exception of Vizcaya (p. 69) in Coconut Grove. Metrorail operates daily from about 6am to midnight. The fare is $2.

Metromover, a 4½-mile elevated line, circles the downtown area and connects with Metrorail at the Government Center stop. Riding on rubber tires, the single-car train winds past many of the area's most important attractions and its shopping and business districts. You may not go very far on the Metromover, but you will get a beautiful perspective from the towering height of the suspended rails. System hours are daily from about 6am to midnight, and the ride is free.

BY BUS Miami's suburban layout is not conducive to getting around by bus. Lines operate and maps are available, but instead of getting to know the city, you'll find that relying on bus transportation will acquaint you only with how it feels to wait at bus stops. In short, a bus ride in Miami is grueling. You can get a bus map by mail, either from the Greater Miami Convention and Visitor's Bureau (see "Visitor Information," earlier in this chapter) or by writing the Metro-Dade Transit System, 3300 NW 32nd Ave., Miami, FL 33142. In Miami, call ✆ **305/770-3131** for public-transit information. The fare is $2. When on South Beach, however, consider the **South Beach Local,** a shuttle bus that runs every 15 to 20 minutes from First Street all the way to Collins Park at 21st Street and Park Avenue for just 25 cents a ride. Look for signs that say South Beach Local. Buses run every 12 minutes Monday through Saturday from 10am to 6pm, and every 20 minutes from 7:45 to 10am and from 6pm to 1am. On Sundays, the bus will come every 12 minutes from noon to 6pm, and every 20 minutes from 10am to noon and from 6pm to 1am. It makes several stops, but it's a lot cheaper than a cab.

By Car

Tales circulate about vacationers who have visited Miami without a car, but they are very few indeed. If you are counting on exploring the city, even to a modest degree, a car is essential. Miami's restaurants, hotels, and attractions are far from one another, so any other form of transportation is relatively impractical. You won't need a car, however, if you are spending your entire vacation at a resort, are traveling directly to the Port of Miami for a cruise, or are here for a short stay centered on one area of the city, such as South Beach, where everything is within walking distance and parking is a costly nightmare.

When driving across a causeway or through downtown, allow extra time to reach your destination because of frequent drawbridge openings. Some bridges open about every half-hour for large sailing vessels to make their way through the wide bays and canals that crisscross the city, stalling traffic for several minutes.

RENTALS It seems as though every car-rental company, big and small, has at least one office in Miami. Consequently, the city is one of the cheapest places in the world to rent a car. Many firms regularly advertise prices in the neighborhood of $150 per week for their economy cars. You should also check with your airline: There are often special discounts when you book a flight and reserve your rental car simultaneously. A minimum age, generally 25, is usually required of renters; some rental agencies have also set maximum ages! A national car-rental broker, **Car Rental Referral Service** (☎ 800/404-4482), can often find companies willing to rent to drivers between the ages of 21 and 24 and can also get discounts from major companies as well as some regional ones.

National car-rental companies, with toll-free numbers, include **Alamo** (www.alamo.com; ☎ 877/222-9075), **Avis** (www.avis.com; ☎ 800/331-1212), **Budget** (www.budget.com; ☎ 800/527-0700), **Dollar** (www.dollar.com; ☎ 800/800-4000), **Hertz** (www.hertz.com; ☎ 800/654-3131), **National** (www.nationalcar.com; ☎ 877/222-9058), and **Thrifty** (www.thrifty.com; ☎ 800/847-4389). One excellent company that has offices in every conceivable part of town and offers extremely competitive rates is **Enterprise** (www.enterprise.com; ☎ 800/261-7331).

Comparison shop before you make any decisions—car-rental prices can fluctuate more than airfares. Many car-rental companies also offer cellular phones or electronic map rentals. It might be wise to opt for these additional safety features (the phone will definitely come in handy if you get lost), although the cost can be exorbitant.

Finally, think about splurging on a convertible. Convertibles offer one of the best ways to see the beautiful surroundings, while getting a tan!

PARKING   Always keep plenty of quarters on hand to feed hungry meters, most of which have been removed in favor of those pesky parking payment stations where you feed a machine and get a printed receipt to display on your dash. Or, on Miami Beach, stop by the chamber of commerce at 1920 Meridian Ave. or any Publix grocery store to buy a magnetic **parking card** in denominations of $10, $20, or $25. Parking is usually plentiful (except on South Beach and Coconut Grove), but when it's not, be careful: Fines for illegal parking can be stiff, starting at $18 for an expired meter and going way up from there.

In addition to parking garages, valet services are commonplace and often used. Because parking is such a premium in bustling South Beach as well as in Coconut Grove, prices tend to be jacked up—especially at night and when there are special events (day or night). You can expect to pay an average of $5 to $15 for parking in these areas.

LOCAL DRIVING RULES   Florida law allows drivers to make a right turn on a red light after a complete stop, unless otherwise indicated. In addition, all passengers are required to wear seat belts, and children 3 and under must be securely fastened in government-approved car seats.

By Taxi

If you're not planning on traveling much within the city (and especially if you plan on spending your vacation within the confines of South Beach's Art Deco District), an occasional taxi is a good alternative to renting a car and dealing with the parking hassles that come with renting your own car. Taxi meters start at about $2.50 for the first quarter-mile and cost around $2.40 for each additional mile. You can blame the rate hikes on the gas crunch. There are standard flat-rate charges for frequently traveled routes—for example, Miami Beach's Convention Center to Coconut Grove will cost about $25. Many cabs have a fuel surcharge costing $1 extra per person. For specifics on rate increases and surcharges, go to www.taxifarefinder.com.

Major cab companies include **Yellow Cab** (☎ 305/444-4444) and, on Miami Beach, **Central** (☎ 305/532-5555).

By Bike

Miami is a biker's paradise, especially on Miami Beach, where the hard-packed sand and boardwalks make it an easy and scenic route. However, unless you are a former New York City bike messenger, you won't want to use a bicycle as your main means of transportation.

[FastFACTS] MIAMI

Area Code   The original area code for Miami and all of Dade County is 305. That is still the code for older phone numbers, but all phone numbers assigned since 1998 have the area code 786 (SUN). For all local calls, even if you're just calling across the street, you must dial the area code (305 or 786) first. Even though the Keys still share the Dade County area code of 305, calls to there from Miami are considered long distance and must be preceded by 1-305. (Within the Keys, simply dial the seven-digit number.) The area codes for Fort Lauderdale are 954 and 754; for Palm Beach, Boca Raton, Vero Beach, and Port St. Lucie, it's 561.

Business Hours   Banking hours vary, but most banks are open weekdays from 9am to 3pm. Several stay open until 5pm or so at least 1 day during the week, and most banks feature automated teller machines (ATMs) for 24-hour banking. Most stores are open daily from 10am to 6pm; however, there are many exceptions (noted in "Practical Matters: The Shopping Scene," in chapter 7). As far as business offices are concerned, Miami is generally a 9-to-5 town.

Dentists   If you're in absolute need of a dentist, go to www.1800dentist.com. Or call Dr. Edderai, who specializes in emergency dental work and features a 24/7 call dental service at (www.northmiami beachdentist.com; ✆ **305/798-7799**).

Doctors   In an emergency, call an ambulance by dialing ✆ **911** (a free call) from any phone. The Dade County Medical Association sponsors a **Physician Referral Service** (✆ **305/324-8717**), weekdays from 9am to 5pm.

Emergencies   To reach the police, an ambulance, or the fire department, dial ✆ **911** from any phone. No coins are needed. Emergency hot lines include **Crisis Intervention** (✆ **305/358-HELP** [4357] or 305/358-4357) and the **Poison Information Center** (✆ **800/222-1222**).

Internet Access   Internet access is available via free Wi-Fi in many parts of the city, including downtown and Miami Beach, as well as at Starbucks and at **Cybr Caffe,** 1574 Washington Ave., South Beach (www.cybrcaffe.com; ✆ **305/534-0057**).

Liquor Laws   Only adults 21 or older may legally purchase or consume alcohol in the state of Florida. Minors are usually permitted in bars, as long as the bars also serve food. Liquor laws are strictly enforced; if you look young, carry identification. Beer and wine are sold in most supermarkets and convenience stores. Most of the city of Miami's liquor stores are closed on Sunday. Liquor stores in the city of Miami Beach are open daily.

Lost Property   If you lost something at the airport, call the **Airport Lost and Found** office (✆ **305/876-7377**). If you lost something on the bus, Metrorail, or Metromover, call **Metro-Dade Transit Agency** (✆ **305/770-3131**). If you lost something anywhere else, phone the **Dade County Police Lost and Found** (✆ **305/375-3366**). You may also want to fill out a police report for insurance purposes.

Newspapers & Magazines   The *Miami Herald* is the city's only English-language daily. It is especially known for its extensive Latin American coverage and has a decent Friday "Weekend" entertainment guide. The most respected alternative weekly is the giveaway tabloid, **New Times,** which contains up-to-date listings and reviews of food, films, theater, music, and whatever else is happening in town. Also free, if you can find it, is **Ocean Drive,** an oversize glossy magazine that's limited on text (no literary value) and heavy on ads and society photos. It's what you should read if you want to know who's who and where to go for fun; it's available at a number of chic South Beach boutiques and restaurants. It is also available at newsstands. In the same vein: **Miami Magazine** has a bit more literary value in addition to the gloss and is free and available throughout the city.

For a large selection of foreign-language newspapers and magazines, check with any of the large bookstores or try **News Cafe,** 800 Ocean Dr., South Beach (✆ **305/538-6397**). Also check out **Eddie's News,** 1096 Normandy Dr., Miami Beach (✆ **305/866-2661**).

Pharmacies **Walgreens Pharmacy** has countless locations all over town, including 1845 Alton Rd. (✆ **305/531-8868**), in South Beach; and 6700 Collins Ave. (✆ **305/861-6742**), in Miami Beach. Then there's **CVS,** which is usually located wherever there's a Walgreens.

Police For emergencies, dial ✆ **911** from any phone. No coins are needed for this call. For other police matters, call ✆ **305/595-6263.**

Post Office The **Main Post Office,** 2200 Milam Dairy Rd., Miami, FL 33152 (✆ **800/275-8777**), is located west of the Miami International Airport. Conveniently located post offices include 1300 Washington Ave. in South Beach and 3191 Grand Ave. in Coconut Grove. There is one central number for all post offices: ✆ **800/275-8777.**

Restrooms Stores rarely let customers use their restrooms, and many restaurants offer their facilities only for their patrons. However, most malls have restrooms, as do many fast-food restaurants. Public beaches and large parks often provide toilets, though in some places you have to pay or tip an attendant. Most large hotels have clean restrooms in their lobbies.

Safety As always, use your common sense and be aware of your surroundings at all times. Don't walk alone at night, and be extra wary when walking or driving though downtown Miami and surrounding areas.

Reacting to several highly publicized crimes against tourists several years ago, local and state governments alike have taken steps to help protect visitors. These measures include special highly visible police units patrolling the airport and surrounding neighborhoods, and better signs on the state's most tourist-traveled routes.

Taxes A 6% state sales tax (plus 1% local tax, for a total of 7% in Miami–Dade

County [from Homestead to North Miami Beach]) is added on at the register for all goods and services purchased in Florida. In addition, most municipalities levy special taxes on restaurants and hotels. In Surfside, hotel taxes total 11%; in Bal Harbour, 11%; in Miami Beach (including South Beach), 13%; and in the rest of Dade County, a whopping 13%. Food and beverage tax in Miami Beach, Bal Harbour, and Surfside is 9%; in Miami-Dade restaurants not located inside hotels, it's 8%, and in restaurants located in hotels, 9%.

Time Zone Miami, like New York, is in the Eastern Standard Time (EST) zone. Between the second Sunday of March and the first Sunday of November, daylight saving time is adopted, and clocks are set 1 hour ahead. America's eastern seaboard is 5 hours behind Greenwich Mean Time. To find out what time it is, call ✆ **305/324-8811.**

Transit Information For Metrorail or Metromover schedule information, surf over to www. miamidade.gov/transit or call ✆ **305/770-3131.**

Weather Hurricane season in Miami runs June through November. For an up-to-date recording of current weather conditions and forecast reports, call ✆ **305/ 229-4522.** Also see the "When to Go" section in chapter 2 for more information on the weather.

EXPLORING MIAMI

I f there's one thing Miami doesn't have, it's an identity crisis—multiple personalities, maybe, but hardly a crisis. In fact, it's the city's vibrant, multifaceted personality that attracts millions each year from all over the world. South Beach may be on the top of many Miami to-do lists, but the rest of the city—a fascinating assemblage of multicultural neighborhoods, some on the verge of a popularity explosion—should not be overlooked. Once considered "God's Waiting Room," the Magic City now attracts an eclectic mix of old and young, celebs and plebes, American and international, and geek and chic with an equally varied roster of activities.

For starters, Miami boasts some of the world's most natural beauty, with dazzling blue waters, fine sandy beaches, and lush tropical parks. The city's man-made brilliance, in the form of crayon-colored architecture, never seems to fade in Miami's unique Art Deco district. For cultural variation, you can experience the tastes, sounds, and rhythms of Cuba in Little Havana.

As in any metropolis, though, some areas aren't as great as others. Downtown Miami, for instance, is still in the throes of a major, albeit slow, renaissance, in which the sketchier warehouse sections of the city are being transformed into hubs of all things hip. In contrast to this development, however, are the still-poverty-stricken areas of downtown such as Overtown, Liberty City, and Little Haiti (though Overtown is striving to transform itself into the Overtown Historic Village, showcasing its landmarks such as the famous Lyric Theater and the home of DA Dorsey, Miami's first African-American millionaire). While we obviously advise you to exercise caution when exploring the less traveled parts of the city, we would also be remiss if we were to tell you to bypass them completely.

Lose yourself in the city's nature and its neighborhoods and, best of all, its people—a sassy collection of artists and intellectuals, beach bums and international transplants, dolled-up drag queens and bodies beautiful.

MIAMI'S BEACHES

Perhaps Miami's most popular attraction is its incredible 35-mile stretch of beachfront, which runs from the tip of South Beach north to Sunny Isles, then circles Key Biscayne and numerous other pristine islands dotting the Atlantic. The characteristics of Miami's many beaches are as varied as the city's population: There are beaches for swimming, socializing, or serenity; for family, seniors, or gay singles; some to make you forget you're in the city, others darkened by huge condominiums. Whatever type of beach vacation you're looking for, you'll find it in one of Miami's two distinct beach areas: Miami Beach and Key Biscayne. And in keeping with today's technology, Miami Beach is now officially a hot spot—as in a wireless hot spot, offering free Wi-Fi with 95% coverage outdoors (70% indoors) throughout the entire city and, yes, even on the sand.

MIAMI BEACH'S BEACHES   Collins Avenue fronts more than a dozen miles of white-sand beach and blue-green waters from 1st to 192nd streets. Although most of this stretch is lined with a solid wall of hotels and condos, beach access is plentiful. There are lots of public beaches here, wide and well maintained, complete with lifeguards, restroom facilities, concession stands, and metered parking (bring lots of quarters). Except for a thin strip close to the water, most of the sand is hard packed—the result of a $10-million Army Corps of Engineers Beach Rebuilding Project meant to protect buildings from the effects of eroding sand.

   Lummus Park Beach (✆ **305/673-7714**), also known simply as South Beach, runs along Ocean Drive from about 6th to 14th streets in South Beach. It's the best place to go if you're seeking entertainment as well as a great tan. On any day of the week, you might spy models primping for a photo shoot, scantily clad sun-worshippers avoiding tan lines (going topless is legal here), and an assembly line of washboard abs off of which you could (but shouldn't) bounce your bottle of sunscreen. Bathrooms and changing facilities are available on the beach, but don't expect to have a Gisele Bündchen encounter in one of these. Most people tend to prefer using the somewhat drier, cleaner bathrooms of the restaurants on Ocean Drive.

   South Beach's **12th Street Beach** (✆ **305/673-7714**) is *the* place to be for Miami's gay beach scene. Here you'll observe the strutting, kibitzing, and gossiping of Miami's beautiful gay population. You might even find yourself lucky enough to happen upon a feisty South Beach party while you're soaking up some rays here. If you can hold it, skip the public bathroom and head over to The Palace on Ocean Drive to use their bathroom.

   In general, the beaches on this barrier island (all on the eastern, ocean side of the island) become less crowded the farther north you go. A wooden boardwalk runs along

   From Desert Island to Fantasy Island

Miami Beach wasn't always a beachfront playground. In fact, it was a deserted island until the late 1800s, when a developer started a coconut farm there. That action sparked an interest in many other developers, including John Collins (for whom Collins Ave. is named), who began growing avocados. Other visionaries admired Collins's success and eventually joined him, establishing a ferry service and dredging parts of the bay to make the island more accessible. In 1921, Collins built a 2½-mile bridge linking downtown Miami to Miami Beach, creating accessibility *and* the longest wooden bridge in the world. Today Miami Beach has six links to the mainland.

Miami's Best Beaches

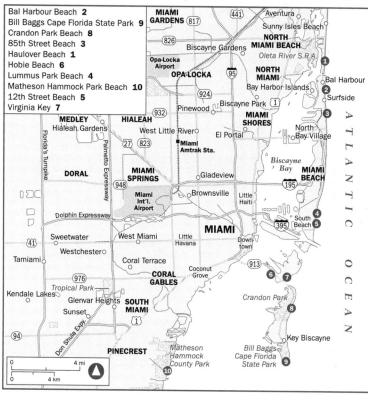

Bal Harbour Beach **2**
Bill Baggs Cape Florida State Park **9**
Crandon Park Beach **8**
85th Street Beach **3**
Haulover Beach **1**
Hobie Beach **6**
Lummus Park Beach **4**
Matheson Hammock Park Beach **10**
12th Street Beach **5**
Virginia Key **7**

the hotel side of the beach from 21st to 46th streets—about 1½ miles—offering a terrific sun-and-surf experience without getting sand in your shoes. Miami's lifeguard-protected public beaches include 21st Street, at the beginning of the boardwalk; 35th Street, popular with an older crowd; 46th Street, next to the Fontainebleau Hotel; 53rd Street, a narrower, more sedate beach; 64th Street, one of the quietest strips around; and 72nd Street, a local old-timers' spot.

KEY BISCAYNE'S BEACHES   If Miami Beach doesn't provide the privacy you're looking for, try Virginia Key and Key Biscayne. Crossing the Rickenbacker Causeway ($1.50 toll), however, can be a lengthy process, especially on weekends, when beach bums and tan-o-rexics flock to the key. The 5 miles of public beach there, however, are blessed with softer sand and are less developed and more laid-back than the hotel-laden strips to the north. In 2008, Key Biscayne reopened the historic **Virginia Key Beach Park,** 4020 Virginia Beach Dr. (✆ **305/960-4600**), the former "colored only" beach that opened in 1945 and closed in 1982 because of high maintenance costs. After an $11-million renovation, the 83-acre historic site features picnic tables and grills, shoreline renourishment, a playground for children with special needs, and a miniature railroad. It's open from sunrise to sunset daily, with free admission.

SOUTH BEACH & THE ART DECO DISTRICT

South Beach's 10 miles of beach are alive with a frenetic, circuslike atmosphere and are center stage for a motley crew of characters, from eccentric locals, seniors, snowbirds, and college students to gender-benders, celebrities, club kids, and curiosity seekers. Individuality is as widely accepted on South Beach as Visa and MasterCard.

Although the beautiful people do flock to South Beach, the models aren't the only sights worth drooling over. The thriving Art Deco District within South Beach has the largest concentration of Art Deco architecture in the world (in 1979, much of South Beach was listed in the National Register of Historic Places). The district is roughly bounded by the Atlantic Ocean on the east, Alton Road on the west, 6th Street to the south, and Dade Boulevard (along the Collins Canal) to the north. Most of the finest examples of the whimsical Art Deco style are concentrated along three parallel streets—Ocean Drive, Collins Avenue, and Washington Avenue—from about 6th to 23rd streets.

Simply put, Art Deco is a style of architecture that, in its heyday of the 1920s and 1930s, used to be considered ultramodern. Today, fans of the style consider it retro fabulous. According to the experts, Art Deco made its debut in 1925 at an exposition in Paris in which it set a stylistic tone, with buildings based on early neoclassical styles with the application of exotic motifs such as flora, fauna, and fountains based on geometric patterns. In Miami, Art Deco is marked by the pastel-hued buildings that line South Beach and Miami Beach. But it's a lot more than just color. If you look carefully, you will see the intricacies and impressive craftsmanship that went into each building in Miami back in the '20s, '30s, '40s, and today, thanks to intensive restoration.

After years of neglect and calls for the wholesale demolition of its buildings, South Beach got a new lease on life in 1979. Under the leadership of Barbara Baer Capitman, a dedicated crusader for the Art Deco region, and the Miami Design Preservation League, founded by Baer Capitman and five friends, an area made up of an estimated 800 buildings was granted a listing on the National Register of Historic Places. Designers then began highlighting long-lost architectural details with soft sherbet shades of peach, periwinkle, turquoise, and purple. Developers soon moved in, and the full-scale refurbishment of the area's hotels was underway.

Not everyone was pleased, though. Former Miami Beach commissioner Abe Resnick said, "I love old buildings. But these Art Deco buildings are 40, 50 years old. They

---

 ## walking BY DESIGN

The Miami Design Preservation League offers several tours of Miami Beach's historic architecture, all of which leave from the Art Deco Welcome Center at 1001 Ocean Dr., in Miami Beach. A self-guided audio tour (available daily 10am–4pm) turns the streets into a virtual outdoor museum, taking you through Miami Beach's Art Deco district at your own leisure, with tours in several languages for $15. Guided tours conducted by local historians and architects offer an in-depth look at the structures and their history. They will often add specialty tours covering everything from architecture to food; call for details. For those who have no time or patience for group tours, there are self-guided ones and even a cellphone tour. For more information on tours or reservations, log on to www.mdpl.org or call ☏ **305/672-2014.**

South Beach Attractions

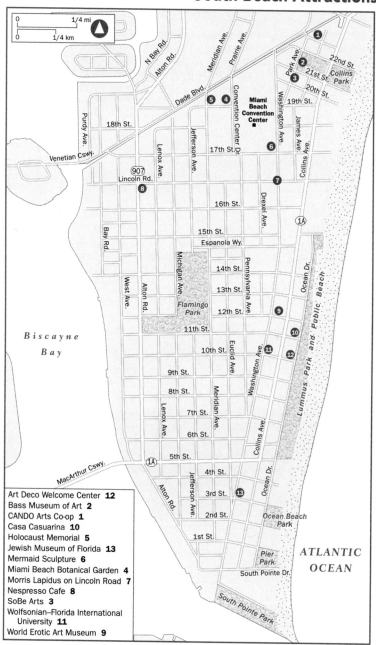

Art Deco Welcome Center **12**
Bass Museum of Art **2**
CANDO Arts Co-op **1**
Casa Casuarina **10**
Holocaust Memorial **5**
Jewish Museum of Florida **13**
Mermaid Sculpture **6**
Miami Beach Botanical Garden **4**
Morris Lapidus on Lincoln Road **7**
Nespresso Cafe **8**
SoBe Arts **3**
Wolfsonian–Florida International
    University **11**
World Erotic Art Museum **9**

On a tiny street in South Beach, there's a piece of Spain that's so vibrant, you almost feel as if you're in Madonna's "La Isla Bonita" video. In 1925, Miami Beach developer NBT Roney hired architect Robert Taylor to design a Spanish village on the property he just purchased on a street called **Española Way.** Today, the historic Mediterranean-Revival-style Spanish Village—or Plaza De España—envisioned by Roney and complete with fountain, stretches from Washington Avenue to Drexel Avenue and features charming boutiques, cafes, and a weekend market.

aren't historic. They aren't special. We shouldn't be forced to keep them." But Miami Beach kept those buildings, and Resnick lost his seat on the commission.

Today hundreds of new establishments—hotels, restaurants, and nightclubs—have renovated these older, historic buildings, putting South Beach on the cutting edge of Miami's cultural and nightlife scene.

Exploring the Area

If you're touring this unique neighborhood on your own, start at the **Art Deco Welcome Center,** 1001 Ocean Dr. (© **305/531-3484**), which is run by the Miami Design Preservation League. The only beachside building across from the Clevelander Hotel and bar, the center gives away lots of informational material, including maps and pamphlets, and runs guided tours around the neighborhood. Art Deco books (including *The Art Deco Guide,* an informative compendium of all the buildings here), T-shirts, postcards, mugs, and other paraphernalia are for sale. It's open daily from 10am to 7:30pm.

Take a stroll along **Ocean Drive** for the best view of sidewalk cafes, bars, colorful hotels, and even more colorful people. Another great place for a walk is **Lincoln Road,** which is lined with boutiques, large chain stores, cafes, and funky art and antiques stores. The Community Church, at the corner of Lincoln Road and Drexel Avenue, was the neighborhood's first church and is one of its oldest surviving buildings, dating from 1921. Then there's the Herzog & de Meuron–designed parking garage at 1111 Lincoln Rd., which is, oddly enough, not only a place to park cars, but an architectural marvel that's also the hub of several trendy new shops and restaurants (including **Nespresso Cafe,** an ultramodern European-style spot serving light fare and coffee). Architecture buffs will love the building. Shopaholics and foodies will love what's in it.

Or, if you prefer to cruise South Beach in a tiny yellow buggy—part scooter, part golf cart—consider **GoCar,** 1661 James Ave. (www.gocartours.com; © **888/462-2755**), a three-wheeled vehicle for two that comes with a GPS device that not only tracks and tells you where to go, but also prompts a recorded tour that kicks on with every site you cruise by. A 1-hour tour is $49, a 3-hour tour is $99, and an all-day tour is $150.

Discovery Miami Beach (www.discoverymiamibeach.com), which likes to call itself the "non Duck tour," is a self-guided walk, bike, or bus audio tour that covers 29 of the most iconic places in South Beach's past and present, featuring commentary by a slew of the city's notables. The tour takes approximately 90 minutes start to finish, but rental periods allow for 4 hours so that you can stop and fully lose—er, immerse—yourself in the experience. The standard rate for a walking tour is $15 per person. Discovery Miami Beach also offers DecoBike cycling tours for $30; tickets are available at the Miami Beach Convention Center Visitor Center, DecoBike Kiosks, and through various hotel concierges.

Bass Museum of Art ★★★ ART MUSEUM   The Bass Museum of Art is Miami's most progressive art museum. World-renowned Japanese architect Arata Isozaki designed the magnificent facility, which features an outdoor sculpture terrace and courtyard. In addition to providing space in which to show the permanent collection, exhibitions of a scale and quality not previously seen in Miami are shown here. Its permanent collection includes Renaissance and Baroque paintings, sculpture, textiles, and an Apulian Vessel Gallery and Egyptian Gallery featuring South Florida's only mummy on view. The Lindemann Family Creativity Center serves as a lab that includes scheduled classes and weekend drop-in art projects. Artists' projects, educational programs, lectures, concerts and free family days complement the works on view. Isozaki also designed an addition to the museum between 1998 and 2002 that doubled its size from 15,000 to 35,000 square feet.

2121 Park Ave. (1 block west of Collins Ave.), South Beach. www.bassmuseum.org. ℂ **305/673-7530.** Admission $8 adults, $6 students and seniors, free for children 6 and under, free 2nd Thurs of the month 6–9pm. Tues–Wed and Fri–Sat 10am–5pm; Thurs 10am–9pm; Sun 11am–5pm.

Holocaust Memorial ★★★ MONUMENT/MEMORIAL   This heart-wrenching memorial is hard to miss and would be a shame to overlook. The powerful centerpiece, Kenneth Treister's *A Sculpture of Love and Anguish,* depicts victims of the concentration camps crawling up a giant yearning hand stretching up to the sky, marked with an Auschwitz number tattoo. Along the reflecting pool is the story of the Holocaust, told in cut marble slabs. Inside the center of the memorial is a tableau that is one of the most solemn and moving tributes to the millions of Jews who lost their lives in the Holocaust we've seen. You can walk through an open hallway lined with photographs and the names of concentration camps and their victims. From the street, you'll see the outstretched arm, but do stop and tour the sculpture at ground level.

1933 Meridian Ave. (at Dade Blvd.), South Beach. www.holocaustmmb.org. ℂ **305/538-1663.** Free admission. Daily 9am–9pm.

Jewish Museum of Florida ★ MUSEUM   Chronicling over 230 years of Jewish heritage and experiences in Florida, the Jewish Museum presents a fascinating look at religion and culture through films, lectures, and exhibits such as "Mosaic: Jewish Life in Florida," which features more than 500 photos and artifacts documenting the Jewish experience in Florida since 1763. Housed in a former synagogue, the museum also delves into the Jewish roots of Latin America. For a little nosh, check out the museum's restaurant, **Bessie's Bistro**, named after Bess Myerson, the first and only Jewish Miss America, whose parents lived around the museum in the '70s. Myerson donated some of her pageant memorabilia, which adorns the Bistro's walls.

301 Washington Ave., South Beach. www.jewishmuseum.com. ℂ **305/672-5044.** Admission $6 adults, $5 seniors and students, $12 families, free Sat. Tues–Sun 10am–5pm. Closed Jewish holidays.

Jungle Island ★ ☺ ZOO   Not exactly an island and not quite a jungle, Jungle Island is an excellent diversion for the kids and for animal lovers. While the island doubles as a protected bird sanctuary, the pricey 19-acre park features an Everglades exhibit, a petting zoo, and several theaters, jungle trails, and aviaries. Living here are hundreds of parrots, macaws, peacocks, cockatoos, and flamingos. Continuous shows star bicycle-riding cockatoos, high-flying macaws, and numerous stunt-happy parrots.

A Japanese Garden

If you ask someone what Japanese influences can be found in Miami, they'll likely point to Nobu, Sushi Siam, Sushi Rock Cafe, and even Benihana. But back in the '50s, well before sushi became trendy, Kiyoshi Ichimura became obsessed with Miami and started sending people and objects from Tokyo, including carpenters, gardeners, and a landscape architect, to design and construct the San-Ai-An Japanese Garden. Originally located in the Jungle Island space, the garden was dismantled during construction and re-created adjacent to the park, at 1101 MacArthur Causeway on Watson Island ((C) **305/960-4639;** http://friendsofjapanesegarden.com). The completed 1-acre garden was renamed **Ichimura Miami–Japan Garden** in honor of its original benefactor, and its sculptures and Japanese artifacts are managed by a coalition of city organizations. Japanese holidays and festivals are celebrated here.

One of the most popular shows is "Tale of the Tiger," featuring awesome animals. Jungle Island also features the only African penguins in South Florida as well as a liger—part lion, part tiger—and endangered baby lemurs. There are also tortoises, iguanas, and a rare albino alligator on exhibit. *Tip:* The park's website sometimes offers downloadable discount coupons, so take a look before you visit because you definitely won't want to pay full price for this park. If you do get your money's worth and see all the shows and exhibits, expect to spend upwards of 4 hours here. *Note:* The former South Miami site of (Parrot) Jungle Island is now known as **Pinecrest Gardens,** 11000 Red Rd. ((C) **305/669-6942**), which features a petting zoo, a mini–water park, lake, natural hammocks, and banyan caves. It's open daily from 8am until sunset; admission is free.

1111 Parrot Jungle Trail, Watson Island (on the north side of MacArthur Causeway/I-395). www.jungle island.com. (C)**305/400-7000.** Admission $33 adults, $31 seniors, $25 children 3–10, free for military personnel with valid ID. Parking $8 per vehicle. Mon–Fri 10am–5pm; Sat–Sun 10am–6pm. From I-95, take I-395 E. (MacArthur Causeway); make a right on Parrot Jungle Trail, which is the 1st exit after the bridge. Follow the road around and under the causeway to the parking garage on the left side.

Miami Children's Museum ★★ ☺MUSEUM   The Children's Museum, located on the MacArthur Causeway, across from Jungle Island, is a modern, albeit odd-looking, 56,500-square-foot facility that includes 14 permanent galleries, traveling exhibits, classrooms, a parent/teacher resource center, the Gloria Martin Kid Smart educational gift shop, a 200-seat auditorium, a Subway restaurant, and two outdoor, interactive play areas. The museum offers hundreds of bilingual, interactive programs, classes, camps, and learning materials related to arts, culture, diversity, community, and communication. There's also a re-creation of a Carnival cruise ship and a gallery of teddy bears from around the world. Children can explore their artistic talents in the Art Gallery. But perhaps the coolest thing of all is the World Music Studio, in which aspiring rock stars can lay down a few tracks and play instruments. The Museum is truly a place where all children can play, learn, imagine and create together. Even as an adult, I have to say I was tempted to participate in some kids-only activities and exhibitions, such as the miniature Bank of America and the Publix Supermarket.

980 MacArthur Causeway, Miami. www.miamichildrensmuseum.org. (C)**305/373-5437.** Admission $15 adults and children 13 months and over, $12 Florida residents. Daily 10am–6pm.

Wolfsonian–Florida International University ★★★ 🏛 MUSEUM   Mitchell Wolfson, Jr., heir to a family fortune built on movie theaters, was known as an eccentric, but we'd call him a pack rat. A premier collector of propaganda and advertising art, Wolfson was spending so much money storing his booty that he decided to buy the warehouse that was housing it. It ultimately held more than 70,000 of his items, from controversial Nazi propaganda to King Farouk of Egypt's match collection. Thrown in the eclectic mix are also zany works from great modernists such as Charles Eames and Marcel Duchamp. Wolfson then gave this incredibly diverse collection to Florida International University. The former 1927 storage facility has

---

roadside ATTRACTIONS

The following examples of public art and prized architecture are great photo opportunities and worth visiting if you're in the area.

○ **Casa Casaurina, also known as Versace Mansion (Amsterdam Palace):** Morbid curiosity has led hordes of people—tourists and locals—to this, once the only private home (now a country club) on Ocean Drive. Legendary Italian designer Gianni Versace bought the home in 1992 and spent $33 million on bringing it up to his standards. Sadly, he was gunned down on his front steps by a deranged stalker in 1997. In 2012, the home was put up for sale for an astounding $125 million. If you can get past the fact that the late designer was murdered on the steps of this palatial estate, you should definitely observe the intricate Italian architecture that makes this house stand out from its streamlined Deco neighbors. Built in the 1930s as a replica of Christopher Columbus's son's palace in Santo Domingo, the house was originally called Casa Casaurina (House of the Pine), but was rechristened the Amsterdam Palace in 1935 when George Amsterdam purchased it. After several stints as a private country club and hotel, it's now a hotel, **The Villa** by **Barton G.** (p. 185), open to the public and run by restaurateur and events planner Barton G. Weiss. It's located at the northwest corner of Ocean Drive and 11th Street, South Beach.

○ **Mermaid Sculpture:** A pop-art masterpiece designed by Roy Lichtenstein, this sculpture captures the buoyant spirit of Miami Beach and its environs. It's in front of the Jackie Gleason Theater of the Performing Arts, at 1700 Washington Ave., Miami Beach.

○ **Morris Lapidus on Lincoln Road:** Famed designer/architect, the late Morris Lapidus—the "high priest of high kitsch"—who is best known for the Fontainebleau Hotel, created a series of sculptures that are angular, whimsical, and quirky, competing with the equally amusing mix of pedestrians who flock to Lincoln Road. In addition to the sculptures on Lincoln Road (at Washington Ave.), which you can't miss, Lapidus also created the **Colony Theater,** 1040 Lincoln Rd., which was built by Paramount in 1943; the 1928 **Sterling Building,** 927 Lincoln Rd., whose glass blocks and blue neon are required evening viewing; and the **Lincoln Theater,** 555 Lincoln Rd., which features a remarkable tropical bas-relief.

For a few Days in December, Miami becomes a cultural mecca as arts lovers from around the world flock here for Switzerland's Art Basel. The focal point of Art Basel is **Collins Park Cultural Center** (www.collinspark.us), which comprises a trio of arts buildings on Collins Park and Park Avenue (off Collins Ave.), bounded by 21st to 23rd streets—these are the **Bass Museum of Art** (p. 59), the new Arquitectonica-designed home of the Miami City Ballet, and the Miami Beach Regional Library, an ultramodern building designed by architect Robert A. M. Stern. Collins Park is an open space that extends to the Atlantic and is home to a series of large sculptural installations. A few cultural institutions that are part of the emerging Collins Park neighborhood are local arts organization **SoBe Arts** at the Carl Fisher complex; the **Miami Beach Botanical Garden;** the **CANDO Arts Co-Op,** 309 23rd St., a 5,000-square-foot gallery that's free and open to the public, featuring over a dozen resident artists; and the **Holocaust Memorial.**

been transformed into a museum that is the envy of curators around the world. The museum is unquestionably fascinating and hosts lectures and rather swinging events surrounding particular exhibits. **The Dynamo,** the museum's cafe and shop, is a fun and funky spot serving coffee, wine, beer, and nibbles, whose focal point is a large library shelving system from the late 19th century. The design represents the first modular book-stacking system ever created.

1001 Washington Ave., South Beach. www.wolfsonian.org. ©**305/531-1001.** Admission $7 adults; $5 seniors, students with ID, and children 6–12; free after 6pm Fri. Sat–Tues noon–6pm; Thurs–Fri noon–9pm.

World Erotic Art Museum ★ MUSEUM   The Hustler store across the street has nothing on this wacky, X-rated museum. Opened in 2005 by then-70-year-old grandmother Naomi Wilzig, the museum features Wilzig's collection of more than 4,000 pieces of erotic art, including Kama Sutra temple carvings from India, peeka-boo Victorian figurines that flash their booties, and a prop from the sexual thriller *A Clockwork Orange.* The 12,000-square-foot museum is located above Mansion, a club that's no stranger to erotic art—that is, performance art. This is a great place to spend an hour or two on a rainy day, and more than anything, the stuff is more amusing than sexy or racy.

1205 Washington Ave., South Beach. www.weam.com. © **305/532-9336.** Admission $15 adults, $14 seniors, $14 students. Children 17 and under not admitted. Mon–Thurs 11am–10pm; Fri–Sun 11am–midnight.

MIAMI BEACH

Museum of Contemporary Art (MOCA) ★★★ ART MUSEUM   MOCA
boasts an impressive collection of internationally acclaimed art with a local flavor. It is also known for its forward thinking and ability to discover and highlight new artists. Film presentations and lectures complement changing exhibitions. Permanent collection includes works by John Baldessari, Dan Flavin, Dennis Oppenheim, Alex Katz, Louise Nevelson, Edward Ruscha, Gabriel Orozco, Julian Schnabel, Zoe Leonard, Nam June Paik, Uta Barth, Teresita Fernandez, Garry Simmons, Jose Bedia, Anna

Miami Area Attractions

American Airlines Arena **9**
Barnacle State Historic Site **19**
Casino Miami, Jai Alai **6**
Coral Castle **25**
Coral Gables Museum **17**
Crandon Park Family Amusement Center **21**
Fairchild Tropical Garden **22**
Freedom Tower **10**
Jungle Island **7**
Kampong **5**
Lowe Art Museum **20**
Marjory Stoneman Douglas Biscayne Nature Center **14**
Miami Art Museum at the Miami-Dade Cultural Center **11**

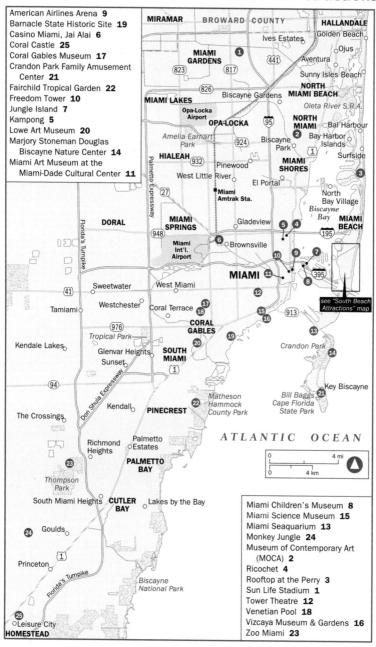

Miami Children's Museum **8**
Miami Science Museum **15**
Miami Seaquarium **13**
Monkey Jungle **24**
Museum of Contemporary Art (MOCA) **2**
Ricochet **4**
Rooftop at the Perry **3**
Sun Life Stadium **1**
Tower Theatre **12**
Venetian Pool **18**
Vizcaya Museum & Gardens **16**
Zoo Miami **23**

Gaskel, Thomas Hirschhorn, Mariko Mori, John Bock, Pierre Huyghe, Philippe Parreno, Edward Kienholz, Raymond Pettibon, Matthew Ritchie, and Sterling Ruby. Exhibitions feature artists such as Yoko Ono, Ed Ruscha, Bruce Weber, Ragnar Kjartansson, and Tracey Emin. Guided tours are offered in English, Spanish, French and Creole by appointment. Free outdoor jazz concerts attract hundreds of music lovers on the last Friday night of each month. The museum's upcoming expansion, expected to be completed in 2014, will triple its overall size, double its gallery space, and include an education wing, a new art storage facility, and enhanced public areas.

770 NE 125th St., North Miami. www.mocanomi.org. ✆ **305/893-6211.** Admission $5 adults, $3 students with ID, free for children 12 and under, Tues by donation. Tues and Thurs–Sat 11am–5pm; Wed 1–9pm; Sun noon–5pm. Closed major holidays.

Patricia and Phillip Frost Art Museum ★★ ART MUSEUM Housed in a 46,000-square-foot state of the art building designed by architect Yann Weymouth, the Patricia and Phillip Frost Art Museum, located on the campus of Florida International University, opened in this space in 2008. The museum has a 35-year history of presenting world-renowned exhibitions. Among the permanent collections is the General Collection, which holds a strong representation of American printmaking from the 1960s and 1970s, photography, pre-Columbian objects dating from A.D. 200 to 500, and a growing number of works by contemporary Caribbean and Latin American artists. The museum, a Smithsonian affiliate, is the only museum in South Florida to offer free daily admission.

Florida International University, 10975 SW 17th St. http://thefrost.fiu.edu. ✆ **305/348-2890.** Free admission. Tues–Sat 10am–5pm; Sun noon–5pm.

KEY BISCAYNE

Miami Seaquarium ★ ☺ ✋ AQUARIUM If you've been to Orlando's SeaWorld, you may be disappointed with Miami's version, which is considerably smaller and not as well maintained. It's hardly a sprawling aquarium, but you will want to arrive early to enjoy the effects of its mild splash. You'll need at least 3 hours to tour the 35-acre oceanarium and see all four daily shows, starring a number of showy ocean mammals. You can cut your visit to 2 hours if you limit your shows to the better, albeit corny, *Flipper Show* and *Killer Whale Show.* The highly regarded Dolphin Encounter allows visitors to touch and swim with dolphins in the Flipper Lagoon. The program costs $139 per person, $45 per adult observer, and $36 per child observer ages 3 to 9, and is offered daily at 12:15 and 3:15pm. Children must be at least 52 inches tall to participate. Reservations are necessary for this program. Call ✆ 305/365-2501 in advance for reservations. The Seaquarium also debuted a new sea lion show and a stingray touch pool.

4400 Rickenbacker Causeway (south side), en route to Key Biscayne. www.miami seaquarium.com. ✆ **305/361-5705.** Admission $36 adults, $27 children 3–9, free for children 2 and under. Parking $8. Daily 9am–6pm (ticket booth closes at 4pm).

A Carousel by the Sea

At the **Crandon Park Family Amusement Center,** 4000 Crandon Blvd., Key Biscayne (✆ **305/361-5421**), there's an outdoor roller rink, a dolphin-shaped splash fountain and marine sculptures, and an old-fashioned carousel, crafted in 1949 by the Alan Herschell Company and restored to its former glory. Even the music—provided by an old-fashioned organ—is historic. The amusement area is open from 10:30am to 5:30pm on weekends, and three rides on the carousel cost $2.

Marjory Stoneman Douglas Biscayne Nature Center ★ ☺ 🎇 NATURE RESERVE If you only have time for one activity on Key Biscayne, skip the Seaquarium and head to the Marjory Stoneman Douglas Biscayne Nature Center for Sea Grass Adventures, in which a naturalist from the center introduces kids and adults to an amazing variety of creatures that live in the sea-grass beds of the Bear Cut Nature Preserve near Crandon Beach on Key Biscayne. You will be able to wade in the water with your guide and catch an assortment of sea life in nets provided by the guides. At the end of the program, participants gather on the beach while the guide explains what everyone has just caught, passing the creatures around in miniature viewing tanks. Call for available dates, times, and reservations. The center and grounds themselves are worth a visit, even if you opt not to participate in one of the scheduled programs.

6767 Crandon Blvd., Key Biscayne. www.biscaynenaturecenter.org. ✆ **305/361-6767.** Free admission to the center; $12 for Sea Grass Adventures. Daily 10am–4pm.

DOWNTOWN

Miami Art Museum ★★★ ART MUSEUM The Miami Art Museum (MAM) features an eclectic mix of modern and contemporary works by such artists as Eric Fischl, Max Beckmann, Jim Dine, Robert Rauschenberg, Chuck Close, James Rosenquist, Jose Bedia, Marcel Duchamp, and Stuart Davis. Rotating exhibitions span ages and styles, and often focus on Latin-American or Caribbean artists. JAM at MAM is the museum's popular happy hour, which takes place on the third Thursday of the month and is tied in to a particular exhibit. Almost as artistic as the works inside the museum is the composite sketch of the people—young and old—who attend these events.

The Miami-Dade Cultural Center, where the museum is housed, is a fortresslike complex designed by Philip Johnson. In addition to the acclaimed Miami Art Museum, the center houses the main branch of the Miami-Dade Public Library,

---

freedom TOWER

Driving north on Biscayne Boulevard in downtown Miami, some may be distracted by the traffic, the neon lights coming from the Bayside Marketplace, or the behemoth cruise ships docked at the port. But perhaps the most dramatic presence on this heavily trafficked stretch of downtown is the Freedom Tower, 600 Biscayne Blvd. at NE Sixth Street, built in 1925 and modeled after the Giralda Tower in Spain. Once home to the now-defunct *Miami Daily News* and *Metropolis* newspapers, the Freedom Tower was sold in 1957 to the U.S. General Services Administration, which used the building to process over 500,000 Cubans fleeing the island once Castro took over.

Considered the Ellis Island of the Cuban exile community, Miami's Freedom Tower has remained largely vacant over the years (the government left the building in 1974), despite hopes and unfulfilled plans to turn it into a museum reflecting its historical significance. In 2004, developers donated the tower to Miami Dade College, which has since used the space for hosting various exhibitions and cultural programs. In 2008, the tower was designated a U.S. National Historic Landmark.

digging MIAMI

Until the controversial discovery of the archaeological site known as the Miami River Circle, the oldest existing artifacts in the city were presumed to have existed in the closets of Miami's retirement homes. In September 1998, during a routine archeological investigation on the mouth of the Miami River, several unusual and unique features were discovered cut into the bedrock: a prehistoric circular structure, 38 feet in diameter, with intentional markings of the cardinal directions as well as a 5-foot-long shark and two stone axes, suggesting the circle had ceremonial significance to Miami's earliest inhabitants—the Tequesta Indians. Radiocarbon tests confirm that the circle is about 2,000 years old.

While some have theorized that the circle is a calendar or Miami's own version of Stonehenge, most scholars believe that the discovery represents the foundation of a circular structure, perhaps a council house or a chief's house. Expert scientists, archeologists, and scholars who have made visits to the site indicate that the circle is of local, regional, and national significance. Local preservationists formed an organization, Save the Miami Circle, to ensure that developers didn't raze the circle to make way for condominiums. As a result, the circle remains put, albeit surrounded by the EPIC and Viceroy/Icon hotels and condos, and the mystery continues. See www. miamicircle.org for more information.

which sometimes features art and cultural exhibits, and the Historical Museum of Southern Florida, which highlights the fascinating history of the area. Keep in mind that the plaza onto which the complex opens is a gathering place for many of those in downtown Miami's homeless population, which makes it a bit off-putting but not dangerous. Work has yet to begin on Museum Park, a $200-plus-million project on an underused 29-acre property on the bay in downtown Miami that will become MAM's new home; estimated completion is sometime in 2013. To check on its status—or lack thereof—go to www.miamiartmuseum.org/museum_park.asp.

101 W. Flagler St., Miami. www.miamiartmuseum.org. © **305/375-3000.** Admission $8 adults, $4 seniors, free for children 11 and under. Tues–Fri 10am–5pm; 3rd Thurs of each month 10am–9pm; Sat–Sun noon–5pm. Closed major holidays. From I-95 south, exit at Orange Bowl–NW 8th St. and continue south to NW 2nd St.; turn left at NW 2nd St. and go 1½ blocks to NW 2nd Ave.; turn right.

THE DESIGN DISTRICT

Rubell Family Collection ★★★ 🏛 ART MUSEUM One of the world's great collections of cutting-edge contemporary art (including Jean-Michel Basquiat, Maurizio Cattelan, Keith Haring, Damien Hirst, Cady Noland, Charles Ray, Cindy Sherman and Andy Warhol) is owned by the Rubell family, Miami hoteliers, and is housed in a 40,000-square-foot former Drug Enforcement Agency facility 10 minutes from South Beach. The museum regularly changes exhibitions such as the well-known show "30 Americans," and there is a seasonal program of lectures, artist talks, and performances as well as a public research library, bookshop, and sculpture garden.

Impressions
You don't find inspiration in Miami; it finds you.
—Pepe Mar, sculptor

95 NW 29th St. (on the corner of NW 1st Ave. adjacent to the Design District and

A cultural gem in Little Havana, the **Tower Theatre**, 1508 SW Eighth St. (*© 305/237-6180*), is one of Miami's oldest cultural landmarks, opening in 1926 as the finest state-of-the-art theater in the south. After the Cuban influx in the 1960s, the theater started showing English-language programming with Spanish subtitles, eventually switching to all Spanish. After years of closings and changing hands, the theater was purchased by the City of Miami and in 1993 added to the National Register as a historic site. After a complete renovation in 1997, the Tower Theatre was back to its Deco glory and is currently managed by Miami-Dade College, which continues the theater's history with various cultural and arts programming, including films and exhibitions of Cuban art by highly regarded artists such as Carlos Navarro.

midtown), Miami. www.rubellfamilycollection.com. *© **305/573-6090.*** Admission $10 adults, $5 students. Nov 30–July 27 Tues–Sun 10am–6pm; by private appointment otherwise.

CORAL GABLES

Coral Gables Museum MUSEUM   This museum is housed in a restored version of the city's original 1930 coral rock police and fire station and pays homage to the City Beautiful with a 3,000-square-foot gallery, a 5,000-square-foot public plaza, and a permanent, evolving exhibit examining Coral Gables's history. Among its exhibitions: George Merrick and His Vision for Coral Gables, Art and Architecture in Coral Gables During the New Deal, and Coral Gables' Sister Cities. If you're interested in architecture and city planning, this is for you. If not, just take your own scenic tour through the city instead.

285 Aragon Ave., Coral Gables. www.coralgablesmuseum.org. *© **305/910-3996.*** Admission $7 adults, $4 children 6 and under, free for members. Tues–Thurs noon–6pm; Fri noon–8pm; Sat 11am–5pm; Sun noon–5pm.

Lowe Art Museum ★★ ART MUSEUM   Located on the University of Miami campus, the Lowe Art Museum has a dazzling collection of 8,000 works that include American paintings, Latin-American art, Navajo and Pueblo Indian textiles, and Renaissance and baroque art. Traveling exhibits, such as *Wine Spectator* magazine's classic posters of the Belle Epoque, also stop here. For the most part, the Lowe is known for its collection of Greek and Roman antiquities, and, as compared to the more modern MOCA, Bass, and Miami Art Museum, features mostly European and international art hailing back to ancient times. Its newest wing, the Myrna and Sheldon Palley Pavilion for Contemporary Glass and Studio Arts, gives the museum a more modern twist with a $3.5-million glass collection featuring masterpieces by Dale Chihuly, Richard Jolley, William Carlson, and others, as well as 3-D art by various contemporary artists.

University of Miami, 1301 Stanford Dr. (at Ponce de León Blvd.), Coral Gables. www.lowemuseum. org. *© **305/284-3603.*** Admission $10 adults, $5 seniors and students with ID; by donation 1st Tues of the month. Tues–Wed and Fri–Sat 10am–5pm; Thurs noon–7pm; Sun noon–5pm.

Venetian Pool ★★★ ☺ HISTORIC SITE   Miami's most beautiful and unusual swimming pool, dating from 1924, is hidden behind pastel stucco walls and is honored with a listing in the National Register of Historic Places. Two underground wells feed the free-form lagoon, which is shaded by three-story Spanish porticos and has both fountains and waterfalls. It can be cold in the winter months. During summer, the pool's 820,000 gallons of water are drained and refilled nightly, thanks to an underground aquifer, ensuring a cool, *clean* swim. Visitors are free to swim and sunbathe here, just as Esther Williams and Johnny Weissmuller did decades ago. For a modest fee, you or your children can learn to swim during special summer programs.

2701 DeSoto Blvd. (at Toledo St.), Coral Gables. www.venetianpool.com. © **305/460-5306.** Admission Apr–Oct $11 adults, $6.30 for children 3–12; Nov and Feb–Mar $7.35 adults, $3.95 for children 3–12. Children must be at least 3 (parents must provide proof of child's age with birth certificate) or 38 in. tall to enter. May–Sept Mon–Fri 11am–5:30pm, Sat–Sun 10am–4:30pm; Oct–Nov and Feb–Apr Tues–Sun 10am–4:30pm.

COCONUT GROVE

Barnacle State Historic Site ★★ HISTORIC HOME   The former home of naval architect and early settler Ralph Middleton Munroe is now a museum in the heart of Coconut Grove. It's the oldest house in Miami and it rests on its original foundation, which sits on 5 acres of natural hardwood forest and landscaped lawns. The house's quiet surroundings, wide porches, and period furnishings illustrate how Miami's first snowbird lived in the days before condomania and luxury hotels. Enthusiastic and knowledgeable state park employees provide a wealth of historical information to those interested in quiet, low-tech attractions such as this one. On Wednesdays from 6 to 7:30pm, they have sunset yoga by the sea. Call for details on the fabulous monthly moonlight concerts during which folk, blues, or classical music is presented and picnicking is encouraged.

3485 Main Hwy. (1 block south of Commodore Plaza), Coconut Grove. © **305/442-6866.** Fax 305/448-7484. Admission $2. Tours $3 adults, $1 children 6–12. Concerts $7 adults, $3 children 6–9, free for children 5 and under. Fri–Mon 9am–4pm. Tours Fri–Mon at 10am, 11:30am, 1pm, and 2:30pm. From downtown Miami, take U.S. 1 south to 27th Ave., make a left, and continue to S. Bayshore Dr.; then make a right, follow to the intersection of Main Hwy., and turn left.

Miami Science Museum ★★ ☺ MUSEUM/PLANETARIUM   The Miami Science Museum features more than 140 hands-on exhibits that explore the mysteries of the universe. Live demonstrations and collections of rare natural history specimens make a visit here fun and informative. Many of the demos involve audience participation, which can be lots of fun for willing and able kids and adults alike. There is also the Wildlife Center, with more than 175 live reptiles and birds of prey. The adjacent Space Transit Planetarium projects astronomy and laser shows as well as interactive demonstrations of upcoming computer technology and cyberspace features. Call or visit the website for a list of upcoming exhibits and laser shows. The

---

A Glimpse into the Past

Coconut Grove's link to the Bahamas dates from before the turn of the 20th century, when islanders came to the area to work in a newly opened hotel called the Peacock Inn. Bahamian-style wooden homes built by these early settlers still stand on Charles Street. Goombay, the lively annual Bahamian festival, celebrates the Grove's Caribbean link and has become one of the largest black-heritage street festivals in America.

museum's $275-million home at Museum Park (see above), built in 2010, is a tri-level natural light and solar-powered homage to high-tech science and technology, including a cone-shaped aquarium tank and an egg-shaped planetarium with views of Biscayne Bay.

3280 S. Miami Ave. (just south of the Rickenbacker Causeway), Coconut Grove. www.miamisci.org. © **305/646-4200.** Admission $15 adults; $11 seniors, students, and children 3–12; free for children 2 and under. Daily 10am–6pm; 1st Fri of every month 10am–10pm; call for show times (last show 4pm Mon–Fri and 5pm Sat–Sun). Closed Thanksgiving and Christmas.

Vizcaya Museum and Gardens ★★★ HISTORIC HOME Sometimes referred to as the "Hearst Castle of the East," this magnificent villa is more Gatsby-esque than anything else you'll find in Miami. It was built in 1916 as a winter retreat for James Deering, cofounder and former vice president of International Harvester. The industrialist purchased art and architectural objects spanning 2,000 years for his ornate mansion, which took 1,000 artisans 2 years to build, and the estate became a celebration of the Gilded Age. Most of the original furnishings, including dishes and paintings, are still intact. You will also see examples of technology available in the early 20th century, including a telephone switchboard, central vacuum-cleaning system, elevators, and fire sprinklers. A free guided tour of the 34 furnished rooms on the first floor takes about 45 minutes. The second floor, which consists mostly of bedrooms, is open to tour on your own. The spectacularly opulent villa wraps itself around a central courtyard. Outside, lush formal gardens, accented with statuary, balustrades, and decorative urns, front an enormous swath of Biscayne Bay. Definitely take the tour of the rooms, but immediately thereafter, you will want to wander and get lost in the resplendent gardens.

3251 S. Miami Ave. (just south of Rickenbacker Causeway), Coconut Grove. www.vizcayamuseum. org.© **305/250-9133.** Admission $15 adults, $10 seniors, $6 children 6–12, free for children 5 and under. Wed–Mon 9:30am—4:30pm.

SOUTH MIAMI–DADE COUNTY

Coral Castle ★ 📷 HISTORIC SITE There's plenty of competition, but Coral Castle is probably the strangest attraction in Florida. In 1923, the story goes, a 26-year-old crazed Latvian, suffering from the unrequited love of a 16-year-old who left him at the altar, immigrated to South Miami and spent the next 25 years of his life carving huge boulders into a prehistoric-looking roofless "castle." It seems impossible that one rather short man could have done all this, but there are scores of affidavits on display from neighbors who swear it happened. Apparently, experts have studied this phenomenon to help figure out how the great pyramids and Stonehenge were built. Rocker Billy Idol was said to have been inspired by this place to write his song "Sweet 16." An interesting 25-minute audio tour guides you through the spot, now on the National Register of Historic Places. Although Coral Castle is overpriced and undermaintained, it's worth a visit when you're in the area (probably en route or coming from the Keys), which is about 37 miles from Miami.

28655 S. Dixie Hwy., Homestead. www.coralcastle.com. © **305/248-6345.** Admission $15 adults, $12 seniors, $7 children 7–12. Group rates available. Sun–Thurs 8am–6pm; Fri–Sat 8am–8pm. Take 836 W (Dolphin Expwy.) toward Miami International Airport. Merge onto 826 S. (Palmetto Expwy.) and take it to the Florida Tpk. toward Homestead. Take the 288th St. exit (no. 5) and then take a right on S. Dixie Hwy., a left on SW 157th Ave., and then a sharp left back onto S. Dixie Hwy. Coral Castle is on the left side of the street.

A berry GOOD TIME

South Florida's farming region has been steadily shrinking in the face of industrial expansion, but you'll still find several spots where you can get back to nature while indulging in a local gastronomic delight—picking your own produce at the "U-Pic-'Em" farms that dot south Dade's landscape. Depending on what's in season, you can get everything from fresh herbs and vegetables to a mélange of citrus fruits and berries. During berry season—January through April—it's not uncommon to see hardy pickers leaving the groves with hands and faces that are stained a tale-telling crimson. On your way through south Dade, keep an eye out for the bright red U-PIC signs.

There are also a number of fantastic fruit stands in the region. **Burr's Berry Farms,** 12741 SW 216th St. ((**C** **305/251-0145**), located in the township of Goulds, about an hour from downtown Miami, has created a sensation with its fabulous strawberry milkshakes. To get there, go south on U.S. 1 and turn right on SW 216th Street. The fruit stand is about 1 mile west. It's open daily from 9am to 5:30pm.

For fresh fruit in a tasty pastry or tart, head over to **Knaus Berry Farm,** at 15980 SW 248th St. ((**C** **305/247-0668**), in an area known as the Redlands. Some people erroneously call this farm an Amish farm, but in actuality, it's run by a sect of German Baptists. The stand offers items ranging from fresh flowers to homemade ice cream, but be sure to indulge in one of their famous homemade cinnamon buns. Be prepared to wait in a long line to stock up—people flock here from as far away as Palm Beach. Head south on U.S. 1 and turn right on 248th Street. The stand is 2½ miles farther on the left side, and is open Monday through Saturday from 8am to 5:30pm.

Monkey Jungle ZOO   Personally, we think this place is nasty. It reeks, the monkeys are either sleeping or in heat, and it's really far from the city, even farther than the zoo. But if primates are your thing and you'd rather pass on the zoo, you'll be in paradise. You'll see rare Brazilian golden lion tamarins and Asian macaques. There are no cages to restrain the antics of the monkeys as they swing, chatter, and play their way into your heart. Screened-in trails wind through acres of "jungle," and daily shows feature the talents of the park's most progressive pupils. People who come here are not monkeying around—many of the park's frequent visitors are scientists and anthropologists. In fact, an interesting archaeological exhibition excavated from a Monkey Jungle sinkhole displays 10,000-year-old artifacts, including human teeth and animal bones. A somewhat amusing attraction here, if you can call it that, is the Wild Monkey Swimming Pool, a show in which you get to watch monkeys diving for food. If you can stand the humidity, the smell, and the bugs (flies, mosquitoes, and so on), expect to spend about 2 hours here. The park's website sometimes offers downloadable discount coupons.

14805 SW 216th St., South Miami. www.monkeyjungle.com. (**C** **305/235-1611.** Admission $30 adults, $28 seniors and active-duty military, $24 children 4–12. Daily 9:30am–5pm (tickets sold until 4pm). Take U.S. 1 south to SW 216th St., or from Florida Tpk., take exit 11 and follow the signs.

Zoo Miami ★★ ☺ ZOO   This 330-acre complex is quite a distance from Miami proper and the beaches—about 45 minutes—but worth the trip. Isolated and never really crowded, it's also almost completely cageless—most animals are kept at bay by cleverly designed moats. This is a fantastic spot to take younger kids; there are wonderful play areas, and safari cycles for rent, and the zoo offers several daily programs designed to educate and entertain, like the "Wildlife Show" and "Animal Tales." Residents include lions, chimpanzees, Komodo dragons, koalas, emus, and meerkats. The air-conditioned monorail and tram tours offer visitors a nice overview of the park. The zoo is always upgrading its facilities, including the impressive aviary, Wings of Asia. Cool activities include the Samburu Giraffe Feeding Station, where, for $3, you get to feed the giraffes veggies; the Kaziranga Camp Rhino Encounter, where you can feed an Indian rhino for $3; and Humpy's Camel Rides, where you can hop on a camel for $5. Amazon & Beyond features jaguars, anacondas, giant river otters, harpy eagles, a stingray touch tank, an interactive water-play area, the Flooded Forest building with a unique display of a forest before and during flood times, and an indoor Cloud Forest that houses reptiles. At 27 acres and a cost of $50 million, this exhibit is massive and makes Zoo Miami the third zoo in the country to have giant river otters, one of its keystone species. Wings Down Under: A Parrot Feeding Adventure is a fun, interactive experience where, for $3, you can enter an aviary with approximately 400 free-flying budgies, cockatiels, and rosellas (all Australian types of parrots) and experience them flying down to your hands to feast on seeds from a cup. There's a Dr. Seuss–inspired Wacky Barn in the children's zoo where you'll have an opportunity to hand feed and touch barn animals such as sheep, minihorses, ponies, goats, pot-bellied pigs, and more. Private tours and overnights are available for those who really want to commune with nature. **Note:** The distance between animal habitats can be great, so you'll do *a lot* of walking here. There are benches, shaded gazebos, cool misters, a water-shooting mushroom, and two water-play areas strategically positioned throughout the zoo so you can escape the heat when you need to. Also, because the zoo can be miserably hot during summer months, plan these visits in the early morning or late afternoon. Expect to spend all day here if you want to see it all.

12400 SW 152nd St., Miami. www.zoomiami.org. ℭ **305/251-0400.** Admission $16 adults, $12 children 3–12. Daily 9:30am–5:30pm (ticket booth closes at 4pm). Free parking. From U.S. 1 south, turn right on SW 152nd St., and follow signs about 3 miles to the entrance. From Florida Tpk. S., take exit 16 west to the entrance.

NATURE PRESERVES, PARKS & GARDENS

The Miami area is a great place for outdoor types, with beaches, parks, nature preserves, and gardens galore. Although South Beach is more known for its sand than its greenery, **South Pointe Park,** 1 Washington Ave. (ℭ **305/673-7730**), reopened after a $22.4-million renovation that transformed the formerly shabby spot into 18 waterfront acres of green space, walkways, a playground, and an observation deck.

Though the historic **Hialeah Park ★**, 2200 E. 4th Ave. (www.hialeahparkracing. com; ℭ **305/885-8000**), is primarily known for horse racing, it's also known for its legendary flock of neon-pink flamingos, which still roam the property and are definitely worth a photo op. After decades of decay, the park was renovated and reopened in 2009, although experts say the restoration of the National Historic Landmark to its former glory will take years and $100 million to complete. Open only for races for now, admission is free. For those who prefer a more historic look, Miami's resident historian Dr. Paul George (see "Organized Tours," p. 80) offers guided tours of the park for $25 per person. To book a tour, call ℭ **305/375-1621** or e-mail citytours@historymiami.org.

At the historic **Bill Baggs Cape Florida State Park ★**, 1200 Crandon Blvd. (www.floridastateparks.org/capeflorida; ✆ **305/361-5811**), at the southern tip of Key Biscayne about 20 minutes from downtown Miami, you can explore the unfettered wilds and enjoy some of the most secluded beaches in Miami. There's also a historic lighthouse that was built in 1825, which is the oldest lighthouse in South Florida. The lighthouse was damaged during the Second Seminole War (1836) and again in 1861 during the Civil War. Out of commission for a while, it was restored to working lighthouse condition in 1978 by the U.S. Coast Guard. The park is also recognized as a site within the U.S. National Park Service's National Underground Railroad Network to Freedom commemorating the trip to the British Bahamas by escaped slaves before the lighthouse was constructed. A rental shack leases bikes, hydrobikes, kayaks, and many more water toys. It's a great place to picnic, but there are also two restaurants on-site: the Lighthouse Cafe, which serves homemade Latin food, including great fish soups and sandwiches, and the Boater's Grill, offering casual waterfront dining. Just be careful that the raccoons don't get your lunch. Bill Baggs has been consistently rated as one of the top 10 beaches in the U.S. for its 1¼ miles of wide, sandy beaches and its secluded, serene atmosphere. Admission is $8 per car with up to eight people (or $4 for a car with only one person; $2 to enter by foot or bicycle). It's open daily from 8am to sunset. Tours of the lighthouse are available every Thursday through Monday at 10am and 1pm. Arrive at least half an hour early to sign up—there is room for only 10 people on each tour. Take I-95 to the Rickenbacker Causeway and take that all the way to the end.

Fairchild Tropical Garden ★★★, at 10901 Old Cutler Rd., in Coral Gables (www.ftg.org; ✆ **305/667-1651**), is the largest of its kind in the continental United States. A veritable rainforest of both rare and exotic plants, as well as 11 lakes and countless meadows, are spread across 83 acres. Palmettos, vine pergola, palm glades, and other unique species create a scenic, lush environment. More than 100 species of birds have been spotted at the garden (ask for a checklist at the front gate), and it's home to a variety of animals. In fact, bird lovers will go batty over the Keys Coastal Habitat, a 4-acre paradise featuring a densely planted collection of plants native to South Florida that was designed to attract migratory birds and other wildlife. You should not miss the 30-minute narrated tram tour (tours leave on the hour 10am–3pm Mon–Fri and 10am–4pm Sat–Sun) to learn about the various flowers and trees on the grounds. There is also a museum, a cafe, a picnic area, and a gift shop with edible gifts and fantastic books on gardening and cooking. Fairchild often hosts major art exhibits by the likes of Dale Chihuly and Roy Lichtenstein. The 2-acre rainforest exhibit, Windows to the Tropics, will save you a trip to the Amazon. New in 2012: the Jason Vollmer Butterfly Laboratory and the Clinton Family Conservatory featuring an exhibit of rare butterflies, birds, hummingbirds, orchids, fish, and tropical plants. Expect to spend a minimum of 2 hours here. Admission is $25 for adults, $18 for seniors, $12 for children ages 6 to 17, and free for children 5 and under. It's open daily, except Christmas, from 9:30am to 4:30pm. Take I-95 south to U.S. 1, turn left onto Le Jeune Road, and follow it straight to the traffic circle; from there, take Old Cutler Road 2 miles to the park.

Named after the late champion of the Everglades, the **Marjory Stoneman Douglas Biscayne Nature Center ★**, 6767 Crandon Blvd., Key Biscayne (www.biscaynenaturecenter.org; ✆ **305/361-6767**; p. 65), is housed in a $4-million facility and offers hands-on marine exploration, hikes through coastal hammocks, bike trips, and beach walks. Local environmentalists and historians lead intriguing trips through the local habitat. Call to reserve a spot on a regularly scheduled weekday or weekend programs. Be sure to wear comfortable, closed-toe shoes for hikes through wet or rocky terrain. It's open daily 10am to 4pm. The park has a $6 per car parking fee; admission to the nature center is free. Special programs and tours cost $12 per person. Call for weekend programs. To get there, take I-95 to the Rickenbacker Causeway exit (no. 1) and take the causeway all the way until it becomes Crandon Boulevard. The center is on the east side of the street (the Atlantic Ocean side) and about 15 minutes from downtown Miami.

Because so many people are focused on the beach itself, the **Miami Beach Botanical Garden,** 2000 Convention Center Dr., Miami Beach (© **305/673-7256**), remains a secret garden. The lush, tropical 4½-acre garden is a fabulous natural retreat from the hustle and bustle of the silicone-enhanced city. It's open Tuesday through Sunday from 9am to 5pm; admission is free.

The **Oleta River State Recreation Area ★★**, 3400 NE 163rd St., North Miami (www.floridastateparks.org/oletariver; © **305/919-1846**), consists of 993 acres—the largest urban park in the state—on Biscayne Bay. The beauty of the Oleta River, combined with the fact that you're essentially in the middle of a city, makes this park especially worth visiting. With miles of bicycle and canoe trails, a sandy swimming beach, kayak- and mountain-bike-rental shop, Blue Marlin Fish House Restaurant, shaded picnic pavilions, and a fishing pier, Oleta River State Recreation Area allows for an outstanding outdoor recreational experience cloistered from the confines of the big city. There are 14 rustic cabins on the premises that sleep four people. The cost is $55 per night, and guests are required to bring their own linens. Bathrooms and showers are outside, as is a fire circle with a grill for cooking. For reservations, call © **800/326-3521.** It's open daily from 8am to sunset. Admission for pedestrians and cyclists is $2 per person. By car, the driver plus car costs $4; the driver plus one to seven passengers and car costs $6. Take I-95 to exit 17 (S.R. 826 E.) and go all the way east until just before the causeway. The park entrance is on your right. Driving time from downtown Miami is about a half-hour.

A testament to Miami's unusual climate, the **Preston B. Bird and Mary Heinlein Fruit and Spice Park ★**, 24801 SW 187th Ave., Homestead (www.fruitandspice park.org; © **305/247-5727**), harbors rare fruit trees that cannot survive elsewhere in the country. If a volunteer is available, you'll learn some fascinating things about this 30-acre living plant museum, where the most exotic varieties of fruits and spices—ackee, mango, Ugli fruits, carambola, and breadfruit—grow on strange-looking trees with unpronounceable names. There are also original coral rock buildings dating back to 1912. The Strawberry Folk Festival in February and an art festival here in January are among the park's most popular—and populated—events. The best part? You're free to take anything that has *naturally* fallen to the ground (no picking here). If the ground is bare, don't worry. The Mango Café in the park's historic Bauer-Mitchell-Neill House features indoor and outdoor garden seating and is open for lunch and late-afternoon dining and serves "Florida Tropical" cuisine—fruit salads, lots of dishes with mango, smoothies, shakes, and, our fave, the Florida lobster roll. You'll also find samples of interesting fruits and jellies made from the park's bounty, as well as exotic ingredients and cookbooks in the gift store. Admission to the spice park is $8 for adults and $2 for children 6 to 11. It's open daily from 9am to 5pm (closed on Christmas). Tours are included in the price of admission and are offered at 11am, 1:30pm, and 3pm. Take U.S. 1 south, turn right on SW 248th Street, and go straight for 5 miles to SW 187th Avenue. The drive from Miami should take 45 minutes to an hour.

ESPECIALLY FOR KIDS

Miami is a lot more kid-friendly than people realize. Toss aside the images of scantily clad sunbathers, inebriated reality stars, and nightlife in general, and you've got yourself the ideal place to bring children. Warm weather and tons of outdoor activities and restaurants make Miami one of the more child-friendly cities—as long as you know where to go. Because of Miami's mostly magnificent weather, there are ample strolling opportunities for the antsiest kids, from Lincoln Road Mall on South Beach to Aventura Mall in North Miami Beach. What's particularly unique about Miami is that parents tend to take their kids out with them everywhere—even at night. This is especially true on Lincoln Road. As touristy as it may be, Bayside Marketplace is another good kids' spot, but during the day only. Kids love the boats coming in and out of the marina there and in Coconut Grove. When all else fails, grab a pail, shovel, and umbrella and hit the beach. Sand and surf almost never ceases to amuse. Here are some of the most kid-friendly attractions in Miami:

Aventura Mall (p. 138)
Bayside Marketplace (p. 139)
Coral Castle (p. 169)
Fruit and Spice Park (p. 173)
Jungle Island (p. 159)
Lincoln Road (p. 58)
Miami Children's Museum (p. 60)
Miami Seaquarium (p. 64)
Miami Science Museum (p. 68)
Monkey Jungle (p. 70)
Sea Grass Adventures (p. 65)
Venetian Pool (p. 67)
Wolfsonian–Florida International University (p. 61)
Zoo Miami (p. 70)

OUTDOOR ACTIVITIES

BIKING　The cement promenade on the southern tip of South Beach is a great place to ride. Biking up the beach (either on the beach or along the beach on a cement pathway—which is a lot easier!) is great for surf, sun, sand, exercise, and people-watching—just be sure to keep your eyes on the road, as the scenery can be most distracting. Most of the big beach hotels rent bicycles, as does the **Miami Beach Bicycle Center,** 601 5th St., South Beach (www.bikemiamibeach.com; ☎ 305/674-0150), which charges $8 per hour, $24 for up to 24 hours, and $80 weekly. It's open Monday through Saturday from 10am to 7pm, Sunday from 10am to 5pm.

For those looking to literally power-bike, **The Electric Bicycle Store,** 1622 Alton Rd., South Beach (www.theelectricbicyclestore.com; ☎ 305/508-4040), has just what you need. Choose from either a completely motorized form of cycling or a mix of pedaling and motor power known as "pedal-assist," which is especially easy on the knees. Rates are $65 per day.

Bikers can also enjoy more than 130 miles of paved paths throughout Miami. The beautiful and quiet streets of Coral Gables and Coconut Grove (several bike trails are spread throughout these neighborhoods) are great for bicyclists, where old trees form canopies over wide, flat roads lined with grand homes and quaint street markers.

A Whole New World

Every Columbus Day, Biscayne Bay becomes a veritable mob scene of boaters celebrating the discovery of another day off of work. The unofficial Columbus Day Regatta has become a tradition in which people take to the water for a day of boating, sunning, and, literally, the bare necessities, as they often strip down to their birthday suits in an eye-opening display of their appreciation for Columbus's discovery of the nude, er, new world.

The terrain in Key Biscayne is perfect for biking, especially along the park and beach roads. If you don't mind the sound of cars whooshing by your bike lane, **Rickenbacker Causeway** is also fantastic, as it is one of the only bikeable inclines in Miami from which you get fantastic elevated views of the city and waterways. However, be warned that this is a grueling ride, especially going up the causeway. **Key Cycling,** 61 Harbor Dr., Key Biscayne (www.keycycling.com; © **305/361-0061**), rents mountain bikes for $15 for 2 hours, $24 a day, or $80 a week. It's open Tuesday through Friday from 10am to 7pm, Monday and Saturday from 10am to 6pm, and Sunday from 10am to 3pm.

If you want to avoid the traffic altogether, head out to **Shark Valley** in the Everglades National Park—one of South Florida's most scenic bicycle trails and a favorite haunt of city-weary locals.

Biking note: Children 15 and under are required by Florida law to wear a helmet, which can be purchased at any bike store or retail outlet selling biking supplies.

BOATING   Private rental outfits include **Boat Rental Plus,** 2400 Collins Ave., Miami Beach (© **305/534-4307**), where powerboats rent for some of the best prices on the beach. Here, you can rent a 21-footer for $69 per hour not including tax or gas, with a 2-hour minimum. A 4-hour rental will get you a free hour. Cruising is permitted only in and around Biscayne Bay (ocean access is prohibited), and renters must be 21 or older to rent a boat. The rental office is at 23rd Street, on the inland waterway in Miami Beach. It's open daily from 10am to sunset. If you want a specific type of boat, call ahead to reserve. Otherwise, show up and take what's available.

For those planning on staying in town a bit longer or more frequently, **Easy Boating Club,** 3301 Rickenbacker Causeway (www.easyboatingclub.com; © **305/856-8229**), is a members-only club that lets you hit the high seas for $199 a month plus a $2,500 initiation fee. You get unlimited access to a fabulous fleet of boats without the hassle of maintenance . . . and, like your best friend or ex-girlfriend, boats are notorious for being high maintenance. With a fleet composed of boats 21 to 23 feet long, the Easy Boating Club has something for everyone, even those whose inner GPS has them a little dazed and confused. An orientation will provide you with explicit instructions on how to maneuver the boat, where to maneuver the boat, good seamanship, and where to find sandbars, canals, restaurants, and other water-based attractions. Also included: basic gear for fishing, tubing, snorkeling, and more.

FISHING   Fishing licenses are required in Florida. If you go out with one of the fishing charter boats listed below, you are automatically accredited because the companies are. If you go out on your own, however, you must have a Florida fishing license, which costs $17 for 3 days and $30 for a week. Visit www.wildlifelicense.com or call © **888/FISH-FLO** (347-4356) for more information.

Some of the best surf-casting in the city can be had at **Haulover Beach Park** at Collins Avenue and 105th Street, where there's a bait-and-tackle shop right on the pier. **South Pointe Park,** at the southern tip of Miami Beach, is another popular fishing spot and features a long pier, comfortable benches, and a great view of the ships passing through Government Cut, the deep channel made when the port of Miami was dug.

You can also do some deep-sea fishing in the Miami area. One bargain outfitter, the **Kelley Fishing Fleet,** at the Haulover Marina, 10800 Collins Ave. (at 108th St.), Miami Beach (www.miamibeachfishing.com; ℂ 305/945-3801), has half-day, full-day, and night fishing aboard diesel-powered "party boats." The fleet's emphasis on drifting is geared toward trolling and bottom-fishing for snapper, sailfish, and mackerel. Half-day and night-fishing trips are $43 for adults and $33 for children up to 10 years old, and full-day trips are $64 for adults and $52 for children. Daily departures are scheduled at 9am and 1:45 and 8pm, and there is a late-night trip departing Saturday at 1am that costs $50 for adults and $38 for children; reservations are recommended.

Also at the Haulover Marina is the charter boat *Helen C,* 10800 Collins Ave. (www.fishmiamibeach.com; ℂ **305/947-4081**). Although there's no shortage of private charter boats here, Captain Dawn Mergelsberg is a good pick, because she puts individuals together to get a full boat. The *Helen C* is a twin-engine 55-footer, equipped for big-game fish such as marlin, tuna, mahimahi, shark, and sailfish. The cost is $160 per person. Private, full-day trips are available for groups of six people per vessel and cost $1,350; half-days are $750. Group rates and specials are also available. Trips are scheduled for 8am to noon and 1 to 5pm daily; call for reservations. Beginners and children are always welcome.

For a serious fishing charter, Captain Charlie Hotchkiss's *Sea Dancer* (www. seadancercharter.com; ℂ **305/775-5534**) offers a first-class experience on a 38-foot Luhrs boat complete with tuna tower and air-conditioned cabin. If you're all about big game—marlin, dolphin, tuna, wahoo, swordfish, and sailfish—this is the charter for you. Catch and release, or fillet your catch to take home. The *Sea Dancer* also offers two fun water adventures, including a 6-hour Bar Cruz, covering the finest watering holes in Miami and Fort Lauderdale, or a Sandbar Cruz, where the boat drops anchor out by Biscayne Bay's historic Stiltsville, where you'll swim, bounce on a water trampoline, and play sports—all in the middle of the bay. Auto transportation is available to wherever the boat may be docked. Rates are $700 for a half-day and $1,100 for a full day, and $500 for the specialty tours. Tours are also available to Bimini. Call for pricing.

Key Biscayne offers deep-sea fishing to those willing to get their hands dirty and pay a bundle. The competition among the boats is fierce, but the prices are basically the same, no matter which you choose. The going rate is about $400 to $500 for a half-day and $600 to $900 for a full day of fishing. These rates are usually for a party of up to six, and the boats supply you with rods and bait as well as instruction for first-timers. Some will also take you out to the Upper Keys if the fish aren't biting in Miami.

You might also consider the following boats, all of which sail out of the Key Biscayne marina and are in relatively good shape and nicer than most out there: *Sunny Boy* (www.sonnyboysportfishing.com; ℂ **305/361-2217**), *Top Hatt* (ℂ **305/361-2528**), and *L & H* (www.landhsportfishing.com; ℂ **305/361-9318**). Call for reservations.

Bridge fishing in Biscayne Bay is also popular in Miami; you'll see people with poles over almost every waterway. But look carefully for signs telling you whether it's legal to do so wherever you are: Some bridges forbid fishing.

Outdoor Activities

EXPLORING MIAMI

GOLF   There are more than 50 private and public golf courses in the Miami area. Contact the **Greater Miami Convention and Visitor's Bureau** (www.miamiand beaches.com; ✆ 800/933-8448) for information.

The best hotel courses in Miami are found at the **Doral Golf Resort and Spa** (p. 211), home of the legendary Blue Monster course, as well as the Gold Course, designed by Raymond Floyd; the Great White Shark Course; and the newest course, the former Silver Course, refinished by Jim McLean and known as the Jim McLean Signature course, which, according to experts, has one of the toughest starting holes in the entire state.

Other hotels with excellent golf courses include the **Turnberry Isle Miami** (p. 199), with two Robert Trent Jones, Sr.–designed courses for guests and members, and the **Biltmore Hotel ★★★** (p. 207), which is our pick for best public golf course because of its modest greens fees and an 18-hole, par-71 course located on the hotel's spectacular grounds. It must be good: Despite his penchant for privacy, former president Bill Clinton prefers teeing off at this course more than any other in Miami!

Otherwise, the following represent some of the area's best public courses. **Crandon Park Golf Course,** formerly known as the Links, 6700 Crandon Blvd., Key Biscayne (www.crandongolfclub.com; ✆ 305/361-9129), is the number-one-ranked municipal course in the state and one of the top five in the country. The park is situated on 200 bayfront acres and offers a pro shop, rentals, lessons, carts, and a lighted driving range. The course is open daily from dawn to dusk; greens fees (including cart) range from $100 to $180, depending on the season, for nonresidents and include a cart. Special twilight rates are also available. Golf club rental is available for $55.

One of the most popular courses among real enthusiasts is the **Doral Park Golf and Country Club,** 5001 NW 104th Ave., West Miami (www.doralpark.org; ✆ 305/ 591-8800); formerly known as the Silver Course, the redesigned Jim McLean Signature Course is managed by the Doral Golf Resort and Spa. Call to book in advance, as this challenging, semiprivate 18-holer is extremely popular with locals. The course is open from 6:30am to 6pm during the winter and until 7pm during the summer. Cart and greens fees vary, so call ✆ 305/592-2000, ext. 2104, for information.

Known as one of the best in the city, the **Country Club of Miami,** 6801 Miami Gardens Dr., at NW 68th Avenue, North Miami (www.golfmiamicc.com; ✆ 305/829-8456), has three 18-hole courses of varying degrees of difficulty. You'll encounter lush fairways, rolling greens, and some history, to boot. The west course, designed in 1961 by Robert Trent Jones, Sr., and updated in the 1990s by the PGA, was where Jack Nicklaus played his first professional tournament and Lee Trevino won his first professional championship. The course is open daily from 7am to sunset. Cart and greens fees are $29 to $58, depending on the season and tee times. Special twilight rates are available.

The recently renovated **Miami Beach Golf Club,** 2301 Alton Rd., South Beach (www.miamibeachgolfclub.com; ✆ 305/532-3350), is a gorgeous, 79-year-old course that, par for the, er, course in Miami Beach, received a $10-million face-lift. Miami Heat players and Matt Damon have been known to tee off here. Greens fees range from $100 to $200, depending on the season.

JET SKIS/WAVERUNNERS   Don't miss a chance to tour the islands on the back of your own powerful watercraft. Bravery is, however, a prerequisite, as Miami's waterways are full of speeding jet skiers and boaters who think they're in the Indy 500. Many beachfront concessionaires rent a variety of these popular (and loud) water scooters. The latest models are fast and smooth. **American Watersports,** at the Miami Beach Marina, 300 Alton Rd. (www.jetskiz.com; © **305/538-7549**), is the area's most popular spot for jet-ski rental. Rates begin at $60 for a half-hour and $89 for an hour, not including gas. They also offer fun jet-ski tours past celebrity homes beginning at $109 an hour.

KAYAKING The **Blue Moon Outdoor Center** rents kayaks at 3400 NE 163rd St., in Oleta River Park (www.bluemoonmiami.com; © **305/957-3040**). Kayak rentals for self-guided tours include single or tandem kayaks and canoes. All rates are for the first 1½ hours. Rates are $18 for single kayak, $26 for tandem kayak. Canoes are $30. Paddle down several calm water routes and spot blue herons, bottlenose dolphin, and possibly manatees. Kayak instructional classes are offered by instructors certified by the ACA (American Canoe Association). There's also stand-up paddleboarding, if that's what you're into. Rentals start at $22. The park offers 16 miles of mountain bike trails rated green for easy, blue for intermediate, and black for difficult. Rates for full-suspension mountain bikes begin at $24. Guided eco-tours are available with advance reservation. There are also some really cool monthly full-moon kayak and bike trips, including a bonfire on the beach. Adventure on either a kayak or a bike, or do the combination deal for $75. Afterward, eat at the famous waterfront Blue Marlin Fish House Restaurant for some smoked fish or fresh lobster burgers. The center is open daily from 9am to sunset. Blue Moon has a second location, **The Loggerhead,** in Broward County at John U. Lloyd Beach State Park in Dania Beach, 6503 N. Ocean Blvd. (© **954/923-6711**), offering kayak, canoe, and standup paddleboard rentals daily from 10am to 5pm. They also offer catering on the beach.

SAILING You can rent sailboats and catamarans through the beachfront concessions desks of several top resorts, such as the Doral Golf Resort and Spa (p. 211).

  Aquatic Rental Center, at northern Biscayne Bay in the Pelican Harbor Marina, 1275 NE 79th St. (www.arcmiami.com; © **305/751-7514** days, 305/279-7424 evenings), can also get you out on the water. A 22-foot sailboat rents for $85 for 2 hours, $125 for 3 hours, $150 for a half-day, and $225 for a full day. A Sunfish sailboat for two people rents at $35 per hour. If you've always had a dream to win the America's Cup but can't sail, the able teachers here will get you started. They offer a 10-hour course over 5 days for $400 for one person, or $500 for two.

SCUBA DIVING & SNORKELING In 1981, the U.S. government began a wide-scale project designed to increase the number of habitats available to marine organisms. One of the program's major accomplishments has been the creation of nearby artificial reefs, which have attracted all kinds of tropical plants, fish, and animals. In addition, **Biscayne National Park** (p. 228) offers a protected marine environment less than an hour's drive south of downtown.

  Several dive shops around the city offer organized weekend outings, either to the reefs or to one of more than a dozen old shipwrecks around Miami's shores. Check "Divers" in the Yellow Pages for rental equipment and for a full list of undersea tour operators.

  Diver's Paradise of Key Biscayne, 4000 Crandon Blvd. (www.keydivers.com; © **305/361-3483**), offers one dive expedition per day during the week and two per day on the weekends to the more than 30 wrecks and artificial reefs off the coast of Miami Beach and Key Biscayne. You can take a 3-day certification course for $499, which includes all the dives and gear. If you already have your C-card, a dive trip costs about $100 if you need equipment, and $60 if you bring your own gear. It's open Tuesday through Friday from 10am to 6pm, and Saturday and Sunday from 8am to

6pm. Call ahead for times and locations of dives. For snorkeling, they will set you up with equipment and maps on where to see the best underwater sights. Rental for mask, fins, and snorkel is $60.

South Beach Divers, 850 Washington Ave., Miami Beach (www.southbeach divers.com; © **305/531-6110**), will also be happy to tell you where to go under the sea and will provide you with scuba rental equipment as well for $65. You can rent snorkel gear for about $12. They also do dive trips to Key Largo three times a week and do dives off Miami on Sunday at $120 for a two-tank dive or $85 if you have your own equipment. Night dives and trips to the USS *Spiegel Grove,* a dive site in Key Largo, are $10 extra.

The most amusing and apropos South Beach diving spot has to be the **Jose Cuervo Underwater Bar,** located 150 yards southeast of the 2nd Street lifeguard station—a 22-ton concrete margarita bar that was sunk on May 5, 2000. Nicknamed "Sinko De Mayo," the site is designed with a dive flag roof, six bar stools, and a protective wall of tetrahedrons.

SWIMMING   There is no shortage of water in the Miami area. See the Venetian Pool listing (p. 67) and the "Miami's Beaches" section on p. 53 for descriptions of good swimming options.

TENNIS   Hundreds of tennis courts in South Florida are open to the public for a minimal fee. Most courts operate on a first-come, first-served basis and are open from sunrise to sunset. For information and directions, call the **City of Miami Beach Recreation, Culture, and Parks Department** (© **305/673-7730**) or the **City of Miami Parks and Recreation Department** (© **305/575-5256**). Of the 590 public tennis courts throughout Miami, the three hard courts and seven clay courts at the **Crandon Tennis Center,** 6702 Crandon Blvd. (© **305/361-5263**), are the best and most beautiful. Because of this, they often get crowded on weekends. You'll play on the same courts as Lendl, Graf, Evert, McEnroe, Federer, the Williams sisters, and other greats; this is also the venue for one of the world's biggest annual tennis events, the Sony Ericsson Open. There's a pleasant, if limited, pro shop, plus many good pros. Only four courts are lit at night, but if you reserve at least 24 to 48 hours in advance, you can usually take your pick. Hard courts cost $4 person per hour during the day, $6 per person per hour at night. Clay courts cost $7 per person per hour during the day. Grass courts are $11 per person per hour. There are no night hours on the clay or grass courts. The courts are open Monday through Friday from 8am to 9pm, Saturday and Sunday until 6pm.

Other courts are pretty run-of-the-mill and can be found in most neighborhoods. We do, however, recommend the **Miami Beach public courts at Flamingo Park,** 1001 12th St., in South Beach (© **305/673-7761**), where there are 19 clay courts that cost $5 per person an hour for Miami Beach residents and $10 per person an hour for non-residents. Playing at night adds an extra $1.50 "light fee." It's first-come, first-served, and is open 8am to 9pm Monday through Friday, 8am to 8pm Saturday and Sunday.

Hotels with the best tennis facilities are the Biltmore (p. 207), Turnberry Isle Miami (p. 190), Doral Golf Resort and Spa (p. 211), and Inn and Spa at Fisher Island Club (p. 180).

WINDSURFING   Many hotels rent windsurfers to their guests, but if yours doesn't have a watersports concession stand, head for Key Biscayne. **Sailboards Miami,** Rickenbacker Causeway, Key Biscayne (www.sailboardsmiami.com; © **305/361-SAIL** [7245]), operates out of two big yellow trucks on Windsurfer Beach, the most popular (though our pick for best is Hobie Beach) windsurfing spot in the city. For those who've never ridden a board but want to try it, they offer a 2-hour lesson for $79 that's guaranteed to turn you into a wave warrior, or you get your money back. After that, you can rent a board for $25 to $30 an hour. If you want to make a day of it, a 10-hour prepaid card costs $240 to $290. These cards reduce the price by about $70 for the day. You can use the card year-round, until the time on it runs out. Sailboards Miami is open Tuesday through Sunday from 10am to 5:30pm. Make your first right after the tollbooth ($\frac{7}{10}$ of a mile after the tollbooth at the beginning of the causeway—you can't miss it) to find the outfitters. They also rent kayaks.

ORGANIZED TOURS

In addition to the tours listed below, a great option for seeing the city is a tour led by **Dr. Paul George.** Dr. George is a history teacher at Miami-Dade Community College and a historian at the Historical Museum of Southern Florida. There's a variety of tours (including the "Ghostly, Ghastly Vice & Crime Coach Tour," detailed below), all fascinating to South Florida buffs. Tours focus on such neighborhoods as Little Havana, Brickell Avenue, or Key Biscayne, and on themes such as Miami cemeteries, the Miami River, and Stiltsville, the "neighborhood" of houses on stilts in the middle of Biscayne Bay. There are also eco-history coach, walking, boat, and bike tours. The often-long-winded discussions can be a bit much for those who just want a quick look around, but Dr. George certainly knows his stuff. The cost is $25 to $49, and reservations are required (www.historymiami.org; ✆ 305/375-1621). Tours leave from the Historical Museum at 101 W. Flagler St., downtown. Call for a schedule.

Design District and Midtown Experience   As the Design District and Midtown Miami areas continue to grow, someone saw fit to create a tour to the neighborhoods. More than a tour, however, it's really just a shuttle bus that ferries visitors from their hotels to shops, restaurants, and galleries. Cost is $89 a person and includes round-trip transportation, a three-course lunch or dinner at participating restaurants, and merchant discounts. Sounds good in theory, but we kind of think it's easier—and cheaper—to take a cab.

www.designdistrictexperience.com. ✆ **786/237-7567.**

Eco-Adventure Tours ★★★   For the eco-conscious traveler, the Miami-Dade Parks and Recreation Department offers guided nature, adventure, and historic tours involving biking, canoeing, snorkeling, hiking, and bird-watching all over the city.

www.miamiecoadventures.com. ✆ **305/365-3018.**

Gray Line Miami ★   Take a tour and get tan as the double-decker buses cruise you through Miami Beach, downtown Miami, Coconut Grove, Little Havana, and Coral Gables from 9am to 6pm daily. A 24-hour hop-on, hop-off pass for the Miami Beach or Grove/Gables loops costs $34 for adults and $24 for kids ages 3 to 13; a 48-hour hop-on, hop-off pass for all routes costs $49 for adults and $39 for kids 3 to 13.

www.graylinemiami.com. ✆ **877/643-1258.**

"Ghostly, Ghastly Vice & Crime Coach Tour" ★★★   Visit the past by video and bus to Miami-Dade's most celebrated crimes and criminals from the 1800s to the present, including some sites where the '80s TV series *Miami Vice* was filmed. From the murder spree of the Ashley Gang to the most notorious murders and crimes of the last century, including the murder of designer Gianni Versace, historian Paul George conducts a most fascinating 3-hour tour of scandalous proportions.

Leaves from the Dade Cultural Center, 101 W. Flagler St., Miami. Advance reservations required; call ©**305/375-1621.** Tickets $44. Held twice a year, usually in Apr and Oct.

"Hispanic Heritage Tour" This is offered during October only (Hispanic Heritage Month). For those looking to immerse themselves in Miami's rich Latin-American culture, the "Herencia Hispana Tour" is the ideal way to explore it all. Hop on a bus and zoom past such hotbeds of Latin activity as downtown's Flagler Street, the unavoidable Elián González house, and Little Havana's Domino Park and Tower Theater, among others. Not just a sightseeing tour, this one includes two very knowledgeable, albeit corny, guides who know just when to infuse a necessary dose of humor into the Elián saga, a segment of history that some people may not consider so amusing.

Tours depart from the Steven P. Clark Government Center, 111 NW 1st St. ©**305/770-3131.** Tours (in Spanish or English, but you must specify which one you require) are free, but advance reservations are required. Tours depart at 9, 9:30, and 10am every Sat in Oct.

"Little Havana Cuban Cuisine & Culture Walking Tour" ★★★ A historian will guide you through a savory tour of Little Havana, stopping for samples of local cuisine and coffee and even stopping to play dominoes with the locals. Tour also includes a visit to the Bay of Pigs Museum, area social clubs, and a *botanica,* a shop that caters to followers of the Santeria or Voudon religions.

www.historymiami.org. ©**305/375-1621.** Tour $30.

Miami Culinary Tours ★★★ There once was a time when Miami was synonymous with early-bird specials and models who didn't eat. Things have changed. Now you can eat your way through the city's most savory neighborhoods, leaving with a few extra pounds to prove it. Miami-as-melting-pot takes on a completely edible meaning thanks to these custom-crafted, specialized tours. Ten years ago, it was inconceivable to eat your way through the Art Deco District, but now you can do just that and marvel at the architecture. And while Little Havana has always been a mouthwatering mecca of Cuban food, thanks to Miami Culinary Tours it's like having your own private Rosetta stone without all the repetition. Choose from 2½-hour tours of South Beach's or Little Havana's best bites, or the "Miami Food Tasting Tour," a 3½-hour Cuban-inspired epicurean adventure throughout the city.

 Venice in Miami

You don't have to endure jet lag and time-zone differences to enjoy the beauty of Italy. Located just off Miami Beach, Florida's own Venetian Islands (NE 15th St. and Dade Blvd.) were joined together in 1926 by a bascule bridge known as the **Venetian Causeway.** A series of 12 bridges connecting the Venetian Islands and stretching between Miami and Miami Beach feature octagonal concrete entrance towers, which give you a great view of the water. The oldest causeway in metropolitan Miami, the Venetian is rickety in a charming way, with fantastic views of the city and the mammoth cruise ships docked at the port, not to mention glimpses of some of Miami's most beautiful waterfront homes. Bikers and joggers especially love the Venetian Causeway, thanks to its limited traffic and beautiful scenery.

Vintage Miami

Although it's hardly Napa Valley, Miami does have an actual winery: **Schnebly Redland's Winery**, 30205 SW 217th Ave., Homestead (www.schneblywinery. com; © **888/717-WINE** [9463]), in whose $1.5-million tasting room you can sample from various vintages. We've tried some, and while they're too fruity for our taste, it's still worth a trip down just to see the press deck where fruit becomes juice and eventually wine. There are 30- to 40-minute tours on weekends for $7 per person and daily tastings for $7 to $ 10 per person. On Friday and Saturday nights, there's live music starting at 6pm for $10 per person. It's open 10am to 5pm Monday to Friday, 10am to 8pm Saturday, and noon to 7pm Sunday.

www.miamiculinarytours.com. © **855/642-3663.** South Beach or Little Havana tours $59; "Miami Food Tasting Tour" $95.

Miami Duck Tours   Hands down, this is the corniest, kookiest tour in the entire city. In fact, the company prefers to call these tours the "quackiest" way to visit Miami and the beaches. Whatever you call it, it's weird. The *Watson Willy* is the first of several Miami Duck Tours "vesicles," not a body part, but a hybrid name that means part vessel, part vehicle (technical name: Hydra Terra Amphibious Vehicle). Each vesicle seats 49 guests, plus a captain and tour guide, and leaves from Watson Island behind Jungle Island, traveling through downtown Miami and South Beach. If you're image-conscious, you may want to reconsider traveling down Ocean Drive in a duck. That's right, a duck, which is what the vesicle looks like. After driving the streets in the duck, you'll end up cruising Biscayne Bay, past all the swank houses.

1661 James Ave., South Beach. www.ducktoursmiami.com. © **305/673-2217.** Tickets $32 adults, $26 seniors and military, $18 children 12 and under.

Redland Tropical Trail Tours ★★★   Check out South Florida farmlands—yes, they do exist in an area near Homestead called the Redlands—on this tour featuring a circuit of stops, tastings, and sightseeing that will take you from gardens and jungles to an orchid farm, an actual working winery (see below), a fruit stand, and more. There's no cost to follow the trail with a map (available on the website) on your own, but call for pricing information for certain attractions found on the trail.

www.redlandtrail.com. © **305/245-9180.**

SIGHTS & ATTRACTIONS BY THEME

5

EXPLORING MIAMI | Sights & Attractions by Theme

WHERE TO EAT IN MIAMI

D on't be fooled by the plethora of superlean model types you're likely to see posing throughout Miami. Contrary to popular belief, dining in this city is as much a sport as plastic surgery and beach yoga. With more than 6,000 restaurants to choose from, dining out in Miami has become a passionate pastime for locals and visitors alike. Our star chefs have fused Californian-Asian with Caribbean and Latin elements to create a world-class flavor all its own: **Floribbean.** Think mango chutney splashed over fresh swordfish or a spicy sushi sauce served alongside Peruvian ceviche.

Miami's new-wave cuisine now rivals that of San Francisco—or even New York. Nouveau Cuban chef Douglas Rodriguez returned to his roots with a few fabulous South Beach nouveau Latino eateries. In addition, other stellar chefs—such as Michael Schwartz and Michelle Bernstein—remain firmly planted in the city's culinary scene, fusing local ingredients into edible masterpieces. Florida foodies rolled out the red carpet for the arrival of Daniel Boulud, just as they did for Scott Conant and Alfred Portale at the swanky Fontainebleau, Jean Georges Vongerichten at the St. Regis Bal Harbour Resort, and soon enough, Jose Andres at the SLS Hotel South Beach. A new rumor is cooked up daily about which megachef plans to open in Miami next. Be prepared to splurge for this stellar New World cuisine.

Thanks to a thriving cafe society in both South Beach and Coconut Grove, you can also enjoy a moderately priced meal and linger for hours without having a waiter hover over you. In Little Havana, you can chow down on a meal that serves about six for less than $10. Because seafood is plentiful, it doesn't have to cost you an arm and a leg to enjoy the appendages of a crab or lobster. Don't be put off by the looks of our recommended seafood shacks in places such as Key Biscayne—often, these spots get the best and freshest catches.

Whatever you're craving, Miami's got it—with the exception of decent, affordable Chinese food and a New York–style slice of pizza. If you're craving a scene with your steak, then South Beach is the place to be. Like many cities in Europe and Latin America, it is fashionable to dine late in South Beach, preferably after 9pm, sometimes as late as midnight. Service on South Beach is notoriously slow and arrogant, but it comes with the turf. (Of course, it is possible to find restaurants that defy the notoriety and actually pride themselves on friendly service.) On the mainland—especially in Coral Gables and, more recently, downtown, Midtown, and on Brickell Avenue— you can also experience fine dining without the pretense.

The biggest complaint when it comes to Miami dining isn't the haughtiness, but rather the dearth of truly moderately priced restaurants, especially in South Beach and Coral Gables. It's either really cheap or really expensive; the in-between somehow gets lost in the culinary shuffle. Quick-service diners don't exist here as they do in other cosmopolitan areas. We've tried to cover a range of cuisine in a range of prices. But with new restaurants opening on a weekly basis, you're bound to find an array of savory dining choices for every budget.

Many restaurants keep extended hours in high season (roughly Dec–Apr) and may close for lunch and/or dinner on Monday, when the traffic is slower. Always call ahead, as schedules do change. During the month of August, many Miami restaurants participate in Miami Spice, where three-course lunches and dinners are served at affordable prices. Check out **www.miamirestaurantmonth.com**. Also, always look carefully at your bill—many Miami restaurants add a 15% to 18% gratuity to your total due to the enormous influx of European tourists who are not accustomed to tipping. Keep in mind that this amount is the *suggested* amount and can be adjusted, either higher or lower, depending on your assessment of the service provided. Because of this tipping-included policy, South Beach waitstaff are best known for their lax or inattentive service. *Feel free to adjust it* if you feel your server deserves more or less.

best MIAMI RESTAURANT BETS

- **Best Splurge: Prime One Twelve** on Miami Beach (p. 92) is where everyone from Gorbachev and Clinton to Madonna and Beyoncé come to satisfy their carnivorous sides, with fare such as $25 Kobe beef hot dogs, dried sticks of bacon at the bar in lieu of peanuts, and the best truffle-infused macaroni and cheese you'll ever eat. The **Forge Restaurant | Wine Bar** (p. 103) is another place to splurge on excellent steaks and seafood.

- **Most Romantic Restaurant: Casa Tua,** in South Beach (📞 **305/673-1010**), offers exquisite Italian cuisine in a Mediterranean villa that's hidden from the street with lush landscaping and an iron gate, resplendent outdoor garden, cozy Hamptons-esque dining room, communal kitchen, and intimate upstairs lounge and patio. See p. 89.

- **Best Value:** Some of the best, heartiest meal deals can be found right on the street corner, in bodegas and no-frills Cuban eateries such as **Versailles** (p. 125) in Little Havana and **Puerto Sagua** (p. 102) and **David's Cafe II** (p. 100) on South Beach, where everything from *arroz con pollo* and Cuban sandwiches to simple eggs and toast won't set you back your next vacation.

- **Best for Families:** If massive movie screens and pizza aren't enough to keep the young 'uns entertained, **Andiamo** (p. 121) has a car wash that may do the trick. Back on South Beach, the reigning kid-friendly foodie spot is **Big Pink** (p. 96), where the monstrous menu is guaranteed to satisfy the pickiest of children and where the volume is almost always on max, so more vocal kids will feel right at home.

- **Best Service:** Service in South Florida is typically less than stellar, but at the Biltmore's **Palme d'Or** (p. 126) and at the Mandarin Oriental's **Azul** (p. 110), service is impeccable (as it should be at those prices). At **Joe's Stone Crab** (p. 90), career servers are throwbacks to the day and age when service was as paramount as food to the fine dining experience.

- **Best Waterfront Dining:** It's a tossup between Biscayne Bay and the Atlantic Ocean, but whichever you prefer, there are two restaurants that provide front-row seats to both. The Mandarin Oriental Hotel's global fusion restaurant, **Azul** (p. 110), faces the Miami skyline and beautiful, tranquil Biscayne Bay, while **Garcia's** (p. 114) faces the scenic Miami River. Tough decisions, but both are winners.

o **Best Cuban Restaurant:** There's always a debate on who has the best, most authentic Cuban cuisine, but for those of you who have never been to Havana, Miami's **Versailles,** in Little Havana (p. 125), is *the* quintessential Cuban diner, featuring enormous portions at paltry prices. For an even more frenetic, freshly squeezed Cuban dining experience, check out **El Palacio de los Jugos** (p. 125).

o **Best Seafood:** In downtown Miami, **The River Seafood & Oyster Bar** (p. 114), **Area 31** (p. 110), and **Garcia's Seafood Grille & Fish** (p. 114) are three of your best catches. Sunny Isles' stellar **NAOE Miami** (p. 112) has a Hollywood vibe and serves up fresh sushi with star power.

o **Best Sunday Brunch: Michael's Genuine Food & Drink** (p. 119) in the Design District could win every one of our "best of" categories thanks to its locally sourced, organic seasonal cuisine; out-of-control desserts; buzzy bar scene; and colorful crowd of foodies, hipsters, celebrities, and assorted culinary dignitaries. The brunch, however, is truly in a category of its own. In a few words: kimchi Benedict and strawberry and *yuzu* Pop-Tarts.

o **Best People-Watching:** The **News Cafe,** in South Beach (p. 101), practically invented the sport of people-watching, encouraging its customers to sit at an out-door table all day if they want, lingering over the passing parades of people while sipping a cappuccino. Lincoln Road's Euro-fabulous **Segafredo Espresso** cafe (p. 160) provides a front-row seat to the hordes of people who parade along the pedestrian mall.

SOUTH BEACH

The renaissance of South Beach started in the early '90s and is still continuing as classic cuisine gives in to modern temptation by inevitably fusing with more chic, nouveau developments created by faithful followers and devotees of the Food Network school of cooking. The ultimate result has spawned dozens of first-rate restaurants. In fact, big-name restaurants from across the country have capitalized on South Beach's international appeal and have continued to open branches here with great success. A few old standbys remain from the *Miami Vice* days, but the flock of newcomers dominates the scene, with places going in and out of style as quickly as the tides.

On South Beach, new restaurants are opening and closing as frequently as Emeril says "Bam!" Despite an economic downturn, when it comes to restaurants, things always seem to be in an upswing, at least according to one poll that said Miamians dine out more than anyone else in the country. And, ironically, most are upscale. As it's impossible to list them all, we recommend strolling and browsing. Most restaurants post a copy of their menu outside. With very few exceptions, the places on Ocean Drive are crowded with tourists and priced accordingly. You'll do better to venture a little farther onto the pedestrian-friendly streets just west of Ocean Drive.

Very Expensive

Asia de Cuba ★ ASIAN/LATIN   Located within the remarkably stunning lobby of the Mondrian hotel, this stylish Asian/Latin import from N.Y.C. and L.A. is the latest Miami offering from the China Grill empire. A fusion of Latin and Asian cuisines, the menu features some familiar favorites tweaked from other China Grill eateries and

A La Folie **26**
Altamare **5**
Asia de Cuba **25**
Balan's **12**
Barton G.
　The Restaurant **24**
Bianca **19**
Big Pink **43**
BLT Steak **30**
Bond St. Lounge **21**
Burger & Beer Joint **3**
The Cafe at Books
　& Books **9**
Casa Tua **18**
China Grill **41**
Clarke's **46**
David's Cafe II **15**
The Dutch **22**
11th Street Diner **35**
Escopazzo **33**
Front Porch Cafe **31**
Grillfish **29**
Haven **6**
Icebox Cafe **13**
Jerry's Famous Deli **28**
Jimmy'z Kitchen **23**
Joe's Stone Crab
　Restaurant **47**
Juvia **7**
Larios on the Beach **36**
La Sandwicherie **32**
Macaluso's **4**
Meat Market **8**
Monty's Sunset
　Seafood Bistro **40**
Mr Chow **22**
News Cafe **37**
Nexxt Cafe **16**
Nobu **20**
Osteria del Teatro **27**
Philippe **44**
Piola **10**
Prime One Twelve **45**
Pubbelly **1**
Puerto Sagua **38**
Quattro **12**

Red, the
　Steakhouse **42**
Sardinia **2**
Shake Shack **7**
Smith &
　Wollensky **48**
Spiga **34**
STK **22**
Sushi Samba
　Dromo **17**
Tap Tap **39**
Van Dyke Cafe **14**
Yardbird Southern
　Table & Bar **11**

served as new here, including the calamari salad Asia de Cuba, featuring the same crispy calamari as China Grill, only this time with more of a tropical twist with ingredients such as chayote, hearts of palm, and banana. Main courses include succulent Cuban barbecue chicken with Thai coconut sticky rice, avocado cilantro fruit salsa, and tamarind sauce; as well as coconut mustard-seed sustainable Chilean sea bass with crab and corn flan, cilantro chimichurri, and jalapeño plum coulis. Prices are steep, but you are paying for prime real estate. Now if only you could just move in.

In the Mondrian, 1100 West Ave., South Beach. www.chinagrillmgt.com. ℂ **305/673-1010.** Reservations required. Main courses $35–$76. AE, DC, MC, V. Daily 7am–10:45pm.

Barton G. The Restaurant ★ AMERICAN   Set on the quieter west side of South Beach, Barton G.—named after its owner, one of Miami's most famous, over-the-top event planners—is a place that looks like a trendy restaurant but eats like a show. Here, presentation is paramount. A popcorn-shrimp appetizer is served on a plateful of, yes, popcorn and stuffed into an actual popcorn box. A light, flavorful grilled sea bass is served in a brown paper bag with laundry clips preserving the steam until your server releases the flavor within. Desserts are equally outrageous: A giant plume of cotton candy reminiscent of drag diva Dame Edna's hair is surrounded by white-, dark-, and milk-chocolate-covered popcorn and chocolate-dipped pretzels. There's nothing ordinary about it, which is why athletes and celebrities such as LeBron James, Tom Cruise, and Will Smith are regulars. An elegant, orchid-laden indoor dining room is popular with members of the socialite set, for whom Barton G. has done many an affair, while the bar area and outdoor garden is the place to be for younger trend seekers.

Note: Another show-stopping production, **Prelude by Barton G.,** 1300 Biscayne Blvd. (ℂ **305/576-8888**), opened within the Adrienne Arsht Center and features a supper-clubby vibe. Choose your own three-course prix-fixe pre- and post-theater dinners. From swell to swanky, don't miss **The Dining Room at the Villa By Barton G.,** 1116 Ocean Dr. (ℂ **305/576-8003;** www.thevillabybartong.com), for impeccable decor and amazing food in the form of the truffled asparagus salad with morels and vodka-cured salmon with mustard caviar and dill pearls.

1427 West Ave., South Beach. ℂ **305/672-8881.** www.bartong.com. Reservations suggested. Main courses $21–$50. AE, DC, DISC, MC, V. Daily 6pm–midnight.

Bianca ★ ITALIAN   Unveiled in early 2012, Bianca is the Delano's latest offering, serving up swanky Italian fare. The menu features local, organic ingredients and participates in the very conscientious, yet very trendy Slow Food Movement. Signature dishes include wood-grilled langoustines, house-made pasta with fresh truffles (shaved table side), whole fish such as branzino and snapper, and an all-natural New York sirloin. The service here is exceptional and the ambience is classy and sophisticated. It's a mature restaurant, much like Bianca's best customers.

In the Delano Hotel, 1685 Collins Ave., South Beach. www.delano-hotel.com. ℂ **305/674-6400.** Reservations recommended for dinner. Main courses $25–$58. AE, DC, MC, V. Daily 7am–4pm and 7pm–midnight (bar until 3am).

BLT Steak ★★★ STEAKHOUSE   Just when we thought we'd had enough meat, BLT Steak opened its doors in the colonial-chic Betsy Hotel, and then we changed our minds. Unlike other steakhouses, this one by Laurent Tourondel is unpretentious and unstuffy, with superb service and a serene setting. The food is outstanding, from the minute they put down the complimentary plate of puffy, fluffy cheesy popovers and chicken liver pâté to your last lingering moment before forcing yourself to leave. Head straight for a selection of fresh and briny East and West Coast oysters, or consider the fantastic *hamachi* with avocado, hearts of palm, and *yuzu* vinaigrette. As for the steaks: They're exceptional, no matter which cut you order. The rib-eye is huge and seasoned perfectly, with marbling so perfect it would have made Liberace cry. Thanks to the meat, side dishes are almost unnecessary, though the creamed spinach–jalapeño mashed potatoes are rather irresistible. For mushroom fans, a side order of hard-to-find-in-these-parts hen of the woods mushrooms are a must, too.

1440 Ocean Dr. (in the Betsy Hotel), South Beach. © **305/673-0044.** Reservations recommended. Main courses $26–$75. AE, DC, MC, V. Daily 6–11pm.

Casa Tua ★★ ITALIAN   The stunning Casa Tua is a sleek and chic, country Italian-style establishment set in a refurbished 1925 Mediterranean-style house-cum-hotel (see p. 178). It has several dining areas, including a resplendent outdoor garden, comfy Ralph Lauren–esque living room, and a communal eat-in kitchen whose conviviality does not translate to some of the staff who have been known to turn up a nose at customers. If you're in the market to splurge, the whole Branzino is a huge hit, though we prefer the seared version with black olives, cherry tomatoes, roasted artichokes, and asparagus. Risottos are also highly recommended. Service is, as always with South Beach eateries, inconsistent, ranging from ultraprofessional to absurdly lackadaisical. For these prices, they should be wiping our mouths for us. What used to be a fabulous lounge upstairs is now a members-only club, so don't even try to get in.

1700 James Ave., South Beach. www.casatualifestyle.com/miami. © **305/673-1010.** Reservations required. Main courses $20–$100. AE, DC, MC, V. Mon–Sat 7pm–midnight.

China Grill ★ PAN-ASIAN   If ever a restaurant could be as cavernous as, say, the Asian continent, this would be it. Formerly a hub of hype and pompous circumstance, China Grill has calmed on the coolness meter despite the infrequent appearance of the likes of J-Lo and Enrique Iglesias, but its cuisine is still sizzling. With a dizzying array of amply portioned dishes (such as the outrageous crispy spinach, wasabi mashed potatoes, crispy calamari salad, spicy beef dumplings, lobster pancakes, and a sinfully delicious dessert sampler complete with sparklers), this epicurean journey into the world of near-perfect Pan-Asian cuisine is well worth a stop on any foodie's itinerary. Keep in mind that China Grill is a family-style restaurant and dishes are for sharing. For those who can't stay away from sushi, China Grill also has Dragon, a 40-seat "sushi den" in a private back room with such one-of-a-kind rolls as the Havana Roll—yellowtail snapper, rum, coconut, avocado, and red tobiko—and cocktails such as the Lemongrass Saketini.

404 Washington Ave., South Beach. www.chinagrillmgt.com. © **305/534-2211.** Reservations strongly recommended. Main courses $27–$59. AE, DC, MC, V. Mon–Thurs 11:45am–midnight; Fri 11:45am–1am; Sat 6pm–1am; Sun 6pm–midnight.

Escopazzo ★★★ ITALIAN   *Escopazzo* means "I'm going crazy" in Italian, but the only sign of insanity in this externally unassuming Northern Italian eatery is the fact that it seats only 90 and it's one of the best restaurants in town. The restaurant's cellar holds 1,000 bottles of various vintages. Escopazzo bills itself as an "Organic Italian Restaurant," serving fresh ingredients in all its dishes as well as a menu of raw vegan and vegetarian dishes. Should you be so lucky as to score a table at this romantic local favorite (choose one in the back dining room that's reminiscent of an Italian courtyard, complete with fountain and faux windows; it's not cheesy at all), you'll have trouble deciding between dishes. Standouts are the ravioli with salt-cured ricotta, honey, and lemon zest in tomato sauce; or grass-fed rib-eye with oyster-mushroom sauce. The hand-rolled pastas and risotto are near perfection. Eating here is like dining with a big Italian family—it's never boring (the menu changes five or six times a year), the service is excellent, and nobody's happy until you are blissfully full.

1311 Washington Ave., South Beach. www.escopazzo.com. ✆ **305/674-9450.** Reservations required. Main courses $26–$45; tasting menus $50-$125. AE, MC, V. Mon–Fri 6pm–midnight; Sat 6pm–1am; Sun 6–11pm.

Joe's Stone Crab Restaurant ★ SEAFOOD   Unless you grease the palms of one of the stone-faced maitre d's with some stone-cold cash, you'll be waiting for those famous claws for up to 2 hours—if not more. As much a Miami landmark as the beaches themselves, Joe's is a microcosm of the city, attracting everyone from T-shirted locals to a bejeweled Ivana Trump. Whatever you wear, however, will be eclipsed by a kitschy, unglamorous plastic bib that your waiter will tie on you unless you say otherwise. Open only during stone crab season (Oct–May), Joe's reels in the crowds with the freshest, meatiest stone crabs and their essential accoutrements: creamed spinach and excellent sweet-potato fries. The claws come in medium, large, and jumbo. Some say size doesn't matter; others swear by the jumbo (and more expensive) ones. Whatever you choose, pair them with a savory mustard sauce (a perfect mix of mayo and mustard) or hot butter. Not feeling crabby? The fried chicken and liver and onions on the regular menu are actually considered by many as far superior—they're definitely far cheaper—to the crabs. Oh yes, and save room for dessert. The Key lime pie here is the best in town. If you don't feel like waiting, try **Joe's Takeaway,** which is next door to the restaurant—it's a lot quicker and just as tasty.

11 Washington Ave. (at Biscayne St., just south of 1st St.), South Beach. www.joesstonecrab.com. ✆ **305/673-0365** or 673-4611 for takeout. Reservations not accepted. Market price varies but averages $45–$65. AE, DC, DISC, MC, V. Sun 11:30am–2pm and 4–10pm; Mon–Thurs 11:30am–2pm and 5–10pm; Fri–Sat 11:30am–2pm and 5–11pm. Closed mid-May to mid-Oct.

Juvia ★★★ ASIAN/FRENCH   A 10,000-square-foot St. Barth import, Juvia is set in a visually arresting location, with a vertical rainforest-inspired (but dry, don't worry) garden designed by internationally acclaimed botanist Patrick Blanc. Views of the city are stellar, but then again, so is the food, which mixes Asian, French, South American, and Florida influences. Signature dishes include Salmon Nashi with truffle oil, dry miso, and micro arugula; Hamachi Espumawith Yuzu Kosho Espuma (a spicy sauce) and cilantro; and milk-fed pork confit with sour cabbage, shiitake, and honey-ginger glaze. It's not cheap—meals average about $70 per person—but then again, they don't call St. Barth the Monaco of the Caribbean for nothing.

1111 Lincoln Rd. South Beach. www.juviamiami.com. ✆ **305/763-8272.** Reservations required. Main courses $35–$76. AE, DC, MC, V. Daily 6pm–midnight.

Meat Market ★★★ STEAKHOUSE   As unoriginal yet as telling as its name is, this bustling Lincoln Road steakhouse is one of the city's best—for many things. Thanks to its sexy, loungey vibe, it's a great bar scene and, at times, a bona fide pickup joint (or, rather, a meat market). And thanks to a talented chef/co-owner, Sean Brasel, it's also a serious eating place. Raw bar selections such as oysters on the half shell with delicious dipping sauces (habanero cocktail sauce is a favorite) or mahimahi with lime, jalapeño, cilantro, and tequila will prepare your taste buds for an epicurean journey that differentiates this meat market from the rest. Seafood appetizers such as crispy crab tail bathed in egg batter and pan-fried with passion fruit–butter sauce and sesame-and-*aji-panca* oil make you wonder why they didn't call it Fish Market. That said, the steaks are indeed delicious, too, but we especially love almost each and every one of the 21 side dishes offered—especially the Gouda-filled tater tots.

915 Lincoln Rd., South Beach. www.meatmarketmiami.com. © **305/532-0088.** Reservations required. Main courses $20–$84. AE, MC, V. Daily 6pm–midnight.

Mr Chow ★ ✋ CHINESE   For whatever reason, celebrities love Michael Chow's exorbitantly priced Chinese cuisine. And we may have liked it as well if it didn't have less flavor than PF Chang's and if our bill for two wasn't pushing $400. Yes, $400 for Chinese food. Of course, you're paying for location, scene, and reputation, which, whether you like it or not, is somewhat stellar. Food critics disagree, but the A-listers of the world don't care. Pushy, tuxedoed waiters trained in upselling offer you customized prix-fixe menus upwards of $60 a person as they try to snatch the actual menu out of your hand. Don't fall for it. Order what you want, but order wisely. And maybe eat before. Portions are tiny. Skip the signature green shrimp—they have no taste. Crispy beef is mushy and the white rice should have gold flecks in it at $12 a bowl. As for our one-star rating? It's for those celebrities who continue to confound us by calling Mr Chow their favorite restaurant.

At the W South Beach, 2201 Collins Ave., South Beach. www.mrchow.com. © **305/695-1695.** Reservations required. Main courses $28–$45 and above. AE, MC, V. Sun–Wed 6–11:30pm; Thurs–Sat 6pm–12:30am.

Nobu ★★ SUSHI   When Lady Gaga ate here, no one really noticed. The same thing happened when Jay-Z and Beyoncé canoodled here. Okay, well, they noticed, but not for long. It's not because people were purposely trying not to notice, but because the real star at Nobu is the sushi. The raw facts: Nobu has been hailed as one of the best sushi restaurants in the world, with always-packed eateries in New York, London, and Los Angeles. The Omakase, or Chef's Choice—a multicourse menu entirely up to the chef for $135 per person—gets consistent raves. Some people, however, say Nobu is overpriced and mediocre. Although you won't wait long for your food to be cooked, you will wait forever to score a table here—even if you have a reservation.

At the Shore Club Hotel, 1901 Collins Ave., South Beach. www.noburestaurants.com. © **305/695-3232.** Reservations suggested. Main courses $26 and above. AE, MC, V. Sun 7–11pm; Mon–Thurs 7pm–midnight; Fri–Sat 7pm–1am.

Osteria del Teatro ★★★ ITALIAN   Located in an unassuming storefront beneath the flashy Cameo nightclub, it's hard to believe that Osteria del Teatro is the best Italian bistro on the beach. What it might be lacking in decor is certainly not absent in the elaborate cuisine. Regulars who swear by this place won't even bother looking at the menu; instead they concentrate on the enormous changing list of specials on the blackboard. You will definitely be faced with some tough choices: homemade green and egg noodles with fresh mushrooms, garlic, tomatoes, and basil; filet of salmon with arugula, cream, and white wine; or homemade ravioli stuffed with scallops and crab in lobster sauce. The regulars here are on a first-name basis with the waiters, who always seem to know what you're in the mood for.

1443 Washington Ave. (at Española Way), South Beach. www.osteriadelteatromiami.com. © **305/538-7850.** Reservations recommended. Main courses $17–$31. AE, DC, MC, V. Mon–Sat 6pm–midnight. Closed Sept.

Philippe ★ CHINESE   Located in the South of Fifth 'hood, Philippe was the first on the block with pricey Chinese, with an upscale white-against-black motif and a noodle-master/showman who wows the crowds with his noodle-making skills with the enthusiasm of a Vegas magician. Gimmicks aside, Philippe's food is fickle, ranging from good to bland. Signature neon-orange chicken satay skewers are dyed in carrot juice and *look* as if they may boast the flavor of a zesty Buffalo wing, but no such luck. The rest of the menu features all the classics—duck, prawns, beef in all sorts of sauces, dumplings—albeit gussied up (price wise, not flavor wise). Stick with noodle dishes. If you're going to drop a second mortgage on Chinese food, head to Hakkasan instead, a place where even Mr Chow has been known to frequent from time to time.

36 Ocean Dr., South Beach. www.philippechow.com. ℂ **305/674-0250.** Reservations required. Main courses $29–$60. AE, DC, MC, V. Mon–Sat noon–4pm; Sun 1:30–4pm; Sun–Wed 6pm–midnight; Thurs–Sat 6pm–1am.

Prime One Twelve ★★ STEAKHOUSE   This frenzied, celebrity-saturated sleek steakhouse is part of the ever-expanding culinary empire of Big Pink and Prime Italian, and is the media darling of the exclusive group of restaurants in the hot South of Fifth Street area of South Beach. Its clubby ambience and bustling bar (complete with dried strips of bacon in lieu of nuts) play second fiddle to the beef, which is arguably the best in the entire city—although some carnivores prefer BLT Steak, Bourbon Steak, and Capital Grille. The 12-ounce filet mignon is seared to perfection and can be enhanced with optional dipping sauces (for a price): truffle, garlic herb, foie gras, and chipotle. The 22-ounce bone-in rib-eye is a good choice if you can afford it, as is the gigantic 48-ounce porterhouse. Prime One Twelve also features a $25 Kobe-beef hot dog, Kobe-beef sliders, and a $30 Kobe burger that is sheer ecstasy. Should you be lucky enough to score such a "prime" reservation, take it.

Note: Also consider Prime's sister restaurant across the street, **Prime Italian,** 101 Ocean Dr. (ℂ **305/695-8484**), a pricey red-sauce restaurant that's not nearly as much of a scene, but features swift service, outdoor seating, and, yes, an easier reservation to snag.

112 Ocean Dr. (in the Prime Hotel), South Beach. www.prime112.com. ℂ **305/532-8112.** Reservations recommended. Main courses $20–$88. AE, DISC, MC, V. Mon–Fri noon–3pm; Sun–Thurs 5:30pm–midnight; Fri–Sat 5:30pm–1am.

Red, the Steakhouse ★★ STEAKHOUSE   When this high-styled, black-, red-, and stone-walled, clubby-contemporary meatery from Cleveland opened 2 blocks away from Prime One Twelve, people laughed. But it was no joke. Red proved itself and has held its own in the glitzy shadows of its neighbor, thanks to spectacularly seasoned steaks that don't taste like those found anywhere else. Purists may sneer at it, but those looking for mad flavor revel in this magical seasoning that is composed of oil, kosher salt, and black peppercorns. Don't fill up too much on the delicious bread and hearty starters like the savory trio of green peppers stuffed with sweet Italian sausage, but don't pass on them either. And if it's good enough for Rosie O' Donnell and Michael Jordan, who is usually holed up in the glass-enclosed private room with flatscreen TVs to watch games on, it's good enough for us.

119 Washington Ave., South Beach. www.redthesteakhouse.com. ℂ **305/534-3688.** Reservations strongly suggested. Main courses $28–$89. AE, DC, MC, V. Sun–Fri 5:30pm–midnight; Sat 5:30pm–2am.

Smith & Wollensky ★ STEAKHOUSE   Although it's a chain steakhouse, Miami Beach's Smith & Wollensky has a waterfront view that separates it from the rest.

Inside seating is typical steakhouse—dark woods and so on—but make sure to request a table by the window so you can watch the cruise ships pass by as they leave the port. Outdoor seating, weather permitting, is resplendent, with a bar that doubles as command central for the happy-hour set on Friday nights. The menu here is a lot more basic than the priceless views, with a few chicken and fish choices and beef served about a dozen ways. The classic is the sirloin, seared lightly and served naked. The veal chop is of Flintstonian proportion. Mediocre side dishes such as asparagus, baked potato, onion rings, creamed spinach, and hash browns are sold a la carte. Service is erratic, from highly professional to rudely aloof. You'll find much tastier steaks (at comparable prices) at BLT Steak and Capital Grille (p. 88 and 111).

1 Washington Ave. (in South Pointe Park), South Beach. www.smithandwollensky.com. © **305/673-2800.** Reservations recommended. Main courses $20–$50. AE, DC, DISC, MC, V. Mon–Sat noon–2am; Sun 11:30am–2am.

STK ★ STEAKHOUSE   This see-and-be-seen meatery is a bright spot off the lackluster lobby of the Perry South Beach (or the hotel formerly known as the Gansevoort). Sexy it is, featuring sleek decor, second-floor catwalk perfect for being seen, and a glazed screen spanning the restaurant's two stories depicting an abstract shape of a woman's body reflecting off the glass. Some Miami-inspired dishes include seared big-eye tuna with roasted pineapple, habanero chili pepper, and *congri* basmati rice; and pork *mojo cazuela*, with citrus chili *maduros* and yuca. And then there are the steaks, signature cuts of meat in small, medium, and large. As for whether to choose this place over the 400 other sceney steakhouses in Miami, it has one (dis) advantage: that DJ. So if you want your steak with a side of sonic boom, this is the meatery for you.

In the Perry South Beach, 2377 Collins Ave., South Beach. http://togrp.com/stkmiami. © **305/604-6988.** Reservations required. Main courses $24–$65. AE, DC, MC, V. Daily 5:30pm–2am.

Expensive

Altamare ★★★ SEAFOOD   Strangely, excellent seafood restaurants in Miami are rarer than your seared tuna, but then there's Altamare, the most low-key, star-studded seafooder on South Beach. Altamare features the stellar new American seafood cuisine of talented chef Simon Stojanovic, who takes whatever is caught that day and transforms it into something simply exquisite. Among his specialties: local hogfish carpaccio with shaved hearts of palm, cara cara orange, chive, and sea salt; snapper ceviche; pan-seared hogfish in a roasted butternut squash sauce with exotic mushrooms and sunchoke chips; and grass-fed beef liver pate with rendered Hudson Valley foie gras, heirloom tomato chutney, and grilled ciabatta. The grilled pork belly with house chili sauce and pickled fennel is another excellent nonseafood dish, but we keep coming back for the seafood, which is truly this restaurant's best catch.

1233 Lincoln Rd., South Beach. www.altamarerestaurant.com. © **305/532-3061.** Reservations recommended. Main courses $19–$42. AE, MC, DC, V. Sun–Thurs 5–11pm; Fri–Sat 5pm–midnight.

The Dutch ★★ AMERICAN   A NYC import from chef Andrew Carmellini, the Dutch features what the chef calls "a roots-inspired menu for Miami Beach." On that menu: seafood and dishes influenced by a range of flavors from the Caribbean to Morocco, the Gulf Coast to the West Coast, and Cuba to Italy. The Dutch's lauded oyster bar, on a central marble counter, is the focal point of the restaurant. Entrees pay homage to the local cafes, corner taverns, neighborhood bistros, seaside shacks, roadside joints, and all the cultural riches of Miami, says the chef, who creates dishes such as steamed yellowtail snapper in a Southeast Asian–style ginger broth with peppers and mussels, as well as spice-glazed pork chop with roasted apple and mustard greens. Prime meats include a 28-ounce veal porterhouse with gremolata. However, we prefer the snacks, hearty fare in their own rights, including little oyster sandwiches and succulent St. Louis ribs with a hoisin–black bean glaze. A stellar crowd of celebrities and hipsters spilling over from the W's bars and club makes for excellent people-watching.

W South Beach, 2201 Collins Ave., South Beach. http://thedutchmiami.com. ✆ **305/938-3111.** Reservations recommended. Entrees $18–$40. AE, MC, V. Mon–Wed 7–11am, noon–4pm, and 6–11:30pm; Thurs–Fri 7–11:30am, noon–4pm, and 6pm–midnight; Sat noon–4pm and 6pm–midnight; Sun 7:30am–4pm and 6–11:30pm.

Haven ★★ MODERN AMERICAN/SUSHI If you've ever wondered what it's like to eat in a high-tech nightclub amidst pulsating lights and music, this is it. Despite what it sounds like, it's a multisensory sensation, thanks to chef Todd Erickson, whose organic small plates are delicious demos of molecular gastronomy. You'll find imaginative dishes like succulent stone crabs served with tomato water and avocado-buttermilk cream, or an "everything" sushi roll with sockeye salmon, cream cheese, chives, bagel, sesame, and poppy. You have to try it to get it. And judging by the crowds, that's exactly what people are doing. As expected with a place like this, the scene really starts in the wee hours, when bartenders transform into mad scientists, mixing cocktails you'd only expect in a science-fiction novel.

1237 Lincoln Rd., South Beach. http://havenlounge.com. ✆ **305/987-8885.** Reservations recommended. Small plates $10–$21. AE, MC, V. Daily 6pm–5am.

Pubbelly ★★★ LATIN/ASIAN A small restaurant that has become an enormous South Beach—and South Floridian—sensation, Pubbelly evokes a Brooklyn-esque, gastropubby vibe with food-loving, beer-savvy hipsters packing in for the delicious mix of northern Asian, Puerto Rican, and Spanish cuisines. Though some compare the place to NYC's hailed Momofuku, Pubbelly is wholly original. The so-called "swine happy menu" features signature dishes like potted rilletes, duck confit, pork belly, and soy-onion marmalade; pork belly dumplings with scallions, *su-shoyu,* and sesame oil; and Pubbelly Ramen with pork belly, shoulder, lemon grass broth, and poached egg. There's also a raw bar and about 20 beers and 100 wines under $80 a bottle. Following the success of Pubbelly, the owners opened nearby eateries **Pubbelly Sushi,** 1424 20th St. (www.pubbellysushi.com; ✆ 305/531-9282), and **Barceloneta,** 1400 20th St. (www.barcelonetarestaurant.com; ✆ 305/538-9299), a Catalonian-inspired small-plate tapas place.

1418 20th St., South Beach. http://pubbelly.com. ✆ **305/532-7555.** Reservations not accepted. Small and larger plates $6–$35. AE, DC, MC, V. Tues–Thurs and Sun 6pm–midnight; Fri–Sat 6pm–1am.

Quattro ★★ ITALIAN Quattro is a Northern Italian standout, thanks to its chefs—30-something-year-old twin brothers hailing from the Piedmont region of Italy who barely speak English, but speak pasta fluently. Signature dishes on the menu include homemade fontina ravioli with white-truffle oil and veal wraps with melted Parmesan cheese and bread crumbs. The wine list is all Italian and reasonably priced. The room is gorgeous, with dramatic lighting, chandeliers, and an all-glass bar that buzzes with *la dolce vita.* Try the cheese plate if you're not too hungry—it's a meal in itself and features that salami you wished you had smuggled back home the last time you returned from Italy. Located across the road from Quattro is its sister restaurant, **Sosta Pizzeria,** 1025 Lincoln Rd. (✆ **305/722-5454**), serving pretty good thin-crust brick oven pizzas.

1014 Lincoln Rd., South Beach. www.quattromiami.com. ✆ **305/531-4833.** Reservations recommended. Main courses $31–$50. AE, MC, V. Sun–Thurs noon–4pm and 6pm–midnight; Fri–Sat noon–4pm and 6pm–1am.

Sardinia ★★ ITALIAN A quiet sensation in South Beach terms, Sardinia doesn't need celebrity sightings and publicists to boost its business. And it's not your typical caprese salad and fusilli pasta factory, either. For starters, the cheese and salumi plates will transport you—or at least your palate—to Italy, as will the rest of the innovative menu, including dishes such as oriechette with wild boar, crunchy fried sweetbreads with Brussels sprouts, and rabbit with Brussels sprouts and beets. Sure, the food's a bit heavy, but it's worth it. As for the scene here, it's all about the food, although the bar is always bustling with people waiting for highly coveted tables. For seafood lovers, don't miss the branzino baked in salt crust.

1801 Purdy Ave., South Beach. www.sardinia-ristorante.com. ✆ **305/531-2228.** Reservations highly suggested. Main courses $17–$43. AE, DC, MC, V. Daily noon–midnight.

Sushi Samba Dromo ★ SUSHI/CEVICHE It's Brazilian, it's Peruvian, it's Japanese, it's . . . super sushi! This multinational New York City import is a hipster's paradise. This stylish, sexy restaurant charges a pretty penny for some exotic sushi rolls. And while the sushi is top notch, the sashimi ceviches are even better. An assortment—your choice of either salmon, yellowtail, tuna, *kanpachi,* and shrimp—is somewhat of a deal at $33, considering the fact that separately each can run you from $13 to $17. For main plates, try the *churrasco à Rio Grande,* a divine assortment of meats served with rice, beans, collard greens, and chimichurri sauce.

600 Lincoln Rd., South Beach. www.sushisamba.com. ✆ **305/673-5337.** Reservations recommended. Main courses $21–$44; sushi rolls $12–$17. AE, MC, V. Mon–Wed noon–midnight; Thurs 11:30am–1am; Fri–Sat noon–2am; Sun brunch 11:30am–3:30pm, dinner 3:30pm–1am.

Yardbird Southern Table & Bar ★★★ SOUTHERN Former *Top Chef* contestant Jeff McInnis grew up in the Florida Panhandle, which is so much more Southern than Miami will ever be. McInnis combined an old genteel sensibility with modern cooking techniques to create this restaurant, which has a cool, buzzy vibe. The menu offers completely addicting Southern edamame (steamed peas with Atlantic sea salt and spicy chili butter); a phenomenal fried green tomato BLT; lick-the-plate good fried chicken biscuits with pepper jelly; sweet tea–brined barbecue ribs; and, the crown jewel for many, Llewelyn's Fine Fried Chicken served with savory cheddar and waffle, spicy honey, and citrus-pepper watermelon. Everything's pretty sensational here, including the bar scene and the bourbon-based cocktails. Saturday and Sunday brunch is a fun scene; don't miss the chicken and waffles.

1600 Lenox Ave., South Beach. http://runchickenrun.com. ✆ **305/538-5220.** Reservations strongly recommended. Plates $6–$42. AE, MC, DC, V. Mon–Fri noon–3pm; daily 5:30–11pm; Sat–Sun brunch 11am–4pm.

Moderate

Balan's ★ MEDITERRANEAN Balan's provides undeniable evidence that the Brits actually do know a thing or two about cuisine. A direct import from London's Soho, Balan's draws inspiration from various Mediterranean and Asian influences, labeling its cuisine "Mediterrasian." With a brightly colored interior straight out of a mod '60s flick, Balan's is a favorite among the gay and arty crowds, especially on weekends during brunch hours. The moderately priced food is rather good here—especially the double-baked cheese soufflé, citrus tossed mixed greens, Thai red curry, and pan-fried tilapia with Indian garbanzo bean curry and mint yogurt. When in doubt, the restaurant's signature US1 Burger is always a good choice. Adding to the ambience is the restaurant's people-watching vantage point on Lincoln Road. In 2009, Balan's expanded over the causeway and opened a second location at 901 S. Miami Ave., in the bustling Brickell area. In 2010, they opened a third at Biscayne Boulevard and 67th Street in the Upper East Side neighborhood.

1022 Lincoln Rd. (btw. Lenox and Michigan), South Beach. www.balans.co.uk. ℂ **305/534-9191.** Reservations accepted, except for weekend brunch. Main courses, sandwiches, salads $9–$30 (breakfast and dinner specials Mon–Fri). AE, DISC, MC, V. Sun–Thurs 8am–midnight; Fri–Sat 8am–1am; Sat–Sun brunch noon–3:30pm.

Big Pink ★ ☺ AMERICAN "Real Food for Real People" is the motto to which this restaurant strictly adheres. Set on what used to be a gritty corner of Collins Avenue, Big Pink—owned by the folks at the higher-end Prime 112—is quickly identified by a whimsical Pippi Longstocking–type mascot on a sign outside. Scooters and motorcycles line the streets surrounding the place, which is a favorite among beach bums, club kids, and those craving Big Pink's comforting and hugely portioned pizzas, sandwiches, salads, and hamburgers. The fare is above average, at best, and the menu is massive, but it comes with a good dose of kitsch, such as the "gourmet" spin on the classic TV dinner, which is done perfectly, right down to the compartmentalized dessert. Televisions line the bar area, and the family-style table arrangement (there are several booths too) promotes camaraderie among diners. Outdoor tables are available. Even picky kids will like the food here, and parents can enjoy the family-friendly atmosphere (not the norm for South Beach) without worrying whether their kids are making too much noise.

157 Collins Ave., South Beach. www.mylesrestaurantgroup.com. ℂ **305/532-4700.** Salads, sandwiches, burgers, pizzas, main courses $7–$23. AE, DC, MC, V. Sun–Wed 8am–midnight; Thurs 8am–2am; Fri–Sat 8am–5am.

Bond St. Lounge ★ SUSHI A New York City import, the sceney, subterranean Bond St. Lounge is in the basement of the shabby-chic Townhouse Hotel and is packing in hipsters as tightly as the crabmeat in a California roll. Despite its tiny—or, rather, intimate—size, Bond St. Lounge's superfresh nigiri and sashimi, and funky sushi rolls such as the sun-dried tomato and avocado or the arugula crispy potato, are worth cramming in here for. As the evening progresses, however, Bond St. becomes more of a bar scene than a restaurant, but sushi is always available at the bar to accompany your sake bloody mary.

Townhouse Hotel, 150 20th St., South Beach. www.townhousehotel.com. ℂ **305/398-1806.** Reservations recommended. Sushi $6–$20. AE, MC, V. Daily 6pm–2am.

Burger & Beer Joint AMERICAN A refreshing alternative to the throngs of high-end eateries that opened in the area over the past few years, B&B is a down-home, family-friendly, well, *burger and beer joint* with no attitude, just great, thick, juicy burgers; fabulously salted skinny fries; beer; cocktails; and adult shakes. Hip without trying too hard, B&B offers all sorts of burgers, from plain and classic iterations (all perfectly cooked at medium rare unless otherwise specified) to those with rock-'n'-roll-inspired monikers: the $32 Stairway to Heaven, 10 ounces of Wagyu beef, 3 ounces of Hudson Valley foie gras, and black-truffle demi on a brioche bun; or the $12 Fly Like an Eagle, two turkey patties with homemade stuffing, brown gravy, and cranberry sauce. You can also create your own burgers, with an intimidating list of cheeses, buns, veggies, sauces, and bells and whistles. Before you start with burgers, you may want to try the sassy tempura fried pickles or braised Buffalo wings, which are unlike the ones found in your typical sports bar—these feature meat marinated in a spicy, zippy sauce and falling off the bone. After dinner, check out the back sports bar, which tends to be a bit smoky. A second location of B&B, as it's known by locals, opened at 900 S. Miami Ave. (© **305/523-2244**), in Mary Brickell Village.

1766 Bay Rd., South Beach. www.burgernbeerjoint.com. © **305/672-3287.** Reservations suggested. Burgers $10–$39. AE, DC, MC, V. Daily noon–5pm; Sun–Thurs 5pm–1am; Fri–Sat 5pm–2am.

The Cafe at Books & Books ★ AMERICAN   This sidewalk cafe offers not only some of the best, freshest breakfasts and lunches in town—the egg-and-tuna salad combo is our favorite, as are the amazing yucca-and-leek homemade hash browns—but gourmet dinners as well. This is not your chain bookstore's prefab tuna sandwich. Sadly, in 2009, the bookstore became a Diesel store, but the cafe stayed. Sandwiches, salads, and burgers are good, but after 5pm the real gourmand comes out in Chef Bernie Matz with specials that change often and include things like a juicy flank steak marinated in espresso and brown sugar, seared, sliced, and served with a pineapple-and-onion salsa and a pair of plantain nests smothered in garlicky mojo. The menu also features an impressive selection of vegetarian and vegan options. If you're still inspired to buy a cookbook after your meal, Books & Books set up a small, cozy annex in the back of the courtyard.

927 Lincoln Rd., South Beach. © **305/695-8898.** Main courses $7–$25. AE, MC, V. Daily 9am–11pm.

Clarke's ★ IRISH   There's more to this neighborhood pub than pints of Guinness. With a warm, inviting ambience and a gorgeously rich wood bar as the focal point, Clarke's is the only true gastropub in Miami, with excellent fare that goes beyond bangers and mash and delicious burgers, and delves into the gourmet. Highlights include Sazerac House crab cakes, whose secret recipe hails from owner Laura Cullen's father's New York City landmark, the Sazerac House; Irish spring rolls; sesame-crusted tuna; and the New York–style pretzel, served on a spike with mustard on the side. The vibe here is very friendly and low key. The a la carte Sunday brunch features all sorts of egg fare, jazzy music, and the best bloody mary in Miami, for a mere $5 each.

840 1st St., South Beach. www.clarkesmiamibeach.com. © **305/538-9885.** Main courses $6–$27. AE, MC, V. Mon 5pm–midnight; Tues–Sat noon–midnight; Sun 11am–11pm.

Grillfish ★ SEAFOOD   Grillfish is one of the longest-lasting seafood restaurants in South Beach. From the beautiful Byzantine-style mural and the gleaming oak bar, you'd think you were eating in a much more expensive restaurant, but Grillfish manages to pay the exorbitant South Beach rent yet remain reasonably priced with the help of a loyal following of locals who come for fresh, simple seafood in a relaxed but upscale atmosphere. The servers are friendly and know the simple menu well. For starters, have the mussels or the blackened Grillfish cakes, and for a main opt for the seafood over pasta, grilled or sautéed seafood with a side of corn on the cob, or surf and turf. At these affordable prices, it's worth a visit to try some local fresh seafood, including mako shark, swordfish, tuna, marlin, and wahoo.

1444 Collins Ave. (corner of Española Way), South Beach. www.grillfish.com. © **305/538-9908.** Reservations accepted for parties of 6 or more only. Main courses $13–$28. AE, DC, DISC, MC, V. Daily 11:30am–4pm and 5:30pm–midnight.

Jerry's Famous Deli ★ DELI Jerry's Famous Deli, which is actually a Los Angeles import, is a New York–style deli on South Beach. The decadent menu features over 700 monstrously portioned items, from your typical corned beef on rye to your atypical brisket burrito. While the quality of the food is excellent, the service pales in comparison: This 24-hour deli is not a place to go if you're in a rush. The modern cafeteria, complete with full bar, is dimly lit with a disco soundtrack. People come here to linger over sandwiches that can feed at least two people, if not more. Should you be craving a Reuben sandwich after a night of clubbing at 5am, Jerry's is command central for that set as well as the original early birders who are first waking at 5am and will have their dinner at 5pm. One thing, though: This is *not* your grandfather's deli, where sandwiches were only a few bucks. Prepare to shell out at least $10 and up for one of Jerry's.

1450 Collins Ave., South Beach. www.jerrysfamousdeli.com. © **305/532-8030.** Main courses $8–$34. AE, DC, DISC, MC, V. Daily 24 hr.

Larios on the Beach ★ ♨ CUBAN If you're a fan of singer Gloria Estefan, you will definitely want to check out this restaurant, which she and her husband Emilio own; if not, you may want to reconsider, as the place is an absolute mob scene, especially on weekends. The classic Cuban dishes get a so-so rating from the Cubans, but a better one from those who aren't as well versed in the cuisine. The portions here are larger than life, as are some of the restaurant's patrons, who come here for the sidewalk scenery and the well-prepared black beans and rice. Inside, the restaurant turns into a makeshift salsa club, with music blaring over the animated conversations and the sounds of English clashing with Spanish. There are locations on Ocean Drive, at the Seminole Hard Rock Hotel & Casino in Hollywood, and in downtown Miami at the American Airlines Arena.

820 Ocean Dr., South Beach. www.bongoscubancafe.com. © **305/532-9577.** Reservations recommended. Main courses $13–$50; sandwiches before 5pm $9–$12. AE, MC, V. Sun–Thurs 11:30am–midnight; Fri–Sat 11:30am–1am.

Macaluso's ★★ ITALIAN This restaurant epitomizes the Italians' love for—and mastery of—savory, plentiful, down-home Staten Island–style food. While the storefront restaurant is intimate and demure in nature, there's nothing delicate about the bold mix of flavors in every meat and pasta dish here. Catch the fantastic clam pie when in season—the portions are huge. Pricier items vary throughout the season but will likely feature fresh fish hand-picked by chef (and owner) Michael. Everyone will recommend favorites such as the rigatoni and broccoli rabe. There are also delicious desserts ranging from homemade anisette cookies to gooey pastries. The wine list is also good. Keep your eyes peeled, as this is a major celeb hot spot.

1747 Alton Rd., South Beach. www.macalusosmiami.com. © **305/604-1811.** Main courses $15–$40; pizza $10–$20. MC, V. Tues–Sat 6pm–midnight; Sun 6–11pm. After 10:30pm, only pies are served.

Monty's Sunset Seafood Bistro ★ SEAFOOD Boasting the best sunset views in South Beach, this recently refurbished restaurant has gone from ordinary to anything but. With the recent entrance of *Top Chef* alum Josie Smith-Malave as executive chef, guests can expect an impressive selection of culinary offerings, including a 20-foot raw bar featuring the largest selection of oysters in Miami Beach. While continuing to provide guests with a laid-back atmosphere, the decor at Monty's has experienced a complete overhaul, with indoor/outdoor bistro-style seating and 20 flatscreen televisions. Monty's offers Ibiza-inspired soirees with live music during the Saturday Brunch and a daily "Sunset Hour" from 4 to 7pm.

300 Alton Rd., South Beach. www.montyssobe.com. © **305/672-1148.** Reservations recommended. Main courses $20–$40. AE, DC, MC, V. Sun–Thurs 11:30am–10pm; Fri 11:30am–midnight; Sat 11:30am–11pm.

Nexxt Cafe AMERICAN   Locals joke that this lively, always-packed outdoor cafe should be called Nexxt Year to reflect the awfully slow service that has become its unfortunate trademark. Service aside, however, Nexxt has made quite a splash on South Beach, attracting an evening crowd looking for nighttime revelry and a morning crowd on the weekends for a standing-room-only brunch sensation. The fresh food comes in lavish portions that could easily feed two; the salads are an especially good bargain and are big enough for more than one person or more than one meal. The burgers and sandwiches are similarly big. They have coffees in tall, grande, and "maxxi." There are also plenty of coffee cocktails, mixed drinks, frozen beverages, and wines, giving this place a nice bar life, too, but buyer beware: Drink prices, like much of the menu, are on the outrageous-for-a-cafe side.

700 Lincoln Rd. (off Euclid Ave.), South Beach. www.nexxtcafe.com. © **305/532-6643.** Main courses $10–$30. AE, MC, V. Daily 9am–1am.

Spiga ★ 🍴 ITALIAN   Spiga is a cozy and low-key Italian restaurant serving simple yet delicious fare. The simple gnocchi with tomato and basil is a garlicky sensation, not to mention a filling entree. The fresh asparagus baked in Parmesan cheese is so fresh that gourmands insist that Alice Waters, the queen of organic cooking, had something to do with it; and the red snapper with kalamata olives, fresh tomatoes, capers, and onions is a refreshingly simple departure from the fusion variety that can be found in almost any area restaurant. The place is extremely romantic and vaguely reminiscent of a Florentine trattoria, and it's not at all sceney.

Prime Hotel Impala, 1228 Collins Ave., South Beach. www.spigarestaurant.com. © **305/534-0079.** Reservations accepted. Main courses $15–$32. AE, DC, MC, V. Daily 6pm–midnight.

Tap Tap ★ HAITIAN   The whole place looks like an overgrown *tap tap*, a brightly painted jitney common in Haiti before the devastating 2010 earthquake. But pre-quake Haiti is alive and well in this restaurant that pays homage to the recovering island nation. Every inch is painted in vibrant neon hues (blue, pink, purple, and so on), and the atmosphere is always fun. It's where the Haiti-philes and Haitians, from journalists to politicians, hang out. There's often live music or other cultural programs happening here. The *lanbi nan citron*, a tart, marinated conch salad, is perfect with a tall tropical drink and maybe some lightly grilled goat tidbits, which are served in a savory brown sauce and are less stringy than typical goat dishes. Another supersatisfying choice is the pumpkin soup, a rich brick-colored purée of subtly seasoned pumpkin with a dash of pepper. Shrimp in Creole sauce is another standout. An excellent salad of avocado, mango, and watercress is a great finish. Soda junkies should definitely try the watermelon soda.

819 5th St. (between Jefferson and Meridian aves., next to the Shell Station), South Beach. © **305/672-2898.** Reservations accepted. Main courses $8–$20. AE, DC, DISC, MC, V. Mon–Thurs 5–11pm; Fri–Sat 5pm–midnight; Sun 5–10pm. Closed July.

Van Dyke Cafe ★ AMERICAN   News Cafe's younger, less harried sibling, Van Dyke, is a locals' favorite, at which people-watching is also premium but attitude is practically nonexistent. The menu here spans a variety of cuisines—sandwiches, panini, burgers, Middle Eastern specialties, pasta, seafood, salads, eggs, and so on—but the Van Dyke's warm, wood-floored interior, upstairs jazz bar, accessible parking, and intense chocolate soufflé make it a less taxing alternative. Also, unlike News, Van Dyke turns into a sizzling nightspot featuring live jazz nearly every night of the week. Outside there's a vast tree-lined seating area that's ideal for people-watching. Those allergic to or afraid of dogs might reconsider eating here, as Van Dyke is also a canine hot spot.

846 Lincoln Rd., South Beach. www.thevandykecafe.com. ℂ**305/534-3600.** Main courses $8–$24. AE, DC, MC, V. Daily 8am–2am.

Inexpensive

A La Folie ★★ FRENCH   The Left Bank took a wrong turn and ended up on the quiet(er) end of Española Way in the form of A La Folie. A La Folie is an authentic French cafe in which wooden booths and walls full of foreign newspapers and magazines make you have to take a second look at your plane ticket to make sure you're still in Miami. In addition to the affected, über-French waitstaff (not snotty, but aloof), A La Folie features some of the best cafe fare in Miami, including delicious, hugely portioned sandwiches such as the French fave *croque monsieur,* salads, crepes, and, of course, cafe au lait and plenty of wine. Indoor and outdoor seating are equally conducive to whiling away many hours sipping coffee, reading a magazine, and reflecting on that whole Freedom Fry controversy of last decade. A tiny outpost opened at 1701 Sunset Harbor Dr. (ℂ 305/672-9336), but stick with the original, it's much more *charmant.*

516 Española Way, South Beach. ℂ **305/538-4484.** Main courses $5–$15. MC, V. Daily 9am–midnight.

David's Cafe II ★ CUBAN   The furthest thing from a trendy spot, David's Cafe's Cuban food is good, cheap, and available 24 hours a day in case you need a jolt of Cuban coffee at, say, 4am. Enjoy supercheap breakfasts (two eggs, home fries or grits, coffee, and toast is $4.75), Cuban sandwiches (ham, pork, Swiss, pickles, and mustard), midnight *arroz con pollo,* fantastic cheeseburgers, a wonderful grilled-cheese sandwich, *ropa vieja* habanera (shredded sirloin and sauce), and pretty much anything you can think of—even, oddly enough, brown rice. Hey, this is South Beach, what can you expect? David's has a huge, more modern second location at 1058 Collins Ave. (ℂ 305/534-8736), also open 24 hours.

1654 Meridian Ave., South Beach. www.davidscafe.com. ℂ**305/672-8707.** Main courses $4–$20. AE, MC, V. Daily 24 hr.

11th Street Diner AMERICAN   The only real diner on the beach, the 11th Street Diner is the antidote to a late-night run to Denny's. Some of Miami's most colorful characters, especially the drunk ones, convene here at odd hours, and your greasy-spoon experience can quickly turn into a three-ring circus. Uprooted from its 1948 Wilkes-Barre, Pennsylvania, foundation, the actual structure was dismantled and rebuilt on a busy—and colorful (a gay bar is right next door, so be on the lookout for flamboyant drag queens)—corner of Washington Avenue. Although it can use a good window cleaning, it remains a popular round-the-clock spot that attracts all walks of life and happens to serve breakfast all day. For heartier fare, the fried chicken or the pork chops with apple and raisins are the way to go. If you're craving French fries, order them smothered in mozzarella with a side of gravy—a tasty concoction that we call disco fries because of its popularity among starving clubbers.

1065 Washington Ave., South Beach. www.eleventhstreetdiner.com. ℂ **305/534-6373.** Main courses $8–$19. AE, MC. Daily 24 hr.

Front Porch Cafe ★ AMERICAN   Even after moving from a dreary Art Deco hotel to the more modern Z Ocean Hotel next door, the Front Porch Cafe is a relaxed local hangout known for cheap breakfasts and, with the new location, drink specials, happy hour, and a bigger dinner menu. Some of the servers tend to be a bit attitudinal and lackadaisical (many are bartenders or club kids by night), so this isn't the place to be if you're in a hurry, especially on the weekends, when the place is packed all day long and lines are the norm. Enjoy home-style French toast with bananas and walnuts, omelets, fresh fruit salads, pizzas, and granola pancakes. If you're starving, order the Breakfast Bonanza, three scrambled eggs with cheddar, mushrooms, and scallions and a choice of fruit, tomatoes, potatoes, or salad with raisin pumpernickel toast. This is where the locals eat for breakfast, lunch, and even dinner.

In the Z Ocean Hotel, 1458 Ocean Dr., South Beach. © **305/531-8300.** Main courses $6–$19. AE, DC, DISC, MC, V. Daily 7am–11pm.

Icebox Cafe ★ AMERICAN   Locals love this place for its homey comfort food—tuna melts, potpies, and eggs for breakfast, lunch, and dinner. Oprah Winfrey singled it out for its desserts, which is really why people raid the Icebox whenever that sweet tooth calls. In the Icebox, you'll discover the best chocolate cake, pound cake, and banana cream pies outside of your grandma's kitchen.

1657 Michigan Ave., South Beach. www.iceboxcafe.com. © **305/538-8448.** Main courses and desserts $3–$10. AE, MC, V. Daily 8am–10:30pm.

Jimmy'z Kitchen ★★ LATIN   Chef Jimmy Carey's impressive culinary pedigree includes stints at the now-defunct Miami sister restaurant to NYC's lauded Le Bernadin, but his heart is clearly in the down home, hearty, no-frills food he cooks in his two Miami restaurants—the first, a stamp-size storefront in a South Beach strip mall and the second, a hipper, bigger Wynwood space built after the first one proved to be such a huge hit (2700 N. Miami Ave.; © **305/573-1505**). A huge menu of panini, sandwiches, and salads tempts, but the main draw at Jimmy'z is the *mofongo*, the signature Puerto Rican dish of fried plantains, garlic, oil and some secret ingredients to which only Carey, his team, and some very keen culinarians are able to decipher. Don't miss the daily specials and, at the Wynwood location, live music.

1542 Alton Rd., South Beach. www.jimmyzkitchen.com. © **305/534-8216.** Sandwiches, salads, entrees $7.50–$16. AE, DC, DISC, MC, V. Sat–Thurs 11am–10pm; Fri 11am–11pm.

La Sandwicherie ★ SANDWICHES   You can get mustard, mayo, or oil and vinegar on sandwiches elsewhere in town, but you'd be missing out on all the local flavor. This gourmet sandwich bar, open until the crack of dawn, caters to ravenous club kids, biker types, and the body artists who work in the tattoo parlor next door. For many people, in fact, no night of clubbing is complete without capping it off with a turkey sub from La Sandwicherie.

229 14th St. (behind the Amoco station), South Beach. www.lasandwicherie.com. © **305/532-8934.** Sandwiches and salads $5–$9. AE, MC, V. Daily 9am–5am. Delivery 9:30am–11pm.

News Cafe ★ AMERICAN   The quintessential South Beach experience, News Cafe is still au courant, albeit swarming with mostly tourists. Unless it's appallingly hot or rainy out, you should wait for an outside table. Service is abysmal and often arrogant (perhaps because the tip is included), but the menu is reliable, running the gamut from sandwiches and salads to pasta dishes and omelets. Our favorite here is the Middle Eastern platter, a dip lover's paradise, with hummus, tahini, tabbouleh, baba ghanouj, and fresh pita bread. If it's not too busy, feel free to order just a cappuccino—your server may snarl, but that's what News is all about; creative types like to bring their laptops and sit here all day (or all night—this place is open 24 hr. a day). If you're alone and need something to read, there's an extensive collection of national and international newspapers and magazines at the in-house newsstand.

800 Ocean Dr., South Beach. www.newscafe.com. ✆ **305/538-6397.** Main courses $7–$20. AE, DC, MC, V. Daily 24 hr.

Piola ★ PIZZA   This hip Italian import turns pizza into a fun, sit-down meal that's hard to beat for the price, quality, and quantity. An unabridged menu of nearly 80 different kinds of pizzas for one that are really enough to share between two people is mind numbing and mouthwatering. I suggest that you order several pizzas, depending on how many people you are dining with (two is more than enough for two, for example). Start with the *quattro formaggio* pizza—brie, Gorgonzola, Parmesan, and mozzarella—and then consider a funkier version, say, smoked salmon and caviar. All pizzas are thin crust and full of flavor. Waitstaff is extremely friendly, too, but be prepared for a lengthy wait, especially on weekend nights when the movie-going crowds next door spill over for a snack. Capitalizing on its South Beach success, Piola is now a minichain, with locations all over the country, and another in Miami, in the Brickell area at 1250 S. Miami Ave. (✆ **305/374-0031**).

1625 Alton Rd., South Beach. www.piola.it. ✆ **305/674-1660.** Reservations accepted. Main courses $10–$16. AE, DC, MC, V. Daily 6pm–1am.

Puerto Sagua ★ CUBAN/SPANISH   This brown-walled diner is one of the only old holdouts on South Beach. Its steady stream of regulars ranges from *abuelitos* (little old grandfathers) and local politicos who meet here every Tuesday morning to hipsters who stop in after clubbing. It has endured because the food is good, if a little greasy. Some of the less heavy dishes are a superchunky fish soup with pieces of whole flaky grouper, chicken, and seafood paella, or marinated kingfish. Also good are most of the shrimp dishes, especially the shrimp in garlic sauce, which is served with white rice and salad. This is one of the most reasonably priced places left on the beach for simple, hearty fare. Our fave? Roast chicken with rice, black beans, and fried plantains. Don't be intimidated by the hunched, older waiters in their white button-down shirts and black pants. If you don't speak Spanish, they're usually willing to do charades. Anyway, the extensive menu, which ranges from BLTs to grilled lobsters to yummy fried plantains, is translated into English. Hurry, before another boutique goes up in its place.

700 Collins Ave., South Beach. ✆ **305/673-1115.** Main courses $10–$39; sandwiches and salads $4.75–$8.75. AE, DC, MC, V. Daily 7:30am–2am.

Shake Shack ★ AMERICAN   Yet another NYC import, this fast-food burger joint modeled after a roadside burger stand, located on a Lincoln Road side street, isn't your typical fast food. The burgers are really good—a mix of sirloin and brisket—and the shakes, floats, and frozen custards are tasty treats. There are also hot dogs, French fries, and a vegetarian burger for those who don't do meat.

1111 Lincoln Rd., South Beach. www.shakeshack.com. ✆ **305/538-8448.** Burgers and hot dogs $4–$8 AE, MC, V. Sun–Thurs 11:30am–11pm; Fri–Sat 11:30am–midnight.

MIAMI BEACH TO NORTH MIAMI BEACH

The area north of the Art Deco District—from about 21st Street to 163rd Street—had its heyday in the 1950s, when huge hotels and gambling halls blocked the view of the ocean. Now many of the old hotels have been converted into condos or budget lodgings, and the bayfront mansions have been renovated by and for wealthy entrepreneurs, families, and speculators. The area has many more residents, albeit seasonal, than visitors. On the culinary front, the result is a handful of superexpensive, traditional establishments as well as a number of value-oriented spots.

Very Expensive

Christine Lee's ★ CHINESE   This Cantonese restaurant is a 35-year-old Miami staple that serves excellent but overpriced Chinese-style dishes featuring steak, shrimp, and lobster sauce, as well as a good rendition of steak *kew*, a Cantonese dish with oyster sauce and hot bean paste. Considering the dearth of good Chinese restaurants in Miami, this is a fine choice if you absolutely *must* satisfy your cravings for Chinese, but it will definitely cost you more than it should, especially since it moved to its swank new location at the Gulfstream Racing and Casino.

Gulfstream Racing and Casino, 901 S. Federal Hwy., Hallandale. www.christinelees.com. ⓒ **954/457-6255.** Reservations recommended. Main courses $12–$43. AE, DISC, MC, V. Daily 11:30am–3pm and 4–10:30pm (not open for lunch May–Sept).

The Forge Restaurant | Wine Bar ★★★ STEAK   Like many of its most loyal, uh, seasoned customers, the Forge underwent a major nip/tuck and traded its dark roots for a lighter, blonder look and a menu that focuses on organic, locally sourced foods. The bar is stunning in a refreshingly rich, not stark, way, and its electronic dispensing wine system turns oenophiles into kids on a video game bender at the Chuck E. Cheese's, only with booze. Good booze, of course. Thankfully, the old-school wine cellar, one of the country's best, still remains just that. The menu by chef Dewey LoSasso, featuring a whopping 65 items, offers a modern, largely organic twist on everything, from seafood and salads to pastas and steaks. The classic Forge Super Steak is still on the menu to the delight of many.

432 Arthur Godfrey Rd. (41st St.), Miami Beach. www.theforge.com. ⓒ **305/538-8533.** Reservations recommended. Main courses $25–$60. AE, DC, MC, V. Sun–Thurs 6pm–midnight; Fri–Sat 6pm–1am.

Gotham Steak ★ STEAK   NYC's Gotham Bar & Grill chef/owner Alfred Portale's Miami offering is a stunning, bi-level, photo-worthy restaurant complete with a chandelier of hand-blown glass and glass-enclosed wine tower. Steaks include a gigantic 16-ounce prime bone-in filet grilled over hardwood charcoal and finished on a 1,200-degree broiler ($58), an 8-ounce filet mignon that you can get pretty much anywhere these days ($40), and the bargain $27 plate of barbecued pork ribs. It's pricey, yes, but if it's meat you are craving in a very dramatic ambiance, Gotham's your place.

In the Fontainebleau, 4441 Collins Ave., Miami Beach. www.fontainebleau.com. ⓒ **305/674-4780.** Reservations required. Main courses $24–$64. AE, DC, MC, V. Daily 6–10:30pm.

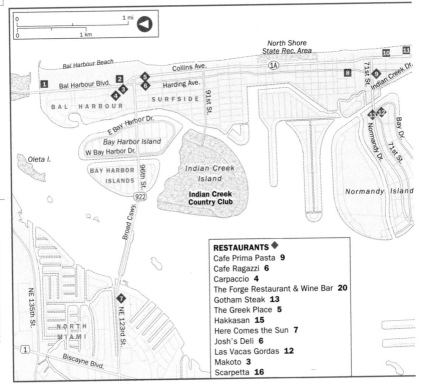

RESTAURANTS ◆
Cafe Prima Pasta **9**
Cafe Ragazzi **6**
Carpaccio **4**
The Forge Restaurant & Wine Bar **20**
Gotham Steak **13**
The Greek Place **5**
Hakkasan **15**
Here Comes the Sun **7**
Josh's Deli **6**
Las Vacas Gordas **12**
Makoto **3**
Scarpetta **16**

Hakkasan ★★★ CHINESE   A flashy bastion of the luxe life, this higher-than-high-end haute Chinese restaurant, owned by Michelin-starred chef Alan Yau of London's Hakkasan fame, is a sight to be seen and tasted. Tucked away on the fourth floor of the labyrinthine Fontainebleau, Hakkasan exudes a nightclubby, Vegas vibe with thumping music, scantily clad diners who think they're in Vegas, and screened-off nooks of semiprivate dining areas. This is some seriously good, gourmet food. Signature dishes include a fabulous filet of roasted silver cod over tender stalks of *gai lan* (Chinese broccoli) in honey and champagne, roasted duck served in bite-size slices with crisped skin with a savory soy sauce, and red snapper with a spicy scallion soy sauce. For the big splurge, try the Peking duck with 30 grams of Russian Osetra caviar at a whopping $198. Go with a group of people if you can so you can share dishes. Not widely advertised is the somewhat affordable (relatively speaking, of course), exceedingly delicious $28 per person dim sum brunch on Saturdays and Sundays from noon to 3pm.

In the Fontainebleau, 4441 Collins Ave., Miami Beach. www.fontainebleau.com. ✆ **786/276-1388.** Reservations required. Main courses $10–$198. AE, DC, MC, V. Sun and Tues–Wed 6–11pm; Thurs–Sat 6pm–12:30am.

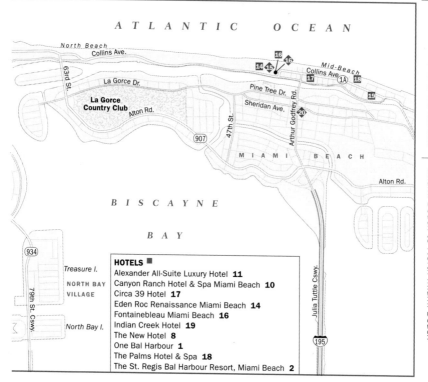

HOTELS ■
Alexander All-Suite Luxury Hotel **11**
Canyon Ranch Hotel & Spa Miami Beach **10**
Circa 39 Hotel **17**
Eden Roc Renaissance Miami Beach **14**
Fontainebleau Miami Beach **16**
Indian Creek Hotel **19**
The New Hotel **8**
One Bal Harbour **1**
The Palms Hotel & Spa **18**
The St. Regis Bal Harbour Resort, Miami Beach **2**

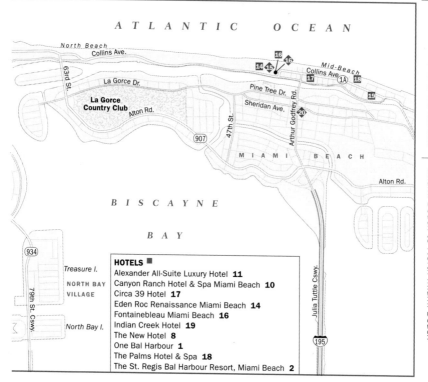

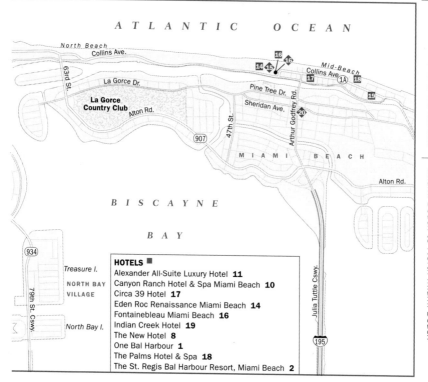

Il Mulino New York ★ ITALIAN   New York's veritable Greenwich Village Italian hot spot opened in Sunny Isles to mixed reviews. An ornate restaurant located in the even more ornate Acqualina Resort, Il Mulino is a saucy affair, with signature dishes such as spaghettini Bolognese, a cartoon-size rack of lamb, veal chop, and more. Service ranges from spotty to spectacular, but there's something about the tuxedoed waiters that makes it all so elegant and romantic. But again, there's that sauce issue. When I ate here, my dish was so covered in sauce I forgot what I had ordered. This restaurant is hit or miss, but when it does hit, it's a fancy Italian pleasure.

In Acqualina, 17875 Collins Ave., Sunny Isles. www.ilmulino.com. ✆ **305/466-9191.** Reservations recommended. Main courses $25–$60. AE, MC, V. Mon–Thurs 5–10:30pm; Fri–Sat 5–11:30pm.

Makoto ★★ JAPANESE   Chef Makoto Okuwa has worked with Iron Chef Morimoto, but he has clearly carved out a fantastic niche of his own here in his eponymous Bal Harbour Shops restaurant, where raw and cooked are treated equally and exceptionally. Udon noodles, black cod, toro tartare, tuna tataki, and possibly the best fried rice you'll ever eat are among the favorites here. Staff is insanely knowledgeable about food, and the scene with its ladies who lunch, assorted celebrities, and locals is up to par with the food. We prefer the outdoor seats for that reason, but if you sit inside, you'll get to watch the chef in action, which is almost as good, if not better, than the people-watching.

In the Bal Harbour Shops, 9700 Collins Ave., Miami Beach. www.makotorestaurant.me. ℂ **305/864-8600.** Reservations required. Sushi $6–$24; main courses $18–$55. AE, DC, MC, V. Mon–Thurs 11:30am–11pm; Fri–Sat 11:30am–midnight; Sun 11:30am–10pm.

Michael Mina's Bourbon Steak ★★ STEAK Although there's no shortage of steakhouses in Miami, there's nothing like this one. Reminiscent of something out of Las Vegas, everything here is massive—from the stunning all-glass wine cellar that takes up an entire wall, to the sheer size of the place at 7,600 square feet. And then there are the prices. But if you don't mind splurging, a meal at the star chef's first and only South Florida location is worth it. Start off with some oysters on the half shell, and then continue with the all-natural farm-raised Angus beef and American Kobe beef. Side dishes are delicious—jalapeño creamed corn, truffled mac and cheese, and a bourbon steak trio with duck fat fries. Not in the mood for steak? Try the whole crispy chicken with truffled mac and cheese. Share it—it's for two. Some say Mina's bar burgers, including the lamb version with yogurt raita, feta, tomato, and arugula, are the best in town.

19999 W. Country Club Dr. (in the Turnberry Isle Miami), Aventura. www.michaelmina.net. ℂ **786/279-6600.** Reservations recommended. Main courses $27–$60; small plates $12–$16. AE, DC, DISC, MC, V. Mon–Thurs 6–10pm; Fri–Sat 6–11pm; Sun 5–9pm.

Scarpetta ★★★ ITALIAN Miami Beach's very own version of the wildly popular NYC Italian restaurant of the same name, Scarpetta has consistently been one of the city's hottest reservations since it opened in late 2008. Chef Scott Conant is a talent and, unlike many star chefs too busy to cook in their own kitchens, he is often found massaging his homemade pasta right here, in his Miami Beach kitchen. And while that kitchen is indeed high tech, the dining room is a showpiece, with ambient lighting, beautiful chandeliers, banquettes, and an aura that's reminiscent of the first-class dining room in an Old World ocean liner that sailed into the 21st century. Once you are seduced by the room, you may not notice that you're paying $23 for a bowl of the chef's signature spaghetti *pomodoro*. The polenta served in a silver ramekin alongside a fricassee of mushrooms with a hint of truffle oil will have you wishing you could sail away on this gastronomical vessel and massage pasta as you sail into the sunset.

In the Fontainebleau, 4441 Collins Ave., Miami Beach. www.fontainebleau.com. ℂ **305/672-4660.** Reservations required. Main courses $23–$42. AE, DC, MC, V. Sun–Thurs 6–11pm; Fri–Sat 6pm–midnight.

Expensive

Carpaccio ★ ITALIAN A favored spot for the ladies who lunch, Carpaccio's location in the ritzy Bal Harbour Shops is its tastiest aspect: It's definitely a place to see and be seen. Ask for specials rather than ordering off the regular menu; they're much more interesting—linguine lobster, snapper piccata, and veal chop any style—though they may be a bit pricier. Wear sunglasses to block the blinding glare of all the diamonds.

9700 Collins Ave. (97th St., in Bal Harbour Shops), Bal Harbour. www.carpaccioatbalharbour.com. ℂ **305/867-7777.** Reservations recommended. Main courses $16–$36; pastas $16–$19; pizzas $14–$17. AE, MC, V. Daily 11:30am–11pm.

Timo ★★★ ITALIAN/MEDITERRANEAN Located in Sunny Isles, Timo is a stylish and hip restaurant catering to mostly North Miami Beach locals. Among the

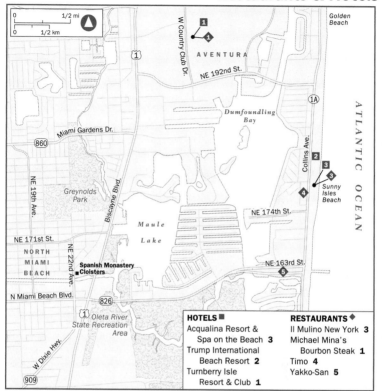

HOTELS ■	RESTAURANTS ◆
Acqualina Resort & Spa on the Beach **3**	Il Mulino New York **3**
Trump International Beach Resort **2**	Michael Mina's Bourbon Steak **1**
Turnberry Isle Resort & Club **1**	Timo **4**
	Yakko-San **5**

specialties, try the handcrafted pastas, including Burrata ravioli; black grouper with borlotti beans, calamari, clams, and aged sherry vinegar; and a phenomenal porcini-dusted veal scaloppini. Less pricey, less heavy items are also available, such as a delicious ricotta and fontina wood-fired pizza with white-truffle oil—perfect for lunch or a happy-hour snack. At Timo, a bistro-meets-lounge atmosphere gives way to a decidedly cool vibe, something that was always conspicuously lacking at Tony Roma's.

17624 Collins Ave., Sunny Isles. www.timorestaurant.com. ℂ **305/936-1008.** Reservations required. Main courses $21–$38; pizza $12–$16. AE, DC, MC, V. Sun–Thurs 11:30am–3pm and 6–10:30pm; Fri–Sat 11:30am–3pm and 6–11pm.

Moderate

Cafe Prima Pasta ★ ITALIAN   Cafe Prima Pasta has gathered quite a bit of fanfare: Because a massive waiting line always spilled out onto the street, the cafe expanded to include ample outdoor seating. The pasta here is homemade, and the kitchen's choice ingredients include ripe, juicy tomatoes; imported olive oil that would cost you a boatload if you bought it in the store; fresh, drippy mozzarella; and fish that tastes as if it has just been caught right out back. The zesty, spicy garlic and oil that is brought out as dip for the bread should be kept with you during your meal, for it doubles as extra seasoning for your food—not that it's necessary. Though tables are packed in, the atmosphere still manages to be romantic. Due to the chef's fancy for garlic, this is a three-Altoid restaurant, so be prepared to pop a few or request that they go light on the garlic.

414 71st St. (half a block east of the Byron movie theater), Miami Beach. www.primapasta.com. ℭ **305/867-0106.** Reservations accepted for parties of 6 or more. Main courses $17–$24; pastas $16–$22. MC, V. Mon–Thurs noon–midnight; Fri noon–1am; Sat 1pm–1am; Sun 5pm–midnight.

Cafe Ragazzi ★★ ITALIAN   This diminutive Italian cafe, with its rustic decor and a swift, knowledgeable waitstaff, enjoys great success for its tasty, simple pastas. The spicy *puttanesca* sauce with a subtle hint of fish is perfectly prepared. Also recommended is the salmon with radicchio. You can choose from many decent salads and carpaccio, too. Ragazzi has a faithful following of regulars, so be prepared for the crowd spilling out on the street—especially on weekend nights.

9500 Harding Ave. (on the corner of 95th St.), Surfside. http://caferagazzi.com. ℭ **305/866-4495.** Reservations accepted for parties of 3 or more. Main courses $10–$25. MC, V. Mon–Fri 11:30am–3pm; daily 5–11:30pm.

Josh's Deli DELI   Joshua Marcus is the former executive sous chef at China Grill and BLT Steak and a former general manager of La Sandwicherie. The guy's got experience. So, he decided to convert his übersuccessful Asian eatery, Chow Down Grill, into a deli serving house-made and hand-cut meats (corned beef, tongue, roasted turkey, salami, pastrami, and more), matzo ball and other soups, fish, potato knishes, *gribenes* (chicken skin fried in chicken fat), and more.

9517 Harding Ave., Surfside. http://chowdowngrill.com. ℭ **305/397-8494.** Reservations not accepted. Main courses $11–$23. Mon–Thurs 11am–10pm; Fri–Sat 11am–11pm; Sun 5–10pm.

Las Vacas Gordas ★★ ARGENTINE/STEAK   You may need a translator at this popular Argentine steakhouse, where service doesn't dillydally, nor do they typically speak understandable English. But don't worry, the culture shock wears off once they start to bring out your meat—and then more meat. Then you'll understand why the name of this restaurant translates to "The Fat Cows." It's a fun experience, as long as you hold off on your food coma. Specialties are the marinated and grilled steaks. All meats are served with a divine chimichurri sauce, but sauces aren't really needed. Neither are sides and salads, but sometimes you'll need something more than red wine to wash your meat down with.

933 Normandy Dr., Miami Beach. www.lasvacasgordas.com. ℭ **305/867-1717.** Reservations highly suggested. Main courses $15–$25. MC, V. Daily 6pm–midnight.

Inexpensive

The Greek Place GREEK   This little hole-in-the-wall diner with sparkling white walls and about 10 wooden stools serves fantastic Greek and American diner-style food. Daily specials like *pastitsio*, chicken *alcyone*, and roast turkey with all the fixings are big lunchtime draws for locals working in the area. Typical Greek dishes like shish kabob, souvlakia, and gyros are cooked to perfection as you wait. Even the hamburger, prime ground beef delicately spiced and freshly grilled, is wonderful. If you're not in the mood for heavy entrees, appetizers and salads are big enough and make for hearty meals, too.

233 95th St. (between Collins and Harding aves.), Surfside. http://greekplacesurfside.com. ℭ **305/866-9628.** Main courses $8–$16; appetizers $5–$12. No credit cards. Mon–Sat 11am–8pm.

Here Comes the Sun ★ AMERICAN/HEALTH FOOD One of Miami's first health-food spots (and it still looks like it did when it opened in 1970, yikes), this bustling grocery store–turned-diner serves hundreds of plates a night, mostly to blue-haired locals. It's noisy and hectic but worth it. Fresh grilled fish and chicken entrees are reliable and served with a nice array of vegetables. The miso burgers with "sun sauce" are a vegetarian's dream.

2188 NE 123rd St. (west of the Broad Causeway), North Miami. ✆ **305/893-5711.** Reservations recommended in season. Main courses $8–$20; sandwiches and salads $5–$15. AE, DC, DISC, MC, V. Mon–Sat 11am–8:30pm.

Yakko-San ★★★ ASIAN If you want to spot Anthony Bourdain, a Food Network star chef, or pretty much any chef in Miami late night, this venerable Asian hot spot is where you'll likely find them. Why here, in a strip mall of all places? Because this is possibly the only place in the city with the exception of maybe NAOE (p. 112) to serve authentic, unpretentious Japanese comfort food the way they do in Japan. Black pork belly, grilled smelt fish, chicken gizzards with chives, and bean sprouts don't even scratch the surface. The menu is something you won't find anywhere else in town (and at exceptionally reasonable prices, too) and the fact that they're open until 3am with full bar makes this place a must in many a foodie's and a night owl's book.

> ### Impressions
>
> *What's really exciting about Miami is its growth as an international destination. We don't have many restrictions as to what our neighborhoods should look like, and that's reflected in our food . . . It's very open and exciting.*
> —Chef Allen Susser

3381 NE 163rd St., North Miami Beach. http://yakko-san.com. ✆ **305/947-0064.** Reservations recommended on weekends. Noodles and entrees $8–$15; sushi $7–$15. AE, DC, DISC, MC, V. Sun–Thurs 5:30–11pm; Fri–Sat 5:30pm–midnight.

KEY BISCAYNE

Key Biscayne is home to the **Ritz-Carlton,** 455 Grand Bay Dr. (www.ritzcarlton.com; ✆ **305/365-4500**), and some of the world's nicest beaches and parks, yet it is not known for great food. Locals, or "Key rats" as they're known, tend to go off-island for meals or takeout, but here are some of the best on-the-island choices.

For a map of restaurants in this section, see p. 111.

Expensive

Rusty Pelican ★★ INTERNATIONAL Reopened just in time for its 40th birthday, Key Biscayne landmark Rusty Pelican is rusty no more after a $9-million renovation. The new menu, by chef Michael Gilligan, includes small plates, seafood, steaks and more. A revamped bar scene offers 1,500 vintages, a variety of microbrews, and creative signature cocktails. Signature dishes include eel and foie gras with tostones and soy-truffle glaze; crispy whole fried snapper with udon noodles and soy-honey sauce; and duck fat–fried Colorado lamb wrapped in phyllo pastry and served with sweet potato puree and mint *jus.* There's a great happy hour from Monday through Friday from 4 to 7pm, with bar food such as baked crab cakes, avocado fries, and sea scallop tiradito.

3201 Rickenbacker Causeway, Key Biscayne. http://miami.therustypelican.com. ✆ **305/361-3818.** Reservations recommended. Main courses $16–$30. AE, DC, MC, V. Sun–Thurs 11:30am–4pm and 5–11pm; Fri–Sat 11:30am–4pm and 5pm–midnight.

Inexpensive

Oasis Sandwich Shop 🍴 CUBAN   Everyone, from the city's mayor to the local handymen, meet for delicious paella and Cuban sandwiches at this little shack. They gather outside, around the little takeout window, or inside at the few tables for super-powerful *cafecitos* and rich *croquetas*. The Cuban sandwich is pretty exceptional. It's slightly dingy, but the food is good and cheap.

19 Harbor Dr. (on corner of Crandon), Key Biscayne. © **305/361-5709.** Main courses $4–$15; sandwiches $5–$10. No credit cards. Daily 6am–9pm.

DOWNTOWN MIAMI

Thanks to the urban renaissance taking place in downtown, a lot more hip, chichi, and bona fide foodie-caliber restaurants are starting to pop up. **The Shops at Midtown Miami,** 3401 N. Miami Ave. (www.shopmidtownmiami.com; © **305/573-3371**), for instance, is the quintessence of urban revival, featuring anchor stores like Target and Marshall's and some really good restaurants, including a branch of NYC's mod Mexican spot **Mercadito** and Sushi Samba's hipper sister, the tapas-oriented **Sugarcane Raw Bar Grill.** That said, while it's safe(ish) to walk the Shops at Midtown, surrounding areas not so much. Perhaps one day soon, it'll be safe to walk through the city at night from one hot spot to the next. Wishful thinking, perhaps, but then again, South Beach used to be unsafe as well.

Very Expensive

Area 31 ★★ SEAFOOD   Miami's very first sustainable seafood restaurant, Area 31 is named after a U.N.-designated, ecologically sustainable area of the Western Central Atlantic Ocean encompassing the coastal waters of Florida, Central America, and northern South America. Area 31 is a gorgeous, 65-seat restaurant on the 16th floor of the EPIC hotel featuring a spectacular outdoor terrace with views of the water and skyline. Executive chef E. Michael Reidt takes his seafood seriously, with seamless, simple, and locally inspired dishes such as yellowfin tuna with green apple and yellow pepper juice; Key West pink shrimp with olive oil, Key lime juice, and chili; fresh shucked oysters; and an assortment of grilled, fresh catches of the day served with mix-and-match sauces. A five-course chef's tasting is highly recommended at $55 per person.

At the EPIC, 270 Biscayne Blvd. Way, Miami. www.area31restaurant.com. © **305/424-5234.** Reservations strongly recommended. Main courses $17–$39. AE, DC, DISC, MC, V. Mon–Sat 5–11pm; Sun 5–10pm.

Azul ★★★ INTERNATIONAL   Azul is one of the most upscale, prettiest—and priciest—waterfront restaurants in town. Located in the Mandarin Oriental, the restaurant's décor is gorgeous, with its waterfront view, high ceilings, walls burnished in copper, and silk-covered chairs. The menu fuses modern European cuisine with American and Asian accents, as seen in dishes such as almond gazpacho with foie gras powder, Argan oil and orange essence; and "Eggs, Bacon & Toast," a 12-hour suckling pig with tempura duck egg, black truffle pomme puree, speck emulsion and red Wine jus.

At the Mandarin Oriental, 500 Brickell Key Dr., Miami. www.mandarinoriental.com. © **305/913-8538.** Reservations strongly recommended. Main courses $24–$80. AE, DC, DISC, MC, V. Mon–Sat 7–11pm.

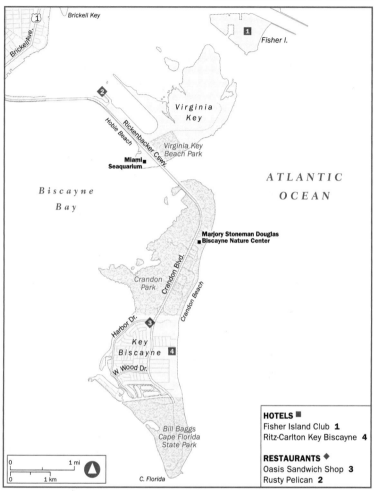

Brickell Key

Fisher I.

Virginia Key

Rickenbacker Cswy.

Hobie Beach

Virginia Key Beach Park

Miami Seaquarium

Biscayne Bay

ATLANTIC OCEAN

Marjory Stoneman Douglas Biscayne Nature Center

Crandon Park

Crandon Blvd.

Crandon Beach

Harbor Dr.

Key Biscayne

W. Wood Dr.

Bill Baggs Cape Florida State Park

C. Florida

0   1 mi
0   1 km

HOTELS ■
Fisher Island Club **1**
Ritz-Carlton Key Biscayne **4**

RESTAURANTS ◆
Oasis Sandwich Shop **3**
Rusty Pelican **2**

Capital Grille ★★ STEAKHOUSE   The best of all the chain steakhouses, Capital Grille is a serious power spot. Wine cellars are filled with high-end classics, and the dark-wood paneling, pristine white tablecloths, chandeliers, and marble floors all contribute to the clubby atmosphere. For an appetizer, start with the lobster and crab cakes. If you're not in the mood for beef or lobster, try the pan-seared red snapper and asparagus covered with hollandaise. You're surrounded by wine cellars filled with about 5,000 bottles of wine—too extensive and rare to list. While some people prefer the more stalwart style and service of Morton's up the block, others find Capital to be a bit livelier. The food's pretty much the same between the two, though I find the steaks at Morton's to be a notch better; however, the atmosphere at the Capital Grille is *much* more inviting. Complimentary valet parking here (as opposed to Morton's, which charges a fee) is another reason to visit this carnivorous capital.

444 Brickell Ave., Miami. www.thecapitalgrille.com. © **305/374-4500.** Reservations recommended. Main courses $25–$39. AE, DC, DISC, MC, V. Mon–Thurs 11:30am–3pm and 5–10:30pm; Fri 11:30am–3pm and 5–11pm; Sat 6–11pm; Sun 5–10pm.

db Bistro Moderne ★★★ BISTRO   Another Manhattan import, db Bistro Moderne, located on the ground floor of the JW Marriott Marquis, is the more casual offering from star chef Daniel Boulud, a modern French American eatery where "traditional French cuisine meets the flavors of the American market." In other words: hanger steak with oxtail ragout, sun-dried tomatoes, celery root, squash, and garlic pomme purée in a red-wine onion compote; or the phenomenal Original db Burger, a stop-you-in-your-tracks sirloin burger filled—yes filled—with braised short ribs on a Parmesan bun. Of course, there's lighter fare, from tartes and salads to terrines, charcuterie, raw bar, and pâtés, catering to the ladies-who-lunch crowd. The elegant, dramatic dining room with soaring 16-foot ceilings and cozy banquettes is also conducive to power lunches, celebratory dinners, and dates.

At the JW Marriott Marquis, 345 Ave. of the Americas, Miami. www.danielnyc.com. © **305/421-8800.** Reservations strongly recommended. Main courses $29–$45. AE, DC, DISC, MC, V. Mon–Fri noon–2:30pm; Sun–Mon 5–10pm; Tues–Thurs 5–11pm; Fri–Sat 5pm–midnight; Sun brunch 11am–3pm.

Il Gabbiano ★★ ITALIAN   Owned by the same folks who own Il Mulino in NYC, the similarities at this high-end Italian restaurant are striking, from the fresh-shaved Parmesan and fried zucchini brought to the table with your bread, to the serious demeanors of what seems to be a mostly Italian waitstaff. The menu is intimidating—written mostly in Italian to describe a slew of pasta, meat, and fish dishes—and should come with a translator if you don't have the iPhone app for that. But the menu is secondary to the specials, lots of them, recited verbally by your charming waiter with the thick accent. Listen carefully unless you expect to spend the entire night there, which isn't such a bad thing considering the water views of Biscayne Bay. While the bustling, buzzy dining room has water views, you can't beat the alfresco seating. Food is high quality with a heavy emphasis on pastas such as fettuccine Alfredo or *pollo alla Valdostano* with prosciutto, foie gras, fontina cheese, and wild mushrooms. Order the double veal chop at your own risk—while the presentation is impressive and the meat tender, I'm not necessarily sure it's worth $65.

335 S. Biscayne Blvd., Miami. www.ilgabbianomia.com. © **305/373-0063.** Reservations necessary. Main courses $26–$55. AE, DC, MC, V. Daily noon–11:30pm.

NAOE Miami ★★★ SUSHI   Simply put, NAOE is Japanese for "OMG *omakase*." Okay, not really, but chef Kevin Cory sure makes you think so with his exquisitely prepared, hyperfresh sushi and Japanese fare. This may be the closest Miami gets to Tokyo. Take the motto: "It's not fresh, it's alive." Open only Wednesday through Sunday, NAOE serves the chef choice menu ($26) every night. All menus are prepared daily and if you have a special request, you need to make it at least a week in advance. Among the items you may find on your plate or in your bento box: smooth egg custard with soft freshwater eel bits; fresh giant clam sashimi in a tangy *shiso* vinaigrette; in-shell conch dressed in simple soy sauce; sweet, chilled corn-miso soup; salmon belly; saltwater and freshwater eel; *uni* so creamy it's been known to silence even the pickiest of reviewers; and horse mackerel with vinegary soy sauce.

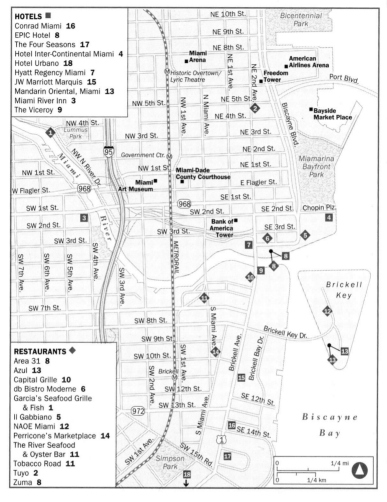

HOTELS ■
Conrad Miami **16**
EPIC Hotel **8**
The Four Seasons **17**
Hotel Inter-Continental Miami **4**
Hotel Urbano **18**
Hyatt Regency Miami **7**
JW Marriott Marquis **15**
Mandarin Oriental, Miami **13**
Miami River Inn **3**
The Viceroy **9**

RESTAURANTS ◆
Area 31 **8**
Azul **13**
Capital Grille **10**
db Bistro Moderne **6**
Garcia's Seafood Grille
   & Fish **1**
Il Gabbiano **5**
NAOE Miami **12**
Perricone's Marketplace **14**
The River Seafood
   & Oyster Bar **11**
Tobacco Road **11**
Tuyo **2**
Zuma **8**

It's as authentic as it gets here. Be careful about what you ask for, though, as extras can add up quickly; they charge for fresh grated wasabi. That's not the tubed stuff, but still.

605 Brickell Key Dr., Miami. www.naoemiami.com. ✆ **305/947-6263.** Reservations recommended. Tasting menus $26. AE, MC, V. Wed–Sun seatings 6:30 and 9:30pm (times may change, so call ahead).

Tuyo ★★ SPANISH/INTERNATIONAL   Located on the roof of Miami Dade College's new Culinary Institute and led by Miami's own culinary trailblazer chef Norman Van Aken, Tuyo is all about farm-to-table fabulousness. The menu includes suckling pig–stuffed empanadas, pan-cooked filet of Key West yellowtail with roasted cauliflower and mashed potatoes, and black grouper sous vide with Serrano ham and avocado. To go along with the fantastic food are the views of downtown and the Miami city skyline.

415 NE 2nd Ave., Miami. http://tuyomiami.com. © **305/237-3200.** Reservations recommended. Main courses $29–$42. AE, DC, DISC, MC, V. Tues–Sat 6–10:30pm.

Zuma ★★★ JAPANESE   A stunning space bolstered by even more stunning cuisine where traditional Japanese meets modern, Zuma is not your typical sushi and noodle spot. The brainchild of German star chef Rainer Becker, who chose Miami as the city of choice for the restaurant's stateside debut, Zuma is constantly at the top of the "best of" lists, including the exclusive S. Pellegrino list, which rated the restaurant as one of the *world's* best and rightfully so. Based on the traditional Japanese school of cooking known as Izakaya with dishes cooked on a traditional robata (wood) grill, menu highlights include prawn and black cod dumplings; sea bass sashimi with yuzu, truffle oil, and salmon roe; yellowtail sashimi with green-chili relish, ponzu, and pickled garlic; sliced seared beef with pickled daikon and fresh truffle dressing; pork-belly skewer with *yuzu* mustard miso; beef skewers with shishito pepper and smoked chili soy; and miso marinated black cod, wrapped in hoba leaf. A $65, $95, or $130 tasting menu features the chef's selection of seasonal signature dishes. And, finally, because desserts aren't exactly a Japanese strong point, Zuma's pastry chef hails from . . . drum roll . . . France. Welcome to Miami.

In the EPIC Hotel, 270 Biscayne Blvd. Way, Miami. www.zumarestaurant.com. © **305/577-0277.** Reservations necessary. Main courses $26–$55. AE, DC, MC, V. Mon–Sat noon–3pm, 3—6pm for light snacks, and 6pm–midnight; Sun noon–2:30pm and 6–10pm.

Moderate

Garcia's Seafood Grille & Fish ★ 🍴 SEAFOOD   A good catch on the banks of the Miami River, Garcia's has a great waterfront setting and a fairly simple yet tasty menu of fresh fish cooked in a number of ways—grilled, broiled, fried, or, the best in our opinions, in garlic or green sauce. Meals are quite the deal here, all served with green salad or grouper soup, and yellow rice or French fries. The complimentary fish-spread appetizer is also a nice touch. Because of this, not to mention the great, gritty ambience that takes you away from neon, neo-Miami in favor of the old seafaring days, there's usually a wait for a table. If so, hang out at the bar and order an appetizer of inexpensive stone crabs or famous conch fritters. They also recently opened an upstairs bar and lounge overlooking the river.

398 NW N. River Dr., Miami. http://garciasseafoodgrill.com. © **305/375-0765.** Reservations recommended. Main courses $12–$26. AE, DC, DISC, MC, V. Sun–Thurs 11am–10pm; Fri–Sat 11am–11pm.

The River Seafood & Oyster Bar ★★ SEAFOOD   A small, yet always packed seafood hot spot next door to Tobacco Road, the River is a buzzy and unpretentious spot for some of the best oysters in town—shipped fresh from all over the world daily—as well as some delicious dishes, including pan-fried snapper filet with avocado–heirloom tomato salad, lemon vinaigrette, plantain chips, and sea salt; and, for the landlubber, duck three ways: glazed duck breast, duck confit salad, and a duck foie gras spring roll. There's also bacon-wrapped meatloaf. A great spot for happy hour, the River Oyster Bar is a lively one, where you can suck down some oysters with some seriously stiff drinks or excellent wines. In fact, the bar is the focal point of the restaurant, considering there are so few tables, it's usually standing room only. Good thing is, service at the bar is swift and oftentimes people end up eating there as they wait for that elusive table.

15 SE 10th St. (corner of S. Miami Ave.), Miami. www.therivermiami.com. © **305/374-9693.** Oysters $2.50–$3; main courses $19–$36. AE, MC, V. Mon–Fri 11:30am–5pm; Mon–Thurs 6–10:30pm; Fri 6pm–midnight; Sat 5:30pm–midnight.

Inexpensive

Perricone's Marketplace ★ ITALIAN   A large selection of groceries and wine, plus an outdoor porch and patio for dining, makes this one of the most welcoming spots downtown. Its rustic setting in the midst of downtown is a fantastic respite from city life. Sunday offers buffet brunches and all-you-can-eat dinners, too. But the place is most popular on weekdays at noon, when the "suits" show up for delectable sandwiches, quick and delicious pastas, and hearty salads.

15 SE 10th St. (corner of S. Miami Ave.), Miami. © **305/374-9693.** Sandwiches $6 and up; pastas $14 and up. AE, MC, V. Sun–Mon 7am–10pm; Tues–Sat 7am–11pm.

Tobacco Road AMERICAN   Miami's oldest bar is a bluesy, Route 66–inspired institution favored by barflies, professionals, and anyone else who wishes to indulge in good and greasy bar fare—chicken wings, nachos, and so on—at reasonable prices in a down-home, gritty-but-charming atmosphere. The burgers are also good—particularly the Death Burger, a deliciously unhealthful combo of choice sirloin topped with grilled onions, jalapeños, and pepper-jack cheese (bring on the Tums!). Also a live-music venue, the Road, as it's known by locals, is well traveled, especially during Friday's happy hour and Tuesday's Lobster Night, when 100 1¼-pound lobsters go for only $13 apiece.

626 S. Miami Ave, Miami. www.tobacco-road.com. © **305/374-1198.** Main courses $13–$17; burgers and sandwiches $6–$7. AE, DC, MC, V. Mon–Sat 11:30am–5am; Sun noon–5am. Cover $5–$10 Fri–Sat nights.

MIDTOWN & WYNWOOD

Expensive

Mercadito Midtown ★ MEXICAN   An outpost of a popular New York restaurant, Mercadito has a reputation for serving great fish tacos (pan-seared tilapia, chile poblano, and tomatillo-garlic mojo). In addition to 10 kinds of tacos, Mercadito has a massive menu of gussied-up Mexican, meant to be shared by the table, and not cheap. For one, you pay for condiments via an open guacamole, salsa, and ceviche bar offering a variety of house-made sauces from mole poblano to manzana (apple, tomatillo, almonds, and habanero). There are also big dishes, like chile relleno, but we say stick with the tacos. Margaritas are individually muddled and made with 100% blue-agave tequila, and cocktails are quite creative, seamlessly blending all sorts of ingredients from hot sauce to mango—the way that, say, the chef should be doing in the kitchen. There's a more casual taqueria located adjacent to the main restaurant.

In the Shops at Midtown Miami, 3252 NE 1st Ave. www.mercaditorestaurants.com. © **305/369-0430.** Reservations recommended. Main courses $10–$29. AE, DC, MC, V. Mon–Sat 11:30am–5pm; Sun–Tues 5pm–midnight; Wed–Thurs 5pm–1am; Fri–Sat 5pm–2am.

Sugarcane Raw Bar Grill ★★★ SOUTH AMERICAN/ASIAN   The darling of Midtown dining, Sugarcane is a sensational small-plates restaurant that beat Zuma to

Roasting to the Occasion

If you find yourself in Wynwood looking for a coffee, don't miss **Panther Coffee**, 2390 NW 2nd Ave. (www.panthercoffee. com; © **305/677-3952**), a boho beanery where the beans are roasted right on site, focusing on small-batch coffees and specialty drinks. Nearby at 2519 NW 2nd Ave. is **Lester's** (© **305/456-1784**), a jolty coffee and wine bar that's reminiscent of an artist's living room.

the punch with Miami's first-ever robata grill. Talented chef Timon Balloo presides over three kitchens—one for cooking meats, one for everything else—and a raw bar, seamlessly fusing South American, Asian, and global cuisine into tidy little (and not so little) plates of palate-pleasing excellence. Loud and bustling, the 4,000-plus-square-foot hip, warehouse-style eatery packs in crowds with potent cocktails and signature dishes such as chicken yakitori cooked on the robata grill, veal meatballs in sherry-fueled demi-glace, fried goat-cheese croquettes, white pork buns with apple kimchi and cilantro; and grilled, spicy Shishito peppers with sea salt and lemon. Most small plates are $10 or less, but be careful; they're so good, and after a few cocktails to boot, you can be looking at a hefty bill. A huge cocktail crowd gathers at the indoor/outdoor bar and patio area after work and late on weekend nights. Sunday brunch is also extremely popular.

In the Shops at Midtown Miami, 3250 NE 1st Ave. www.sugarcanerawbargrill.com. © **786/369-0353.** Reservations recommended. Small plates $5–$10. AE, DC, MC, V. Sun–Wed 11:30am–midnight; Thurs 11:30am–1am; Fri–Sat 11:30am–2am.

Moderate

City Hall ★ AMERICAN   An American-style brasserie, this two-story, 6,000-square-foot restaurant serves comfort-food dishes including mac 'n' cheese, meatloaf, and Australian lamb rack with potato pancakes and homemade applesauce. There's also a great lunch (try the Reuben), brunch, and pre- and post-theater scene featuring some of Miami's movers, shakers, and politicians.

2004 Biscayne Blvd., Miami. www.cityhalltherestaurant.com. © **305/764-3130.** Reservations recommended. Main courses $19–$30; lunch, burgers, and sandwiches $12–$15. AE, DC, DISC, MC, V. Mon–Thurs 11:30am–11pm; Fri–Sat 11:30am–1am; Sun 10am–10pm.

Gigi ★ ASIAN   Although Gigi considers itself a noodle bar, there are only three noodle dishes on the tiny menu. But it doesn't matter. Swarms of foodies and hipsters pack this casual-chic Wynwood spot into the wee hours, when 3 items to decipher from are better than 30. And while the noodles are admittedly deelish—the steak *chow fun* with mushroom, eggplant, and cabbage broth is a favorite—be sure to check out one of the three rice bowls; crispy soft-shell crab with red coconut curry, basil, mango, and jasmine rice; and any of the many "snacks," including the crispy chicken skin, chicken drumsticks, and pork buns. Portions are small, so prices add up. Gigi serves beer and wine only.

3470 N. Miami Ave., Miami. www.giginow.com. © **305/573-1520.** Reservations not required. Main courses $12–$16. AE, DC, DISC, MC, V. Mon–Thurs 6pm–3am; Fri–Sat 6pm–5am.

Jean Paul's House Restaurant and Market ★ PERUVIAN   A cozy, rustic house worthy of a design magazine photo shoot, Jean Paul's House serves New World

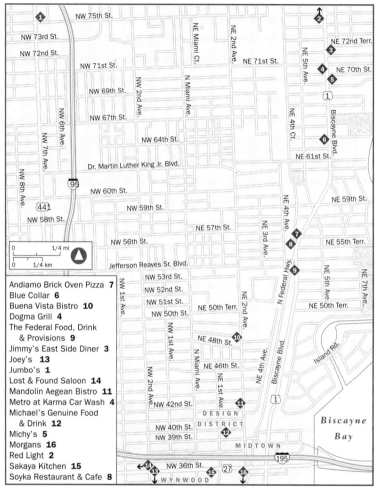

Andiamo Brick Oven Pizza **7**
Blue Collar **6**
Buena Vista Bistro **10**
Dogma Grill **4**
The Federal Food, Drink
& Provisions **9**
Jimmy's East Side Diner **3**
Joey's **13**
Jumbo's **1**
Lost & Found Saloon **14**
Mandolin Aegean Bistro **11**
Metro at Karma Car Wash **4**
Michael's Genuine Food
& Drink **12**
Michy's **5**
Morgans **16**
Red Light **2**
Sakaya Kitchen **15**
Soyka Restaurant & Cafe **8**

cuisine with a Peruvian touch, thanks to its chef/owner Jean Paul Desmaison. The seasonally changing menu offers fantastic fresh fare. Signature dishes include crispy pork belly braised in grapes and Pisco 100 and served with sweet-potato purée; beef tenderloin served with onions, tomato, Aji Amarillo, and Pisco 100; and a hearty, flavorful bouillabasse. Lunch is lighter, with sandwiches such as nicoise, roast turkey, or roasted pork leg. There's a great weekday happy hour featuring small plates.

2426 NE 2nd Ave., Miami. www.jeanpaulshouse.com. © **305/573-7373.** Reservations suggested. Main courses $16–$29; sandwiches $9–$12. AE, DC, DISC, MC, V. Mon–Fri 11:30am–3pm and 3:30–5:30pm; Mon–Thurs 6–10pm; Fri–Sat 6–11pm.

Joey's ★★ 👔 ITALIAN   Sometimes you have to go out of your way for good pizza in Florida, even if that means driving into the still-dodgy-yet-arty Wynwood area for it. Joey's is a cozy, minimalistic, industrial-style concrete-floored eatery with an open kitchen, a few tables inside, and an outdoor patio. A full-blown menu of pastas and meat and seafood entrees includes dishes like baked cod with eggplant and tomato *gremolata* or lamb chops with juniper-berry reduction, but we personally go there for the pizza, from classic Margherita to a pie dotted with figs, Gorgonzola, honey, and hot pepper. There are also some nice, reasonably priced Italian wines by the glass. As for the neighborhood, Joey's insists it's on its way. We say take a cab or car straight there, hand the keys to the valet, and enter an oasis of urban evolution.

2506 NW 2nd Ave., Miami. www.joeyswynwood.com. ℭ **305/438-0488.** Reservations recommended. Main courses and pizzas $7–$24. AE, DC, DISC, MC, V. Mon–Wed 11:30am–9:30pm; Thurs 11:30am–10:30pm; Fri–Sat 11:30am–11:30pm.

Wynwood Kitchen & Bar ★ LATIN   Wynwood Kitchen & Bar is groundbreaking. The restaurant is part of an art campus that also houses Wynwood Walls, an art park with a collection of more than 18 murals by leading international street artists. Adding to the already successful Goldman-owned Joey's, WKB is another reason besides art galleries to go to the Wynwood neighborhood. The 5,000-square-foot, warehousey WKB features a menu of Latin-inspired global small plates such as bacon-wrapped dates, ropa vieja empanadas, and octopus skewers, and larger plates such as pan-seared scallops and crispy polenta; murals (and drinks inspired) by acclaimed graffiti artists Shepard Fairey and Christian Awe; and the requisite hipster bar with creative cocktails named after artists whose works have adorned Wynwood and its surroundings.

2550 NW 2nd Ave., Miami. http://wynwoodkitchenandbar.com. ℭ **305/722-8959.** Small plates $7–$15; main courses $11–$15. AE, MC, V. Mon–Sat 11am–midnight. Bar open until 1am.

Inexpensive

Lost & Found Saloon ★ 👔 SOUTHWESTERN   Located in the heart of Wynwood, this rough-and-tumble cowboy-style eatery is the OK Corral for area artists, hipsters, and fans of Tex-Mex and Southwestern food. There are lots of options for vegetarians, with dishes such as tofu sampler with pine nuts and sun-dried tomatoes and grilled and marinated portobello mushrooms. But we'll stick with the meat and seafood dishes, including a chipotle-seared mahimahi with grilled asparagus and fresh-made pico de gallo. Tacos and sandwiches are good, too, especially during the Giddy Up Happy Hours from 4 to 7pm weeknights and 5 to 10pm on Sundays, when food, wine, and beer are all discounted and a taco will set you back about $5.

185 NW 36th St., Miami. www.thelostandfoundsaloon-miami.com. ℭ **305/576-1008.** Tacos, burritos, sandwiches $5–$10, main courses $11–$18. AE, MC, V. Daily 11am–3am.

Morgans ★ 👔 BISTRO   Located on a sketchy stretch of up-and-coming Wynwood across from the Shops at Midtown Miami, the cozy, charming Morgans is a welcome respite from the hype and circumstance surrounding this neighborhood. Housed in a two-story lavender house with striped black-and-white awnings and a large wraparound terrace, Morgans is where Miamians go for modern comfort food like Voluptuous Grilled Cheese, sensational skinny fries, brioche French toast, mac and cheese, and meatloaf with "smokey mash." Morgans serves three meals a day, but we prefer the daytime vibe for breakfast, brunch, and lunch. A tiny indoor dining room is minimal, clean, and IKEA-esque, but when weather permits we highly recommend grabbing a table on the porch and marveling at the paradox of gritty surroundings and oh-so-cozy confines and cuisine.

28 NE 29th St., Miami. http://themorgansrestaurant.com. ✆ **305/573-9678.** Breakfast, brunch, and lunch $9–$21; dinner main courses $14–$28. AE, DC, MC, V. Tues–Thurs 11am–10pm; Fri 11am–11pm; Sat 8am–5pm and 6–11pm; Sun 8am–5pm.

Sakaya Kitchen ★★★ ASIAN   The best no-frills, counter-service spot in the city, Sakaya Kitchen is in a class of its own, serving seriously gourmet Asian fare from traditional and street-hawker dishes to modern twists on classics. Chef/owner Richard Hales cooks up divine pork buns starring meat that marinates for 24 hours in a mix of brown sugar, toasted spices, and sesame oil before roasting for yet another 8 hours; Korean-style chicken wings marinated in a spicy Korean chili sauce; baby back ribs with a honey-and-orange glaze; and more. Sure, you stand in line (the wait is well worth it), order off a chalkboard, and use plastic utensils, but Sakaya Kitchen is the closest thing to Asia in Miami. For those on the go, Sakaya's food truck, **Dim Ssam a Go Go,** is a great meal if you can catch it, and another location of Sakaya opened in downtown Miami at 125 SE 3rd Ave. (✆ **305/371-2511**).

In the Shops at Midtown Miami, 3401 N. Miami Ave., Miami. www.sakayakitchen.com. ✆ **305/576-8096.** Main courses $5–$19. AE, DC, MC, V. Sun noon–9pm; Mon–Sat noon–10pm.

DESIGN DISTRICT

For a map of restaurants in this section, see p. 117.

Expensive

Michael's Genuine Food & Drink ★★★ NEW AMERICAN   The sleek yet unassuming dining room and serene courtyard seating are constantly abuzz with Design District hipsters, foodies, and celebrities. It's all thanks to chef/owner Michael Schwartz's fresh vision for fabulous food—a stellar, fresh mix of all organic products, some from Schwartz's own stash, including eggs laid by hens at Lake Meadow Farms in Ocoee, Florida, and by chickens at PNS Farm in Homestead. With an emphasis on products sourced from local growers, fishermen, and ranchers, the menu, which changes daily, is divided into small, medium, large, and extralarge plates. There are also excellent pizzas, such as the shiitake mushroom pizza with cave-aged Gruyère, caramelized onion, fresh thyme, and Lucini extra virgin oil. We love the $4-to-$6 bar menu, featuring crispy hominy with chili and lime, deviled eggs, kimchi, and chicken liver crostini. Book early for Michael's, as it's always crowded. The Sunday brunch is enormously popular. There's a great weekday happy hour.

> **Impressions**
>
> *Bliss is a locally grown ingredient.*
> —Hedy Goldsmith, pastry chef at Michael's Genuine Food & Drink

130 NE 40th St., Miami. www.michaelsgenuine.com. ✆ **305/573-5550.** Reservations recommended. Main courses $14–$59. AE, DC, DISC, MC, V. Mon–Fri 11:30am–3pm; Mon–Thurs 5:30–11pm; Fri–Sat 5:30pm–midnight; Sun 11am–2:30pm and 5:30–10pm.

Moderate

Buena Vista Bistro ★ FRENCH   This is a neighborhood favorite of artists, business folk, and people who appreciate the delicious, mostly French fare offered off the tiny eatery's chalkboard. A few utilitarian tables inside, some out front and others in a side garden area, are almost always full. The menu's short, but the portions are large. Among the best: a deliciously spicy curry chicken, grouper with beurre blanc, roast salmon, and rib-eye and fries. A sister restaurant, the **Buena Vista Deli,** opened up the block at 4590 NE 2nd Ave. (http://buenavistadeli.com; **305/576-3945**), serving delicious sandwiches, salads, and fresh made breads.

4582 NE 2nd Ave., Miami. www.buenavistabistro.com. ✆ **305/456-5909.** Reservations not accepted. Main courses $10–$20. AE, DC, DISC, MC, V. Daily 11am–midnight.

Mandolin Aegean Bistro ★ GREEK   The Greek food is good here, really good, but all people rave about is the ambiance. As if a piece of Santorini or Mykonos landed in, of all places, the Design District, Mandolin is one of the most resplendent, albeit smallest, spots in the city. Although there are a few seats indoors, you will want to sit outside in the garden, shaded by trees illuminated by gas lanterns. There aren't many tables out here either, so come early. As for that food, the owners pride themselves on serving the finest peasant fare, featuring locally caught fish; the purest olive oil; fresh herbs and vegetables; farm-raised meats; and homemade breads, cheeses, and yogurt.

4312 NE 2nd Ave., Miami. www.mandolinmiami.com. ✆ **305/576-6066.** Reservations strongly recommended. Main courses $15–$28; meze $8–$18. AE, DC, DISC, MC, V. Mon–Sat noon–11pm; Fri–Sun noon–10pm.

BISCAYNE CORRIDOR

For a map of restaurants in this section, see p. 117.

Expensive

Michy's ★★ 🍴 LATIN   Star chef Michelle Bernstein's homey 50-seat eatery started a foodie renaissance on Miami's burgeoning Upper East Side. If you drive too fast, you'll miss the small storefront restaurant, a deceiving facade for a whimsical retro orange-and-blue interior where stellar small plates such as ham-and–blue cheese croquettes are consumed in massive quantities because they're that good. Best of all, everything on the menu comes in half and full portions, so you can either control—or channel—the gluttony. There's also a zingy ceviche that changes daily; pan-seared sole with sunchoke purée, baby artichokes, preserved lemon, and olive nage (flavored broth); short ribs "falling off the bone," which it is, with mashed potatoes and butter-braised Brussels sprouts; and, for those whose appetites call for it, on Wednesday nights, all-you-can-eat fried chicken. Fabulous fried chicken. There's nothing ordinary about Michy's, except for the fact that a reservation here is nearly impossible to score if not made weeks in advance. For a more casual experience, check out Bernstein's fantastic lunch spot, **Crumb on Parchment,** 3930 NE 2nd Ave. (✆ **305/572-9444**), featuring soups, salads, sandwiches, and amazing pastries; it's open Monday to Friday 8:30am to 5:30pm.

Impressions
Miami's cuisine is fearless; there are no boundaries.
—Chef Michelle Bernstein, Michy's/Sra. Martinez

6927 Biscayne Blvd. www.michysmiami.com. ✆ **305/759-2001.** Reservations recommended. Main courses $15–$30. AE, DC, MC, V. Tues–Thurs noon–3pm and 6–10:30pm; Fri noon–3pm and 6–11pm; Sat 6–11pm; Sun 6–10:30pm.

Moderate

Blue Collar ★ AMERICAN Contemporary comfort food served in a comfy, cozy space on Biscayne has officially classified Miami's foodies as Blue Collar. With 20 seats inside and 18 outside, the cozy spot serves, among other things, pork and beans smoky bacon; Berkshire sausage, white beans, fried egg, and toast; shrimp and grits with Trugole cheese, Neuske bacon, and New Orleans–style barbecue sauce; and crispy-skin snapper with rock shrimp, vegetable fried rice, and red curry. There's also a selection of homemade pastas and a rotation of over 20 vegetables from the VEG Chalkboard, offered daily. Don't miss chef/owner Daniel Serfer's Chanukah latkes with homemade applesauce, served year-round, and wisely so.

6370 Biscayne Blvd., Miami. www.bluecollarmiami.com. ✆ **305/756-0366.** Reservations recommended. Main courses $12–$18. AE, DC, DISC, MC, V. Sun–Thurs 11:30am–10pm; Fri–Sat 11:30am–11pm.

The Federal Food, Drink & Provisions ★★ PUB FARE Modern gastropub fare doesn't get more creative—or down to earth—than it does at this Biscayne Boulevard storefront hot spot, better known as the Fed. This isn't your typical beer-and-wings sort of place. The smaller plates tout items such as crispy tripe dusted with barbecue powder and maple syrup dipping sauce; buffalo pig wings with blue cheese mousse, pickled carrots, and celery; and biscuits and gravy crowned with crispy sweetbreads and served with peas, carrots, and country gravy. Larger plates include a sensational iron-roasted porterhouse with bone marrow, bacon onion marmalade, and fatted-duck-liver butter, and an equally excellent plate of Grove Farms grilled lamb chops with roasted baby fennel, beet greens, and lamb reduction. Add to it an excellent selection of wines, craft beers, and cocktails, and you've got yourself a place where you will be well Fed.

5132 Biscayne Blvd., Miami. www.thefederalmiami.com. ✆ **305/758-9559.** Main courses $13–$35. AE, DC, DISC, MC, V. Mon–Thurs 11:30am–10:30pm; Fri–Sat 11:30am–1am.

Red Light ★★ 🏠 CAJUN/CREOLE This one takes the award for the most offbeat location in town, as the on-site restaurant for one of Biscayne Boulevard's grittier motels (which since the restaurant opened is in the process of its own revitalization). If you can ignore the location, not to mention some of the motel's more, uh, colorful clientele, consider Chef Kris Wessell's daring menu instead. Although the place looks like a greasy spoon with vinyl booths and an old-diner vibe, it serves fine gourmet fare with Southern accents. The barbecue shrimp are outstanding, and the quail is an excellent entree—a full order features two birds, deboned except for wings and legs, perfectly roasted, and served with Bing cherry peppercorn and Gruyère grits. After dinner, head downstairs and have a cocktail on the shore of the very pungent Little Miami River. It's just par for the offbeat course.

In the Motel Blu, 7700 Biscayne Blvd., Miami. www.redlightmiami.com. ✆ **305/757-7773.** Reservations recommended on weekends. Main courses $9–$20. AE, DC, MC, V. Tues–Sat 6pm–2am.

Inexpensive

Andiamo Brick Oven Pizza ★ PIZZA Leave it to visionary Mark Soyka (News Cafe, Van Dyke Cafe, Soyka) to turn a retro-style 1960s carwash into one of the city's best pizza places. The brick-oven pizzas are to die for, whether you choose the simple Andiamo pie (tomato sauce, mozzarella, and basil) or the designer combos of pancetta and caramelized onions; hot and sweet sausage with broccoli rabe; or portobello mushrooms with truffle oil and goat cheese. Pizzas come in three sizes: 10-, 13-, and 16-inch. There are also excellent panini and salads. Though the pizza is undeniably delicious here, the most talked-about aspect of Andiamo is the fact that while you're washing down slice after slice, you can get your car washed and detailed at Leo's, the space's original and still-existing occupant out back.

5600 Biscayne Blvd., Miami. www.andiamopizzamiami.com. ⓒ **305/762-5751.** Main courses $9–$18. MC, V. Sun–Thurs 11am–11pm; Fri–Sat 11am–midnight.

Dogma Grill ★★ HOT DOGS   A little bit of L.A. comes to a gritty stretch of Biscayne Boulevard in the form of this very tongue-in-cheek hot dog stand whose motto is "A Frank Philosophy." The brainchild of a former MTV executive, Dogma will change the way you view hot dogs, offering a plethora of choices, from your typical chili dog to Chicago style, with celery salt, hot peppers, onions, and relish. The tropical version with pineapple is a bit funky but fitting for this stand, which attracts a very colorful, arty crowd from the nearby Design District. The buns here are softer than feather pillows, and the hot dogs are grilled to perfection. Try the garlic fries and the lemonade, too.

7030 Biscayne Blvd., Miami. www.dogmagrill.com. ⓒ **305/759-3433.** Main courses $3–$4. No credit cards. Daily 11am–9pm.

Jimmy's East Side Diner ★ DINER/BREAKFAST   The only thing wrong with this quintessential, consummate greasy-spoon diner is that it's not open 24 hours. Other than that, for the cheapest breakfasts in town, not to mention lunches and early dinners, Jimmy's is a dream come true. Try the banana pancakes, corned-beef hash, roasted chicken, or Philly cheesesteak. Jimmy's is a very neighborhoody place, where the late Bee Gee Maurice Gibb used to dine every Sunday. Adding to the aging regulars is a new, eclectic contingency of hung-over hipsters for whom Jimmy's is a sweet—and cheap—morning-after salvation.

7201 Biscayne Blvd., Miami. ⓒ **305/759-3433.** Main courses $3–$11. No credit cards. Daily 6:30am–4pm.

Jumbo's ★★★ 🍴 SOUL FOOD   Open 24 hours daily, this Miami institution is the kind of place where you'll see everyone from Rastafarian musicians and cabdrivers to Lenny Kravitz. It's in a shady neighborhood—Carol City—so if you go there, you're going for only one reason—Jumbo's. Family owned for more than 50 years, Jumbo's is known for its world-famous fried shrimp, fried chicken, catfish fingers, and collard greens. Its motto—"Life is to be enjoyed, not to be endured . . . Making friends is our business"—is spot on. The service is friendly and fun, and there's history here, too. Jumbo's was the first restaurant in Miami to integrate, in 1966, and the first to hire African-American employees, in 1967.

7501 NW 7th Ave., Miami. ⓒ**305/751-1127.** Main courses $5–$15. AE, DC, MC, V. Daily 24 hr.

Metro at Karma Car Wash ★ 🍴 BISTRO   The funkiest thing to hit Biscayne Boulevard since Dogma, this carwash-cum-bistro is a big hit with the locals who love their SUVs as much as their hot spots. Put your car in for a wash and relax on the outdoor patio, reminiscent of your best friend's backyard, where you can sip from an impressive number of micro beers, wines, and coffees, and snack on delicious organic fare, including sandwiches, salads, and a very good burger made with grass-fed filet mignon. DJs and cocktail parties make it a happening spot from Thursday on, and while we don't encourage you to drink and drive, of course, there's never been a better excuse to shine your car (it's pricey, but they do a spotless job!) while waxing social at the same time.

7010 Biscayne Blvd., Miami. www.metrobistromiami.com. ☎ **305/759-1392.** Sandwiches $12–$14; entrees $12–$22. AE, DC, MC, V. Tapas bar/cafe Wed–Sat 8am–1am. Car wash daily 8am–8pm.

Soyka Restaurant & Cafe ★ AMERICAN   Brought to us by the same man who owned the News and Van Dyke cafes in South Beach, Soyka, like its former siblings, was catalyst to the Biscayne Corridor revival. The motif inside is industrial chic, reminiscent of a souped-up warehouse. Lunches focus on burgers, sandwiches, and wood-fired-oven pizzas. Dinners include simple fare, such as an excellent, massive Cobb salad, or more elaborate dishes such as the delicious meatloaf. The bar area provides a few comfy couches and bar stools and tables at which to dine, if you prefer not to sit in the open dining room. A children's menu is available for both lunch and dinner. A lively crowd of bohemian Design District types, professionals, and singles gather here for a taste of urban life. On weekends, the place is packed and very loud. Do not expect an after-dinner stroll around the neighborhood—it's still too dangerous for pedestrian traffic. Head over the causeway to South Beach and stroll there.

5556 NE 4th Court (Design District, off Biscayne Blvd. and 55th St.), Miami. www.soykarestaurant. com. ☎ **305/759-3117.** Reservations recommended for parties of 8 or more. Main courses $10–$28. AE, MC, V. Sun–Thurs 11am–11pm (bar open until midnight); Fri–Sat 11am–midnight (bar open until 1am). Happy hour Mon–Fri 4–7pm.

LITTLE HAVANA

The main artery of Little Havana is a busy commercial strip called SW Eighth Street, or Calle Ocho. Auto-body shops, cigar factories, and furniture stores line this street, and on every corner there seems to be a pass-through window serving superstrong Cuban coffee and snacks. In addition, many of the Cuban, Dominican, Nicaraguan, Peruvian, and other Latin American immigrants have opened full-scale restaurants ranging from intimate candlelit establishments to bustling stand-up lunch counters.

For a map of restaurants in this section, see p. 133.

CUBAN coffee

Despite the more than a dozen Starbucks that dot the Miami landscape, locals still rely on the many Cuban cafeterias for their daily caffeine fix. Beware of the many establishments throughout Miami that serve espresso masked as Cuban coffee. For the real deal, go to the most popular—and most animated—Cuban cafeterias: **La Carreta** and **Versailles** (see below).

Cuban coffee is a longstanding tradition in Miami. You'll find it served from the takeout windows of hundreds of cafeterías or loncherías around town, especially in Little Havana, downtown, Hialeah, and the beaches. Depending on where you are and what you want, you'll spend between 40¢ and $1.50 per cup.

The best café cubano has a rich layer of foam on top formed when the hot espresso shoots from the machine into the sugar below. The result is the caramelly, sweet, potent concoction that's a favorite of locals of all nationalities.

To partake, you've just got to learn how to ask for it en español.

FROM CEVICHE TO PICADILLO: latin cuisine AT A GLANCE

In Little Havana for dinner? Many restaurants list menu items in English for the benefit of *norteamericano* diners. In case they don't, though, here are translations and suggestions for filling and delicious meals:

Arroz con pollo: Roast chicken served with saffron-seasoned yellow rice and diced vegetables.

Café cubano: Very strong black coffee, served in thimble-size cups with lots of sugar. It's a real eye-opener.

Camarones: Shrimp.

Ceviche: Raw fish seasoned with spice and vegetables and marinated in vinegar and citrus to "cook" it.

Croquetas: Golden-fried croquettes of ham, chicken, or fish.

Paella: A Spanish dish of chicken, sausage, seafood, and pork mixed with saffron rice and peas.

Palomilla: Thinly sliced beef, similar to American minute steak, usually served with onions, parsley, and a mountain of french fries.

Pan cubano: Long, white, crusty Cuban bread. Ask for it *tostado*—toasted and flattened on a grill with lots of butter.

Picadillo: A rich stew of ground meat, brown gravy, peas, pimientos, raisins, and olives.

Plátano: A deep-fried, soft, mildly sweet banana.

Pollo asado: Roasted chicken with onions and a crispy skin.

Ropa vieja: A shredded beef stew whose name literally means "old clothes."

Sopa de pollo: Chicken soup, usually with noodles or rice.

Tapas: A general name for Spanish-style hors d'oeuvres, served in grazing-size portions.

Expensive

Casa Juancho ★ SPANISH   A generous taste of Spain comes to Miami in the form of the cavernous Casa Juancho, which looks like it escaped from a production of *Don Quixote*. The numerous dining rooms are decorated with traditional Spanish furnishings and enlivened nightly by strolling Spanish musicians who tend to be annoying and expect tips—do not encourage them to play at your table; you'll hear them loud and clear from other tables, trust me. Try not to be frustrated with the older staff members who don't speak English or respond quickly to your subtle glance—the food is worth the frustration. Your best bet is to order lots of tapas, such as the mixed seafood vinaigrette, fresh shrimp in hot garlic sauce, and fried calamari rings. A few entrees stand out, such as roast suckling pig, baby eels in garlic and olive oil, and Iberian-style snapper.

2436 SW 8th St. (just east of SW 27th Ave.), Little Havana. www.casajuancho.com. ✆ **305/642-2452.** Reservations recommended (not accepted Fri–Sat after 8pm). Main courses $25–$42; tapas $8–$40. AE, DC, DISC, MC, V. Sun–Thurs noon–midnight; Fri–Sat noon–1am.

Moderate

Hy-Vong ★ VIETNAMESE   This place is a must in Little Havana, so expect to wait hours for a table and don't even think of mumbling a complaint. This Vietnamese cuisine combines the best of Asian and French cooking with spectacular results. Food at Hy-Vong is elegantly simple and superspicy. Appetizers include small, tightly packed Vietnamese spring rolls and kimchi, a spicy, fermented cabbage. Star entrees include pastry-enclosed chicken with watercress–cream cheese sauce and fish in tangy mango sauce. Unfortunately, service here is not typically friendly or stellar—in fact, it borders on abysmal, but once you finally get your food, all will be forgotten.

3458 SW 8th St. (btw. 34th and 35th aves.), Little Havana. www.hyvong.com. © **305/446-3674.** Reservations accepted for parties of 5 or more. Main courses $7–$20. AE, DISC, MC, V. Sun–Thurs 6–11pm; Fri–Sat 6–11:30pm. Closed 2 weeks in Aug.

Inexpensive

El Palacio de los Jugos ★ CUBAN   Although the original is on West Flagler Street, this Little Havana outpost of the Cuban culinary landmark is just as good, if not better, serving fresh squeezed juices (guava, papaya, sugar cane, mango), tropical shakes, and some of the most authentic Cuban fare this side of Havana at prices that go back to the days when Havana was a bustling hot spot. Here, you'll find everything from oxtail to roasted chicken, pork ribs, and roast pork, and pretty much anything comes dished from a steam table with a heaping helping of either *arroz con pollo* or red beans and rice. You also get a generous hunk of boiled yuca with its traditional accompaniment of garlic and citrus mojo sauce. They also serve a fantastically cheap breakfast. It's loud, it's frenzied, it's almost 100% in Spanish, and it's one of the most delicious Miami experiences you will have for around five bucks.

14300 SW 8th St., Little Havana. © **305/221-1615.** Juices and main courses $2–$5. No credit cards. Mon–Sat 7am–9pm; Sun 7am–8pm.

La Carreta ★ CUBAN   This cavernous family-style restaurant is filled with relics of an old farm and college kids eating *medianoches* (midnight sandwiches with ham, cheese, and pickles) after partying all night. Waitresses are brusque but efficient and will help Anglos along who may not know the lingo. The menu is vast and very authentic, but is known for its sandwiches and smaller items. Try the *sopa de pollo,* a rich golden stock loaded with chunks of chicken and fresh vegetables, or the *ropa vieja,* a shredded beef stew in thick brown sauce. Because of its immense popularity and low prices, La Carreta has opened seven branches throughout Miami, including a counter in the Miami airport.

3632 SW 8th St., Little Havana. www.lacarreta.com. © **305/444-7501.** Main courses $5–$25. AE, DC, DISC, MC, V. Daily 24 hr.

Latin American Cafeteria ★★ CUBAN   The name may sound a bit generic, but this no-frills indoor-outdoor cafeteria has the best Cuban sandwiches in the entire city. They're big enough for lunch and a doggie-bagged dinner, too. Service is fast, prices are cheap, but be forewarned: English is truly a second language at this chain, so have patience—it's worth it.

6820 SW 40th St., Miami. © **305/663-2600.** Main courses $5–$10. AE, MC, V. Daily 7:30am–11pm.

Versailles ★ CUBAN   Versailles is the meeting place of Miami's Cuban power brokers, who meet daily over *café con leche* to discuss the future of the Cuban exiles' fate. A glorified diner that celebrated its 40th anniversary in 2011, the place sparkles with glass, chandeliers, murals, and mirrors meant to evoke the French palace. There's nothing fancy here—nothing French, either—just straightforward food from the home country. The menu is a veritable survey of Cuban cooking and includes specialties such as Moors and Christians (flavorful black beans with white rice), *ropa* *vieja* (shredded beef stew), and fried whole fish. Versailles is the place to come for *mucho* helpings of Cuban kitsch. It's also the place where politicians and aspiring presidents of the United States come to mingle and schmooze with the Cuban contingency. With its late hours, it's also the perfect place to come after spending your night in Little Havana.

3555 SW 8th St., Little Havana. www.versaillesrestaurant.com. © **305/444-0240.** Main courses $5–$20. DC, DISC, MC, V. Mon–Thurs 8am–2am; Fri 8am–3am; Sat 8am–4:30am; Sun 9am–1am.

CORAL GABLES

Coral Gables is a foodie's paradise—a city in which you certainly won't go hungry. What Starbucks is to most major cities, excellent gourmet and ethnic restaurants are to Coral Gables, where there's a restaurant on every corner, and everywhere in between.

Very Expensive

Christy's ★ STEAK/AMERICAN Christy's is the kind of place where conversations are at a hush and no one seems to care whom they're sitting next to. The selling point here, rather, is the broiled lamb chops, prime rib of beef with horseradish sauce, teriyaki-marinated filet mignon, herb-crusted sea bass, crab cakes, and perfectly tossed Caesar salad. Baked sweet potatoes and a sublime blackout cake are also yours for the taking. For a little drama, order the baked Alaska. It livens things up. Just like a fine wine or the typical Christy's customer, the meat here is aged a long time. A landmark since 1978, Christy's has thrived amid the comings and goings of neighboring nouveau Coral Gables restaurants. It's located on a nondescript corner, and you'll know you've arrived at the right place if you can count the Rolls-Royces parked out front. There's live jazz at the piano bar starting at 7pm every Thursday through Saturday.

3101 Ponce de León Blvd., Coral Gables. www.christysrestaurant.com. ©**305/446-1400.** Reservations recommended. Main courses $19–$41. AE, DC, MC, V. Mon–Thurs 11:30am–10pm; Fri 11:30am–11pm; Sat 5–11pm; Sun 5–10pm.

Palme d'Or ★★★ FRENCH Don't be fooled by the ornate setting—yes, it's rich; yes, it's fancy, oozing with Old World elegance, but the cuisine and the service are far from stuffy. Hailed by many as the city's top restaurant, Palme d'Or's New French cuisine is made utterly delicious and accessible via a unique tasting menu showcasing innovative interpretations of classic Continental cuisine, featuring exceptional local ingredients with specialties flown in directly from France and elsewhere. You can order a la carte, but we suggest you go with the prix-fixe menus—three plates at $43, four plates at $64, or five plates at $78. And choosing is tough with the always changing, evolving dishes such beef carpaccio with shaved cured foie gras and sweet Indian curry; poached Atlantic hake filet with Spanish olive oil, purple potato, baby fennel, and baby garlic confit; or grilled buffalo tenderloin with crispy fingerling

---

Impressions

Miami is the same place that New Orleans was a hundred years ago in the emergence of different cultures. It's fascinating because in the same way North Americans have come to understand the difference between Northern Italian and Southern Italian, we're coming to understand the difference between Peruvian, Venezuelan, and Brazilian cuisine.

—Chef Norman Van Aken

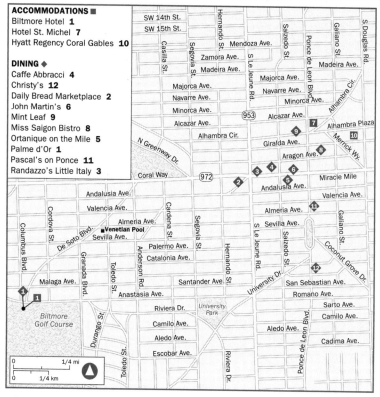

ACCOMMODATIONS ■
Biltmore Hotel **1**
Hotel St. Michel **7**
Hyatt Regency Coral Gables **10**

DINING ◆
Caffe Abbracci **4**
Christy's **12**
Daily Bread Marketplace **2**
John Martin's **6**
Mint Leaf **9**
Miss Saigon Bistro **8**
Ortanique on the Mile **5**
Palme d'Or **1**
Pascal's on Ponce **11**
Randazzo's Little Italy **3**

potatoes and vine-ripe tomato in a traditional Béarnaise foam—essentially and utterly nontraditional, and there's the rub. Service is equally exceptional, making this one of Miami's best, if not the best, upscale dining experiences.

At the Biltmore Hotel, 1200 Anastasia Ave., Coral Gables. www.biltmorehotel.com. ✆ **305/913-3201.** Reservations recommended. Tasting menus $43–$78; a la carte $14–$24. AE, DC, MC, V. Tues–Sat 6–10:30pm.

Pascal's on Ponce ★★★ FRENCH   Straight from the tutelage of world-renowned chef Alain Ducasse, chef Pascal Oudin has established himself as a star student at his very own restaurant that takes French food to another level. Rack of lamb chops with Picholine olive tapanade, coco-bean purée, Mediterranean condiment, and *jus Corséare;* or roasted duck breast with date compote, corn pudding, and root vegetable in a Dolce Forte reduction are just a few outstanding examples of how Oudin combines classical French techniques with the ingredients of the Americas. Check out the tasting menus and three-course, $22 bistro menus, which is an excellent, inexpensive way to get the full foodie experience.

2611 Ponce de León Blvd., Coral Gables. www.pascalmiami.com. ✆ **305/444-2024.** Reservations recommended. Main courses $20–$40. AE, DISC, MC, V. Mon–Thurs 11:30am–3pm; Sun–Thurs 6–10pm; Fri–Sat 6–11pm.

Expensive

Caffe Abbracci ★★ ITALIAN   You'll understand why this restaurant's name means "hugs" in Italian the moment you enter the dark, romantic enclave: Your appetite will be embraced by the savory scents of fantastic Italian cuisine wafting through the restaurant. The homemade black-and-red ravioli filled with lobster in pink sauce, risotto with porcini and portobello mushrooms, and the house specialty—grilled veal chop topped with fresh sage—are irresistible and perhaps the culinary equivalent of a warm, embracing hug. A cozy bar and lounge were added recently to further encourage the warm and fuzzy feelings.

318 Aragon Ave. (1 block north of Miracle Mile, btw. Salzedo St. and Le Jeune Rd.), Coral Gables. www.caffeabbracci.com. ✆ **305/441-0700.** Reservations recommended for dinner. Main courses $22–$35; pastas $16–$22. AE, DC, MC, V. Sun 6–11:30pm; Mon–Thurs 11:30am–3pm and 6–11:30pm; Fri 11:30am–3pm and 6pm–12:30am; Sat 6pm–12:30am.

Ortanique on the Mile ★★★ CARIBBEAN   Chef Cindy Hutson has truly perfected tantalizing New World Caribbean cuisine. For starters, ask if the pumpkin bisque with a hint of pepper sherry is on the menu. If not, a spicy fried calamari salad is exceptional. Afterward, move on to the tropical mango salad with fresh marinated sable hearts of palm, julienne mango, baby field greens, toasted Caribbean candied pecans, and passion-fruit vinaigrette. For an entree, we recommend the pan-sautéed Bahamian black grouper marinated in teriyaki and sesame oil. It's served with an *ortanique* (an orangelike fruit) orange liqueur sauce and topped with steamed seasoned chayote, zucchini, and carrots on a lemon-orange *boniato*—sweet plantain mash. For dessert, try the chocolate mango tower: layers of brownie, chocolate mango mousse, meringue, and sponge cake, accompanied by mango sorbet and tropical-fruit salsa. Entrees may not be cheap, but they're a lot less than airfare to the islands, which is where most, if not all, of the ingredients hail from.

278 Miracle Mile (next to Actor's Playhouse), Coral Gables. www.cindyhutsoncuisine.com. ✆ **305/446-7710.** Reservations requested. Main courses $21–$44. AE, DC, MC, V. Mon–Tues 6–10pm; Wed–Sat 6–11pm; Sun 5:30–9:30pm.

Moderate

John Martin's ★ IRISH PUB   Forest-green and dark-wood walls provide a very intimate, publike atmosphere in which local businesspeople and barflies alike come to hoist a pint or two. The menu offers some tasty British specialties, such as bangers and mash and shepherd's pie, as well as Irish lamb stew and corned beef and cabbage. Of course, to wash it down, you'll want to try one of the ales on tap or one of the more than 20 single-malt scotches. The crowd is upscale and chatty, as is the young waitstaff. Check out happy hour on weeknights, plus the Sunday brunch with loads of hand-carved meats and seafood.

253 Miracle Mile, Coral Gables. www.johnmartins.com. ✆ **305/445-3777.** Reservations recommended on weekends. Main courses $13–$20; sandwiches and salads $9–$12. AE, DC, DISC, MC, V. Sun–Thurs 11:30am–midnight; Fri–Sat 11:30am–2am.

Mint Leaf ★ INDIAN   Straight from London is this cozy (read: tiny) modern Indian eatery, where Bollywood films play on the flatscreen and the congenial owner runs around making sure everyone's happy. And you will be happy as long as you score a table here—there are only about 15 inside and a miniature bar with two stools. Cuisine is authentic if not particularly spicy, with all traditional tandoori favorites, samosas, naans, and *dosas*.

276 Alhambra Circle, Coral Gables. www.mintleafib.com. ✆ **305/443-3739.** Reservations strongly recommended. Main courses $14–$25. AE, DC, DISC, MC, V. Daily noon–3pm and 6–10:30pm.

Randazzo's Little Italy ★★★ ITALIAN   This old-school, *Godfather*-influenced, *Goodfellas*-inspired, *Sopranos*-style Italian restaurant is a guaranteed knockout, and not just because the owner is a former professional boxer, either. Come hungry and leave with your pants unbuttoned as this bustling, fun, and phenomenally garlicky restaurant has a way of making Little Italy seem mammoth, thanks to huge portions of traditional favorites—sausage and peppers, meatballs and spaghetti, and rigatoni with vodka sauce, which one critic said was so good it could "bring any homesick Italian American to tears." The house specialty is spaghetti with Sunday gravy—al dente strands of pasta studded with meatballs the size of wrecking balls and large chunks of sweet and hot sausage.

385 Miracle Mile, Coral Gables. www.randazzoslittleitaly.com. ✆ **305/448-7002.** Reservations strongly recommended. Main courses $20–$39. AE, DC, DISC, MC, V. Mon–Fri 11:30am–2:30pm; Mon–Thurs 6–10pm; Fri–Sat 6–11pm.

Red Fish Grill ★ SEAFOOD   Hidden away at the edge of the saltwater lagoon in lush and tropical Matheson Hammock Park, Red Fish Grill is a decent seafood restaurant, but people don't come here for the food. Judging by the ambience alone, the restaurant deserves four stars, but because the food is just okay (fish is either greasy or dry), it only gets one. But that's okay. A new owner (Christy's steakhouse) promises better things to come. In the meantime, romantic, hard to find, and truly reminiscent of Old Miami, Red Fish Grill makes up for its lack of flavor with its hard-to-beat, majestic setting.

In Matheson Hammock Park, 9610 Old Cutler Rd., Coral Gables. www.redfishgrill.net. ✆ **305/668-8788.** Reservations accepted. Main courses $23–$39. AE, DC, DISC, MC, V. Tues–Thurs 6–10pm; Fri–Sun 5–10pm. Enter Matheson Hammock Park; stay on the main road until you see the restaurant's parking lot.

Inexpensive

Daily Bread Marketplace GREEK   This place is great for takeout food and homemade breads. The falafel and gyro sandwiches are large, fresh, and filling. The spinach pie for less than $1 is also recommended, though it's short on spinach and heavy on pastry. Salads and spreads, including luscious tabbouleh, hummus, and eggplant, are also worth a go. To eat in or take out, the Middle Eastern fare here is a real treat, especially in an area so filled with fancy French and Cuban fare. Plus, you can pick up groceries such as grape leaves, fresh olives, couscous, fresh nuts, and pita bread.

2400 SW 27th St. (off U.S. 1 under the monorail), Coral Gables. www.dailybreadmarketplace.com. ✆ **305/856-0363** or 856-0366. Sandwiches and salads $4–$10. MC, V. Mon–Sat 9am–8pm; Sun 11am–5pm.

Miss Saigon Bistro ★★ VIETNAMESE   Unlike Alain Boublil and Claude-Michel Schönberg's bombastic Broadway show, this Miss Saigon is small, quiet, and not at all flashy. Servers at this family-run restaurant will graciously recommend dishes or even have something custom-made for you. The menu is varied and reasonably priced, and the portions are huge—large enough to share. Noodle dishes and soup bowls are hearty and flavorful; caramelized prawns are fantastic, as is the whole snapper with lemon grass–and-ginger sauce. Despite the fact that there are few tables inside and a hungry crowd usually gathers outside in the street, you won't be rushed through your meal, which is worth savoring. There is also a larger location at 9503 S. Dixie Hwy., in South Miami's Pinecrest (© **305/661-2911**).

148 Giralda Ave. (at Ponce de León and 37th Ave.), Coral Gables. www.misssaigonbistro.com. © **305/446-8006.** Main courses $10–$22. AE, DC, DISC, MC, V. Mon and Wed–Thurs 11:30am–3pm and 5:30–10pm; Tues 11:30am–3pm and 6:30–10pm; Fri 11:30am–3pm and 5:30–11pm; Sat 5:30–11pm; Sun 5:30–10pm.

COCONUT GROVE

Coconut Grove was long known as the artists' haven of Miami, but the rush of developers trying to cash in on the laid-back charm of this old settlement has turned it into something of an overgrown mall. Still, there are several great dining spots both inside and outside the confines of Mayfair and CocoWalk.

Expensive

George's in the Grove ★ FRENCH   When the former owner of Le Bouchon du Grove opened his own bistro around the corner, shouts of *"mon Dieu!"* were heard loud and clear. But there's really no comparison. Whereas Le Bouchon is a traditional French bistro, George's is a modern version, with sleek decor and a sleeker champagne-sipping clientele. Entrees range from such classics as French onion soup, ratatouille, and steak *frites* to a very Miami mango *tarte tatin*. For something unusually good, try the pizza with duck confit, onion jam, aged Gruyère, and fresh shiitake mushrooms. For dessert, people plotz over the Nutella pizza. As the night goes on, the music gets louder, champagne corks start a-popping, and a party scene ensues. If you want romance, go to Le Bouchon; if you want a *Sex and the City* scene, George's is *le place*. In 2010, George's opened in South Miami at 1549 Sunset Dr. (© **305/284-9989**).

3145 Commodore Plaza, Coconut Grove. www.georgesrestaurants.com. © **305/444-7878.** Main courses $13–$40. AE, DC, MC, V. Sun and Tues–Wed 6–11pm; Thurs–Sat 6pm–1am.

Le Bouchon du Grove ★ FRENCH   This very authentic bistro is French right down to the waitstaff, who may speak only French to you, forgetting they're in the heart of Coconut Grove, U.S.A. But it matters not. The food, prepared by an animated French (what else?) chef, is good. It used to be superb, but it has fallen off a bit. Still, a delicious starter that's always reliable is the *gratinée Lyonnaise* (traditional French onion soup). Fish is brought in fresh daily; try the pan-seared sea bass *(dos de loup de mer roti)* when it's in season. Though slightly heavy

---

Getting Back Into the Grove

Aging hippies may recall **Coconut Grove** as a hub of all things peace and love. When the '60s ended, the beatniks made the Grove a retro-fab kind of town. Then came the '80s, and the Grove was as dead as Joplin and Hendrix. The '90s saw a resurgence with **CocoWalk,** whose sole purpose was to attract tourists, locals, and college students to its open-air debauchery, which is home to a **Fat Tuesday's** (© 305/534-1328), **Hooters** (© 305/442-7283), and **Chili's** (© 305/772-5472). It's nothing innovative or spectacular, but it may suit this town well, like an old Crosby, Stills & Nash song.

HOTELS■
Hampton Inn **7**
Mayfair Hotel & Spa **4**
Mutiny Hotel **5**
Ritz-Carlton Coconut Grove **6**
Sonesta Bayfront Hotel
  Coconut Grove **3**

RESTAURANTS◆
George's in the Grove **1**
Le Bouchon du Grove **2**

on the oil, it is delivered with succulent artichokes, tomato confit, and seasoned roasted garlic, and it is a gastronomic triumph. The *carre d'agneau roti* (roasted rack of lamb with Provence herbs) is served warm and tender, with a perfect amount of seasoning. There's also an excellent selection of pricey, but drinkable, French and American red and white wines.

3430 Main Hwy., Coconut Grove. www.lebouchondugrove.com. ✆ **305/448-6060.** Reservations recommended. Main courses $20–$30. AE, MC, V. Mon–Thurs 10am–3pm and 5–11pm; Fri 10am–3pm and 5pm–midnight; Sat 8am–3pm and 5pm–midnight; Sun 8am–3pm and 5–11pm.

SOUTH MIAMI–DADE COUNTY & WEST MIAMI

Though mostly residential, these areas nonetheless have several eating establishments worth the drive.

Expensive

Tropical Chinese ★ CHINESE This strip-mall restaurant, way out in West Miami–Dade, is hailed as the best Chinese restaurant in the city. While the food is indeed very good—certainly more interesting than at your typical beef-and-broccoli place—it still seems overpriced. But because good Chinese food in Miami is almost an oxymoronic statement save for some of the fancier restaurants, locals are known to make the trek west for a trip to Tropical. Garlic spinach and prawns in a clay pot are delicious, with the perfect mix of garlic cloves, mushrooms, and fresh spinach. But this isn't your typical Chinese takeout. It's not cheap. Unlike most Chinese restaurants, the dishes here are not large enough to share. Sunday-afternoon dim sum, with all sorts of dumplings, pork buns, and traditional bite-size items carted around to your table, is extremely popular, and lines often snake around the shopping center.

7991 Bird Rd., West Miami. www.tropicalchinesemiami.com. © **305/262-7576.** Reservations highly recommended on weekends. Main courses $10–$53. AE, DC, MC, V. Mon–Fri 11:30am–10:30pm; Sat 11am–11:30pm; Sun 10:30am–10pm. Take U.S. 1 to Bird Rd. and go west on Bird, all the way down to 78th Ave. The restaurant is btw. 78th and 79th on the north side of Bird Rd.

Moderate

Town Kitchen & Bar ★ AMERICAN   A lively neighborhood breakfast, lunch, dinner, and late-night bistro with a great bar scene, Town is where locals gather for good food—everything from Kobe sliders and seafood tacos to meal-worthy salads, ceviches, mussel pots, brick-oven pizza, and main plates such as bacon-wrapped prawns, steaks, and hearty pasta dishes. Though we wouldn't necessarily make a special trip to South Miami for a meal at Town, if and when we *are* there, this is the place to eat.

7301 SW 57th Court, South Miami. www.townkitchenbar.com. © **305/740-8118.** Reservations highly recommended on weekends. Burgers, salads, and pizzas $9–$14; main courses $12–$42. AE, DC, MC, V. Mon–Fri 11:30am–2am; Sat–Sun 8am–2am.

Inexpensive

Crepe Maker Cafe ★ ☺ CREPES/FRENCH   Create your own delicious crepes at this little French cafe. You can choose from ham, tuna, black olives, red peppers, capers, artichoke hearts, and pine nuts. Some of the best include a Philly cheesesteak with mushrooms, and a classic chicken *cordon bleu*. Delicious dessert crepes include ice cream, strawberries, peaches, walnuts, and pineapples. Enjoy your crepe fresh off the griddle at the counter or from a bar stool. The soups are delicious. Kids can run around in a small play area.

8269 SW 124th St., South Miami. ©**305/233-4458** or 233-1113. Crepes $1.50–$8.50. AE, DC, MC, V. Sun–Thurs 11:30am–9:30pm; Fri–Sat 11:30am–10:30pm. Take U.S. 1 south to 124th St. and make a left. The restaurant is on the north side of the street, across from the park.

Shiver's BBQ ★ 📖 AMERICAN   Family owned and operated for over 50 years, Shiver's is all about the pig, specializing in slow-smoked meats such as baby back ribs, pork spare ribs, beef ribs, chicken, beef brisket, pork, and more. The zingy house-made barbecue sauce is worthy of taking home with you (ask for the new, secret Martha's Sauce), and the down-home service here is also something we'd like to bring back to Miami proper with us.

28001 S. Dixie Hwy., Homestead. http://shiversbbq.com. ©**305/248-2272.** Main courses $5–$15. AE, DISC, MC, V. Daily 11am–9pm.

Shorty's ★ BARBECUE   A Miami tradition since 1951, this honky-tonk of a log cabin still serves some of the best ribs and chicken in South Florida. People line up

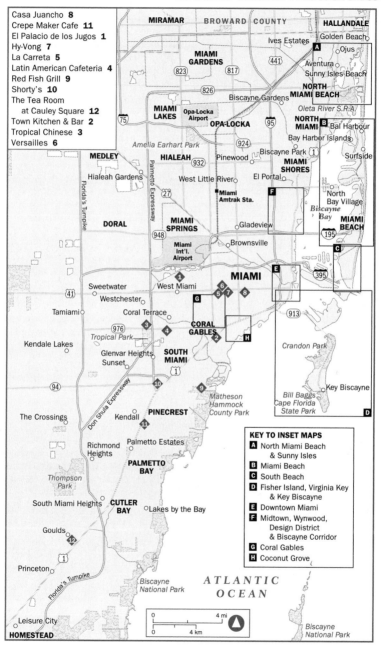

Casa Juancho **8**
Crepe Maker Cafe **11**
El Palacio de los Jugos **1**
Hy-Vong **7**
La Carreta **5**
Latin American Cafeteria **4**
Red Fish Grill **9**
Shorty's **10**
The Tea Room
   at Cauley Square **12**
Town Kitchen & Bar **2**
Tropical Chinese **3**
Versailles **6**

KEY TO INSET MAPS

A North Miami Beach
& Sunny Isles

B Miami Beach

C South Beach

D Fisher Island, Virginia Key
& Key Biscayne

E Downtown Miami

F Midtown, Wynwood,
Design District
& Biscayne Corridor

G Coral Gables

H Coconut Grove

Perhaps because of its location at the bottom of the map, Miami is often last in receiving trends that have already swept the nation several times over. In 2009, a welcome, albeit minor, congestion of food trucks clogged our arteries both literally and figuratively. The first is **gastroPod Mobile Gourmet** (www. twitter.com/gastropodmiami), a customized, vintage 1962 Airstream with ultramodern kitchen serving up some serious street food—triple-decker sliders stuffed with shaved pork belly on a potato bun, and short-rib hot dogs. Joining this retro-fab, nomadic kitchen on wheels on the streets of Miami are about 100 food trucks or more, including a few of the original pioneers: **Latin**

Burger and Taco (www.twitter.com/ latinburger); **A Chef's Burger** (© 786/ 344-5825), a greasy spoon on wheels; a grilled cheese truck cheekily called **Ms. Cheezious; Sakaya Kitchen's Dim Ssam a go go;** and more. And, racking up mileage, albeit in a Scion instead of a truck, is **Feverish Ice Cream** (www. twitter.com/feverishmiami), a hipster's version of the old-school ice-cream truck serving gourmet frozen treats. For the definitive guide to Miami food trucks and their locations, go to **www. miamifoodtrucks.com**. Look for these trucks everywhere from downtown and the beaches to Coral Gables and Coconut Grove.

for the smoke-flavored, slow-cooked meat that's so tender it seems to fall off the bone. The secret, however, is to ask for your order with sweet sauce. The regular stuff tastes bland and bottled. All of the side dishes, including the coleslaw, corn on the cob, and baked beans, look commercial but complete the experience. This is a jeans-and-T-shirt kind of place, but you may want to wear jeans with an elastic waistband, as overeating is not uncommon.

9200 S. Dixie Hwy. (btw. U.S. 1 and Dadeland Blvd.), South Miami. www.shortys.com. ©**305/670-7732.** Main courses $7–$18. DISC, MC, V. Sun–Thurs 11am–10pm; Fri–Sat 11am–11pm.

The Tea Room at Cauley Square ★ ENGLISH TEA   Do stop in for a spot of tea at this cozy tearoom in historic Cauley Square, off U.S. 1. The little lace-curtained room is an unusual sight in this heavily industrial area better known for its warehouses than its doilies. Try one of the simple sandwiches, such as the turkey club with potato salad or French onion soup. The ambrosia with finger sandwiches or banana-nut bread is an interesting choice, served with a blend of pineapple, mandarin oranges, miniature marshmallows, and sour cream. Daily specials (such as spinach-and-mushroom quiche) and delectable desserts are musts before you begin your explorations of the old antiques and art shops in this little enclave of civility down south. Oh, and remember to put your pinky up while sipping your tea.

12310 SW 224th St. (at Cauley Sq.), South Miami. www.tearoombakery.com. © **305/258-0044.** Sandwiches and salads $6–$14; desserts $5. AE, DISC, MC, V. Daily 11am–4pm. Take 836 W. (Dolphin Expwy.) toward Miami International Airport. Take Palmetto Expwy. S. ramp toward Coral Way. Merge onto 826 S. Follow signs to Florida Tpk. toward Homestead. Take the turnpike south and exit at Caribbean Blvd. (exit 12). Go about 1 mile on Caribbean Blvd. and turn left on S. Dixie Hwy. and then right at SW 224th St. Then turn left onto Old Dixie Hwy. and take a slight right onto SW 224th St. The restaurant is at Cauley Square Center.

White Lion Cafe ★ 🎁 AMERICAN   The quintessence of a quaint off-the-beaten-path eatery in not-so-quaint Miami, the White Lion Cafe is a hidden gem serving Southern-style blue-plate specials, including delicious meatloaf and fried chicken. There's also an extensive entertainment calendar here, with everything from live jazz to karaoke. If you're in the Homestead area en route to or coming from the Keys, it's definitely worth a stop here, where time seems to stand still, at least until the band starts playing.

146 NW 7th St., Homestead. www.whitelioncafe.com. ℭ **305/248-1076.** Main courses $10–$22. AE, DISC, MC, V. Daily 5pm until "the fat lady sings." Take 836 E. to 826 S.; at exit 6 make a left and head West on 8th St. (Campbell Dr.); after crossing Krome Ave. take a left at 1st Ave. (the very next light), and turn right on 7th St. The cafe is on the left.

MIAMI
SHOPPING

7

Miami is one of the world's premier shopping cities; more than 12 million visitors come every year and typically spend, well, billions. People come to Miami from all over—from Latin America to Hong Kong—in search of some products that are all-American (in other words, Levi's, Nike, and such).

So if you're not into sunbathing and outdoor activities, or you just can't take the heat, you'll be in good company in one of Miami's many malls—and you are not likely to emerge empty-handed. In addition to the strip malls, Miami offers a choice of megamalls, from the upscale Village of Merrick Park and the mammoth Aventura Mall to the ritzy Bal Harbour Shops and touristy, yet scenic, Bayside Marketplace (just to name a few).

Miami also offers more unique shopping spots, such as the up-and-coming area near downtown known as the Biscayne Corridor, where funky boutiques dare to defy the Gap, and Little Havana, where you can buy hand-rolled cigars and *guayabera* shirts (loose-fitting cotton or gauzy shirts).

You may want to order the Greater Miami Convention and Visitors Bureau's "Shop Miami: A Guide to a Tropical Shopping Adventure." Although it is limited to details on the bureau's paying members, it provides some good advice and otherwise unpublished discount offers. The glossy little pamphlet is printed in English, Spanish, and Portuguese and provides information about transportation from hotels, translation services, and shipping. Call ✆ **888/76-MIAMI** (766-4264) or 305/447-7777 for more information.

SHOPPING AREAS

Most of Miami's shopping happens at the many megamalls scattered from one end of the county to the other. However, excellent boutique shopping and browsing can be found in the following areas (see "The Neighborhoods in Brief," on p. 45, for more information):

(see "The Neighborhoods in Brief," on p. 45, for more information):

Impressions
Someday . . . Miami will become the great center of South American trade. —Julia Tuttle, Miami's founder, 1896

AVENTURA On Biscayne Boulevard between Miami Gardens Drive and the county line at Hallandale Beach Boulevard is a 2-mile stretch of major retail stores including Target, Best Buy, DSW, Bed Bath & Beyond,

Loehmann's, Marshall's, Old Navy, Sports Authority, and more. Also here is the mammoth Aventura Mall, housing a fabulous collection of shops and restaurants. Nearby in Hallandale Beach, the Village at Gulfstream Park is a new outdoor dining, shopping, and entertainment complex at the ever-expanding racetrack.

BISCAYNE CORRIDOR ★   Amid the ramshackle old motels of yesteryear exist several funky, kitschy, and arty boutiques along the stretch of Biscayne Boulevard from 50th Street to about 79th Street known as the Biscayne Corridor. Everything from hand-painted tank tops to expensive Juicy Couture sweat suits can be found here, but it's not just about fashion: Several furniture stores selling antiques and modern pieces exist along here as well, so look carefully, as you may find something that would cause the appraisers on *Antiques Road Show* to lose their wigs. For more mainstream creature comforts—Target, PetSmart, Loehmann's, Marshall's, Homegoods, and West Elm—check out the Shops at Midtown Miami, a sprawling outdoor shopping and dining destination on a gritty yet developing street at North Miami Avenue and NE 36th Street.

CALLE OCHO   For a taste of Little Havana, take a walk down 8th Street between SW 27th Avenue and SW 12th Avenue, where you'll find some lively street life and many shops selling cigars, baked goods, shoes, furniture, and record stores specializing in Latin music. For help, take your Spanish dictionary.

COCONUT GROVE   Downtown Coconut Grove, centered on Main Highway and Grand Avenue, and branching onto the adjoining streets, is one of Miami's most pedestrian-friendly zones. The Grove's wide sidewalks, lined with cafes and boutiques, can provide hours of browsing pleasure. Coconut Grove is best known for its chain stores (Gap, Victoria's Secret, Bath & Body Works, and so on) and some funky holdovers from the days when the Grove was a bit more bohemian, plus some good sidewalk cafes and lively bars.

> ### Impressions
>
> *Miami's culture inspires my couture. Fashion without a foundation is just posing.*
> —Rene Ruiz, Miami-based fashion designer

DESIGN DISTRICT   Although it's still primarily an interior design, art, and furniture hub, Design District is slowly adding retail to its roster with a few funky and fabulous boutiques catering to those who don't necessarily have to ask, "How much?"

DOWNTOWN MIAMI   If you're looking for discounts on all types of goods—especially watches, fabric, buttons, lace, shoes, luggage, and leather—Flagler Street, just west of Biscayne Boulevard, is the best place to start. I wouldn't necessarily recommend buying expensive items here, as many stores seem to be on the shady side and do not understand the word *warranty*. However, you can still have fun here as long as you are a savvy shopper and don't mind haggling. Most signs are printed in English, Spanish, and Portuguese; however, many shopkeepers may not be entirely fluent in English. Mary Brickell Village, a 192,000-square-foot urban entertainment center west of Brickell Avenue and straddling South Miami Avenue between 9th and 10th streets downtown, hasn't been so quick to emerge as a major shopping destination as much as it is a dining and nightlife one with a slew of trendy restaurants, bars, a few boutiques, and the requisite Starbucks—a sure sign that a neighborhood has been revitalized.

MIRACLE MILE (CORAL GABLES)   Actually only a half-mile long, this central shopping street was an integral part of George Merrick's original city plan. Today the strip still enjoys popularity, especially for its bridal stores, ladies' shops, haberdashers, and gift shops. Recently, newer chain stores, such as Barnes & Noble, Old Navy, and Starbucks, have been appearing on the Mile. The hyperupscale **Village of Merrick Park,** a mammoth, 850,000-square-foot outdoor shopping complex between Ponce de León Boulevard and Le Jeune Road, just off the Mile, houses Nordstrom, Neiman Marcus, Armani, Gucci, Jimmy Choo, and Yves St. Laurent, to name a few.

SOUTH BEACH ★   South Beach has come into its own as far as trendy shopping is concerned. While the requisite stores such as the Gap and Banana Republic have anchored here, several higher-end stores have also opened on the southern blocks of Collins Avenue, which has become the Madison Avenue of Miami. For the hippest clothing boutiques (including Armani Exchange, Ralph Lauren, Intermix, Benetton, Levi's, Barneys Co-Op, Diesel, Guess, Club Monaco, Kenneth Cole, and Nicole Miller, among others), stroll along this pretty strip of the Art Deco District.

For those who are interested in a little more fun with their shopping, consider South Beach's legendary Lincoln Road. This pedestrian mall, originally designed in 1957 by Morris Lapidus, is home to an array of clothing, books, tchotchkes, and art, as well as a menagerie of sidewalk cafes flanked on one end by a multiplex movie theater and, at the other, by the Atlantic Ocean.

MALLS

There are so many malls in Miami and more being built all the time that it would be impossible to mention them all. What follows is a list of the biggest and most popular.

You can find any number of nationally known department stores, including Saks Fifth Avenue, Macy's, Bloomingdale's, Sears, and JCPenney, in the Miami malls listed below. Miami's own Burdines is now a Macy's, too, located at 22 E. Flagler St., downtown, and 1675 Meridian Ave. (just off Lincoln Rd.) in South Beach.

Aventura Mall ☺   A multimillion-dollar makeover has made this spot one of the premier places to shop in South Florida. With more than 2.3 million square feet of space, this airy, Mediterranean-style mall has a 24-screen movie theater and more than 280 stores, including megastores Nordstrom, Macy's, JC Penney, and Sears. Specialty stores are impressive and high end, including Calvin Klein, Missoni, Ted Baker, Lily Pulitzer, Apple, Betsey Johnson, Hugo Boss, Coach, Diesel, Miss Sixty, Henri Bendel, Herve Leger by Max Azria, 7 for All Mankind, True Religion, and more. A large indoor playground, Adventurer's Cove, is a great spot for kids, and the mall frequently offers activities and entertainment for children. There are numerous restaurants, including Cheesecake Factory, Grand Lux Cafe, Paul Maison de Qualite, the Grill on the Alley, and Sushi Siam, and a food court that eschews the usual suspects in favor of local operations. 19501 Biscayne Blvd. (at 197th St. near the Dade–Broward County line), Aventura. www.shopaventuramall.com. ✆ **305/935-1110.**

Bal Harbour Shops   One of the most prestigious fashion meccas in the country, Bal Harbour offers the best quality goods from the finest names. Giorgio Armani, Dolce & Gabbana, Christian Dior, Fendi, Harry Winston, Pucci, Krizia, Rodier, Gucci, Agent Provocateur, Carolina Herrera, Celine, Chanel, Chloe, Diane Von Furstenberg, Brooks Brothers, Kiton, Stella McCartney, Waterford, Cartier, H. Stern, Hublot, Tourneau, and many others are sandwiched between Neiman Marcus and a newly expanded Saks Fifth Avenue. Well-dressed shoppers stroll in a pleasant open-air emporium featuring several good cafes, covered walkways, and lush greenery. Parking costs $1.50 an hour with a validated ticket, $5 without. *Tip:* You can stamp your own at the entrance to Saks Fifth Avenue, even if you don't make a purchase. 9700 Collins Ave. (on 97th St., opposite the Sheraton Bal Harbour Hotel), Bal Harbour. www.bal harbourshops.com. *℃* **305/866-0311.**

Malls

Bayside Marketplace A popular stop for cruise-ship passengers, this touristy waterfront marketplace is filled with the usual suspects of chain stores (Gap, Guess, Victoria's Secret) as well as a slew of tacky gift shops and carts hawking assorted junk in the heart of downtown Miami. The second-floor food court is stocked with dozens of fast-food choices and bars. Most of the restaurants and bars stay open later than the stores. There's Bubba Gump Shrimp Co., Hooters, Hard Rock Cafe, Chili's, the Knife, and the best spot for drinks and snacks, Largo Seafood & Grill. Parking ranges from $3 to $10, depending on the days and times. While we wouldn't recommend you necessarily drop big money at Bayside, you should go by just for the view (of Biscayne Bay and the Miami skyline) alone. There are tons of tour boats here in case you feel like throwing yourself in the water to avoid the crowds. Beware of the adjacent amphitheater known as Bayfront Park, which usually hosts large-scale concerts and festivals, causing major pedestrian and vehicle traffic jams. 401 Biscayne Blvd., downtown. www.baysidemarketplace.com. *℃* **305/577-3344.**

CocoWalk CocoWalk is a lovely outdoor Mediterranean-style mall with the usual fare of Americana: Gap, Victoria's Secret, and so on. Its open-air architecture is inviting not only for shoppers but also for friends or spouses of shoppers who'd prefer to sit at an outdoor cafe while said shopper is busy in the fitting room. In 2010, the shopping center went bankrupt after the movie theater closed and is currently in the throes of coming up with its own stimulus plan which includes a cushy Paragon Movie Theater. 3015 Grand Ave., Coconut Grove. www.cocowalk.net. *℃* **305/444-0777.**

Dadeland Mall One of the county's first malls, Dadeland features more than 185 specialty shops, anchored by four large department stores: Macy's, JCPenney, Nordstrom, and Saks Fifth Avenue. The mall also boasts the country's largest Limited/Express store. Sixteen restaurants serve from the adjacent food court. New retail stores are constantly springing up around this centerpiece of South Miami suburbia. If you're not in the area, however, the mall is not worth the trek. 7535 N. Kendall Dr. (intersection of U.S. 1 and SW 88th St., 15 min. south of downtown), Kendall. *℃* **305/665-6226.**

Dolphin Mall As if Miami needed another mall, this $250-million megamall is similar to Broward County's monstrous Sawgrass Mills outlet, albeit without the luxury stores. The 1.4-million-square-foot outlet mall features outlets such as Off Fifth (Saks Fifth Avenue), plus several discount shops, a 28-screen movie theater, and a bowling alley. Florida Tpk. at S.R. 836, West Miami. www.shopdolphinmall.com. *℃* **305/365-7446.**

The Falls Traffic to this mall borders on brutal, but once you get there, you'll feel a slight sense of serenity. Tropical waterfalls are the setting for this outdoor shopping center with dozens of moderately priced and slightly upscale shops. Miami's first Bloomingdale's is here, as are Polo, Ralph Lauren, Caswell-Massey, and more than 95 other specialty shops. Also there: Macy's, Crate & Barrel, Brooks Brothers, and Pottery Barn, among others. If you are planning to visit any of the nearby attractions, which include Metrozoo and Monkey Jungle, check with customer service for information on discount packages. 8888 Howard Dr. (at the intersection of U.S. 1 and 136th St., about 3 miles south of Dadeland Mall), Kendall. www.shopthefalls.com. *℃* **305/255-4570.**

Sawgrass Mills   Just as some people need to take a tranquilizer to fly, others need one to traipse through this mammoth mall—the largest outlet mall in the country. Depending on what type of shopper you are, this experience can either be blissful or overwhelming. If you've got the patience, it is worth setting aside a day to do the entire place. Though it's located in Broward County, it is a phenomenon that attracts thousands of tourists and locals sniffing out bargains. For a lot more upscale fashion not necessarily at bargains (so buyer beware), Colonnade Outlets features outlet versions of Theory, Coach, Miss Sixty USA, Salvatore Ferragamo, and other luxury stores that allegedly offering savings of up to 70%. When driving, take I-95 north to 595 west to Flamingo Road. Exit and turn right, driving 2 miles to Sunrise Boulevard. You can't miss this monster on the left. Parking is free, but don't forget where you parked your car or you might spend a day looking for it. 12801 W. Sunrise Blvd., Sunrise (west of Fort Lauderdale). www.simon.com. ✆ **954/846-2300.**

Shoppes at Mayfair in the Grove   This sleepy, desolate, labyrinthine shopping area conceals a movie theater, several shops (Ann Taylor Loft and Bath & Body Works are the two most recognizable), a bookstore, and the Improv Comedy Club. It was meant to compete with the CocoWalk shopping complex (just across the street), but its structure is very mazelike. Though it is open air, it is not wide open like CocoWalk and pales in comparison to that somewhat more populated neighbor. 2911 Grand Ave. (just east of Commodore Plaza), Coconut Grove. www.mayfairinthegrove.com. ✆ **305/448-1700.**

The Shops at Midtown Miami   Located just off Biscayne Boulevard in a gritty yet transitional neighborhood near the Design District and Wynwood, the Shops at Midtown Miami is more of a locals' spot, with Target, West Elm, Loehmann's, Marshall's, and PetSmart. There are also some great dining options here, including Five Guys Burgers and Fries, the Cheese Course, Lime Fresh Mexican Grill, Mercadito, 100 Montaditos (featuring literally 100 varieties of a Spanish-style sandwich), and Sugarcane Raw Bar. If later-night Target shopping makes you crave a drink, head to Ricochet, Midtown's hipster hangout and lounge. Go here at your own risk, as the area is still a bit sketchy. 3401 N. Miami Ave, Midtown Miami. www.shopmidtownmiami.com. ✆ **305/573-3371.**

The Shops at Sunset Place   This sprawling outdoor shopping complex offers more than just shopping. Visitors experience high-tech special effects, such as daily tropical storms (minus the rain) and the electronic chatter of birds and crickets. In addition to a 24-screen movie complex and an IMAX theater, there's a Splitsville bowling alley and a video arcade, as well as mall standards such as Victoria's Secret, Gap, Hollister, American Eagle Outfitters, Urban Outfitters, bebe, and so on. 5701 Sunset Dr. (at 57th Ave. and U.S. 1, near Red Rd.), South Miami. www.simon.com. ✆ **305/663-0482.**

The Village at Gulfstream Park   Gulfstream Park's outdoor dining and entertainment venue, on the border of Miami-Dade and Broward counties near Aventura in Hallandale Beach, features an expanding list of businesses—Crate & Barrel, Pottery Barn, Williams-Sonoma, and West Elm, among other clothing and accessories boutiques; restaurants including Yard House, BRIO Tuscan Grill, and American Pie Brick Oven Pizza; and bars including a branch of South Beach's popular Playwright Irish Pub, Cadillac Ranch, and more. 501 S. Federal Hwy., Hallandale Beach. www.the villageatgulfstreampark.com. ✆ **954/458-0145.**

Village of Merrick Park   Giving Bal Harbour Shops a run for its money is this Coral Gables Mediterranean-style outdoor mall consisting of extremely high-end stores such as Jimmy Choo, Sonia Rykiel, Neiman Marcus, Miami's very first Nordstrom, and upscale eateries such as the Palm. In fact, the owner of Bal Harbour Shops was so paranoid he'd lose his business to Merrick Park that he shoveled a ton of cash in an ad campaign making sure people wouldn't forget that Bal Harbour was here first. People who can afford it won't be forgetting about either anytime soon. 4425 Ponce de León Blvd., Coral Gables. ✆ **305/529-0200.**

SHOPPING A TO Z
Antiques & Collectibles

Miami's antiques shops are scattered in small pockets around the city. Many that feature lower-priced furniture can be found in North Miami, in the 1600 block of NE 123rd Street, near West Dixie Highway. About a dozen shops sell china, silver, glass, furniture, and paintings. But you'll find the bulk of the better antiques in Coral Gables and in Southwest Miami along Bird Road between 64th and 66th avenues and between 72nd and 74th avenues. For international collections from Bali to France, check out the burgeoning scene in the Design District centered on NE 40th Street west of 1st Avenue. Miami also hosts several large antiques shows each year. In October and November, the most prestigious one—the **Original Miami Beach Antique Show**—hits the Miami Beach Convention Center (www.originalmiami beachantiqueshow.com; ✆ **305/673-7311**). Exhibitors from all over come to display their wares, including jewelry. Miami's huge concentration of Art Deco buildings from the '20s and '30s makes this the place to find the best selections of Deco furnishings and decorations. A word to the serious collectors: Dania Beach, up in Broward County (see chapter 12), about half an hour from downtown Miami, is the best place for antiques (it's known as the antiques capital of South Florida), so you may want to consider browsing in Miami and shopping up there.

Alhambra (Antiques)   This fabulous store specializes in 18th-, 19th-, and 20th-century French and European antiques, furniture, accessories, lighting, and art. They also have a garden collection of antique jars and pots, as well as a really cool collection of vintage bird cages. The store prides itself on the fact that it does not use outsourced buyers or wholesalers. Every piece in the store has been purchased by the owners on their quarterly trips to Europe. 2850 Salzedo St., Coral Gables. www.alhambra antiques.com. ✆ **305/446-1688.**

Industrian   What's a retro-fabulous Charles Eames chair doing sitting next to an ultramodern 21st-century, Jetsonian piece of furniture? The answer is Industrian, where vintage and new furniture live in harmony. 5580 NE 4th Court, Miami. ✆ **305/754-6070.**

Miami Twice   Retro has different meanings to different age groups, and to embrace that, Miami's best retro retail has an ever-changing collection of vintage clothing, designer purses, accessories, and jewelry. There's also an excellent selection of new lines of clothing, jewelry, costuming, and masquerade masks that have that retro feel. Miami Twice also has antiques and collectables dating from 1850 to 1970. During the month of October, it turns into one big costume shop for Halloween. 6562 Bird Rd., South Miami. www.miami-twice.com. ✆ **305/666-0127.**

Modernism Gallery   Specializing in 20th-century furnishings from Gilbert Rohde, Noguchi, and Heywood Wakefield, this shop has some of the most beautiful examples of Deco goods from France and the United States. If it doesn't have what you're looking for, ask. The staff possesses the amazing ability to find the rarest items. 1500 Ponce de León Blvd., Coral Gables www.modernism.com. By appointment only. ☏ **305/442-8743.**

Senzatempo 🎁 If the names Charles Eames, George Nelson, or Gio Ponti mean anything to you, this is where you'll want to visit. In addition to, say, a $13,000 1940s chrome food warmer, there's retro, Euro-fabulous designer furniture and decorative arts from 1930 to 1960 here, as well as collectible watches, timepieces, and clocks. 1655 Meridian Ave., 2nd floor (at Lincoln Rd.), South Beach. www.senzatempo.com. ☏ **305/534-5588.**

Stone Age Antiques 🎁 Movie posters, military memorabilia, tribal masks, cowboy hats—you name it, they probably have it, but nautical antiques are their specialty. Looking for a certain ship's wheel? Stone Age most likely has it. 3236 NW S. River Dr. at NW 32nd St. N. Miami. www.stoneage-antiques.com. ☏ **305/633-5114.**

Worth Galleries A great place to browse—if you don't mind a little dust—this huge warehouse has an impressive stash of very large antique lighting and contemporary chandeliers as well as modern art and antique oil paintings. The furniture is hand selected in Europe. And for a different era, it offers a large selection of fine contemporary furniture that includes Midcentury Modern and Art Deco periods. 2520 SW 28th Lane (just west of U.S. 1), Miami. www.miamiantique.com. ☏ **305/285-1330.**

Art Galleries

Bernice Steinbaum Gallery Check out the modern multimedia exhibits here by contemporary artists including Hung Liu, Glexis Novoa, and Maria Gonzalez. 3550 N. Miami Ave. www.bernicesteinbaumgallery.com. ☏ **305/573-2700.** Mon–Sat 10am–6pm.

CIFO An outstanding nonprofit gallery established by Ella Fontanals Cisneros and her family to foster cultural exchange among the visual arts, CIFO is dedicated to the support of emerging and midcareer contemporary multidisciplinary artists from Latin America. 1018 N. Miami Ave. at NW 10th St. www.cifo.org. ☏ **305/445-3880.** Mon–Thurs 10am–4pm during exhibitions or by appointment.

Diana Lowenstein Fine Arts One of Miami's preeminent modern art collectors, Lowenstein's gallery in the burgeoning Wynwood area of downtown Miami is a hot spot for serious collectors and admirers. 2043 N. Miami Ave. www.dlfinearts.com. ☏ **305/576-1804.** Tues–Sat 10:30am–6pm.

Dorsch Gallery An expansive gallery known for hosting some fabulous parties for the who's who in the art world, Dorsch is known for some seriously funky exhibitions. 151 NW 24th St. at N. Miami Ave. www.dorschgallery.com. ☏ **305/576-1278.** Thurs–Sat 1–5pm.

Fredric Snitzer Gallery The catalyst to the explosion of the Wynwood arts scene, this warehouse pays homage to works by local stars and New World School of the Arts grads, as well as artists from Cuba's legendary '80s Generation. 2247 NW 1st Place at N. Miami Ave. www.snitzer.com. ☏ **305/448-8976.** Tues–Sat 11am–5pm.

Gary Nader Fine Art If you're into Latin American art by the likes of Botero, Matta, and Lam, this is the place for you. In addition, there are monthly exhibits of emerging artists. 62 NE 27th St. at N. Miami Ave. www.garynader.com. ☏ **305/576-0256.** Mon–Sat 10am–6pm.

Margulies Collection 🎁 This massive, 45,000-square-foot Wynwood warehouse is the city's crown jewel, showcasing contemporary and vintage photography, video, sculpture, and installations in various genres, including pop art, minimalism,

The Last Holdout

As all the galleries move to the Design District and Wynwood, one original South Beach holdout exists, and it may seem very familiar to you. **Britto Central,** 818 Lincoln Rd., South Beach (www.britto.com; © **305/531-8821**), featuring the works of Brazilian artist Romero Britto, is the only one that can afford the rent considering he is constantly commissioned by the city for various public works of art. Some people liken Britto to Andy Warhol because of his colorful, whimsical paintings of young children and animals, among other things. Serious art lovers, however, consider Britto's cartoonish works more along the lines of a second-rate Walt Disney. You decide.

and expressionism. 591 NW 27th St. at 6th Ave. www.margulieswarehouse.com. © **305/576-1051**. Wed–Sat 11am–4pm.

Books

You can find local branches of **Barnes & Noble** at 152 Miracle Mile (© 305/446-4152), 5701 Sunset Dr. (© 305/662-4770), 18711 NE Biscayne Blvd. (© 305/935-9770), 7710 N. Kendall Dr. (© 305/598-7292), and 12405 N. Kendall Dr. (© 305/598-7727).

Books & Books A dedicated following turns out to browse at this warm and wonderful little independent shop. Enjoy the upstairs antiquarian room, which specializes in art books and first editions. If that's not enough intellectual stimulation for you, the shop hosts free lectures from noted authors, experts, and personalities almost nightly. At another location, 933 Lincoln Rd. (© **305/532-3222**), you'll rub elbows with tanned and buffed South Beach bookworms sipping cappuccinos at the Russian Bear Cafe inside the store. This branch stocks a large selection of gay literature and also features lectures. And if you happen to be at the ritzy Bal Harbour Shops and not in the mood to do the Gucci thing, there's another Books & Books here, too (© **305/864-4241**). 265 Aragon Ave., Coral Gables. www.booksandbooks.com. © **305/442-4408.**

Beauty & Cosmetics

Brownes & Co. Apothecary Since 1991 Brownes & Co. has been the go-to beauty destination in Miami, where the young and the young at heart peruse antique display cases filled with glass jars of anti-aging serums, delicious French soaps, lotions, and potions. An incredible selection of makeup, hair-care, skin-care, and bath/body products include Darphin, Skinceuticals, Molton Brown, Nars, Dr. Hauschka, and Diptyque. Feel free to browse and sample here, as persistent perfume-spritzing salespeople do not work here. If you do need help, the staff are experts when it comes to all things beauty, especially in the salon/spa where you can get fabulously coiffed, colored, buffed, and waxed by true beauty experts. Signature treatments include the Kneipp deluxe manicure/pedicure, Caudalie facial, and the Well-being massage. There's a second outpost in the Design District at 87 NE 40th Street. 1688 Jefferson Rd., South Beach. www.brownesbeauty.com. © **305/538-7544.**

MAC Viva glam! The innovative brand of makeup is all here, and if you're lucky you may get a free makeover. 650 Collins Ave., South Beach. www.maccosmetics.com. © **305/604-9040.**

Sephora The Disney World of makeup, Sephora offers a dizzying array of cosmetics, perfumes, and styling products. Unlike Brownes & Co., however, personal service and attentiveness is at a minimum. Because there are so many products, shopping here can be a harrowing experience. www.sephora.com. 721 Collins Ave., South Beach (🕿 **305/532-0904**); 19575 Biscayne Blvd., Aventura (🕿 **305/931-9579**); Dadeland Mall, 7535 SW 88th St., Miami (🕿 **305/740-3445**).

Cigars

Although it is illegal to bring Cuban cigars into the United States, somehow, forbidden *Cohibas* show up at every dinner party and nightclub in town. Not that I condone it, but if you hang around the cigar smokers in town, no doubt one will be able to tell you where you can get some of the highly prized contraband. Be careful, however, of counterfeits, which are typically Dominican cigars posing as Cubans. Cuban cigars are illegal and unless you go down a sketchy alley to buy one from a dealer (think of it as shady as a drug deal), you are going to be smoking Dominican ones.

The stores listed below sell excellent hand-rolled cigars made with domestic- and foreign-grown tobacco. Many of the *viejitos* (old men) got their training in Cuba working for the government-owned factories in the heyday of Cuban cigars.

El Credito Cigar Factory This tiny storefront shop employs about 45 veteran Cuban rollers who sit all day rolling the very popular torpedoes and other critically acclaimed blends. They're usually back-ordered, but it's worth stopping in: They will sell you a box and show you around. 1106 SW 8th St., Little Havana. 🕿 **305/858-4162.**

Mike's Cigars 🏪 Mike's may have abandoned its old digs for a bigger, newer location, but it's one of the oldest and best smoke shops in town. Since 1950, Mike's has been selling the best from Honduras, the Dominican Republic, and Jamaica, as well as the very hot local brand, La Gloria Cubana. Many say it has the best prices, too. Mike's has the biggest selection of cigars in town and the employees speak English. They also have fun in-store events that dudes love involving cigars, football, and booze. 1030 Kane Concourse (at 96th St.), Bay Harbor Island. www.mikescigars.com. 🕿 **305/866-2277.**

Clothing & Accessories

Miami didn't become a fashion capital until—believe it or not—the pastel-hued, Armani-clad cops on *Miami Vice* had their close-ups on the tube. Before that, Miami was all about old men in white patent leather shoes and well-tanned women in bikinis. How things have changed! Miami is now a fashion mecca in its own right, with some of the same high-end stores you'd find on Rue de Faubourg St. Honore in Paris or Bond Street in London. You'll find all the chichi labels, including Prada and Gucci, right here at the posh Bal Harbour Shops or further south at the Village of Merrick Park. For funkier frocks, South Beach is the place, where designers such as Nicole Miller, Ralph Lauren, and Giorgio Armani—well, Armani Exchange—compete for window shoppers with local up-and-coming designers, some of whom design for drag queens and club kids only. Miami's edgy Upper East Side and Design District neighborhoods also slowly but surely are developing as hot spots for hipwear. The strip on Collins Avenue between 7th and 10th streets has become quite upscale, including such shops as Armani Exchange, True Religion, Ugg Australia, and Intermix, along with the inescapable Gap and Banana Republic. Then there's the Herzog & de Meuron-designed parking garage at 1111 Lincoln Rd., which is the quintessence of multitasking, featuring shops, restaurants, and places to park your cars so you can enjoy them. A great spot to load up on shopping energy is the very modern, very European **Nespresso Cafe**, a Technicolor homage to caffeine and light fare. Of course, there's also more mainstream (and affordable) shopping in the plethora of malls and outdoor shopping and entertainment complexes that are sprinkled throughout the city (see "Malls," earlier).

UNISEX

Atrium Young Hollywood always makes Atrium a stop on their South Beach shopping list. With designer brands at designer prices, don't be surprised if you see that $200 white T-shirt on an Olsen twin in the latest issue of *Us Weekly*. 1925 Collins Ave., South Beach. ©**305/695-0757.**

Barneys Co-Op An outpost of Barneys New York, only this time, it's more "affordable." Hooey. If you think a T-shirt for $150 is affordable, then this store is for you. Otherwise, Barneys Co-Op is always great for browsing and marveling over the fashion victims who actually do pay such absurd prices for a cotton T-shirt. 832 Collins Ave., South Beach. ©**305/421-2010.**

Base USA A hipster hangout, featuring clothing that's fashionable, and, of course, pricey. Base is also known for its cool and funky CD collection (all for sale, of course), coffee-table books, and nice smelling candles. 939 Lincoln Rd., South Beach. ©**305/531-4982.**

En Avance If you couldn't get into LIV or SET last night, consider plunking down some major pocket change for the au courant labels that En Avance is known for. One outfit bought here and the doormen have no ground to stand on when it comes to high-fashion dress codes. 161 NE 40th St., Design District. ©**305/576-0056.**

Original Penguin Store Remember the Izod alligator? Forget it for a second and consider this, the hippest retro men's line since, well, Izod, featuring sweaters, polo shirts, T's, and more sporting a penguin logo. 925 Lincoln Rd., South Beach. www.originalpenguin.com. ©**305/673-0722.**

Urban Outfitters It took a while for this urban outpost to hit Miami, but once it did, it became a favorite for the young hipster set who favor T-shirts that say "Princess" instead of Prada. Cheapish, utilitarian, and funky, Urban Outfitters is an excellent place to pick up a pair of cool jeans or some funky tchotchkes for your apartment. www.urbanoutfitters.com. 653 Collins Ave., South Beach (©**305/535-9726**); Shops at Sunset, 5701 SW 72nd St., South Miami (©**305/663-1536**); Aventura Mall (©**305/936-8358**).

The Webster A Parisian-style couture emporium straight out of *Women's Wear Daily*, Webster features runway-ready *prêt a porter* for men and women by all those boldface names you read in the fashion magazines. It's so swanky, there's even a champagne and caviar bar, Caviar Kaspia, inside. Recession, what? 1220 Collins Ave., South Beach. www.thewebstermiami.com. ©**305/674-7899.**

Y-3 A collaboration between couture designer Yohji Yamamoto and Adidas, Y-3 chose Miami's Design District as its first freestanding store ever, but bigger news than that is that it's the district's first-ever clothing store, featuring a full range of funky men's and women's apparel, shoes, and accessories. The two-story store prides itself on fusing style and sport and often hosts very fabulous art and culture events. www. adidas.com. 150 NE 40th St., Design District (📞 **305/535-9726** or 305/573-1603); 1111 Lincoln Rd. (📞 305/538-9302).

WOMEN'S

Belinda's Designs   This German designer makes some of the most beautiful and intricate teddies, nightgowns, and wedding dresses. The styles are a little too Stevie Nicks for me, but the creations are absolutely worth admiring. The prices are appropriately high. 917 Washington Ave., South Beach. www.belindasdesigns.net. 📞 **305/532-0068.**

Christian Louboutin   What the Beatles are to music, Christian Louboutin may be to women's shoes. The French shoe god, immortalized on the feet of every well-heeled celebrity and socialite and in a Jennifer Lopez song, chose the Miami Design District as the place for his very first Miami outpost. As gorgeous as the shoes, so is the store, so if it's not in the budget to buy, just go browse. If you can handle it. 155 NE 40th St., Design District. 📞 **305/576-6820.**

HiHo Batik   Hand-painted tank tops, adorable accessories, and funky jewelry is what you'll discover in this colorful North Miami boutique, which also hosts make-your-own batik parties. Although they also sell boy's clothing, it's much more of a girlie thing. 2174 NE 123rd St., North Miami. www.hihobatik.com. 📞 **305/754-8890.**

Intermix   Pretty young things can get all dolled up thanks to Intermix's fun assortment of hip women's fashions, from Stella McCartney's pricey rhinestone T-shirts to the latest jeans worn by everyone at the MTV Awards. 634 Collins Ave., South Beach. www. intermixonline.com. 📞 **305/531-5950.**

Kore Boutique   A high-fashion Biscayne Corridor boutique with dressy and chic-casual wear as well as shoes, jewelry, and bags. 2925 Biscayne Blvd., Biscayne Corridor. 📞 **305/573-8211.**

La Perla   The only store in Florida that specializes in superluxurious Italian intimate apparel. Of course, you could fly to Milan for the price of a few bras and a nightgown, but you can't find better quality. 342 San Lorenzo Ave., Coral Gables. 📞 **305/864-2070.**

Marni   Looking for the Miami fashionista set? Look no further than this gorgeous flagship store that, like the Webster, looks as if it jumped out of a *Women's Wear Daily* photo shoot, with prices to boot. 3930 NE 2nd Ave., Design District. www.marni.com. 📞 **305/764-3357.**

Place Vendome   This shop is for cheap and funky club clothes from zebra-print pants to bright, shiny tops. 934 Lincoln Rd., South Beach (📞 **305/673-4005**); Aventura Mall, North Miami Beach (📞 **305/932-8931**).

Rebel   Fashionable and funky clothing for mom and daughter is what you'll find in this fabulous Biscayne Corridor boutique that carries labels not found anywhere else. Superfriendly help is a bonus, too. 6669 Biscayne Blvd., Biscayne Corridor. 📞 **305/758-2369.**

Savvy Girl   A small South Miami boutique sandwiched between a tire center and a supermarket with not a whole lot of merchandise, but a nice selection of jeans, dresses, and what I like to call "disco tops," or, nightclub wear. 5781 SW 40th St., South Miami. www.shopsavvygirl.com. 📞 **305/665-9833.**

Scoop Here's the real scoop: The Shore Club hotel boutique hails from New York City and is the shop of choice for visiting celebs who just walk in and don't have to ask the price of the latest from Diane Von Furstenberg, Helmut Lang, Marc Jacobs, Paul Smith, Malo, and Jimmy Choo. The Shore Club, 1901 Collins Ave. ✆ **305/532-5929.**

MEN'S

Duncan Quinn Saville Row and James Bond meet Miami at this dapper, dashing British-style men's store featuring custom-made, swanky suits, ties, and hankies. Even if you're not in the market to buy, you have to take a look at this store, which features classic Ducattis and a vintage 1962 Maserati as decor. 4040 NE 2nd Ave., Design District. www.duncanquinn.com. ✆ **305/671-3820.**

La Casa de las Guayaberas 👔 Miami's premier purveyor of the traditional yet retro-hip Cuban shirt known as the *guayabera*—a loose-fitting, pleated, button-down shirt—was founded by Ramon Puig, who emigrated to Miami over 40 years ago and, until his death at the age of 90 in 2011, used the same scissors he did back then. Today there's a team of seamstresses who hand sew 20 shirts a day in all colors and styles. Prices range from $15 to $375. 5840 SW 8th St., Little Havana. ✆ **305/266-9683.**

Pepi Bertini European Men's Clothing Coral Gables men's store features a complete selection of men's designer shirts, as well as custom-made shirts. 315 Miracle Mile, Coral Gables. www.pepibertini.com. ✆ **305/461-3374.**

CHILDREN'S

Most department stores have extensive children's sections. But if you can't find what you are looking for, consider one of the many Baby Gaps or Gap Kids outlets around town or try one of the specialty boutiques listed here.

Genius Jones In addition to the requisite, adorable, and pricey kids' threads, Genius Jones has high-end kids' furniture by the likes of Agatha Ruiz de la Prada, David Netto, and other brands that will set you back some serious bucks. www.genius jones.com. 1661 Michigan Ave., South Beach (✆ **305/534-7622);** 49 NE 30th St., Design District (✆ **305/571-2000**); Mizner Park, 417 Plaza Real, Boca Raton (✆ **561/300-4004**).

ACCESSORIES

Me & Ro Jewelry This place offers fun and not-so-cheap baubles. Their designs are popular with stars like Sarah Jessica Parker and Julia Roberts. In the Shore Club, 1901 Collins Ave., South Beach. www.meandrojewelry.com. ✆ 305/672-3566.

MIA Jewels This store carries fun and funky necklaces, bracelets, rings, and accessories in all price ranges. http://miajewels.com. 1439 Alton Rd., South Beach (✆ **305/53-6064**); Aventura Mall (✆ **305/931-2000**).

SEE This fantastic eyewear store features an enormous selection of stylish specs at decent prices. The staff is patient and knowledgeable. 921 Lincoln Rd., South Beach. ✆ **305/672-6622.**

Turchin Love and Light Collections Besides the fact that we saw Jennifer Aniston shopping here, we love this tiny Design District jewel box for its collection designed using unique artifacts made in Tibet, Nepal, Africa, India, Bhutan, and Pakistan. 130 NE 40th St., Design District. www.turchinjewelry.com. ✆ **305/573-7117.**

HIGH-END JEWELRY

For name designers like Gucci and Tiffany & Co., go to the Bal Harbour Shops (see "Malls," earlier).

Seybold Building   Jewelers who specialize in an assortment of goods (diamonds, gems, watches, rings, and such) gather here daily to sell diamonds and gold. With 300 jewelry stores located inside this independently owned and operated multilevel treasure chest, the glare is blinding as you enter. You'll be sure to see handsome and up-to-date designs, but not too many bargains. 36 NE 1st St., downtown. www.seyboldjewelry.com. ℂ **305/374-7922.**

Food & Drink

There are dozens of ethnic markets in Miami, from Cuban bodegas (little grocery stores) to Jamaican import shops and Guyanese produce stands. I've listed a few of the biggest and best markets in town that sell prepared foods as well as staple items. On Saturday mornings, vendors set up stands loaded with papayas, melons, tomatoes, and citrus, as well as cookies, ice creams, and sandwiches on South Beach's Lincoln Road.

Epicure Market   This is the closest thing Miami Beach has to the famed Balducci's or Dean & DeLuca. Here, you'll find not only fine wines, cheeses, meats, fish, and juices, but some of the best produce, such as portobello mushrooms the size of a yarmulke. This neighborhood landmark is best known for supplying the Jewish residents of the beach with all their Jewish favorites, such as matzo ball soup, gefilte fish, and deli items. Prices are steep, but generally worth it. There's a much larger, newer Epicure Market at 17190 Collins Ave. in Sunny Isles Beach (ℂ **305/936-7703**), featuring an expansive outdoor cafe (in a former parking lot) and bar which often hosts wine tastings. 1656 Alton Rd., Miami Beach. ℂ **305/672-1861.**

Gardner's Market   Anything a gourmet or novice cook could desire can be found here. One of the oldest and best grocery stores in Miami, Gardner's now has three locations, all of which offer great takeout and the freshest produce. http://gardnersmarkets.com. 7301 Red Rd., South Miami (ℂ **305/667-9953**); 8287 SW 124th St., Pinecrest (ℂ **305/255-2468**); 3117 Bird Ave., Miami (ℂ **305/476-9900**).

Joe's Takeaway   If you don't want to wait 2 hours to get your paws on Joe's Stone Crab's meaty claws, let Joe's, Miami's stone-crab institution (p. 90), ship you stone crabs anywhere in the country (but only during the season, which runs from mid-Oct through mid-May). 11 Washington Ave., South Beach. ℂ **800/780-CRAB** (2722) or 305/673-0365.

La Brioche Doree   This tiny storefront off 41st Street is packed most mornings with French expatriates and visitors who crave the real thing. There are luscious pastries and breads, plus soup and sandwiches at lunch. No one makes a better croissant. 4017 Prairie Ave., Miami Beach. ℂ **305/695-3477.**

La Estancia Argentina   The best of edible Buenos Aires is found at this small but comprehensive gourmet Argentine and Latin market. There are two locations. www.laestanciaweb.com. 17870 Biscayne Blvd., North Miami Beach (ℂ **305/932-6477**); 4425 Ponce de León Blvd., Coral Gables (ℂ **305/445-3933**).

Laurenzo's Italian Center   Anything Italian you want—homemade ravioli, hand-cut imported Romano cheese, plus fresh fish and meats—can be found here. Laurenzo's also offers one of the most comprehensive wine selections in the city. Be sure to see the neighboring store full of just-picked herbs, salad greens, and vegetables from around the world. A daily farmer's market is open from 7am to 6pm. Incredible daily specials lure thrifty shoppers from all over the city. If you can't wait to eat the stuff when you get back to your hotel, there's a cafe here too. 16385 and 16445 W. Dixie Hwy., North Miami Beach. www.laurenzosmarket.com. ℂ **305/945-6381** or 305/944-5052.

Marky's   Shopping here is sort of like shopping at the deli owned by the Sopranos, only in Russian. Here, you'll find the finest caviar, cheeses, and pretty much anything else you can't get in Miami that's edible—but make sure to ask about the secret back room. 687 NE 79th St., Biscayne Corridor. www.markys.com. ℒ **305/758-9288.**

Music Stores

If you are one of the few who still buys music in stores, believe it or not, there are not one but three that sell everything from vintage vinyl to soon-to-be-extinct CDs.

Casino Records Inc.   The young, hip salespeople here speak English and tend to be music buffs. This store has the largest selection of Latin music in Miami. Their slogan translates to "If we don't have it, forget it." Believe me, they've got it. 2290 SW 8th St., Little Havana. ℒ **786/394-8899.**

Sweat Records 👔   If Miami had basements, this place would be like that basement where your coolest friend hangs out, where undiscovered indie music that will soon play on radio stations' constant rotation (or not) plays before anyone else hears it. Founded by a DJ and a DJ-turned criminal defense attorney, Sweat is also a fully vegan coffee and treat bar with free Wi-Fi. It also sells magazines, books, and gifts, and hosts cool events and parties on a constant basis. 5505 NE 2nd Ave., Miami. http://sweatrecordsmiami.com. ℒ **786/693-9309.**

Yesterday and Today Records 👔   This is Miami's most unique and well-stocked store for vinyl—you know, the audio dinosaur that went out with the Victrola? Y & T, as it's known, is a collector's heaven, featuring every genre of music imaginable on every format. Chances are, you could find some eight-track tapes, too. 9274 SW 40th St., Miami. http://vintagerecords.com. ℒ **305/554-1020.**

Sporting Goods

People-watching seems to be the number-one sport in South Florida, but for the more athletic pursuits, consider the shops listed below. One of the area's largest sports-equipment chains is the **Sports Authority,** with at least six locations throughout the county. Check the White Pages for details.

Alf's Golf Shop   This is the best pro shop around. The knowledgeable staff can help you with equipment for golfers of every level, and the neighboring golf course offers discounts to Alf's clients. There are four locations. www.alfsgolf.com. 524 Arthur Godfrey Rd., Miami Beach (ℒ **305/673-6568**); 15369 S. Dixie Hwy., Miami (ℒ **305/378-6086**); 1180 S. Dixie Highway, Coral Gables (ℒ **305/663-4653**); 2600 NW 87th Ave., in Doral near the Miami International Airport (ℒ **305/470-0032**).

Bass Pro Shops Outdoor World   Fishing and sports enthusiasts must head north to Broward County to see this huge retail complex, which offers demonstrations in such sports as fly-fishing and archery, classes in marine safety, and every conceivable gadget you could ask for. 200 Gulf Stream Way (west side of I-95), Dania Beach. www.basspro.com. ℒ **954/929-7710.**

Edwin Watts Golf Shops   One of 30 Edwin Watts shops throughout the Southeast, this full-service golf retail shop is one of the most popular in Miami. You can find it all here, including clothing, pro-line equipment, gloves, bags, balls, videos, and books. Plus, you can get coupons for discounted greens fees on many courses. There are two locations. www.edwinwattsgolf.com. 15100 N. Biscayne Blvd., North Miami Beach (ℒ **305/944-2925**); 8484 NW 36th St., in Doral (ℒ **305/591-1220**).

Island Water Sports   You'll find everything from booties to gloves to baggies and tanks. Check in here before you rent that WaveRunner or windsurfer. 16231 Biscayne Blvd., North Miami. www.iwsmiami.com. ☏ **305/944-0104.**

South Beach Dive and Surf Center   Prices are slightly higher at this beach location, but you'll find the hottest styles and equipment. It also offers surfboard rental. You can get a free surf report at ☏ **305/534-7873.** 850 Washington Ave., South Beach. ☏ **305/673-5900.**

Thrift Stores/Resale Shops

C. Madeleine's   The best, most couture-istic vintage store in town, brands from Gucci, Pucci, Fiorucci, and even Chanel and Balenciaga are usually snatched up by the likes of Jessica Simpson, Lenny Kravitz, or their stylists, who call this fashion emporium home. 13702 Biscayne Blvd., North Miami. www.cmadeleines.com. ☏ **305/945-0010.**

The Children's Exchange ☺   Selling everything from layettes to overalls, this pleasant little shop is chock-full of good Florida-style stuff for kids to wear to the beach and in the heat. 1415 Sunset Dr., Coral Gables. http://thechildrenexchange.com. ☏ **305/666-6235.**

Douglas Gardens Jewish Home and Hospital Thrift Shop   Prices here are no longer the major bargain they once were, but for housewares and books, you can do all right. It's in a not so great neighborhood, so this store is truly for the die-hard thrifters. Call to see if it's offering any specials for seniors or students. 5713 NW 27th Ave., North Miami Beach. ☏ **305/638-1900.**

Out of the Closet   The chain of thrift stores from Northern and Southern California owned and operated by AIDS Healthcare Foundation has several So Flo locations. www.outofthecloset.org. 1510 Alton Rd., South Beach (☏ 305/531-6800); 2900 N. Biscayne Blvd., Biscayne Corridor (☏ **305/764-3773**); 2097 Wilton Dr., Wilton Manors (☏ **954/358-5590**).

Red White & Blue Thrift Store 🎁   Miami's best-kept thrift secrets are these two mammoth stores that are typically meticulously organized and well stocked. You've got to search for great stuff, but it is there. There are especially good deals on children's clothes and housewares. 12640 NE 6th Ave., North Miami. www.redwhiteandblue thriftstore.com. ☏ **305/893-1104.** 901 E. 10th Ave., Hialeah. ☏ **305/887-5351.**

PRACTICAL MATTERS: THE SHOPPING SCENE

As a general rule, shop hours are Monday through Saturday from 10am to 6pm, and Sunday from noon to 5pm. Many stores stay open late (until 9pm or so) 1 night of the week, usually Thursday. Shops in Coconut Grove are open until 9pm Sunday through Thursday, and even later on Friday and Saturday. South Beach's stores also stay open later—as late as midnight. Department stores and shopping malls keep longer hours as well, with most staying open from 10am to 9 or 10pm Monday through Saturday, noon to 6pm on Sunday. With all these variations, you may want to call specific stores to find out their hours.

The 7% state and local sales tax is added to the price of all nonfood purchases. In Surfside, hotel taxes total 11%; in Bal Harbour, 11%; in Miami Beach (including South Beach), 13%; and in the rest of Dade County, a whopping 13%. Food and beverage tax in Miami Beach, Bal Harbour, and Surfside is 9%; in Miami-Dade restaurants not located inside hotels it's 8%; and in restaurants located in hotels, 9%.

Most Miami stores can wrap your purchase and ship it anywhere in the world via United Parcel Service (UPS). If they can't, you can send it yourself, either through FedEx (© **800/463-3339**), UPS (© **800/742-5877**), or through the U.S. Mail (see "Fast Facts: South Florida" on p. 347).

Practical Matters: The Shopping Scene

MIAMI ENTERTAINMENT & NIGHTLIFE

8

With all the hype, you'd expect Miami to have long outlived its 15 minutes of fame by now. But you'd be wrong. Miami's nightlife, in South Beach and, slowly but surely, downtown and its urban environs, is hotter than ever before—and getting cooler with the opening of each funky, fabulous watering hole, lounge, and club. Not always cool, however, is the presence of ubiquitous, closely guarded velvet ropes used to often erroneously create an air of exclusivity. Don't be fooled or intimidated by them—*anyone* can go clubbing in the Magic City, and throughout this section, I've provided tips to ensure that you gain entry to your desired venue.

South Beach is certainly Miami's uncontested nocturnal nucleus, but more and more diverse areas, such as the Design District, Midtown/Wynwood, Brickell, South Miami, and even Little Havana, are increasingly providing fun alternatives without the ludicrous cover charges, "fashionably late" hours of operation (things don't typically get started on South Beach until after 11pm), lack of sufficient self-parking, and outrageous drink prices that are standard in South Beach.

While South Beach dances to a more electronic beat, other parts of Miami dance to a Latin beat—from salsa and merengue to tango and cha-cha. However, if you're looking for a less frenetic good time, Miami's bar scene has something for everyone, from haute hotel bars to sleek, loungey watering holes.

Parts of downtown, such as the Biscayne Corridor, the Miami River, Midtown, Wynwood, and the Design District, are undergoing a trendy makeover a la New York City's Meatpacking District. Cool lounges, bars, and clubs are popping up and providing the "in" crowds with a newer, more urban-chic nocturnal pasture. To get a feel for Wynwood's emerging hipster vibe, check out the Wynwood Art Walk, held the second Saturday of every month, in which local galleries, artists, bars, and restaurants are typically packed and the usually desolate neighborhood is brimming with pedestrians. For more information, go to http://wynwoodartwalk.com.

But if the possibility of a celebrity sighting in one of the city's lounges, bars, or clubs doesn't fulfill your cultural needs, Miami also provides a variety of first-rate diversions in theater, music, and dance, including a world-class ballet (under the aegis of Edward Villella), a recognized symphony, and a talented opera company. The **Adrienne Arsht Center for the Performing Arts** (p. 156) and the **New World Center** (p. 156), a stunning, sonically stellar, $154-million Frank Gehry–designed training facility, performance space, and outdoor park, are the focal points for the arts. About 15% of the music events at New World Center are free to the public.

For up-to-date listing information, and to make sure the club of the moment hasn't expired, check the *Miami Herald*'s "Weekend" section, which runs on Friday, or the more comprehensive listings in *New Times*, Miami's free alternative weekly, available each Wednesday; or visit www.miami.com online.

THE PERFORMING ARTS

Highbrows and culture vultures complain that there is a dearth of decent cultural offerings in Miami. What do locals tell them? Go back to New York! However, in recent years, Miami's performing arts scene has improved greatly. The city's Broadway Series features Tony Award–winning shows (the touring versions, of course), which aren't always Broadway caliber, but usually pretty good and not nearly as pricey. Local arts groups such as the Miami Light Project, a not-for-profit cultural organization that presents performances by innovative dance, music, and theater artists, have had huge success in attracting big-name artists such as Nina Simone and Philip Glass to Miami. Also, a burgeoning bohemian movement in Little Havana has given way to performance spaces that are nightclubs in their own right.

Theater

The **Actors' Playhouse,** a musical theater at the newly restored Miracle Theater at 280 Miracle Mile, Coral Gables (www.actorsplayhouse.org; ✆ **305/444-9293**), is a grand 1948 Art Deco movie palace with a 600-seat main theater and a smaller theater/rehearsal hall that hosts a number of excellent musicals for children throughout the year. In addition to these two theaters, the Playhouse recently added a 300-seat children's balcony theater. Tickets run from $10 to $52.

The **GableStage,** at the Biltmore Hotel (p. 207), Anastasia Avenue, Coral Gables (www.gablestage.org; ✆ **305/445-1119**), is a well-regarded and award-winning theater that usually secures the rights to Broadway and off-Broadway plays and is known for its edgy productions. Tickets cost $38 to $50.

The **Jerry Herman Ring Theatre** is on the main campus of the University of Miami in Coral Gables (✆ **305/284-3355**). The University's Department of Theater Arts uses this stage for advanced-student productions of comedies, dramas, and musicals. Faculty and guest actors are regularly featured, as are contemporary works by local playwrights. Performances are usually scheduled Tuesday through Saturday during the academic year. In the summer, don't miss "Summer Shorts," a selection of superb one-act plays. Tickets sell for $10 to $18.

The **New Theatre,** at the Roxy Performing Arts Center, 1645 SW 107th Ave. (www.new-theatre.org; ✆ **305/443-5909**), prides itself on showing renowned works from America and Europe. As the name implies, you'll find mostly contemporary plays, with a few classics thrown in. Performances are staged Thursday through Sunday year-round. Tickets are $40 on Friday, Saturday, and Sunday matinee, and $35 on Thursday and Sunday evenings. If tickets are available on the day of the performance—and they usually are—students pay half price.

Classical Music

In addition to a number of local orchestras and operas (see below), which regularly offer quality music and world-renowned guest artists, each year brings a slew of classical-music special events and touring artists to Miami. The **Concert Association of Florida** (**CAF;** www.concertassociation.org; © **877/433-3200**) produces one of the most important and longest-running series. Known for more than a quarter of a century for its high-caliber, star-packed schedules, CAF regularly arranges the best "serious" music concerts for the city. Season after season, the schedules are punctuated by world-renowned dance companies and seasoned virtuosi such as Itzhak Perlman, Andre Watts, and Kathleen Battle. Because CAF does not have its own space, performances are usually scheduled at the New World Center or the Fillmore at the Jackie Gleason Theater of the Performing Arts (see the "Major Venues" section below). The season lasts October through April, and ticket prices range from $20 to $70.

New World Symphony   This organization, led by artistic director Michael Tilson Thomas, is a steppingstone for gifted young musicians seeking professional careers. The orchestra specializes in innovative, energetic performances and often features renowned guest soloists and conductors. The season lasts from October to May, during which time there are many free concerts. In the fall of 2010, the NWS moved to the spectacular Frank Gehry–designed campus at the **New World Center** (p. 156). 500 17th St., South Beach. www.nws.org. © **305/673-3330.** Tickets free–$60. Rush tickets (remaining tickets sold 1 hr. before performance) $20. Students $10 (1 hr. before concerts; limited seating).

Opera

Florida Grand Opera   Around for more than 60 years, this company regularly features singers from top houses in both America and Europe. All productions are sung in their original language and staged with projected English supertitles. Tickets become scarce when Placido Domingo comes to town. The season runs roughly from November to April, with five performances each week. In 2007, the opera moved into more upscale headquarters in the Sanford and Dolores Ziff Ballet Opera House at the **Arsht Center for the Performing Arts.** Box office: 1300 Biscayne Blvd., Miami. www.fgo. org. © **305/949-6722.** Tickets $19–$175. Student discounts available.

Dance

Several local dance companies train and perform in the Greater Miami area. In addition, top traveling troupes regularly stop at the venues listed below. Keep your eyes open for special events and guest artists.

Ballet Flamenco La Rosa   For a taste of local Latin flavor, see this lively troupe perform impressive flamenco and other styles of Latin dance on Miami stages. (They also teach Latin dancing—see the "The Rhythm Is Gonna Get You" box later in this chapter.) 13126 W. Dixie Hwy., North Miami. www.balletflamencolarosa.com. © **305/899-7729.** Tickets $20 at door; $15 in advance; $8 for students and seniors.

South Beach Entertainment & Nightlife

The Abbey **16**
Bar 721 **12**
Burger & Beer Joint **14**
Cameo **20**
Clevelander **30**
Cozy **36**
FDR **8**
Fillmore Miami Beach at the Jackie Gleason Theater **7**
Jazid **22**
Jerry's Famous Deli **21**
Lucky Strike Lanes **13**
Mac's Club Deuce **23**
Mango's Tropical Café **31**
Mansion **24**
Miami City Ballet **3**
Mondrian **28**
Mova **18**
Mynt **5**
News Cafe **32**
New World Center **10**
Nikki Beach **35**
The Palace **27**
Playwright Irish Pub **25**
The Purdy Lounge **15**
The Rooftop at the Perry **1**
The Room **34**
Rose Bar at the Delano **6**
Score **11**
Segafredo Espresso **17**
SET **9**
Skybar at the Shore Club **4**
Twist **29**
Upstairs at the Van Dyke Café **19**
WALL **2**
Wet Bar at the W South Beach **26**
Wet Willie's **33**

Miami City Ballet This artistically acclaimed and innovative company, directed by Edward Villella, features a repertoire of more than 60 ballets, many by George Balanchine, and has had more than 20 world premieres. The company's three-story center features eight rehearsal rooms, a ballet school, a boutique, and ticket offices. The City Ballet season runs from September to April with major performances at the Arsht Center, Broward Center, and Kravis Center. 2200 Liberty Ave., South Beach. www. miamicityballet.org. ✆ **305/929-7000** or 929-7010 for box office. Tickets $20–$169.

Major Venues

Architecturally and aurally groundbreaking, the **New World Center**, 500 17th St., South Beach (✆ **305/673-3330**), the new Frank Gehry–designed campus of the New World Symphony (p. 154), features practice rooms, rehearsal rooms, technology suites, and a grand performance space. Even if you're not into the music, this is something to see. Don't miss the $2.50 miniconcerts or the outdoor WALLCAST concerts that take place on the campus, featuring incredible audio effects and visuals projected onto a 7,000-square-foot wall. During these events, most people spread out on the lawn with a blanket and a picnic basket.

The **Colony Theater,** 1040 Lincoln Rd. in South Beach (✆ **305/674-1040**), which has become an architectural showpiece of the Art Deco District, opened in 2006 after a $4.3-million renovation that added wing and fly space, improved access for those with disabilities, and restored the lobby to its original Art Deco look.

At the 1,700-seat **Gusman Center for the Performing Arts,** 174 E. Flagler St., downtown Miami (✆ **305/372-0925**), seating is tight and so is funding, but the sound is superb. In addition to hosting the Miami Film Festival, the elegant Gusman Center features pop concerts, plays, film screenings, and special events. The auditorium was built as the Olympia Theater in 1926, and its ornate palace interior is typical of that era, complete with fancy columns, a huge pipe organ, and twinkling "stars" on the ceiling.

Not to be confused with the Gusman Center (above), the **Gusman Concert Hall,** 1314 Miller Dr., at 14th Street, Coral Gables (✆ **305/284-6477**), is a roomy 600-seat hall that gives a stage to the Miami Chamber Symphony and a varied program of university recitals.

The **Fillmore Miami Beach at the Jackie Gleason Theater,** located in South Beach at Washington Avenue and 17th Street (✆ **305/673-7300**), may be a mouthful, but when it comes to live music, it truly rocks. The venue's decor is very modern Hard Rock–meets–Miami Beach, complete with requisite bars, chandeliers, and an homage to the original legendary Fillmore in San Francisco. The Fillmore, which was taken over by Live Nation, brings major talent to the beach, from Lenny Kravitz and Snow Patrol to comedians Lewis Black and Lisa Lampanelli. Fillmore also hosts various awards shows, from the Food Network Awards to the Fox Sports Awards.

The **Adrienne Arsht Center for the Performing Arts,** 1300 Biscayne Blvd. (www.arshtcenter.org; ✆ **786/468-2000**), opened in late 2006 after a whopping $446-million tab. Included: The 2,400-seat **Sanford and Dolores Ziff Ballet Opera House** and the 2,200-seat **Knight Concert Hall** are Miami venues for the **Concert Association of Florida, Florida Grand Opera, Miami City Ballet,** and **New World Symphony,** as well as premier venues for a wide array of local, national, and international performances, ranging from Broadway musicals and visiting classical artists to world and urban music, Latin concerts, and popular entertainment from many cultures. The **Studio Theater,** a flexible black-box space designed for up to 200 seats, hosts intimate performances of contemporary theater, dance, music, cabaret, and other entertainment. The **Peacock Education Center** acts as a catalyst for arts education and enrichment programs for children and adults. Finally, the **Plaza for the Arts** is a magnificent setting for outdoor entertainment, social celebrations, and informal community gatherings.

Designed by world-renowned architect Cesar Pelli, the Carnival Center is the focal point of a planned Arts, Media, and Entertainment District in mid-Miami. The complex is wrapped in limestone, slate, decorative stone, stainless steel, glass curtain walls, and tropical landscaping, and was completed in mid-2006. Newly opened within the complex is a bona fide restaurant, **Prelude by Barton G.** (www.prelude bybartong.com; ✆ **305/357-7900**), an old-school yet modern supper club featuring prix-fixe pre- and post-theater menus. There are no parking facilities, so valet parking is available for $10 to $20 or you can park at lots across the street or the Marriott nearby; to make things easy, just take a cab.

BARS & LOUNGES

There are countless bars and lounges in and around Miami (most require proof that you are 21 or older to enter), with the highest concentration on trendy South Beach. The selection here is a mere sample. Keep in mind that many of the popular bars—and the easiest to get into—are in hotels (with a few notable exceptions—see below). For a clubbier scene, if you don't mind making your way through hordes of inebriated club kids, a stroll on Washington Avenue will provide you with ample insight into what's hot and what's not. Just hold on to your bags. It's not dangerous, but occasionally a few shady types manage to slip into the crowd. Another very important tip when in a club: *Never put your drink down out of your sight*—there have been unfortunate incidents in which drinks have been spiked with illegal chemical substances. For a less hard-core, more collegiate nightlife, head to Coconut Grove. Oh, yes, and when going out in South Beach, make sure to take a so-called disco nap, as things don't get going until at least 11pm. If you go earlier, be prepared to face an empty bar or club. Off of South Beach and in hotel bars in general, the hours are fashionably earlier, with the action starting as early as, say, 7pm.

The Abbey   Dark, dank, and hard to find, this local microbrewery is a favorite for locals looking to escape the $20 candy-flavored martini scene. Best of all, there's never a cover and it's always open until 5am, perfect for those pesky and insatiable hops cravings that pop up at 3 or 4am. 1115 16th St., South Beach. ✆ **305/538-8110.**

Bardot 👬   Modeled after the basement of a 1970s rock star, Bardot is Miami proper's hottest new scene despite the fact that it prides itself on being the antithesis of being sceney. A mixed crowd of young and old, gay and straight, and everything in between is what you'll find at this off-the-beaten-path lounge-cum–speak-easy located in the back of a Midtown furniture store. Shag carpeting, comfy couches, and decor straight out of *That '70s Show* make for a very comfy backdrop for cocktailing, listening to live music, and watching what may be, at the time of this writing, Miami's most colorful hipster crowd. 3456 N. Miami Ave., Miami. www.bardotmiami.com. ✆ **305/ 576-5570.**

Bar 721   Hidden behind bustling Lincoln Road is this bar that looks as if the 1970s took a time machine to the 21st century and got off for a bathroom break in the 1950s. Whatever decade you may be in mentally or otherwise, the bar is great fun, something guys would want as their man rooms and women wouldn't mind visiting for a drink or two. 721 N. Lincoln Lane, South Beach. ☎305/532-1342.

Blackbird Ordinary It's hard to locate, but once you do find this oddly named drinking den, you'll be happy you did. Reminiscent of what locals describe as "a real big-city lounge," Blackbird is cavernous, featuring a huge bar with a very creative cocktail list, tons of cozy couches and tables, board games, a funky crowd, and, hallelujah, live music. Plus, it's open until 5am every night, or morning, rather. 1729 SW 1st Ave., Miami. www.blackbirdordinary.com. ☎305/377-4628.

The Blue Piano This tiny, tiny storefront packs a loud punch, especially when its co-owner, Latin Grammy Award–winning Bacilos frontman Jorge Villamizar, is in the house jamming with his pals. A wine, beer, and tapas bar with very few tables, Blue Piano is a hipster hot spot where you never know who may show up and put on an impromptu jam session. 4600 NE 2nd Ave., Miami. www.thebluepiano.com. ☎305/576-7919.

Burger & Beer Joint Although downstairs at this bustling, well, burger and beer joint is more about food, in back is a sports bar complete with flatscreen TVs to catch the latest game. Not in the mood for athletics? Consider the lounge upstairs where a chilled-out scene attracts everyone from barflies and models to overly full diners from downstairs looking to veg out on the couches. 1766 Bay Rd., South Beach. www.burgern beerjoint.com. ☎305/672-3287.

Cafeina The only true lounge in Wynwood, Cafeina is a buzzy, kicky hot spot that prides itself on its tapas and its creative caffeine-infused cocktails. An outdoor garden lounge area is amazing in the cooler months, and the warehouse art gallery–cum–bar and lounge indoors serves as a sleek space to strike a pose. 297 NW 23rd St., Miami. www.cafeinamiami.com. ☎305/438-0792.

> ### Impressions
>
> *There are two shifts in South Beach. There's 9 to 5. And then there's 9 to 5.*
> —South Beach artist Stewart Stewart

Clevelander If wet-T-shirt contests and a fraternity-party atmosphere are your thing, then this Ocean Drive mainstay is your kind of place. Popular with tourists and locals who like to pretend they're tourists, the Clevelander, which was the recent recipient of much-needed renovations, attracts a lively, sporty crowd of only adults (the burly bouncers *will* confiscate fake IDs) who have no interest in being part of a scene, but, rather, like to take in the very revealing scenery. A great time to check out the Clevelander is on a weekend afternoon, when beach Barbies and Kens line the bar for a post-tanning beer or frozen cocktail. 1020 Ocean Dr., South Beach. www.clevelander.com. ☎305/531-3485.

Club 50 at the Viceroy If you're afraid of heights, you may want to bypass this stunning, swanky lounge located 50 stories above Brickell Avenue. But you may want to conquer your fear, as Club 50 is entirely worth it if you're looking for a sophisticated swilling spot that caters to Miami's elite. Indoors is reminiscent of a lounge in an old-school, first-class ocean liner, while outside is more L.A. with lap pool, bar, and panoramic views of the downtown skyline. 485 Brickell Ave., Miami. www.viceroymiami.com. ☎305/503-4400.

Cozy A very French, very expensive piano bar in the South of Fifth neighborhood right next door to the zillion-dollar Apogee condo, where the likes of actor Michael Caine and basketball's Pat Riley call home, Cozy lives up to its name in ambience

Stargazing

The most popular places for celebrity sightings include Mansion, LIV, SET, WALL, Mondrian, FDR, Skybar at the Shore Club, and, when it comes to stars gazing at other stars, Miami Heat basketball games. Edgier, under-the-radar celebs can be spotted at Mac's Club Deuce around 5 in the morning.

with blood-red walls and chandeliers. But when it comes to the check, there's nothing cozy about it, with a cheese plate coming in at a whopping $50 and glasses of wine starting at $20. But if you're in the mood for a nightcap—and we mean just one—and some great live piano and surprise celebrity musicians (the Gypsy Kings love dropping in and jamming out here when in town), Cozy (or Sarkozy, as we like to call it) is entirely worth the splurge. 500 South Pointe Dr., South Beach. www.thecozybar.com. ☏ **305/ 532-2699.**

DRB Miami A tiny spot across the street from the performing arts center, DRB— Democratic Republic of Beer—is where Miami meets Williamsburg, Brooklyn, with an unabridged list of microbrews from all over the world, a better-than-average bar menu, and a crowd of hops-loving hipsters sporting ironic facial hair and quoting Kafka. 255 NE 14th St., Miami. www.drbmiami.com. ☏ **305/372-4565.**

Electric Pickle A tiny bar with upstairs lounge and a parking lot out back that doubles as its outdoor area, Electric Pickle is the unofficial clubhouse of Miami's indie music scene, where the long-running Brit-pop, hipster-happy one-nighter Pop Life takes up residence every Saturday. We completely recommend the place if that's your scene, but go at your own risk as its host neighborhood is still very dodgy. 2826 N. Miami Ave., Wynwood. www.electricpicklemiami.com. ☏ **305/456-5613.**

FDR FDR is a dimly chandelier-lit den of old-school Florida decor meets swanky cruise-ship lounge, where everyone from young hipsters and swanky sophisticates to the Golden Girls would go for a fancy night out. Operated by Las Vegas nightlife innovators the Light Group, the interior of this subterranean speak-easy is the antithesis of the sleek, stark hotel in which it resides, and for that, we love it. 1685 Collins Ave. (in the Delano), South Beach. www.delano-hotel.com. ☏ **305/672-2000.**

Fox's Sherron Inn 🍸 The spirit of Frank Sinatra is alive and well at this dark and smoky watering hole that dates back to 1946. Everything down to the vinyl booths and the red lights make Fox's a retro-fabulous dive bar. Cheap drinks, couples cozily huddling in booths, and a seasoned staff of bartenders and barflies make Fox's the perfect place to retreat from the trenches of trendiness. Oh, and the food's actually good here, too. 6030 S. Dixie Hwy. (at 62nd Ave.), South Miami. ☏ **305/661-9201.**

Mac's Club Deuce Standing amid an oasis of trendiness, Mac's Club Deuce is the quintessential dive bar, with cheap drinks and a cast of characters ranging from your typical barfly to your atypical drag queen. It's got a well-stocked jukebox, friendly bartenders, and a pool table. It's an insomniac's dream, open daily from 8am to 5am. 222 14th St., South Beach. ☏ **305/673-9537.**

Mondrian If you can only stop at one South Beach bar for a beverage, we say this one should be it thanks to its jaw-dropping views of Biscayne Bay and an equally impressive interior surrealist decor (even more so after a few) in which Alice in Wonderland Spring Breaks on South Beach. Drinks are delicious and you'll pay a pretty price for it, but save some money for either a bottle in the lobby's tiny, couchy, VIP Sunset Lounge, a snack at Asia de Cuba, or for the automated vending machines hawking Bentleys and assorted luxuries. 1100 West Ave., South Beach. www.mondrian-miami.com. ☏ **305/514-1500.**

Mynt A massive 6,000-square-foot place, Mynt is a huge living room in which some models, D-list celebrities, locals, and assorted hangers-on bask in the green glow to the beat of very loud lounge and dance music. If you want to dance—or move, for that matter—this is not the place in which to do so. It's all about striking a pose in here. Unless you know the person at the door, be prepared to be ridiculed and socially shattered, as you may be forced to wait outside upward of an hour. If that's the case, forget it; it's not worth it. 1921 Collins Ave., South Beach. www.myntlounge.com. ☏ **786/276-6132.** Cover $10–$20.

Playwright Irish Pub Bono came here once when U2 was in town, not because it's such an authentic Irish pub, but because the bar was showing some European soccer match—and serves pints of Guinness. A great pre- or postclub spot, Playwright is one of the few places in town that also features live music from time to time. 1265 Washington Ave., South Beach. www.playwrightirishpub.com. ☏ **305/534-0667.**

The Purdy Lounge Purdy is not unlike your best friend's basement, featuring a pool table and a slew of board games such as Operation to keep the attention-deficit-disordered from getting bored. The cocktails are relatively cheap at this no-nonsense bar. With no cover, no DJ, and no attitude, a line is inevitable (it gets crowded inside), so be prepared to wait. Saturday night has become the preferred night for locals, while Friday night's happy hour draws a young professional crowd on the prowl. 1811 Purdy Ave. at Sunset Harbor, South Beach. www.purdylounge.com. ☏ **305/531-4622.**

Ricochet Located in Midtown Miami, Ricochet is an "art and music venue," with live bands (both local and bigtime), famous comedians (Gilbert Gottfried, Tommy Davidson), backgammon, and a curated video art collection. 3250 Buena Vista Blvd., Midtown. http://ricochetlounge.com. ☏ **786/353-0846.**

The Rooftop at the Perry Possibly the best thing about the Perry (formerly known as the Gansevoort) is the hotel's rockin' rooftop pool lounge, where on any given day or night, scantily clad scene (and bikini) chasers can be found either in or out of the water, sipping colorful cocktails to the tune of DJ-spun music. 2399 Collins Ave., South Beach. www.perrysouthbeachhotel.com. ☏ **305/604-1000.**

The Room It's beer and wine only at this South of Fifth hideaway, where locals come to get away from the insanity just a few blocks away. The beer selection is comprehensive, with brews from almost everywhere in the world. The wine is not so great, but there's no whining here at this tiny, industrial-style, candlelit spot. 100 Collins Ave., South Beach. www.theotheroom.com. ☏ **305/531-6061.**

Rose Bar at the Delano If every rose has its thorn, the thorn at this painfully chic hotel bar is the excruciatingly high price of cocktails. The crowd here is dominated by so-called glitterati and assorted poseurs who view life through (Italian-made) rose-colored glasses. 1685 Collins Ave., South Beach. www.delano-hotel.com. ☏ **305/672-2000.**

Segafredo Espresso Although Segafredo is technically a cafe, it has become an integral part of Miami's nightlife as command central for Euros who miss that very special brand of European cafe society. European lounge music, tons of outdoor tables on a prime corner of Lincoln Road, and always a mob scene make 'Fredo one of our favorite nocturnal diversions. Although South Beach boasts the original, there

SWANK hotel bars

Long gone are the days of the old-school Holiday Inn lounges. In fact, some hotels seem to spend more money on their bars than they do on their bedding. That aside, hotel bar-hopping is very popular in Miami. The fabulous **W South Beach** has several watering holes, from the Living Room lobby bar and poolside Wet Bar to the bars in their star-studded Mr Chow and Soleà restaurants. Here's my list of the rest of the best:

Rose Bar at the Delano (p. 160): For seeing and being seen.

Skybar at the Shore Club (below): Also for seeing and being seen.

Mondrian (p. 159): Picture Alice in Wonderland going through the wrong mouse hole and ending up in South Beach. Trippy.

Bond St. Lounge at the Townhouse (p. 96): A tiny bar/lounge that also serves food. A New York import, it's known for excellent sushi and a hip, chic, jet-set crowd.

Martini Bar at the Raleigh Hotel (p. 183): A true throwback to the days of Deco set to the tunes of Edith Piaf, Tony Bennett, Sinatra, and more.

Club 50 at the Viceroy (p. 150): There are lofty spots in Miami and then there's this, located high above the city on the 50th floor with some of the best views—and people-watching—in Miami.

The Bar at the Setai (p. 184): The bar formerly known as the Champagne and Crustacean Bar may be a thing of more liquid economic times, but this simply named club (and Pool & Beach Bar) at the Setai still offer pricey drinks in stunning settings. This time, however, cocktails look like drinks but eat like meals. Huh? Try the one with the bacon-infused bourbon and see what we mean.

are other Segafredo locations, with different owners, in the Brickell Area (at 1421 S. Miami Ave.), on Espanola Way on South Beach, and in South Miami (at 5800 SW 73rd St). 1040 Lincoln Rd., South Beach. ⓒ **305/673-0047.**

Skybar at the Shore Club   Once popular on any given night, Skybar was yet another brilliant example of how hotelier Ian Schrager managed to control the hipsters in a most Pavlovian way. But Skybar finally dropped the loftiness when the A-list dropped them. That being said, this former celebrity hot spot is on the rise again, so beware. For those of you who can't get in, the Skybar is basically the entire backyard area of the Shore Club, consisting of several areas, including the Moroccan-themed garden area, the hip-hop–themed indoor Red Room, the Sand Bar by the beach, and the Rum Bar by the pool. At the Shore Club, 1901 Collins Ave., South Beach. www.shoreclub. com. ⓒ **305/695-3100.**

The Stage   Just as its name says, the Stage is a premiere venue for local and national talent and, on days when that stage is dark, a great spot for lounging to the tune of DJs spinning everything from lounge and down tempo to rock. 170 NE 38th St., Design District. http://thestagemiami.com. ⓒ **305/576-9577.**

Wet Bar at the W South Beach   As wholly unoriginal as the name is, the poolside Wet Bar along with the secret-garden Grove and lobby-level Living Room at the fabulous W South Beach are among the city's most stylish, creative, and buzzworthy nightspots, thanks to a stellar combo of master mixologists who shake and stir up some of the most creative—and pricey—cocktails you'll ever drink, celebrities and

LATE-NIGHT bites

Although some dining spots in Miami stop serving at 10pm, many are open very late or even around the clock—especially on weekends. So, if it's 4am and you need a quick bite after clubbing, don't fret. There are a vast number of pizza places lining Washington Avenue in South Beach that are open past 6am. Especially good are **La Sandwicherie**, 229 14th St. (behind the Amoco station; (✆ **305/532-8934**), which serves up a great late-night sandwich until 5am. Nearby is the **BK Whopper Bar,** 1101 Washington Ave. (✆ **305/673-4560**), Burger King's spin on a hip burger joint, open 24 hours a day, serving beer and as gourmet a burger as BK can make. Another place of note for night owls is the **News Cafe,** 800 Ocean Dr. (✆ **305/538-6397**), a trendy and well-priced cafe that has an enormous

menu offering great all-day breakfasts, Middle Eastern platters, fruit bowls, or steak and potatoes—and everything is served 24 hours a day. If you're craving a corned beef on rye at 5am, **Jerry's Famous Deli,** 1450 Collins Ave. (✆ **305/534-3244**), is open 24/7. If your night out was at one of the Latin clubs around town, stop in at **Versailles,** 3555 SW 8th St. (✆ **305/444-0240**), in Little Havana. What else but a Cuban *medianoche* (midnight sandwich) will do? It's not open all night, but its hours extend well past midnight—usually until 3 or 4am on weekends—to cater to gangs of revelers, young and old. Over the causeway near Midtown, **Gigi,** 3470 N. Miami Ave. (✆ **305/573-1520**), is a late-night noodle bar open until 3am weekdays and 5am on weekends. For a more thorough listing of Miami's most notable restaurants, see chapter 6.

locals who drink them, and resplendent settings with Facebook-worthy photo-op backdrops. 2201 Collins Ave., South Beach. ✆ **305/938-3000.**

Wet Willie's   With such telling drinks as Call a Cab, this beachfront oasis is not the place to go if you have a long drive ahead of you. A well-liked pre- and postbeach hangout, Wet Willie's inspires serious drinking. Popular with the Harley-Davidson set, tourists, and beachcombers, this bar is best known for its rooftop patio (get there early if you plan to get a seat) and its half-nude bikini beauties. 760 Ocean Dr., South Beach. ✆ **305/532-5650.**

THE CLUB & MUSIC SCENE
Dance Clubs

Clubs are as much a cottage industry in Miami as is, say, cheese in Wisconsin. Clubland, as it is known, is a way of life for some. On any given night in Miami, there's something going on—no excuses are needed to throw a party here. Short of throwing a glamorous event for the grand opening of a new gas station, Miami is very party hearty, celebrating everything from the fact that it's Tuesday night to the debut of a hot new DJ. Within this very bizarre after-dark community, a colorful assortment of characters emerges, from (a)typical 9-to-5ers to shady characters who have reinvented themselves as hot shots on the club circuit. While this see-and-be-seen scene may not be your cup of Absolut, it's certainly never boring.

The club music played on Miami's ever-evolving social circuit is good enough to get even the most rhythmically challenged wallflowers dancing. For aspiring DJs, a branch of the renowned **Scratch DJ Academy,** 2 NE 40th St. (www.scratch.com; © **305/535-2599**), opened; for $350 a session, you, too, can become a master of the turntables.

To keep things fresh in Clubland, local promoters throw one-nighters, which are essentially parties with various themes or motifs, from funk to fashion. Because these change so often, we can't possibly list them here. Word of mouth, local advertising, and listings in the free weekly *New Times,* www.miami.citysearch.com, or the "Weekend" section of the *Miami Herald* are the best ways to find out about these ever-changing events.

Before you get all decked out to hit the town as soon as the sun sets, consider the fact that Miami is a very late town. Things generally don't get started here before 11pm. The Catch-22 is that if you don't arrive on South Beach early enough, you may find yourself driving around aimlessly for parking, as it is very limited outside of absurd $20+ valet charges. Municipal lots fill up quickly, so your best bet is to arrive on South Beach somewhat early and kill time by strolling around, having something to eat, or sipping a cocktail in a hotel bar. Another advantage of arriving a bit earlier than the crowds is that some clubs don't charge a cover before 11pm or midnight, which could save you a wad of cash over time. Most clubs are open every night of the week, though some are open only Thursday to Sunday and others are open only Monday through Saturday. Call ahead to get the most up-to-date information possible: Things change very quickly around here, and a call in advance can help you make sure that the dance club you're planning to go to hasn't become a video arcade. Cover charges are very haphazard, too. If you're not on the ubiquitous guest list (ask your

 GROUND RULES: stepping out IN MIAMI

o Nightlife on South Beach doesn't really get going until after 11pm. As a result, you may want to consider taking what is known as a disco nap so that you'll be fully charged until the wee hours.

o If you're unsure of what to wear out on South Beach, your safest bet is anything black.

o Do *not* try to tip the doormen manning the velvet ropes. That will only make you look desperate, and you'll find yourself standing outside for what will seem like an ungodly amount of time. Instead, try to land your name on the ever-present guest list by calling the club early in the day yourself or, better yet, having the concierge at your hotel do it for you. If you don't have connections and you find yourself

without a concierge, then act assertive, not surly, at the velvet rope, and your patience will usually be rewarded with admittance. If all else fails—for men, especially—surround yourself with a few leggy model types and you'll be noticed quicker.

o If you are a man going out with a group of men, unless you're going to a gay bar, you will most likely not get into any South Beach hot spot unless you are with women.

o Finally, have fun. It may look like serious business when you're on the outside, but once you're in, it's another story. Attacking Clubland with a sense of humor is the best approach to a successful, memorable evening out.

concierge to put you on the list—he or she usually has the ability to do so, which won't help you with the wait to get in, but will eliminate the cover charge), you may have to fork over a ridiculous $20 to walk past the ropes. Don't fret, though. There are many clubs and bars that have no cover charge—they just make up for it by charging $20 for a martini!

Bongos Cuban Café Gloria Estefan's latest hit in the restaurant business pays homage to the sights, sounds, and cuisine of pre-Castro Cuba. Bongos is a mammoth restaurant attached to the American Airlines Arena in downtown Miami. On Friday after 11pm and Saturday after 11:30pm, it's transformed from a friendly-family restaurant into the city's hottest 21-and-over salsa nightclub. Cover charges can be hefty, but consider it your ticket to an astounding show of some of the best salsa dancers in the city. Prepare yourself for standing room only. Salsa lessons are also available for those with two left feet. At the American Airlines Arena, 601 Biscayne Blvd., Downtown. www.bongoscubancafe.com. ✆**786/777-2100.** Cover Fri–Sat; women free until 11pm, $20 after 11pm; men $20.

Cameo Still haunted by the ghost of clubs past, the space formerly known as crobar has undergone much-needed renovations and reopened as Cameo. Under Opium's direction, Cameo, which boasts a supersonic sound system, star DJs, and plenty of VIP seating, once again is another must-stop on the nocturnal itineraries of any die-hard or erstwhile clubber. It's open Thursday through Monday from 10pm to 5am. 1445 Washington Ave., South Beach. www.cameomiami.com. ✆ **305/531-8225.** Cover Thurs, Sun–Mon $20–$40; Fri–Sat $25–$50.

Club Space Clubland hits the mainland with this cavernous downtown warehouse of a club. With more than 30,000 square feet of dance space, you can spin around a la Stevie Nicks (albeit to a techno beat) without having to worry about banging into someone. On Saturday and Sunday nights, the party usually extends to the next morning, sometimes as late as 10am. It's quite a sight to see club kids rushing off to work straight from Space on a Monday morning. Known as the venue of choice for world-renowned DJs, Club Space sometimes charges ludicrous admission fees to cover its hefty price tags. *Note:* Club Space doesn't really get going until around 3am. Call for more information, as it doesn't have a concrete schedule. 34 NE 11th St., Miami. www.clubspace.com. ✆**305/372-9378.** Cover up to $50.

LIV The biggest in Miami's celebrity-saturated nightlife, LIV (as in, "celebrities live for LIV") is the Fontainebleau's flashy dance club. Go early even if it means lining up in the lobby. In the cavernous LIV, expect to see celebs ensconced in visible VIP areas. 4441 Collins Ave., South Beach. www.livnightclub.com. ✆ **305/538-2000.** Cover $10–$50.

> **Impressions**
>
> Working the door teaches you a lot about human nature.
>
> —A former South Beach doorman

Mansion This place is a massive multilevel lounge that, according to the owners and promoters, is entirely "VIP," meaning you'd best know someone to get in or else you'll be among the masses outside. DJs, models, and celebrities galore—Rihanna, Beyoncé, Jay-Z, and more—not to mention high ceilings, wood floors, brick walls, and a stellar light-and-sound system—make this place a *must* on the list of see-and-be-scenesters. It's open Tuesday through Sunday from 11pm to 5am. 1235 Washington Ave., South Beach. www.theopium group.com. ✆**305/531-5535.** Cover $10–$40.

WINTER music CONFERENCE

Every March, Miami is besieged by the most unconventional conventioneers the city has ever seen. These fiercely dedicated souls descend upon the city in a very audible way, with dark circles under their eyes and bleeps, blips, and scratches that can wake the dead. No, we're not talking about a *Star Trek* convention, but, rather, the **Winter Music Conference** (WMC), the world's biggest and most important gathering of DJs, remixers, agents, artists, and pretty much anyone who makes a dime off of the booming electronic music industry hailing from more than 60 countries from all over the world. But unlike most conventions, this one is completely interactive and open to the paying public as South Beach and Miami's hottest clubs transform into showcases for the various audio wares. For 5 consecutive days and nights, DJs, artists, and software producers play for audiences composed of A&R reps, talent scouts, and locals just along for the ride. Parties take place everywhere, from hotel pools to street corners. There's always something going on every hour on the hour, and most people who really get into the throes of the WMC get little or no sleep. Energy drinks become more important than water, and, for the most part, if you see people popping pills, they're not likely vitamins.

At any rate, the WMC is worth checking out if you get ecstatic over names such as David Guetta, Swedish House Mafia, Peter Rauhoffer, Roger Sanchez, Frankie Knuckles, Hex Hector, Paul Oakenfold, Deep Dish, and Armand Van Helden, among many, many others. For more information on WMC events, go to **www.wmcon.com**.

Nikki Beach   What the Playboy Mansion is to L.A., the Nikki Beach is to South Beach—but if you want a locals scene, you won't find it here. The allure is mostly for visiting tourists who love to gawk at their fellow half-naked ladies and men actually venturing into the daylight on Sunday (around 4pm, which is ungodly in this town) to see, be seen, and, at times, be obscene. At night, it's very "Brady Bunch Goes to Hawaii," with a sexy Tiki hut/Polynesian theme, albeit rated R. Also located within this bastion of hedonism is the second-floor nightclub for those who want to dance on an actual dance floor and not sand. 101 Ocean Dr., South Beach. www.nikkibeach.com. © **305/538-1111.** Cover $10–$20.

SET   The Opium Group's undisputed "it" child, SET is still *the* place to be, at least amongst the jet set and Euro-types who can't get enough of it. A luxurious lounge with chandeliers and design mag–worthy decor is always full of trendsetters, celebs, and wannabes. Where you really want to be, however, is upstairs, in the private VIP room. SET is known for a ruthless door policy; ask your hotel concierge to get you in. 320 Lincoln Rd., South Beach. www.setmiami.com. © **305/531-2800.** Cover $20.

WALL   The W South Beach's requisite velvety roped-off hip nightclub, WALL has a VIP scene complete with couches reserved for only those dropping thousands on booze even in a recession. With its mirrored walls and flashy ambience, a night in WALL is not unlike what we think it would feel like to spin around inside a disco ball. 2201 Collins Ave., South Beach. © **305/938-3000.**

Live Music

Unfortunately, Miami's live music scene is not thriving. Instead of local bands garnering devoted fans, local DJs are more admired, skyrocketing much more easily to fame—thanks to the city's lauded dance-club scene. However, there are still several places that strive to bring Miami up to speed as far as live music is concerned. You just have to look—and listen—for it a bit more carefully. The following is a list of places where you can catch some live acts.

Churchill's Hideaway British expatriate Dave Daniels couldn't live in Miami without a true English-style pub, so he opened Churchill's Hideaway, the city's premier space for live rock music. Filthy and located in a rather unsavory neighborhood, Churchill's is committed to promoting and extending the lifeline of the lagging local music scene. A fun no-frills crowd hangs out here. It is deafening once the music starts. Monday is open-mic night, while Wednesday is reserved for ladies' wrestling. 5501 NE 2nd Ave., Little Haiti. www.churchillspub.com. ℂ305/757-1807. Cover up to $6.

Grand Central The newest addition to Miami's ever-burgeoning yet still somewhat underground indie music scene, Grand Central is, indeed, the Grand Central of live indie acts who flock here from around the world to perform for adoring hipster fans. 697 N. Miami Ave., downtown. www.grandcentralmiami.com. ℂ305/377-2277. Cover varies.

Jazid Smoky, sultry, and illuminated by flickering candelabras, Jazid is the kind of place where you'd expect to hear Sade's "Smooth Operator" on constant rotation. Instead, however, you'll hear live jazz (sometimes acid jazz), soul, and funk. An eclectic mix of mellow folk convenes here for a much-needed respite from the surrounding Washington Avenue mayhem. 1342 Washington Ave., South Beach. www.jazid.net. ℂ305/673-9372. Cover free–$10.

Tobacco Road Al Capone used to hang out here when it was a speak-easy. Now locals flock here to see local bands perform, as well as national acts such as George Clinton and the P-Funk All-Stars, Koko Taylor, and the Radiators. Tobacco Road (the proud owner of Miami's very first liquor license) is small and gritty, and meant to be that way. Escape the smoke and sweat in the backyard patio, where air is a welcome commodity. The downright-cheap nightly specials, such as the $13 lobster on Tuesday, are quite good and served until 2am; the bar is open until 5am. 626 S. Miami Ave. (over the Miami Ave. Bridge, near Brickell Ave.), downtown. www.tobacco-road.com. ℂ305/374-1198. Cover Thurs–Sat $5–$10.

Upstairs at the Van Dyke Cafe The cafe's jazz bar, located on the second floor, resembles a classy speak-easy in which local jazz performers play to an intimate, enthusiastic crowd of mostly adults and sophisticated young things, who often huddle at the small tables until the wee hours. 846 Lincoln Rd., South Beach. www.thevandykecafe. com. ℂ305/534-3600. Cover Sun–Thurs $5, Fri–Sat $10 for a seat; no cover at the bar.

Latin Clubs

Considering that Hispanics make up a large part of Miami's population and that there's a huge influx of Spanish-speaking visitors, it's no surprise that there are some great Latin nightclubs in the city. Plus, with the meteoric rise of the international music scene based in Miami, many international stars come through the offices of MTV Latino, SONY International, and a multitude of Latin TV studios based in Miami—and they're all looking for a good club scene on weekends. Most of the Anglo clubs also reserve at least 1 night a week for Latin rhythms.

THE rhythm IS GONNA GET YOU

Are you feeling shy about hitting a Latin club because you fear your two left feet will stand out? Then take a few lessons from one of the following dance companies or dance teachers. They offer individual and group lessons to dancers of any origin who are willing to learn. These folks have made it their mission to teach merengue and flamenco to non-Latinos and Latino left foots, and are among the most reliable, consistent, and popular ones in Miami. So what are you waiting for?

Thursday and Friday nights at **Bongo's Cuban Café,** American Airlines Arena, 601 Biscayne Blvd., downtown ((C) **786/777-2100**), are amazing showcases for some of the city's best salsa dancers, but amateurs need not be intimidated, thanks to the instructors from Latin Groove Dance Studios who are on hand to help you with your two left feet. Lessons are free.

At **Ballet Flamenco La Rosa** in the Performing Arts Network (PAN) building,

13126 W. Dixie Hwy., North Miami (www. panmiami.org; (C) **305/899-7730**), you can learn to flamenco, salsa, or merengue. This is the only professional flamenco company in the area. They charge $15 per class.

Nobody teaches salsa like **Luz Pinto** (www.latin-heat.com; (C) **786/281-9747**). She teaches 7 days a week and, trust us, with her, you'll learn cool turns easily. She charges $50 for a private lesson and is the only instructor who doesn't charge extra if you want to share the lesson with a partner or friends. She teaches everything from classic to hip wedding dances to ballroom, disco, and merengue, as well as L.A.-style and Casino-style salsa, popularized in the 1950s in Cuba. You will be impressed with how well and quickly Luz can teach you to have fun and feel great dancing.

Hoy Como Ayer Formerly known as Cafe Nostalgia, the Little Havana hangout dedicated to reminiscing about Old Cuba, Hoy Como Ayer is like the Brady Bunch of Latin hangouts—while it was extremely popular with old-timers in its Cafe Nostalgia incarnation, it is now experiencing a resurgence among the younger generation seeking its own brand of nostalgia. Its Thursday-night party, Fuacata (slang for "Pow!"), is a magnet for Latin hipsters, featuring classic Cuban music mixed in with modern DJ-spun sound effects. It's open Thursday to Sunday from 9pm to 4am. 2212 SW 8th St. (Calle Ocho), Little Havana. www.hoycomoayer.us. (C) **305/541-2631.** Cover Thurs–Sun $10.

La Covacha 🏠 This hut, located virtually in the middle of nowhere (West Miami), is the hottest Latin joint in the entire city. Sunday features the best in Latin rock, with local and international acts. But the shack is really jumping on weekend nights, when the place is open until 5am. Friday is *the* night here, so much so that the owners had to place a red velvet rope out front to maintain some semblance of order. It's an amusing sight—a velvet rope guarding a shack—but once you get in, you'll understand the need for it. Do not wear silk here, as you *will* sweat. 10730 NW 25th St. (at NW 107th Ave.), West Miami. www.lacovacha.com. (C) **305/594-3717.** Cover up to $20.

Mango's Tropical Cafe Claustrophobic types do not want to go near Mango's—ever. One of the most popular spots on Ocean Drive, this outdoor enclave of Latin liveliness shakes with the intensity of a Richter-busting earthquake. Mango's is *Cabaret,* Latin-style. Nightly live Brazilian and other Latin music, not to mention scantily clad male and female dancers, draws huge gawking crowds in from the sidewalk. But pay attention to the music, if you can: Incognito international musicians often lose their anonymity and jam with the house band on stage. It's open daily from 11am to 5am. 900 Ocean Dr., South Beach. www.mangostropicalcafe.com. © **305/673-4422.** Cover $5–$15.

THE GAY & LESBIAN SCENE

Miami and the beaches have long been host to what is called a "first-tier" gay community. Similar to the Big Apple, the Bay Area, or LaLa land, Miami has had a large alternative community since the days when Anita Bryant used her citrus power to boycott the rise in political activism in the early '70s. Well, things have changed, and Miami-Dade now has a gay-rights' ordinance.

Newcomers intending to party in any bar, whether downtown or certainly on the beach, will want to check ahead for the schedule, as all clubs must have a gay or lesbian night to pay their rent. Miami Beach, in fact, is a capital of the gay circuit party scene, rivaling San Francisco, Palm Springs, and even the mighty Sydney, Australia, for tourist dollars. However, ever since South Beach got bit by the hip-hop bug, many of Miami's gays have been crossing county lines into Fort Lauderdale, where there are, surprisingly, many more gay establishments.

Mova Just off Lincoln Road, Mova (formerly Halo) is the beach's newer, boutiquey gay lounge. Smoke-free and überstylish, Mova is open nightly until 3am and features DJs and a daily buy-one-get-one-free happy hour from 3 to 6pm. 1625 Michigan Ave., South Beach. No phone.

The Palace Just steps away from the men preening on the predominantly gay 12th Street Beach is this gay bar and drag-show venue, which loudly and proudly plants its rainbow flag on the Ocean Drive sidewalk, much to the curiosity of the guests quietly lounging at the Tides hotel next door. Snag a sidewalk table before a show (usually Fri–Sat 6pm and Sun 11am and 4pm) if you want Tiffany Fantasia to get all up in your Cobb salad. 1200 Ocean Dr. www.palacesouthbeach.com.

Score There's a reason this Lincoln Road hotbed of gay activity is called Score. In addition to the huge pickup scene, Score offers a multitude of bars, dance floors, lounge areas, and outdoor tables, in case you need to come up for air. You should have been there when Lady Gaga stopped by to sing a few bars of *Bad Romance*. Sunday afternoon tea dances are legendary. 727 Lincoln Rd., South Beach. www.scorebar.net. © **305/535-1111.**

Twist One of the most popular bars (and hideaways) on South Beach, this recently expanded bar (which is literally right across the street from the police station) has a casual yet lively atmosphere. 1057 Washington Ave., South Beach. www.twistsobe.com. © **305/538-9478.**

ALTERNATIVE ENTERTAINMENT
Bowling Alleys

Think of it as the Big Lebowski meets Studio 54, because in Miami, this is not your Sunday-afternoon ESPN bowling tournament. As much a fun rainy-day activity as it is with the kids, bowling in Miami gives new meaning to partying in the gutter.

Lucky Strike Lanes South Beach's only bowling alley is a pricey blast for adults and children, with 14 lanes, two pool tables, free Wi-Fi, a pulsating nightclub-esque soundtrack, a full bar, TVs, and a restaurant. Kids are allowed only up until 9pm, after which time Lucky Strike turns into a 21-and-over scene. 1691 Michigan Ave. www.bowl luckystrike.com. © **305/532-0307.** $45–$55 per hr. depending on day and time, including shoe rental. Mon–Thurs 11:30am–1am; Fri 11:30am–2am; Sat 11am–2am; Sun 11am–1am.

Splitsville Luxury Lanes & Dinner Lounge Located at Sunset Place, Splitsville is South Miami's Lucky Strike, with 12 lanes, 6 pool tables, a full-service restaurant, TVs, and multiple bars. Like Lucky Strike, no youth age 20 and under are allowed after 8pm, when the place turns into a thumping club scene until 5am. Unlike Lucky Strike, Splitsville is affordable, and because of that, there's usually a wait list for a lane. Luckily, there are plenty of other distractions to keep you busy while you wait. 5701 Sunset Dr. www.splitsvillelanes.com. © **305/665-5263.** Mon–Thurs $3.50 per person per game, $2 for shoe rental; Fri–Sun $6 per person per game, $4 for shoe rental. Mon–Thurs 4pm–2am; Fri–Sat 11am–5am; Sun 11am–2am.

Strike Miami Located at the Dolphin Mall, this one is Miami's biggest bowling alley, with 34 lanes and a nightclub setting. This one, owned by NYC's famed Bowlmor, even has glow-in-the-dark bowling. Food, bars, TVs—you get the picture. It's 18 and over after 9pm. In the Dolphin Mall, 11401 NW 12 St. www.bowlmor.com. ©**305/594-0200.** $30–$40 per hr. depending on day and time, including shoe rental. Mon–Thurs 4pm–1am; Fri noon–3am; Sat 11am–3am; Sun 11am–1am.

Gambling

Although gambling is technically illegal in Miami, there are plenty of loopholes that allow all kinds of wagering. Gamblers can try their luck at offshore casinos or on shore at bingo, jai alai, card rooms, horse tracks, dog races, and Native American reservations. The newly reopened **Hialeah Park Racing** (www.hialeahparkracing.com) has thoroughbred and quarter horse racing and, sometime in the near future, because no racetrack in Florida is complete without it, poker and slot machines. For slots and poker, you can check out the **Magic City Casino,** 5 minutes from the airport and downtown Miami at 450 NW 37th Ave. (www.magiccitycasino.com; © **888/56-MAGIC** [566-2442]), but we recommend you stick with the casino at **Calder Casino & Race Course,** located by Sun Life Stadium at 21001 NW 27th Ave. in Miami Gardens (www.calderracecourse.com; © **305/625-1311**), featuring 1,200 slot machines, poker, and horse racing. You can also drive up to Broward County, where the **Seminole Hard Rock Hotel and Casino** (www.seminolehardrock. com), **Seminole Casino Coconut Creek** (www.seminolecoconutcreekcasino. com), **Mardi Gras Racetrack and Gaming** (www.playmardigras.com), **Isle Casino & Racing** (www.pompano-park.isleofcapricasinos.com), and the new and still expanding **Gulfstream Park Casino and Racing** (www.gulfstreampark.com) in Hallandale offer slots, poker, and, in the cases of Hard Rock and Gulfstream, blackjack too.

Despite the Hard Rock in Hollywood's behemoth presence on the gambling circuit (and its many imitators), some people prefer the less flashy **Miccosukee Indian Gaming,** 500 SW 177th Ave. (off S.R. 41, in West Miami, on the outskirts of the Everglades; © **800/741-4600** or 305/222-4600), where a touch of Vegas meets West Miami. This tacky casino isn't Caesar's Palace, but you can play tab slots, high-speed bingo, and even poker. With more than 85,000 square feet of playing space,

Alternative Entertainment

the complex even provides overnight accommodations for those who can't get enough of the thrill and don't want to make the approximately 1-hour trip back to downtown Miami. Take the Florida Turnpike south toward Florida City/Key West. Take the SW 8th Street exit (no. 25) and turn left onto SW 8th Street. Drive for about 3½ miles and then turn left onto Krome Avenue, and left again at 177th Street; you can't miss it.

SPECTATOR SPORTS

Check the *Miami Herald*'s sports section for a daily listing of local events and the paper's Friday "Weekend" section for comprehensive coverage and in-depth reports. For last-minute tickets, call the venue directly, as many season ticket holders sell singles and return unused tickets. Expensive tickets are available from brokers or individuals listed in the classified sections of the local papers. Some tickets are also available through **Ticketmaster** (© 305/358-5885; www.ticketmaster.com).

BASEBALL The 2003 World Champion **Florida Marlins** shocked the sports world in 1997 when it became the youngest expansion team to win a World Series, but then floundered as its star players were sold off by former owner Wayne Huizenga. The team shocked the sports world again in 2003 by winning the World Series, and turned many of Miami's apathetic sports fans into major-league ball fans. The Marlins are not as good as they were anymore after trading their best players, but in April 2012 moved to their new home in the zillion-dollar (actually $525 million and counting) baseball stadium in the space formerly known as the Orange Bowl. Anyway, if you're interested in catching a game, *be warned:* The summer heat in Miami can be unbearable, even in the evenings. The new stadium features a retractable roof to make things more bearable.

In the meantime, home games are held at **Sun Life Stadium,** 2269 NW 199th St., North Miami Beach (© 305/623-6200). Tickets cost from $4 to $50. Box office hours are Monday to Friday from 8:30am to 5:30pm and before games; tickets are also available through Ticketmaster. The team currently holds spring training in Melbourne, Florida.

BASKETBALL The **Miami Heat** (© 786/777-1000) is one of Miami's hottest tickets, especially since the team won the NBA championship in 2006 and thanks to the powerhouse trifecta composed of Dwyane Wade, LeBron James, and Chris Bosh, who led the team into the 2012 playoffs against the Oklahoma Thunder. Courtside seats are full of visiting celebrities. The season lasts from October to April, with most games beginning at 7:30pm. The team plays in the waterfront **American Airlines Arena,** downtown on Biscayne Boulevard. Tickets are $10 to $100 or much more. Box office hours are Monday through Friday from 10am to 5pm (until 8pm on game nights); tickets are also available through Ticketmaster (© 305/358-5885).

CAR RACING **Homestead-Miami Speedway,** One Speedway Blvd., Homestead (www.homesteadmiamispeedway.com; © 866/409-7223 or 866/409-RACE [7223]), made history in 2009 when it become the first venue ever to host all of North America's premier motorsports championships: the IndyCar, Grand-Am, and Firestone Indy Lights Series; and NASCAR's Sprint Cup, Nationwide, and Camping World Truck Series. Even when the major races aren't going on here, you can channel your inner speed demon via open-to-the-public events that allow regular folk to put the pedal to the metal, including Hooked on Driving (www.hookedondriving.com) and Florida Track Days (www.floridatrackdays.com). The track also features private club–level seating. Tickets to all events vary.

FOOTBALL Miami's golden boys are the **Miami Dolphins,** the city's most recognizable team, followed by thousands of "dolfans." The team plays at least eight home games during the season, between September and December, at **Sun Life Stadium,** 2269 NW 199th St., Miami Gardens (✆ **305/620-2578**). Hit-maker Jimmy Buffett has a heavy presence at games, as do an impressive roster of celebrity "co-owners," including local faves Gloria and Emilio Estefan, Jennifer Lopez and Marc Anthony, and Fergie from the Black Eyed Peas. Because of this, the home games now feature an "orange carpet," on which owners and their famous friends prance before star-struck fans. Free concerts before games also bring big names thanks to the Buffett connection. In May 2012, HBO announced that it would spotlight the Dolphins on its popular reality show "Hard Knocks," and in June 2012 the team signed wide receiver Chad Ochocinco (soon to be plain old Chad Johnson again). Tickets cost $20 and much, much more. The box office is open Monday through Friday from 8:30am to 5:30pm; tickets are also available through Ticketmaster (www.ticketmaster.com; ✆ **305/358-5885**).

HORSE RACING Located on the Dade–Broward County border in Hallandale (just north of North Miami Beach/Aventura) is **Gulfstream Racing & Casino,** at U.S. 1 and Hallandale Beach Boulevard (www.gulfstreampark.com; ✆ **305/454-7000**), South Florida's very own version of Churchill Downs, but without the hats. This horse track is a haven for serious gamblers and voyeurs alike. Large purses and important races are commonplace at this sprawling suburban course, and the track is typically crowded, especially after receiving a multimillion-dollar face-lift that has added to the park a brand-new flashy casino, nightclubs, restaurants (including **The Cheese Course,** a sushi spot, pizza place, and a popular beer restaurant, **Yard House**), and stores in the massive work in progress known as the **Village at Gulfstream Park** (www.thevillageatgulfstreampark.com). Admission and parking are free. January through April, post times are 1:15pm Wednesday through Sunday. The track is closed Mondays and Tuesdays, though the casino remains open. If you're hungry, South Florida's venerable **Christine Lee's** Chinese restaurant is housed here. **Hialeah Park,** 2200 E. 4th Ave. (www.hialeahparkracing.com; ✆ **305/885-5000**), is a National Historic Landmark that reopened in 2009 with a 20-day race season in November and another one in December. Though initially limited to shorter—and less glamorous—quarter horse races, Hialeah Park aspires to add thoroughbred events in the future. Fans of racing have been patient and will wait it out. After all, it is the racetrack where champions like Seabiscuit, who made his racing debut at Hialeah Park on January 19, 1935, made history. Then there's **Calder Casino & Race Course,** located by Sun Life Stadium at 21001 NW 27th Ave. in Miami Gardens (www.calderracecourse.com; ✆ **305/625-1311**). Owned by the venerable Churchill Downs, Calder first opened as a horse-racing track back in 1971 and has been one of the most successful parimutuel franchises in the state's history. While horse racing and simulcast wagering are its mainstays, in order to keep up with the competition, Calder added a casino in January 2010. And while not exactly racing, a newish event that takes place on the sands of South Beach is the **Miami Beach Polo Cup,** featuring hard-core sand-kicking polo matches, a parade of the ponies down the beach, and chic parties. General admission to matches throughout the weekend is free to the public, while VIP tickets are available for those seeking more than a view from the sidelines and for coveted events outside of the arena. Visit www.miamipolo.com.

JAI ALAI Jai alai, sort of a Spanish-style indoor lacrosse, was introduced to Miami in 1924 and is regularly played in two Miami-area frontons (the buildings in which jai alai is played). Although the sport has roots stemming from ancient Egypt, the game, as it's now played, was invented by Basque peasants in the Pyrenees mountains during the 17th century. Players use *cesetas,* curved wicker baskets strapped to their wrists, to hurl balls, called *pelotas,* at speeds that sometimes exceed 170 mph. Spectators, who are protected behind a wall of glass, place bets on the evening's players. The Florida Gaming Corporation owns the jai alai operations throughout the state, making betting on this sport as legal as buying a lottery ticket.

The **Casino Miami Jai Alai,** 3500 NW 37th Ave., at NW 35th Street (www. casinomiamijaialai.com; © **305/633-6400**), is America's oldest fronton, dating from 1926. It schedules 13 games per night, which typically last 10 to 20 minutes, but can occasionally go much longer. Admission is free. There are year-round games. On Wednesday, Thursday, and Sunday, there are matinees only, which run from noon to 5:30pm. Friday, Saturday, and Monday, there are matinees in addition to evening games, from 7pm to midnight. This is the main location where jai alai is played in Miami. In keeping up with the Joneses, they added the word "casino" to the name with the addition of over a thousand slot machines as well as poker and dominoes tables. The other South Florida jai alai venue is in Dania, near the Fort Lauderdale–Hollywood International Airport.

Jai Alai Explained

Jai alai originated in the Basque country of northern Spain, where players used church walls as their courts. The game looks something like lacrosse, with rules similar to handball or tennis. It's played on a court with numbered lines. What makes the game unique, however, is the requirement that the ball must be returned in one continuous motion. The server must bounce the ball behind the serving line and, with the basket, must hurl the ball to the front wall, with the aim being that, upon rebound, the ball will bounce between lines four and seven. If it doesn't, it is an under- or overserve and the other team receives a point.

WHERE TO STAY IN MIAMI

As much a part of the landscape as the palm trees, many of Miami's hotels are on display as if they were contestants in a beauty pageant. The city's long-lasting status on the destination A-list has given rise to an ever-increasing number of upscale hotels, and no place in Miami has seen a greater increase in construction than Miami Beach. Since the area's renaissance, which began in the late 1980s, the beach has turned what used to be a beachfront retirement community into a sand-swept hot spot for the Gucci and Prada set—even in a recession. Contrary to popular belief, however, the beach does not discriminate, and it's the juxtaposition of the chic elite and the hoi polloi that contributes to its allure.

Many of the old hotels from the 1930s, 1940s, and 1950s have been totally renovated, giving way to dozens of boutique hotels. Keep in mind that when a hotel claims that it was just renovated, it can mean that they've completely gutted the building—or just applied a coat of fresh paint or hung a new picture on the wall. Always ask what specific changes were made during a renovation, and be sure to ask if a hotel will be undergoing construction while you're there. You should also find out how near your room will be to the center of the nightlife crowd; trying to sleep directly on Ocean Drive or Collins and Washington avenues, especially during the weekend, is next to impossible, unless your lullaby of choice happens to include throbbing salsa and bass beats.

While South Beach may be the nucleus of all things hyped and hip, it's not the only place with hotels. The advantage to staying on South Beach as opposed to, say, Coral Gables or Coconut Grove is that the beaches are within walking distance, the nightlife and restaurant options are aplenty, and, basically, everything you need is right there. However, staying there is definitely not for everyone. If you're wary, don't worry: South Beach is centrally located and only about a 15- to 30-minute drive from most other parts of Miami.

For a somewhat less expensive stay that's only a 10-minute cab ride from South Beach, Miami Beach proper (the area north of 23rd St. and Collins Ave. all the way up to 163rd St. and Collins Ave.) offers a slew of reasonable stays, right on the beach, that won't cost you your kids' college education funds.

What *will* cost you a small fortune are the luxury hotels in the city's financial Brickell Avenue district, the area of choice for expense-account

PRICE CATEGORIES

Very Expensive	$400 and up	Moderate	$150–$250
Expensive	$250–$400	Inexpensive	Under $150

business travelers and camera-shy celebrities trying to avoid the South Beach spotlight.

For a less frenetic, more relaxed, and more tropical experience, the ritzy resort on Key Biscayne exudes an island feel, even though just across the water is the spectacular Miami skyline.

Those who'd rather bag the beach in favor of shopping bags will enjoy North Miami Beach's proximity to the Aventura Mall. For Miami with an Old World European flair, Coral Gables and its charming hotels and exquisite restaurants provide a more prim and proper, well-heeled perspective of Miami than the trendy boutique and condo hotels on South Beach.

best HOTEL BETS

o **Best Splurge:** For the most decadent splurges in the city, the brand-new **St. Regis Bal Harbour** (p. 198) and its butler service will make you feel like a real VIP. Same goes for **The Setai** (p. 184), where you can rub elbows with the likes of Beyoncé and Jay-Z.

o **Best Value:** Affordable and hip, **The Catalina Hotel & Beach Club** (p. 191) is a retro fab stay with stylish rooms, Swedish Tempur-Pedic mattresses, a hot bar, and VIP hookups at all the clubs in South Beach. It's hard to find a hotel on South Beach with both good value and excellent service, but the **Chesterfield Hotel, Suites & Day Spa** (p. 192) is one of Miami's best bargains as well as coolest hotels.

o **Best for Families:** On South Beach, the **Loews** (p. 181) is known for its Loews Loves Kids program of activities for kids and kids at heart including Dive-in Movies at the pool, salsa lessons, and bingo.

o **Most Romantic:** The Moorish-style **Biltmore** (p. 207) and its stunning and sprawling swimming pool is the quintessence of Old World romance. On the completely other end of the spectrum is the **Miami River Inn** (p. 207), which is romantic in a rustic way, transporting you back to a time when things were simpler, yet no less scenic. On South Beach, the **Raleigh** (p. 183) is a romantic Art Deco darling with lush, tropical outdoor areas.

o **Best Service:** In addition to the obvious choices—**Four Seasons** (p. 203), **Mandarin Oriental** (p. 204), and **St. Regis Bal Harbour** (p. 198)—excellent service can be found at less frou frou stays such as **The Angler's Resort** (p. 176), where staff is uncharacteristically friendly, and **Lords South Beach** (p. 175), the area's first gay-owned, mostly gay hotel, where service is friendly and accommodating without being too doting and annoying.

o **Best Celebrity-Saturated Hotel:** Although it's hardly the first in the chain of hip, trendy hotels, the **W South Beach** (p. 186) is considered the brand's signature showpiece, and for good reason. All rooms in this visually arresting, Bali-meets–Miami Beach resort boast ocean views and all the trappings of modern hipster society. The hotel's bar and restaurant scene are among the city's hottest, thanks to a celebrity clientele who flock to Mr Chow and Wall nightclub.

○ **Best Art Deco Hotel:** The **Raleigh Hotel** (p. 183) is the reigning diva of Deco, dating back to 1940. It features one of the most photographed palm-lined swimming pools, reminiscent of the days of Esther Williams.

○ **Best Spa Hotel: The Standard Spa, Miami Beach** (p. 190) is a wholly holistic experience located right on Biscayne Bay. In addition to dolphin sightings, there are Turkish hammams, an outdoor yoga lounge, and even a mud lounge, where getting dirty was never so cleansing.

○ **Best Beach Hotel:** Miami's **Ritz-Carlton South Beach** (p. 183) is a lot more than just a drop in the sand thanks to its DiLido Beach Club, providing stellar food, drink, entertainment, and beach toys whenever and wherever you feel like it. Coming in at a close second is its Key Biscayne sibling, the **Ritz-Carlton Key Biscayne, Miami** (p. 202).

○ **Best Hotel for Foodies: The Fontainebleau Miami Beach** (p. 200) has not one, but three star-chef-helmed restaurants: Scott Conant's **Scarpetta,** Alfred Portale's **Gotham Steak,** and Alan Yau's **Hakkasan,** the first Michelin-starred haute Chineserie outside of the U.K.

SOUTH BEACH

On South Beach, it's all about atmosphere. The hotel rooms are generally overpriced, but you're paying for the South Beach vibe. Though rooms of some hotels may *look* ultrachic, they are as comfortable as sleeping on a concrete slab. Once you decide how much atmosphere you want, the choice will be easier. Fortunately, for every chichi hotel in South Beach—and there are many—there are just as many moderately priced, more casual options.

If status is important to you, as it is to many South Beach visitors, then you will be quite pleased with the number of haute hotels in the area. But the times may be a-changin': **Courtyard by Marriott** (📞 **800/321-2211** or 305/604-8887) maintains a 90-room, moderately priced hotel on a seedy stretch of Washington Avenue, smack in the middle of Clubland, a horror to many a South Beach trend seeker. In 2011, the very jet-setty chain known as the **Room Mate Hotel** opened at the formerly old and dingy Waldorf Towers, 860 Ocean Dr. (www.room-matehotels.com; 📞 **786/439-1600**). The Spanish-brand chain features 44 mod rooms with wooden floors at affordable rates—or, as they prefer to call it, "sexy prices and plans"—starting at around $155 in high season. In other words, it's an upscale hostel for young travelers.

For the gay traveler, the 53-room **Lords South Beach,** 1120 Collins Ave. (www.lordssouthbeach.com; 📞 **877/4484754**), has taken over the defunct Hotel Nash with a sleek, stylish, and playful vibe featuring requisite bar, restaurant, and a massive fiberglass polar bear holding a beach ball to greet guests in the lobby.

Meanwhile, as a result of the economic downturn, two very popular South Beach hotels faced foreclosure in late 2009 and early 2010. Amid financial disaster, the swanky **Sagamore** (p. 184) was about to team up with the Playboy Club. That deal fell through and in 2011 the hotel also seemed to be bouncing back slowly. The Gansevoort Miami Beach had accumulated construction debt and looked on the brink of foreclosure—and was rescued in February 2010 by the capable Coral

Management (Casa Ybel in Sanibel Island and Sandpearl in Clearwater Beach, among others), but in 2012, the hotel dropped the Gansevoort and became **The Perry** (p. 182), a move that the owners hope is for the best, especially after major, much needed renovations.

The hotel scene could be even better if Sir Richard Branson has his way and brings Virgin Hotels and some of its $500 million to South Beach. Word is the company is looking for 150- to 400-room "urban properties" to transform into four-star hotels and appealing to the "creative class of high-income, well-educated metropolitan travelers." Along similar lines: the **SLS South Beach,** 1701 Collins Ave., a $65-million Philippe Starck–designed, 142-room boutique hotel from billionaire hotelier Sam Nazarian. Expected in late 2012, the hotel will feature a branch of L.A. hot spot **Katsuya** and world-class eatery by star-chef José Andrés. Over at the historic Royal Palm, 1545 Collins Ave., a hotel that never seems to make it, the Chicago and NYC-based James Hotel has taken over that space and plans a $42.6-million renovation of the 70-some-odd-year-old hotel. Hopefully the **James Royal Palm** will stay for a while. Renovations are expected to be completed by early 2013. Thompson Hotels took over the former Hotel Victor at 1144 Ocean Dr., are renovating the property, and rebranding it as **Thompson Ocean Drive** (www.thompsonhotels.com); completion is slated for late 2012.

Note: Art Deco hotels, while pleasing to the eye, may be a bit run-down inside. It's par for the course on South Beach, where appearances are, at times, deceiving.

Very Expensive

The Angler's Resort ★ Veiled by lush landscaping, this Mediterranean revival is a welcome escape from the neighboring chaos and bright lights of busy Washington Avenue. This luxury boutique is a mere 2-block walk from the Atlantic Ocean, and only minutes away from the airport. Designed by Wallace Tutt, whose previous work includes the Versace Mansion, the property is a unique collection of four very different buildings—two completely restored and two new buildings—offering a variety of accommodations from suites and duplexes to triplex villas. Rooms in each category are large and feature the typical luxury comforts of Wi-Fi, flatscreen TVs, and iPod. Not so typical: One remote control works on all of these features—even the internal and external lights. Most rooms offer a terrace or balcony, and some even come equipped with Jacuzzis. The restaurant, **660 at the Angler's,** offers fantastic contemporary American fare. There's an outdoor pool, but if you prefer the beach, stop by the front desk to pick up a beach bag for the day, complete with towels, water, sunscreen, toys, and novels (upon request).

Greater Miami Hotels

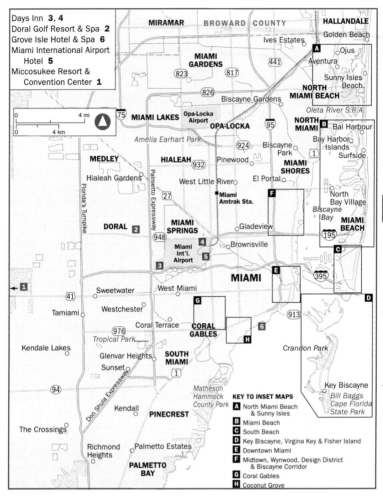

Days Inn **3, 4**
Doral Golf Resort & Spa **2**
Grove Isle Hotel & Spa **6**
Miami International Airport
   Hotel **5**
Miccosukee Resort &
   Convention Center **1**

KEY TO INSET MAPS
A North Miami Beach
   & Sunny Isles
B Miami Beach
C South Beach
D Key Biscayne, Virgina Key & Fisher Island
E Downtown Miami
F Midtown, Wynwood, Design District
   & Biscayne Corridor
G Coral Gables
H Coconut Grove

660 Washington Ave., South Beach, FL 33139. www.theanglersresort.com. ✆ **305/534-9600.** Fax 305/532-3099. 45 fully furnished units, including suites and villas. Winter $329–$495 studio suites; $469–$699 duplex suites; off season $230–$245 studio suites; $255–$699 duplex suites. AE, DISC, MC, V. Valet parking $29 per night. Pets accepted. **Amenities:** Restaurant; poolside dining cabanas; beach concession; 24-hr. concierge; pool; room service; indoor and poolside spa services; private rooftop terraces and gardens. *In room:* A/C, TV/DVD, hair dryer, minibar, MP3 docking station, Wi-Fi.

Bentley Hotel ★   The biggest coup the Bentley Hotel pulls off is its ability to remain immune to the throngs of pedestrians on the well-traveled Ocean Drive. A private front entrance leads, via elevator, to the main lobby. Inside this enclave of Old

World luxury you will find a charming ambience and an overly accommodating, professional staff. The hotel's 40 suites are both hotel rooms and condos; some of them can be rented year-round. Rooms come complete with marble floors, well-stocked kitchens, and roomy bathrooms. Try not to get a corner room, though, or you will learn more about your neighbors than you'd ever want to. A rooftop pool and beach club across the street are two excellent amenities. Because it is located on South Beach's bustling strip of neon and nightlife, the Bentley, despite its efforts to stand apart from the rest of its neighbors, isn't impervious to noise. However, if you want luxe in the midst of all the action, the Bentley is a great choice.

510 Ocean Dr., South Beach, FL 33139. www.thebentleyhotel.com. © **800/236-8510** or 305/538-1700. Fax 305/532-4865. 40 units. Winter $195–$625 double; off season $145–$265 double. AE, DC, DISC, MC, V. **Amenities:** Concierge; rooftop pool; room service. *In room:* A/C, TV/DVD, hair dryer, high-speed Internet, kitchen, minibar.

The Betsy Hotel ★   The Betsy is the lone surviving example of Florida Georgian architecture on the famous byway, Ocean Drive. Behind its plantation-style shutters and columned facade, the Betsy Hotel offers a tropical colonial beachside haven. Each room and suite in the oceanfront hotel is a nod to the stately colonial rooms of yesteryear blended with the modern aesthetic of South Beach. The Betsy boasts the South Florida installment of New York's **BLT Steak** (p. 88) restaurant by A-list chef Laurent Tourondel; a roof-deck solarium with Zen garden for sunning, spa services, drinks, and light fare; a well-heeled lobby bar scene; and a private basement lounge that bills itself as the anti-celebrity bar, where guests enter by invitation only and reality stars are strictly prohibited, as well they should be. While the beach is a few steps away, the hotel also offers a serene outdoor pool scene.

1440 Ocean Dr., Miami Beach, FL 33139. www.thebetsyhotel.com. © **866/531-8950** or 305/531-3934. Fax 305/531-9009. 63 units. Winter $409–$879 double, $979–$4,000 suite; off season $309–$779 double, $879–$3,500 suite. AE, DC, DISC, MC, V. Valet parking $30. **Amenities:** Restaurant; bar; babysitting; concierge; outdoor pool; room service; roof-deck solarium w/spa services. *In room:* A/C, TV/DVD, CD player, hair dryer, MP3 docking station, Wi-Fi.

Casa Tua   This outrageous boutique offers custom-tailored amenities (from toiletries to snacks) for each of its guests, who fill out a detailed profile when booking one of Casa Tua's five suites. Styled like a glorious Mediterranean beach house, Casa Tua also has a posh restaurant with an Italian-accented menu and a second-floor lounge for afternoon tea and evening cocktails. The hotel's management is very cagey as far as hotel details are concerned, expressing a deep concern for "keeping its clientele extremely exclusive." Enough said, I suppose. Rather than fork over the money to stay here—there's no pool anyway—I do suggest that you absolutely splurge at Casa Tua, the restaurant (p. 89), which happens to be one of South Beach's most exquisite.

1700 James Ave., Miami Beach, FL 33139. www.casatualifestyle.com. © **305/673-1010.** 5 suites. Winter $750–$1,050; off-season $400–$600. Rates include daily breakfast. **Amenities:** Restaurant; bar. *In room:* A/C, TV/DVD, hair dryer; minibar; MP3 docking station; free Wi-Fi.

Delano ★   This was South Beach's original see-and-be-seen hotel. The stunning pool area, Rose Bar, Agua Spa, Lenny Kravitz–designed speak-easy FDR, and Bianca restaurant are still studded with the boldface and the beautiful. But today, the Delano, a place where smiles from staffers were once as rare as snow in Miami, is somewhat kinder and gentler. The hotel is still pleasantly amusing to look at—with 40-foot sheer white billowing curtains hanging outside, mirrors everywhere, Adirondack

South Beach Hotels

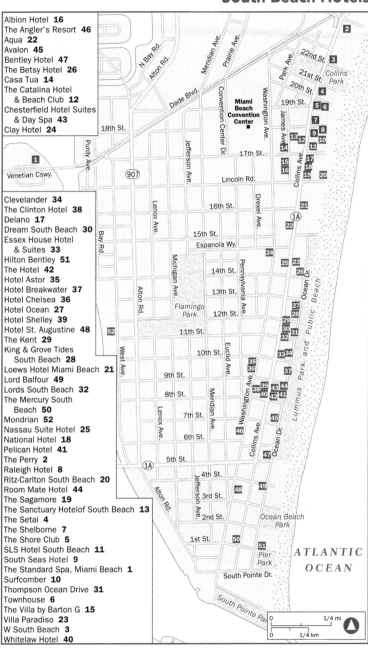

Albion Hotel **16**
The Angler's Resort **46**
Aqua **22**
Avalon **45**
Bentley Hotel **47**
The Betsy Hotel **26**
Casa Tua **14**
The Catalina Hotel
   & Beach Club **12**
Chesterfield Hotel Suites
   & Day Spa **43**
Clay Hotel **24**

Clevelander **34**
The Clinton Hotel **38**
Delano **17**
Dream South Beach **30**
Essex House Hotel
   & Suites **33**
Hilton Bentley **51**
The Hotel **42**
Hotel Astor **35**
Hotel Breakwater **37**
Hotel Chelsea **36**
Hotel Ocean **27**
Hotel Shelley **39**
Hotel St. Augustine **48**
The Kent **29**
King & Grove Tides
   South Beach **28**
Loews Hotel Miami Beach **21**
Lord Balfour **49**
Lords South Beach **32**
The Mercury South
   Beach **50**
Mondrian **52**
Nassau Suite Hotel **25**
National Hotel **18**
Pelican Hotel **41**
The Perry **2**
Raleigh Hotel **8**
Ritz-Carlton South Beach **20**
Room Mate Hotel **44**
The Sagamore **19**
The Sanctuary Hotel of South Beach **13**
The Setai **4**
The Shelborne **7**
The Shore Club **5**
SLS Hotel South Beach **11**
South Seas Hotel **9**
The Standard Spa, Miami Beach **1**
Surfcomber **10**
Thompson Ocean Drive **31**
Townhouse **6**
The Villa by Barton G **15**
Villa Paradiso **23**
W South Beach **3**
Whitelaw Hotel **40**

Miami
Beach
Convention
Center ■

**ATLANTIC
OCEAN**

chairs, and faux fur–covered beds. But if you're not eating or sleeping here, you may have a hard time getting in for a peek. New management from Vegas wants to keep it exclusive for better or for worse. Rooms that were once done up sanitarium style, sterile yet terribly trendy, received a revamp that boasts a splash of color and reworked bathrooms that went from spartan to spacious.

1685 Collins Ave., South Beach, FL 33139. www.delano-hotel.com. ℂ **800/555-5001** or 305/672-2000. Fax 305/532-0099. 194 units, including 1 penthouse. Winter from $495 city view, $1,250 suite, $2,200 bungalow, $4,000 penthouse; off season from $345 city view, $950 suite, $1,000 bungalow, $3,100 penthouse. Extra person $50. AE, DC, DISC, MC, V. Valet parking $37. **Amenities:** 3 restaurants; 3 bars; children's program (seasonal); concierge; state-of-the-art gym; large outdoor pool; room service; Agua spa. *In room:* A/C, TV/DVD, CD player, hair dryer, minibar, MP3 docking station, Wi-Fi.

Fisher Island Club ★★★ 🛅 Located on an exclusive island just off Miami Beach, this hotel is a luxurious fusion of *Fantasy Island, Lifestyles of the Rich and Famous,* and *Survivor.* Just minutes from South Beach, it feels worlds away. The only way to get there is by private ferry, which shuttles guests to and from the mainland every 15 to 20 minutes. It can be a hassle, but it does run on a very regular schedule. The ferry lets residents on first, so if there's no room after all the Bentleys roll on, you'll have to wait for the next one. Don't worry if you are carless—golf carts are the island's preferred mode of transportation. Rooms vary in size and shape, and cottages come with hot tubs. There's also a world-class spa, restaurants, tennis, golf, and pretty much everything to entertain the island's offbeat millionaires and billionaires—you know, the kind who tug their Gucci-clad pooches around in their Rolls-Royce golf carts.

1 Fisher Island Dr., Fisher Island, FL 33190. www.fisherislandclub.com. ℂ **800/537-3708** or 305/535-6020. Fax 305/535-6003. 60 units. Winter $405–$495 double, $890–$2,040 suite or cottage; off season $325–$395 double, $450–$1,630 suite or cottage. Golf, tennis, and spa packages available seasonally. 20% gratuity added to all food and beverages. AE, DC, MC, V. **Amenities:** 3 restaurants; 3 bars; airport transportation; babysitting; concierge; golf course; 2 marinas; limited room service; world-class spa; 18 tennis courts. *In room:* A/C, TV/DVD, hair dryer, minibar.

Hilton Bentley ★ Reality-TV junkies may recognize the Hilton Bentley as the place where two of the ubiquitous Kardashian sisters stayed during their show *Kourtney and Khloe Take Miami.* Hotel fans will recognize the place as haute Hilton, sitting directly on the ocean in the swank South of Fifth neighborhood and featuring 100 suites, ranging from studios to one- and two-bedroom quasi-apartments with full kitchens, spacious marble bathrooms, and private balconies. Although there's a pool, a private beach club provides guests with prime sunning opportunities. Although it's located directly across from one of the busiest restaurants in town (Prime One Twelve, whose sister Prime Italian resides here) and also features Cuban seafood hot spot D. Rodriguez Cuba on Ocean, the hotel maintains a sense of quiet and serenity that's paramount in these parts.

101 Ocean Dr., Miami Beach, FL 33139. www.bentleymiamisouthbeach.hilton.com. ℂ **800/236-8510** or 305/938-4600. Fax 305/938-4601. 100 units. Winter $399–$3,500 double; off-season $229–$2,500 double. AE, DC, DISC, MC, V. **Amenities:** Private beach club; concierge; exercise facilities; pool; spa. *In room:* A/C, TV/DVD, fax, hair dryer, Wi-Fi.

Hotel Breakwater ★ Reopened in 2011 after a much needed renovation, this crown jewel of Ocean Drive features sleek rooms, lounges, and concierge services offering what management likes to call the "100% Wish Guarantee." Standard rooms,

parlor; babysitting; children's programs; concierge; health club; Jacuzzi; sprawling outdoor pool; room service; sauna; spa; watersports equipment/rentals. *In room:* A/C, TV, hair dryer, high-speed Internet access, minibar.

Mondrian ★★   The Mondrian is painfully trendy, but it's also refreshingly different. For one, it's located on the western, residential bay side of South Beach, where its neighbors (and its former incarnation) are high-rise condos. Panoramic views of the bay and skyline are stunning. Rooms have been done up with the usual chic trappings and are comfy enough. World-famous design star and *Elle Decor*'s 2006 International Designer of the Year, Marcel Wanders, envisioned the property as Sleeping Beauty's castle, with whimsical adult-playground-style environs. The hotel's so-called "Modern Resort" concept features an **agua spa** (of Delano fame) and Jeffrey Chodorow's **Asia de Cuba** restaurant. And while the indoor spaces are swell, it's the outdoor pool area that really must be seen, especially at sundown. Don't miss the lobby's futuristic, ridiculous vending machine from which, if you slide your credit card in, you can actually buy yourself a Bentley. Shop at your own risk.

1100 West Ave., Miami Beach, FL 33139. www.mondrian-miami.com. ⓒ **800/606-6090** or 305/514-1500. Fax 305/514-1800. 335 units. Winter $350 studio, $950 deluxe 2-bedroom suite; off season $195 studio, $795 deluxe 2-bedroom suite. AE, DC, DISC, MC, V. Valet parking $37. **Amenities:** Restaurant; 3 bars; babysitting; concierge; fitness center; pool; room service; agua spa; watersports equipment/rentals. *In room:* A/C, TV, high-speed Internet access, kitchenette.

National Hotel ★   Sceney it's not, but scenic? Absolutely. With its towering ceilings, sultry furnishings, and massive gilded mirrors, the elegant 1940s-style National is a Deco darling. At 11 stories, the main building offers grand views of the ocean. Guest rooms and suites were designed as a tranquil and elegant refuge from bustling South Beach. Rooms are divided into two distinctive buildings: the **Historic Tower** and the **Cabana Wing,** which feature their own balconies overlooking the spectacular Infinity Pool. While all the rooms in the main hotel are comfortable and plush, the best rooms are the 32 ultramodern poolside cabana rooms. The hotel's historic Deco lobby and bar known for amazing cocktails is a rarity in a town where all vestiges of the good old days have given way to sterile minimalism. The pool, however, is the hotel's crown jewel. It's Miami's longest pool (205 ft.) and almost too sleek (rivaling even the Delano's pool) for splashing.

1677 Collins Ave., South Beach, FL 33139. www.nationalhotel.com. ⓒ **800/327-8370** or 305/532-2311. Fax 305/534-1426. 152 units. Winter $380–$480 double; off season $270–$350 double. AE, DC, DISC, MC, V. Valet parking $25. **Amenities:** Restaurant; 2 bars; concierge; exercise room; large outdoor pool; room service; watersports equipment/rentals. *In room:* A/C, TV/DVD, hair dryer, high-speed Internet, minibar, stereo.

The Perry   Formerly known as the Gansevoort, this hotel is trying hard to remain hipster central, despite being in the throes of a major identity crisis. In 2010, it faced foreclosure and auction, fired much of its staff, and ended up in the capable management hands of Coral Hospitality, which has seemingly returned the hotel to a sense of stability. The hotel is currently undergoing a $100-million renovation, slated to be completed sometime in 2014. Guest rooms are decorated in hot pink, magenta, and yellow tones, set against charcoal-gray suede walls, and most rooms have balconies overlooking the ocean. The 26,000-square-foot rooftop playground (complete with a 110-ft. elevated swimming pool, bar, and lounge) offers divine views of the ocean, the bay, and downtown. On the main level is a 40,000-square-foot oceanfront pool plaza with an infinity-edge pool and cabanas. There's also a David Barton Gym and Spa,

available with city or ocean views, each feature a foyer, king-size bed, sitting area, flatscreen TV, and bathrooms with rejuvenating rainforest showers. Private penthouses for high rollers boast spectacular ocean views, living rooms, and secluded terraces, with select Penthouse terraces featuring their own private plunge pools. A rooftop lounge offers day beds, love seats, and unobstructed panoramic views of the Atlantic Ocean. At night, the candlelit deck, accented with soft lighting and music, slowly transforms into an adults-only tropical oasis. Two floors below is the Wellness Garden, where you can relax in cabanas, unwind with poolside massages, and wade in the floating lap pool. The hotel's guest-only beach zone is located directly across Ocean Drive, offering lounge service along with a variety of watersports activities.

940 Ocean Dr., Miami Beach, FL 33139. www.breakwatersouthbeach.com. ☏ **305/532-2362.** Fax 305/672-7665. 100 units. Winter $409–$879 double, $979–$4,000 suite; off season $309–$779 double, $879–$3,500 suite. AE, DC, DISC, MC, V. Valet parking $33. **Amenities:** Restaurants; bar; concierge; outdoor pool; room service; roof deck. *In room:* A/C, TV/DVD, CD player, hair dryer, minibar, MP3 docking station, Wi-Fi.

King & Grove Tides South Beach ★★★
This 10-story Art Deco masterpiece reminiscent of a gleaming ocean liner with porthole windows received a massive makeover and complete transformation that redesigned the hotel's public spaces and guest rooms. The stylish luxury suites all offer expansive ocean views and are spacious, ranging from oceanfront studio suites of 550 square feet to the 2,600 square foot Tides Suite. The penthouses on the 9th and 10th floors are situated at the highest point on Ocean Drive, allowing for a priceless panoramic view of the ocean, the skyline, and the beach. The restaurant and bar at King & Grove Tides has a well-deserved reputation as "South Beach's Living Room," featuring a resplendent outdoor terrace and Deco-chic Coral Bar. A full selection of spa services is available in rooms and poolside. The hotel also has "Personal Assistants" to greet you upon check in and assist you throughout your stay. Welcome to South Beach.

1220 Ocean Dr., South Beach, FL 33139. www.kingandgrove.com. ☏ **800/439-4095** or 305/604-5070. Fax 305/503-3275. 44 units. Winter $595 studio suites, $1,500–$5,000 penthouse suites; off season $395 studio suites, $1,000–$4,000 penthouse suites. Extra person $100. AE, DC, DISC, MC, V. Valet parking $35. Pets $150 1-time fee including new "Paws" program. **Amenities:** Restaurant; lounge and bar; concierge; fitness room; outdoor heated pool; room service. *In room:* A/C, TV/DVD, CD player, hair dryer, minibar, Wi-Fi.

Loews Miami Beach Hotel ★ ☺
The Loews is one of the largest hotels on South Beach, consuming an unprecedented 900 feet of oceanfront. This 790-room behemoth is considered an eyesore by many, an architectural triumph by others. In 2010, the resort completed a $50-million renovation, which whisked the resort from stale to stellar, introducing a new retail area, a wall-size aquarium, an old-fashioned ice-cream parlor, boutique, water features along the hotel's driveway, and updated public spaces and guest rooms. Rooms are still a bit boxy and bland, but they are clean and have new carpets and bedspreads. If you can steer your way past all the conventioneers in the lobby, you can escape to the equally massive pool (with an undisputedly gorgeous, landscaped entrance). The hotel hosts fun activities for both kids (the Loews Loves Kids program), and adults (Dive-in Movies at the pool, salsa lessons, and bingo). *Tip:* Rooms facing away from Collins Avenue are much quieter.

1601 Collins Ave., South Beach, FL 33139. www.loewshotels.com. ☏ **800/23-LOEWS** (235-6397) or 305/604-1601. 790 units. Winter from $499 double; off season from $289 double. AE, DC, DISC, MC, V. Valet parking $30. Pets accepted. **Amenities:** 5 restaurants; 2 bars; coffee bar; ice-cream

trendy meatery **STK,** VIP bar and lounge by the Opium Group, and a shark tank with 27 types of fish and sharks that spans 50 feet of the lobby.

2377 Collins Ave., South Beach, FL 33139. www.perrysouthbeachhotel.com.© **305/604-1000.** Fax 305/604-6886. 340 units. $250–$595 deluxe double or king; $685–$1,000 suite. AE, DC, DISC, MC, V. Valet parking $15 per night. **Amenities:** 2 restaurants; bar and lounge; beachfront lounge; concierge; fitness center; infinity-edge rooftop pool; room service; spa. *In room:* A/C, TV/DVD, CD player, hair dryer, minibar, MP3 docking station, Wi-Fi.

Raleigh Hotel ★★   The Raleigh is quintessential old-school Miami Beach with a modern twist. Polished wood, original terrazzo floors, and an intimate martini bar add to the fabulous atmosphere that's favored by fashion photographers. One look at the hotel's fleur-de-lis pool and you'll expect Esther Williams to splash up in a dramatic, aquatic plié. The entire outdoor area is a stunning oasis that elicits oohs and aahs from even the most jaded jet-setters. The cozy bar off the lobby is reminiscent of a place where Dorothy Parker and her Algonquin Round Tablers would have gathered for spirited musings. Rooms, which underwent a makeover in 2012, feature period furnishings and terrazzo floors; rooms overlooking the pool and ocean are the most peaceful. The massive penthouse is a favorite among visiting celebrities and authors. In 2012, Miami's top chef Michael Schwartz took over the food and beverage operations at the hotel—meaning the food is reason alone to come here.

Desi Was Here

During the Raleigh Hotel's opening-night white-tie ball in 1940, a sick band member was replaced by a then-unknown local drummer. You may have heard of him: Desi Arnaz.

1775 Collins Ave., Miami Beach, FL 33139. www.raleighhotel.com.© **800/848-1775** or 305/534-6300. Fax 305/538-8140. 104 units. Winter $500–$800 double, $925–$2,175 suite; off season $345–$720 double, $750–$2,000 suite. AE, DC, DISC, MC, V. Valet parking $35. **Amenities:** Restaurant; bar; coffee bar; concierge; pool; room service. *In room:* A/C, TV/DVD, hair dryer, minibar, MP3 docking station, Wi-Fi.

Ritz-Carlton South Beach ★★ ☺   Far from ostentatious, the Ritz-Carlton South Beach moves away from gilded opulence in favor of the more soothing pastel-washed touches of Deco. Though South Beach is better known for its trendy boutique hotels, the Ritz-Carlton provides comfort to those who might prefer 100% cotton Frette sheets and goose-down pillows to high-style minimalism. The best rooms, by far, are the 72 poolside and oceanview lanai rooms. There's also a trade-marked "Tanning Butler" who will spritz you with SPF and water whenever you want. There's impeccable service, an elevated pool with unobstructed views of the Atlantic and live entertainment on weekends, an impressive stretch of sand with a fabulous beach club, and a world-class 16,000-square-foot spa and wellness center. Parents love the Ritz Kids program for kids ages 5 through 12; and for gourmands, there's the Ritz's amazing Sunday champagne brunch.

1 Lincoln Rd., South Beach, FL 33139. www.ritzcarlton.com.© **800/241-3333** or 786/276-4000. Fax 786/276-4001. 375 units. Winter $479 standard, $769 junior suite; off season $269 standard, $489 junior suite. AE, DISC, MC, V. Valet parking $36 (overnight), $24 (daily). **Amenities:** 2 restaurants; 2 bars; babysitting; children's program; fitness center; outdoor heated pool; room service; spa; extensive watersports equipment/rentals. *In room:* A/C, TV, hair dryer, high-speed Internet access, minibar.

The Sagamore ★★ Just two doors down from the Delano hotel is the Sagamore, fabulous in its own right, with an ultramodern lobby-cum–art gallery–cum-restaurant that's infinitely warmer than your typical pop-art exhibit at the Museum of Modern Art. The hotel doesn't take itself too seriously and boasts a tongue-in-cheek sense of humor that was evidenced when it hosted a Lox and Botox party—no, we're not kidding. Although the lobby and its requisite restaurant, bar, and lounge areas have become command central for the international chic elite and celebrities, the Sagamore's all-suite, apartment-like rooms are havens from the hype, with all the cushy comforts of home and then some. The sprawling outdoor lawn, dotted with cabanas with plasma TVs screening everything from Japanese anime to digital art, pool, and beachfront, makes you realize you're not in Kansas anymore. A branch of Miami's coiffeur to the stars, **Rik Rak,** opened in one of the outdoor bungalows.

1671 Collins Ave., South Beach, FL 33139. www.sagamorehotel.com. © **877/SAGAMORE** (724-2667) or 305/535-8088. Fax 305/535-8185. 93 units. Winter $395–$4,500 suite; off season $195–$1,500 suite. AE, DC, DISC, MC, V. Valet parking $37. **Amenities:** Restaurant; bar; pool bar; concierge; fitness center; pool; room service; spa. *In room:* A/C, TV/VCR/DVD, hair dryer, kitchenette, minibar, MP3 docking station, Wi-Fi.

The Sanctuary Hotel of South Beach ★ Set a bit off the beaten path is this modern, all-suite resident hotel (meaning people can actually rent or buy rooms and live here) that takes luxury very seriously, even if it does resemble a souped-up motel, with its ground-floor rooms only accessible from a communal outdoor courtyard area. Flying into town? Let the Sanctuary's Range Rover pick you up at the airport. Soothingly modern, all rooms have full state-of-the-art Italian kitchens, flatscreen TVs, and Wi-Fi. In addition, bathrooms come with Jacuzzi tubs, and in-room fridges are stocked with everything you specify before checking into the hotel. A roof-deck "bedroom" allows you to relax in the sun or slink around in the wading pool. Star chef Douglas Rodriguez's **Ola,** a fashionable Latin eatery and hot spot, is situated smack in the middle of the very posh, albeit tiny, lobby.

1745 James Ave., South Beach, FL 33139. www.sanctuarysobe.com. © **305/673-5455.** Fax 305/673-3113. 30 units. Winter $375–$1,500 suite; off-season $215–$1,050 suite. AE, DC, DISC, MC, V. Valet parking $18. **Amenities:** Restaurant; bar; pool bar; concierge; fitness center; rooftop pool; room service; spa. *In room:* A/C, TV/VCR/DVD, CD player, hair dryer, kitchen, minibar, Wi-Fi.

The Setai ★★★ Asian-inspired Setai is truly for that 1% of society who can afford it—but if you want to splurge, this is where to do it. All of the suites—some are actually condos participating in the condo-hotel program—are gorgeous apartments with floor-to-ceiling windows, full kitchens, and Jacuzzi bathtubs bigger than a small swimming pool. There are 85 regular hotel rooms that are an average of 600 square feet. All are adorned in sleek Asian decor with over-the-top comforts, including illy coffee makers, Asprey Purple Water luxe bathroom amenities, and washer/dryers in the tower units. The courtyard area with plush seating and reflective pool is lovely, but not as cool as the pool area with its **Pool & Beach Bar.** There's also **The Grill,** which features European-inspired small plates with French and Spanish accents, and **The Restaurant,** its proper name, featuring far-out Far East–meets-West cuisine, with stainless-steel tandoori ovens—out of this world, really, but with these steep prices and small portions, you may as well buy a ticket to Asia.

2001 Collins Ave., South Beach, FL 33139. www.setai.com. © **305/520-6000.** Fax 305/520-6600. 130 units. Winter $775 studio suite, $30,000 penthouse; off season $575 studio suite, $30,000 penthouse. AE, DC, DISC, MC, V. Valet parking $40. **Amenities:** 4 restaurants; 2 bars; concierge;

fitness center; 3 pools; room service; spa. *In room:* A/C, TV/DVD, hair dryer, kitchen (1-, 2-, and 3-bedroom suites only), minibar, Wi-Fi.

The Shelborne ★   This 1940s Art Deco darling finally caught up to speed with the 21st century after a 2-year, $20-million renovation that added the requisite sheen, shine, and sleekness needed to compete with its neighbors. The young and fabulous come here for its James Bond–inspired steakhouse, **Vesper American Brasserie;** a top-notch poolside taco spot and watering hole, **Lucy's Cantina Royale;** a sushi bar featuring the rolling skills of Chef Hiroyuki "Zama" Tanaka, **Bar Tanaka;** and lobby lounge. Rooms have either city or ocean views and feature clean, modern decor with marble bathrooms and flatscreen HD TVs. For higher rollers, there's a 2,500-square-foot penthouse with its own bar and sweeping views of the Atlantic. For those traveling en masse, townhouses feature washers and dryers. Pool and beach areas offer tricked-out cabanas with private bathrooms and showers.

1801 Collins Ave., South Beach, FL 33139. www.shelborne.com. © **305/531-1271.** Fax 305/531-2206. 200 units. Winter $199–$499 double; off season $169–$399 double. AE, DC, DISC, MC, V. Valet parking $35. **Amenities:** 3 restaurants; 3 bars; pool bar; concierge; fitness center; pool; room service; spa. *In room:* A/C, TV/VCR/DVD, hair dryer, kitchenette in some units, minibar, Wi-Fi.

Shore Club ★   In the fickle world of hot hotels, the Shore Club struggles to hold on to its place at the top, but does okay thanks to Florida's only **Nobu** sushi restaurant and, on certain nights, a celebrity clientele that would fill up an entire issue of *Us Weekly*. During high seasons and Spring Break, it's party central here. An outpost of L.A.'s celebrity-laden SkyBar is still stellar even if its clientele may not be, with a Marrakech-meets-Miami motif that stretches throughout the hotel's sprawling pool, patio, and garden areas. Another draw is the recently added **Terrazza,** Shore Club's new signature restaurant, featuring indoor/outdoor dining spaces with views of the iconic pool and known for authentic Italian cooking with an edge. The rooms—most of which have an ocean view—are loaded with state-of-the-art amenities and, frankly, have a bit more personality than those at Delano.

1901 Collins Ave., Miami Beach, FL 33139. www.shoreclub.com. © **877/640-9500** or 305/695-3100. Fax 305/695-3299. 309 units, including 8 bungalows. From $285 superior, $490 suite, $1,500 bungalow. AE, DC, MC, V. Valet parking $42. **Amenities:** 2 restaurants; bar; concierge; 2 outdoor swimming pools; room service; spa. *In room:* A/C, TV, CD player, high-speed Internet access, minibar, MP3 docking station.

SLS Hotel South Beach   Debuting in late 2012, the SLS Hotel South Beach, rebuilt on the site of the former Ritz Plaza hotel, marks star designer Philippe Starck's long-awaited return to South Beach (he arrived in the early '90s with the Delano and has been AWOL ever since). The 140 guestrooms are softly lit and feature plush pillow-top beds, whimsical furniture, and wall-covering designs a la Starck. Restaurants will be stellar, from **The Bazaar,** the world-renowned restaurant from culinary icon and James Beard award-winning chef José Andres, to traditional Japanese cuisine at L.A.-import **Katsuya.** The pool area, Hyde Beach, will feature "artful mixology" and a first: José Andrés's first-ever "food truck," a stationary kitchen to service the pool area with food.

1701 Collins Ave., Miami Beach, FL 33139. www.sbe.com/southbeach. © **305/674-1701.** 140 units. From $300 double. **Amenities:** 2 restaurants; bars; nightclub; state-of-the-art fitness center; 2 pools; spa; *In room:* A/C, TV/DVD, CD player, hair dryer, Wi-Fi.

The Villa By Barton G.   The former Versace Mansion got a new name and a new attitude in 2010 when party planner/restaurateur/Miami's PT Barnum Barton G.

9

WHERE TO STAY IN MIAMI

South Beach

Weiss signed a 20-year lease to run the all-suite hotel, restaurant, and special-events space. Restyled as the Villa By Barton G., Weiss channels his inner Versace in the decor of the manse's 10 ornate rooms. The restaurant—Weiss's third—dishes up redefined continental cuisine on (what else?) Versace china in the late designer's dining room. A $75 tasting menu there makes it somewhat affordable for those not able to swank it up overnight. Also still intact: the manse's mosaic pool, the bottom of which has Versace's signature Medusa icon created from a thousand mosaic tiles.

1116 Ocean Dr., South Beach, FL 33139. www.thevillabybartong.com. ℂ **305/587-8003.** Fax 305/357-7960. 10 suites. From $895 suite. AE, DISC, MC, V. Valet parking $45 overnight, $25 daily. **Amenities:** Restaurant; private lounge; pool; personal butler service. *In room:* A/C, TV/DVD, hair dryer, iPad, Wi-Fi.

W South Beach ★★★ South Beach's "it" girl, the W is stunning and cool. A work of art in itself, the property features a Bali-meets–Miami Beach sensibility, with breathtaking landscape design by conceptual design garden artist Paula Hayes and exclusive artwork by rock-'n'-roll photographer Danny Clinch. W South Beach's stylish guest rooms and suites are soothing in shades of teal and white, enhanced by a fusion of white-ceramic wood tiles, soft linens, and glossy acrylic accents. All rooms have a W signature bed with plush pillow-top mattress and feather bed overlay, goosedown duvet and pillows, and 350-thread-count cotton-blend sheets. Expansive glass balconies offer unparalleled and unobstructed views of the beach and ocean. And then there are the amenities, including Florida's first-ever **Mr Chow** restaurant; a branch of NYC's fab oyster bar **The Dutch;** three "destination" bars, including the award-winning **Living Room Bar**, known for its avant garde cocktail menu; a secret garden gathering spot for cocktails; celeb-saturated **Wall** nightclub; and Bliss Spa.

2201 Collins Ave., Miami Beach, FL 33139. www.wsouthbeach.com. ℂ **305/938-3000.** Fax 305/938-3005. 312 units. Winter $459–$1,209 studio, $859–$1,289 suite; off season $389–$799 studio, $599–$1,209 suite. AE, DC, DISC, MC, V. Valet parking $35. **Amenities:** 2 restaurants; 3 bars; nightclub; state-of-the-art fitness center; 2 pools; spa; tennis and basketball courts. *In room:* A/C, TV/DVD, CD player, hair dryer, Wi-Fi.

Expensive

Albion Hotel ★ An architectural masterpiece on Lincoln Road originally designed in 1939 by internationally acclaimed architect Igor Polevitzky (of Havana's legendary Hotel Nacional fame), this sleek, modern, nautical-style hotel was once the local headquarters for Abbie Hoffman and the Students for a Democratic Society during the 1972 Democratic National Convention in Miami. Though the Albion has fallen off the hipster radar somewhat and is in desperate need of a sprucing-up of its lobby and pool areas, its location 2 blocks from the beach is key. Rooms have been fully renovated—no longer are they sterile and industrial chic, but much warmer and with color, taking a little of the edge off. While there is no restaurant in the hotel, for lighter fare, the mezzanine-level Pantry provides snacks and continental breakfast items. The Albion is a hotel for quiet, hip, intellectual types rather than those who prefer to be on parade.

1650 James Ave. (at Lincoln Rd.), Miami Beach, FL 33139. www.rubellhotels.com. ℂ **877/RUBELLS** (782-3557) or 305/913-1000. Fax 305/674-0507. 100 units. Winter $250–$395 double; off season $175–$205 double. AE, DC, DISC, MC, V. Valet parking $30. Pets accepted. **Amenities:** Bar; airport limo service; babysitting; concierge; small exercise room; large outdoor heated pool. *In room:* A/C, TV/DVD, stereo w/CD player, hair dryer, minibar, free Wi-Fi.

Hotel Dining

Although travelers don't necessarily choose a hotel by its dining options, a number of Miami's best restaurants can be found inside hotels. Some of the city's most hailed cuisine can be had at the W's **The Dutch** and **Mr Chow** (p. 93 and p. 91), the Setai's **Grill** and **Restaurant,** Delano's **Bianca** (p. 88), Mondrian's **Asia de Cuba** (p. 86) **Casa Tua's** eponymous eatery (p. 89), and Mandarin Oriental's **Azul** (p. 110), The Perry's **STK,** the Betsy Hotel's **BLT Steak,** the Sanctuary's **Ola** (p. 184), JW Marriott Marquis' **db Bistro Moderne** (p. 112), EPIC's **Area 31** (p. 110), Fairmont Turnberry's **Bourbon Steak** (p. 106), and the reigning king on the cuisine scene: **Nobu** (p. 91), a New York import at The Shore Club. See chapter 6 for reviews of these and other hotel restaurants.

Dream South Beach ★ With the economy holding up construction of this NYC import for what seemed to be years, the hotel—which has taken over two landmark Art Deco hotels, the Tudor and the Palmer House—could have changed its name to Nightmare, but instead, it chugged on and became a pleasant reality when it opened in June 2011, featuring 108 rooms, requisite rooftop pool lounge, small full-service Ayurvedic spa, **Tudor House** restaurant by Food Network celebrity chef Geoffrey Zakarian, and hipster-approved mood lighting. Decor of the hotel is definitely something out of a sound sleep: modern Moroccan meets late-'70s, Halston-inspired sleek. All rooms feature Bluetooth-enabled smart phones, MP3 docking station, 380-plus thread count Egyptian cotton linens, and, of course, Wi-Fi.

1111 Collins Ave., Miami Beach, FL 33139. www.dreamsouthbeach.com. © **888/376-7623.** Fax 305/673-4749. 108 units. Winter $279–$599 double, $70 extra for junior suite; off season $199–$299 double, $70 extra for junior suite. AE, DC, DISC, MC, V. Valet parking $35. **Amenities:** Restaurant; bar; babysitting; concierge; rooftop lounge and pool; room service; full service spa. In room: A/C, TV/DVD, CD player, hair dryer, MP3 docking station, Wi-Fi.

The Hotel ★ Kitschy fashion designer Todd Oldham whimsically restored this 1939 gem (formerly the Tiffany Hotel) as he would have restored a vintage piece of couture. He laced it with lush, cool colors, hand-cut mirrors, and glass mosaics from his studio, then added artisan detailing, while preserving the terrazzo floors and porthole windows. The small, soundproof rooms are very comfortable and incredibly stylish, though the bathrooms are a bit cramped. Nevertheless, the showers are irresistible, with fantastic rain-shower heads. There's no need to pay more for an oceanfront view here—go up to the rooftop, where the hip and funky Spire Bar and emerald-shaped pool are located, and you'll have an amazing view of the Atlantic. The hotel added an oceanfront annex, with 20 new deluxe rooms and two new 850-square-foot oceanfront terrace suites located at 800 Ocean Dr., above News Cafe. Here, Oldham-designed rooms feature warm tones of browns, grays, and orange; flatscreen TVs; glass-enclosed showers with oversize shower heads; thick windows to block out the inevitable noise; and separate rates—$225 to $415 off season, $265 to $625 in winter. The addition shares facilities with its sister property.

801 Collins Ave., South Beach, FL 33139. www.thehotelofsouthbeach.com. © **877/843-4683** or 305/531-2222. Fax 305/531-3222. 53 units. Winter $225–$545 suite; off season $195–$415 suite. AE, DC, DISC, MC, V. Valet parking $25 per day. **Amenities:** Bar; pool bar; concierge; gym; small pool; room service. In room: A/C, TV, hair dryer, MP3 docking station, free Wi-Fi.

THE best HOTEL SPAS

- **Agua Spa at the Delano,** 1685 Collins Ave., Miami Beach (℃ **305/673-2900**), is resplendently situated on the rooftop of the hotel, overlooking the Atlantic, and features stellar treatments such as the milk-and-honey massage that make it popular with celebs and laywomen alike. Lose yourself in a tub of fragrant oils, algae, or minerals for a 20-minute revitalization, or try the collagen, mud, and hydrating masks.

- **Bliss Spa at the W South Beach,** 2201 Collins Ave. (℃ **305/938-3000**), the hippest spa in town, Bliss offers rad treatments including the Ginger Rub, Hangover Herbie, Betweeny Wax, and Triple Oxygen Treatment.

- **The Ritz-Carlton Key Biscayne, Miami, Spa,** 415 Grand Bay Dr., Key Biscayne (℃ **305/648-5900**), is a sublime 20,000-square-foot West Indies–colonial style Eden in which you can treat yourself to over 60 treatments, including Shea Mango Body Buff, Seawater Therapy, Coco-Luscious Body Treatment, and Vichy Rain revitalization in which sprays of hot and cold water are said to stimulate circulation, energize the body, and bring satisfaction to your psyche.

- **The Standard,** 40 Island Ave., Miami Beach (℃ **305/673-1717**), is an updated version of an old-school, Borscht Belt–style Miami Beach spa, featuring authentic Turkish hammam, cedar sauna room, and resplendent bayfront pool.

- **Turnberry Isle Miami,** 19999 W. Country Club Dr., Aventura (℃ **305/932-6200**), offers a sprawling 25,000-square-foot spa with a massive menu of treatments, Finnish saunas, Turkish steam rooms, turbulent whirlpools, and bracing cold-plunge tubs that are sure to give you an uplifting jolt.

- **Spa Internazionale at Fisher Island,** 1 Fisher Island Dr., Fisher Island (℃ **800/537-3708**), is the city's poshest spa, known for its picturesque setting and the Guinot Paris Hydradermie facial—a 75-minute moisturizing and cleansing facial that leaves the skin silky smooth.

- **The Spa at Mandarin Oriental,** 500 Brickell Key Dr., Miami (℃ **305/913-8288**), is a luxe, tri-level spa preferred by the likes of Jennifer Aniston and Jennifer Lopez, best known for its innovative and restorative treatments inspired by the ancient traditions of Chinese, ayurvedic, European, Balinese, and Thai cultures. The 17 private treatment rooms are done up in bamboo, rice paper, glass, and natural linens, and two of the spa's split-level suites include a

Hotel Ocean ★   This Mediterranean enclave, located smack in the middle of crazy Ocean Drive, remains somehow protected from the disarray, perhaps due to the lovely French-style courtyard in which live jazz is often performed. The European-style hotel's 27 suites are great, with soundproofed windows, terraces facing the ocean, massive bathrooms with French toiletries, and original fireplaces that add to the coziness, even if you're not likely to use them. Funky and comfy furniture, wood

personal multijet tub overlooking Biscayne Bay.

○ **Canyon Ranch Hotel & Spa Miami Beach,** 6801 Collins Ave., Miami Beach (☏ **304/742-9000**), is a spa's spa. The largest in Miami with over 54 treatment rooms, Canyon Ranch's methods of pampering are among the most high tech in the biz, from traditional massages, scrubs, and treatments to ultimate health and wellness programs regulated by medical professionals.

○ **Lapis at the Fontainebleau Miami Beach,** 4441 Collins Ave., Miami Beach (☏ **304/538-2000**), may be located in the most massive hotel in the city, but once you're inside, you'll feel like you're the only one in the universe, with highlights including a mineral water-jet pool with red-seaweed extract and heated hammam benches and a light massage that, combined with a series of electrical currents, is like a nip/tuck without the nipping.

○ **ESPA at Acqualina,** 17875 Collins Ave., Miami Beach (☏ **304/918-6844**), the first of its kind in the United States, offers the latest facials, advanced massages, and ayurvedic experiences. The luxurious two-story spa overlooks the glistening Atlantic Ocean.

○ **Exhale Spa at EPIC Hotel,** 270 Biscayne Blvd. Way (☏ **305/424-5226**), has 12,000 square feet devoted to what they call "lifestyle, mind and body," with treatments such as laser eye-lifts (!), core fusion mind and body classes and, we kid you not, canine massages.

○ **Sports Club/LA at the Four Seasons,** 1435 Brickell Ave., Miami (☏ **305/358-3535**). Although this 44,000-square-foot musclehead hangout is a cardio and weight-lifting-obsessed paradise, there's also a spa consisting of 10 treatment rooms, including a couple's massage room and wet treatment room with Vichy showers.

○ **The Spa at Icon Brickell at Viceroy,** 485 Brickell Ave., Miami (☏ **305/503-4400**), Designed by the master of minimalism Philippe Starck, the spa looks like a cozy library with bookshelves, sofa, and fireplaces. But this isn't your professor's study. Also inside: hot and cold sunken marble baths. Treatment rooms feature billowing white curtains, a Starck-ian trademark. Stunning.

○ **The Spa at the Setai,** 2001 Collins Ave. (☏ **305/520-6500**), a stellar, Asian-style spa where the philosophy of relaxation is derived from an ancient Sanskrit legend, natural elixirs, eternal youth, and Asian treatments and ingredients such as green tea.

flooring, and Spanish-tile bathrooms with 20-square-foot showers are the latest additions to the hotel's rooms. Room 504 is the hotel's best kept secret, with ocean view and private balcony. The hotel's restaurant, Mia Bella Roma, is known for its superb service, rustic decor, and big plates of Italian food. There's no pool, but since the beach is directly across the street, it really shouldn't stop you from staying at this excellent spot.

1230 Ocean Dr., Miami Beach, FL 33139. www.hotelocean.com. ✆ **800/783-1725** or 305/672-2579. Fax 305/672-7665. 27 units. Winter $230–$280 double, $330–$515 suite, $750 penthouse; off season $199–$245 double, $290–$460 suite, $555 penthouse. Rates include continental breakfast. AE, DC, DISC, MC, V. Valet parking $33. Pets accepted for $15 per day. **Amenities:** Restaurant; concierge; limited room service. *In room:* A/C, TV/DVD, CD player, fridge, hair dryer, minibar, Wi-Fi.

Lord Balfour ★ 🏨

Located in the quiet but very chic South of Fifth neighborhood is this formerly run-down hotel that, after a major renovation, now features a lobby bar and lounge and updated guest rooms. Rooms feature sustainable bamboo hardwood floors; oversize windows with views of the courtyard, Ocean Drive, or the neighborhood; custom writing desks and chairs; leather lounge seating; ETRO bath products; luxurious bed linens; plush robes and towels; iPod docking stations; flatscreen TVs; and complimentary Wi-Fi. It doesn't have a pool or a restaurant, but it's located near the ocean in one of the hottest dining 'hoods in the area.

350 Ocean Dr., Miami Beach, FL 33139. www.lordbalfourmiami.com. ✆ **800/501-0401** or 305/673-0401. Fax 305/674-9634. 64 units. Winter from $299 double; off season from $199 double. AE, DC, DISC MC, V. **Amenities:** Bar. *In room:* A/C, TV, hair dryer, Wi-Fi (free).

Pelican Hotel ★★

Owned by the same creative folks behind the Diesel Jeans company, the fashionable Pelican is South Beach's only self-professed "toy-hotel," in which each of its 30 rooms and suites is decorated as outrageously as some of the area's more colorful drag queens. Each room has been designed daringly and rather wittily by Swedish interior decorator Magnus Ehrland. Countless trips to antiques markets, combined with his wild imagination, have turned room no. 309, for instance, into the "Psychedelic(ate) Girl"; room no. 201 into the "Executive Fifties" suite; and no. 209 into the "Love, Peace, and Leafforest" room. But the most popular room is the tough-to-score no. 215, or the "Best Whorehouse," which is said to have made even former Hollywood madam Heidi Fleiss red with envy. The Ocean Drive location and the hotel's cafe make the Pelican a very popular people-watching spot.

826 Ocean Dr., Miami Beach, FL 33139. www.pelicanhotel.com. ✆ **800/7-PELICAN** (773-5422) or 305/673-3373. Fax 305/673-3255. 30 units. Winter $280–$450 double, $480–$800 oceanfront suite; off season $165–$220 double, $330–$540 oceanfront suite. AE, DC, MC, V. Valet parking $22. **Amenities:** Restaurant; bar; concierge; access to area gyms; room service; Wi-Fi. *In room:* A/C, TV, CD player, fridge w/complimentary water, hair dryer.

The Standard Spa, Miami Beach ★★

The quintessential spa resort, the Standard, owned by hip hotelier André Balazs, is housed in Miami Beach's legendary Lido Spa spot, a place that was swinging back in the days when women still wore bathing caps. Today, the hotel is full of all the modern trappings of a swank spa resort, with a bayfront view and a serene location on the Venetian Causeway—walking distance to all the South Beach craziness. Remnants of the atomic age of the fabulous '50s still exist here—the lobby's white-marble walls, terrazzo floors, and stainless-steel elevators. Add to that a touch of Scandinavian retro modernism. Whitewashed guest rooms are serviced by roaming carts offering herbal teas and aromatherapy foot baths. There's a cedar sauna; a Turkish hammam; a chlorine-free plunge pool, with a 12-foot-tall waterfall and DJ-spun music piped beneath the water; clothing-optional mud baths; and a waterfront restaurant with glorious views. Anything but standard.

40 Island Ave., Miami Beach, FL 33139. www.standardhotels.com. ✆ **305/673-1717.** Fax 305/673-8181. 105 units. $189–$1,350 suite. AE, DC, DISC, MC, V. Valet parking $37. **Amenities:** 2 restaurants; bar; concierge; fitness center; pool; 24-hour room service; sauna; spa. *In room:* A/C, TV/DVD, CD player, hair dryer, minibar, WiFi.

Surfcomber Miami, South Beach ★★   Recently acquired by hip hotel chain Kimpton Hotels & Restaurants, this once-schlocky Art Deco landmark has been returned to its glory and to the 21st century with a top-to-bottom renovation that added a little bit of European boho chic into the mix. Guest rooms feature luxurious bed linens and bath products by European fashion designer, Etro. Guests will also enjoy a diverse mix of dining and lounge options, including Lantao Kitchen + Cocktails and Lantao Social Club, an ode to Southeast Asian cuisine served in a sleek atmosphere. The oceanfront pool is a fantastic place to either sun, sleep under the shade of the palm trees, or hole up in a cabana. As with all Kimptons, this one's totally pet-friendly.

1717 Collins Ave., Miami Beach, FL 33139. www.surfcomber.com. © **800/994-6103** or 305/532-7715. Fax 305/532-7280. 186 units. High-season starting rate $365, low season $229 for a king deluxe or double deluxe room. AE, DC, DISC, MC, V. Valet parking $36 per night. **Amenities:** 2 restaurants; bar; concierge; fitness center; pool; 24-hour room service; in-room spa services. *In room:* A/C, TV/DVD, CD player, hair dryer, minibar, Wi-Fi.

Moderate

Aqua ★ 🐾   It's been described as the Jetsons meets Jaws, but the Aqua isn't all Hollywood. Animated, yes, but with little emphasis on special effects and more on a friendly staff, Aqua is a good catch for those looking to stay in style without compromising their budget. Rooms are ultramodern in an IKEA sort of way—in other words, cheap chic. There are apartment-like junior suites, suites, and a really fabulous penthouse, but the standard deluxe rooms aren't too shabby either, with decent-size bathrooms and high-tech amenities. It's a favorite among Europeans and young hipsters on a budget. This '50s-style boutique motel has definitely been spruced up and its sundeck, courtyard garden, and small pool are popular hangouts for those who prefer to stay off the nearby sand. A small yet sleek lounge inside is a good place for a quick cocktail, breakfast, or snack. Welcome complimentary cocktails are offered Thursdays through Saturdays.

1530 Collins Ave., Miami Beach, FL 33139. www.aquamiami.com. © **305/538-4361.** Fax 305/673-8109. 45 units. Winter $160 double, $200–$400 suite; off season $95 double, $125–$395 suite. $7.50 nightly resort fee includes free Wi-Fi in public areas, beach towels, and continental breakfast. AE, DISC, MC, V. Valet parking $25. **Amenities:** Lounge; bar; small pool. *In room:* A/C, TV, CD player, minibar.

The Catalina Hotel & Beach Club ★★   The Catalina is something straight out of an Austin Powers movie. Groovy, indeed! The hotel took over the space next door and added 60 more rooms, a rooftop pool, and a funky sushi restaurant, Kung Fu Kitchen & Sushi. The mod-squad lobby decor gives way to rooms glazed in white with hints of bright colors featuring Tempur-Pedic Swedish mattresses, 300-thread-count Mascioni sheets, goose-down comforters and pillows, iPods, and, of course, flatscreen TVs. The three-building hotel has a happening bar and lounge scene and features a 24-hour restaurant, **Maxine's Bistro & Bar,** with a decidedly European jet-set vibe and a splashy beach club where you can get poolside manicures and pedicures. Request a room in the recently upgraded Maxine building featuring marble bathrooms and espresso wood floors. Free passes to nightclubs and free transportation to and from Miami International are among the many perks here.

1732 Collins Ave., South Beach, FL 33139. www.catalinahotel.com. © **305/674-1160.** Fax 305/672-8216. 136 units. Winter $225–$290 double; off season $125–$250 double. Rates include unlimited happy-hour cocktails daily 7–8pm, daily beach-chair passes at beach club. AE, DC, MC, V. Valet

Two Good-Value South Beach Hotels

For a taste of South Beach action without breaking the bank, check out the **South Seas Hotel,** 1751 Collins Ave. (www.southseashotel.com; ✆ **800/345-2678** or 305/538-1411), or the **Avalon,** 700 Ocean Dr. (www.avalonhotel.com; ✆ **800/933-3306** or 305/538-0133). Both offer good deals on their websites for clean, functional rooms. The South Seas common areas may be bland, but the hotel sits on a stretch of Collins between the Delano and Raleigh—a great location if you want to hang at either hotel's happening poolside bar. The Avalon is smack in the middle of Ocean Drive's *Girls Gone Wild* scene; thumping bass and wet T-shirt contests might rage around you, but the hotel maintains an aura of Art Deco calm—as does its excellent restaurant, **A Fish Called Avalon.**

—Kelly Regan

parking $35. **Amenities:** 2 restaurants; 3 bars; complimentary bike cruisers; 2 pools. *In room:* A/C, TV/VCR, CD player, hair dryer, minibar, free Wi-Fi.

Chesterfield Hotel & Suites ★   This charismatic sliver of a property has won the loyalty of fashion industrialists and romantics alike. Unfortunately, not everyone loves it. Some have complained of the constant construction, apathetic service, and run-down or complete lack of amenities. But if you're in a partying mood, this place is for you. The very central location (1 block from the ocean) and the newly added rooftop sun deck are a plus, especially because the hotel lacks a pool. Most of the rooms are immaculate and reminiscent of a loft apartment; large bathrooms with big, deep tubs are especially enticing. Rooms have been upgraded with the addition of the Lily & Leon Hotel. The Chesterfield has several different room types, but some rooms are dark and have not had upgrades; do not hesitate to ask for a room change. Note that if you're staying on Collins or Washington avenues, you're going to hear noise: South Beach isn't known for its quiet, peaceful demeanor. For R&R, try the hotel's day spa, and for good and fast sushi, try the hotel's new sushi bar, **I Love Sushi.**

841 Collins Ave., South Beach, FL 33139. www.thechesterfieldhotel.com. ✆ **305/673-3767.** Fax 305/535-9665. 90 units. Winter $175–$245 suite, $395 penthouse; off season $125–$195 suite, $335 penthouse. Extra person $20. AE, DC, MC, V. Valet parking $30. Well-behaved pets accepted. **Amenities:** Restaurant; 2 bars; concierge; reduced rates at local gym; spa. *In room:* A/C, TV, CD player, hair dryer, high-speed Internet access, minibar.

The Clinton Hotel ★   The former president has nothing to do with this chic boutique hotel, but once he gets a gander of the model types who hang here, he may want to endorse it as his own. The Clinton Hotel brings a Space Age–meets–South Beach vibe to the area, thanks to funky furniture, a somewhat sedate lobby bar, and a restaurant that has changed hands several times. Freebies including drinks every night from 7 to 8pm, Wi-Fi, shuttle to and from MIA, and nightclub passes make up for what the hotel lacks. This boutique hotel manages to stand out from the rest, thanks to its inner sanctum of serenity that includes a sleek (but tiny) pool, private sunning deck, and rooftop spa.

825 Washington Ave., South Beach, FL 33139. www.clintonsouthbeach.com. ✆ **305/938-4040.** Fax 305/538-1472. 88 units. Winter $215–$450 suite; off season $69–$189 suite. AE, DC, DISC, MC, V. Valet parking $22. **Amenities:** Restaurant; coffee and sandwich bar; bar; pool bar; concierge; fitness center and spa; pool; room service. *In room:* A/C, TV, hair dryer, minibar.

Essex House Hotel & Suites ★   The Essex House Hotel was created by Deco pioneer Henry Hohauser in 1938 and has received numerous awards for its authentic restoration. The hotel's whimsically created shiplike architecture rises from the shore with decks that are designed to take in succulent ocean breezes. The sleek Bauhaus interiors add to the distinct charm of the place. All suites feature solid-oak furnishings and have a fridge, wet bar, and Jacuzzi. Although the hotel is right on the pulse of South Beach's constant activity, the new double-glazed, sound-absorbing windows provide an acoustical barrier to the street noise. A spa pool graces the south patio and gardens. In an area where the infamous Al Capone used to play cards, there is now an intimate dining area where complimentary breakfast is served and evening cocktails can be enjoyed.

1001 Collins Ave., Miami Beach, FL 33139. www.essexhotel.com. © **800/553-7739** or 305/534-2700. Fax 305/532-3827. Year-round $99–$299. Rates include breakfast. AE, DC, DISC, MC, V. **Amenities:** Bar; concierge; outdoor pool. *In room:* A/C, TV, fridge, hair dryer, Wi-Fi.

Hotel Astor ★   This venerable Deco hotel has gone through an identity crisis over the past few years, but we think it may be over. A cool retreat from the madness of South Beach, Hotel Astor has been around the block, so to speak, but remains as one of South Beach's tried and true. Rooms are decorated in soothing tones of taupe with blonde oak and chrome accents, hardwood floors, and large marble bathrooms. Other new additions to the hotel include a spa, and Astor Cuba, a restaurant serving classic Cuban cuisine and cocktails. No pool here anymore, but it's 2 blocks from the beach.

956 Washington Ave., South Beach, FL 33139. www.hotelastor.com. © **800/270-4981** or 305/531-8081. Fax 305/531-3193. 40 units. Winter $155–$220 double, $340–$700 suite; off season $125–$170 double, $220–$500 suite. $12 daily resort fee includes beach chairs, umbrellas, newspaper. AE, DC, MC, V. Valet parking $20. **Amenities:** Restaurant; 2 bars; babysitting; 24-hr. concierge; gym; room service; spa. *In room:* A/C, TV, hair dryer, minibar, free Wi-Fi.

The Kent ★ ✦   For a funky boutique hotel in the heart of South Beach, the Kent is quite a deal. All rooms feature blond-wood floors and ultramodern steel furnishings and accessories, which surprisingly aren't cold but rather inviting and whimsical. The staff is eager to please and the clientele comes largely from the fashion industry. The decor is high on the kitsch factor, heavy on multicolored Lucite with toys and other assorted articles of whimsy, and even if you can't afford to stay in it, the very James Bond–esque Lucite Suite is a must-see. There's no pool or sundeck, but you're only 1 block from the beach here. There's also a restaurant named after a play on the city's name: Mayame, serving American fare with an excellent selection of French wines and champagnes.

1131 Collins Ave., South Beach, FL 33139. www.thekenthotel.com. © **866/826-KENT** (5368) or 305/604-5068. Fax 305/403-7592. 59 units. Winter $145–$250 double; off season $79–$250 double. Additional person $20. AE, DISC, MC, V. Valet parking $20; self-parking $6. **Amenities:** Restaurant; bar; garden. *In room:* A/C, TV/DVD, CD player, hair dryer, minifridge, MP3 docking stations, free Wi-Fi.

The Mercury South Beach ★ ♙   Another South of Fifth hot spot, the Mercury is an upscale, modern, all-suite resort that combines Mediterranean charm with trendy South Beach flair. The hotel is also attached to (but not affiliated with) a lively cantina and tequila bar which also provide the hotel's room service. A small outdoor heated pool and Jacuzzi are located in a courtyard that's shared with the restaurant (yes, diners can see you swim). Accommodations are ultrastylish, with sleek light-wood furnishings, Mascioni cotton bedding, European kitchens, and spacious bathrooms with spa tubs. If you're able to splurge, the penthouse here is hypercool, with wraparound terrace and massive living and bedroom areas and kitchen. If you're looking to stay in style without the hassle of the South Beach hustle and bustle, this is the place for you.

100 Collins Ave., Miami Beach, FL 33139. www.themercurysouthbeach.com. © **877/786-2732** or 305/398-3000. Fax 305/398-3001. 44 units. Seasonal rates $159–$239. AE, DC, MC, V. Valet parking $25. **Amenities:** Concierge; access to local fitness center (Crunch); Jacuzzi; heated pool; room service. *In room:* A/C, TV/DVD, CD player/stereo, hair dryer, kitchen, minibar, Wi-Fi.

Nassau Suite Hotel ★★ Stylish and reasonably priced, this 1937 hotel feels more like a modern apartment building with its 22 suites (studios or one-bedrooms) featuring wood floors, modern furniture, and fully equipped open kitchens. Beds are king size or queen size and rather plush, but the bed isn't the room's only place to rest: Each room also has a sitting area that's quite comfortable. Registered as a National Historic Landmark, the Nassau Suite Hotel may exist in an old building, but both rooms and lobby are fully modernized. The Nassau Suite caters to a young, hip crowd of both gay and straight guests and it's also ideal for families looking for a great location and the convenience of a small apartment. Continental breakfast is included in the rate, as are beach chairs and towels, beach toys for kids, wireless Internet, access to a business center and gym, and a private movie theater.

1414 Collins Ave., South Beach, FL 33139. www.nassausuite.com. © **866/859-4177** or 305/532-0043. Fax 305/534-3133. 22 units. Winter from $209 studio suite, from $259 1-bedroom suite; off season from $149 studio suite, from $199 1-bedroom suite. Parking $20 per day. **Amenities:** Concierge; gym; daily maid service; private movie theater. *In room:* A/C, flatscreen TV, large closets, hair dryer, high-speed Internet, fully equipped kitchen, minibar, MP3 dock.

Townhouse ★★ New York hipster Jonathan Morr felt that Miami Beach had lost touch with the bons vivants who gave the city its original cachet, so he decided to take matters into his own hands. His solution: this five-story so-called shabby-chic hotel. The charm of this hotel is in its clean and simple yet chic design with quirky details: exercise equipment that stands alone in the hallways, and a fantastic rooftop lounge that's perfect for sunning during the day and cocktail sipping at night. Comfortable, shabby-chic rooms boast L-shaped couches for extra guests (for whom you aren't charged). Though the rooms are all pretty much the same, consider the ones with the partial ocean view. The hotel also offers a rooftop lounge and beach access, with chair and umbrella rentals available. The hotel's basement features the hot sushi spot **Bond St. Lounge**.

150 20th St., South Beach, FL 33139. www.townhousehotel.com. © **877/534-3800** or 305/534-3800. Fax 305/534-3811. 69 units. Winter $195–$395 double, $395–$450 penthouse; off season $105–$215 double, $295–$390 penthouse. Rates include Parisian-style (coffee and pastry) breakfast. AE, MC, V. Valet parking $25. **Amenities:** Restaurant; bar; bike rental; workout stations; free Wi-Fi. *In room:* A/C, TV/VCR, CD player, fridge, hair dryer.

Whitelaw Hotel ★ With a slogan that reads, "Clean sheets, hot water, and stiff drinks," the Whitelaw Hotel stands apart from other boutique hotels with its fierce sense of humor. Only half a block from Ocean Drive, this hotel, like its clientele, is full of distinct personalities, pairing such disparate elements as luxurious Belgian sheets with shag carpeting to create an innovative setting. All-white rooms manage to be homey and plush, and not at all antiseptic, with white-wood floors, a much-needed improvement from the old linoleum. Bathrooms are pretty small and not that well stocked, and towels are sometimes in short supply, but those who stay here aren't really looking for luxury—they just want to party. Complimentary cocktails in the lobby every night from 7 to 8pm contribute to a very social atmosphere.

808 Collins Ave., Miami Beach, FL 33139. www.whitelawhotel.com.© **305/398-7000.** Fax 305/398-7010. 49 units. Winter $145–$225 double/king; off season $95–$145 double/king. Rates subject to change during special events. Rates include complimentary continental breakfast and free cocktails in the lobby (7–8pm daily). AE, DC, MC, V. Parking $32. **Amenities:** Lounge; free airport pickup (to and from MIA); concierge. *In room:* A/C, TV, CD player, hair dryer, free Wi-Fi.

Inexpensive

Clay Hotel ★ 🏷   A former youth hostel (they turned it over in 2011), the Clay occupies a beautiful 1920s-style Spanish Mediterranean building at the corner of historic Española Way. An eclectic smattering of Australians, Europeans, and other budget travelers makes it Miami's best clearinghouse of "insider" travel information. All deluxe single, double, and family rooms come with private bathrooms, telephones, air-conditioning, ceiling fans, refrigerators, satellite TV, and free Wi-Fi. If you love the historic Art Deco vibe that has come to symbolize South Beach, then Española Way is the spot for you, with open-air markets, live music, and entertainment as well as one-of-a-kind eateries. It truly is a gem of a location, if a bit loud at times. Reservations for private rooms are essential in season and recommended year-round.

1438 Washington Ave. (at Española Way), South Beach, FL 33139. www.clayhotel.com.© **800/379-2529** or 305/534-2988. Fax 305/673-0346. 147 units. Year-round $75–$250 double. MC, V, DISC. Valet parking $19. **Amenities:** Concierge; access to nearby health club; night-club passes. *In room:* A/C, TV, fridge, hair dryer, Wi-Fi (free).

Clevelander ★   A South Beach institution favored by the beer-swilling set, the Clevelander is best known for its neon- and glass-blocked poolside and bar used in countless photo shoots and Budweiser commercials. Its reputation as a hotel has improved, thanks to a major face-lift in the form of new lobby and guest rooms with Wi-Fi, 300-thread-count Egyptian cotton bedding, high-definition plasma TVs, blackout curtains, noise-reducing systems, and, of course, more bars and a rooftop lounge. Despite the noise-reducing systems, the makeover hasn't really changed the noise level, which on Ocean Drive can be deafening. Party animals don't mind at all. But if your idea of a party doesn't involve drinking challenges and wet T-shirt contests, visit the Clevelander for a cocktail and stay elsewhere.

1020 Ocean Dr., Miami Beach, FL 33139. www.clevelander.com. © **877/532-4006** or 305/532-4006. Fax 305/534-4707. 60 units. Winter $189–$269 double; off season $129–$209 double. AE, DC, MC, V. Valet parking $20. **Amenities:** Restaurant; 5 bars; concierge; gym; outdoor pool; rooftop decks. *In room:* A/C, TV, Wi-Fi.

Hotel Chelsea ★   This funky Art Deco property is a boutique hotel with a bit of a twist, with accents and decor based on the principles of feng shui. Soft amber lighting, bamboo floors, full-slate bathrooms, and Japanese-style furniture arranged in a way that's meant to refresh and relax you are what separate the Chelsea from just about any other so-called boutique hotel on South Beach. Chelsea also serves free

9

WHERE TO STAY IN MIAMI

South Beach

drinks at happy hour, and, in case you've had enough relaxation, free passes to South Beach's hottest nightclubs are added bonuses.

944 Washington Ave. (at 9th St.), Miami Beach, FL 33139. www.thehotelchelsea.com. ✆ **305/534-4069.** Fax 305/672-6712. 42 units. Winter $95–$225 double, $125–$245 king, $165–$300 minisuite; off season $75–$125 double, $95–$145 king, $115–$165 minisuite excluding special event and holiday time periods. Rates include cocktails 7–8pm daily. AE, DC, MC, V. Valet parking $20. **Amenities:** Bar; free shuttle to and from MIA; concierge; discounted pass to local gym. *In room:* A/C, TV, CD player, hair dryer, minibar, free Wi-Fi.

Hotel Shelley ★

The renovated Hotel Shelley has a laid-back beach atmosphere, yet cutting-edge style. The architecturally sound boutique hotel built in 1931 in the heart of the Art Deco District of Miami Beach has reinvented itself with a complete $1.5-million renovation of its 49 guest rooms. Complete with Mascioni 300-thread-count linens, goose-down pillows and comforters, LCD plasma TVs, and custom-built cabinetry, the guest rooms at the Shelley allow you to chill out after a long day at the beach or rock out before a big night of partying. The subtle purple hues in the rooms and public areas are in true Art Deco style. The bar in the lobby offers free drinks from 7 to 8pm every night and VIP passes to area nightclubs.

844 Collins Ave., Miami Beach, FL 33139. www.hotelshelley.com. ✆ **305/531-3341.** Fax 305/535-9665. 49 units. Winter $145–$225 double, $165–$245 king, $165–$300 minisuite; off season $75–$125 double, $95–$145 king, $115–$165 minisuite. Rates are subject to change for special events and holidays. Rates include cocktails in the lobby. AE, DC, MC, V. Parking $30. **Amenities:** Lounge; free airport pickup (to and from MIA); concierge; free passes to area nightclubs. *In room:* A/C, TV, CD player, hair dryer, minibar.

Hotel St. Augustine ★★ 🏠

Proving that good things do, indeed, come in small packages is this diminutive, South of Fifth boutique hotel that's part spa, part hotel, and part haven for hipsters seeking refuge from the more mainstream boutique hotel–cum-hangouts. The lobby is minute, with an equally miniature bar, and the rooms are smallish but designed like cosmopolitan lofts, with maple-wood beds and banquettes, and outstanding, spacious bathrooms with glass-enclosed spa cabinets with steam baths and European-engineered multijet spray showers. Seriously, if you're into bathrooms, this is nirvana. Dimmable lighting in the bathroom and a spa bar that offers aromatherapy oils, cooling eye masks, invigorating shower gels, body buffers, and protective sun products make it hard to leave the room.

347 Washington Ave., Miami Beach, FL 33139. www.hotelstaugustine.com. ✆ **800/310-7717** or 305/532-0570. Fax 305/532-8493. 24 units. Year-round $155–$175 double. Rates include continental breakfast. AE, DC, MC, V. Self-parking $15. **Amenities:** Bar; 24-hr. concierge; discounted use of nearby health club; video/CD library. *In room:* A/C, TV/DVD, CD player, hair dryer, minibar, Wi-Fi.

Villa Paradiso ★★ 🏠

This guesthouse is more like a cozy apartment house than a hotel. There's no elegant lobby or restaurant, but the amicable staff is happy to give you a room key and advice on what to do. The spacious apartments are simple, beachy and elegant—hardwood floors, French doors, and stylish wrought-iron furniture—and are remarkably quiet considering their location, 1 block to the beach, and a few blocks from Lincoln Road and all of South Beach's best clubs. All have full kitchens, and guests have a choice of a large studio with either one or two queen beds or a one-bedroom suite. All rooms overlook the hotel's pretty courtyard garden.

1415 Collins Ave., Miami Beach, FL 33139. www.villaparadisohotel.com. ✆ **305/532-0616.** Fax 305/673-5874. 17 units. Winter $129–$235 apt; off season $89–$159 apt. Additional person $15. AE, DC, MC, V. Parking nearby $15. *In room:* A/C, TV, complimentary coffee, complimentary local calls, equipped kitchen, free Wi-Fi.

MIAMI BEACH, NORTH BEACH, SURFSIDE, BAL HARBOUR & SUNNY ISLES

The area of Miami Beach north of South Beach encompasses North Beach, Surfside, Bal Harbour, and Sunny Isles. Unrestricted by zoning codes throughout the 1950s, 1960s, and especially 1970s, area developers went crazy, building ever bigger and more brazen structures, especially north of 41st Street, known as "Condo Canyon." Consequently, there's now a glut of medium-quality condos, with a few scattered holdouts of older hotels and motels casting shadows over the newer, swankier stays emerging on the beachfront.

The western section of the neighborhood used to be inundated with Brooklyn's elderly Jewish population during the season. Though the area still maintains a religious preference, visiting tourists from Argentina to Germany, replete with Speedos and thong bikinis, are clearly taking over.

Miami Beach, as described here, runs from 24th Street to 192nd Street, a long strip that varies slightly from end to end. Staying in the southern section, from 24th to 42nd streets, can be a good deal—it's still close to the South Beach scene, but the rates are more affordable. The North Beach area begins at 63rd Street and extends north to the city limit at 87th Terrace and west to Biscayne Bay (at Bay Dr. W.). Bal Harbour and Bay Harbor are at the center of Miami Beach and retain their exclusivity and character. The neighborhoods north and south of here, such as Surfside and Sunny Isles, have nice beaches and some shops, but are a little worn around the edges.

For maps of hotels in this section, see p. 104 and p. 107.

Very Expensive

Acqualina Resort & Spa on the Beach ★★★ ☺
Once you step inside this resort, you forget that you're in Miami and feel as if you're on the Italian Riviera. On 4½ beachfront acres, with more than 400 feet of Atlantic coastline, Acqualina is a Mediterranean-style resort towering over all the others, with its baroque fountains, impeccably appointed suites, and a branch of NYC's acclaimed **Il Mulino** restaurant. The Acqualina Spa by ESPA is one of Miami's priciest and poshest spas, and while there are three pools just steps away from the beach, the outdoor area is uninspiring. The hotel's **AcquaMarine Program** has a splashy array of marine-biology activities for kids and adults. Best of all, the chance of some teeny-bopper tabloid figure partying here is unlikely. In fact, there's really no scene here at all, which, for some, is bliss.

17875 Collins Ave., Sunny Isles Beach, FL 33160. www.acqualina.com. © **305/918-8000.** Fax 305/918-8100. 97 units. Winter $850–$1,050 double, $1,600–$3,350 suite; off season $475–$675 double, $1,025–$2,000 suite. AE, DC, DISC, MC, V. Valet parking $30. **Amenities:** 2 restaurants; bar; babysitting; concierge; 3 outdoor pools; room service; state-of-the-art spa. *In room:* A/C, TV, CD player, fax, hair dryer, minibar, Wi-Fi.

Canyon Ranch Hotel & Spa Miami Beach ★
Located on an unseemly stretch of Collins Avenue, the Miami version of the famous Tucson, Arizona, and Lenox, Massachusetts, spa and wellness hotel is located directly on the beach. If you're looking to drop in excess of, say, $345 for a Japanese bathing ritual or $500 for

an "Optimal Health" consultation with a doctor, then this place is for you. The main draw here is a 70,000-square-foot health club that includes a two-story rock-climbing wall as well as equipment for testing oxygen saturation and bone density. The hotel has a full-time medical staff of 15, including a Chinese medicine specialist/acupuncturist, nutritionist, and physical therapist. Because the place operates as a condo as well, every suite—spacious one- and two-bedrooms starting at 720 square feet—has fine furnishings, top electronics, and a designer kitchen. The oceanfront Canyon Ranch Grill features all healthy fare. In addition to 750 feet of beach, there are four pools, a reading garden overlooking the ocean, and water-therapy programs. To preserve the tranquil vibe, cellphone use is prohibited in many of the hotel's public areas.

6801 Collins Ave., Miami Beach, FL 33141. www.canyonranch.com/miamibeach. © **800/742-9000** or 305/514-7000. Fax 305/864-2744. 150 units. Winter from $605 suite; off season from $315 suite. AE, DISC, MC, V. Valet parking $35. **Amenities:** 3 restaurants; juice and smoothie bar; babysitting; fitness center; 4 outdoor pools; room service; spa. In room: A/C, TV, high-speed Internet, kitchen.

One Bal Harbour ★★★ ☺

This oceanfront resort may have no big-name affiliation, but it's still big-time luxe. The luxurious suites are resplendent, with mahogany floors, leather walls, panoramic views of the ocean, and bathrooms with 10-foot floor-to-ceiling windows and a free-standing tub overlooking the ocean. Elevators take you directly into your suite, like a luxury apartment building. A kids' program pays special attention to trendy tots with all sorts of amenities and classes, mini-manicures and pedicures, and a VIP card good for sodas and ice cream. The hotel is pet-friendly and treats pets like celebrities via their Posh Pets program. A swanky spa, butler service, spectacular pool, and 750 feet of beachfront will cost you a pretty penny, but if you're looking to be doted on hand and foot without lifting a finger, this is the place.

10295 Collins Ave., Bal Harbour, FL 33154. www.oneluxuryhotels.com. © **877/545-5410** or 305/455-5400. Fax 305/866-2419. 124 units. Winter from $700 double, off season from $375 double; year-round $9,000 penthouse suite. AE, MC, V. Valet parking $32. **Amenities:** Restaurant; bar; kids programs; concierge; outdoor pool; room service; spa. In room: A/C, TV/DVD/CD player, hair dryer, minibar, Wi-Fi.

The St. Regis Bal Harbour Resort, Miami Beach ★★★ ☺

The St. Regis Bal Harbour is the embodiment of swank. Its 243 luxe rooms all include spacious glass-enclosed balconies with floor-to-ceiling panoramic views of the ocean, marble bathrooms, and smart technology. Studios and suites have kitchenettes and all suites include dining and living areas as well as a separate bathroom. The beach club has 1,000 feet of white sand, cabanas, and beach services. After you finish playing at the beach, soak in the two amazing pools and enjoy special poolside freebies, like cocktail samples, frozen grapes, and sunscreen-spritzing services. There's also a "Spa Without Walls" where you can experience Remède Spa treatments in a private cabana or on the beach. The St. Regis Childrens' Club ensures that the little ones won't be bored. The St. Regis Athletic Club features personal training on the beach. A restaurant by star chef Jean Georges Vongerichten, J&G Grill, is yet another reason why the St. Regis is a must for those seeking a stylish and sophisticated stay.

9703 Collins Ave., Bal Harbour FL 33154. www.stregisbalharbour.com. © **305/993-3300.** Fax 305/993-3305. 243 units. Year-round $850–$1,250 deluxe ocean view, $2,000–$42,000 1- or 2-bedroom oceanfront suite. AE, DC, DISC, MC, V. Valet parking $38. **Amenities:** 3 restaurants; concierge; 2 outdoor pools; room service; state-of-the-art spa and fitness center; watersports equipment/rentals. In room: A/C, TV/VCR, CD player, fax, fridge (upon request), hair dryer, minibar.

Trump International Beach Resort ✪

Donald, Donald, Donald, what were you thinking when you opened this uninspiring 32-story, 390-room beach resort? Yes, the Trump International sits on a prime piece of beachfront property, but I've seen rooms in Holiday Inns that have more personality than these. Completely bland with no style whatsoever, the Trump International is a folly of massive proportions despite a recent renovation that added a pool and increased the beachfront, which I must say are lovely. But still. With a cavernous, blasé lobby in which you can hear a pin drop, elevators slower than you can imagine, and views of T-shirt shops and Denny's, this hotel is a travesty.

18001 Collins Ave., Sunny Isles Beach, FL 33160. www.trumpmiami.com. © **800/628-1197** or 305/692-5600. Fax 305/692-5601. 360 units. Winter $296–$445 double, $445–$1,100 suite; off season $299–$350 double, $420–$1,080 suite. AE, DC, DISC, MC, V. Valet parking $18. **Amenities:** 2 restaurants; 2 bars and lounges; air-conditioned cabanas on pool and beach; children's program (ages 4–12); concierge; 2 outdoor pools; room service; full-service spa; watersports equipment/rentals. In room: A/C, TV, CD player, hair dryer, high-speed Internet, microwave, minibar, radio, washer/dryer (suites only).

Turnberry Isle Miami ★★★ One of Miami's classiest resorts (along the lines of the Mandarin Oriental), this gorgeous 300-acre retreat has every possible facility for relaxation seekers and active guests, particularly golfers. You'll enjoy spacious rooms and suites, golf courses, restaurants, the spa and fitness center, heated pools, a tennis center, and a private beach club, plus a great kids' program. The main attractions are two Raymond Floyd championship courses, available only to members and guests of the hotel; a Laguna Pool with a water slide, lazy river, and private cabanas; and **Bourbon Steak,** a restaurant by star Chef Michael Mina. Be sure to check out the chef's garden along the pathways of the resort. The Spa & Fitness Center offers an unabridged menu of treatments. A location in the well-manicured residential and shopping area of Aventura appeals to those who want peace, quiet, and a great mall. A complimentary shuttle takes guests to and from the Beach Club and Aventura Mall.

19999 W. Country Club Dr., Aventura, FL 33180. www.turnberryislemiami.com. © **866/612-7739** or 786/279-6770. Fax 305/933-6560. 392 units. Winter $349–$899 double, $649–$5,600 suite; off season $169–$509 double, $463–$3,000 suite. AE, DC, DISC, MC, V. Valet parking $30. **Amenities:** 4 restaurants; 5 bars and lounges; concierge; 2 golf courses; 3 outdoor pools; room service; state-of-the-art spa and fitness center; 4 clay hydro tennis courts; watersports equipment/rentals. In room: A/C, TV/VCR, CD player, fax, fridge (upon request), hair dryer, minibar.

Expensive

Alexander All-Suite Luxury Hotel ★ Just a few miles from happening South Beach or ritzy Bal Harbour, the Alexander is pricey, but worth it for the size of the suites and the doting attention. Like staying at a rich grandparent's condo, suites are spacious one- and two-bedroom miniapartments with private balconies overlooking the Atlantic Ocean and Miami's Intracoastal Waterway. Each contains a living room, a fully equipped kitchen, *two* bathrooms (one with just a shower and the other with a shower/tub combo), and a balcony. The hotel itself is well decorated, with sculptures, paintings, antiques, and tapestries, most of which were garnered from the Cornelius Vanderbilt mansion. Two oceanfront pools are surrounded by lush vegetation; one of these "lagoons" is fed by a cascading waterfall. Shula's Steak House, owned by former Dolphins football coach Don Shula, is open for lunch and dinner daily.

5225 Collins Ave., Miami Beach, FL 33140. www.alexanderhotel.com. © **800/327-6121** or 305/865-6500. Fax 305/341-6553. 150 units. Winter $399 1-bedroom suite, $599 2-bedroom suite; summer $239 1-bedroom suite, $399 and up 2-bedroom suite. Packages available. AE, MC, V. Parking $25. Very small pets accepted ($250 nonrefundable deposit). **Amenities:** 3 restaurants; 2 bars;

concierge; small fitness center; Jacuzzis; 2 large outdoor pools; limited room service; sauna; spa; watersports equipment/rentals. *In room:* A/C, TV, hair dryer, kitchen, Wi-Fi.

Eden Roc Renaissance Miami Beach ★★   Just next door to the mammoth Fontainebleau, this Morris Lapidus–designed flamboyant hotel, which originally opened in 1956, has been restored to its former glamour. In 2008, the Eden Roc received a $225-million face-lift that added a new 21-story oceanfront tower and utterly transformed the look and feel of the hotel. Despite having a whopping 631 guest rooms, the Eden Roc Renaissance Miami Beach has the distinct and intimate feel of a boutique hotel. The sleek outdoor space is expansive, with four pools, water features, and gardens threaded with walkways and intimate seating areas. For even more relaxation and serenity, take a treatment in the first ever **ELLE Spa,** featuring whitewashed walls and natural elements like stone and wood. The sceney, swanky steakhouse, **1500°,** features the farm-to-table cuisine of executive chef Paula DaSilva, a *Hell's Kitchen* finalist. If we had a choice between Eden Roc Renaissance and Fontainebleau, we'd choose the Eden Roc Renaissance for its seamless service and a more relaxed, much less Las Vegasy vibe than its neighbor.

4525 Collins Ave., Miami Beach, FL 33140. www.edenrocmiami.com. © **800/327-8337** or 305/531-0000. Fax 305/674-5555. 631 units. Winter $339–$425 double, $394 suite, $750–$1,500 bungalow suites, $2,500–$3,500 penthouse; off season $199–$274 double, $239–$409 suite, $450–$750 bungalows, $1,500 penthouse. Extra person $15. Packages available. AE, DC, DISC, MC, V. Valet parking $24. Pets accepted for a fee. **Amenities:** 2 restaurants; lounge; bar; babysitting; concierge; health club; 4 outdoor pools; room service; spa; watersports equipment/rentals. *In room:* A/C, TV, hair dryer, high-speed Internet, kitchenettes (in suites and penthouse), minibar.

Fontainebleau Miami Beach ★   Big changes—$1 *billion* worth—are afoot at Miami Beach's legendary hotel. This grand, Morris Lapidus–designed monolith that once symbolized *Old* Miami decadence reemerged in 2008 as a modern Vegas-style hotel, entertainment, and dining complex featuring all the trappings of a luxury hotel. Choose from the main property or the modern, new all-suite hotel tower, where rooms are plush and posh. The 40,000-square-foot Lapis spa and a dramatic oceanfront poolscape are among the many highlights. And while it's a magnet for celebrities who like to disappear into its hugeness, the hotel also brought celebrity chefs as well—with Alfred Portale's **Gotham Steak** (p. 103), Scott Conant's Italian outpost **Scarpetta** (p. 106), and London's acclaimed Chinese restaurant **Hakkasan** (p. 104) There's also two hotter-than-hot nightclubs, LIV and Arkadia. Bottom line here: It's huge. This place is so spread out you may feel like you're in an airport terminal. Yet the bars, clubs, and restaurants are almost always packed, so if you're looking for a one-stop hot spot, this is the place to be.

4441 Collins Ave., Miami Beach, FL 33140. www.fontainebleau.com. © **800/548-8886** or 305/538-2000. Fax 305/535-3286. 1,504 units. Winter from $399 double, from $509 suite; off season from $229 double, from $299 suite. AE, DISC, MC, V. Valet parking $36. Pets accepted. **Amenities:** 12 restaurants and lounge; concierge; fitness center; 10 pools w/cabanas; room service; spa. *In room:* A/C, TV/DVD, fax, hair dryer, iMac w/high-speed Internet, kitchenette (in suites), minibar.

Moderate

Circa39 Hotel ★ 🎒   Circa 39 Hotel is located close to the SOBE action, but far enough away to actually get some sleep when you want it. This stylish yet affordable boutique hotel has 100 funky guest rooms featuring wood floors and a cool crisp look with white furnishings dotted with pale-blue pillows; a swimming pool and sundeck complete with cabanas and umbrella-shaded chaises; the Play Bar & Lounge with board games and daily happy hour; and Bistro 39, which served breakfast, lunch, and dinner 7 days a week. If you're looking to stay in a hip hotel but don't want to deal with the frenzy of South Beach, this is a great option.

3900 Collins Ave., Miami Beach, FL 33139. www.circa39.com. © **800/550-0505** or 305/538-4900. Fax 305/538-4998. 100 units. Winter $189–$299 double; off season $119–$199 double. Additional person $15. AE, MC, V. Self-parking $25 per day. Dog-friendly (under 30 lbs). **Amenities:** Bistro 39; Play Bar & Lounge; beach chairs and umbrellas; concierge; tropical courtyard; fitness room; outdoor pool. In room: A/C, TV, hair dryer, Wi-Fi.

Indian Creek Hotel ★ 🏨   Located off the beaten path, the Indian Creek Hotel is a meticulously restored 1936 building with one of the first operating elevators in Miami Beach. Because of its location, which faces the Indian Creek waterway, and its lush landscaping, this place feels like an old-fashioned Key West bed-and-breakfast. The revamped rooms are outfitted in Art Deco furnishings, such as antique writing desks, pretty tropical prints, and small but spotless bathrooms. Just 1 block from a good stretch of sand, the hotel also has a landscaped pool area in the back garden. A welcome new, hip, shabby-chic and young vibe has taken over from the formerly stuffy atmosphere, with a superb staff in lieu of all the bells and whistles of other area stays. The hotel's bar, **The Broken Shaker,** is one of Miami's best-kept secrets, featuring a boozy homage to the art of the classic—and futuristic—cocktail.

2727 Indian Creek Dr. (1 block west of Collins Ave. and the ocean), Miami Beach, FL 33140. www. indiancreekhotel.com. © **800/491-2772** or 305/531-2727. Fax 305/531-5651. 61 units. Winter $149–$199 double, $269–$289 suite; off season $69–$199 double, $179–$249 suite. Extra person $25. Group packages and summer specials available. AE, DC, DISC, MC, V. **Amenities:** Restaurant; bar; concierge; pool; limited room service. In room: A/C, TV/VCR, CD player (in suites), fridge (in suites), hair dryer, Wi-Fi.

The New Hotel ★ 🏨   If you drive too fast on Harding Avenue, you will miss this charming, funky boutique hotel located amid North Beach's ramshackle, Art Deco, motel-like apartment buildings. But don't be dismayed by its neighbors, because inside is a secret oasis of all things eco-conscious, stylish, and economically savvy, too. The tiny, 10-room New Hotel is located a block from the beach and features comfortably modern rooms with wood floors; IKEA-chic furniture; spacious, colorful bathrooms; and in-room recycling systems. Out back is a nice pool complete with a great gastropub called **Lou's Beer Garden,** which attracts local hipsters as well as visitors. Staff is extremely friendly and accommodating. If you don't mind being off the beaten path and close to the beach and can snag a room here, do so.

7337 Harding Ave., Miami Beach, FL 33140. www.thenewhotelmiami.com. © **305/704-7879.** Fax 305/647-0636. 10 units. Winter $150–$200 double; off season $99–$129 double. AE, DC, MC, V. Public parking nearby $10 a day. **Amenities:** Restaurant; poolside bar; lounge; bike rental; concierge; pool; room service; spa; free Wi-Fi. In room: A/C, TV, hair dryer, free high-speed Internet, kitchenette, minibar, MP3 docking station.

The Palms Hotel & Spa ★   Just a stone's throw away from Miami Beach's entertainment district, the Palms Hotel & Spa is ideally located on the beach on the northern, more tranquil side of South Beach. This sophisticated oceanfront resort underwent $20 million worth of enhancements, and features lush gardens landscaped with palms and other tropical plants and a large pool as its centerpiece. Luxurious accommodations were recently redone and feature fabulous spa-inspired bathrooms. Service is warm and caring. The hotel boasts the Palms Spa, a luxury-lifestyle Aveda spa offering a highly personalized experience through Aveda's holistic treatments in five multipurpose treatment rooms and one outdoor treatment cabana, as well as hair, nail, and makeup services. In its quest to provide a natural and wholesome experience for every guest, the hotel also features an excellent restaurant—**Essensia Restaurant & Lounge,** focusing on utilizing local, organic, and seasonal ingredients. The Palms was recognized by Florida's Green Lodging Program for demonstrating a commitment to protecting Florida's natural resources.

3025 Collins Ave., Miami Beach, FL 33140. www.thepalmshotel.com.✆ **800/550-0505** or 305/534-0505. Fax 305/534-0515. 251 units. Winter $239–$639 double, $799 suite; off season $179–$600 double, $659 suite. AE, DC, MC, V. Valet parking $29. **Amenities:** Restaurant; lounge; poolside bar; bike rental; concierge; fitness room; pool; 24-hour room service; spa. *In room:* A/C, plasma TV, hair dryer, minibar, MP3 docking station, Wi-Fi.

KEY BISCAYNE

Locals call it the Key, and technically, Key Biscayne, a barrier island, isn't even part of the Florida Keys. A relatively unknown area until Richard Nixon bought a home here in the '70s, Key Biscayne, at 1¼ square miles, is an affluent but hardly lively residential and recreational island known for its pricey homes, excellent beaches, and actor Andy Garcia, who makes his home here. The island is far enough from the mainland to make it feel semiprivate, yet close enough to downtown for guests to take advantage of everything Miami has to offer.

Very Expensive

Ritz-Carlton Key Biscayne, Miami ★★★ ☺ The Ritz-Carlton takes Key Biscayne to the height of luxury with 44 acres of tropical gardens, a 20,000-square-foot destination spa, and a world-class tennis center under the direction of tennis pro Cliff Drysdale. Decorated in British colonial style, the Ritz-Carlton is straight out of Bermuda, with its impressive flower-laden landscaping. The Ritz Kids programs provide children ages 5 to 12 with fantastic activities, including quality time with the resort's affectionate blue-and-gold macaw mascot. The 1,200-foot beachfront offers everything from pure relaxation to fishing, boating, or windsurfing. Spacious and luxuriously appointed rooms feature new decor that embodies the resort's island-destination feel and large balconies that overlook the ocean or lush gardens. The oceanview Italian restaurant **Cioppino** is excellent for formal dining and an exquisite all-you-can-eat Sunday champagne brunch. If you prefer casual dining, the oceanfront **Cantina Beach** serves great authentic Mexican food and even has a "tequlier"—a sommelier for tequila. The St. Tropez–inspired **Dune Oceanfront Burger Lounge** is ideal for lazy afternoons on the sand with one of their gourmet burgers and a glass of champagne, while the resort's nighttime spot **RUMBAR** evokes Old Havana with an impressive rum selection. The hotel's remote location—just a 10-minute drive from the hustle and bustle—makes it a favorite for those who want to avoid the hubbub.

455 Grand Bay Dr., Key Biscayne, FL 33149. www.ritzcarlton.com. ✆ **800/241-3333** or 305/365-4500. Fax 305/365-4501. 402 units. Winter $629 double, $909 junior suite; off season $379 double, $579 junior suite. AE, DC, DISC, MC, V. Valet parking (call for fees). **Amenities:** 4 restaurants; 3 bars; children's programs; concierge; fitness center; 2 outdoor heated pools; room service; spa; tennis center w/lessons available; watersports equipment/rentals. *In room:* A/C, TV, hair dryer, high-speed Internet, minibar.

DOWNTOWN

If you've ever read Tom Wolfe's *Bonfire of the Vanities,* you may understand what downtown Miami is all about. If not, it's this simple: Take a wrong turn and you could find yourself in some serious trouble. Desolate and dangerous at night, downtown is trying to change its image, but it's been a long, tedious process. Recently, however, part of the area has experienced a renaissance in terms of nightlife, with several popular dance clubs and bars opening in the environs of NE 11th Street, off Biscayne Boulevard. If you're the kind of person who digs an urban setting, you may enjoy downtown, but if you're looking for shiny, happy Miami, you're in the wrong place (for now). As posh, pricey lofts keep going up faster than the nation's deficit, downtown is about to experience the renaissance it has been waiting for. Keep your eye on this area, and remember that you read it here first: Downtown Miami will be the new South Beach. Eventually. Although business hotels can be expensive, quality and service are of a high standard. Look for discounts and packages on weekends, when offices are closed and rooms often go empty.

Most downtown hotels cater primarily to business travelers and cruise passengers, although with the slower-than-slow downtown renaissance in progress, a few higher-end luxury hotels opened in the area in late 2010, including a **JW Marriott Marquis,** 55 Biscayne Boulevard Way (www.jwmarriottmarquismiami.com; © **305/350-0750**), the hotel chain's hyperluxe hybrid featuring an indoor basketball court, hauter-than-thou hotel within a hotel (**Beaux Arts**), and **db Bistro Moderne,** Miami's very first culinary offering from star chef **Daniel Boulud.**

For a map of hotels in this section, see p. 113.

Very Expensive

EPIC Hotel ★★★   The Green Seal and Green Lodging–certified EPIC, a Kimpton hotel, makes guests feel as if they are residents in a posh, plush high-rise with stunning views of the Miami skyline and Biscayne Bay. The dramatic hotel lobby features 26-foot-high vaulted ceilings, a beautiful white-onyx registration desk, glass walls, and shimmering pools, not to mention the first U.S.-based **Zuma** (p. 114) restaurant, serving informal (yet überpricey) Japanese dining known as Izakaya. A new lobby lounge, Kyma, opened in 2012. The guest rooms and suites are full of open space and light, offering breathtaking views and a huge bathroom with open cutout into the bedroom area. Luxury services include an on-site hotel spa by exhale, an expansive outdoor 16th-floor pool deck with private cabanas, two infinity pools, and an excellent seafood restaurant/lounge, **Area 31** (p. 110). The hotel is extremely pet-friendly, offering pet sitting and grooming services as well as beds, bones, and bottled water for your furry friend.

270 Biscayne Blvd. Way, Miami, FL 33131. www.epichotel.com. © **305/424-5226.** Fax 305/424-5232. 411 units. Winter $399–$499 Cityview King or Cityview Double; off season $199–$399 Cityview King or Cityview Double. AE, DC, DISC, MC, V. Valet parking $36 per night. **Amenities:** 2 restaurants; lobby lounge; concierge; club-level rooms; fitness center; 2 outdoor pools; room service; full-service spa. *In room:* A/C, TV, hair dryer, MP3 docking station, Wi-Fi.

The Four Seasons ★★★ ☺   Deciding between the hyperluxe Mandarin Oriental and the equally luxe, albeit somewhat museum-like Four Seasons is almost like trying to tell the difference between Ava and Zsa Zsa Gabor. There are some obvious differences and some similarities, but they're kind of subtle. While the architecturally striking Mandarin is located on the semiprivate Brickell Key, the 70-story Four Seasons resembles an office building and is smack in the middle of the business district, making it more of a business hotel than a resort, per se. Service here is paramount. A 2011 renovation added plush window seats, vibrant colors, and inspiring artwork to the cushy rooms, most of which overlook Biscayne Bay. The best rooms are the corner suites with views facing both south and east over the water. There are three gorgeous pools spread out on more than 2 acres. Poolside amenities include fully loaded Kindles and mini–spa treatments. Guests at the hotel all have access to Sports Club/LA. **Edge, Steak & Bar** serves farm-to-table fare (check out the chef's garden by the pool) and a sophisticated bar scene.

1435 Brickell Ave., Miami, FL 33131. www.fourseasons.com/miami. © **305/358-3535.** Fax 305/358-7758. 260 units. Winter $429–$519 double; $800 suite; off season $329–$419 double, $600 suite. AE, DC, DISC, MC, V. Valet parking $34. **Amenities:** 2 restaurants; 2 bars; concierge; the Sports Club/LA fitness center; outdoor Jacuzzi; 3 outdoor pools; full-service spa. *In room:* A/C, TV, hair dryer, minibar, Wi-Fi.

JW Marriott Marquis ★ Although there are no shortages of Marriotts in the area, the newest offering from the chain dares to defy the stereotypes by merging two successful brands—the JW Marriott and the Marriott Marquis—into an all-in-one swanky downtown destination that doesn't only cater to business travelers. A unique feature is the 19th and 20th "Entertainment Floors," featuring a Jim McLean Golf School, golf simulators, putting greens, pro shop, NBA-approved full-size indoor basketball court, virtual bowling alley, and outdoor heated pool. Rooms are nice and roomy, featuring city or bay views, marble bathrooms, and, our fave, TVs embedded in bathroom mirrors. The hotel is home to star chef Daniel Boulud's **db Bistro Moderne** (p. 112). There's a hotel within a hotel here: **Hotel Beaux Arts,** a glorified concierge level located on the 39th floor, with private check-in to 44 lavishly decorated guest rooms and suites with state-of-the-art video and sound systems throughout, hardwood floors, and Italian-marble bathrooms. Marriott, is that you?

255 Biscayne Blvd. Way, Miami, FL 33131. www.jwmarriottmarquismiami.com. © **305/421-8600.** Fax 305/421-8601. 313 units. Winter $365–$500 double, from $679 suite; off season $259–$459 double, $539 suite. AE, DC, DISC, MC, V. Valet parking $32. **Amenities:** 2 restaurants; 2 bars; concierge; fitness center; outdoor Jacuzzi; heated outdoor pool; full-service spa. *In room:* A/C, TV, hair dryer, minibar, Wi-Fi.

Mandarin Oriental, Miami ★★★ Catering to business travelers, big-time celebrities (Jennifer Aniston; J-Lo; the late, great Jacko; Will Smith; and so on), and the leisure traveler who doesn't mind spending big bucks, the swank Mandarin Oriental features a waterfront location, recently renovated residential-style rooms with Asian touches (all with balconies), upscale dining, and bathrooms equipped with Aromatherapy Associates products. The waterfront view of the city is the hotel's best asset. The hotel's high-end restaurant **Azul** (p. 110) is one of Miami's best, as is the 15,000-square-foot spa, the only official five-star spa in the state, in which traditional Thai massages and ayurvedic treatments are the norm. The hotel is also home to a 20,000-foot white-sand beach club complete with beach butlers and beachside cabana treatments, which is nice, considering that the hotel is 15 minutes from the beach. For those who want to venture out, the Mandarin offers the city's only official "nightlife guide" to lead you to the hot spots. The hotel is also very pet-friendly.

500 Brickell Key Dr., Miami, FL 33131. www.mandarinoriental.com/miami. © **305/913-8383.** Fax 305/913-8300. 326 units. Year-round $435–$900 double; $1,300–$6,500 suite. AE, DC, DISC, MC, V.

Valet parking $36. Pets welcome. **Amenities:** 2 restaurants; 3 bars; concierge; nearby golf; state-of-the-art fitness center; outdoor Jacuzzi; infinity pool; full-service holistic spa; nearby tennis. *In room:* A/C, TV, hair dryer, minibar, Wi-Fi.

Expensive

Casa Moderna Miami   Located in the (mostly empty) 67-story Marquis condo building overlooking the MacArthur Causeway and close to the performing arts center and the arena, this plush, 56-room hotel has a spa, Amuse Restaurant & Lounge, the 14th-floor Sky Pool Deck, and unparalleled views of Biscayne Bay and downtown Miami. Much like a condo, there are six different room types and all feature floor-to-ceiling windows (request a room that faces Miami Beach and not I-95), plush linens, and soaking tubs with views (again, make sure you get a room with one). Formerly known as Tempo Miami, this hotel took a big leap of faith opening in this section of downtown, a haven for vehicular—not pedestrian—traffic (in fact, its former management, the swank Rock Resorts, dumped 'em in 2011).

1100 Biscayne Blvd., Miami, FL 33129. www.casamodernamiami.com. © **888/687-3859** or 786/369-0300. Fax 786/369-1052. 56 units. Winter $259–$774 double; off season $223–$574 double. AE, DC, DISC, MC, V. Valet parking $20. **Amenities:** Restaurant; bar; pool; spa. *In room:* A/C, TV/DVD, hair dryer, Wi-Fi.

Conrad Miami ★   Although you won't find ubiquitous Hilton heiresses Paris and Nicky at this business-oriented hotel (they hang out on South Beach), you will find luxury lovers who have no interest in minimalism or celebrity spottings. In this 203-room, 36-floor skyscraper located in the heart of Miami's financial district, you may feel as if you're in an office building, but once you walk over the bridge across a sparkling pool, visions of cramped cubicles and bad lighting will immediately disappear. Located on the 25th floor, the lobby is illuminated by a magnificent atrium that shares the attention with a restaurant, lounge, and private event room—it splits the difference between the 203 guest rooms and the 116 fully serviced luxury apartments. All rooms have illy Espresso machines. There's a superb gym, spa, and two tennis courts.

1395 Brickell Ave., Miami, FL 33131. www.conradmiami.com. © **305/503-6500.** Fax 305/533-7177. 203 units. Winter $279–$509 double; off season $189–$369 double. AE, DC, DISC, MC, V. Valet parking $37. **Amenities:** Restaurant; 2 bars; babysitting; concierge; fitness center; outdoor Jacuzzi; rooftop pool; full-service spa. *In room:* A/C, TV/DVD, hair dryer, high-speed Internet, minibar.

Hotel Inter-Continental Miami ★   This hotel presents a serious Catch-22: It's got a front-row view of all of Miami Beach, Biscayne Bay, the Miami River, and the Atlantic Ocean, but it is also located in downtown Miami, which still hasn't quite gotten there as a destination. If it's a view that you want, stay here; but if it's location you want, reconsider. With the decidedly threatening presence of the EPIC around the corner and the hyperluxurious Mandarin Oriental and Viceroy just over the Brickell Bridge, the Inter-Continental had no choice but to keep up with the competition. A $34-million renovation brought it up to speed with the rest, but it's still a bit old-fashioned. It boasts more marble than the Liberace Museum, but it is warmed by bold colors and a fancified Florida flavor. Rooms are a tad nicer than those in a typical chain hotel, with marble bathrooms and sit-in windowsills. Ten treatment rooms and a Vichy shower are among the amenities at the excellent mySPA.

100 Chopin Plaza, Miami, FL 33131. www.icmiamihotel.com. © **800/327-3005** or 305/577-1000. Fax 305/577-0384. 641 units. Winter $179–$389 double, off season $139–$339 double; year-round $550–$3,000 suite. Additional person $30. Weekend and other packages available. AE, DC, DISC, MC, V. Valet parking $20. **Amenities:** 3 restaurants; 2 lounges; concierge; access to nearby golf course; Olympic-size outdoor heated pool; room service; spa. *In room:* A/C, TV/DVD, CD player, hair dryer, minibar.

Hyatt Regency Miami The Hyatt Regency is located just off the Miami River in the heart of downtown Miami. It shares space with the Miami Convention Center, the James L. Knight Convention Center Theater, an exhibition hall, and a 5,000-seat auditorium and concert hall. This hotel is perfect for large groups, business travelers, or basketball fanatics in town to see the Miami Heat play at the nearby American Airlines Arena. The People Mover and Metrorail are just blocks away, and water taxis are available at the front steps. Most of the spacious, recently renovated guest rooms have great bathrooms, products, and a balcony with a view of either the city or the bay.

400 SE 2nd Ave., Miami, FL 33131. www.miami.hyatt.com. © **800/233-1234** or 305/358-1234. Fax 305/374-1728. 612 units. Winter $209–$369 double, suite $379–$409; off season $125–$159 double, $169–$269 suite. AE, DC, DISC, MC, V. Valet parking $29. **Amenities:** Restaurant; health club; outdoor pool. *In room:* A/C, TV, hair dryer, high-speed Internet.

The Viceroy ★ One of the few condo-hotel combos to open before the bust, the trendy Kelly Wearstler–designed Viceroy is located on prime real estate on Biscayne Bay between downtown Miami and trendy Brickell Avenue. The hotel itself occupies its own tower within a three-tower structure and houses a 162-room hotel in conjunction with residences. All rooms are full of the modern trappings—Wii and PlayStation gaming systems, DVD players, portable printers, 42-inch flatscreen TVs, and hair- and body-care products by Neil George. Residents and guests alike share exclusive access to the 15th-floor outdoor podium's sweeping recreation area—lounge and deck space, sun deck with cabanas, and a 310-foot infinity pool overlooking the bay. The signature restaurant **Eos** serves an updated Mediterranean menu, with a dining room overlooking the 15th-floor pool, alfresco tables, a fireplace, and waterfront views. **Café Icon** is available for quickie bites in the pool deck. Even better is **Club 50,** the upscale rooftop lounge/restaurant on the 50th floor.

485 Brickell Ave., Miami, FL 33131. www.viceroymiami.com. © **866/720-1991.** 162 units. Winter $200–$400 double; off season $150 double. AE, DC, DISC, MC, V. Valet parking $35. **Amenities:** 2 restaurants; lounge; 500-sq.-ft. state-of-the-art fitness facility; 2 outdoor pools; room service; full-service spa. *In room:* A/C, TV, hair dryer, kitchen or kitchenette, Wi-Fi.

Moderate

Hotel Urbano A boutique hotel on the southern, more residential end of Brickell Avenue, Hotel Urbano is a welcome addition to all the haughty high-rises, with just three stories and a lot of style and personality. The Urbano features contemporary decor and a gorgeous, free-form pool with poolside lounge surrounded by private cabanas with a fire pit. Rooms feature city or pool views with big walk-in showers. The seasonally displayed artwork throughout the hotel is selected by William Braemer, curator of Art Fusion Galleries in Miami's Design District, and all artwork displayed is available for purchase. Browse the latest collection while sipping on cocktails or enjoy alfresco dining featuring South Florida–inspired fare at the **Bistro Urbano Restaurant.** Although geared to business travelers, its location just feet away from Key Biscayne's Rickenbacker Causeway and Vizcaya Museum and Gardens, and close to downtown Miami and Brickell nightlife, makes this urban oasis an excellent, and surprisingly affordable, place to be.

2500 Brickell Ave., Miami, FL 33129. www.hotelurbano.com. ✆ **877/499-5265** or 305/854-2070. Fax 305/856-5055. 65 units. Winter $209–$299 double; off season $129–$169 double. AE, DC, DISC, MC, V. Valet parking $24. Pet-friendly. **Amenities:** Restaurant; bar; fitness center; pool. *In room:* A/C, TV/DVD, fridge, hair dryer, free Wi-Fi.

Miami River Inn ★★★ 👔 The Miami River Inn, listed on the National Register of Historic Places, is a quaint, country-style hideaway (Miami's *only* bed-and-breakfast), consisting of four cottages smack in the middle of developing downtown Miami. In fact, it's so hidden that most locals don't even know it exists, which only adds to its panache. Every room has hardwood floors and is uniquely furnished with antiques dating from 1908. In one room, you might find a hand-painted bathtub, a Singer sewing machine, and an armoire from the turn of the 20th century, restored to perfection. Thirty-eight rooms have private bathrooms. One- and two-bedroom apartments are available as well. In the foyer, you can peruse a library filled with books about Old Miami. It's close to public transportation, restaurants, and museums, and is only 5 minutes from the business district.

118 SW S. River Dr., Miami, FL 33130. www.miamiriverinn.com. ✆ **800/468-3589** or 305/325-0045. Fax 305/325-9227. 38 units. Winter $149–$299 double; off season $89–$149 double. Rates include continental breakfast and parking. Extra person $15. AE, DC, DISC, MC, V. Free parking. Pets accepted for $25 per night. **Amenities:** Babysitting; access to nearby gym facilities; Jacuzzi; small pool. *In room:* A/C, TV, hair dryer (upon request).

CORAL GABLES

The Gables, as it's affectionately known, was one of Miami's original planned communities and is still among the city's prettiest, most pedestrian-friendly (albeit preservation-obsessed) neighborhoods. Pristine with a European flair, Coral Gables is best known for its wide array of excellent upscale restaurants of various ethnicities, as well as a hotly contested shopping megacomplex, with upscale stores such as Nordstrom.

If you're looking for luxury, Coral Gables has a number of wonderful hotels, but if you're on a tight budget, you may be better off elsewhere. One well-priced chain in the area is the **Holiday Inn,** 1350 S. Dixie Hwy. (✆ **800/HOLIDAY** [465-4329] or 305/667-5611), with rates between $100 and $225, depending on the time of year. It's directly across the street from the University of Miami and is popular with families and friends of students.

For a map of hotels in this section, see p. 127.

Biltmore Hotel ★★★ A romantic sense of Old World glamour combined with a rich history permeates the Biltmore. Built in 1926, it's the oldest Coral Gables hotel and is a National Historic Landmark—one of only two operating hotels in Florida to receive that designation. Rising above the Spanish-style estate is a majestic 300-foot copper-clad tower, modeled after the Giralda bell tower in Seville and visible throughout the city. Large Moorish-style rooms are decorated with tasteful decor, European feather beds, Egyptian cotton duvets, writing desks, and some high-tech amenities. The landmark 23,000-square-foot winding pool area has private cabanas, an alfresco bar, and a restaurant. For aspiring chefs, there's a serious culinary academy here where you can take classes, or for those who just want to chill, a fantastic, full service spa. Always a popular destination for golfers, including former president Bill Clinton (who stays in the Al Capone suite), the Biltmore is situated on a lush, rolling, 18-hole Donald Ross course that is as challenging as it is beautiful.

1200 Anastasia Ave., Coral Gables, FL 33134. www.biltmorehotel.com. ℂ **800/727-1926** or 305/445-1926. Fax 305/442-9496. 273 units. Winter $395–$895 double, off season $229–$499 double; year-round $659–$6,500 specialty suites. Extra person $20. Special packages available. AE, DC, DISC, MC, V. Valet parking $25; self-parking free. **Amenities:** 4 restaurants; 4 bars; concierge; 18-hole golf course; state-of-the-art health club; outdoor pool; room service; sauna; full-service spa; 10 lit tennis courts. *In room:* A/C, TV, VCR (upon request), fax, hair dryer, high-speed Internet, minibar.

9

Hotel St. Michel ★   This European-style hotel, in the heart of Coral Gables, is one of the city's most romantic options. The accommodations and hospitality are straight out of Old World Europe, complete with dark-wood-paneled walls, cozy beds, beautiful antiques, and a quiet elegance that seems startlingly out of place in trendy Miami. Everything here is charming—from the brass elevator and parquet floors to the paddle fans. One-of-a-kind furnishings make each room special. Of course, the antiquity is countered with modernity in the form of flatscreen TVs in all rooms. Bathrooms are on the smaller side, but are hardly cramped. All have tub/shower combinations except for two, which have one or the other. If you're picky, request your preference. Guests are treated to fresh fruit upon arrival and enjoy seamless service throughout their stay. For a little *Italia* with your *Francais*, there's **Gaetano Ristorante,** serving, strangely, rustic Italian cuisine.

162 Alcazar Ave., Coral Gables, FL 33134. www.hotelstmichel.com. ℂ **800/848-HOTEL** (4683) or 305/444-1666. Fax 305/529-0074. 28 units. Winter $169 double, $199 suite; off season $119 double, $149 suite. Extra person $10. Rates include continental breakfast and fresh fruit daily. AE, DC, MC, V. Self-parking $9. **Amenities:** Bar; lounge; concierge; access to nearby health club; room service; free Wi-Fi in all public areas. *In room:* A/C, TV, hair dryer.

Hyatt Regency Coral Gables ★★   Depart from the ordinary to a stunning Spanish-style Miami luxury hotel set in the heart of Coral Gables. The building itself is inspired by Spain's famed 14th-century Alhambra Castle, featuring pink stone, arched entrances, grand courtyards, and tile roofs. Most recently, the courtyard and pool were beautifully renovated. Inside you'll find overstuffed chairs on marble floors surrounded by opulent antiques and chandeliers. The guest rooms are large and comfortable. Some rooms have balconies or terraces. The hotel underwent a $10-million room renovation that added a little more pizzazz to the rooms, which all feature Mediterranean-inspired decor, comfy beds, and a marble bath with great amenities. Though the hotel fails to authentically mimic something much older and much farther away, the high level of personalized service, modern amenities, and ideal location in the "Beverly Hills of Miami" make this hotel perfect for your getaway

50 Alhambra Plaza, Coral Gables, FL 33134. www.coralgables.hyatt.com. ℂ **800/233-1234** or 305/441-1234. Fax 305/441-0520. 250 units. Winter $339–$399 double, $409–$629 suite; off season $159–$199 double, $200–$250 suite. Additional person $25. Packages and senior discounts available. AE, MC, V. Valet parking $22; self-parking $16. **Amenities:** Restaurant; bar; concierge; nearby

WHERE TO STAY IN MIAMI

golf course; health club; Jacuzzi; large outdoor heated pool; room service; 2 saunas. *In room:* A/C, TV, hair dryer, high-speed and wireless Internet access, minibar.

COCONUT GROVE

This waterfront village hugs the shores of Biscayne Bay, just south of U.S. 1 and about 10 minutes from the beaches. Once a haven for hippies, head shops, and artsy bohemian characters, the Grove succumbed to the inevitable temptations of commercialism and has become a Gap nation, featuring a host of theme and chain restaurants, bars, a megaplex, and lots of stores. Outside the main shopping area, however, you'll find the beautiful remnants of Old Miami in the form of flora, fauna, and, of course, water.

For a map of hotels in this section, see p. 131.

Very Expensive

Mayfair Hotel and Spa ★★   Coconut Grove's alternative to cookie-cutter hotel brands, the Mayfair Hotel and Spa is an eclectic, Art Deco/Nouveau retreat. Complimentary Wi-Fi, terry robes, 300-thread-count sheets, and plasma TVs are in every room. Located on the rooftop is a bar and lounge, a serpentine bench built into the parapet which winds around a fire feature, and billowing white curtains surrounding eight private cabanas with L-shaped sofas, flatscreen TVs, and private safes. There's also an excellent, pizza restaurant, Spartico, and Jurlique spa, which exclusively utilizes its own line of organic products and follows a holistic approach to outer beauty and inner health.

3000 Florida Ave., Coconut Grove, FL 33133. www.mayfairhotelandspa.com. ✆ **800/433-4555** or 305/441-0000. Fax 305/447-9173. 179 units. Winter $279–$679 suite; off-season $149–$579 suite; year-round $3,000 penthouse. Packages available. AE, DC, DISC, MC, V. Valet parking $26. Pets accepted. **Amenities:** Restaurant; rooftop bar; concierge; Jacuzzi; outdoor pool; room service. *In room:* A/C, TV/DVD, CD player, hair dryer, minibar, Wi-Fi.

Mutiny Hotel ★   En route to the center of the Grove, docked along Sailboat Bay and the marina, lies this revamped hotel best known as the hangout for the *Miami Vice* set—drug kingpins, undercover cops, and other shady characters—during the mid-'80s. Now it caters to a much more legitimate clientele. Service and style are bountiful at the Mutiny, which somehow has avoided the Nouveau-hotel hype and managed to stand on its own quiet merits without becoming part of the scene. The newly converted condos were voted by the *Miami Herald* as "the second best kept secret among hotels" in South Florida (first was Kona Kai). The suites' British Colonial motif is warmed up with soft drapes, comfortable mattresses, and regal Old English furnishings. Each suite comes with a large bathroom (executive and two-bedroom suites have two bathrooms), full kitchen complete with china and complimentary coffee, and all the usual amenities associated with this class of hotel.

2951 S. Bayshore Dr., Miami, FL 33133. www.mutinyhotel.com. ✆ **888/868-8469** or 305/441-2100. Fax 305/441-2822. 120 suites. Winter $239–$799 1- and 2-bedroom suites; off season $119–$599 1- and 2-bedroom suites. AE, DC, DISC, MC, V. Valet parking $21. **Amenities:** Restaurant; babysitting; concierge; health club; small outdoor heated pool w/whirlpool; limited room service; spa. *In room:* A/C, TV/DVD, hair dryer, kitchen, Wi-Fi.

Ritz-Carlton Coconut Grove   The third and smallest of Miami's Ritz-Carlton hotels is the most intimate of its properties, surrounded by 2 acres of tropical gardens and overlooking Biscayne Bay and the Miami skyline. Decorated in the likeness of an

Italian villa, the hotel's understated luxury is a welcome addition to an area known for its gaudiness. A room renovation in 2008 saw the addition of Italian damask patterns, Carrara marble bathrooms, and dark Emperador marble-topped dressers that create the feeling of being in a luxurious, private villa. That said, this is more of a business hotel than a vacation or resort property. In addition to the usual Ritz-Carlton standard of service and comfort, the hotel has a tranquil Boutique Spa, and an excellent, cozy Italian trattoria, **Bizcaya** (with footstools for women to put their purses on—how classy!), also known for its sublime Sunday Brunch.

3300 SW 27th Ave., Coconut Grove, FL 33133. www.ritzcarlton.com.© **800/241-3333** or 305/644-4680. Fax 305/644-4681. 115 units. Winter $379 double, $479 suite; off season $209 double, $279 suite. AE, DC, DISC, MC, V. Valet parking $24. **Amenities:** Restaurant; pool grill; 2 bars; babysitting; concierge; fitness center; outdoor heated pool; room service; spa. *In room:* A/C, TV, hair dryer, high-speed Internet access, minibar.

Expensive

Grove Isle Hotel and Spa ★   Hidden away in the bougainvillea and lushness of the Grove, the Grove Isle Hotel and Spa is off the beaten path on its own lushly landscaped 20-acre island, just outside the heart of Coconut Grove. The isolated exclusivity of this resort contributes to a country-club vibe, though for the most part, the people here aren't snooty, but just value their privacy and precious relaxation time. You'll step into suites that are elegantly furnished, with canopy beds and a patio or balcony overlooking the bay. You'll need to reserve early here—rooms go very fast. The 6,000-square-foot, Indonesian-inspired Spa at Grove Isle is top-notch. Introduced in early 2010, **Gibraltar,** a haute-cuisine restaurant, serves fresh seafood and other regional specialties in a spectacular, elegant dining room, or, better yet, outside on the water.

4 Grove Isle Dr., Coconut Grove, FL 33133. www.groveisle.com.© **800/884-7683** or 305/858-8300. Fax 305/854-6702. 50 units. Winter $299–$399 double, $379–$529 suite; off season $179–$279 double, $279–$399 suite. Packages available. AE, DC, MC, V. Valet parking $17. **Amenities:** Restaurant; babysitting; concierge; large outdoor heated pool; room service; full-service spa; 12 tennis courts. *In room:* A/C, TV/VCR, CD player, hair dryer, high-speed Internet, minibar.

Moderate

Hampton Inn   This very standard chain hotel is a welcome reprieve in an area otherwise known for very pricey accommodations. The rooms are nothing exciting, but the freebies, like local phone calls, parking, in-room movies, breakfast buffet, and hot drinks around the clock, make this a real steal. Although there is no restaurant or bar, it is close to lots of both—only about half a mile to the heart of the Grove's shopping and retail area and about as far from Coral Gables. Rooms are brand new, sparkling clean, and larger than that of a typical motel. Located at the residential end of Brickell Avenue, it's a quiet, convenient location 15 minutes from South Beach and 5 minutes from Coconut Grove. If you'd rather save your money for dining and entertainment, this is a good bet.

2800 SW 28th Terrace (at U.S. 1 and SW 27th Ave.), Coconut Grove, FL 33133. www.hampton-inn.com. © **305/448-2800.** Fax 305/442-8655. 137 units. Winter $150–$209 double; off season $100–$179 double. Rates include continental breakfast buffet and local calls. AE, DC, DISC, MC, V. Free parking. **Amenities:** Exercise room; Jacuzzi; large outdoor pool. *In room:* A/C, TV, fridge and microwave (on request).

Sonesta Bayfront Hotel Coconut Grove ★   With a great location offering panoramic views of Biscayne Bay, the marina and the Miami skyline, the Sonesta is more than just a chain hotel—it's a condo, too! And because of that, it's meticulously maintained and features 205 contemporary styled guest rooms, all with flatscreens and balconies and many with ocean views. The fantastic eighth-floor pool and Sky Lounge, which received a $500,000 renovation, overlooks the water and the hustle and bustle down below in the Grove, while the restaurant, Panorama, serves delicious Peruvian cuisine. Ask about the hotel's cool packages, including swimming with the dolphins and learning how to sail.

2889 McFarlane Rd., Coconut Grove, FL 33133. www.sonesta.com/coconutgrove. ✆ **305/529-2828.** Fax 305/529-2008. 205 units. Winter $239–$399 double, $319–$659 suite; off-season: $169–$259 double, $269–$389 suite. AE, DC, DISC, MC, V. Valet parking $23. **Amenities:** Restaurant; sky bar; concierge; state-of-the-art fitness center; pool; spa; squash courts. *In room:* A/C, TV/DVD, CD player, hair dryer, Wi-Fi.

WEST MIAMI & AIRPORT AREA

As Miami continues to grow at a rapid pace, expansion has begun westward, where land is plentiful. Several resorts have taken advantage of the space to build world-class tennis and golf courses. While there's no sea to swim in, a plethora of facilities can definitely make up for the lack of an ocean view.

If you must stay near the airport, consider any of the dozens of moderately priced chain hotels. You'll find one of the cheapest and most recommendable options at either of the **Days Inn** locations at 7250 NW 11th St. and 4767 NW 36th St. (✆ **800/329-7466** for both, or 305/888-3661 or 305/261-4230, respectively), each about 2 miles from the airport. Prices include free transportation from the airport.

For a map of hotels in this section, see p. 177.

Expensive

Doral Golf Resort & Spa ★ ☺   In 2011, Donald Trump announced that he was purchasing this sprawling, 650-acre resort for $170 million with plans to put at least $150 million in much-needed upgrades into it. In the meantime, this resort remains a landmark both for the city of Miami and the game of golf. There are five championship courses here, including the **TPC Blue Monster** and the **Great White Course** (designed by Greg Norman). Learn from a pro at the **Jim McLean Golf School,** then take on his **Signature Course,** featuring what many claim as the toughest starting holes in golf. All of the rooms at the iconic Doral are spacious and feature private balconies, many overlooking a golf course or garden. The accommodations reveal plantation-style decor with accents of wicker and wood, and large marble bathrooms. After a day of golf, relax at **The Spa at Doral,** then feast on a hand-cut steak at the Latin-inspired **Mesazul Steakhouse.** Kids of all ages will enjoy the **Blue Lagoon Water Park,** featuring two 80,000-gallon pools with cascading waterfalls, a rock facade, and a 125-foot water slide. For a spa or golf vacation, the Doral is a great choice. Otherwise, consider investing your money in a hotel that's better located.

4400 NW 87th Ave., Miami, FL 33178. www.doralresort.com. ✆ **800/71-DORAL** (713-6725) or 305/592-2000. Fax 305/594-4682. 693 units. Winter rates starting at $279 double; off season $129 double. Extra person $35. Golf and spa packages available. AE, DC, DISC, MC, V. Valet parking $17. **Amenities:** 7 restaurants; babysitting; concierge; 5 golf courses, driving range and instructional school; jogging/fitness trail; health club; kid's camp; 6 pools; room service; world-class spa w/33 treatment rooms. *In room:* A/C, TV, hair dryer, high-speed Internet access.

Moderate

Miami International Airport Hotel ★   I don't know of a nicer airport hotel, and you can't beat the convenience—it's actually in the airport at Concourse E. Every amenity of a first-class tourist hotel is here. The rooms are modern, clean, and spacious, with newly renovated furnishings, mattresses, fixtures, and carpeting. You might think you'd be deafened by the roar of the planes, but all of the rooms have been soundproofed and actually allow in very little noise. In addition, the hotel has modern security systems and is extremely safe. Top of the Port Restaurant located on the seventh floor offers panoramic views of the runways and city skyline, and a sushi restaurant on terminal level is quite good.

Airport Terminal Concourse E (at the intersection of NW 20th St. and Le Jeune Rd.; P.O. Box 997510), Miami, FL 33299-7510. www.miahotel.com. ✆ **800/327-1276** or 305/871-4100. Fax 305/871-0800. 260 units. Winter $169–$219 double; off season $129–$259 double. Additional person $10. AE, DC, MC, V. Parking $15. **Amenities:** Restaurant; cocktail lounge; concierge; limited room service. *In room:* A/C, TV, hair dryer, Wi-Fi.

Miccosukee Resort & Convention Center ★   Located on the edge of the Everglades, about 30 to 40 minutes west of the airport, the Miccosukee Resort is the closest thing South Florida's got to Las Vegas, but accommodations really are just a step above a Holiday Inn. The Miccosukee tribe was originally part of the lower Creek Nation, which lived in areas now known as Alabama and Georgia. After the final Seminole War in 1858, the last of the Miccosukees settled in the Everglades. Following the lead set recently by many other Native American tribes, they built the resort to accumulate gambling revenue. Although many tourists go out to the resort solely to gamble, it also has expansive meeting and banquet facilities, spa services, great children's programs, entertainment, and excursions to the Florida Everglades. Guest rooms are standard, furnished with custom pieces made exclusively for the resort, but if you're here, you're not likely to spend that much time in your room.

500 SW 177th Ave. (at intersection with SW 8th St.), Miami, FL 33194. www.miccosukee.com. ✆ **877/242-6464** or 305/221-8623. Fax 305/925-2556. 309 units. Year-round $149 double; $189 suite. All rooms sleep up to 3 people; suites sleep 4–6 people. AE, DC, DISC, MC, V. Free parking. **Amenities:** 5 restaurants; 24-hr. deli; state-of-the-art health club and spa; indoor heated pool; room service. *In room:* A/C, TV, in-room movies, hair dryer, minibar, Wi-Fi; whirlpool and wet bar in some suites.

PRACTICAL MATTERS: THE MIAMI HOTEL SCENE

SEASONS & RATES   South Florida's tourist season is well defined, beginning in mid-November and lasting until Easter, though if you ask the city's most ardent spin doctors, the season in So Flo now lasts year-round. It all depends on where and when you're here and what's going on at the time. Hotel prices escalate until about March, after which they begin to decline. During the off season, hotel rates are typically 30% to 50% lower than their winter highs. But timing isn't everything. Rates also depend on your hotel's proximity to the beach and how much ocean you can see from your window. Small motels a block or two from the water can be up to 40% cheaper than similar properties right on the sand.

The rates listed below are broken down into two broad categories: winter (generally, Thanksgiving through Easter) and off season (about mid-May through Aug). The months in between, the shoulder season, should fall somewhere in between the highs and lows, while rates always go up on holidays. Remember, too, that state and city taxes can add as much as 12.5% to your bill in some parts of Miami. Some hotels, especially those in South Beach, also tack on additional service charges, and don't forget that parking is a pricey endeavor.

LONG-TERM STAYS   If you plan to visit Miami for a month, a season, or more, think about renting a condominium apartment or a room in a long-term hotel. Long-term accommodations exist in every price category, from budget to deluxe, and in general are extremely reasonable, especially during the off season. Check with the reservation services below, or write a short note to the chamber of commerce in the area where you plan to stay. In addition, many local real estate agents handle short-term rentals (meaning less than a year).

RESERVATION SERVICES   Central Reservation Service (www.reservation-services.com; ✆ **800/950-0232** or 305/274-6832) works with many of Miami's hotels and can often secure discounts of up to 40%. It also gives advice on specific locales, especially in Miami Beach and downtown. During holiday time, there may be a 3- to 5-day minimum stay required to use their services. Call for more information.

For bed-and-breakfast information throughout the state, contact **Florida Bed and Breakfast Inns** (www.florida-inns.com; ✆ **800/524-1880**). For information on the ubiquitous boutique hotels, check out the **Greater Miami Convention and Visitor's Bureau**'s slick website, **www.miamiboutiquehotels.com**.

THE EVERGLADES & BISCAYNE NATIONAL PARK

The vast ecosystem of Everglades National Park—and most of South Florida, really—is a shallow, 40-mile-wide, slow-moving river. Its current 1.5 million acres (less than 20% of its mass when preserved in 1947) remain one of few places to see endangered American crocodiles, leatherback turtles, and West Indian manatees. Take your time: The rustling of a bush might be a tiny, red-throated anole lizard; that splash of purple might be a mule-ear orchid.

10

Active Pursuits   Popular day hikes like the **Coastal Prairie** and **Gumbo Limbo** trails wend their way through canopies of cypress and gumbo-limbo trees and past waterways with alligators and pink-hued roseate spoonbills. Shark Valley is South Florida's most scenic bicycling trail, a flat, paved route frequented by sunbathing alligators and turtles. Canoeing through the Everglades allows serene, close-up views of this junglelike ecosystem.

Flora & Fauna   A river of saw grass marks Everglades National Park, punctuated with islands of gumbo-limbo hammocks, royal palms, and pale, delicate orchids. The **Anhinga Trail** teems with native wildlife: the swallowtail butterfly, American crocodile, leatherback turtle, West Indian manatee, and, rarely, the Florida panther.

Tours   Shallow-draft, fan-powered airboats careen through bayous, rising ever so slightly above swaying saw grass and alongside flocks of snowy egrets. The high-speed runabouts operate just outside park boundaries, including **Gator Park** and **Coopertown Airboat Tours.** At the Shark Valley entrance **Shark Valley Tram Tours** transport visitors on 2-hour, naturalist-led explorations through the heart of the Everglades. A highlight is the climb up a 65-foot observation tower for a bird's-eye view of the "river of grass."

THE best EVERGLADES & BISCAYNE NATIONAL PARK EXPERIENCES

o **Biking Shark Valley:** Anyone who's ever been on a bicycle knows all about bumps in the road. But when it comes to biking in this Everglades natural treasure, a 15-mile paved road full of sights, smells, and sounds, those bumps could very well be alligators.

o **Cooling Off with Some Cold War History, 'Glades-Style:** History buffs will love the **Nike Hercules Missile Base HM-69** (p. 221), a military base that arose out of very real Cold War fears. The base was turned back over to the park in 1979 but wasn't open to the public until 2009.

o **Canoeing Through the Everglades:** The **Noble Hammock Canoe Trail** (p. 222) is a 2-mile loop that's perfect for beginners. Hardier canoers will want to try the **Hell's Bay Canoe Trail** (p. 223), a 3- to 6-mile course, depending on how far you choose to go. It got its name for a reason: Fans of this trail like to say, "It's hell to get in and hell to get out."

o **Stuffing Your Face at the Everglades Seafood Festival:** Every February, Everglades City, the tiny town at the edge of the Ten Thousand Islands, is a seafood lover's dream come true, complete with live country music, crafts, and characters.

o **Sleeping in the Everglades:** Spending the night in the Everglades is truly an experience. Some prefer camping, but we prefer the **Ivey House B&B** (p. 227), where you'll feel at home and, best of all, like a local.

EVERGLADES NATIONAL PARK ★★

Though many people think of the Everglades as one big swamp swarming with ominous creatures, the Everglades isn't really a swamp at all, but one of the country's most fascinating natural resources.

For first-timers or those with dubious athletic skills, the best way to see the 'Glades is probably via airboats, which aren't actually allowed in the park proper, but which cut through the saw grass on the park's outskirts, taking you past the amazing flora and fauna. A walk on one of the park's many trails will provide you with a different vantage point: up-close interaction with an assortment of tame wildlife. But the absolute best way to see the 'Glades is via canoe, which allows you to get incredibly close to nature. Whichever method you choose, you will marvel at the sheer beauty of the Everglades.

This vast, unusual ecosystem is actually a 40-mile-wide, slow-moving river. Rarely more than knee-deep, the water is the lifeblood of this wilderness, and the subtle shifts in water level dictate the life cycles of the native plants and animals. In 1947, 1.5 million acres—less than 20% of the Everglades' wilderness—were established as Everglades National Park. At that time, few lawmakers understood how neighboring

The Everglades

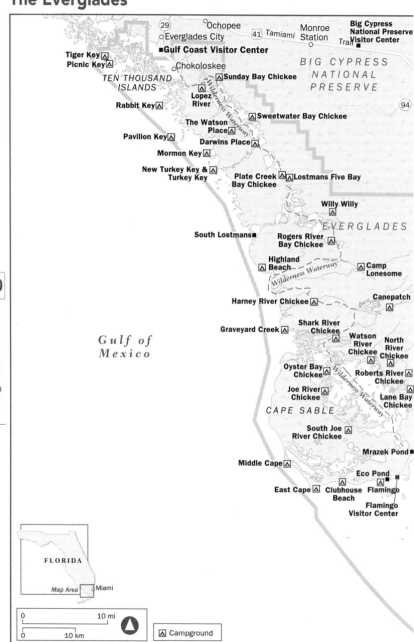

29
Ochopee
Everglades City
41 Tamiami
Monroe Station
Trail
Big Cypress National Preserve Visitor Center

Gulf Coast Visitor Center

BIG CYPRESS NATIONAL PRESERVE

Tiger Key
Picnic Key
TEN THOUSAND ISLANDS
Chokoloskee
Sunday Bay Chickee
Lopez River
Rabbit Key
94
Sweetwater Bay Chickee
The Watson Place
Pavilion Key
Darwins Place
Mormon Key
New Turkey Key & Turkey Key
Plate Creek Bay Chickee
Lostmans Five Bay
Willy Willy
EVERGLADES
South Lostmans
Rogers River Bay Chickee
Highland Beach
Wilderness Waterway
Camp Lonesome
Canepatch
Harney River Chickee
Gulf of Mexico
Graveyard Creek
Shark River Chickee
Watson River Chickee
North River Chickee
Oyster Bay Chickee
Roberts River Chickee
Joe River Chickee
Wilderness Waterway
Lane Bay Chickee
CAPE SABLE
South Joe River Chickee
Mrazek Pond
Middle Cape
Eco Pond
East Cape
Clubhouse Beach
Flamingo
Flamingo Visitor Center

FLORIDA
Map Area
Miami

0   10 mi
0   10 km

Campground

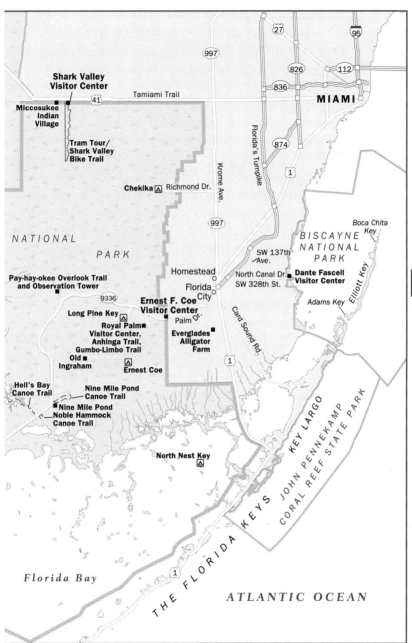

Lazy River
It takes a month for 1 gallon of water to move through Everglades National Park.

ecosystems relate to each other. Consequently, the park is heavily affected by surrounding territories and is at the butt end of every environmental insult that occurs upstream in Miami.

While there has been a marked decrease in the indigenous wildlife, Everglades National Park remains one of the few places where you can see dozens of endangered species in their natural habitat, including the swallowtail butterfly, American crocodile, leatherback turtle, Southern bald eagle, West Indian manatee, and Florida panther.

Take your time on the trails, and a hypnotic beauty begins to unfold. Follow the rustling of a bush, and you might see a small green tree frog or tiny brown anole lizard, with its bright-red spotted throat. Crane your neck to see around a bend, and discover a delicate, brightly painted mule-ear orchid.

The slow and subtle splendor of this exotic land may not be immediately appealing to kids raised on video games, but they'll certainly remember the experience and thank you later. There's enough dramatic fun around the park, such as airboat rides, hiking, and biking, to keep them satisfied for at least a day.

Beware of the multitude of mosquitoes who live in the Everglades (the bugs seem to be immune to repellent)—wear long pants and cover your arms.

Essentials

GETTING THERE & ACCESS POINTS   Although the Everglades may seem overwhelmingly large, it's easy to get to the park's two main areas: the northern section, accessible via Shark Valley and Everglades City, and the southern section, accessible through the Ernest F. Coe Visitor Center, near Homestead and Florida City.

NORTHERN ENTRANCES   A popular day trip for Miamians, **Shark Valley,** a 15-mile paved loop road (with an observation tower in the middle of the loop) overlooking the pulsating heart of the Everglades, is the easiest and most scenic way to explore the park. Just 25 miles west of the Florida Turnpike, Shark Valley is best reached via the Tamiami Trail, South Florida's preturnpike, two-lane road, which cuts across the southern part of the state along the park's northern border. Roadside attractions (boat rides and alligator farms, for example) along the Tamiami Trail are operated by the Miccosukee Indian Village and are worth a quick, fun stop. An excellent tram tour (leaving from the Shark Valley Visitor Center) goes deep into the park along a trail that's also terrific for biking. Shark Valley is about an hour's drive from Miami.

A little less than 10 miles west along the Tamiami Trail from Shark Valley, you'll discover **Big Cypress National Preserve,** in which stretches of vibrant green cypress and pine trees make for a fabulous Kodak moment. If you pick up S.R. 29 and head south from the Tamiami Trail, you'll hit a modified version of civilization in the form of Everglades City (where the Everglades meet the Gulf of Mexico), where there's another entrance to the park and the **Gulf Coast Visitor Center.** From Miami to Shark Valley, go west on I-395 to S.R. 821 South (Florida Tpk.). Take the U.S. 41/Southwest 8th Street (Tamiami Trail) exit. The Shark Valley entrance is just 25 miles west. To get to Everglades City, continue west on the Tamiami Trail and head south on S.R. 29. Everglades City is approximately a 2½-hour drive from Miami, but because it is scenic, it may take longer if you stop or slow down to view your surroundings.

SOUTHERN ENTRANCE (VIA HOMESTEAD & FLORIDA CITY) If you're in a rush to hit the 'Glades and don't care about the scenic route, this is your best bet. Just southeast of Homestead and Florida City, off S.R. 9336, the southern access to the park will bring you to the Ernest F. Coe Visitor Center. Inside the park, 4 miles beyond the Ernest F. Coe Visitor Center, is the Royal Palm Visitor Center, the starting point for the two most popular walking trails, Gumbo Limbo and Anhinga, where you'll witness a plethora of birds and wildlife roaming freely. Thirteen miles west of the Ernest F. Coe Visitor Center, you'll hit Pa-hay-okee Overlook Trail, which is worth a trek across the boardwalk to reach the observation tower, over which vultures and hawks hover protectively amid a resplendent, picturesque, bird's-eye view of the Everglades. From Miami to the southern entrance, go west on I-395 to S.R. 821 South (Florida Tpk.), which will end in Florida City. Take the first right through the center of town (you can't miss it) and follow signs to the park entrance on S.R. 9336. The Ernest F. Coe Visitor Center is about 1½ hours from Miami.

VISITOR CENTERS & INFORMATION Contact the **Everglades National Park Headquarters,** 40001 S.R. 9336, Homestead, FL 33034 (℃ **305/242-7700**), for information. Ask for a copy of *Parks and Preserves,* a free newspaper that's filled with up-to-date information about goings-on in the Everglades. Headquarters is staffed by helpful phone operators daily from 8:30am to 4:30pm. You can also try **www.nps.gov/ever**.

Note that all hours listed are for the high season, generally November through May. During the slow summer months, many offices and outfitters keep abbreviated hours. Always call ahead to confirm hours of operation.

The **Ernest F. Coe Visitor Center,** at the park headquarters entrance, west of Homestead and Florida City, is the best place to gather information. In addition to details on tours and boat rentals, and free brochures outlining trails, wildlife, and activities, you will find state-of-the-art educational displays, films, and interactive exhibits. A gift shop sells postcards, film, an impressive selection of books about the Everglades, unusual gift items, and a supply of your most important gear: insect repellent. The shop is open daily from 9am to 5pm.

The **Royal Palm Visitor Center,** a small nature museum located 3 miles past the park's main entrance, is a smaller information center. The museum is not great (its displays are equipped with recordings about the park's ecosystem), but the center is the departure point for the popular Anhinga and Gumbo Limbo trails. It's open daily from 8am to 4pm.

Knowledgeable rangers, who provide brochures and personal insight into the park's activities, also staff the **Flamingo Visitor Center,** 38 miles from the main entrance, at the park's southern access, with natural-history exhibits and information on visitor services, and the **Shark Valley Visitor Center,** at the park's northern entrance. Flamingo is open daily from 9am to 4:30pm, while Shark Valley is open daily from 9:15am to 5:15pm.

ENTRANCE FEES, PERMITS & REGULATIONS Permits and passes can be purchased only at the main park or Shark Valley entrance station. Even if you are just visiting for an afternoon, you'll need to buy a 7-day permit, which costs $10 per vehicle. Pedestrians and cyclists are charged $5 each. An **Everglades Park Pass,** valid for a year's worth of unlimited admissions, is available for $25. You may also purchase a 12-month America the Beautiful National Parks and Federal Recreation Lands Pass–Annual Pass for $80, which is valid for entrance into any U.S. national park. U.S. citizens ages 62 and older pay only $10 for the America the Beautiful National Parks and Federal Recreation Lands Pass–Senior Pass that's valid for life. An America the Beautiful National Parks and Federal Recreation Lands Pass–Access Pass is free to U.S. citizens with disabilities.

Permits are required for campers to stay overnight either in the backcountry or at the primitive campsites. See "Camping in the Everglades," on p. 226.

Those who want to fish without a charter captain must obtain a State of Florida saltwater fishing license. These are available in the park, or at any tackle shop or sporting-goods store nearby. Nonresidents pay $30 for a 7-day license or $17 for a 3-day license. Florida residents pay $17 for an annual fishing license. A snook license must be purchased separately at a cost of $10; a lobster permit is $5. For more information on fishing licenses, go to **http://myfwc.com/license**.

Charter captains carry vessel licenses that cover all paying passengers, but ask to be sure. Freshwater fishing licenses are available at various bait-and-tackle stores outside the park at the same rates as those offered inside the park. A good one nearby is **Don's Bait & Tackle,** 1108 N. Homestead Blvd. (www.donsbaitandtackle.com; ✆ **305/247-6616**). *Note:* Most of the area's freshwater fishing, limited to murky canals and artificial lakes near housing developments, is hardly worth the trouble when so much good saltwater fishing is available.

SEASONS There are two distinct seasons in the Everglades: high season and mosquito season. High season is also dry season and lasts from late November to May. Most winters here are warm, sunny, and breezy—a good combination for keeping the bugs away. This is the best time to visit because low water levels attract the largest variety of wading birds and their predators. As the dry season wanes, wildlife follows the receding water; by the end of May, the only living things you are sure to spot will make you itch. The worst, called no-see-ums, are not even swattable. If you choose to visit during the buggy season, be vigilant in applying bug spray. Also, realize that many establishments and operators either close or curtail offerings in summer, so always call ahead to check schedules.

RANGER PROGRAMS More than 50 ranger programs, free with entry, are offered each month during high season and give visitors an opportunity to gain an expert's perspective. Ranger-led walks and talks are offered year-round from the Royal Palm, Flamingo, and Gulf Coast visitor centers, as well as Shark Valley Visitor Center during winter months. Park rangers tend to be helpful, well informed, and good humored. Some programs occur regularly, such as Royal Palm Visitor Center's "Glade Glimpses," a walking tour on which rangers point out flora and fauna, and discuss issues affecting the Everglades' survival. Tours are scheduled at 1:30pm daily. The Anhinga Amble, a similar program that takes place on the Anhinga Trail, starts at 10:30am daily and lasts about 50 minutes. Because times, programs, and locations vary from month to month, check the schedule, available at any of the visitor centers.

SAFETY There are many dangers inherent in this vast wilderness area. *Always* let someone know your itinerary before you set out on an extended hike. It's mandatory that you file an itinerary when camping overnight in the backcountry (which you can do when you apply for your overnight permit at either the Flamingo Visitor Center or the Gulf Coast Visitor Center). When you're on the water, watch for weather changes; thunderstorms and high winds often develop rapidly. Swimming is not recommended because of the presence of alligators, sharks, and barracudas. Watch out for the region's four indigenous poisonous snakes: diamondback and pygmy rattle-snakes, coral snakes (identifiable by their colorful rings), and water moccasins (which swim on the surface of the water). Bring insect repellent to ward off mosquitoes and biting flies. First aid is available from park rangers. The nearest hospital is in Home-stead, 10 miles from the park's main entrance.

Seeing the Highlights

Shark Valley, a 15-mile paved road (ideal for biking) through the Everglades, pro-vides a fine introduction to the wonders of the park, but don't plan on spending more than a few hours here. Bicycling (p. 222) and taking a guided tram tour (p. 225) are fantastic ways to cover the highlights.

If you want to see a greater array of plant and animal life, make sure that you venture into the park through the main entrance, pick up a trail map, and dedicate at least a day to exploring from there.

Stop first along the Anhinga and Gumbo Limbo trails, which start right next to each other, 3 miles from the park's main entrance. These trails provide a thorough introduction to the Everglades' flora and fauna and are highly recommended to first-time visitors. Each is a half-mile round-trip. **Gumbo Limbo Trail** (my pick for best walking trail in the Everglades) meanders through a gorgeous, shaded, junglelike hammock of gumbo-limbo trees, royal palms, ferns, orchids, air plants, and a general blanket of vegetation, though it doesn't put you in close contact with much wildlife. **Anhinga Trail** is one of the most popular trails in the park because of its abundance of wildlife: There's more water and wildlife in this area than in most parts of the Everglades, especially during dry season. Alligators, lizards, turtles, river otters, her-ons, egrets, and other animals abound. Arrive early to spot the widest selection of exotic birds, such as the anhinga bird, the trail's namesake, a large black fishing bird so accustomed to humans that many of them build their nests in plain view. Take your time—at least an hour is recommended for each trail. Both are wheelchair accessible. If you treat the trails and modern boardwalk as pathways to get through quickly, rather than destinations to experience and savor, you'll miss out on the still beauty and hidden treasures that await you.

To get closer to nature, a few hours in a canoe along any of the trails allows pad-dlers the chance to sense the park's fluid motion and to become a part of the eco-sphere. Visitors who choose this option end up feeling more like explorers than observers. (See "Outdoor Activities," below.)

No matter which option you choose, I strongly recommend staying for the 7pm program, available during high season at the Long Pine Key Amphitheater. This ranger-led talk and slide show will give you a detailed overview of the park's history, natural resources, wildlife, and threats to its survival.

And while the nature tours and talks are fascinating, so are the tours of **Nike Hercules Missile Base HM-69 ★**, a product of collective thinking by President John F. Kennedy and his advisors that arose out of very real Cold War fears. The base was turned back over to the park in 1979 but wasn't open to the public until 2009. From January to March, free ranger-led tours take visitors on a 90-minute driving and walking tour of the missile assembly building, three barns where 12 missiles were stored, the guardhouse, and the underground control room. Tours depart from the Ernest Coe Visitor Center at 2pm Saturday and Sunday and at 10am and 2pm Tues-day. The tour is free but the $10 park admission still applies. Definitely call for res-ervations (☏ 305/242-7700).

Outdoor Activities

BIKING   The relatively flat, 38-mile paved **Main Park Road** is great for biking because of the multitude of hardwood hammocks (treelike islands or dense stands of hardwood trees that grow only a few inches above land) and a dwarf cypress forest (stunted and thinly distributed cypress trees, which grow in poor soil on drier land).

Shark Valley, however, is the best biking trail by far. If the park isn't flooded from excess rain (which it often is, especially in spring), this is South Florida's most scenic bicycle trail. Many locals haul their bikes out to the 'Glades for a relaxing day of wilderness-trail riding. You'll share the flat, paved road only with other bikers, trams, and a menagerie of wildlife. (Don't be surprised to see a gator lounging in the sun or a deer munching on some grass.) There are no shortcuts, so if you become tired or are unable to complete the 15-mile trip, turn around and return on the same road. Allow 2 to 3 hours to bike the entire loop.

Those who love to mountain-bike and who prefer solitude might check out the **Southern Glades Trail,** a 14-mile unpaved trail lined with native trees and teeming with wildlife, such as deer, alligators, and the occasional snake. The trail runs along the C-111 canal, off S.R. 9336 and Southwest 217th Street.

Bicycles are available from **Shark Valley Tram Tours,** at the park's Shark Valley entrance (www.sharkvalleytramtours.com; ☎ **305/221-8455**), for $8 per hour; rentals can be picked up anytime between 8:30am and 4pm and must be returned by 5pm.

BIRD-WATCHING   More than 350 species of birds make their home in the Everglades. Tropical birds from the Caribbean and temperate species from North America can be found, along with exotics that have flown in from more distant regions. Eco and Mrazek ponds, located near Flamingo, are two of the best places for birding, especially in early morning or late afternoon in the dry winter months. Pick up a free birding checklist from one of the visitor centers (p. 219) and inquire about what's been spotted in recent days. In late 2009, a survey revealed that there were more than 77,000 nests in the Everglades. The endangered woo stork increased its nesting activity 1,776% from the previous year. For a guided birding tour, consider the **Everglades Area Tours** (www.evergladesareatours.com; ☎ **239/695-9107**) "**National Park and Grand Heritage Birding Tour,**" a comprehensive, 6- to 7-hour naturalist-led tour with multiple forms of transportation—powerboats, kayaks, and even a beach walk, so you don't miss any of the spectacular feathered (among others) species who call the park home. The tour is a steep $250 per person and limited to six per tour.

CANOEING   Canoeing through the Everglades may be one of the most serene, diverse adventures you'll ever have. From a canoe (where you're incredibly close to the water level), your vantage point is priceless. Canoers in the 'Glades can coexist with the gators and birds in a way no one else can; the creatures behave as if you're part of the ecosystem—something that won't happen on an airboat. A ranger-guided boat tour is your best bet, and oftentimes they are either free or very inexpensive at around $7 to $12 per person. As always, a ranger will help you understand the surroundings and what you're seeing. They don't take reservations, but for more information on the various boat tours, call ☎ **239/695-3311.**

Everglades National Park's longest "trails" are designed for boat and canoe travel, and many are marked as clearly as walking trails. The **Noble Hammock Canoe Trail,** a 2-mile loop, takes 1 to 2 hours and is recommended for beginners. The

Hell's Bay Canoe Trail, a 3- to 6-mile course for hardier paddlers, takes 2 to 6 hours, depending on how far you choose to go. Park rangers can recommend other trails that suit your abilities, time limitations, and interests.

You can rent a canoe at the **Ivey House B&B** (www.evergladesadventures.com; ✆ **877/577-0679**) for $62 for 24 hours, $35 per full day (any 8-hr. period), or for $25 per half-day (1–5pm only). Kayaks and tandem kayaks are also available. The rental agent will shuttle your party to the trail head of your choice and pick you up afterward. Rental facilities are open daily from 8am to 5pm.

During ideal weather conditions (stay away during bug season!), you can paddle right out to the Gulf and camp on the beach. However, Gulf waters at beach sites can be extremely rough, and people in small watercraft such as a canoe should exercise caution.

You can also take a canoe tour from the Parks Docks on Chokoloskee Causeway on S.R. 29, ½ mile south of the traffic circle at the ranger station in Everglades City. Call **Everglades National Park Boat Tours** (✆ **800/445-7724**) for information. And for an eco-tour of the 'Glades, **Everglades Area Tours** (www.evergladesarea tours.com; ✆ **239/695-9107**) offers not only guided fishing charters, but also guided kayak eco-tours, customized bird-watching and photo expeditions, and full-moon/sunset paddling, as well as bicycle and aerial tours of the Everglades. Their signature "Boat Assisted Kayak Eco Tour" puts six kayaks and six passengers into a dedicated motorboat for a trip out to the Wilderness Waterway deep within Everglades National Park, where you will paddle in absolute wilderness, spotting birds, dolphins, manatees, sea turtles, alligators, and perhaps even the elusive American crocodile. The shuttle then brings you back to Everglades City/Chokoloskee. The trip costs $140 and includes transportation, guide, kayaks, and all safety equipment.

FISHING   About a third of Everglades National Park is open water. Freshwater fishing is popular in brackish **Nine-Mile Pond** (25 miles from the main entrance) and other spots along the Main Park Road, but because of the high mercury levels found in the Everglades, freshwater fishers are warned not to eat their catch. Before casting, check in at a visitor center, as many of the park's lakes are preserved for observation only. Fishing licenses are required; see p. 220 for more information.

Saltwater anglers will find snapper and sea trout plentiful. For an expertly guided fishing trip through the backcountry, **Adventures in Backwater Fishing** (www.fishing-florida.com/adventures; ✆ **239/643-1261**) will send you out with Capt. Dave Harding and Capt. George LeClair, who promise unique fishing—fly-fishing and spin casting, among other things—without breaking the bank. Six-hour trips will set you back around $385. A great list of charters and guides can be found at the Flamingo Marina or at **www.fishing-florida.com/adventures**.

MOTORBOATING   Motorboating around the Everglades seems like a great way to see plants and animals in remote habitats, and, indeed, it's an interesting and fulfilling experience as you throttle into nature. However, environmentalists are taking stock of the damage inflicted by motorboats (especially airboats) on the delicate ecosystem. If you choose to motor, remember that most of the areas near land are "no wake" zones and that, for the protection of nesting birds, landing is prohibited on most of the little mangrove islands. Motorboating is allowed in certain areas, such as Florida Bay, the backcountry toward Everglades City, and the Ten Thousand Islands area. In all the freshwater lakes, however, motorboats are prohibited if they're above

5 horsepower. There's a long list of restrictions and restricted areas, so get a copy of the park's boating rules from park headquarters before setting out.

The Everglades' only marina—accommodating about 50 boats with electric and water hookups—is **Flamingo Marina,** 1 Flamingo Lodge Hwy., Everglades City (© **239/695-3101**). The marina is the only remnant of the now-demolished Flamingo Lodge, which suffered terrible damage from hurricanes Katrina and Wilma in 2005. Word is that if enough funds can be rounded up, it'll be replaced with a hurricane-resistant lodging complex featuring a small hotel, cottages, and eco-tents. The well-marked channel to the Flamingo is accessible to boats with a maximum 4-foot draft and is open year-round. Reservations can be made through the marina store (http://evergladesnationalparkboattoursflamingo.com/canoe.php; © **239/695-3101**). Seventeen-foot skiffs with 15-horsepower motors are available for rent. These low-power boats cost $80 for 2 hours, $150 for 4 hours, $195 for 8 hours, and $390 for 24 hours. A $100 deposit is required.

Organized Tours

AIRBOAT TOURS   Shallow-draft, fan-powered airboats were invented in the Everglades by frog hunters who were tired of poling through the brushes. Airboats cut through the saw grass, sort of like hydraulic boats; at high enough speeds, a boat actually rises above the saw grass and into the air. Even though airboats are the most efficient (not to mention fast and fun!) way to get around, they are not permitted in the park—these shallow-bottom runabouts tend to inflict severe damage on animals and plants. Just outside the boundaries of the Everglades, however, you'll find a number of outfitters offering rides. *Tip:* Consider bringing earplugs, as these high-speed boats are *loud.* Sometimes operators provide plugs, but bring a pair just in case.

One of the best outfitters is **Gator Park,** 12 miles west of the Florida Turnpike at 24050 SW Eighth St. (www.gatorpark.com; © **305/559-2255;** daily 9am–5pm), which happens to be one of the most informative and entertaining airboat-tour operators around, not to mention the only one to give out free earplugs. Some of the guides deserve a medal for getting into the water and poking around a massive alligator, even though they're not really supposed to. After the boat ride, there's a free interactive wildlife show that features alligator wrestling and several other frightening acts involving scorpions. Take note of the peacocks that live in the trees here. Admission for the boat ride and show is $23 for adults, $12 for children 6 to 11. They also offer $45 airboat tours, $35 for children 6 to 11, that depart every 20 minutes, which include transportation to and from hotels on Miami Beach, Bal Harbour, Surfside, and Sunny Isles.

Another recommended outfitter is **Coopertown Airboat Tours** (www.coopertownairboats.com; © **305/226-6048**), about 11 miles west of the Florida Turnpike on the Tamiami Trail (U.S. 41). The superfriendly staff has helped the company garner the title of "Florida's Best" by the *Miami Herald* for 40 years in a row. You never know what you're going to see, but with great guides, you're sure to see *something* of interest on the 40-minute, 8-mile round-trip tours. There are also a restaurant and a small gator farm on the premises. Airboat rides cost $22 for adults, $11 for children 7 to 11. Private airboat tours are $50 per hour per person. Discounts can be found on the website. The company is open daily from 8am to 6pm; tours leave frequently.

The **Everglades Alligator Farm,** 4 miles south of Palm Drive on Southwest 192nd Avenue (www.everglades.com; © **305/247-2628**), offers half-hour guided airboat tours daily from 9am to 6pm. The price, which includes admission to the park, is $23 for adults and $16 for children 4 to 11.

Another reputable company is **Captain Doug's,** 35 miles south of Naples and 1 mile past the bridge in Everglades City (ⓒ **800/282-9194**).

CANOE TOURS   Slink through the mangroves, slide across saw grass prairies, and walk the sands of the unfettered Ten Thousand Islands—a canoe tour is a great way to explore the Everglades backcountry. Contact **Everglades Adventures** (www. evergladesadventures.com; ⓒ **877/567-0679**) at the Ivey House B&B (p. 227) for an expert guide.

ECO-TOURS   Although it's fascinating to explore on your own, it would be a shame for you to tour the Everglades without a clue about what you're seeing. **Everglades Adventures** (see "Canoe Tours," above) can guide and entertain you, as well as explain such key issues as the differences between alligators and crocodiles, or between swamps and the Everglades.

MOTORBOAT TOURS   Both Florida Bay and backcountry tours are offered Thursday to Monday at the **Flamingo Marina** (see "Motorboating," above). Florida Bay tours cruise nearby estuaries and sandbars, while six-passenger backcountry boats visit smaller sloughs. Passengers can expect to see birds and a variety of other animals (I once saw a raccoon and some wild pigs). Both cost $27 for adults, $13 for children 5 to 12. Tours depart throughout the day; reservations are recommended. Charter-fishing and sightseeing boats can also be booked through the resort's main reservation number (ⓒ **239/695-3101**). If you're on the Gulf Coast side of things, the naturalist-guided Gulf Coast boat tour of the Ten Thousand Islands departs from the **Gulf Coast Marina** (located in the **Gulf Coast Visitor Center,** 5 miles south of Hwy. 41/Tamiami Trail on S.R. 29, in the Everglades City area; ⓒ **239/695-2591**) and lasts an hour and a half. There's also a mangrove wilderness tour through the swampier part of the park. Tour prices are the same as the tours at the Flamingo Marina.

TRAM TOURS   At the park's Shark Valley entrance, open-air tram buses take visitors on 2-hour naturalist-led tours that delve 7½ miles into the wilderness and are the best quick introduction you can get to the Everglades. At the trail's midsection, passengers can disembark and climb a 65-foot observation tower with good views of the 'Glades (though the tower on the Pa-hay-okee Trail is better). Visitors will see plenty of wildlife and endless acres of saw grass. Tours run December through April, daily on the hour between 9am and 4pm, and May through November at 9:30am, 11am, 1pm, and 3pm. The tours are sometimes stalled by flooding or particularly heavy mosquito infestation. Reservations are recommended from December to March. The cost is $19 for adults, $18 for seniors, and $12 for children 3 to 12. For further information, contact **Shark Valley Tram Tours** (www.sharkvalleytramtours.com; ⓒ **305/221-8455**).

Where to Eat in & Around the Park

Here for nearly a quarter of a century, **El Toro Taco Family Restaurant,** 1 S. Krome Ave., near Mowry and Campbell drives, Homestead (ⓒ **305/245-8182**), opens daily at 9:30am and stays crowded until at least 9pm most days. The fresh grilled meats, tacos, burritos, salsas, guacamole, and stews are all mild and delicious. No matter how big your appetite, it's hard to spend more than $15 per person at this Mexican outpost. Bring your own beer or wine.

Housed in a one-story, windowless building that looks something like a medieval fort, the **Capri Restaurant,** 935 N. Krome Ave., Florida City (www.dinecapri.com; ✆ **305/247-1542**), has been serving hearty Italian-American fare since 1958. Great pastas and salads complement a menu of meat and fish dishes; portions are big. Lunch and dinner are served Monday through Friday until 9:30pm and Saturday until 10:30pm. The **White Lion Café,** 146 NW 7th St., Homestead (www.white lioncafe.com; ✆ **305/248-1076**), is a quaint home-and-gardens-cum-cafe with live blues, jazz, and swing music at night, and a menu with blue-plate specials and cheekily named appetizers and entrees such as Dirty Little Shrimp and Garlic Romanian, which is actually delicious skirt steak sliced thin and served with fresh mushrooms, spinach, and garlic over real mashed potatoes and gravy. Entree prices range from $10 to $22. Dinner is served Tuesday through Saturday from 5pm until "the fat lady sings."

The **Miccosukee Restaurant,** just west of the Shark Valley entrance on the Tamiami Trail/U.S. 41 (✆ **305/223-8380**), serves authentic pumpkin bread, fry bread, and fish, and not-so-authentic Native American interpretations of tacos and fried chicken. It's worth a stop for brunch, lunch, or dinner.

Near the Miccosukee reservation is the **Pit Bar-B-Q,** 16400 SW 8th St. (www. thepitbarbq.com; ✆ **305/226-2272**), a total pit of a place known for some of the best smoked ribs, barbecued chicken, and corn bread this side of the Deep South. It's open daily from 11am to 8pm.

In Everglades City, the **Oyster House,** on Chokoloskee Causeway, S.R. (the locals call it Hwy.) 29 S. (www.oysterhouserestaurant.com; ✆ **239/695-2073**), is a large, homey seafood restaurant with modest prices, excellent service, and a fantastic view of the Ten Thousand Islands. Try the hush puppies. For more authentic local flavor, try the **Camellia Street Grill,** 208 Camellia St. (✆ **239/695-2003**), an off-the-beaten-path, rusty waterfront fish joint fusing Southern hospitality with outstanding seafood served with a gourmet twist. An on-site herb and veggie garden provides the freshest ingredients and stellar salads. Everything is homemade, including the Key lime pie, and there's live music on Fridays and Saturdays.

Where to Stay

There is no lodging within Everglades National Park proper unless you count your tent as lodging. However, there are a few accommodations just outside the park that are clean and reasonably priced. A $45-million casino hotel, **Miccosukee Resort** (www.miccosukee.com; ✆ **877/242-6464**), is adjacent to the Miccosukee bingo and gaming hall on the northern edge of the park. Although bugs can be a major nuisance, especially in the warm months, camping (the best way to fully experience South Florida's wilderness) is really the way to go in this very primitive environment.

CAMPING IN THE EVERGLADES

Campgrounds are open year-round in Flamingo and Long Pine Key. Both have drinking water, picnic tables, charcoal grills, restrooms, and tent and trailer pads, and welcome RVs (Flamingo allows up to 40-ft. vehicles, while Long Pine Key accepts up to 60-footers), though there are no electrical hookups. Flamingo has cold-water showers; Long Pine Key does not have showers or hookups for showers. Private ground fires are not permitted, but supervised campfire programs are conducted during winter months. Long Pine Key and Flamingo are popular and require reservations in advance, which can be made through the National Park Reservations Service (www. nps.gov; ℭ **800/365-CAMP** [2267]). Campsites are $16 per night; during winter season (Nov–Apr), there's a 14-day consecutive-stay limit, and a maximum of 30 days a year.

Camping is also available year-round in the **backcountry** (those remote areas accessible only by boat, foot, or canoe—basically, most of the park), on a first-come, first-served basis. Campers must register with park rangers and get a permit in person or by phone no less than 24 hours before the start of their trip. The permit costs $10 plus $2 per camper per night. For more information, contact the **Gulf Coast Visitor Center** (ℭ **239/695-3311**) or the **Flamingo Visitor Center** (ℭ **239/695-2945**), which are the only two places that sell the permits. Once you have one, camping sites cost $16 (with a maximum of 8 people per site), or $30 for a group site (maximum of 15 people). In 2011, Flamingo added 41 new sites with electrical hookup at $30 per site. Campers can use only designated campsites, which are plentiful and well marked on maps.

Many backcountry sites are **chickee huts**—covered wooden platforms (with toilets) on stilts. They're accessible only by canoe and can accommodate free-standing tents (without stakes). Ground sites are located along interior bays and rivers, and beach camping is also popular. In summer especially, mosquito repellent is necessary gear.

LODGING IN EVERGLADES CITY

As Everglades City is 35 miles southeast of Naples and 83 miles west of Miami, many visitors choose to explore this western entrance to Everglades National Park, located off the Tamiami Trail, on S.R. 29. An annual seafood festival held the first weekend in February is a major event that draws hordes of people. Everglades City (the gateway to the Ten Thousand Islands), where the 'Glades meet the Gulf of Mexico, is the closest thing you'll get to civilization in South Florida's swampy frontier, with a few touristy shops, a restaurant, and one bed-and-breakfast.

Ivey House B&B ★★ 🏠 The first certified Green Lodging in Collier County, the Ivey House offers a variety of accommodations: the Ivey House Inn, featuring spacious rooms with private bathrooms, TVs, phones and small refrigerators located around the courtyard pool and waterfall; the Ivey House Lodge, housed in what used to be a recreational center for the men who built the Tamiami Trail, featuring 11 small rooms (no TVs, phone, or heat in these rooms) with communal living area and bathrooms (one each for women and men); and the Ivey House Cottage, with living room, two bedrooms, a full kitchen, a private bathroom, and a screened-in porch. Owners Sandee and David Harraden are extremely knowledgeable about the Everglades and assist guests, providing a variety of daily excursions. A full hot breakfast is provided during peak season. Box lunches are available year-round for $13. *Note:* There is no smoking in any of the buildings.

107 Camellia St., Everglades City, FL 34139. www.iveyhouse.com. ℭ **877/567-0679** or 239/695-3299. Fax 239/695-4155. 30 units. Winter $169–$209 in inn, $99–$114 in lodge, $229 in cottage; off season $99–$139 in inn, $89–$104 in lodge, $179 in cottage. 2-night minimum in all facilities during Everglades Seafood Festival in Feb (higher rates apply). Rates include continental breakfast. MC, V. **Amenities:** Restaurant (breakfast only); pool; free Wi-Fi. *In room:* A/C and heat, TV, fridge (in inn and cottage), kitchen (in cottage).

Rod & Gun Lodge ★ Set on the banks of the sleepy Baron River, this rustic old white-clapboard house has plenty of history and all kinds of activities for sports enthusiasts, including a pool, bike rentals, a tennis center, and nearby boat rentals and private fishing guides. Hoover vacationed here after his 1928 election victory, and Truman flew in to sign Everglades National Park into existence in 1947 and stayed over as well. Other guests have included Richard Nixon, Burt Reynolds, and Mick Jagger. The public rooms are beautifully paneled and hung with tarpon, wild boar, deer antlers, and other trophies. Guest rooms in this single-story building are unfussy but comfortable. All have porches looking out on the river. Out by the pool, a screened veranda with ceiling fans is a pleasant place for a libation. The excellent seafood **restaurant** serves breakfast, lunch, and dinner. The entire property is smoke-free.

Riverside Dr. and Broadway (P.O. Box 190), Everglades City, FL 34139. www.evergladesrodandgun. com. *℃* **239/695-2101.** 17 units. Winter $110–$140 double; off season $95 double. No credit cards. Closed after July 4 for the summer. **Amenities:** Restaurant; bike rental; pool; tennis courts. *In room:* A/C, TV.

LODGING IN HOMESTEAD & FLORIDA CITY

Homestead and Florida City, two adjacent towns that were almost blown off the map by Hurricane Andrew in 1992, have come back better than before. About 10 miles from the park's main entrance, along U.S. 1, 35 miles south of Miami, these some-what rural towns offer several budget options, including chain hotels. There is a **Days Inn** (*℃* **305/245-1260**) in Homestead and a **Ramada Inn** (*℃* **800/272-6232** or 305/247-8833) right off the turnpike in Florida City. The best options are in Florida City: **The Best Western Gateway to the Keys,** 411 Krome Ave. (U.S. 1; www.bestwestern.com; *℃* **800/528-1234** or 305/246-5100), **Florida City Travelodge,** 409 SE 1st Ave. (www.tlflcity.com; *℃* **305/248-5995**); and the **Everglades International Hostel,** 20 SW 2nd Ave. (www.evergladeshostel.com; *℃* **305/248-1122**).

BISCAYNE NATIONAL PARK ★

With only about 500,000 visitors each year (mostly boaters and divers), the unusual Biscayne National Park is one of the least crowded parks in the country. Perhaps that's because the park is a little more difficult than most to access—more than 95% of its 181,500 acres is underwater.

The park's significance was first formally acknowledged in 1968 when, in an unprecedented move (and despite intense pressure from developers), President Lyndon B. Johnson signed a bill to conserve the barrier islands off South Florida's east coast as a national monument—a protected status just a rung below national park. After being twice enlarged, once in 1974 and again in 1980, the waters and land surrounding the northernmost coral reef in North America became a full-fledged national park—the largest of its kind in the country.

To be fully appreciated, Biscayne National Park should be thought of as more preserve than destination. Use your time here to explore underwater life, but also to relax. The park's small mainland mangrove shoreline and keys are best explored by boat. Its extensive reef system is great for diving and snorkeling.

The park consists of 44 islands, but only a few are open to visitors. The most popular is **Elliott Key,** which has campsites and a visitor center, plus freshwater showers (cold water only), restrooms, trails, and a buoyed swim area. It's about 9 miles from **Convoy Point,** the park's official headquarters on land. During Columbus Day weekend, there is a very popular regatta for which a lively crowd of party people gathers—sometimes in the nude—to celebrate the long weekend. If you'd prefer to rough it a little more, the 29-acre island known as **Boca Chita Key,** once an exclusive haven for yachters, has now become a popular spot for all manner of boaters. Visitors can camp and tour the island's restored historic buildings, including the county's second-largest lighthouse and a tiny chapel.

Essentials

GETTING THERE & ACCESS POINTS Convoy Point, the park's mainland entrance, is 9 miles east of Homestead. To reach the park from Miami, take the Florida Turnpike to the Tallahassee Road (SW 137th Ave.) exit. Turn left, then left again at North Canal Drive (SW 328th St.), and follow signs to the park. Another option is to rent a speedboat in Miami and cruise south for about 1½ hours. From U.S. 1, whether you're heading north or south, turn east at North Canal Drive (SW 328th St.). The entrance is approximately 9 miles away. The rest of the park is accessible only by boat.

Because most of Biscayne National Park is accessible only to boaters, mooring buoys abound, as it is illegal to anchor on coral. When no buoys are available, boaters must anchor on sand or on the docks surrounding the small harbor off Boca Chita. Boats can also dock here overnight for $20. Even the most experienced boaters should carry updated nautical charts of the area, which are available at Convoy Point's Dante Fascell Visitor Center. The waters are often murky, making the abundant reefs and sandbars difficult to detect—and there are more interesting ways to spend a day than waiting for the tide to rise. There's a boat launch at adjacent Homestead Bayfront Park and 66 slips on Elliott Key, available free on a first-come, first-served basis.

Round-trip transportation to and from the visitor center to Elliott Key costs $50 (plus tax) round-trip per person and takes about an hour. This is a convenient option, *available only if you have six people to fill a boat,* ensuring that you don't get lost on some deserted island by boating there yourself. If you don't have six people, you can charter the boat to and from the key for $300. Round-trip transportation to and from Boca Chita Key, however, is $50 per person regardless of how many people are going out. Call ✆ **305/230-1100** for the seasonal schedule.

VISITOR CENTERS & INFORMATION Open daily from 9am to 5pm, the **Dante Fascell Visitor Center** (often referred to by its older name, Convoy Point Visitor Center), 9700 SW 328th St., Homestead, FL 33033-5634, at the park's main entrance (www.nps.gov/bisc; ✆ **305/230-7275;** fax 305/230-1190), is the natural starting point for any venture into the park without a boat. It provides comprehensive information about the park; on request, rangers will show you a short video on the park.

For information on transportation, glass-bottom boat tours, and snorkeling and scuba-diving expeditions, contact the park concessionaire, **Biscayne National Underwater Park, Inc.,** P.O. Box 1270, Homestead, FL 33030 (www.biscayne underwater.com; ✆ **305/230-1100;** fax 305/230-1120). It's open daily from 8:30am to 5pm.

ENTRANCE FEES & PERMITS Park entrance is free, but there is a $20 overnight docking fee at both Boca Chita Key Harbor and Elliott Key Harbor, which includes a campsite. Campsites are $15 for those staying without a boat. Group camping costs $30 a day and covers up to six tents and 25 people. See p. 220 for information on fishing permits. Backcountry camping permits are free and can be picked up from the Dante Fascell Visitor Center. For more information on fees and permits, call the park ranger at ☏ **305/230-1144.**

Seeing the Highlights

Because the park is primarily underwater, the only way to truly experience it is with snorkel or scuba gear. Beneath the surface of Biscayne National Park, the aquatic universe pulses with multicolored life: abounding bright parrotfish and angelfish, gently rocking sea fans, and coral labyrinths. (See the "Snorkeling & Scuba Diving" section, below, for more information.) Afterward, take a picnic out to Elliott Key and taste the crisp salt air blowing off the Atlantic. Or head to Boca Chita, an intriguing island that was once the private playground of wealthy yachters.

Sports & Outdoor Activities

CANOEING & KAYAKING   Biscayne National Park affords excellent canoeing, both along the coast and across the open water to nearby mangroves and artificial islands dotting the longest uninterrupted shoreline in the state. Because tides can be strong, only experienced canoeists should attempt to paddle far from shore. If you do plan to go far, first obtain a tide table from the visitor center and paddle with the current. Free ranger-led canoe tours are scheduled from 9am to noon on the second and fourth Saturdays of the month between mid-January and late April; phone for information. You can rent a canoe at the park's concession stand for $16 to $25 for the 90 minutes, and 50% of the initial cost per additional hour. Paddleboats are also available for $30 to $40 for the 90 minutes, and 50% of the initial cost per additional hour. Call ☏ **305/230-1100** for reservations, information, ranger tours, and boat rentals. You can also visit the website of the park's concession at www.biscayne underwater.com.

FISHING   Ocean fishing is excellent year-round at Biscayne National Park; many people cast their lines from the breakwater jetty at Convoy Point. A fishing license is required (p. 220). Bait is not available in Biscayne National Park, but it is sold in adjacent Homestead Bayfront Park. Stone crabs and Florida lobsters can be found here, but you're allowed to catch these only on the ocean side when they're in season. There are strict limits on size, season, number, and method of take (including spearfishing) for both freshwater and saltwater fishing. The latest regulations are available at most marinas, bait-and-tackle shops, and the park's visitor centers; or you can contact the **Florida Fish and Wildlife Conservation Commission,** Bryant Building, 620 S. Meridian St., Tallahassee, FL 32399-1600 (☏ **850/488-0331**). For those looking to learn a little about fishing, Biscayne National Park offers a free Fisheries Awareness Class on the third Wednesday of every month (during even-numbered months, classes are in Spanish) from 6 to 9:30pm at Suniland Park, 12855 S. Dixie Hwy. (☏ **305/230-1144,** ext. 3089), in Miami.

HIKING & EXPLORING   As the majority of this park is underwater, hiking is not the main attraction here, but there are some interesting sights and trails nonetheless. At Convoy Point, you can walk along the 370-foot boardwalk and along the half-mile jetty that serves as a breakwater for the park's harbor. From here, you can usually see brown pelicans, little blue herons, snowy egrets, and a few exotic fish.

Elliott Key is accessible only by boat, but once you're there, you have two good trail options. True to its name, the Loop Trail makes a 1.5-mile circle from the bayside visitor center, through a hardwood hammock and mangroves, to an elevated oceanside boardwalk. You'll likely see land crabs scurrying around the mangrove roots.

Boca Chita Key was once a playground for wealthy tycoons, and it still has the peaceful beauty that attracted elite anglers from cold climates. Many of the historic buildings are still intact, including an ornamental lighthouse that was never put to use. Take advantage of the 3-hour tours, including a boat trip, that usually are led by a park ranger and available every Sunday in winter at 1:30pm. The price is $35 for adults, $25 for seniors, and $20 for children 11 and under. However, call in advance to see if the sea is calm enough for the trip—the boats won't run in rough waters. See "Glass-Bottom Boat Tours," below, for information about daily trips.

SNORKELING & SCUBA DIVING   The clear, warm waters of Biscayne National Park are packed with colorful tropical fish that swim in the offshore reefs. If you didn't bring your own gear, you can rent or buy snorkeling and scuba gear at the full-service dive shop at Convoy Point. Rates are in line with those at mainland dive shops.

The best way to see the park from underwater is to take a snorkeling or diving tour operated by **Biscayne National Underwater Park, Inc.** (www.biscayneunderwater.com; ☎ 305/230-1100). The "Snorkel Mangrove Eco Adventure" takes you inside the barrier islands of Elliott Key at 10am daily; it's $80 for adults, $40 for seniors and children. The other tour, the "Snorkel Reef Adventure," takes you inside the Biscayne Bay and around the shoreline of the barrier islands and the finger channels at 10am and 1:30pm daily for $45 per person. There are also private two-tank dives for certified divers; the price is $99, including two tanks and weights. Make your reservations in advance. The shop is open daily from 9am to 5pm.

Before entering the water, be sure to apply waterproof sunblock—once you begin to explore, it's easy to lose track of time, and the Florida sun is brutal, even during winter.

SWIMMING   You can swim off the protected beaches of Elliott Key, Boca Chita Key, and adjacent Homestead Bayfront Park, but none of these matches the width or softness of other South Florida beaches. Check the water conditions before heading into the sea: The strong currents that make this a popular destination for windsurfers and sailors can be dangerous, even for strong swimmers. Homestead Bayfront Park is really just a marina next to Biscayne National Park, but it does have a beach and picnic facilities, as well as fishing areas and a playground. It's located at Convoy Point, 9698 SW 328th St., Homestead (☎ **305/230-3034**).

Glass-Bottom Boat Tours

If you prefer not to dive, the best way to see the sights is on a glass-bottom boat. **Biscayne National Underwater Park, Inc.** (www.biscayneunderwater.com; ☎ **305/230-1100**), has daily trips to view some of the country's most beautiful reefs and tropical fish. Boats depart year-round from Convoy Point at 10am and last about 3 hours. At $45 for adults, $35 for seniors, and $30 for children 12 and under, the scenic, informative tours are pricey, but if you don't enjoy the trip, they promise a full refund. Boats carry fewer than 50 passengers; reservations are almost always necessary.

Where to Stay

Besides campsites, there are no facilities available for overnight guests to this watery park. Most noncamping visitors come for an afternoon, on their way to the Keys, and stay overnight in nearby Homestead (see p. 228 for listings). The good news is that

Biscayne National Park boasts some of the state's most pristine **campsites**. Because they are inaccessible by motor vehicle, you'll be sure to avoid the mass of RVs so prevalent in many of the state's other campgrounds. The sites on Elliott Key and Boca Chita can be reached only by boat. If you don't have your own boat, call *©* **305/230-1100** to arrange a drop-off. Transportation to Elliott Key from the visitor center costs $50 (plus tax). They do not provide transportation to Boca Chita, so you'll have to rent a boat. Boca Chita has only saltwater toilets (no showers or sinks); Elliott Key has freshwater, cold-water showers and toilets, but is otherwise no less primitive. If you didn't pay for the overnight docking fee, campsites are $15.

With a backcountry permit, available free from the visitor center, you can pitch your tent somewhere even more private. Ask for a map and be sure to bring plenty of bug spray. Sites cost $15 a night for up to six persons staying in one or two tents. Backcountry camping is allowed only on Elliott Key, which is a very popular spot (accessible only by boat) for boaters and campers. It is approximately 9 miles from the Dante Fascell Visitor Center and offers hiking trails, fresh water, boat slips, showers, and restrooms. While there, don't miss the Old Road, a 7-mile tropical hammock trail that runs the length of Elliott Key. This trail is one of the few places left in the world to see the highly endangered Schaus swallowtail butterfly, recognizable by its black wings with diagonal yellow bands. These butterflies are usually out from late April to July.

THE KEYS & THE DRY TORTUGAS

The drive from Miami to the Keys is a slow descent into an unusual but breathtaking American ecosystem: On either side, for miles ahead, are nothing but emerald waters. (On weekends, however, you will also see plenty of traffic in front of and in back of you.) Strung out across the Atlantic Ocean like loose strands of cultured pearls, more than 400 islands make up this 150-mile-long necklace.

Despite the usually calm landscape, these rocky islands can be treacherous, as tropical storms, hurricanes, and tornadoes are always possibilities. The exposed coast poses dangers to those on land as well as at sea.

When Spanish explorers Juan Ponce de León and Antonio de Herrera sailed amid these craggy, dangerous rocks in 1513, they and their men dubbed the string of islands "Los Martires" (The Martyrs) because they thought the rocks looked like men suffering in the surf. It wasn't until the early 1800s that rugged and ambitious pioneers, who amassed great wealth by salvaging cargo from ships sunk nearby, settled the larger islands (legend has it that these shipwrecks were sometimes caused by "wreckers," who removed navigational markers from the shallows to lure unwitting captains aground). At the height of the salvaging mania (in the 1830s), Key West boasted the highest per-capita income in the country.

However, wars, fires, hurricanes, mosquitoes, and the Depression took their toll on these resilient islands in the early part of the 20th century, causing wild swings between fortune and poverty. In 1938, the spectacular Overseas Highway (U.S. 1) was finally completed atop the ruins of Henry Flagler's railroad (which was destroyed by a hurricane in 1935, leaving only bits and pieces still found today), opening the region to tourists, who had never before been able to drive to this sea-bound destination. These days, the highway connects more than 30 of the populated islands in the Keys. The hundreds of small, undeveloped islands that surround these "mainline" Keys are known locally as the "backcountry" and are home to dozens of exotic animals and plants. Therein lie some of the most renowned outdoor sporting opportunities, from bonefishing to spearfishing and—at appropriate times of the year—diving for lobsters and stone crabs. To get to the backcountry, you must take to the water—a vital part of any trip to the Keys. Whether you fish, snorkel, dive, or cruise, include some time on a boat in your itinerary; otherwise, you haven't truly seen the Keys.

11 | The Florida Keys

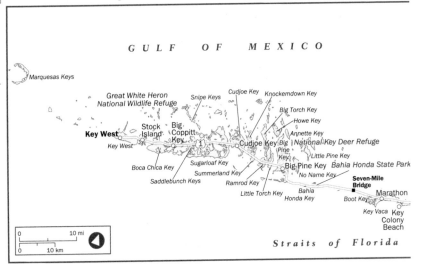

Of course, people go to the Keys for the peaceful waters and year-round warmth, but the sea and the teeming life beneath and around it are the main attractions here: Countless species of brilliantly colored fish can be found swimming above the ocean's floor, and you'll discover a stunning abundance of tropical and exotic plants, birds, and reptiles.

The warm, shallow waters (deeper and rougher on the eastern/Atlantic side of the Keys) nurture living coral that supports a complex, delicate ecosystem of plants and animals—sponges, anemones, jellyfish, crabs, rays, sharks, turtles, snails, lobsters, and thousands of types of fish. This vibrant underwater habitat thrives on one of the few living tropical reefs on the entire North American continent. As a result, anglers, divers, snorkelers, and watersports enthusiasts of all kinds come to explore.

Heavy traffic has taken its toll on this fragile eco-scape, but conservation efforts are underway (traffic laws are strictly enforced on Deer Key, for example, due to deer crossings that have been contained, thanks to newly installed fences). In fact, environmental efforts in the Keys exceed those in many other high-traffic visitor destinations.

Although the atmosphere throughout the Keys is that of a laid-back beach town, don't expect many impressive beaches. Nice beaches are mostly found in a few private resorts, though there are some small, sandy strips in John Pennekamp Coral Reef State Park, Bahia Honda State Park, and Key West. One great exception is Sombrero Beach, in Marathon (p. 241), which is well maintained by Monroe County and is larger and considerably nicer than other beaches in the Keys.

The Keys are divided into three sections, both geographically and in this chapter. The Upper and Middle keys are closest to the Florida mainland, so they are popular with weekend warriors who come by boat or car to fish or relax in such towns as Key Largo, Islamorada, and Marathon. Farther on, just beyond the impressive Seven-Mile Bridge (which actually measures 6½ miles), are the Lower Keys, a small, unspoiled

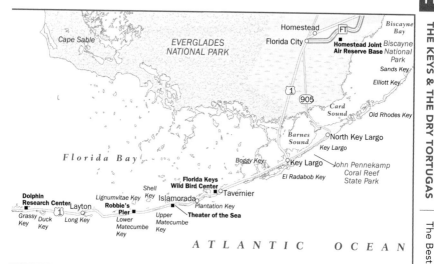

swath of islands teeming with wildlife. Here, in the protected regions of the Lower Keys, is where you're most likely to catch sight of the area's many endangered animals—with patience, you may spot the rare eagle, egret, or Key deer. You should also keep an eye out for alligators, turtles, rabbits, and a huge variety of birds.

Key West, the most renowned—and last—island in the Lower Keys, is the southernmost point in the continental United States (made famous by Ernest Hemingway). This tiny island is the most popular destination in the Florida Keys, overrun with cruise-ship passengers and day-trippers, as well as franchises and T-shirt shops. More than 1.6 million visitors pass through it each year. Still, this "Conch Republic" has a tightly knit community of permanent residents who cling fiercely to their live-and-let-live attitude—an atmosphere that has made Key West famously popular with painters, writers, and free spirits, despite the recent influx of money-hungry developers who want to turn Key West into Palm Beach South.

The last section in this chapter is devoted to the Dry Tortugas, a national park located 68 nautical miles from Key West.

THE best KEYS & THE DRY TORTUGAS EXPERIENCES

- **Starting (or Capping) Off Your Keys Trip at Alabama Jack's:** This venerable road house way off the beaten path is a ritual for pre-and post-Keys visitors. With amazing views of the water (look out for manatees!), mediocre food, country music, and cold drinks, Alabama Jack's is the living, breathing version of a Zac Brown or Jimmy Buffett song that's truly of another place and era.
- **Swimming with Dolphins:** The eco-culture and consciousness of the Florida Keys are unparalleled, which is why if you're going to swim with dolphins (everyone

should do it at least once in their lives), you'll want to do it here, with trained professionals who respect the animals.

- **Snorkeling in the Looe Key National Marine Sanctuary:** What Key West's Duval Street is to wacky people-watching, Looe Key is to coral-watching. Here, you'll see 150 varieties of hard and soft coral—some centuries old—as well as every type of tropical fish, including gold and blue parrotfish, moray eels, barracudas, and French angels.

- **Hiring a Captain at Old Charter Boat Row, Key West:** The kind of captains reality shows are made about are found right here at historic Charter Boat Row, home to over 30 charter-fishing and party boats. Not only will you get the cruise of a life-time, but you may end up with a friend for life, too.

- **Happy Hour Anywhere, Anytime:** That song, "It's 5 O'Clock Somewhere"? Definitely written about the Keys, where when it comes to boozing, it's 5 o'clock all day, any day. Belly up to a bar, a boat, or anywhere for that matter, order a cocktail, and breathe. This is what it's all about.

EXPLORING THE KEYS BY CAR

After you've left the Florida Turnpike and landed on U.S. 1, which is also known as the Overseas Highway (see "Getting There" under "Essentials," below), you'll have no trouble negotiating these narrow islands, as only one main road connects the Keys. The scenic, lazy drive from Miami can be very enjoyable if you have the patience to linger and explore the diverse towns and islands along the way. If you have the time, we recommend allowing at least 2 days to work your way down to Key West, and 3 or more days once there.

Encouraging you to slow down is the new $21-million, 106-mile **Florida Keys Overseas Heritage Trail,** a work in progress that is creating a scenic, multiuse paved trail for bikers, hikers, runners, fishermen, and sightseers running parallel to the Overseas Highway and extending from Key Largo all the way down to Key West. With 66 of the 106 miles already completed and 12 miles of trail and five bridges under construction, the rest of the trail is still under design and scheduled for completion by 2013.

 Alabama Jack's: Card Sound's Favorite Dive

On its own, there's not much to the waterfront shack that is **Alabama Jack's,** 5800 Card Sound Rd., Card Sound (© **305/248-8741**). The bar serves beer and wine only, and the restaurant specializes in delicious, albeit greasy, bar fare. But this quintessential Old Floridian dive, in a historic fishing village called Card Sound between Homestead and Key Largo, is a colorful "must" on the drive south, especially on Sunday, when bikers mix with barflies, anglers, line dancers, and Southern belles in all their fabulous frills. There's live country music, so pull up a bar stool, order a cold one, and take in the sights—in the bay and at the bar. The views of the mangroves are spectacular. To get here, pick up Card Sound Road (the old Rte. 1) a few miles after you pass Homestead, heading toward Key Largo. Alabama Jack's is on the right side and can't be missed.

Most of U.S. 1 is a narrow two-lane highway, with some wider passing zones along the way. The speed limit is usually 55 mph (35–45 mph on Big Pine Key and in some commercial areas). There has been talk of expanding the highway, but plans have not been finalized. Even on the narrow road, you can usually get from downtown Miami to Key Largo in just over an hour. If you're determined to drive straight through to Key West, allow at least 3½ hours. Weekend travel is another matter entirely: When the roads are jammed with travelers from the mainland, the trip can take upwards of 5 to 6 hours (when there's an accident, traffic is at an absolute standstill). We *strongly* urge you to avoid driving anywhere in the Keys on Friday afternoon or Sunday evening.

Most addresses in the Keys (except in Key West and parts of Marathon) are delineated by **mile markers** (MM), small green signs on the roadside that announce the distance from Key West. The markers start at no. 127, just south of the Florida mainland. The zero marker is in Key West, at the corner of Whitehead and Fleming streets. Addresses in this chapter are accompanied by a mile marker (MM) designation when appropriate.

THE UPPER & MIDDLE KEYS

58 miles SW of Miami

The Upper Keys are a popular year-round refuge for South Floridians, who take advantage of the islands' proximity to the mainland. This is the fishing and diving capital of America, and the swarms of outfitters and billboards never let you forget it.

Key Largo, once called Rock Harbor but renamed to capitalize on the success of the 1948 Humphrey Bogart film (which wasn't filmed here), is the largest Key and is more developed than its neighbors to the south. Dozens of chain hotels, restaurants, and tourist information centers service the water enthusiasts who come to explore the nation's first underwater state park, **John Pennekamp Coral Reef State Park,** and its adjacent marine sanctuary. **Islamorada,** the unofficial capital of the Upper Keys, has the area's best atmosphere, food, fishing, entertainment, and lodging. It's an unofficial "party capital" for mainlanders seeking a quick tropical excursion. Here (Islamorada is actually composed of four islands), nature lovers can enjoy walking trails, historic exploration, and big-purse fishing tournaments. For a more tranquil, less party-hearty experience, other Keys besides Key West and Islamorada are better choices. **Marathon,** smack in the middle, is known as the heart of the Keys and is one of the most populated. But don't judge it by its main drag. To appreciate Marathon you need to go beyond U.S. 1. It is part fishing village, part tourist center, part nature preserve. This area's highly developed infrastructure includes resort hotels, a commercial airport, and a highway that expands to four lanes.

Essentials

GETTING THERE　From Miami International Airport (there is also an airport in Marathon), take Le Jeune Road (NW 42nd Ave.) to Route 836 West. Follow signs to the Florida Turnpike South, about 7 miles. The turnpike extension connects with U.S. 1 in Florida City. Continue south on U.S. 1. For a scenic option, take Card Sound Road, south of Florida City, a backcountry drive that reconnects with U.S. 1 in upper Key Largo. The view from Card Sound Bridge is spectacular and well worth the $1 toll.

If you're coming from Florida's west coast, take Alligator Alley to the Miami exit and then turn south onto the turnpike extension. The turnpike ends in Florida City, at which time you will be dumped directly onto the two-lane U.S. 1, which leads to the Keys. Have around $15 for the tolls. If you take U.S. 1 straight down and bypass the turnpike, it's free, but a lot longer.

Greyhound (www.greyhound.com; ✆ **800/231-2222**) has three buses leaving Miami for Key West every day, with stops in Key Largo, Tavernier, Islamorada, Marathon, Big Pine Key, Cudjoe Key, Sugarloaf, and Big Coppit on the way south. Prices range from $40 to $56 one-way and $81 to $110 round-trip; the trip takes from 1 hour and 40 minutes to 4 hours and 40 minutes, depending on how far south you're going. Seats fill quickly in season, so come early. It's first-come, first-served.

Once you've arrived in the Keys, let **Flying Dog Helicopters** (www.flyingdog helicopters.com; ✆ **866/425-4743**) take you on 10- to 20-minute helicopter tours of the Upper and Middle keys from their base at Holiday Isle in Islamorada, featuring aerial views of sandbars, reefs, sharks, and more. Price ranges from $70 to $155 per person.

VISITOR INFORMATION Make sure you get your information from an official not-for-profit center. The **Key Largo Chamber of Commerce,** U.S. 1 at MM 106, Key Largo, FL 33037 (www.keylargo.org; ✆ **800/822-1088** or 305/451-1414; fax 305/451-4726), runs an excellent facility, with free direct-dial phones and plenty of brochures. Headquartered in a handsome clapboard house, the chamber operates as an information clearinghouse for all of the Keys and is open daily from 9am to 6pm.

The **Islamorada Chamber of Commerce,** housed in a little red caboose, U.S. 1 at MM 82.5, P.O. Box 915, Islamorada, FL 33036 (www.islamoradachamber.com; ✆ **800/322-5397** or 305/664-4503; fax 305/664-4289), offers maps and literature on the Upper Keys.

You can't miss the big, blue visitor center at MM 53.5, **Greater Marathon Chamber of Commerce,** 12222 Overseas Hwy., Marathon, FL 33050 (www.florida keysmarathon.com; ✆ **800/262-7284** or 305/743-5417; fax 305/289-0183). Here you can receive free information on local events, festivals, attractions, dining, and lodging.

On your smartphone, check out the **Florida Keys app** available for the iPhone, iPod touch, and iPad. With it, users can access information to weather, events, venues, and maps, as well as GPS and audio driving tours. Best of all, the app is free.

Exploring the Upper & Middle Keys

Crane Point Hammock ★★ ☺ 👘 NATURE RESERVE Crane Point Hammock is a little-known but worthwhile stop, especially for those interested in the rich botanical and archaeological history of the Keys. This privately owned, 64-acre nature area is considered one of the most important historic sites in the Keys. It contains what is probably the last virgin thatch-palm hammock in North America, as well as a rainforest exhibit and an archaeological site with prehistoric Indian and Bahamian artifacts.

Also headquarters for the Florida Keys Land and Sea Trust, the hammock's impressive nature museum has simple, informative displays of the Keys' wildlife, including a walk-through replica of a coral-reef cave and life-size dioramas with tropical birds and Key deer. Kids can make art projects, see 6-foot-long iguanas, climb through a scaled-down pirate ship, and touch a variety of indigenous aquatic and landlubber creatures.

5550 Overseas Hwy. (MM 50), Marathon. www.cranepoint.net. ✆ **305/743-9100.** Admission $13 adults, $11 seniors 66 and over, $8.50 students, free for children 5 and under. Mon–Sat 9am–5pm; Sun noon–5pm.

Dolphin Research Center ★★★ ☺ NATURE RESERVE   Of the several such centers in the continental United States (all located in the Keys), the Dolphin Research Center is a nonprofit facility and one of the most organized and informative. Although some people argue that training dolphins is cruel and selfish, this is one of the most respected of the institutions that study and protect the mammals. Trainers at the center will also tell you that the dolphins need stimulation and enjoy human contact. They certainly seem to. They nuzzle and seem to smile and kiss the people who get to interact with them in daily interactive programs. The "family" of over 20 dolphins and sea lions swims in 90,000-square-feet of natural saltwater pools carved out of the shoreline. If you can't get into an interactive program, you can watch the sessions that cover a variety of topics from fun facts about dolphins, to therapeutic qualities of dolphins, to research projects in progress. Because the Dolphin Encounter swimming program is the most popular, advanced reservations are required and can be made up to 6 months in advance. The cost is $189 per person. If you're not brave enough to swim with the dolphins or if you have a child under 5 (not permitted to swim with dolphins), try the Dolphin Dip program, in which participants stand on a submerged platform from which they can "meet and greet" the critters. A participating adult must hold children younger than 5. Cost for this program is $104 per person (free for children 4 and under).

Note: Swimming with dolphins has both its critics and its supporters. You may want to visit the Whale and Dolphin Conservation Society's website at **www.wdcs. org** for more information.

U.S. 1 at MM 59 (on the bay side), Marathon. www.dolphins.org. ✆ **305/289-1121.** Admission $20 adults, $18 active military and veterans, $15 children 4–12. Daily 9am–4:30pm. Narrated behavior sessions with bottlenose dolphins and sea lions and educational presentations approximately every half-hour.

Florida Keys Wild Bird Center ★ NATURE RESERVE   Wander through lush canopies of mangroves on wooden walkways to see some of the Keys' most famous residents—the large variety of native birds, including broad-wing hawks, great blue and white herons, roseate spoonbills, cattle egrets, and pelicans. This not-for-profit center operates as a hospital for the many birds that have been injured by accident or disease. In 2002, the World Parrot Mission was established here, focusing on caring for parrots and educating the public about the birds. Visit at feeding time, usually about 3:30pm, when you can watch the dedicated staff feed the hundreds of hungry birds.

U.S. 1 at MM 93.6 (bay side), Tavernier. www.fkwbc.org. ✆ **305/852-4486.** Donations suggested. Daily sunrise–sunset.

Pigeon Key ★★ HISTORIC SITE   At the curve of the old bridge on Pigeon Key is an intriguing historic site that has been under renovation since late 1993. This 5-acre island once served as the camp for the crew that built the old railway in the early 20th century, and later served as housing for the bridge builders. From here, the vista includes the vestiges of Henry Flagler's old Seven-Mile Bridge and the one on which traffic presently soars, as well as many old wooden cottages and a tranquil stretch of lush foliage and sea. If you miss the shuttle tour from the Pigeon Key visitor center or would rather walk or bike to the site, it's about 2½ miles. Either way, you may want to bring a picnic to enjoy after a brief self-guided walking tour and a museum visit to what has become an homage to Flagler's railroad, featuring artifacts and photographs of the old bridge. An informative 28-minute video of the island's history is shown every hour starting at 10am. Parking is available at the Knight's Key end of the bridge, at MM 48, or at the visitor center at MM 47, on the ocean side.

East end of the Seven-Mile Bridge near MM 47, Marathon. www.pigeonkey.net. © **305/743-5999.** Admission $12 adults, $9 children 12 and under. Prices include shuttle transportation from the visitor center. Daily 10am–4pm; shuttle tours depart Marathon and run every 90 min. 10am–2:30pm; return trips run 10:30am–4pm.

Robbie's Pier ★★★ 🐟 NATURAL ATTRACTION

One of the best and definitely one of the cheapest attractions in the Upper Keys is the famed Robbie's Pier. Here the fierce steely tarpons, a prized catch for backcountry anglers, have been gathering for the past 20 years. You may recognize these prehistoric-looking giants that grow up to 200 pounds; many are displayed as trophies and mounted on local restaurant walls. To see them live, head to Robbie's Pier, where tens and sometimes hundreds of these behemoths circle the shallow waters waiting for you to feed them. Robbie's Pier also offers ranger-led boat tours and guided kayak tours to Indian Key, where you can go snorkeling or just bask in the glory of your surroundings.

U.S. 1 at MM 77.5, Islamorada. www.robbies.com. © **305/664-9814.** Admission to see the tarpon $1. Bucket of fish to feed them $3. Daily 8am–5pm. Make a hard-right U-turn off the highway, then it's a short drive before you'll see a HUNGRY TARPON restaurant sign. Robbie's driveway is just before the restaurant.

Seven-Mile Bridge ★★★ ICON

A stop at the Seven-Mile Bridge is a rewarding and relaxing break on the drive south. Built alongside the ruins of oil magnate Henry Flagler's incredible Overseas Railroad, the "new" bridge (btw. MMs 40 and 47) is considered an architectural feat. The apex of the wide-arched span, completed in 1985 at a cost of more than $45 million, is the highest point in the Keys. The new bridge and its now-defunct neighbor provide excellent vantage points from which to view the stunning waters of the Keys. In the daytime, you may want to walk, jog, or bike along the 4-mile stretch of old bridge. Or you may join local anglers, who catch barracuda, yellowtail, and dolphin (the fish, not the mammal) on what is known as "the longest fishing pier in the world." Parking is available on both sides of the bridge.

Btw. MMs 40 and 47 on U.S. 1. © **305/289-0025.**

Theater of the Sea ★ ☺ AQUARIUM

Established in 1946, the family-owned Theater of the Sea is one of the world's oldest continually operated marine mammal parks. Recently refurbished, the park's dolphin and sea lion shows are entertaining and informative, especially for children. If you want to swim with dolphins and haven't booked well in advance, you may be able to get into this place with just a few hours' notice, as opposed to the more rigid Dolphin Research Center in Marathon (see above). While the Dolphin Research Center is a legitimate, scientific establishment, Theater of the Sea is more like a theme-park attraction. That's not to say the dolphins are mistreated, but it's not as educational and professional as the Dolphin Research Center. The park's dolphin, parrot, and sea lion shows, and walking tours to visit other indigenous species of reptiles and fish, are entertaining and informative for all ages. If you want to swim with dolphins, sea lions, or southern rays, or do one of the other interactive programs, it is recommended that you call for reservations in advance. With the exception of the Dolphin Wade, all swimmers must be a minimum of 5 yrs old to participate. Other restrictions apply. There are twice-daily 4-hour adventure and snorkel cruises that cost $69 for adults and $45 for children ages 3 to 12, during which you can learn about the history and ecology of the marine environment.

U.S. 1 at MM 84.5, Islamorada. www.theaterofthesea.com. ✆ **305/664-2431.** Admission $29 adults, $20 children 3–12. Dolphin swim $185; dolphin wade $175; sea lion swim $140; sting ray swim $65. Reservations are a must. Daily 10am–5pm (ticket office closes at 3:30pm).

OUTDOOR SIGHTS & ACTIVITIES

Anne's Beach, MM 73.5 (on Lower Matecumbe Key, at the southwest end of Islamorada), is more picnic spot than full-fledged beach, but die-hard tanners congregate on this lovely, tiny strip of coarse sand that was damaged beyond recognition by storms in 1998. The place has been spruced up a bit, even the restrooms, which are (for now) clean and usable.

A better choice for real beaching is **Sombrero Beach ★★**, in Marathon, at the end of Sombrero Beach Road (near MM 50). This wide swath of uncluttered beachfront actually benefited from Hurricane George in 1998, with generous deposits of extra sand and a face-lift courtesy of the Monroe County Tourist Development Council. More than 90 feet of sand is dotted with palms, Australian pines, and royal poincianas, as well as with grills, clean restrooms, and Tiki huts for relaxing in the shade. It's also a popular nesting spot for turtles that lay their eggs at night.

If you're interested in seeing the Keys in their natural, pre–modern development state, you must venture off the highway and take to the water. Two backcountry islands that offer a glimpse of the "real" Keys are **Indian Key** and **Lignumvitae Key ★★★**. Visitors come here to relax and enjoy the islands' colorful birds and lush hammocks (elevated pieces of land above a marsh).

Named for the lignum vitae ("wood of life") trees found there, Lignumvitae Key supports a virgin tropical forest, the kind that once thrived on most of the Upper Keys. Human settlers imported "exotic" plants and animals, irrevocably changing the botanical makeup of many backcountry islands and threatening much of the indigenous wildlife. Over the past 25 years, however, the Florida Department of Natural Resources has successfully removed most of the exotic vegetation from this key, leaving the 280-acre site much as it existed in the 18th century. The island also holds the Matheson House, a historic structure built in 1919 that has survived numerous hurricanes. You can go inside, but it's interesting only if you appreciate the coral rock of which the house is made. It's a museum dedicated to the history, nature, and topography of the area. More interesting are the **Botanical Gardens,** which surround the house and are a state preserve. Lignumvitae Key has a visitor center at MM 88.5 (✆ **305/664-2540**).

Indian Key, a much smaller island on the Atlantic side of Islamorada, was occupied by Native Americans for thousands of years before European settlers arrived. The 10-acre historic site was also the original seat of Dade County before the Civil War. You can see the ruins of the previous settlement and tour the lush grounds on well-marked trails (off Indian Key Fill, Overseas Hwy., MM 79). For more information on Indian Key, check out www.abfla.com/parks/indiankey/indiankey.html or call the Florida Park Service (✆ **305/664-4815**).

If you want to see both islands, plan to spend at least half a day. You can rent your own powerboat from **Robbie's Rent-A-Boat,** U.S. 1 at MM 77.5 (on the bay side), on Islamorada. It's then a $1 admission fee to each island, which includes an hour-long guided tour by park rangers. This is a good option if you're a confident boater. We also recommend Robbie's **ferry service.** A visit to Lignumvitae Key costs $20 for adults and $15 for kids 12 and under, which includes the $1 park admission. For a ride to Indian Key, take the 2½-hour "Florida Bay Eco-Nature Tour," which costs $35 for adults and $20 for children 12 and under. The ferry is a more economical, easier way to enjoy the beauty of the islands. The runabouts, which carry up to six people, usually depart from Robbie's Pier (p. 240) Thursday through Monday at 10am and 2pm for Lignumvitae Key, but when demand is low and mosquitoes are high, the ferry runs only from Friday to Sunday from 10am to 2pm. In high season, you may need to book 2 days before departure. Robbie's also does eco-tours, 2-hour trips through passages among the sea-grass beds that rim the many protected shallow bays. You'll get to cruise among the hundreds of small, uninhabited mangrove and hardwood hammock islands, which host an amazing variety of wildlife and create the island network of the Florida Bay. Call © **305/664-4815** for information from the park service; or call © **305/664-9814** or visit Robbie's.

TWO EXCEPTIONAL STATE PARKS

One of the best places to discover the diverse ecosystem of the Upper Keys is its most famous park, **John Pennekamp Coral Reef State Park ★★★**, located on U.S. 1 at MM 102.5, in Key Largo (www.pennekamppark.com; © **305/451-6300**). Named for a former *Miami Herald* editor and conservationist, the 188-square-mile park, which celebrated its 50th anniversary in 2010, is the nation's first undersea preserve: It's a sanctuary for part of the only living coral reef in the continental United States.

Because the water is extremely shallow, the 40 species of coral and more than 650 species of fish here are accessible to divers, snorkelers, and glass-bottom-boat passengers. To experience this park, visitors must get in the water—you can't see the reef from the shore. Your first stop should be the visitor center, which has a mammoth 30,000-gallon saltwater aquarium that re-creates a reef ecosystem. At the adjacent dive shop, you can rent snorkeling and diving equipment and join one of the boat trips that depart for the reef throughout the day. Visitors can also rent motorboats, sailboats, sailboards, and canoes. The 2½-hour glass-bottom-boat tour is the best way to see the coral reefs if you don't want to get wet. Watch for the lobsters and other sea life residing in the fairly shallow ridge walls beneath the coastal waters. *Remember:* These are protected waters, so you can't remove anything from them.

Canoeing around the park's narrow mangrove channels and tidal creeks is also popular. You can go on your own in a rented canoe or, in winter, sign up for a tour led by a local naturalist. Hikers have two short trails from which to choose: a boardwalk through the mangroves, and a dirt trail through a tropical hardwood hammock. Ranger-led walks are usually scheduled daily from the end of November to April. Call © **305/451-1202** for schedule information and reservations.

Park admission is $8 per vehicle of two to eight passengers, $4 for a single driver, and $2 for pedestrians and bicyclists, plus a 50¢ Monroe County surcharge per person. On busy weekends, there's often a line of cars waiting to get into the park. On your way in, ask the ranger for a map. Glass-bottom-boat tours cost $24 for adults and $17 for children 11 and under. Tours depart three times daily, at 9:15am, 12:15pm, and 3pm. Snorkeling tours are $30 for adults and $25 for children 17 and under; masks, fins, and snorkels cost $7 and the snorkel is yours to keep. Canoes rent for $12 per hour; kayaks are $12 per hour for a single, $17 per hour for a double. For experienced boaters only, four different sizes of reef boats (powerboats) rent for $160 to $210 for 4 hours, and $259 to $359 for a full day; call © **305/451-6325** for information. A minimum $400 deposit (or more, depending on boat size) is required. The park's boat-rental office is open daily from 8am to 5pm (last boat rented at 3pm); phone for tour and dive times. Reservations are recommended for all of the above. Also see below for more options on diving, fishing, and snorkeling off these reefs.

Long Key State Recreation Area ★★★, U.S. 1 at MM 68, Long Key (www. floridastateparks.org/longkey; ✆ 305/664-4815), is one of the best places in the Middle Keys for hiking, camping, snorkeling, and canoeing. This 965-acre site is situated atop the remains of an ancient coral reef. At the entrance gate, ask for a free flyer describing the local trails and wildlife.

Three nature trails can be explored via foot or canoe. The Golden Orb Trail is a 40-minute walk through mostly plants; the Layton Trail is a 15-minute walk along the bay; and the Long Key Canoe Trail glides along a shallow-water lagoon. The excellent 1.5-mile canoe trail is short and sweet, allowing visitors to loop around the mangroves in about an hour. Long Key is also a great spot to stop for a picnic if you get hungry on your way to Key West. Campsites are available along the Atlantic Ocean. The swimming and saltwater fishing (license required) are top-notch here, as is the snorkeling, which is shallow and on the shoreline of the Atlantic. For novices, educational programs on the aforementioned are available, too.

Railroad builder Henry Flagler created the Long Key Fishing Club here in 1906, and the waters surrounding the park are still popular with game fishers. In summer, sea turtles lumber onto the protected coast to lay their eggs. Educational programs are available to view this phenomenon.

Admission is $5 per car of two to eight people, $4 for a single-occupant vehicle, $2 per pedestrian or bicyclist, plus 50¢ per person Monroe County surcharge (except for the Layton Trail, which is free). The recreation area is open daily from 8am to sunset. You can rent canoes at the trail head for about $5 per hour, $10 each additional hour. The nearest place to rent snorkel equipment is the Postcard Inn at Holiday Isle, 84001 U.S. 1, Islamorada (✆ 800/327-7070). Camping is popular, and a construction project completed in July 2012 upgraded the park's campsites.

WATERSPORTS

There are hundreds of outfitters in the Keys who will arrange all kinds of water activities, from cave dives to parasailing. If those recommended below are booked up or unreachable, ask the local chamber of commerce for a list of qualified members.

BOATING   In addition to the rental shops in the state parks, you'll find dozens of outfitters along U.S. 1 offering a range of runabouts and skiffs for boaters of any experience level. Captain Pip's, U.S. 1 at MM 47.5, Marathon (www.captainpips. com; ✆ 800/707-1692 or 305/743-4403), charges $195 to $330 per day. Overnight accommodations are available and include a free boat rental: 2-night minimum $250 to $450 in season and $225 to $415 off season; weekly rates are $1,185 to $2,595. Rooms are Key West comfortable and charming, with ceiling fans, tile floors, and pine paneling. But the best part is that every room comes with an 18- to 21-foot boat for your use during your stay. Robbie's Rent-a-Boat, U.S. 1 at MM 77.5, Islamorada (www.robbies.com; ✆ 305/664-9814), rents 18- to 26-foot motorboats with engines ranging from 60 to 130 horsepower. Boat rentals are $135 to $185 for a half-day and $185 to $235 for a full day.

CANOEING & KAYAKING   We can think of no better way to explore the uninhabited backcountry on the Gulf side of the Keys than by kayak or canoe, as you can reach places that big boats just can't get to because of their large draft. Manatees will sometimes cuddle up to the boats, thinking them to be another friendly species.

Many area hotels rent kayaks and canoes to guests, as do the outfitters listed here. Florida Bay Outfitters, U.S. 1 at MM 104, Key Largo (www.kayakfloridakeys.com;

C **305/451-3018**), rents canoes and sea kayaks for use in and around John Pennekamp Coral Reef State Park for $40 to $75 for a half-day, $50 to $90 for a full day. **Florida Keys Kayak and Sail,** U.S. 1 at MM 75.5, Islamorada (www.robbies.com; *C* **305/664-4878**), at Robbie's Pier, offers backcountry tours, botanical-preserve tours of Lignumvitae Key, historic-site tours of Indian Key, and sunset tours through the mangrove tunnels and saltwater flats. Tour rates are from $39 to $49; rental rates range from $15 per hour to $45 per day for a single kayak, and $20 per hour to $60 per day for a double kayak.

Reflections Nature Tours (www.floridakeyskayaktours.com; *C* **305/872-4668**) is a small mobile company that specializes in kayak tours through the Lower Keys. Guided kayak excursions cost $50 per person for a 3-hour tour, $50 per person for a 2-hour full-moon tour. The 4-hour custom tour with mothership transport of kayaks and paddlers costs $125 per person. All tours are by appointment only. Kayak rentals are $45 for a single kayak all day and $60 for a full-day tandem. For the same price as a single kayak, you can rent a paddleboard. Reflections also offers paddleboard tours, lessons, and custom kayak sailing and fishing excursions.

Nature lovers can slip through the silent backcountry waters off Key West and the Lower Keys in a kayak, discovering the flora and fauna that make up the unique Keys ecosystem, on **Blue Planet Kayak Tours'** (www.blue-planet-kayak.com; *C* **305/294-8087**) starlight tour. All excursions are led by an environmental scientist. The starlight tours last between 2½ and 3 hours. No previous kayaking experience is necessary. Cost for the guided kayak adventure is $50 per person.

FISHING **Robbie's Partyboats & Charters,** U.S. 1 at MM 77.5, Islamorada (www.robbies.com; *C* **305/664-8070** or 664-8498), located at Robbie's Marina on Lower Matecumbe Key, offers day and night deep-sea and reef-fishing trips aboard a 65-foot party boat. Big-game fishing charters are also available, and "splits" are arranged for solo fishers. Party-boat fishing costs about $35 for a half-day morning tour ($3 for rod-and-reel rental); it's $40 if you want to go back out on an afternoon tour. Charters run about $950 to $1,050 for a full day.

Bud n' Mary's Fishing Marina, U.S. 1 at MM 79.8, Islamorada (www.budn marys.com; *C* **800/742-7945** or 305/664-2461), one of the largest marinas between Miami and Key West, is packed with sailors offering backcountry fishing charters. This is the place to go if you want to stalk tarpon, bonefish, and snapper. If the seas are not too rough, deep-sea and coral fishing trips can also be arranged. Charters for two anglers cost $400 for a half-day, $575 for a full day; splits begin at $75 per person. Tarpon trips for two are $425.

JET-SKIING **SeaMonster Watersports,** 3390 Gulfview Ave., Marathon (*C* **305/743-6541**), offers 2-hour jet-ski tours to the Seven-Mile Bridge, Key Vaca, and Pigeon Key. Tours are $130 per jet ski and carry up to three to four passengers, including children.

SCUBA DIVING & SNORKELING Just 6 miles off Key Largo is a U.S. Navy Landing Ship Dock, the latest artificial wreck site to hit the Keys—or, rather, to be submerged 130 feet *below* the Keys.

The **Florida Keys Dive Center,** U.S. 1 at MM 90.5, Tavernier (www.floridakeys divectr.com; *C* **305/852-4599**), takes snorkelers and divers to the reefs of John Pennekamp Coral Reef State Park and environs every day. PADI (Professional Association of Diving Instructors) training courses are available for the uninitiated. Tours leave at 8am and 12:30pm; the cost is $38 per person to snorkel (plus $10 rental fee for mask, snorkel, and fins), and $65 per person to dive (plus an extra $19 if you need to rent all the gear. Add $10 to that $19 if you're going on a major "heavy metal" dive to sites such as *Spiegel Grove,* a landing ship dock that was sunk to create an artificial reef.

At **Hall's Dive Center & Career Institute,** U.S. 1 at MM 50, Marathon (www. hallsdiving.com; ℂ **305/743-5929**), snorkelers and divers can dive at Looe Key, Sombrero Reef, Delta Shoal, Content Key, or Coffins Patch. Tours are scheduled daily at 9am and 1pm. You'll spend 1 hour at each of two sites per tour. It's $40 per person to snorkel (gear included), $35 for children, and $55 to $65 per person (weights included) to dive (tanks $7.50 to $15 each).

The **Key Largo Scuba Shack,** 97684 Overseas Hwy., in the Seafarer Resort at MM 97.8 (www.keylargoscubashack.com; ℂ **305/735-4313**), will take 6 to 10 divers on a 37-foot Burpee dive vessel on once-daily three-tank, dive-master-guided trips to explore the area's reefs and wrecks. Rates range from $40 to $160 per person.

ORGANIZED TOURS

Key Largo Bike and Adventure Tours (www.keylargobike.com; ℂ **305/395-1551**) provides guided bicycle tours, including the "Pigeon Key Biking and Kayaking Tour," a 6-hour, $180 per-person excursion that includes transportation, active gear, entrance fees, and lunch. In addition to biking and kayaking, participants can choose between snorkeling on the beach or taking a 1.5-mile hiking trail. They also conduct rides to Key West that are for experienced cyclists who are used to riding along the road. The tour starts at MM 100 and ends at the southernmost point in the continental United States. Participants can choose to explore Key West for the afternoon, or spend the night for an additional charge. These tours take place on the second Saturday of every month. For a shorter trip focused on history and local culture, the company provides historical trips in Islamorada. The 3-mile tours, which last approximately 2 hours and take place every weekend, proceed at an easy pace and include 10 stops around the island.

Where to Eat

Not known as a culinary hot spot (though it's improving), the Upper and Middle keys do have some excellent restaurants, most of which specialize in seafood. The landmark **Green Turtle Inn** (below) is alive and well, featuring classic and contemporary Florida cuisine, a full bar and tasting station, custom catering, gourmet to go, and a Green Turtle product line, all in a beautiful, rustic environment. The restaurant is flanked by an art gallery and sport-fishing outfitter, making it a one-stop shop for locals and fun-loving tourists.

Often, visitors (especially those who fish) take advantage of accommodations that have kitchen facilities and cook their own meals. Some restaurants will even clean and cook your catch, for a fee.

VERY EXPENSIVE

Atlantic's Edge ★★★ SEAFOOD   Continuing its award-winning culinary tradition, albeit with a modern twist, the 21st-century version of Atlantic's Edge is a welcome addition to the Upper Keys dining scene. Signature dishes include panroasted hogfish with house-made gnocchi, baby vegetables, arugula salad, and Parmesan foam; and whole fried yellowtail snapper with rice, chili aioli, citrus vinaigrette, and house-made tartar sauce. With an emphasis on farm-to-table ingredients and, of course, the freshest seafood possible, Atlantic's Edge puts on an impressive show. The revamped restaurant itself is stunning, with views of its namesake and a gorgeous glassed-in wine cellar featuring an impressive collection of vintages.

Cheeca Lodge, U.S. 1 at MM 82, Islamorada. © **305/664-4651.** Reservations recommended. Main courses $25–$44. AE, DC, MC, V. Daily 7am–5pm and 6–10pm.

Pierre's ★★★ FRENCH   The two-story British West Indies–style plantation home that houses this exquisite French restaurant is only part of the dramatic effect of a dinner at Pierre's. Inside, you'll find more design drama—in a good way—in the form of an eclectic mix of Moroccan, Indian, and African artifacts. Lighting is dim, with candlelight and Tiki torches outside, and it's completely romantic—especially outdoors on the second-floor veranda overlooking the water. The food challenges the setting, with amazing flavors and gorgeous presentation. The lemon butter–poached Maine lobster with sweet corn and chorizo fritters, and the Florida Keys hogfish meunière with roasted creamer potatoes, pattypan squash, and baby zucchini are to die for. Desserts are divine, and if you can't decide what to have, order the Valrhona Chocolate Fondue with biscotti, *pâté a choux,* lemon sugar cookies, strawberries, and mandarin oranges. After dinner, head downstairs to the Green Flash Lounge, where you'll find a laid-back cocktail scene, with locals and visitors marveling at the exquisite, priceless setting. Pierre's also hosts a fabulous, monthly Full Moon Party with its casual-dining sister, Morada Bay Beach Café.

U.S. 1 at MM 81.6 (bay side), Islamorada. www.pierres-restaurant.com. © **305/664-3225.** Main courses $28–$41. AE, MC, V. Sun–Thurs 6–10pm; Fri–Sat 6–11pm. Lounge open at 5pm daily. Restaurant closed Tues during summer.

EXPENSIVE

Barracuda Grill ★ SEAFOOD   This small, casual spot serves good seafood, steaks, and chops, but what you really want here—if you can get it before it sells out—is the local black grouper, pan sautéed and oven roasted and then served with a schmear of Key lime caper butter. Some favorites are the Caicos gold conch, braised pork shank, and mangrove snapper and mango. Try the appetizer of tipsy olives, marinated in gin or vodka, to kick-start your meal. For fans of spicy food, go for the red-hot calamari. Decorated with barracuda-themed art, the restaurant also features a well-priced American wine list with lots of California vintages.

U.S. 1 at MM 49.5 (bay side), Marathon. www.barracudagrillmarathonfl.com. © **305/743-3314.** Main courses $16–$46. AE, MC, V. Wed–Sat 6–10pm.

Butterfly Café ★★★ SEAFOOD   In the stunning Tranquility Bay resort, Butterfly Café is the newest gourmet hot spot in the Middle Keys, with water views and a stellar menu of fresh local seafood. Among the dishes not to miss: horseradish-encrusted grouper, and Cuban-spiced, grilled pork chops with garlic, lime, and cumin and served with black beans and rice. Service is very friendly and knowledgeable, and desserts are to die for. Save room for the sticky toffee pudding and nutty-crust Key lime pie with white-chocolate mousse. It's open for breakfast, lunch, and dinner, but Sunday brunch is especially spectacular. Don't miss the tropical French toast.

2600 Overseas Hwy., in the Tranquility Bay Resort, Marathon. www.tranquilitybay.com. © **305/289-0888.** Main courses $18–$37. AE, MC, V. Daily 7–10am and 11:30am–10pm; Sun brunch 10:30am–2:30pm.

Green Turtle Inn ★★ SEAFOOD   This landmark Keys restaurant serves cuisine cooked with locally farmed vegetables and microgreens for a fabulous dining experience. The restaurant has been expanded and revamped, with a new menu. Some old menu items remain—the famous turtle chowder with pepper sherry and luscious conch chowder—but the new menu items are nothing to sneer at. Small plates, including pan-seared scallops with whipped potatoes, sherry-vinegar brown butter, white-truffle oil, and sizzled leeks, make for satisfying main courses, but don't miss entrees such as fresh seared tuna with shrimp and sweet-pepper hash, wilted spinach, sweet soy glaze, and wasabi mustard. And do not pass up the Green Turtle bread pudding! After dinner, check out the art gallery and gourmet shop. Green Turtle also serves excellent breakfast (try the coconut French toast) and lunch (we love the yellowtail po'boy). For those craving Asian, the Green Turtle's sister restaurant is **Kaiyo Grill and Sushi,** MM 81.7 (www.kaiyokeys.com; ℂ **305/664-5556**), an excellent "island-influenced" Asian restaurant.

81219 Overseas Hwy., at MM 81.2, Islamorada. www.greenturtlekeys.com. ℂ **305/664-2006.** Main courses $20–$38. AE, MC, V. Daily 7–10am and 11:30am–10pm.

Marker 88 ★★★ SEAFOOD   An institution in the Upper Keys, Marker 88 has been pleasing locals and visitors since it opened in the 1970s. New chefs and owners have infused a new life into the place and the menu, which still utilizes fresh fruits, local ingredients, and fish caught in the Keys' waters. Among the menu highlights are the crispy yellowtail meunière, sautéed and finished with a Key lime butter; and mahi Martinique, sautéed and topped with sweet basil, grilled bananas, and garlic butter. The waitresses, who are pleasant enough, require a bit of patience, but the food—not to mention the spectacular Gulf views—is worth it.

U.S. 1 at MM 88 (bay side), Islamorada. www.marker88.info. ℂ **305/852-9315.** Reservations suggested. Main courses $24–$38; burgers and sandwiches $10–$15. AE, DC, DISC, MC, V. Tues–Sun 5–11pm. Closed Sept.

Ziggie and Mad Dog's ★★★ STEAKHOUSE   When former Miami Dolphins player the late Jim Mandich, aka Mad Dog, bought Ziggie's Crab Shack from Sigmund "Ziggie" Stockie, he decided to keep the ex-owner's name up there with his own. These days, people are mad for this fine Florida Keys steak and chop house. Casually elegant, Ziggie and Mad Dog's is quite the Upper Keys scene, attracting everyone from locals and tourists to day-trippers looking for something more than a ramshackle fish shack. If you're starving, we dare you to order the 28-ounce Csonka Porterhouse named after Mandich's fellow 'fins teammate Larry Csonka. People also rave about the bone-in rib-eye and the mac and cheese. Service is friendly and the vibe is fun. Sports fans love it here not because of the games on in the bar, but because many of Mandich's famous athlete friends come here.

83000 Overseas Hwy., Islamorada. www.ziggieandmaddogs.com. ℂ **305/664-3391.** Reservations suggested. Main courses $20–$40. AE, DC, DISC, MC, V. Daily 5:30–10pm.

MODERATE

Island Grill ★ SEAFOOD   If you drive too fast over Snake Creek Bridge, you may miss one of the best Keys dining experiences around. Just under the bridge and on the bay, Island Grill is a locals' favorite, with an expansive outdoor deck and bar and cozy waterfront dining room serving some fresh fare, including their famous tuna nachos, guava barbecued shrimp, and graham cracker–crusted calamari. There are also salads, sandwiches—try the lobster roll—and entrees, including a whole yellow-tail snapper with Thai sweet chili sauce that's out of this world. Bring your own catch, and they'll cook and prepare it for you—served family-style with veggies and rice for only $12. Live entertainment almost every night brings in a great, colorful Keys crowd. Although they serve breakfast too, we say skip the food and just stick to the bloody marys.

MM 88.5 (ocean side at Snake Creek Bridge), Islamorada. www.keysislandgrill.com. ☎ **305/664-8400.** Reservations not necessary. Main courses $14–$40; sandwiches $7–$14. Sun–Thurs 11am–10pm; Fri–Sat 11am–11pm.

Key Largo Conch House Restaurant & Coffee Bar ★★ AMERICAN A funky, cozy, off-the-beaten-path hot spot for breakfast, lunch, and dinner, Key Largo Conch House is exactly that—a house set amid lush foliage, complete with resident dog, parrot, wraparound veranda for outdoor dining, and a warm and inviting indoor dining room reminiscent of your grandma's. Food is fresh and fabulously priced—from the heaping $15 plate of Mom's Andouille Alfredo, to $8-to-$14 twists on the usual eggs Benedict, including our favorite, the crab cakes Benedict. Featured on the Food Network, Conch House should be a feature on everyone's trip down to the Keys, if not just for a cup of excellent coffee and a slice of homemade Key lime pie. It's also one of the few pet-friendly restaurants in the area.

U.S. 1 at MM 100, Key Largo. www.keylargocoffeehouse.com. ☎ **305/453-4844.** Reservations recommended. Main courses $11–$39; wraps and sandwiches $8–$14; breakfast $7–$15. AE, DC, DISC, MC, V. Daily 7am–10pm.

Lazy Days ★ SEAFOOD/BAR FARE   Making good on its name, this laid-back oceanfront eatery is the quintessence of Keys lifestyle. But chef/owner Lupe is far from lazy, preparing excellent fresh seafood, seafood pastas, vegetarian pastas, sandwiches, steaks, and chicken. He'll even cook your own catch. A popular happy hour at the bar from 4 to 6pm features three-for-$1 appetizers (at the bar only). Lazy Days is so popular that Lupe and co-owner Michelle Ledesma have opened **Lazy Days South,** featuring an identical menu and waterfront seating at the Marathon Marina (☎ **305/289-0839**).

79867 Overseas Hwy., Islamorada. www.lazydaysrestaurant.com. ☎ **305/664-5256.** Reservations not usually required. Main courses $15–$28; lighter fare and appetizers $9–$15. AE, DC, DISC, MC, V. Sun–Thurs 11am–9:30pm; Fri–Sat 11am–10pm.

Lorelei Restaurant and Cabana Bar ★ SEAFOOD/BAR FARE   Follow the siren call of the enormous roadside mermaid—you won't be dashed onto the rocks. This big old fish house and bar, with excellent views of the bay, is a great place for a snack, a meal, or a beer. A good-value menu focuses mainly on seafood; in season, lobster is the way to go. Other fare includes the standard clam chowder, fried shrimp, and doughy conch fritters. For those tired of fish, the menu offers a few beef options, but we say the simpler the better. Food is definitely trumped by ambience. The outside bar has live music every evening, and you can order snacks and light meals from a limited menu.

U.S. 1 at MM 82, Islamorada. www.loreleifloridakeys.com. ☎ **305/664-4656.** Reservations not usually required. Main courses $13–$22; sandwiches $9–$11. AE, DC, DISC, MC, V. Daily 7am–10:30pm. Outside bar serves breakfast 7–11am; lunch/appetizer menu 11am–9pm. Bar closes at midnight.

INEXPENSIVE

Calypso's Seafood Grill ★★ 🏠 SEAFOOD

With a motto proudly declaring, "Yes, we know the music is loud and the food is spicy. That's the way we like it!" you know you're in a typical Keys eatery. Thankfully, the food is anything but, with inventive seafood dishes in a casual and rustic waterside setting. Among the house specialties is cracked conch and steamed clams, but if you're not too hot, try the she-crab soup. It's exceptional. If it's offered, try the outstanding deep-fried corn and the hog snapper however they prepare it. The prices are surprisingly reasonable, but the service may be a bit more laid back than you're used to.

1 Seagate Blvd. (near MM 99.5), Key Largo. ✆ **305/451-0600.** Main courses $10–$20. No credit cards. Wed–Thurs and Sun–Mon 11:30am–10pm; Fri–Sat 11:30am–11pm. From the south, turn right at the blinking yellow lights near MM 99.5 to Ocean Bay Dr., and then turn right. Look for the blue-vinyl-sided building on the left.

Islamorada Fish Company ★★ SEAFOOD

Pick up a cooler of stone crab claws in season (mid-Oct to Apr), or try the great fried-fish sandwiches. A few hundred yards up the road (at MM 81.6) is Islamorada Fish Company Restaurant & Bakery, the newer establishment, which looks like an average diner but has fantastic seafood, pastas, and breakfasts. Locals gather here for politics and gossip as well as grits, oatmeal, omelets, and pastries. Keep your eyes open while dining outside—the last time we were here, baby manatees were floating around, waiting for their close-ups.

U.S. 1 at MM 81.5 (up the street from Cheeca Lodge), Islamorada. www.islamoradafishco.com. ✆ **800/258-2559** or 305/664-9271. Reservations not accepted. Main courses $12–$22; sandwiches $10–$15. DISC, MC, V. Sun–Thurs 11am–9pm; Fri–Sat 11am–10pm.

Snapper's ★ SEAFOOD

A locals' waterfront favorite, Snapper's serves fresh seafood caught by local fishermen—or by you, if you dare! The blackened mahimahi is exceptional and a bargain, complete with salad, vegetable, and choice of starch. There's also live music nightly and a lively, colorful—and deliciously casual—crowd. A popular Sunday brunch features live jazz from the barge out back and a make-your-own–bloody mary bar. Kids love feeding the tarpon off the docks, and for those who just can't stay away from work, there's free Wi-Fi, indoors and out. If you caught a big one, clean it and they will cook it for you at $12 for 8 ounces a person. For an even more casual dining experience, check out the Turtle Club, the entirely outdoor, waterfront bar and grill located out back and featuring live music and a more casual menu of sandwiches, snacks, and pub grub.

139 Seaside Ave., at MM 94.5, Key Largo. www.snapperskeylargo.com. ✆ **305/852-5956.** Main courses $13–$28; sandwiches $9–$15. DISC, MC, V. Sun–Thurs 11am–9pm; Fri–Sat 11am–10pm.

Entertainment & Nightlife

Nightlife in the Upper Keys tends to start before the sun goes down, often at noon, as most people—visitors and locals alike—are on vacation. Also, many anglers and sports-minded folk go to bed early.

Hog Heaven, MM 85.3, just off the main road on the ocean side, Islamorada (✆ **305/664-9669**), opened in the early 1990s, the joint venture of young locals tired of tourist traps. This whitewashed biker bar is a welcome respite from the neon-colored cocktail circuit. It has a waterside view and diversions such as big-screen TVs and video games. The food isn't bad, either. The atmosphere is cliquish because most patrons are regulars, so start up a game of pool to break the ice. It's open daily from 11am to 4am.

No trip to the Keys is complete without a stop at the **Tiki Bar at the Postcard Inn Beach Resort & Marina at Holiday Isle,** U.S. 1 at MM 84, Islamorada (☏ 305/664-2321). Hundreds of revelers visit this oceanside spot for drinks and dancing at any time of day, but the live rock starts at 8pm and goes until around 1am. The thatched-roof Tiki Bar draws a mix of thirsty people, all in pursuit of a good time. In the afternoon and early evening (when everyone is either sunburned, drunk, or just happy to be dancing to live reggae), head for the 21-and-over version of Swiss Family Robinson meets the Florida Keys at **Rum Runner's,** also at Holiday Isle and open daily until midnight. For information, call the Postcard Inn Holiday Isle.

Locals and tourists mingle at the outdoor cabana bar at **Lorelei** (see "Where to Eat," above). Most evenings after 5pm, you'll find local bands playing on a thatched-roof stage—mainly rock or reggae, and sometimes blues.

Woody's Saloon and Restaurant, U.S. 1 at MM 82, Islamorada (☏ 305/664-4335), is a lively, loud, raunchy, local legend serving up mediocre pizzas, buck-naked strippers, and live bands almost every night. The house band, Big Dick and the Extenders, showcases a 300-pound Native American who does a lewd, rude, and crude routine of politically incorrect jokes and songs starting at 9pm Tuesday through Sunday. He is a legend. By the way, don't think you're lucky if you're offered the front table: It's the target seat for Big Dick's haranguing. Avoid the lame karaoke on Sunday and Monday evenings. There's a small cover most nights. Drink specials, contests, and Big Dick keep this place packed until 4am almost every night. *Note:* This place is not for the faint of heart, but more for those from the Howard Stern School of Nightlife.

For a more subdued atmosphere, try the stained-glass and mahogany-wood bar and club at **Zane Grey's,** on the second floor of World Wide Sportsman, MM 81.5 (☏ 305/664-4244). Outside, enjoy a view of the calm waters of the bay; inside, soak up the history of real longtime anglers. It's open from 11am to at least 11pm (later on weekends). Call to find out who's playing on Friday and Saturday nights, when there's live entertainment and no cover.

Where to Stay

U.S. 1 is lined with chain hotels in all price ranges. In the Upper Keys, the best moderately priced option is the **Courtyard Marriott Key Largo,** off U.S. 1 at MM 100, Key Largo (www.marriott.com; ☏ 305/451-3939), which has a waterfront heated pool, marina with tour boats and boat rentals and a Tiki bar, and is just 3 miles from John Pennekamp Coral Reef State Park. Another good Upper Keys option is the pet-friendly **Days Inn Islamorada Oceanfront Resort,** U.S. 1 at MM 82.5 (www.daysinnflakeys.com; ☏ 800/DAYS-INN [329-7466] or 305/664-3681). In the Middle Keys, the **Siesta Motel,** 7425 Overseas Hwy., MM 54 in Marathon (www.siestamotel.net; ☏ 305/743-5671), offers reasonably priced, very clean oceanside rooms. The **Holiday Inn Express & Suites,** 13201 Overseas Hwy. (www.hiexpress.com; ☏ 888/465-4329 or 305/289-0222) is a smoke-free and pet-friendly hotel featuring free hot breakfast, marina, Tiki bar, large outdoor pool, and free Wi-Fi.

Because the real beauty of the Keys lies mostly beyond the highways, there is no better way to see this area than by boat. So why not stay in a floating hotel? Especially if you're traveling with a group, houseboats can be economical. To rent a houseboat, contact **Houseboat Vacations,** 85944 Overseas Hwy., Islamorada (www.floridakeys.com/houseboats; ☏ 305/664-4009). Rates are from $1,112 to $1,350 for 3 nights. Boats accommodate up to six people.

Those wondering what may have happened to many of the condos that were built before the real estate bust take the **Islander Bayside,** 81450 Overseas Hwy., Islamorada (www.islanderbayside.com; © **305/664-0082**), a former condo which quickly changed gears and reopened as an extended stay hotel in 2010 featuring 25 two-bedroom, one-and-a-half-bath town homes, a 14-slip marina, and nightly rates beginning at $399 with a 3-night minimum.

VERY EXPENSIVE

Cheeca Lodge & Spa ★★★ ☺ Located on 27 lush acres of beachfront, this rambling resort is home to a full-service spa, 9-hole golf course, and much more. Rooms have the amenities of a world-class resort in a laid-back setting. The historic landmark boasts Premier Suites, 840-square-foot rooms with huge balconies, floor-to-ceiling glass walls opening to ocean or island views, open-air round spa tubs for two, and glass rain showers. Standard guest rooms feature West Indies–style decor, marble bathrooms, flatscreen TVs, and wireless Internet. The lobby includes a bar, 2,400 square feet of retail shops, and the restaurants **Limoncello,** offering rustic Mediterranean dishes, and Cheeca's signature restaurant, **Atlantic's Edge,** featuring fresh seafood, steaks, and organic local produce. **The Spa at Cheeca** offers products from fair-trade sources as well as a variety of massage therapies, skin care, body treatments, a fitness room, and butler-serviced poolside cabanas. Cheeca also offers tennis, a 9-hole Jack Nicklaus–designed golf course, eco-tours, sunset cruises, snorkel excursions, boats with seasoned guides for backcountry fishing, the Camp Cheeca children's environmental program, and much more. The $39 daily resort fee may seem steep, but it's worth it as it includes just about everything.

U.S. 1 at MM 82 (P.O. Box 527), Islamorada, FL 33036. www.cheeca.com. © **305/664-4651.** Fax 305/664-2893. 212 units. In season $599–$1,099 Superior, $599–$1,399 Luxury, $899–$999 Premier; off season $199–$599 Superior, $249–$549 Luxury, $399–$499 Premier. AE, DC, DISC, MC, V. **Amenities:** 2 restaurants; 2 lounges (1 poolside); babysitting; bike rental; children's nature programs; concierge; 9-hole golf course; 5 Jacuzzis; 2 outdoor heated pools; saltwater lagoon; room service; full-service spa; 6 lighted hard tennis courts; watersports equipment/rentals. *In room:* A/C, TV/DVD, CD player, hair dryer, kitchenette (in suites), minibar, Wi-Fi (free).

Hawks Cay Resort ★★★ ☺ Set on its own 60-acre island in the Middle Keys, this resort is far superior to Cheeca Lodge when it comes to activities. In addition to sailing, fishing, snorkeling, diving, SNUBA, water-skiing, kiteboarding, and stand-up paddleboarding, guests have the opportunity to interact directly with dolphins in the resort's Dolphin Connection program. (You'll need to reserve a spot well in advance.) In 2011, the resort added the JetLev flying experience, allowing guests to wear a water-propelled jetpack and soar up to 30 feet into the air. Guest rooms are large, with spacious bathrooms, island-style furniture, and private balconies with ocean or tropical views. There are also 225 waterfront villas with full kitchens. The 7,000-square-foot **Calm Waters Spa** provides stellar treatments. Organized children's activities include marine- and ecology-inspired programs. Fine-dining options include a Nuevo-Latino restaurant and bar featuring hard-to-find rums; **Sand Bar,** a new adults-oriented area that features opulent light fare; **Ocean,** an open-kitchen concept restaurant; and **Island Time,** a gift shop offering a full Starbucks menu.

61 Hawks Cay Blvd., at MM 61, Duck Key, FL 33050. www.hawkscay.com. © **877/667-0763** or 305/743-7000. Fax 305/743-5215. 419 units, including 242 2- and 3-bedroom villas. Winter $329–$659 double, $549–$1,300 suite, $519–$1,400 villa; off season $279–$559 double, $479–$900 suite, $449–$1,000 villa. Packages available. AE, DC, DISC, MC, V. **Amenities:** 4 restaurants; lounge; bike

rental; children's programs ($48–$75 per child); concierge; exercise room; Jacuzzi; 5 outdoor heated pools; room service; full-service spa; 8 tennis courts (6 hard, 2 clay, 2 lighted); watersports equipment/rentals. *In room:* A/C, TV, fridge, hair dryer, Internet access.

EXPENSIVE

Casa Morada ★★ 👜 The closest thing to a boutique hotel in the Florida Keys, Casa Morada is the brainchild of a trio of New York women who used to work for hip hotelier Ian Schrager. This 16-suite property is a hipster haven tucked away off a sleepy street and radiates serenity and style in an area where serenity is aplenty, but style is elusive. Sitting on 1¼ acres of prime bayfront, the hotel features a limestone grotto, a freshwater pool, and poolside beverage service. Each of the cool rooms has either a private garden or a terrace—request the one with the open-air Jacuzzi that faces the bay. While the decor is decidedly island, think St. Barts rather than, say, Gilligan's. There's no on-site restaurant, though a complimentary breakfast is served daily. Enjoy free use of bikes, bocce balls, board games, and morning yoga lessons. Only children 16 and older are allowed.

136 Madeira Rd., Islamorada, FL 33036. www.casamorada.com. ⓒ **888/881-3030** or 305/664-0044. Fax 305/664-0674. 16 units. Winter $329–$659 double; off season $249–$509 double. Rates include continental breakfast. AE, DISC, MC, V. From U.S. 1 S., at MM 82.2, turn right onto Madeira Rd. and continue to the end of the street. The hotel is on the right. Friendly pets welcome. **Amenities:** Complimentary bike use; freshwater pool. *In room:* A/C, TV/DVD, CD player, hair dryer, minibar.

Jules' Undersea Lodge ★★★ 👜 Staying here is an experience of a lifetime—if you're brave enough to take the plunge. Originally built as a research lab, this small underwater compartment, which rests on pillars on the ocean floor, now operates as a two-room hotel. As expensive as it is unusual, Jules' is most popular with diving honeymooners. To get inside, guests swim 21 feet under the structure and pop up into the unit through a 4×6-foot "moon pool" that gurgles soothingly all night long. The 30-foot-deep underwater suite consists of two separate bedrooms that share a common living area. Room service will deliver your meals, daily newspapers, and even a late-night pizza in waterproof containers, at no extra charge. If you don't have time or a desire to spend the night, you can hang out and explore the lodge for 3 hours for $125 to $165 per person.

51 Shoreland Dr., Key Largo, FL 33037. www.jul.com. ⓒ **305/451-2353.** Fax 305/451-4789. 2 units. $375–$475 per person. Rates include breakfast and dinner, as well as all equipment and unlimited scuba diving in the lagoon for certified divers. Packages available. AE, DISC, MC, V. From U.S. 1 S., at MM 103.2, turn left onto Transylvania Ave., across from the Central Plaza shopping mall. *In room:* A/C, kitchenette.

Kona Kai Resort, Gallery & Botanic Garden ★★★ 👜 This little haven is an exquisite, adults-only waterfront property right on Florida Bay, a location offering stunning sunset views overlooking Everglades National Park. Colorful, comfortable, and modern rooms and suites are nestled in a lush 2-acre botanic garden brimming with tropical vegetation. There's also an orchid house and small tropical fruit garden. Guests are encouraged to take a complimentary 90-minute ethnobotanical tour of the gardens with a staff ethnobotanist. A beachfront freshwater pool (heated in winter and cooled in summer), complimentary bottled water and fresh fruit poolside, a Jacuzzi, and one of the largest private beaches on the island make Kona Kai the perfect place for escape and relaxation. Kona Kai's complimentary concierge services will organize Everglades excursions; fishing trips; snorkeling and diving excursions; and parasail, kayak, paddleboard, bicycle, and kiteboard outings. Tennis, beachside ping-pong, kayaks, paddleboats, Wi-Fi, CD/DVD libraries, and parking are all complimentary, and there is no resort fee.

97802 Overseas Hwy. (U.S. 1 at MM 97.8), Key Largo, FL 33037. www.konakairesort.com. © **800/365-7829** or 305/852-7200. 11 units. Winter $299–$629 double and 1-bedroom suite, $699–$989 2-bedroom suite; off season $219–$469 double and 1-bedroom suite, $499–$729 2-bedroom suite. AE, DISC, MC, V. Free parking. Children 16 and under not permitted. **Amenities:** Concierge; Jacuzzi; heated/cooled pool; in-room and on-beach spa treatments; lighted tennis court; watersports equipment/rentals; Wi-Fi (free). *In room:* A/C, TV/DVD, CD player, fridge, hair dryer, full kitchen (suites only), no phone.

The Moorings Village ★★★ 🛗

You'll never see another soul on this 18-acre resort, a former coconut plantation, if you choose not to. There isn't even maid service unless you request it. The whitewashed units, from cozy cottages to three-bedroom houses, are spacious with fully equipped kitchens and rustic, yet modern, decor. Most have washers and dryers, and all have CD players and DVD players; ask when you book. The real reason to come to this resort is to relax on the 1,000-plus-foot beach (one of the only real beaches around). You'll also find a great pool, a hard tennis court, and a few kayaks and sailboards, but no motorized water vehicles in the waters surrounding the hotel. There's no room service or restaurant, but Morada Bay and Pierre's across the street are excellent. This is a place for people who like each other a lot. Leave the kids at home unless they're extremely well behaved and not easily bored.

123 Beach Rd., near MM 81.5, on the ocean side, Islamorada, FL 33036. www.mooringsvillage.com. © **305/664-4708.** Fax 305/664-4242. 18 units. Winter $375 small cottage, $600 1-bedroom house, $850 2-bedroom house, $1,650 3-bedroom oceanfront house; off season $275 small cottage, $425 1-bedroom house, $650 2-bedroom house, $1,200 3-bedroom oceanfront house. AE, MC, V. **Amenities:** Outdoor heated pool; spa; tennis court; watersports equipment. *In room:* A/C, TV/DVD, CD player, hair dryer, kitchen.

Tranquility Bay Beach House Resort ★★★ ☺

Tranquility Bay sits on a tropically landscaped 12 acres on the Gulf of Mexico and worlds away from the busy, not-so-pretty main stretch of Marathon's U.S. 1. You'll feel like you're in your own beach house—literally, with gorgeous two- and three-bedroom conch-style cottages all with water views. All of them come equipped with everything a techno-savvy beach bum needs. Every beach house has spacious porches with French doors, wooden deck chairs, and 180-degree views of the water. The restaurant, **Butterfly Café,** has seasonal seafood menus. The resort has an on-site watersports center featuring jet-skiing, kayaking, and boat rentals, as well as two swimming pools, gazebos, a great lawn with putting green, and a beachfront Tiki bar. Activities from adventure fishing to snorkeling and spa services can be arranged with the front-desk staff. *Note:* This is a smoke-free resort. Smoking is only permitted in designated areas.

2600 Overseas Hwy., Marathon, FL 33036. www.tranquilitybay.com. © **305/289-0888.** Fax 305/289-0667. 87 units. Winter $349–$699 double; off season $249–$599 double. AE, DC, MC, V. **Amenities:** Fitness center; 2 outdoor heated pools; spa services; watersports equipment/rentals. *In room:* A/C, TV/DVD, CD player, hair dryer, kitchen, Wi-Fi.

MODERATE

Banana Bay Resort & Marina ★★ 🛗

Once you enter the lush, 10-acre grounds of Banana Bay, you'll realize you're in one of the most bucolic and best-run properties in the Middle Keys. The resort is a beachfront maze of two-story buildings hidden among banyans and palms, with moderately sized rooms, many with private balconies. An activity area has horseshoe pits, a bocce court, barbecue grills, and tennis courts. The pool is one of the largest freshwater pools in the Keys. The kitschy restaurant serves three meals a day, indoors and poolside. The hotel also has a vendor on-site to rent boats, WaveRunners, kayaks, day-sailing dinghies, and bait and tackle.

U.S. 1 at MM 49.5, Marathon, FL 33050. www.bananabay.com. © **800/BANANA-1** (226-2621) or 305/743-3500. Fax 305/743-2670. 60 units. Winter $185–$245 double; off season $105–$225 double. 3- and 7-night honeymoon and wedding packages available. AE, DC, DISC, MC, V. **Amenities:** Restaurant; bar; Jacuzzi; pool; tennis courts; watersports equipment/rentals. *In room:* A/C, TV, fridge, hair dryer.

Conch Key Cottages ★★ 🎁

Occupying its own private microisland just off U.S. 1, Conch Key Cottages is a place to get away from it all. The cottages exude a sense of bohemian luxury (not an oxymoron) and Old Florida architecture with tin roofs and Dade County pine. The romantic, beachfront cottages are just steps from the ocean. The two-bedroom oceanview stilt cottages, the gardenview cottage, and the marina/sunset cottage are the most spacious and well designed on the property, and are tailor-made for families. There are several other cottages and apartments situated around the pool and property. All units feature full-size kitchens and outdoor grills with all the pots, pans, and utensils you'd need. There's also free use of kayaks, a delicious continental breakfast delivered to your door, and an unlimited supply of fresh Florida oranges that you can juice right in your own cottage.

Private island off U.S. 1 at MM 62.3, Marathon, FL 33050. www.conchkeycottages.com. © **800/330-1577** or 305/289-1377. Fax 305/743-8661. 13 units. $110–$499 cottage, depending on occupancy and time of year. Rates include complimentary continental breakfast daily. AE, DISC, MC, V. **Amenities:** Concierge; heated pool; free Wi-Fi. *In room:* A/C, TV, hair dryer, full kitchen, no phone.

Hilton Key Largo Resort ★

A short drive from Miami, this Hilton-run property is an ideal escape for a weekend or longer, situated on 13 acres of forest and the Gulf. Most rooms have water views. Forget the pools (there are two, a kids' and an adults' pool, in the middle of the parking lot). Instead, spend your time on the private, white-sand beach where you can partake in watersports activities, walk on nature trails, lounge on chairs, or hang out at the Tiki bar. It's very peaceful and beautiful, which you'd never know from its motel-esque facade. There's a restaurant on-site and it's okay—stick to area restaurants if you can or, better yet, bring some snacks and stick them in the in-room fridge. Once you see the beach here, you may not want to leave for a food run.

97000 S. Overseas Hwy., Key Largo, FL 33037. www.keylargoresort.com. © **888/871-3437** or 305/852-5553. Fax 305/852-8669. 200 units. Winter $159–$289 double, $319–$449 suite; off season $129–$259 double, $249–$379 suite. AE, DISC, MC, V. **Amenities:** Restaurant; 3 bars; children's activities; Jacuzzi; 2 outdoor pools; 2 tennis courts; watersports equipment/rentals. *In room:* A/C, TV, fridge, hair dryer, Internet access.

Lime Tree Bay Resort Motel

The only place to stay in the tiny town of Layton (pop. 183), Lime Tree is midway between Islamorada and Marathon and is on a pretty piece of waterfront graced with hundreds of mature palm trees and tropical foliage. It prides itself on its promise of no hustle, no valets, and, most amusingly, no bartenders in Hawaiian shirts! Motel rooms and efficiencies have tiny bathrooms with showers, but are clean and well maintained. The best deal is the two-bedroom bayview suite, with a spacious living area, a large private deck overlooking the Gulf, full kitchen, and two full bathrooms. Fifteen efficiencies and suites have kitchenettes. Pretty cool in its own right is the Zane Grey Suite (named after the famous author and screenwriter, who lived right around the corner), which has fantastic views and a second-story location with private stairs. A renovation in 2011 included the addition of nine Hemingway Suites, which are located 20 feet from the water. The resort's restaurant, which underwent a renovation in 2012, serves seafood, steaks and pasta.

U.S. 1 at MM 68.5, Layton, Long Key, FL 33001. www.limetreebayresort.com. © **800/723-4519** or 305/664-4740. Fax 305/664-0750. 36 units. Winter $117–$375 double; summer $100–$320 double; off season $89–$290 double. AE, DC, DISC, MC, V. **Amenities:** Restaurant; Jacuzzi; small outdoor pool; tennis court; Wi-Fi in business center. *In room:* A/C, TV, fridge, kitchenette (in some).

Pines and Palms ★★ 👬 Looking for a beachfront cottage or, better yet, an oceanfront villa, but don't want to spend your child's college fund? This is the place. Cheery one- to three-bedroom cozy cottages, Atlantic views, and a private beachfront with hammocks and a pool give way to a relaxed, tropical paradise. Service is friendly and accommodating. All rooms and cottages have full kitchens and balconies, and are ideal for extended stays. Although there's no restaurant, the staff will be happy to bring a barbecue to your patio so you can grill out by the beach. There's usually a 2-night minimum.

MM 80.4 (ocean side), Islamorada, FL 33036. www.pinesandpalms.com. © **800/624-0964** or 305/664-4343. 25 units. Year-round $89–$219 double; $129–$299 suite; $159–$459 cottage; $399–$579 villa. AE, MC, V. **Amenities:** Bike rental; heated freshwater pool; watersports equipment/rentals. *In room:* A/C, fridge, kitchen (in most).

Postcard Inn Beach Resort & Marina at Holiday Isle ★★ The landmark rough-and-tumble, rum-saturated Holiday Isle received a much-needed major makeover. This whimsical surfer-chic property touts waterfront rooms washed in white woods and sand-colored stripes. Each room and suite has been personalized with amusing quotes from ocean lovers that have been hand-stenciled on the walls. That said, the renovation may have been hasty, as some remnants of the old Holiday Inn seem evident. Still standing, shockingly, is the resort's World Famous Tiki Bar, which hasn't been touched and still serves those hyperpotent Rumrunners that will make you need a room if you don't have one already. There is also a brand-new Shula Burger, inspired by the Miami Dolphins' legendary coach Don, as well as countless other eating and drinking opportunities. The beachfront has been cleaned up and features lounges and a lawn with Adirondack chairs. Staff is friendly and helpful and will guide you through the Keys if need be, but with all the watersports (and drinking) opportunities on the property, why bother leaving?

MM 84.5 (ocean side), Islamorada, FL 33036. www.holidayisle.com. © **800/327-7070.** Fax 305/664-4681. 151 units. Year-round $169–$500. AE, MC, DC, DISC, V. **Amenities:** 2 restaurants; 3 bars; concierge; pool; watersports equipment/rentals. *In room:* A/C, TV, fridge, hair dryer, Wi-Fi.

INEXPENSIVE

Ragged Edge Resort ★★ This oceanfront property's Tahitian-style units are spread along more than half a dozen gorgeous, grassy waterfront acres. All are immaculately clean and comfortable, and most are outfitted with full kitchens and tasteful furnishings. There's no bar, restaurant, or staff, per se, but the retreat's affable owner is happy to lend bicycles and give advice on the area's offerings. A large dock attracts boaters and a variety of local and migratory birds. An outdoor heated freshwater pool is a bonus for those months when the temperature gets a bit chilly.

243 Treasure Harbor Rd. (near MM 86.5), Islamorada, FL 33036. www.ragged-edge.com. © **800/436-2023** or 305/852-5389. 11 units. Year-round $69–$99 double; $109–$259 suite. AE, MC, V. **Amenities:** Free use of bikes; outdoor pool. *In room:* A/C, fridge, kitchen (in most).

CAMPING

John Pennekamp Coral Reef State Park ★★ One of Florida's best parks (p. 242), Pennekamp has 47 well-separated campsites, half of which are available by advance reservation. The tent sites are small but equipped with restrooms, hot water, and showers. Note that the local environment provides fertile breeding grounds for insects, particularly in late summer, so bring repellent. Two man-made beaches and a small lagoon attract many large wading birds. Reservations are held until 5pm; the park must be notified of late arrival on the check-in date. Pennekamp opens at 8am and closes around sundown.

U.S. 1 at MM 102.5 (P.O. Box 487), Key Largo, FL 33037. www.pennekamppark.com. ✆ **305/451-1202.** Reservations through Reserve America ✆ **800/326-3521.** 47 campsites. $36 (with electricity) per site, 8 people maximum. Park entry $8 per vehicle with driver (plus 50¢ per person Monroe County surcharge). Yearly permits and passes available. AE, DISC, MC, V. No pets.

Long Key State Park ★ The Upper Keys' other main state park is more secluded than its northern neighbor—and more popular. All sites are located oceanside and surrounded by narrow rows of trees and nearby restroom facilities. Reserve well in advance, especially in winter.

U.S. 1 at MM 67.5 (P.O. Box 776), Long Key, FL 33001. www.floridastateparks.org/longkey. ✆ **305/664-4815.** 60 sites. $36 per site for 1–8 people; $5 per vehicle (plus 50¢ per person Monroe County surcharge). AE, DISC, MC, V. No pets.

THE LOWER KEYS

128 miles SW of Miami

Unlike their neighbors to the north and south, the Lower Keys (including **Big Pine, Sugarloaf,** and **Summerland**) are devoid of rowdy Spring Break crowds, boast few T-shirt and trinket shops, and have almost no late-night bars. What they do offer are the best opportunities to enjoy the vast natural resources on land and water that make the area so rich. Stay overnight in the Lower Keys, rent a boat, and explore the reefs—it might be the most memorable part of your trip.

Essentials

GETTING THERE See "Essentials" for the Upper and Middle keys (p. 237) and continue south on U.S. 1. The Lower Keys start at the end of the Seven-Mile Bridge. There are also airports in Marathon and Key West.

VISITOR INFORMATION **Big Pine and Lower Keys Chamber of Commerce,** ocean side of U.S. 1 at MM 31 (P.O. Box 430511), Big Pine Key, FL 33043 (www.lowerkeyschamber.com; ✆ **800/872-3722** or 305/872-2411; fax 305/872-0752), is open Monday through Friday from 9am to 5pm, and Saturday from 9am to 3pm. The pleasant staff will help with anything a traveler may need. Call, write, or stop in for a comprehensive, detailed information packet.

Exploring the Lower Keys

Once the centerpiece (these days, it's Big Pine Key) of the Lower Keys and still a great asset is **Bahia Honda State Park ★★★**, U.S. 1 at MM 37.5, Big Pine Key (www.bahiahondapark.com or www.floridastateparks.org/bahiahonda/default.cfm; ✆ **305/872-2353**), which has one of the most beautiful coastlines in South Florida. Bahia (pronounced *Bah*-ya) Honda is a great place for hiking, bird-watching, swimming, snorkeling, and fishing. The 524-acre park encompasses a wide variety of ecosystems, including coastal mangroves, beach dunes, and tropical hammocks. There are miles of trails packed with unusual plants and animals, plus a small white-sand beach. Shaded seaside picnic areas are fitted with tables and grills. Although the beach is never wider than 5 feet, even at low tide, this is the Lower Keys' best beach area.

True to its name (Spanish for "deep bay"), the park has relatively deep waters close to shore—perfect for snorkeling and diving. Easy offshore snorkeling here gives even novices a chance to lie suspended in warm water and simply observe diverse marine life passing by. Or else head to the stunning reefs at Looe Key, where the coral and fish are more vibrant than anywhere else in the United States. Snorkeling trips go from the Bahia Honda concessions to Looe Key National Marine Sanctuary (4 miles offshore). They depart twice daily (9:30am and 1:30pm) March through September and cost $30 for adults, $25 for children 6 to 17, and $8 for equipment rental. Call © 305/872-3210 for a schedule.

Entry to the park is $8 per vehicle of two to eight passengers, $4 for a solo passenger, $2 per pedestrian or bicyclist, and free for children 5 and under, with a 50¢-per-person Monroe County surcharge. It's open daily from 8am to sunset.

The most famous residents of the Lower Keys are the tiny Key deer. Of the estimated 300 existing in the world, two-thirds live on Big Pine Key's **National Key Deer Refuge ★**. To get your bearings, stop by the rangers' office at the Winn-Dixie Shopping Plaza, near MM 30.5 off U.S. 1. They'll give you an informative brochure and map of the area. The refuge is open Monday through Friday from 8am to 5pm.

If the office is closed, head out to the **Blue Hole,** a former quarry now filled with the fresh water that's vital to the deer's survival. To get there, turn right at Big Pine Key's only traffic light at Key Deer Boulevard (take the left fork immediately after the turn) and continue 1½ miles to the observation-site parking lot, on your left. The .5-mile **Watson Hammock Trail,** about ⅓ mile past the Blue Hole, is the refuge's only marked footpath. The deer are more active in cool hours, so try coming out to the path in the early morning or late evening to catch a glimpse of these gentle dog-size creatures. There is an observation deck from which you can watch and photograph the protected species. Refuge lands are open daily from a half-hour before sunrise to a half-hour after sunset. Don't be surprised to see a lazy alligator warming itself in the sun, particularly in outlying areas around the Blue Hole. If you do see a gator, do not go near it, do not touch it, and do not provoke it. Keep your distance; if you must get a photo, use a zoom lens. Also, whatever you do, do not feed the deer—it will threaten their survival. Call the **park office (© 305/872-2239)** to find out about the infrequent free tours of the refuge, scheduled throughout the year.

OUTDOOR ACTIVITIES

BIKING The Lower Keys are a great place to get off busy U.S. 1 to explore the beautiful back roads. On Big Pine Key, cruise along Key Deer Boulevard (at MM 30). Those with fat tires can ride into the National Key Deer Refuge. Many lodgings offer bike rentals.

BIRD-WATCHING A stopping point for migratory birds on the Eastern Flyway, the Lower Keys are populated with many West Indian bird species, especially in spring and fall. The small, vegetated islands of the Keys are the only nesting sites in the U.S. for the white-crowned pigeon. They're also some of the few breeding places for the reddish egret, roseate spoonbill, mangrove cuckoo, and black-whiskered vireo. Look for them on Bahia Honda Key and the many uninhabited islands nearby.

BOATING Dozens of shops rent powerboats for fishing and reef exploring. Most also rent tackle, sell bait, and have charter captains available. **Florida Keys Boat Rental** (www.keysboat.com; © 305/664-2003) offers an impressive selection of boats from $125 to $450 for a half-day and $105 to $650 for a full day. They also offer kayaks and paddleboats for eco-tours.

CANOEING & KAYAKING The Overseas Highway (U.S. 1) touches on only a few dozen of the many hundreds of islands that make up the Keys. To really see the Lower Keys, rent a kayak or canoe—perfect for these shallow waters. **Reflections Kayak Nature Tours,** operating out of the Old Wooden Bridge Fishing Camp, 1791 Bogie Dr., MM 30, Big Pine Key (www.floridakeyskayaktours.com; © 305/872-4668), offers fully outfitted backcountry wildlife tours, either on your own or with an expert. The expert, U.S.C.G.-licensed Captain Bill Keogh, wrote the book on the subject. *The Florida Keys Paddling Guide* (Countryman Press) covers all the unique ecosystems and inhabitants, as well as favorite routes from Key Biscayne to the Dry Tortugas National Park. The 3-hour kayak tours cost $50 per person. An extended 4-hour backcountry tour for two to six people costs $125 per person and uses a mothership to ferry kayaks and paddlers to the remote reaches of the refuge. Reservations are required.

FISHING A day spent fishing, either in the shallow backcountry or in the deep sea, is a great way to ensure a fresh-fish dinner, or you can release your catch and just appreciate the challenge. Whichever you choose, **Strike Zone Charters,** U.S. 1 at MM 29.5, Big Pine Key (www.strikezonecharter.com; © 305/872-9863), is the charter service to call. Prices for fishing boats start at $650 for a half-day and $850 for a full day with the possibility of a $50 fuel surcharge added to the cost. If you have enough anglers to share the price (they take up to six people), it isn't too steep. The outfitter may also be able to match you with other interested visitors. Strike Zone also offers daily trips to Looe Key National Marine Sanctuary on a glass-bottom boat. The 2-hour trip costs $25 for viewing, $35 for snorkeling, and $45 for scuba diving, all with a $3-per-person fuel charge. Strike Zone's 5-hour **Eco Island** excursion offers a vivid history of the Keys from the glass-bottom boat. The tour stops for snorkeling and light tackle fishing and docks at an island for their famous island fish cookout. Cost is $55 per person plus an additional $3 surcharge for fuel, including mask, snorkel, fins, vests, rods, reel, bait, fishing licenses, food, and all soft drinks.

HIKING You can hike throughout the flat, marshy Keys on both marked trails and meandering coastlines. The best places to trek through nature are **Bahia Honda State Park,** at MM 29.5, and **National Key Deer Refuge,** at MM 30. Bahia Honda Park has a free brochure describing an excellent self-guided tour along the Silver Palm Nature Trail. You'll traverse hammocks, mangroves, and sand dunes, and cross a lagoon. The walk (less than a mile) explores a great cross section of the natural habitat in the Lower Keys and can be done in less than half an hour.

SNORKELING & SCUBA DIVING Snorkelers and divers should not miss the Keys' most dramatic reefs at the **Looe Key National Marine Sanctuary.** Here you'll see more than 150 varieties of hard and soft coral—some centuries old—as well as every type of tropical fish, including gold and blue parrotfish, moray eels, barracudas, French angels, and tarpon. **Looe Key Dive Center,** U.S. 1 at MM 27.5, Ramrod Key (www.diveflakeys.com; © 305/872-2215), offers a mind-blowing 5-hour tour aboard a 45-foot catamaran with two shallow 1-hour dives for snorkelers and scuba divers. Snorkelers pay $44, children 6 and under pay $34; divers pay $84 for three dives, $69 for two. Snorkeling equipment is available for rent for $10;

diving-equipment rental prices range from $14 to $29. On Wednesday and Saturday, you can do a fascinating dive to the *Adolphus Busch, Sr.*, a shipwreck off Looe Key in 100 feet of water, for $50, with $30 per additional diver.

Where to Eat

There aren't many fine-dining options in the Lower Keys, with the exception of the **Dining Room at Little Palm Island,** MM 285, Little Torch Key (℗ **305/872-2551**), where you'll be wowed with gourmet French Caribbean fare that looks like a meal but tastes like a vacation (see the hotel listing below). You need to take a ferry to this chichi private island, where you can indulge at the oceanside restaurant even if you're not staying.

MODERATE

Mangrove Mama's Restaurant SEAFOOD/CARIBBEAN   As the locals who come daily for happy hour will tell you, this is a Lower Keys institution and a dive in the best sense of the word (the restaurant is a shack that used to have a gas pump as well as a grill). Guests share the property with stray cats and some miniature horses out back. It's run-down, but in a charming Keys sort of way—come on, they serve beer in a jelly glass. A handful of tables, inside and out, are shaded by banana trees and palm fronds. Fish is the menu's mainstay, although soups, salads, sandwiches (try the lobster Reuben), and omelets are also good. Grilled-chicken and club sandwiches are tasty alternatives to fish, as are meatless chef's salads and spicy barbecued baby back ribs. The restaurant is under new ownership, which some say has let the place slip a bit, though they still rock their Sunday brunch with amazing crab Benedict.

U.S. 1 at MM 20, Sugarloaf Key. www.mangrovemamasrestaurant.com. ℗ **305/745-3030.** Main courses $18–$30; lunch $9–$15; brunch $5–$15. MC, V. Daily 11am–3pm and 5:30–10pm.

INEXPENSIVE

Coco's Kitchen ★ CUBAN/AMERICAN   This storefront has been dishing out black beans, rice, and shredded beef for more than 10 years. The owners, who are actually from Nicaragua, cook not only superior Cuban food, but also local specialties, Italian dishes, and Caribbean choices. Specialties include fried shrimp, whole fried yellowtail, and Cuban-style roast pork (available only on Sat). The best bet is the daily special, which may be roasted pork or fresh grouper, served with rice and beans or salad and crispy fries. Top off the huge meal with a rich caramel-soaked flan.

283 Key Deer Blvd. (in the Winn-Dixie Shopping Center), Big Pine Key. http://cocoskitchen.com. ℗ **305/872-4495.** Main courses $9.50–$18; breakfast $2.75–$8.50; lunch $4–$7. MC, V. Tues–Sun 7am–3pm. Turn right at the traffic light near MM 30.5; stay in the left lane.

No Name Pub PUB FARE/PIZZA   This hard-to-find funky old bar out in the boondocks (tagline: You Found It) serves snacks and sandwiches until 11pm on most nights, and drinks until midnight. Pizzas are tasty—try one topped with local shrimp. Or consider a bowl of chili with all the fixings. Everything is served on paper plates. Locals hang out at the rustic bar, one of the Keys' oldest bars blanketed with thousands of autographed dollar bills, drinking beer and listening to a jukebox heavy with 1980s tunes.

¼ mile south of No Name Bridge on N. Watson Blvd., Big Pine Key. www.nonamepub.com. ℗ **305/872-9115.** Pizzas $6–$18; subs $5–$9. MC, V. Daily 11am–11pm. Turn right at Big Pine's only traffic light (near MM 30.5) onto Key Deer Blvd. Turn right on Watson Blvd. At the stop sign, turn left. Look for a small wooden sign on the left marking the spot.

Entertainment & Nightlife

Although the mellow islands of the Lower Keys aren't exactly known for wild nightlife, there are some friendly bars and restaurants where locals and tourists gather. **No Name Pub** (listed above) is one of the best. One of the most scenic is **Parrotdise Waterfont,** Barry Avenue near MM 28.5 (www.parrotdisewaterfront.com; ✆ 305/872-9989), the only waterfront restaurant between Key West and Marathon. The place is enclosed with windows looking out onto the water where there's a shark pond. Great food (even sushi) is served from 10:30am to 10pm, and the bar closes around midnight. The place even has its own brand of wine, which is currently being marketed in France, of all places. Parrotdise attracts an odd mix of bikers and blue-hairs daily, and is a great place to overhear local gossip and colorful metaphors. Pool tables are the main attraction, but there's also live music some nights. The drinks are reasonably priced, and the food isn't too bad, either.

Where to Stay

There are a number of cheap, fairly unappealing fish shacks along the highway for those who want bare-bones accommodations. So far, there are no national hotel chains in the Lower Keys. For information on lodging in cabins or trailers at local campgrounds, see "Camping," below.

VERY EXPENSIVE

Little Palm Island Resort & Spa ★★★ This exclusive island escape—host to presidents and royalty—is not just a place to stay while in the Lower Keys; it is a destination all its own. Built on a private 5½-acre island, it's accessible only by boat or seaplane. Guests stay in thatched-roof duplexes amid lush foliage and flowering tropical plants—and Key deer, which are to this island what cats are to Key West. Many bungalows have ocean views and private decks with hammocks. Inside, the romantic suites have all the comforts of a swank beach cottage, but without phones, TVs, or alarm clocks. Mosquitoes can be a problem, even in winter. (Bring spray and lightweight, long-sleeved clothing.) Known for a stellar spa and innovative and pricey food, Little Palm also hosts visitors just for dinner, brunch, or lunch. If you're staying on the island, opt for the full American plan, which includes three meals a day.

Launch is on the ocean side of U.S. 1 at MM 28.5, Little Torch Key, FL 33042. www.littlepalmisland. com. ✆ **800/343-8567** or 305/872-2524. Fax 305/872-4843. 30 units. Winter $840–$1,695 double; off season $640–$1,595 double. Rates include transportation to and from the island and unlimited (nonmotorized) watersports. Meal plans include 2 meals daily for $125 per person per day, 3 meals at $140 per person. AE, DC, DISC, MC, V. No children 15 and under. **Amenities:** Restaurant; bar; courtesy van from Key West or Marathon airport; concierge; health club; 2 pools; limited room service; spa; watersports equipment/rentals. In room: A/C, hair dryer, Internet access, minibar, no phone.

INEXPENSIVE

Parmer's Resort ★ Parmer's, a fixture for more than 20 years, is known for its charming hospitality and helpful staff. This downscale resort offers modest but comfortable cottages, each of them unique. Some are waterfront, many have kitchenettes, and others are just a bedroom. The Wahoo room (no. 26), a one-bedroom efficiency, is especially nice, with a small sitting area that faces the water. All units have been recently updated and are very clean. Many can be combined to accommodate families. The hotel's waterfront location, not to mention the fact that it's only a half-hour from Key West, almost makes up for the fact that you must pay extra for maid service.

565 Barry Ave, MM 28.5, Little Torch Key, FL 33042. www.parmersresort.com. © **305/872-2157.** Fax 305/872-2014. 45 units. Winter $134–$194 double, from $174 efficiency; off season $99–$129 double, from $129 efficiency. Rates include continental breakfast. AE, DISC, MC, V. From U.S. 1, turn right onto Barry Ave. Resort is ½ mile down on the right. **Amenities:** Heated pool. *In room:* A/C, TV.

CAMPING

Bahia Honda State Park ★★★ (www.floridastateparks.org/bahiahonda/default. cfm; © **800/326-3521**) offers some of the best camping in the Keys. It is as loaded with facilities and activities as it is with campers. But don't be discouraged by its popularity—this park encompasses more than 500 acres of land, 80 campsites spread throughout three areas, and three spacious, comfortable duplex cabins. Cabins hold up to eight guests each and come complete with linens, kitchenettes, wraparound terraces, barbecue pits, and rocking chairs. For one to four people, camping costs about $36 per site. Depending on the season, cabin prices range from $120 to $160.

Another excellent value can be found at the **KOA Sugarloaf Key Resort** ★★, near MM 20. This oceanside facility has 200 fully equipped sites, with water, electricity, and sewer, which rent for about $89 a night (no-hookup sites cost about $55). Or you can pitch a tent on the 5 acres of waterfront property. Or stay in a shiny Airstream trailer which sleeps up to four people for $170 a night. This place is especially nice because of its private beaches and access to diving, snorkeling, and boating; its grounds are also well maintained. In addition, the resort rents travel trailers: The 25-foot Dutchman sleeps six and costs about $150 a day. For details, contact the resort at P.O. Box 420469, Summerland Key, FL 33042 (www.koa.com; © **800/562-7731** or 305/745-3549; fax 305/745-9889).

KEY WEST ★★★

159 miles SW of Miami

Key West is the land of the eternal vacation. It seems the sun is always shining here, making the island a perfect destination for sunbathers, fishermen, divers, and motorcyclists. Munch on fresh seafood, watch the jugglers in Mallory Square, and have another margarita.

Things to Do The preferred leisure activity in Key West is relaxing. Visitors inclined toward more active pursuits head to the docks, where divers explore submarine reefs, and anglers head off from **Garrison Bight Marina** in hopes of landing sailfish and tarpon in the azure waters of the Gulf of Mexico.

Shopping You'll soon become convinced the predominant island souvenir is a tacky T-shirt. But if you can make it past the crude shirts, you'll discover a nice supply of bathing suits, strappy sandals, and sunglasses along Duval Street. Head to **Cigar Alley** between Front and Greene streets for a stogie rolled by Cuban immigrants.

Nightlife & Entertainment When the sun begins to drop, Sunset Celebration goes into full swing in **Mallory Square.** Magicians, jugglers, and one-man bands entertain the crowds each evening as the sun tints the sky and waves with orange and purple. After dark, do the **Duval Street** crawl. Favorite bars include Sloppy Joe's, reputed to be an old Hemingway haunt, the Green Parrot, and Hog's Breath Saloon.

Restaurants & Dining For a dinner of "conch fusion cuisine," stop in at Hot Tin Roof, in the Ocean Key Resort. Or head off the beaten track to enjoy a fish dinner at Hogfish Bar and Grill, where tattooed bikers and yacht owners alike gather to eat freshly caught fish at picnic tables.

Essentials

GETTING THERE   For directions by car, see "Essentials" (p. 237) for the Upper and Middle keys and continue south on U.S. 1. When entering Key West, stay in the far-right lane onto North Roosevelt Boulevard, which becomes Truman Avenue in Old Town. Continue for a few blocks and you'll find yourself on **Duval Street ★**, in the heart of the city. If you stay to the left, you'll also reach the city center after passing the airport and the remnants of historic houseboat row, where a motley collection of boats once made up one of Key West's most interesting neighborhoods.

Several regional airlines fly nonstop (about 55 min.) from Miami to Key West. **American Eagle** (✆ 800/433-7300), **Continental** (✆ 800/525-0280), **Delta** (✆ 800/221-1212), and **US Airways Express** (✆ 800/428-4322) land at the recently expanded **Key West International Airport,** South Roosevelt Boulevard (✆ 305/296-5439), on the southeastern corner of the island.

Greyhound (www.greyhound.com; ✆ 800/231-2222) has buses leaving Miami for Key West every day. Prices range from $40 to $56 one-way and $81 to $110 round-trip. Seats fill up in season, so come early. The ride takes about 4½ hours.

You can also get to Key West from Ft. Myers or Marco Island via the **Key West Express** (www.seakeywest.com; ✆ 866/KW-FERRY [593-3779]), a 155-foot-long catamaran that travels to Key West at 40 mph. The Big Cat features two enclosed cabins, sun seated deck, observation deck, satellite TV, and full galley and bar. Prices range from $86 one-way and $146 round-trip per person.

GETTING AROUND   Old Town Key West has limited parking, narrow streets, and congested traffic, so driving is more of a pain than a convenience. Unless you're staying in one of the more remote accommodations, consider trading in your car for a bicycle. The island is small and flat as a board, which makes it easy to negotiate, especially away from the crowded downtown area. Many tourists choose to cruise by moped, an option that can make navigating the streets risky, especially because there are no helmet laws in Key West. Hundreds of visitors are seriously injured each year, so be careful and spend the extra few bucks to rent a helmet.

Rates for simple one-speed cruisers start at about $10 per day. Scooters start at about $20 for 2 hours, $35 per day, and $109 per week. The best shops include the **A&M Scooter and Bicycle Center,** 523 Truman Ave. (www.amscooterskeywest. com; ✆ 305/294-4556); the **Moped Hospital,** 601 Truman Ave. (www.moped hospital.com; ✆ 866/296-1625); and **Tropical Bicycles & Scooter Rentals,** 1300 Duval St. (✆ 305/294-8136). The **Bike Shop,** 1110 Truman Ave. (www. thebikeshopkeywest.com; ✆ 305/294-1073), rents cruisers for $12 per day, $60 per week; a $150 deposit is required.

PARKING   Parking in Key West's Old Town is limited, but there is a well-placed **municipal parking lot** at Simonton and Angela streets, just behind the firehouse and police station. If you've brought a car, you may want to stash it here while you enjoy the very walkable downtown part of Key West.

VISITOR INFORMATION   The **Key West Chamber of Commerce,** 402 Wall St., Key West, FL 33040 (www.keywestchamber.org; ✆ 800/527-8539 or 305/294-2587), provides both general and specialized information. The lobby is open daily from 8:30am to 6pm; phones are answered from 8am to 8pm. Gay travelers may want to call the **Key West Business Guild** (✆ 305/294-4603), which represents more than 50 guesthouses and B&Bs, as well as many other gay-owned businesses (ask for its color brochure).

Check out the **Key West Walking Tours app** from the iTunes store, which will give you a great overview of the island with over 40 sites, including some art galleries and nightlife. Cost is $5. Or, try the **Key West Historic Marker Tour** (📞 **305/507-0300**), a free download at www.keywesthistoricmarkertour.org, featuring over 50 sites from former cigar factories and the home of philosopher John Dewey to Key West's oldest house and the southernmost house in the continental United States

ORIENTATION A mere 2×4-mile island, Key West is simple to navigate, even though there's no real order to the arrangement of streets and avenues. As you enter town on U.S. 1 (Roosevelt Blvd.), you will see most of the moderate chain hotels and fast-food restaurants. The better restaurants, shops, and outfitters are crammed onto Duval Street, the main thoroughfare of Key West's Old Town. On surrounding streets, many inns and lodges are set in picturesque Victorian/Bahamian homes. On the southern side of the island are the coral-beach area and some of the larger resort hotels.

The area called Bahama Village is the furthest thing from a tourist trap, but can be a bit spotty at night if you aren't familiar with the area. With several newly opened, trendy restaurants and guesthouses, this hippie-ish neighborhood, complete with street-roaming chickens and cats, is the roughest and most urban you'll find in the Keys. You might see a few drug deals on street corners, but they're nothing to be overly concerned about: It looks worse than it is, and resident business owners tend to keep a vigilant eye out. The area is actually quite funky and should be a welcome diversion from the Duvalian mainstream.

Exploring Key West

Key West's greenest attraction, the **Florida Keys Eco-Discovery Center,** overlooking the waterfront at the Truman Annex (http://floridakeys.noaa.gov/eco_discovery.html; 35 E. Quay Rd.; 📞 **305/809-4750**), features 6,000 square feet of interactive exhibits depicting Florida Keys underwater and upland habitats—with emphasis on the ecosystem of North America's only living contiguous barrier coral reef, which parallels the Keys. Kids dig the interactive yellow submarine, while adults seem to get into the cinematic depiction of an underwater abyss. Admission is free, and the center is open 9am to 4pm Tuesday through Saturday.

Before shelling out for any of the dozens of worthwhile attractions in Key West, we recommend getting an overview on either of the two comprehensive island tour companies, the **Conch Tour Train** or the **Old Town Trolley** (p. 271). There are simply too many attractions and historic houses to list. We've highlighted our favorites below, but we encourage you to seek out others.

Audubon House and Tropical Gardens ★★ PARK/GARDEN   This well-preserved mid-19th-century home of Capt. John H. Geiger stands as a prime example of early Key West architecture. It is named after renowned painter and bird expert John James Audubon, who visited the Florida Keys in 1832 and who painted and collected specimens in these gardens. The graceful two-story structure is a retreat from the bustle of Old Town. A guide will introduce you to the history of the period and the property. You will then go back in time and visit the two other floors of the house and the tropical gardens on your own. Admire rare Audubon prints, antiques, and historical photos. Even if you don't want to explore the grounds and home, check

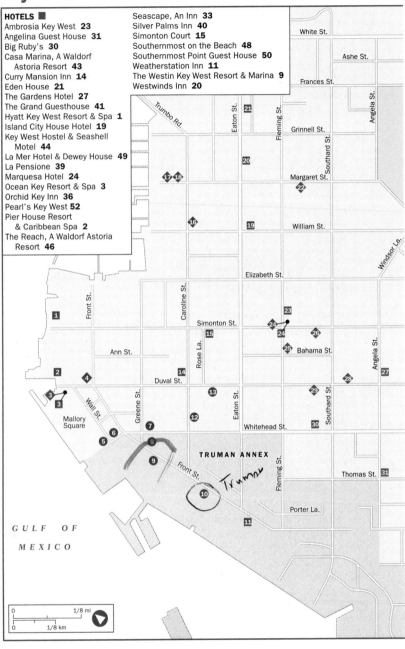

HOTELS ■

Ambrosia Key West **23**
Angelina Guest House **31**
Big Ruby's **30**
Casa Marina, A Waldorf
  Astoria Resort **43**
Curry Mansion Inn **14**
Eden House **21**
The Gardens Hotel **27**
The Grand Guesthouse **41**
Hyatt Key West Resort & Spa **1**
Island City House Hotel **19**
Key West Hostel & Seashell
  Motel **44**
La Mer Hotel & Dewey House **49**
La Pensione **39**
Marquesa Hotel **24**
Ocean Key Resort & Spa **3**
Orchid Key Inn **36**
Pearl's Key West **52**
Pier House Resort
  & Caribbean Spa **2**
The Reach, A Waldorf Astoria
  Resort **46**

Seascape, An Inn **33**
Silver Palms Inn **40**
Simonton Court **15**
Southernmost on the Beach **48**
Southernmost Point Guest House **50**
Weatherstation Inn **11**
The Westin Key West Resort & Marina **9**
Westwinds Inn **20**

White St.

Ashe St.

Frances St.

Angela St.

Trumbo Rd.

Eaton St.

Fleming St.

Grinnell St.

Southard St.

Margaret St.

William St.

Elizabeth St.

Windsor La.

Caroline St.

Front St.

Simonton St.

Ann St.

Rose La.

Duval St.

Greene St.

Wall St.

Mallory
Square

Eaton St.

Bahama St.

Angela St.

Whitehead St.

Southard St.

TRUMAN ANNEX

Front St.

Truman

Thomas St.

Fleming St.

Porter La.

GULF OF

MEXICO

0   1/8 mi
0   1/8 km

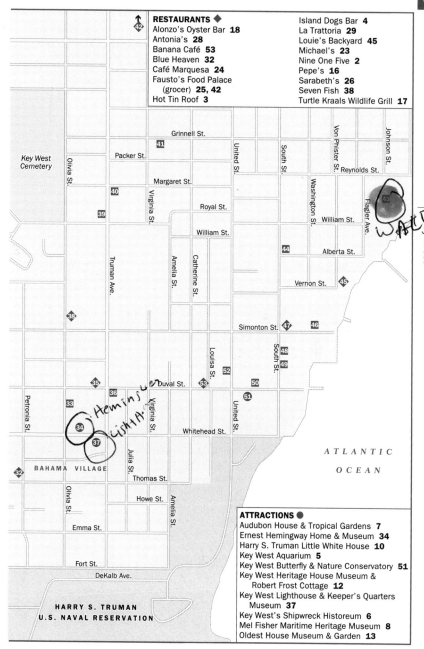

RESTAURANTS ◆
Alonzo's Oyster Bar **18**
Antonia's **28**
Banana Café **53**
Blue Heaven **32**
Café Marquesa **24**
Fausto's Food Palace
  (grocer) **25, 42**
Hot Tin Roof **3**

Island Dogs Bar **4**
La Trattoria **29**
Louie's Backyard **45**
Michael's **23**
Nine One Five **2**
Pepe's **16**
Sarabeth's **26**
Seven Fish **38**
Turtle Kraals Wildlife Grill **17**

Grinnell St.
Packer St.
Key West Cemetery
Olivia St.
Margaret St.
Virginia St.
Royal St.
William St.
William St.
Amelia St.
Catherine St.
Truman Ave.
United St.
South St.
Von Phister St.
Reynolds St.
Johnson St.
Washington St.
William St.
Flagler Ave.
Alberta St.
Vernon St.
Simonton St.
Louisa St.
South St.
United St.
Duval St.
Virginia St.
Whitehead St.
Petronia St.
Julia St.
Thomas St.
BAHAMA VILLAGE
Olivia St.
Howe St.
Amelia St.
Emma St.
Fort St.
DeKalb Ave.
HARRY S. TRUMAN
U.S. NAVAL RESERVATION

ATLANTIC

OCEAN

ATTRACTIONS ●
Audubon House & Tropical Gardens **7**
Ernest Hemingway Home & Museum **34**
Harry S. Truman Little White House **10**
Key West Aquarium **5**
Key West Butterfly & Nature Conservatory **51**
Key West Heritage House Museum &
  Robert Frost Cottage **12**
Key West Lighthouse & Keeper's Quarters
  Museum **37**
Key West's Shipwreck Historeum **6**
Mel Fisher Maritime Heritage Museum **8**
Oldest House Museum & Garden **13**

out the gift shop, which sells a variety of fine mementos at reasonable prices, and the Audubon Gallery, which sells original Audubon hand colored engravings and lithographs from the early to mid-19th century. Expect to spend 30 minutes to an hour.

205 Whitehead St. (btw. Greene and Caroline sts.). www.audubonhouse.com. ☎ **305/294-2116.** Admission $12 adults, $5 children 6–12, $7.50 students of any age. Daily 9:30am–5pm (last entry at 4:30pm).

East Martello Museum and Gallery MUSEUM   Adjacent to the airport, the East Martello Museum is in a Civil War–era brick fort that itself is worth a visit. The museum contains a bizarre variety of exhibits that do a thorough job of interpreting the city's intriguing past. Historic artifacts include model ships, a deep-sea diver's wooden air pump, a crude raft from a Cuban "boat lift," a supposedly haunted doll, and a horse-drawn hearse. Exhibits illustrate the Keys' history of salvaging, sponging, and cigar making. After seeing the galleries (which should take 45–60 min.), climb a steep spiral staircase to the top of the lookout tower for good views over the island and ocean. A member of the Key West Art and Historical Society, East Martello has two cousins: the **Key West Museum of Art and History,** 281 Front St. (☎ **305/295-6616**), and the **Key West Lighthouse Museum** (p. 268). Expect to spend 1 to 2 hours.

3501 S. Roosevelt Blvd. www.kwahs.com/martello.htm. ☎ **305/296-3913.** Admission $6 adults, $5 seniors, $3 children 8–12. Daily 9:30am–4:30pm (last entry at 4pm). Closed Christmas.

Ernest Hemingway Home & Museum ★ HISTORIC HOME   Hemingway's handsome stone Spanish colonial house, built in 1851 and designated a literary landmark by the American Library Association in 2010, was one of the first on the island to be fitted with indoor plumbing and a built-in fireplace. From literary to splashy, the home has the first ever swimming pool built on the island as well as a penny that Hemingway, who owned the home from 1931 until his death in 1961, pressed into the cement just because. And while the ghost of Hemingway may or may not be present here today, descendants of some of the 50 cats he lived with here—including the famed six-toed felines—still roam the grounds. It was during those years that the Nobel Prize–winning author wrote some of his most famous works, including *For Whom the Bell Tolls, A Farewell to Arms,* and *The Snows of Kilimanjaro.* Fans may want to take the optional half-hour house tour to see his study as well as rooms with glass cabinets that store certain artifacts, books, and pieces of mail addressed to him. It's interesting (to an extent) and included in the price of admission. If you don't take the tour or you have no interest in Hemingway, the price of admission is a waste of money, except for the lovely architecture and garden. If you're feline phobic (or allergic), beware: There are cats everywhere. Thirty-minute guided tours are given every 15 minutes, and expect to spend an hour on the property.

907 Whitehead St. (btw. Truman Ave. and Olivia St.). www.hemingwayhome.com. ☎ **305/294-1136.** Fax 305/294-2755. Admission $12 adults, $6 children 6 and over. Daily 9am–5pm. Limited parking.

Harry S. Truman Little White House ★★ HISTORIC HOME   President Truman used to refer to the White House as the "Great White Jail." On temporary leave from the Big House, Truman discovered the serenity of Key West and made his escape to what became known as the Little White House, which is open to the public for touring. The house is fully restored; the exhibits document Truman's time in the Keys. Tours run every 15 minutes and last between 45 and 50 minutes, so plan to spend more than an hour here. For fans of all things Oval Office–related, there's a presidential gift shop on the premises.

111 Front St. www.trumanlittlewhitehouse.com. © **305/294-9911.** Admission $16 adults, $14 seniors, $5.40 children 5–12. Tickets cheaper on website. Daily 9am–4:30pm.

Key West Aquarium ★★ ☺ AQUARIUM   The island's first attraction, the Key West Aquarium is a modest but fascinating place. A long hallway of eye-level displays showcases dozens of varieties of fish and crustaceans. Kids can touch sea cucumbers, hermit crabs, starfish, and horseshoe crabs in the Touch Tank, which allows for a hands-on experience with harmless sea creatures. The Atlantic Shores Exhibit features a cross section of a near-shore mangrove environment and a 50,000-gallon tank that's home to a variety of tropical fish and game fish. At Stingray Bay, visitors can pet cow nosed rays. If possible, catch one of the free guided tours during which time you may be able to witness the dramatic feeding frenzy of the sharks, tarpon, barracudas, stingrays, and turtles. Expect to spend 1 to 1½ hours here.

1 Whitehead St. (at Mallory Sq.). www.keywestaquarium.com. © **305/296-2051.** Admission $15 adults, $13 seniors, $6.45 children $12. Tickets cheaper on website. Look for discount coupons at local hotels, at Duval St. kiosks, and from trolley and train tours. Daily 10am–6pm; tours at 11am and 1, 3, and 4pm.

Key West Butterfly & Nature Conservatory ★★ ☺ NATURE RESERVE In a 13,000-square-foot pavilion, this attraction has nature lovers flitting with excitement, thanks to the 5,000-square-foot, glass-enclosed butterfly aviary as well as a gallery, learning center, and gift shop exploring all aspects of the butterfly world. Inside, more than 1,500 butterflies and 3,500 plants, including rare orchids, and even fish and turtles coexist in a controlled climate. You'll walk freely among the butterflies. Expect to spend an hour here.

1316 Duval St. www.keywestbutterfly.com. © **305/296-2988.** Admission $12 adults, $9 seniors, $8.50 children 4–12. Daily 9am–5pm; last ticket sold at 4:30pm.

Key West Cemetery ★★★ 🏛 CEMETERY   This funky cemetery is the epitome of quirky Key West: irreverent and humorous. Take note of the stacked (dare we say condo-style?) tombs that are that way because digging 6 feet under through rocky soil back in the early settler days was nearly impossible. Best of all, however, is the morbid humor that is alive and well here with such amusing epitaphs as AT LEAST I KNOW WHERE HE'S SLEEPING TONIGHT. Some of the inscriptions are hard to find even with the free walking-tour guide, but this place is fun to explore. Plan to spend 30 minutes to an hour or more, depending on how morbid your curiosity is.

Entrance at the corner of Margaret and Angela sts. Free admission. Daily dawn–dusk.

Key West Lighthouse & Keeper's Quarters Museum ★ MUSEUM   When the Key West Lighthouse opened in 1848, it signaled the end of a profitable era for the pirate salvagers who looted reef-stricken ships. The story of this and other area lighthouses is illustrated in a small museum that was formerly the keeper's quarters. It's worth mustering the energy to climb the 88 claustrophobic steps to the top, where you'll be rewarded with magnificent views of Key West and the ocean. Expect to spend 30 minutes to an hour.

938 Whitehead St. www.kwahs.com. © **305/295-6616.** Admission $10 adults, $9 seniors and locals, $5 children 7–12. Daily 9:30am–4:30pm.

A Smokin' Park

Though Key West has a rich hippie history, a new park pays homage to cigars. **Gato Village Pocket Park,** 616 Louisa St., honors the island's once-flourishing cigar-making industry. Located on the site of a former cigar maker's cottage in what was once called Gatoville—a housing community built by cigar baron Eduardo Gato for his factory workers—the park features a re-creation of the cottage's front porch and facade, a 13-foot-tall metal cigar and signage telling the community's ashy history.

Key West's Shipwreck Historeum MUSEUM   You'll see more impressive artifacts at Mel Fisher's museum, but for the morbidly curious, shipwrecks should rank right up there with car wrecks. For those of you who can't help but look, this museum is the place to be for everything you ever wanted to know about shipwrecks and more. See movies, artifacts, and a real-life wrecker, who will be happy to indulge your curiosity about the wrecking industry that preoccupied the early pioneers of Key West. Depending on your level of interest, you can expect to spend up to 2 hours here.

1 Whitehead St. (at Mallory Sq.). www.shipwreckhistoreum.com. © **305/292-8990.** Fax 305/292-5536. Admission $15 adults, $13 seniors, $6.45 children 4–12. Tickets cheaper on website. Shows daily every half-hour 9:45am–4:45pm.

Mel Fisher Maritime Heritage Museum ★★ MUSEUM   This museum honors local hero Mel Fisher, whose death in 1998 was mourned throughout South Florida and who, along with a crew of other salvagers, found a multimillion-dollar treasure trove in 1985 aboard the wreck of the Spanish galleon *Nuestra Señora de Atocha.* If you're into diving, pirates, and sunken treasures, check out this small museum, full of doubloons, pieces of eight, emeralds, and solid-gold bars. A 1700 English merchant slave ship, the only tangible evidence of the transatlantic slave trade, is on view on the museum's second floor. An exhibition telling the story of more than 1,400 African slaves captured in Cuban waters and brought to Key West for sanctuary is the museum's latest, most fascinating exhibit to date. Expect to spend 1 to 3 hours.

200 Greene St. www.melfisher.org. © **305/294-2633.** Admission $13 adults, $11 students, $6.25 children 6–12. Mon–Fri 8:30am–5pm; Sat–Sun and holidays 9:30am–5pm. Take U.S. 1 to Whitehead St. and turn left on Greene.

Oldest House Museum & Garden ★ HISTORIC HOME   Dating from 1829, this old New England Bahama House has survived pirates, hurricanes, fires, warfare, and economic ups and downs. The one-and-a-half-story home was designed by a ship's carpenter and incorporates many features from maritime architecture, including portholes and a ship's hatch designed for ventilation before the advent of air-conditioning. Especially interesting is the detached kitchen building outfitted with a brick "beehive" oven and vintage cooking utensils. Though not a must-see on the Key West tour, history and architecture buffs will appreciate the finely preserved details and the glimpse of a slower, easier time in the island's life. Plan to spend 30 minutes to an hour.

322 Duval St. www.oirf.org. © **305/294-9501.** Free admission. Daily 10am–4pm.

OUTDOOR ACTIVITIES

BEACHES   Key West actually has a few small beaches, although they don't compare with the state's wide natural wonders up the coast; the Keys' beaches are typically narrow and rocky. Here are your options: Smathers Beach, off South Roosevelt Boulevard, west of the airport; Higgs Beach, along Atlantic Boulevard, between White Street and Reynolds Road; and Fort Zachary Beach, located off the western end of Southard Boulevard.

A magnet for partying teenagers, **Smathers Beach** is Key West's largest and most overpopulated. Despite the number of rowdy teens, the beach is actually quite clean. If you go early enough in the morning, you may notice people sleeping on the beach from the night before.

Higgs Beach is a favorite among Key West's gay crowds, but what many people don't know is that beneath the sand is an unmarked cemetery of African slaves who died while waiting for freedom. Higgs has a playground and tennis courts, and is near the minute Rest Beach, which is actually hidden by the White Street pier. The sand here is coarse and rocky and the water tends to be a bit mucky, but if you can bear it, Higgs is known as a great snorkeling beach. If it's sunbathing you want, skip Higgs and go to Smathers.

Although there is an entrance fee ($6 per car of two to eight, $4 single-occupant vehicle, $2 pedestrians and bicyclists, plus 50¢ per person for Monroe County surcharge), we recommend the beach at **Fort Zachary Taylor State Park,** as it has a great historic fort; a Civil War museum; and a large picnic area with tables, barbecue grills, restrooms, and showers. Large trees scattered across 87 acres provide shade for those who are reluctant to bake in the sun.

BIKING & MOPEDING   A popular mode of transportation for locals and visitors, bikes and mopeds are available at many rental outlets in the city. Escape the hectic downtown scene and explore the island's scenic side streets by heading away from Duval Street toward South Roosevelt Boulevard and the beachside enclaves along the way.

FISHING   As any angler will tell you, there's no fishing like Keys fishing. Key West has it all: bonefish, tarpon, dolphin, tuna, grouper, cobia, and more—sharks, too.

Step aboard a small exposed skiff for an incredibly diverse day of fishing. In the morning, you can head offshore for sailfish or dolphin (the fish, not the mammal), and then by afternoon get closer to land for a shot at tarpon, permit, grouper, or snapper. Here in Key West, you can probably pick up more cobia—one of the best fighting and eating fish around—than anywhere else in the world. For a real fight, ask your skipper to go for the tarpon—the greatest fighting fish there is, famous for its dramatic "tail walk" on the water after it's hooked. Shark fishing is also popular.

You'll find plenty of competition among the charter-fishing boats in and around Mallory Square. You can negotiate a good deal at **Charter Boat Row,** 1801 N. Roosevelt Ave. (across from the Shell station), home to more than 30 charter-fishing and party boats. Just show up to arrange your outing, or call **Garrison Bight Marina** (© 305/292-8167) for details.

The advantage of the smaller, more expensive charter boats is that you can call the shots. They'll take you where you want to go, to fish for what you want to catch. These "light tackles" are also easier to maneuver, which means you can go to backcountry spots for tarpon and bonefish, as well as out to the open ocean for tuna and dolphin fish. You'll really be able to feel the fish, and you'll get some good fights, too. Larger

Historic Charter Boat Row (www.key westfishingboats.com), located in the City Marina at 1801 N. Roosevelt Blvd., has over 35 charter fishing boats to choose from. Choosing is actually an intriguing process as you can stroll through and hear stories of award-winning captains and record-breaking catches. If you are there at the right time (generally noon, 2pm, and 4pm) you will see a proud crew, happy fisherman, and a prized catch. Boats range from 18 to 65 feet and can accommodate all styles of fishing: flats, fly, offshore, inshore, bottom fishing, wreck/reef, trophy, shark, and more. Prices vary based on the type of boat and type of fishing. Party boats are as low as $50 per person. A typical offshore private quarter-day trip starts at $650.

boats, for up to six or seven people, are cheaper and are best for kingfish, billfish, and sailfish. For every kind of fishing charter, from flats and offshore to backcountry and wreck fishing, call **Almost There Sportfishing Charters** (www.almostthere.net; ✆ **800/795-9448**).

The huge commercial party boats are more for sightseeing than serious angling, though you can be lucky enough to get a few bites at one of the fishing holes. Some party boats, however, offer the best of both worlds, offering all the required gear, bait and license. Party boats target snappers, groupers, sharks, and a variety of other bottom fish. One especially good deal is the **Gulfstream IV** in Key West (www.gulfstreamkey west.com; ✆ **305/296-8494**), a 6-hour charter that departs daily at 10am. You'll pay $65 for adults, $60 for seniors, and $40 for kids 6 to 12. Kids under 6 are free. This 60-foot party boat usually has 15 to 30 other anglers. Bring your own lunch or purchase onboard. Beer and wine are allowed.

Serious anglers should consider the light-tackle boats that leave from **Oceanside Marina,** on Stock Island at 5950 Peninsula Ave., 1½ miles off U.S. 1 (✆ **305/294-4676**). It's a 20-minute drive from Old Town on the Atlantic side. There are more than 30 light-tackle guides, which range from flatbed, backcountry skiffs to 28-foot open boats. There are also a few larger charters and a party boat that goes to the Dry Tortugas.

For a light-tackle outing with a very colorful Key West flair, call **Capt. Bruce Cronin** (www.fishbruce.com; ✆ **305/294-4929**) or **Capt. Ken Harris** (www. kwextremeadventures.com; ✆ **305/294-8843**), two of the more famous (and pricey) captains working these docks for more than 20 years. You'll pay from $750 for a full day, usually about 8am to 4pm, and from $500 for a half-day. For a comprehensive list of Florida Keys fishing guides, go to www.ccaflorida.org/guides/keys_guides.html.

GOLF The area's only public golf club is **Key West Golf Club** (www.keywestgolf. com; ✆ **305/294-5232**), an 18-hole course at the entrance to the island of Key West at MM 4.5 (turn onto College Rd. to the course entrance). Designed by Rees Jones, the course has plenty of mangroves and water hazards on its 6,526 yards. It's open to the public and has a new pro shop. Call ahead for tee-time reservations. Rates are $40 to $70 per player during off season and $50 to $95 in season, including cart.

KAYAKING **Lazy Dog Adventure,** 5114 Overseas Hwy. (http://lazydog.com; ✆ **305/295-9898**), operates a first-rate, 2-hour daily kayaking tour through the backcountry of Key West for $35 per person. For the really adventurous, it also offers a 4-hour kayak and snorkel tour combo through the mangroves and backcountry for $60 per person.

SCUBA DIVING   One of the area's largest scuba schools, **Dive Key West, Inc.,** 3128 N. Roosevelt Blvd. (www.divekeywest.com; ℂ **800/426-0707** or 305/296-3823), offers instruction at all levels; its dive boats take participants to scuba and snorkel sites on nearby reefs.

Key West Marine Park (ℂ **305/294-3100**), the newest dive park along the island's Atlantic shore, incorporates no-motor "swim-only" lanes marked by buoys, providing swimmers and snorkelers with a safe way to explore the waters. The park's boundaries stretch from the foot of Duval Street to Higgs Beach.

Wreck dives and night dives are two of the special offerings of **Lost Reef Adventures,** 261 Margaret St. (www.lostreefadventures.com; ℂ **800/952-2749** or 305/296-9737). Phone for regularly scheduled runs and private charters.

In 2009, the *General Hoyt S. Vandenberg,* a 524-foot former U.S. Air Force missile tracking ship, was sunk 6 miles south of Key West to create an artificial reef. For a map of the **Florida Keys Shipwreck Heritage Trail,** an entire network of wrecks from Key Largo to Key West, go to http://floridakeys.noaa.gov/shipwrecktrail/welcome.html.

For hard-core and high-tech wreck divers, check out the **Wreck Trek Passport Program,** www.fla-keys.com/diving/wrecktrek, spotlighting the Florida Keys Shipwreck Trail from Key Largo to Key West and allowing certified divers to explore the trail and be rewarded for logging back-to-back wreck dives through January 1, 2014. The dive passport highlights nine shipwrecks. After completing all nine dives, passport holders are entered into a drawing for grand prizes, including dive equipment and dive-and-stay hotel packages. Even if you don't compete, it's worth a look just for the trail information alone.

ORGANIZED TOURS

BY TRAM & TROLLEY-BUS   Yes, it's more than a bit hokey to sit on this 60-foot tram of yellow cars, but it's worth it—at least once. The island's whole story is packed into a neat, 90-minute package on the **Conch Tour Train,** which covers the island and all its rich, raunchy history. In operation since 1958, the cars are open-air, which can make the ride uncomfortable in bad weather. The engine of the "train" is a propane-powered jeep disguised as a locomotive. Tours depart from both Mallory Square and the Welcome Center, near where U.S. 1 becomes North Roosevelt Boulevard, on the less developed side of the island. For information, call ℂ **305/294-5161** or go to www.conchtourtrain.com. The cost is $29 for adults, $26 for seniors, free for children 12 and under. Tickets are cheaper on the website. Daily departures are every half-hour from 9am to 4:30pm.

The **Old Town Trolley** is the choice in bad weather or if you're staying at one of the hotels on its route. Humorous drivers maintain a running commentary as the enclosed trolley loops around the island's streets past all the major sights. Trolley buses depart from Mallory Square and other points around the island, including many area hotels. For details, visit www.trolleytours.com or call ℂ **305/296-6688.** Tours are $29 for adults, $26 for seniors, and free for children 12 and under. Tickets are cheaper on the website. Departures are daily every half-hour (though not always on the half-hour) from 9am to 4:30pm. New from Old Town Trolley: **"Ghosts & Gravestones Frightseeing Tour,"** a 90-minute look at Key West's scariest sites and stories. Tours depart from 501 Front St. at 6:30 and 8pm. Tickets are $30 per person and children 12 and under are not recommended to attend, but if they do, it's $25 for them. Tickets are cheaper on the website.

Whichever you choose, both of these historic, trivia-packed tours are well worth the price of tickets.

BY AIR   **Conch Republic Air Force,** at Key West Airport, 3469 S. Roosevelt Blvd. (www.keywestbiplanes.com; ✆ **305/294-8687**), offers open-cockpit biplane rides over Key West and the coral reef in a 1942 Waco. The rides accommodate two passengers in the forward cockpit, but true thrill-seekers will also enjoy a spin in a Pitts Special S-2C, which does loops, rolls, and sideways figure eights. For the photographer, they offer a 1941 J-3 Cub for superslow flight over Key West and the coral reef; dual instruction, tail-wheel checkouts, and banner towing in the Cub are also available. For war-bird enthusiasts, there's the 1944 North American T-6 Texan, originally used for advanced fighter training in World War II. Company owner Fred Cabanas was decorated in 1991, after he spotted a Cuban airman defecting to the United States in a Russian-built MIG fighter. Sightseeing flights cost $160 to $335 depending on duration.

BY BIKE   One of the best ways to explore Key West is by bike. Thanks to **Eaton Bikes,** 830 Eaton St. (www.eatonbikes.com; ✆ **305/294-8188**), you can pedal around the Old Town district on a 2-hour bicycle tour led by a knowledgeable guide who will offer insight into everything from Key West's seafaring history to architecture, foliage, and even local gossip. Included in the $30-per-person tour are locally sourced refreshments, bike, and helmet. Tours go three times weekly. Call for time information.

BY BOAT   The catamarans and the glass-bottom boat of **Fury Water Adventures,** 237 Front St. (www.furycat.com; ✆ **305/296-6293**), depart on daytime coral-reef tours and evening sunset cruises (call for times). Reef trips cost $40 per adult, $20 per child 6 to 12; sunset cruises are $49 per adult and $30 per child 6 to 12. Prices are cheaper on the website.

The schooner ***Western Union*** (www.schoonerwesternunion.org; ✆ **305/292-9830**) was built in 1939 and served as a cable-repair vessel until it was designated the flagship of the city of Key West and began day, sunset, and charter sailings. Sunset sailings are especially memorable and include entertainment, cocktails, and cannon fire. Prices vary but range from $59 for adults and $29 for children 4 to 12; inquire for details.

Classic Harbour Line Key West (www.sail-keywest.com), features sightseeing and sunset tours aboard two stunning schooners, the ***Adirondack*** and ***America 2.0,*** a 105-foot tribute ship that just happens to be the winner of the 2011 Great Chesapeake Bay Schooner Race, which actually will race with you on it for $75. It's an awesome experience for speed freaks. Other tours range from $35 and up.

Sunset Culinaire Tours (www.sunsetculinaire.com; ✆ **305/296-0982**) is a cruise aboard the vessel *RB's Lady* and includes a tour of Key West harbor as the sun sinks below the horizon, and a three-course gourmet dinner (including beer or wine) prepared by chef Brian Kirkpatrick. The vessel departs from Sunset Marina, off U.S. 1 at 5555 College Rd., at 5:30pm nightly. Boarding time is 5pm and the cost is $85 per person.

OTHER TOURS   **Sharon Wells** (✆ **305/294-0566**), historian, artist, and owner of the KW Light Gallery, leads a slew of great tours throughout the island, focusing on things as diverse as literature, architecture, and places connected with the island's gay and lesbian culture.

Not necessarily a tour, per se, but a special-interest trip, **Key West Wellness Retreats** offers 5-night stays at **Rose Lane Villas,** 522 Rose Lane (www.roselane villas.com; © **800/294-2170**), a collection of private condos complete with full kitchen, free Wi-Fi, and shared pool. Each stay includes nutrition and fitness evaluations, poolside Pilates, reflexology, yoga, skin-care sessions, and mangrove kayaking excursions. Prices start at $1,499 per person.

For a lively look at Key West, try the **"Key West Pub Crawl"** (www.keywest walkingtours.com; © **305/744-9804**), a tour of the island's most famous bars. It's given on Tuesday and Friday nights at 8pm, lasts 2½ hours, costs $30, and includes five (!) drinks. Another fun option is the 1-mile, 90-minute **ghost tour** (www.haunted tours.com; © **305/294-WALK** [294-9255]), leaving daily at 8 and 9pm from the Holiday Inn La Concha, 430 Duval St. Cost is $15 for adults and $10 for children 11 and under. This spooky and interesting tour gives participants insight into many old island legends.

Key West's **"Ghosts and Legends Tour"** (www.keywestghosts.com; © **866/622-4467** or 305/294-1713) is a fun, 90-minute narrated tour of the island and its spirits. You'll walk through the shadowy streets and lanes of Old Town, stopping at allegedly haunted Victorian mansions, and learning about island pirate lore, voodoo superstitions and rituals, a count who lived with the corpse of his beloved, and other bizarre yet true aspects of this eerie place. Tours depart nightly from the Porter House Mansion on the corner of Duval and Caroline Street. Space is limited and reservations are required. Tickets are $18 for adults and $10 for children.

Since the early 1940s, Key West has been a haven for gay luminaries such as Tennessee Williams and Broadway legend Jerry Herman. The **"Gay and Lesbian Historic Trolley Tour,"** created by the Key West Business Guild, showcases the history, contributions, and landmarks associated with the island's flourishing gay and lesbian culture. Highlights include Williams's house, the art gallery owned by Key West's first gay mayor, and a variety of guesthouses whose gay owners fueled the island's architectural-restoration movement. The 70-minute tour takes place Saturday at 10:50am, starting and ending at City of Key West parking lot, corner of Simonton Street and Angela Street. Look for the trolley with the rainbow flags. The cost is $25. Call © **305/294-4603** or go to www.gaykeywestfl.com/featureevent.cfm?id=16.

Where to Eat

With its share of the usual drive-through fast-food franchises—mostly up on Roosevelt Boulevard—and Duval Street succumbing to the lure of a Hard Rock Cafe and Starbucks, you might be surprised to learn that, over the years, an upscale and high-quality dining scene has begun to thrive in Key West. Just wander Old Town or the newly spruced-up Bahama Village and browse menus after you've exhausted our list of picks below.

If you're staying in a condominium or an efficiency, you may want to stock your fridge with groceries, beer, wine, and snacks from the area's oldest grocer, **Fausto's Food Palace.** Open since 1926, Fausto's has two locations: 1105 White St. and 522 Fleming St. The Fleming Street location will deliver with a $25 minimum order (© **305/294-5221** or 305/296-5663).

VERY EXPENSIVE

Café Marquesa ★★★ CONTEMPORARY AMERICAN If you're looking for fabulous, upscale dining (and service), this is the place. The intimate, 50-seat restaurant is something to look at, but it's really the food that you'll want to admire. Specialties include macadamia-crusted yellowtail snapper, prosciutto-wrapped black Angus filet, and roast duck breast with red curry–coconut sauce. If you're looking to splurge, this is the place.

In the Marquesa Hotel, 600 Fleming St. ✆ **305/292-1919.** Reservations highly recommended. Main courses $21–$39. AE, DC, MC, V. Summer daily 7–11pm; winter daily 6–11pm.

Hot Tin Roof ★★★ FUSION Ever hear of conch fusion cuisine? Neither did we until we experienced it firsthand at Hot Tin Roof, Ocean Key Resort's chichi restaurant which transforms South American, Asian, Italian, and Keys cuisine into an experience unlike any other in this part of the world. The 3,000-square-foot space features both indoor and outdoor deck seating overlooking the harbor. Live jazz/fusion adds to the stunning environment—it's the epitome of casual elegance. Signature dishes include an irresistible lobster tempura with Asian slaw and lemon grass butter; pork ribs with black garlic barbecue sauce and mango slaw; and caramelized mahi with coconut, corn, poblano, and carrots that makes this tin roof very hot, to say the least, especially for Key West. Try the divine polenta fries with truffle aioli. Last time we ate here, Meryl Streep was sitting next to us with her family, looking as impressed as she was impressive.

In the Ocean Key Resort, Zero Duval St. ✆ **305/296-7701.** Reservations highly recommended. Main courses $21–$39. AE, DC, MC, V. Daily 7:30–11am and 5–10pm.

Louie's Backyard ★★ CARIBBEAN Nestled amid blooming bougainvillea on a lush slice of the Gulf, Louie's remains one of the most romantic restaurants on earth. It's off the beaten path, which makes it even more romantic. Star chef Norman Van Aken brought his talents from Miami and started one of the finest dining spots in the Keys. Try the sensational oyster, sweet corn, and shiitake-mushroom potpie for starters, and for a main course, the grilled Berkshire pork chop with beer-braised cabbage and sweet potatoes is to die for. You can't go wrong with the fresh catch of the day, or any seafood dish, for that matter. After dinner, sit at the dockside bar and watch the waves crash, almost touching your feet, while enjoying a cocktail at sunset. The weekend brunches are also great. And a ritual for many in Key West is sunset cocktails at the oceanfront Tiki bar. If you're not in the mood for a full-blown meal, consider the restaurant's stellar **Upper Deck Lounge,** serving tapas, including focaccia, bruschetta, carpaccio, roasted clams, flaming Ouzo shrimp, a daily assortment of cheeses, and pizzas Tuesday through Saturday from 5 to 10pm. It can be hard to get a reservation at Louie's, so call way in advance.

700 Waddell Ave. www.louiesbackyard.com. ✆ **305/294-1061.** Reservations highly recommended. Main courses $30–$55; lunch $10–$20; tapas $5–$25. AE, DC, MC, V. Daily 11:30am–3pm and 6–10:30pm.

EXPENSIVE

Alonzo's Oyster Bar ★ SEAFOOD Alonzo's serves good seafood in a casual setting. It's on the ground floor of the A&B Lobster House, at the end of Front Street in the marina; if you want to dress up, go upstairs for the "fine dining." To start your meal, try the steamed beer shrimp—tantalizingly fresh jumbo shrimp in a sauce of garlic, Old Bay seasoning, beer, and cayenne pepper. A house specialty is white-clam chili, a delicious mix of tender clams, white beans, and potatoes served with a dollop of sour cream. The staff is cheerful and informative, and the service is very good.

700 Front St. www.alonzosoysterbar.com. © **305/294-5880.** Main courses $19–$28. MC, V. Daily 11am–11pm.

Antonia's ★★ REGIONAL ITALIAN   The food is great, but the atmosphere a bit fussy for Key West. If you don't have a reservation in season, don't even bother. Still, if you don't mind paying high prices for dishes that go for much less elsewhere, try this old favorite. From the perfectly seasoned homemade focaccia to an exemplary crème brûlée, this elegant little standout is amazingly consistent. The menu includes a small selection of classics, linguine with shrimp, delicious pillowy gnocchi, and *zuppa di pesce* (fish soup). And don't miss the outstanding warm goat-cheese soufflé served with pan-seared asparagus, baby green beans, carrots, and Belgian endive over a roasted tomato vinaigrette. You can't go wrong with any of the handmade pastas. And the owners, Antonia Berto and Phillip Smith, travel to Italy every year to research recipes, so you can be sure you're getting an authentic taste of Italy in small-town Key West.

615 Duval St. www.antoniaskeywest.com. © **305/294-6565.** Reservations suggested. Main courses $19–$35. AE, DC, MC, V. Daily 6–11pm.

Banana Café ★★★ FRENCH   Banana Café benefits from a French-country-cafe look and feel. The upscale local eatery discovered by savvy visitors on the less congested end of Duval Street has retained its loyal clientele with affordable prices and delightful, light preparations. The crepes are legendary, for breakfast or lunch; the fresh ingredients and French-themed menu bring daytime diners back for the casual, classy, tropical-influenced seafood-heavy dinner menu. We highly recommend the pork chop stuffed with spinach and goat cheese, braised tomato, mashed potato, and port-wine sauce. There's live jazz every Thursday night.

1211 Duval St. www.banana-cafe-key-west.com. © **305/294-7227.** Main courses $20–$30; breakfast and lunch $3–$17. AE, DC, MC, V. Breakfast/lunch daily 8am–3pm; dinner Tues–Sat 6–10pm.

Blue Heaven ★★★ SEAFOOD/AMERICAN/NATURAL   This hippie-run restaurant has become the place to be in Key West—and with good reason. Be prepared to wait in line. The food is some of the best in town—especially at breakfast, which features homemade granola, tropical-fruit pancakes (owner Richard often makes his pancakes with beer), and seafood Benedict. Dinners are just as good and run the gamut from Caribbean barbecue shrimp and Jamaican jerk chicken to curried soups and vegetarian stews. Some people are put off by the dirt floors and roaming cats and birds, but frankly, it adds to the charm. The building used to be a bordello, where Hemingway was said to hang out refereeing boxing matches. It's still lively here, but not *that* lively!

305 Petronia St. www.blueheavenkw.com. © **305/296-8666.** Main courses $20–$30; lunch $6–$15; breakfast $5–$15. AE, DISC, MC, V. Daily 8am–10:30pm; Sun brunch 8am–2pm. Closed mid-Sept to early Oct.

La Trattoria ★ ITALIAN   Have a true Italian feast in a relaxed atmosphere. Each dish here is prepared and presented according to old Italian tradition. Try the delicious bread crumb–stuffed mushroom caps; they're firm yet tender. The stuffed eggplant with ricotta and roasted peppers is light and flavorful. Or have the seafood salad of shrimp, calamari, and mussels, which is fish-market fresh and tasty. The pasta dishes are also great—go for the penne Venezia, with mushrooms, sun-dried tomatoes, and crabmeat. For dessert, don't skip the homemade tiramisu; it's light yet full flavored. The dining room is spacious but still intimate, and the waiters are friendly. Before you leave, visit **Virgilio's,** the restaurant's resplendent indoor/outdoor cocktail lounge with live jazz until 2am. For those looking for a waterfront view, check out **La Trattoria Oceanside,** 3593 S. Roosevelt Blvd. (© **305/295-6789**), which is open every night 5 to 10:30pm.

524 Duval St. www.latrattoria.us. © **305/296-1075.** Main courses $14–$40. AE, DC, DISC, MC, V. Daily 5:30–11pm.

Michael's ★★★ 🎁 STEAKHOUSE Tucked away in a residential neighborhood, Michael's is a meaty oasis in a sea of fish. With steaks flown in from Allen Brothers in Chicago, this is *the* steakhouse for when you're craving meat, from New York strip to porterhouse. Unlike most steakhouses, Michael's exudes a relaxed, tropical ambience with a fabulous indoor/outdoor setting that's romantic but not stuffy. Seafood selections are also highly recommended and change nightly based on the day's catches. A fantastic fondue menu makes for a tasty snack or even a meal, complemented by an excellent, reasonably priced wine list, and for those not starving, check out the "Lite Side" menu, available from 5:30 until 7:30pm.

532 Margaret St. www.michaelskeywest.com. © **305/295-1300.** Reservations recommended. Main courses $15–$40. AE, DC, DISC, MC, V. Daily 5–11pm.

Nine One Five ★★★ ECLECTIC Housed in a restored Victorian mansion, Nine One Five is a cozy, romantic restaurant with such good food that it was selected to host a six-course dinner at the James Beard House in NYC. Twice. The cuisine is simple yet flavorful, with everything from Devils on Horseback (bacon-wrapped dates stuffed with garlic and served with a soy-ginger dipping sauce) to duck liver pâté. A tapas platter can be enjoyed as an appetizer or as a main course up in the restaurant's loft lounge area. For main courses, we suggest the Thai whole fish with sizzling chili garlic sauce and steamed basmati rice, or the Soul Mama Seafood soup, a mix of Key West shrimp, mussels, clams, and black grouper in a Thai green-curry coconut broth with lemon grass, cilantro, and basmati rice. Service is seamless and attentive, although if you sit up on the quaint second-floor porch, you may be there for a while. But this is the kind of place where you want to linger.

915 Duval St. www.915duval.com. © **305/296-0669.** Reservations recommended. Main courses $22–$34. AE, DISC, MC, V. Mon–Sat noon–3pm; daily 6–11pm. Upstairs lounge daily until 2am.

Seven Fish ★★ 🎁 SEAFOOD "Simple, good food" is Seven Fish's motto, but this little secret is much more than simple. One of the most popular restaurants with locals, Seven Fish is a chic seafood spot serving some of the best fish on the island. Sea scallops with pea purée and spinach, and gnocchi with blue cheese and sautéed fish are among the dishes to choose from. For dessert, do not miss the Key lime cake over tart lime curd with fresh berries.

632 Olivia St. www.7fish.com. © **305/296-2777.** Reservations recommended. Main courses $17–$29. AE, MC, V. Wed–Mon 6–10pm.

MODERATE
Ambrosia ★ SUSHI Trendy sushi spot Ambrosia, in the Santa Maria condo turned hotel, features some of the freshest fish in town. Chef-owner Masa offers you expertly prepared sushi—if you're a fan of tuna, try his *toro* (tuna belly). Specialty rolls include the Key West, a mix of stone crab, avocado, and smelt roe, and the Florida,

tempura lobsters wrapped in pink soybean protein. Cooked dishes are also excellent—try the lobster teriyaki or the pork with ginger sauce. Ambrosia is also a vegetarian hot spot, with excellent tofu dishes.

1401 Simonton St. http://keywestambrosia.com. ℭ **305/293-0304.** Sushi $4–$15; main courses $14–$26. AE, DISC, MC, V. Daily 11am–11pm.

Pepe's ★ 🍴 AMERICAN   This old dive has been serving good, basic food for nearly a century. Steaks and Apalachicola Bay oysters are the big draws for regulars, who appreciate the rustic barroom setting and historical photos on the walls. Look for original scenes of Key West in 1909, when Pepe's first opened. If the weather is nice, choose a seat on the patio under a stunning mahogany tree. Burgers, fish sandwiches, and standard chili satisfy hearty eaters. Buttery sautéed mushrooms and rich mashed potatoes are the best comfort foods in Key West. There's always a wait, so stop by early for breakfast, when you can get old-fashioned chipped beef on toast and all the usual egg dishes. In the evening, reasonably priced cocktails are served on the deck.

806 Caroline St. (btw. Margaret and Williams sts.). www.pepescafe.net. ℭ **305/294-7192.** Main courses $11–$30, breakfast $3–$17, lunch $3–$18. DISC, MC, V. Daily 6:30am–10:30pm.

Sarabeth's ★★ 🍴AMERICAN   An offshoot of the New York City breakfast hot spot, Sarabeth's brings a much-needed shot of cosmopolitan comfort food to Key West in the form of delicious breakfasts with Sarabeth's signature homemade jams and jellies. Choose from buttermilk to lemon-ricotta pancakes or almond-crusted cinnamon French toast. For lunch, the traditional Caesar salad, burger, or Key West pink shrimp roll with avocado are all excellent choices. Dinner is simple, but savory, with top-notch dishes from chicken potpie and meatloaf to a divine green-chili-pepper macaroni with three cheeses or meaty shrimp-and-crabmeat cakes. The dining room is cozy and intimate, and it feels like you're eating in someone's house; a few tables are on a small outdoor patio.

530 Simonton St. www.sarabethskeywest.com. ℭ **305/293-8181.** Main courses $15–$26, breakfast $7–$12, lunch $12–$15. MC, V. Mon 8am–3pm; Wed–Sun 8am–3pm and 6–10pm.

Turtle Kraals Wildlife Grill ★ ☺ 🍴 BARBECUE/SEAFOOD   You'll join lots of locals in this out-of-the-way converted warehouse with indoor and dockside seating, which serves innovative seafood at great prices. Try the twin lobster tails stuffed with mango and crabmeat, stone crabs when in season (Oct–May), or any of the big quesadillas or fajitas. There's also a barbecue menu created by an award-winning pit master from Chicago who presides over an on-premise smoker on which ribs, pork butts, beef brisket, and chicken are slow-smoked for up to 14 hours. Kids will like the wildlife exhibits, the turtle cannery, and the very cheesy menu. Blues bands play most nights, and for drinks the restaurant's roof deck, **The Tower Bar,** has fabulous views of the marina.

213 Margaret St. (at Caroline St.). www.turtlekraals.com. ℭ **305/294-2640.** Main courses $10–$26. DISC, MC, V. Mon–Thurs 11am–10:30pm; Fri–Sat 11am–11pm; Sun noon–10:30pm. Bar closes at midnight.

INEXPENSIVE
Hogfish Bar & Grill ★ 🍴 SEAFOOD   A ramshackle, rough-and-tumble seafood bar and grill on Safe Harbor in "downtown" Stock Island (there's no town, just fisheries, boats, and artists and craftsmen working out of shacks), Hogfish is a popular spot for its namesake sandwich. Similar to grouper, hogfish is a delicious, rare fish

with a scalloplike flavor, and the sandwich they make out of it, served on Cuban bread, is so popular it's usually sold out by noon. Key West pink shrimp are aplenty here, so peel and eat is another popular pastime while you're waiting for your hogfish. The fried rock lobster bites are another excellent way to bide your time here. If you're here for breakfast, try the fried hogfish Benedict—it's unlike any Benedict you've ever had. Live music and a lively, salty bar scene created by locals and tourists alike make Hogfish a quintessential Key West experience. Kids especially like feeding the fish in the harbor.

6810 Front St., Stock Island. www.hogfishbar.com. ☏ **305293-4041.** Main courses $10–$24; breakfast $7–$14; sandwiches $7–$15. AE, DISC, MC, V. Daily 11am–10pm. Take U.S. 1 N. out of Key West and across the Cow Key Channel Bridge. At the 3rd stoplight, bear to the right and onto MacDonald Ave. Follow for approx. 1 mile and make a right on 4th Ave. (across from Boyd's Campground). Take your next left on Front St. and drive almost to the end—you'll see the Hogfish Bar and Grill on the right.

Island Dogs Bar ★ AMERICAN   This islandy, Tommy Bahama–esque bar purchased in 2010 by Pat Croce (who owns the popular Rum Barrel bar and restaurant across the street) is a cool spot to throw back a few while catching a game or a live band. But more important is the fare—not typical bar fare, but upscale pub fare including the Island Dog, a bacon-wrapped hot dog topped with pineapple, mango, and banana peppers—and, well, you get the picture. Sit at the bar or at one of the few outdoor tables ideally placed for watching the crowds stumble—literally—off Duval Street.

505 Front St. www.islanddogsbar.com. ☏ **305/295-0501.** Main courses $5–$12. AE, DISC, MC, V. Daily 11am–2am.

Shopping

You'll find all kinds of unique gifts and souvenirs in Key West, from coconut postcards to Key lime pies. On Duval Street, T-shirt shops outnumber almost any other business. If you must get a wearable memento, be careful of unscrupulous salespeople. Despite efforts to curtail the practice, many shops have been known to rip off unwitting shoppers. It pays to check the prices and the exchange rate before signing any sales slips. You are entitled to a written estimate of any T-shirt work before you pay for it.

At Mallory Square, you'll find the **Clinton Street Market,** an overly air-conditioned mall of kiosks and stalls designed for the many cruise-ship passengers who never venture beyond this supercommercial zone. There are some coffee and candy shops, and some high-priced hats and shoes. There's also a free and clean restroom.

Once the main industry of Key West, cigar making is enjoying renewed success at the handful of factories that survived the slow years. Stroll through **Cigar Alley** (while on Greene St., go 2 blocks west and you'll hit Cigar Alley, also known as Pirate's Alley), where you will find *viejitos* (little old men) rolling fat stogies just as they used to do in their homeland across the Florida Straits. Stop at the **Conch Republic Cigar Factory,** 512 Greene St. (www.conch-cigars.com; ☏ **305/295-9036**), for an excellent selection of imported and locally rolled smokes, including the famous El Hemingway. Remember, buying or selling Cuban-made cigars is illegal. Shops advertising "Cuban cigars" are usually referring to domestic cigars made from tobacco grown from seeds that were brought from Cuba decades ago. To be fair, though, many premium cigars today are grown from Cuban seed tobacco—only it is grown in Latin America and the Caribbean, not Cuba.

If you're looking for local or Caribbean art, you'll find nearly a dozen galleries and shops on Duval Street between Catherine and Fleming streets. There are also some excellent shops on the side streets. One worth seeking out is the **Haitian Art Co.,** 1100 Truman Ave. (www.haitian-art-co.com; ✆ **305/296-8932**), where you can browse through room upon room of original paintings from well-known and obscure Haitian artists, in a range of prices from a few dollars to a few thousand. Also check out **Cuba, Cuba!** at 814 Duval St. (www.cubacubastore.com; ✆ **305/295-9442**), where you'll see paintings, sculpture, and photos by Cuban artists, as well as books and art from the island.

From sweet to spicy, **Peppers of Key West,** 602 Greene St. (www.peppersof keywest.com; ✆ **305/295-9333**), is a hot-sauce lover's heaven, with hundreds of variations, from mild to brutally spicy. Grab a seat at the tasting bar and be prepared to let your taste buds sizzle. *Tip:* Bring beer, and they'll let you sit there as long as you want, tasting some of their secret sauces!

Literature and music buffs will appreciate the many bookshops and record stores on the island. **Key West Island Bookstore,** 513 Fleming St. (www.keywestisland books.com; ✆ **305/294-2904**), carries new, used, and rare books, and specializes in fiction by residents of the Keys, including Ernest Hemingway, Tennessee Williams, Shel Silverstein, Judy Blume, Barbara Ehrenreich, Ann Beattie, Richard Wilbur, and John Hersey. The bookstore is open daily from 10am to 9pm.

For anything else, from bed linens to candlesticks to clothing, go to downtown's oldest and most renowned department store, **Fast Buck Freddie's,** 500 Duval St. (✆ **305/294-2007**). For the same merchandise at reduced prices, try **Half Buck Freddie's ★**, 726 Caroline St. (✆ **305/294-2007**), where you can shop for out-of-season bargains and "rejects" from the main store.

Also check out **KW Light Gallery,** 534 Fleming St. (✆ **305/294-0566**), for high-quality contemporary photography as well as historic images and other artwork relating to the Keys or to the concept of light and its varied interpretations. The gallery is open Thursday through Tuesday from 10am to 6pm (10am–4pm in summer). Owner/photographer/painter Sharon Wells also gives historic tours of Key West, so inquire while you're inside.

Entertainment & Nightlife

Duval Street is the Bourbon Street of Florida. Amid the T-shirt shops and clothing boutiques, you'll find bar after bar serving neon-colored frozen drinks to revelers drinking and partying from noon to dawn. Bands and crowds vary from night to night and season to season. Your best bet is to start at Truman Avenue and head up Duval to check them out for yourself. Cover charges are rare, except in gay clubs (see "The Gay & Lesbian Scene," below), so stop into a dozen and see which you like. Key West is a late-night town, and most bars and clubs don't close until around 3 or 4am.

Captain Tony's Saloon   Just around the corner from Duval's beaten path, this smoky old bar is about as authentic as you'll find. It comes complete with old-time regulars who remember the island before cruise ships docked here; they say Hemingway drank, caroused, and even wrote here. The late owner, Capt. Tony Tarracino, was a former controversial Key West mayor—immortalized in Jimmy Buffett's "Last Mango in Paris." 428 Greene St. www.capttonyssaloon.com. ✆ **305/294-1838.**

Cowboy Bill's Honky Tonk Saloon   "The Southernmost Country Bar in the USA" features two boot-scootin' locations of indoor and outdoor bars, pool, darts, video games, 26 TVs, line dancing, live music, and the only mechanical bull in the Keys that gets kicking every Tuesday through Saturday from 10pm to 2am, with a special "sexy" bull-riding competition every Wednesday at 11:30pm. Participate or watch, but note that there are webcams catching all the action. And after several dollar Pabst Blue Ribbons, trust us, there's a lot of action going on here from 10pm to 4am daily. Also check out **Cowboy Bill's Reloaded** at 430 Green Street. 618 Duval St. and 430 Greene St. www.cowboybillskw.com. ⓒ **305/295-8219.**

The Green Parrot Bar A Key West landmark since 1890, the Green Parrot is a locals' favorite featuring stiff drinks, salty drinkers, and excellent live music, from bluegrass and country to Afro-punk. 601 Whitehead St. www.greenparrot.com. ⓒ **305/294-6133.**

Sloppy Joe's You'll have to stop in here just to say you did. Scholars and drunks debate whether this is the same Sloppy Joe's that Hemingway wrote about, but there's no argument that this classic bar's early-20th-century wooden ceiling and cracked-tile floors are Key West originals. There's live music nightly, as well as a cigar room and martini bar. 201 Duval St. www.sloppyjoes.com. ⓒ **305/294-5717,** ext. 10.

THE GAY & LESBIAN SCENE

Key West's live-and-let-live atmosphere extends to its thriving and quirky gay community. Before and after Tennessee Williams, Key West has provided the perfect backdrop to a gay scene unlike that of many large urban areas. Seamlessly blended with the prevailing culture, there is no "gay ghetto" in Key West, where the whole place is fabulous.

In Key West, the best music and dancing can be found at the predominantly gay clubs. While many of the area's other hot spots are geared toward tourists who like to imbibe, the gay clubs are for those who want to rave, gay or not. Covers vary, but are rarely more than $10.

Two popular adjacent late-night spots are the **801 Bourbon Bar/One Saloon,** 801 Duval St. and 514 Petronia St. (www.801bourbon.com; ⓒ **305/294-9349** for both), featuring great drag and lots more disco. A mostly male clientele frequents this hot spot from 9pm to 4am. Another Duval Street favorite is **Aqua,** 711 Duval St. (www.aquakeywest.com; ⓒ **305/292-8500**), where you might catch drag queens belting out torch songs or judges voting on the best package in the wet-jockey-shorts contest.

Sunday nights are fun at La-Te-Da, proper name: **La Terraza de Martí,** 1125 Duval St. (www.lateda.com; ⓒ **305/296-6706**), the former Key West home of Cuban exile José Martí. This is a great spot to gather poolside for the best martini in town—don't bother with the food. Upstairs is the **Crystal Room** (ⓒ **305/296-6706**), with a high-caliber cabaret performance featuring the popular Randy Roberts in winter.

Where to Stay

You'll find a wide variety of places to stay in Key West, from resorts with all the amenities to seaside motels, quaint bed-and-breakfasts, and clothing-optional guesthouses. You can almost always find a place to stay at the last minute, unless you're in town during the most popular holidays: Fantasy Fest (around Halloween), when Mardi Gras meets South Florida for the NC-17 set and most hotels have outrageous rates and 5-night minimums; Hemingway Days (in July), when Papa is seemingly and eerily alive and well; and Christmas and New Year's—or for a big fishing tournament (many are held Oct–Dec) or a boat-racing tourney. However, you may want to book early, especially in winter, when prime properties fill up and many require 2- or 3-night minimum stays. Prices at these times are extremely high. Finding a decent room for less than $100 a night is a real trick.

Another suggestion, and our recommendation, is to call **Vacation Key West** (www.vacationkw.com; ✆ **800/595-5397** or 305/295-9500), a wholesaler that offers discounts of 20% to 30% and is skilled at finding last-minute deals. It represents mostly larger hotels and motels, but can also place visitors in guesthouses. The phones are answered Monday through Friday from 9am to 6pm, and Saturday from 11am to 2pm. **Key West Innkeepers Association** (www.keywestinns.com; ✆ **800/492-1911** or 305/292-3600) can also help you find lodging in any price range from among its members and affiliates.

GLBT travelers may want to call the **Key West Business Guild** (www.gaykey westfl.com; ✆ **305/294-4603**), which represents more than 50 guesthouses and B&Bs in town, as well as many other gay-owned businesses. Be advised that most gay guesthouses have a clothing-optional policy. One of the most elegant and popular is the clothing-optional **Big Ruby's,** 409 Applerouth Lane (www.bigrubys.com; ✆ **800/477-7829** or 305/296-2323), located on a little alley just off Duval Street. Rates start at $186 double in peak season and $129 off season. A low cluster of buildings surrounds a lush courtyard where a hearty breakfast is served each morning and wine is poured at dusk. The all-male guests hang out by the pool, tanning in the buff.

For women mostly (and women only during Womenfest, held in early Sept) and their male friends and/or family members, **Pearl's Key West,** 525 United St. (www. pearlskeywest.com; ✆ **800/749-6696** or 305/292-1450), is a large, fairly well-maintained guesthouse with 38 rooms and suites, full breakfast, two pools (where you may choose to go topless), two hot tubs, a gym, and poolside bar and grill. Rates range from $79 to $369.

VERY EXPENSIVE

Hyatt Key West Resort & Spa ★ Sitting on the bay and nicknamed "the Sanctuary off of Duval," the Hyatt features a waterfront pool, small beach area, and guest rooms with white-porcelain tile floors, flatscreen TVs, and fabulous bathrooms. New spa cabanas allow for outdoor treatments, and a restaurant overlooking the water is great for breakfast, lunch, or dinner. Located right near Duval Street and next door to several lively bars, the Hyatt offers the best of both worlds when it comes to Key West relaxation—and partying. **The Blue Mojito Bar & Grill** is a great spot on the property for a cocktail or three. The property's new signature restaurant, the **SHOR American Seafood Grill,** serves great, well, seafood. You also shouldn't miss a trip to the **Jala Spa** while you are there. Jala offers a variety of natural treatments and uses a new skin-care line, Amala, which is green-certified.

601 Front St., Key West, FL 33040. www.keywest.hyatt.com. ✆ **800/55-HYATT** (554-9288) or 305/809-1234. Fax 305/809-4050. 118 rooms. Winter $485–$550 double; off season $335–$450 double. AE, DC, DISC, MC, V. **Amenities:** Restaurant; bar; fitness center; pool; spa; watersports equipment/rentals. *In room:* A/C, TV, hair dryer, Wi-Fi.

Ocean Key Resort & Spa ★★ You can't beat the location of this 100-room resort, at the foot of Mallory Square, the epicenter of the sunset ritual. Ocean Key also features a Gulf-side heated pool and the lively Sunset Pier, where guests can wind down with cocktails and live music. Guest rooms are huge and luxuriously appointed, with living and dining areas, oversize Jacuzzis, and views of the Gulf, the harbor, or Mallory Square and Duval Street. The two-bedroom suite is 1,200 square feet and has a full kitchen, three beds, and a large private balcony. The property is adorned in classic Key West decor, from the tile floors and hand-painted furniture to the pastel art. The Indonesian-inspired **SpaTerre** is perhaps the best in town. The resort's restaurant, **Hot Tin Roof** (p. 274), is one of Key West's best. **The Liquid Lounge** is a VIP pool lounge featuring private cabanas and nightclub-style bottle service and music.

Zero Duval St. (near Mallory Docks), Key West, FL 33040. www.oceankey.com. © **800/328-9815** or 305/296-7701. Fax 305/292-2198. 100 units. Winter $379–$679 double, $479–$1,149 suite; off season $239–$439 double, $319–$639 suite. AE, DC, MC, V. **Amenities:** 2 restaurants; 3 bars; babysitting; bike rental; concierge; heated pool; room service; watersports equipment/rentals. *In room:* A/C, TV, hair dryer, minibar, Wi-Fi.

The Westin Key West Resort & Marina ★★   In the heart of Old Town, the Westin Key West Resort & Marina is next to Mallory Square and within walking distance of Duval Street. Featuring large rooms with all the modern conveniences, most of the 178 rooms and suites have ocean views and balconies. Bistro 245 serves ample breakfasts, lunches, dinners, and a huge Sunday brunch. Visit the Westin Sunset Pier for the nightly Sunset Celebration, with live performers and outdoor dining.

The Westin's sister property, **Sunset Key Guest Cottages, A Westin Resort** ★★★ (www.westinsunsetkeycottages.com; © **888/477-7SUN** [7786]), features 40 luxurious cottages just 10 minutes by boat from Key West. Check in at the Westin Key West Resort & Marina and take a 10-minute launch ride to the secluded island of Sunset Key, where there is a white-sandy beach, free-form pool, tennis courts, spa, and stunning beachfront Latitudes restaurant. Cottages are equipped with full kitchens, entertainment centers, and one, two, three, or four bedrooms. Guests at Sunset Key have access to all the amenities at the Westin Key West Resort & Marina. For a nominal fee, guests of the Westin Key West Resort & Marina can enjoy the beach on Sunset Key.

245 Front St., Key West, FL 33040. www.westinkeywestresort.com. © **800/221-2424** or 305/294-4000. Fax 305/294-4086. 178 units, 40 cottages. Winter $399–$659 double, $499–$1,149. suite, Sunset Key Guest Cottages $695–$3,695; off season $229–$459 double, $329–$829 suite, Sunset Key Guest Cottages $595–$3,695. AE, DC, DISC, MC, V. Valet parking $22 per day; self-parking $20 per day. Pets up to 40 lb. allowed at the Westin Key West Resort & Marina only. **Amenities:** 5 restaurants; 3 bars; concierge; fitness room; Jacuzzi; outdoor heated pool; limited room service; watersports equipment/rentals. *In room:* A/C, TV, hair dryer, Wi-Fi.

EXPENSIVE

Ambrosia Key West ★★ 🎒   Ambrosia is one of Key West's treasures, a private compound set on 2 lush acres just a block from Duval Street. Two lagoon-style pools, a spa pool, suites, town houses, and a cottage are spread around the grounds. Town houses have living rooms, kitchens, and spiral staircases leading to master suites with vaulted ceilings and private decks. The cottage is a perfect family retreat, with two bedrooms, two bathrooms, a living room, and a kitchen. All rooms have private entrances, most with French doors opening onto a variety of intimate outdoor spaces, including private verandas, patios, and gardens with sculptures, fountains, and pools. The breakfast buffet rocks, with eggs, biscuits, gravy, bacon, and pretty much anything you'd want. There's also complimentary coffee, tea, and bottled water with water filtration systems around the property for free refills. Fantastic service, bolstered by the philosophy that it's better to have high occupancy than high rates, explains why Ambrosia has a 90% year-round occupancy—a record in seasonal Key West.

622 Fleming St., Key West, FL 33040. www.ambrosiakeywest.com. ✆ **800/535-9838** or 305/296-9838. Fax 305/296-2425. 20 units. Winter $309–$649 suite; off season $189–$419 suite. Rates include breakfast buffet. AE, DISC, MC, V. Off- and on-street parking. Pets accepted. **Amenities:** 2 outdoor heated pools, 1 spa pool. *In room:* A/C, TV, CD player, fridge, hair dryer, kitchen (in some), Wi-Fi.

Casa Marina, A Waldorf Astoria Resort ★ ☺ After a dramatic $44-million renovation, Casa Marina is the only resort in Key West to offer a pleasing mix of both historic architecture *and* modern Key West vibe. Supremely located on the south side of the island, spanning more than 1,000 feet of private beach, the Casa Marina features sweeping lawns, a grand veranda, and a new "water walk" leading from the historic lobby to the water's edge. Recently revitalized rooms with sun-soaked balconies overlook the Atlantic and historic Old Town Key West. Elegant artwork and furnishings are complemented by luxurious bedding and soothing earth tones. One- and two-bedroom oceanview suites have stellar views and separate living areas. In addition to the beach itself, there are also two outdoor pools, a full-service spa, and an outdoor restaurant. Nightly movies shown at the pool with free popcorn and snacks cater to families with kids.

1500 Reynolds St., Key West, FL 33040. www.casamarinaresort.com. ✆ **866/397-6342** or 305/296-3535. Fax 305/296-3008. 311 units. Winter $249–$499 double, $349–$799 suite; off season $149–$399 double, $249–$699 suite. AE, DC, MC, V. **Amenities:** Restaurant; bar; bike rental; concierge; fitness center; 2 pools; room service; spa; watersports equipment/rentals. *In room:* A/C, TV, hair dryer, high-speed Internet, minibar.

Curry Mansion Inn ★★ ⛱ This charismatic inn is the former home of the island's first millionaire, a once-penniless Bahamian immigrant who made a fortune as a pirate. Owned today by Al and Edith Amsterdam, the Curry Mansion is now on the National Register of Historic Places, but you won't feel like you're staying in a museum—it's rather like a wonderfully warm home. Rooms are sparsely decorated, with wicker furniture, four-poster beds, and pink walls—call it Key West minimalism meets Victorian. The dining room is reminiscent of a Victorian dollhouse, with elegant table settings and rich wood floors and furnishings. Every morning, there's a delicious European-style breakfast buffet; at night, cocktail parties are held. There's also a really nice patio, on which, from time to time, there's live entertainment.

511 Caroline St., Key West, FL 33040. www.currymansion.com. ✆ **800/253-3466** or 305/294-5349. Fax 305/294-4093. 28 units. Winter $240–$300 double, $315–$365 suite; off season $195–$235 double, $260–$285 suite. Rates include breakfast buffet. AE, DC, MC, V. No children 11 and under. **Amenities:** Dining room; bike rental; concierge; pool. *In room:* A/C, TV, minibar.

The Gardens Hotel ★★★ ⛱ Once a private residence, the Gardens Hotel (whose main house is listed on the National Register of Historic Places) is hidden amid exotic gardens. Behind the greenery is a Bahamian-style hideaway with luxuriously appointed rooms in the main house, garden and courtyard rooms in the carriage house, and one ultrasecluded cottage. Though the place is within walking distance of frenetic Duval Street, you may not want to leave. A free-form pool is centered in the courtyard, where a Tiki bar serves libations. The Jacuzzi is hidden behind foliage. Guest rooms have hardwood floors, plantation beds with Tempur-Pedic mattresses, and marble bathrooms. Winding brick pathways leading to secluded seating areas in the private gardens make for an idyllic getaway. On Sunday afternoons the hotel features a very happening scene with live jazz in the gardens, and on Fridays and Saturday nights there's cabaret in the piano room. There's a wine bar, the

d'Vine Wine Gallery, offering 36 different vintages. *Note:* If you plan to party, do not stay here—guests tend to be on the quieter, more sophisticated side.

526 Angela St., Key West, FL 33040. www.gardenshotel.com. © **800/526-2664** or 305/294-2661. Fax 305/292-1007. 17 units. Winter $300–$415 double, $495–$675 suite; off season $175–$325 double, $225–$395 suite. Rates include continental breakfast. AE, DC, MC, V. **Amenities:** Bar; pool. *In room:* A/C, TV, hair dryer.

Island City House Hotel ★★   The oldest running B&B in Key West, the Island City House consists of three separate charming buildings that share a common junglelike patio and pool. The first building is a historic three-story wooden structure with wraparound verandas on every floor. The warmly outfitted interiors here include wood floors and antiques. The unpainted wooden Cigar House has large bedrooms, similar in ambience to those in the Island City House. The Arch House has newly renovated floors and features six airy Caribbean-style suites. Built of Dade County pine, this house's cozy bedrooms are furnished in wicker and rattan, and come with small kitchens and bathrooms. A shaded brick courtyard and pretty pool are surrounded by lush gardens where, every morning, a delicious continental breakfast is served. *Note:* Those who have an allergy to or dislike of cats should know that there are several friendly "resident" felines who call Island City House home.

411 William St., Key West, FL 33040. www.islandcityhouse.com. © **800/634-8230** or 305/294-5702. Fax 305/294-1289. 24 units. Winter $230–$420 double; off season $150–$300 double. Rates include breakfast. AE, DC, MC, V. **Amenities:** Bike rental; concierge; access to nearby health club; outdoor heated pool. *In room:* A/C, TV, hair dryer, kitchen.

La Mer Hotel & Dewey House ★★★ 🎁   If we were to build a beach house, this is exactly what it would look like. And although it's technically one bed-and-breakfast, La Mer Hotel is Victorian style while the adjoining Dewey House is more quaint and cottagey. Between the two, there are 19 rooms, each with a turn-of-the-19th-century feel but with modern amenities including granite wet bars, Wi-Fi, and luxurious linens that may have you lingering in the comfy beds for longer than you'd like, especially when you look out from your balcony or private patio and check out the views of the ocean. Stunning. Every morning there's a deluxe breakfast of fresh breads, made-to-order waffles, fresh-squeezed juices, and more on the Dewey Terrace overlooking the beach that's shared with La Mer & Dewey House's sister hotel, the more party-hearty Southernmost on the Beach. To keep with the old-school theme, there's a daily **afternoon tea** service, also included in the rates, from 3:30 to 5:30pm.

506 South St., Key West, FL 33040. www.southernmostresorts.com. © **800/354-4455** or 305/296-6577. Fax 305/294-8272. 19 units. Winter $249–$449 double; off season $159–$299 double. Rates include continental breakfast, daily afternoon tea, and parking. AE, DISC, MC, V. **Amenities:** Restaurant; bar; concierge; pool shared w/Southernmost on the Beach. *In room:* A/C, TV, mini-fridge, hair dryer, free Wi-Fi.

Marquesa Hotel ★★★ 🎁   The exquisite Marquesa offers the charm of a small historic hotel coupled with the amenities of a large resort. It encompasses four buildings, two pools, and a three-stage waterfall that cascades into a lily pond. Two of the hotel's buildings are luxuriously restored Victorian homes outfitted with plush antiques and contemporary furniture. The rooms in the two newly constructed buildings are even cushier; many have four-poster wrought-iron beds with bright floral spreads. If you can, try to get a room with its own private porch overlooking the pool. These are sublime. The bathrooms in the new buildings are lush and spacious; those in the older buildings are also nice, but not nearly as huge and luxe. The decor is simple, elegant, and spotless. The hotel also boasts one of Key West's best restaurants, **Café Marquesa.**

600 Fleming St. (at Simonton St.), Key West, FL 33040. www.marquesa.com. ☏ **800/869-4631** or 305/292-1919. Fax 305/294-2121. 27 units. Winter $330–$395 double, $495–$520 suite; off season $190–$290 double, $270–$330 suite. AE, DC, MC, V. No children 14 and under. **Amenities:** Restaurant; bike rental; concierge; access to nearby health club; 2 outdoor pools (1 heated); limited room service. *In room:* A/C, flatscreen TV, fridge, hair dryer, Internet access, minibar.

Parrot Key Resort ★★★   Parrot Key's waterfront Conch-style cottages, suites, and rooms are the epitome of beachy luxury and are the largest available in Key West. Accommodations options include deluxe king or double queen rooms, deluxe one- and two-bedroom suites, and luxury two- and three-bedroom guest cottages. Guest cottages feature gourmet kitchens and all rooms offer private patio, porch, or balcony; flatscreen TVs; premium cable service; and DVD/stereo systems. All rooms are smoke-free. Situated on 5 acres of award-winning tropical landscaping, the resort boasts four private pools (each in its own sculpture-garden setting), private white-sand sunbathing terraces, and the poolside **Café Blue** and Tiki bar. Minutes from the action on Duval Street, Parrot Key is an idyllic retreat.

2801 N. Roosevelt Blvd., Key West, FL 33040. www.parrotkeyresort.com. ☏ **305/809-2200.** Fax 305/292-3322. 104 units. Winter $349–$1,199 double; off season $169–$799 double. AE, DC, DISC, MC, V. **Amenities:** Poolside cafe and Tiki bar; bike rental; concierge; fitness center; high-speed Internet access property-wide; outdoor pools; spa services; watersports equipment/rentals; complimentary Wi-Fi. *In room:* A/C, TV, hair dryer.

Pier House Resort & Caribbean Spa ★   If you're looking for something a bit more intimate than the Reach Resort (see below), Pier House is an ideal choice. Its location—at the foot of Duval Street and just steps from Mallory Docks—is the envy of every hotel on the island. Set back from the busy street, on a short strip of private beach, this place is a welcome oasis of calm. The accommodations vary tremendously—no two rooms are alike—from simple business-style rooms to romantic quarters with whirlpool tubs. Although every unit has a balcony or a patio, not all overlook the water. Our favorites, in the two-story spa building, don't have any view at all. But what they lack in scenery, they make up for in opulence: Each well-appointed spa room has a sitting area and a huge Jacuzzi bathroom.

1 Duval St. (near Mallory Docks), Key West, FL 33040. www.pierhouse.com. ☏ **800/327-8340** or 305/296-4600. Fax 305/296-9085. 142 units. Winter $309–$529 double, $479–$3,000 suite; off season $229–$369 double, $389–$2,000 suite. AE, DC, MC, V. **Amenities:** 3 restaurants; 3 bars; babysitting; bike rental; concierge; fitness center; 2 Jacuzzis; heated pool; limited room service; sauna; full-service spa; watersports equipment/rentals. *In room:* A/C, TV, hair dryer, Internet access, minibar.

The Reach, a Waldorf Astoria Resort ★★★   Fresh from a $41-million renovation, the boutique-style Reach Resort features gingerbread balconies, tin roof accents, and shaded Spanish walkways characteristic of historic Key West. Newly refurbished guest rooms are large, with modernized decor and custom furnishings that are vibrant and crisp. Every room features comfortable sectional sofas and sliding glass doors that open onto balconies, some with ocean views. Sixty-eight boutique and 10 executive suites are also available. A new pool deck and 450-foot natural-sand beach are the perfect settings to enjoy a massive array of watersports, available right on the premises. The resort is also home to the Manhattan-based **Strip House** restaurant, which is as delicious as it is, well, sexy. Unlike most area resorts, which are smallish, this one seems infinitely larger and, in many ways, worlds away from the rest of Key West.

1435 Simonton St., Key West, FL 33040. www.reachresort.com. ✆ **866/397-6427** or 305/296-5000 for reservations. Fax 305/296-3008. 150 units. Winter $249–$499 double, $299–$549 suite; off season $149–$399 double, $199–$449 suite. AE, DC, DISC, MC, V. **Amenities:** 2 restaurants; bar; bike rental; concierge; outdoor heated pool; room service; spa; watersports equipment/rentals. *In room:* A/C, TV, minifridge, hair dryer, high-speed Internet, minibar.

Simonton Court ★★★ 🛅 This is one of our favorite stays in Key West—too bad it's always booked. Once a cigar factory, Simonton Court features meticulously appointed restored historic cottages and suites amid sparkling pools and luxuriant private gardens. There are several options to choose from: bed-and-breakfast, cottages, guesthouse, mansion, and inn. Some cottages even have their own pools. There's no restaurant, but the well-informed concierge will help you with reservations anywhere no matter what you crave. People love the place so much, they book years in advance. Once you stay here, if you're lucky, you'll understand why.

320 Simonton St., Key West, FL 33040. www.simontoncourt.com. ✆ **800/944-2687** or 305/294-6386. Fax 305/293-8446. 30 units. Winter $260–$350 double in mansion, $480–$515 cottage, $260–$400 inn, $330–$440 manor house, $300–$400 town house; off season $160–$270 double in mansion, $360–$395 cottage, $160–$270 inn, $220–$320 manor house, $190–$270 town house. Rates include continental breakfast. AE, DISC, MC, V. **Amenities:** Concierge; 4 outdoor pools; Wi-Fi throughout the 2 acres. *In room:* A/C, TV/VCR/DVD, fridge, hair dryer.

Southernmost on the Beach ★★★ This beachfront hotel—one of the few in Key West—offers rooms with views of the Atlantic, a huge oceanfront pool, and a lively pool bar. The best part about this resort is its location directly on an actually sandy private beach. Grounds have been beautifully landscaped with lush gardens and palm trees. Eighty luxury suites feature flatscreen TVs, MP3 docking stations, sleek mahogany furniture, and blue-and-white decor made to resemble a yacht. The open-air Southernmost **Beach Café** is a nice place for lunch or sunset dinner, but the poolside Tiki bar is where most of the action is. Because of its impressive, beautiful beach, Southernmost is the site of many weddings. In addition to its more subdued, romantic sister bed-and-breakfast La Mer Hotel & Dewey House (p. 284), Southernmost on the Beach has another property across the street, also with a great pool scene, albeit not on the water—the **Southernmost Hotel in the USA,** 1319 Duval St. (✆ **800/354-4455**), where rates range from $159 to $299 in winter and $99 to $199 in summer.

508 South St., Key West, FL 33040. www.southernmosthotels.com. ✆ **800/354-4455** or 305/295-6550. Fax 305/294-8272. 127 units. Winter $279–$475 double; off season $159–$299 double. Rates include parking. AE, DC, DISC, MC, V. **Amenities:** Restaurant; bar; bike rental; concierge; health club; pool; spa; watersports equipment rental. *In room:* A/C, TV, hair dryer, minifridge, free Wi-Fi.

Weatherstation Inn ★ 🛅 Originally built in 1912 as a weather station, this beautifully restored, meticulously maintained, Renaissance-style inn is just 2 blocks from Duval Street but seems worlds away. It's on the tropical grounds of the former Old Navy Yard, now a private gated community. Presidents Truman, Eisenhower, and JFK all visited the station. Spacious and uncluttered, each guest room is uniquely furnished to complement the interior architecture: hardwood floors, tall sash windows, and high ceilings. The large, modern bathrooms are especially appealing. The staff is both friendly and accommodating.

57 Front St., Key West, FL 33040. www.weatherstationinn.com. ✆ **800/815-2707** or 305/294-7277. Fax 305/294-0544. 8 units. Winter $235–$335 double; off season $180–$245 double. Rates include continental breakfast. AE, DISC, MC, V. **Amenities:** Concierge; outdoor pool. *In room:* A/C, TV/VCR, hair dryer.

MODERATE

Eden House ★ 🎁 Owned and operated by Mike Eden for over 34 years, Eden House is a fabulous spot for everyone from budget travelers to those seeking a more private retreat. With a variety of rooms ranging from semiprivate with shared bathrooms to suites with private Jacuzzi, full kitchen, washer, dryer, porch, and private entrance, Eden House does have something for everyone. A free happy hour from 4 to 5pm daily is a great way to meet people, grab a drink, and relax amid the beautifully landscaped grounds complete with waterfalls and porch swings. For those not in the social mood, steal away to a hammock—there are several throughout the property. Other amenities include a pool, Jacuzzi, sun deck, and grill area. Owner Eden is hilarious and if you have a chance, chat with him. As he says, "Key West is a bowl of granola. What's not fruits and nuts, is flakes."

1015 Fleming St., Key West, FL 33040. www.edenhouse.com. ✆ **800/533-5397** or 305/296-6868. Fax 305/294-1221. 40 units. Winter $185–$200 semiprivate, $210–$245 private, $295–$320 deluxe, $385–$450 apt or conch house; off season $155–$180 semiprivate, $150–$175 private, $180–$260 deluxe, $255–$320 apt or conch house. MC, V. **Amenities:** Restaurant; garden pool; Wi-Fi. *In room:* A/C, TV/VCR, fridge, hair dryer.

La Pensione ★★ This classic B&B, set in a stunning 1891 home, is a total charmer. The comfortable rooms all have air-conditioning, ceiling fans, and king-size beds. Many also have French doors opening onto spacious verandas. Although the rooms have no TVs, the distractions of Duval Street, only steps away, should keep you adequately occupied. Breakfast, which includes Belgian waffles, fresh fruit, and a variety of breads or muffins, can be taken on the wraparound porch or at the communal dining table. Recent guests, however, have informed us that service here is not as friendly as it used to be and that the inn's location on U.S. 1 isn't so hot when it comes to the noise and traffic levels.

809 Truman Ave. (btw. Windsor and Margaret sts.), Key West, FL 33040. www.lapensione.com. ✆ **800/893-1193** or 305/292-9923. Fax 305/296-6509. 9 units. Winter $228–$328 double; off season $148–$168 double. Rates include breakfast. Discount of 10% for readers who mention this book. AE, DC, DISC, MC, V. No children. **Amenities:** Bike rental; outdoor pool; Wi-Fi. *In room:* A/C.

Orchid Key Inn ★ What happens to an old-school motor lodge located smack in the middle of Duval Street? It becomes a new-school, trendy motor lodge complete with wine bar and 24 modern, albeit tiny, rooms. And although it's in the middle of the action, the Orchid Key Inn is surprisingly a quiet and peaceful place. We stayed in the very first room right on Duval and heard hardly any noise. Paths lead you through lush tropical landscapes which surround the rooms and suites. Tranquil waterfalls and water features surround the sun deck, heated pool, and spa, all of which are hidden from the main drag. Free daily breakfast and sunset happy hours make it a great place for socializing or just getting your day or party started.

1004 Duval St., Key West, FL 33040. www.orchidkey.com. ✆ **800/845-8384** or 305/296-9915. Fax 305/2924886. 24 units. Winter $189–$289 king deluxe, $209–$309 1-bedroom suite; off season $119–$169 king deluxe, $149–$209 1-bedroom suite. Rates include continental breakfast and happy hour. AE, DISC, MC, V. Pets allowed with advance arrangements. **Amenities:** Bar; concierge; Jacuzzi; heated pool. *In room:* A/C, HDTV, hair dryer, MP3 docking station, Wi-Fi.

Seascape, An Inn ★ This romantic retreat located on a quiet street behind the Hemingway House and within walking distance of the water and the action was built from native pine in the Bahamas in the 1840s and transported by ship to Key West, where it was rebuilt in 1889. Fast-forward to 2012 and you have a splendidly renovated, tropical-style inn with turn-of-the-19th-century charm. Rooms are decorated in colorful, tropical decor and have private bathrooms. Most have French doors that open out to a heated pool and Jacuzzi, upstairs sun deck, or lush gardens and courtyard where guests indulge in a delicious champagne continental breakfast. The two-story Havana Suite has a private entrance as well as a kitchenette.

420 Olivia St., Key West, FL 33040. www.seascapetropicalinn.com. © **800/765-6438** or 305/296-7776. Fax 305/296-6283. 6 units. Winter $199–$229 double, $204–$239 suite; off season $129–$149 double, $169–$199 suite. Rates include champagne breakfast. AE, DISC, MC, V. **Amenities:** Jacuzzi; pool. *In room:* A/C, TV, hair dryer, Internet access.

Silver Palms Inn ★ Emerging from the wreckage of the mom-and-pop El Rancho Motel is this brand-new, affordable 50-room boutique hotel on the edge of Duval Street featuring modern, immaculately clean rooms and suites surrounding a courtyard, deck, and sparkling pool. Amenities are aplenty here, from 40-inch LCD TVs and hypoallergenic pillows and duvets to free Wi-Fi, free parking, and free continental breakfast. Eco-conscious travelers will appreciate the green initiatives, including water and energy conservation and use of eco-friendly insulation and products.

830 Truman Ave., Key West, FL 33040. www.silverpalmsinn.com. © **800/294-8783** or 305/294-8700. 50 units. Winter $209–$369 king, $229–$389 double, $239–$399 suite; off season $189–$289 king, $199–$309 double, $219–$359 suite. AE, DISC, MC, V. Free parking. **Amenities:** Fitness room; heated saltwater swimming pool; free Wi-Fi. *In room:* A/C, TV, hair dryer, microwave, minifridge, Wi-Fi.

Westwinds Inn ★ A close second to staying in your own private 19th-century, tin-roofed clapboard house is this tranquil inn, just 4 blocks from Duval Street in the historic seaport district. And although it looks 19th century, it's got a foot in the 21st with wireless Internet and HDTV. Lush landscaping keeps the place private and secluded; at times, you'll feel as if you're alone. Two pools, one heated in winter, are offset by alcoves, fountains, and the well-maintained whitewashed inn, which is actually composed of five separate buildings. Rooms are Key West comfortable, with private bathrooms, wicker furnishings, and fans. All rooms are smoke-free.

914 Eaton St., Key West, FL 33040. www.westwindskeywest.com. © **800/788-4150** or 305/296-4440. Fax 305/293-0931. 22 units. Winter $185–$220 double, $225–$275 suite; off season $90–$180 double, $140–$195 suite. Rates include continental breakfast. DISC, MC, V. No children 11 and under. **Amenities:** Bike rental; 2 pools (1 heated); Wi-Fi. *In room:* A/C, TV (in some), kitchenette (in some).

INEXPENSIVE

Angelina Guest House ★★ Just 2 blocks off Duval Street, this former bordello and gambling hall–turned–youth hostel guesthouse is one of the cheapest in town—and it's conveniently near a hot hippie restaurant called **Blue Heaven** (p. 275). Though the neighborhood is urban, it's generally safe and full of character. Accommodations are furnished uniquely in a modest style. Of the 13 rooms, 4 have shared bathrooms (there are 2 clean bathrooms in the hallway). There are no TV's and no phones, but there is free Wi-Fi. Don't oversleep and miss the amazing homemade cinnamon rolls served with the daily continental breakfast. A gorgeous lagoon-style heated pool, with waterfall and tropical landscaping, is an excellent addition. Even better are the poolside hammocks—get out there early, as they go quickly! Even though the Angelina is sparse (perfect for bohemian types who don't mind a little grit), it's a great place to crash if you're traveling on the cheap.

302 Angela St. (at Thomas St.), Key West, FL 33040. www.angelinaguesthouse.com. © **888/303-4480** or 305/294-4480. Fax 305/272-0681. 13 units. Winter $109–$199 double; off season $79–$139 double. Rates include continental breakfast. DISC, MC, V. **Amenities:** Concierge; outdoor heated pool; free Wi-Fi. *In room:* A/C, no phone.

The Grand Guesthouse ★★ 🗡 Don't expect cabbies or locals to know about this well-kept secret, in a residential section of Old Town, about 5 blocks from Duval Street. It's got almost everything you could want, including a moderate price tag. Proprietors Jim Brown, Jeffrey Daubman, and Derek Karevicius provide any and all services for their appreciative guests. All units have private bathrooms, air-conditioning, and private entrances. The best deal is room no. 2; it's small and lacks a closet, but it has a porch and the most privacy. Suites are a real steal: The large two-room units come with kitchenettes. This place is the best bargain in town.

1116 Grinnell St. (btw. Virginia and Catherine sts.), Key West, FL 33040. www.grandkeywest.com. 📞 888/947-2630 or 305/294-0590. 10 units. Winter $158–$228 double, $198–$248 suite; off season $108–$168 double, $128–$188 suite. Rates include expanded continental breakfast. DISC, MC, V. Free parking. **Amenities:** Bike rental; concierge. *In room:* A/C, TV, CD player, hair dryer, kitchenette (in some), minifridge, MP3 docking station, Wi-Fi.

Key West Hostel & Seashell Motel This well-run hostel, the only one in the Keys, is a 3-minute walk to the beach and Old Town. Very popular with European backpackers, it's a great place to meet people. The dorm rooms are dark and sparse, but livable if you're desperate for a cheap stay. There are all-male, all-female, and co-ed dorm rooms for couples. The higher-priced private motel rooms are a good deal, especially those equipped with kitchens. Amenities include a Tiki hut with TV; bike rentals; a fully equipped outdoor kitchen with barbecue grill; vending machines; and coin-operated laundry. There's also free Wi-Fi access throughout the property.

718 South St., Key West, FL 33040. www.keywesthostel.com. 📞 305/296-5719. Fax 305/296-0672. 30 dorm beds, 16 motel rooms. Year-round $49–$59 dorm room; winter $120–$160 motel room, off season $90–$120 motel room. MC, V. Free parking. **Amenities:** Bike rental. *In room:* Motel rooms have A/C, TV, fridge, hair dryer; dorm rooms have A/C only.

Southernmost Point Guest House ★★ 😊 🎒 One of the few inns here that welcomes children and pets, this romantic guesthouse is a real find. The antiseptically clean rooms are not as fancy as the house's ornate 1885 exterior, but each is unique and includes rattan furniture with Mombasa-style netting on the beds. Room no. 5 is best, with a private porch, an ocean view, and windows that let in lots of light. Every unit comes with fresh flowers, wine, and a full decanter of sherry. There's also a barbecue grill under a grapevine for those in the mood to pretend it's their home and just grill out. Mona Santiago, the kind, laid-back owner, provides chairs and towels for the beach, which is just a block away. Guests can help themselves to free wine as they soak in the 14-seat hot tub. Kids will enjoy the backyard swings and the pet rabbits.

1327 Duval St., Key West, FL 33040. www.southernmostpoint.com. 📞 305/294-0715. Fax 305/296-0641. 6 units. Winter $125–$200 double, $260–$285 suite; off season $75–$120 double, $165–$175 suite. Rates include breakfast. AE, MC, V. Pets accepted ($5 in summer, $10 in winter). **Amenities:** Pool; Wi-Fi. *In room:* A/C, TV/VCR, fridge, hair dryer.

THE DRY TORTUGAS ★★

70 miles W of Key West

Few people realize that the Florida Keys don't end at Key West, as about 70 miles west is a chain of seven small islands known as the Dry Tortugas. Because you've come this far, you might wish to visit them, especially if you're into bird-watching, their primary draw.

Ponce de León, who discovered this far-flung cluster of coral keys in 1513, named them Las Tortugas because of the many sea turtles, which still flock to the area during nesting season in the warm summer months. Oceanic charts later carried the preface "dry" to warn mariners that fresh water was unavailable here. Modern intervention has made drinking water available, but little else.

These undeveloped islands make a great day trip for travelers interested in seeing the natural anomalies of the Florida Keys—especially the birds. The Dry Tortugas are nesting grounds and roosting sites for thousands of tropical and subtropical oceanic birds. Visitors will also find a historic fort, good fishing, and terrific snorkeling around shallow reefs.

Getting There

BY BOAT *Yankee Freedom II* (www.yankeefreedom.com; © **800/634-0939** or 305/294-7009), a high-speed boat complete with A/C, cushioned seats, three restrooms, freshwater rinse shower, and full galley selling snacks, soft drinks, beer, wine, mixed drinks (on return trip only), film, and souvenirs, zips you to and from the Dry Tortugas in 2 hours and 15 minutes. The round-trip fare ($165 for adults, $155 for seniors, $120 for children 4 to 16) includes continental breakfast, water, lunch, and a 40-minute guided tour of the fort led by an expert naturalist. The boat leaves Key West for Fort Jefferson at 8am and returns by 5:15pm.

BY PLANE **Key West Seaplane Adventures** at the Key West International Airport (www.keywestseaplanecharters.com; © **305/293-9300**) offers morning, afternoon, and full-day trips to the Dry Tortugas National Park via 10 passenger DHC-3T Turbine Otter seaplanes. Prices are $265 and $465 for adults, and $212 and $380 for children, not including the $5-per-person park entry fee. Flights include free soft drinks and snorkeling equipment.

Exploring the Dry Tortugas

Of the seven islands that make up the Dry Tortugas, Garden Key is the most visited because it is where Fort Jefferson and the visitor center are located. Loggerhead Key, Middle Key, and East Key are open only during the day and are for hiking. Bush Key is for the birds—literally! It's a nesting area for birds only, though it is open from October to January for special excursions. Hospital and Long keys are closed to the public.

Fort Jefferson, a six-sided, 19th-century fortress, is set almost at the water's edge of Garden Key, so it appears to float in the middle of the sea. The monumental structure is surrounded by 8-foot-thick walls that rise from the sand to a height of nearly 50 feet. Impressive archways, stonework, and parapets make this 150-year-old monument a grand sight. With the invention of the rifled cannon, the fort's masonry construction became obsolete and the building was never completed. For 10 years, however, from 1863 to 1873, Fort Jefferson served as a prison, a kind of "Alcatraz East." Among its prisoners were four of the "Lincoln Conspirators," including Samuel A. Mudd, the doctor who set the broken leg of fugitive assassin John Wilkes Booth. In 1935, Fort Jefferson became a national monument administered by the National Park Service. Today, Fort Jefferson is struggling to resist erosion from the salt and sea, as iron used in the gun openings and the shutters in the fort's walls has accelerated the deterioration, and the structure's openings need to be rebricked. The National Park Service has designated the fort as the recipient of a $15-million face-lift, a project that may take up to a decade to complete.

For more information on Fort Jefferson and the Dry Tortugas, visit www.fort jefferson.com or call the **Everglades National Park Service** (𝄃 **305/242-7700**). Fort Jefferson is open during daylight hours. A self-guided tour describes the history of the human presence in the Dry Tortugas while leading visitors through the fort.

OUTDOOR ACTIVITIES

BIRD-WATCHING   Bring your binoculars and your bird books: Bird-watching is *the* reason to visit this cluster of tropical islands. The Dry Tortugas, in the middle of the migration flyway between North and South America, serve as an important rest stop for the more than 200 winged varieties that pass through annually. The season peaks from mid-March to mid-May, when thousands of birds show up, but many species from the West Indies can be found here year-round.

FISHING   In July 2001, a federal law closed off all fishing in a 90-square-mile tract of ocean called the Tortugas North and a 61-square-mile tract of ocean called the Tortugas South. It basically prohibits all fishing in order to preserve the dwindling population of fish (a result of commercial fishing and environmental factors). However, rules have been alleviated and some sport fishing is now allowed in the Dry Tortugas. We recommend a charter such as **Dry Tortugas Fishing Adventures** (www.tortugasfishing.com; 𝄃 **305/797-6396**), which will take you on a 42-foot sport-fishing catamaran into deep water where you'll catch dolphin (fish, not mammals), tuna, wahoo, king mackerel, sailfish, and an occasional marlin. Trips are overnight and rates are steep: from $3,400 to $3,600 and $1,000 per extra day. If you don't have the money or the time, **Captain Andy Griffiths** (www.fishandy.com; 𝄃 **305/296-2639**) will take you on 3-hour custom fishing trips to the Tortugas at $99 per passenger with a minimum of four anglers.

SCUBA DIVING & SNORKELING   The warm, clear, shallow waters of the Dry Tortugas produce optimum conditions for snorkeling and scuba diving. Four endangered species of sea turtles—green, leatherback, Atlantic Ridley, and hawksbill—can be found here, along with myriad marine species. The region just outside the seawall of Fort Jefferson is excellent for underwater touring; an abundant variety of fish and coral live in 3 to 4 feet of water.

Camping on Garden Key

The rustic beauty of **Garden Key** (the only island of the Dry Tortugas where you can pitch tents) is a camper's dream. There are no RVs or motor homes: They can't get here. The abundance of birds doesn't make it quiet, but the camping—a stone's throw from the water—is as beautiful as it gets.

Picnic tables, cooking grills, and toilets are provided, but there are no showers. All supplies must be packed in and out. Sites are $3 per person per night and available on a first-come, first-served basis. The 10 sites book up fast. For more information, call the **National Park Service** (𝄃 **305/242-7700**).

THE GOLD COAST: HALLANDALE TO THE PALM BEACHES

Named not for the sun-kissed skin of the area's residents, but for the gold salvaged from shipwrecks off its coastline, the Gold Coast embraces more than 60 miles of beautiful Atlantic shoreline—from the pristine sands of Palm Beach to the legendary strip of beaches in Fort Lauderdale.

If you haven't visited the cities along Florida's southeastern coast in the past few years, you'll be amazed at how much has changed. Miles of grassland and empty lots have been replaced with luxurious resorts and high-rise condominiums. Taking advantage of their proximity to Miami, the cities that make up the Gold Coast have attracted millions looking to escape crowded sidewalks, traffic, and the everyday routines of life.

Fortunately, amid all the building, much of the natural treasure of the Gold Coast remains. There are 300 miles of Intracoastal Waterway, Fort Lauderdale's Venetian-inspired canals, and the splendor of the Everglades just a few miles inland.

The most popular areas in the Gold Coast are Fort Lauderdale, Boca Raton, and Palm Beach. While Fort Lauderdale is a favored beachfront destination, Boca Raton and Palm Beach are better known for their country-club lifestyles and shopping. Farther north is the quietly popular Jupiter, best known for spring training at the Roger Dean Stadium. In between these better-traveled destinations are a few things worth stopping for. Driving north along the coastline is one of the best ways to fully appreciate what the Gold Coast is all about—it's a perspective you certainly won't find in a shopping mall.

Tourists come here by the droves, but they aren't the only people coming; thousands of transplants, fleeing the increasing population influx in Miami and the frigid winters up north, have made this area their home. As a result, there was a brief construction boom in the existing cities and even westward, into the swampy areas of the Everglades. The boom is at a standstill now, obviously, though you'll still see construction on some homes contracted before the recession, in Broward County, for instance. There has also been a great revitalization of several downtown areas, including Hollywood, Fort Lauderdale, and West Palm Beach. These once-desolate urban centers have been spruced up and now attract more young travelers and families than ever.

Unfortunately, like its neighbors to the south, the Gold Coast can be prohibitively hot and buggy in summer. The good news is that bargains are plentiful May through October, when many locals take advantage of package deals and uncrowded resorts.

For the purposes of this chapter, the Gold Coast will consist of the towns of Hallandale, Hollywood, Pompano Beach, Fort Lauderdale, Dania, Deerfield, Boca Raton, Delray Beach, Boynton Beach, and Palm Beach.

THE best GOLD COAST EXPERIENCES

○ **Spying on Sea Turtles:** In June and July, the John U. Lloyd Beach is crawling with nature lovers who come for the spectacular Sea Turtle Awareness Program, during which time you may be able to witness a few miraculous sights: the turtles nesting and, sometimes, their eggs hatching.

○ **Imbibing at Cap's Place Island Restaurant:** Although technically you can drive to this Lighthouse Point landmark hideaway, half the fun is taking the boat ride. Once you're "there," you'll experience what was once a raucous rum-running restaurant and casino favored by types immortalized in several HBO dramas. See p. 307.

○ **Finding Japan at the Morikami Museum & Gardens:** This gem is a 200-acre Japanese-style garden filled with serene mile-long paths, koi- and carp-filled moats, a meditation rock garden, a bonsai collection, and more. See p. 320.

○ **Cheering at a Polo Match:** Sure, Palm Beach has a rep for being a stuffy, slack-jawed So Flo hub of haughtiness, but when in Rome—er, Palm Beach, make like a local and take in a polo match. Hats optional, fun required and, frankly inevitable.

○ **Channeling Your Inner Lounge Singer at the Royal Room Cabaret:** Palm Beach's Colony Hotel is command central for old-school singers a la Connie Francis, who perform here to a crowd of regulars who consider the Royal Room their very chic Cheers. See p. 342.

EXPLORING THE GOLD COAST BY CAR

Like most of South Florida, the Gold Coast consists of a mainland and adjacent barrier islands. You'll have to check maps to keep track of the many bridges that allow access to the islands where most tourist activity is centered. Interstate 95, which runs north-south, is the area's main highway. Farther west is the Florida Turnpike, a toll road that can be worth the expense, as the speed limit is higher and it's often less congested than I-95. Also on the mainland is U.S. 1, which generally runs parallel to I-95 (to the east) and is a narrower thoroughfare that is mostly crowded with strip malls and seedy hotels.

We recommend taking Fla. A1A, a slow oceanside road that connects the long, thin islands of Florida's east coast. This is the most scenic road, ushering you properly into the relaxed atmosphere of these resort towns.

FORT LAUDERDALE

Once famous (or infamous) for the annual mayhem it hosted during Spring Break, **Fort Lauderdale** now attracts a more affluent, better-behaved crowd. Its 300 miles of navigable waterways and innumerable canals permit thousands of residents to anchor boats in their backyards. On land, institutions like the Museum of Art Fort Lauderdale and Museum of Discovery & Science give the city cultural resonance.

Things to Do   Spend at least an afternoon or evening cruising Fort Lauderdale's waterways by **water taxi.** Stroll the **Hollywood Beach Boardwalk** for a people-watching extravaganza. Head to **Fort Lauderdale Beach** to sun and swim or hike the nature trails at **Lloyd Beach.** Get in 18 holes at **Emerald Hills** or take a dive off **Pompano Beach.**

Shopping   Bargain hunters scavenge the racks at **Sawgrass Mills,** a mega–outlet center with everything from Swarovski crystals to LEGO with a little Gucci, Prada, and Target thrown in for good measure. Although it's not as vast as it used to be, the arts and antiques district in Dania Beach boasts some good finds. For upscale boutiques, browse **Las Olas Boulevard** and for a place with better views than bargains, peruse the only beachfront mall, the **Gallery at Beach Place.**

Restaurants & Dining   Fort Lauderdale is home to several fine restaurants, and ethnic options now join the legions of surf-and-turf joints in **Pompano Beach** and **downtown. Las Olas Boulevard** is packed with good eateries, from fusion and southwestern to Caribbean and seafood.

Nightlife & Entertainment   Over the years, Fort Lauderdale has vastly improved the quality of its nightlife by welcoming earthy and sophisticated bars and clubs, especially downtown or on **Las Olas Boulevard. The Seminole Hard Rock Hotel & Casino** and **Village at Gulfstream Park** offer gaming *and* clubbing. For a quieter night out, consider **Hollywood.**

Visiting Broward County

But even with the shine of Fort Lauderdale, the city's home county of Broward is less exposed and a lot calmer than highly hyped Miami–Dade County; according to some, it's much friendlier than the Magic City, too. In fact, a friendly rivalry exists between residents of both counties. Miamians consider themselves more sophisticated and cosmopolitan than their northern neighbors, who, in turn, dismiss the alleged sophistication as snobbery and actually prefer their own county's gentler pace.

With more than 23 miles of beachfront and 300 miles of navigable waterways, Broward County is also a great outdoor destination. Scattered amid the shopping malls, condominiums, and tourist traps is a beautiful landscape lined with hundreds of parks, golf courses, tennis courts, and, of course, beaches.

The City of Hallandale Beach is a small, peaceful oceanfront town just north of Dade County's Aventura. Condos are the predominant landmarks in Hallandale, which is still pretty much a retirement community, although the revamped multimillion-dollar **Westin Diplomat Resort & Spa** (p. 312) is slowly trying to revitalize and liven up the area.

Just north of Hallandale is the more energetic, burgeoning city of Hollywood. Once a sleepy community wedged between Fort Lauderdale and Miami, Hollywood is now a bustling area of 1.5 million people with an array of ethnic and racial

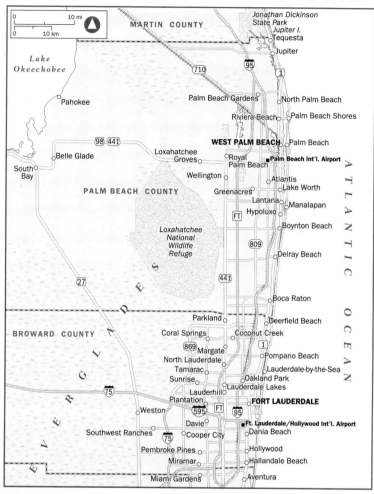

identities, from white and African American to Jamaican, Chinese, and Dominican. (*Money* magazine trumpeted the self-described "City of the Future" as having an ethnic makeup that mirrors what the U.S. will look like by the year 2022.) A spate of redevelopment has made the pedestrian-friendly center along Hollywood Boulevard and Harrison Street, east of Dixie Highway, a popular destination for travelers and locals alike. Some predict Hollywood will be South Florida's next big destination. While the prediction is dubious, Hollywood is awakening from its long slumber. Prices are a fraction of those at other tourist areas, and a quasi-bohemian vibe is apparent in the galleries, clubs, and restaurants that dot the new "strip." Its gritty undercurrent, however, prevents it from becoming too trendy.

Fort Lauderdale, with its well-known strip of beaches, restaurants, bars, and souvenir shops, has undergone a major transformation. Consider the recent hotel openings: Starwood's **W Fort Lauderdale** (p. 312), the swanky **Ritz-Carlton** (p. 311), and the **B Ocean Fort Lauderdale Hotel** (p. 310). And in 2009, Sir Richard Branson debuted his fleet of Virgin America jetliners in Florida with service from Fort Lauderdale, not Miami, to L.A. and San Francisco.

Huge cruise ships also take advantage of Florida's deepest harbor, Port Everglades. The seaport is on the southeastern coast of the Florida peninsula, near the Fort Lauderdale Hollywood International Airport on the outskirts of Hollywood and Dania Beach. And with a $75-million cruise terminal expansion, Port Everglades is on its way to being the busiest cruise port in the world.

Essentials

GETTING THERE   If you're driving from Miami, it's a straight shot north to Hollywood or Fort Lauderdale. Visitors on their way to or from Orlando should take the Florida Turnpike to exit 53, 54, 58, or 62, depending on the location of your accommodations. The **Fort Lauderdale–Hollywood International Airport** is easy to negotiate, and just 15 minutes from both of the downtown areas it services. However, its user-friendliness may not last much longer: Due to its popularity, the airport is *still* undergoing a $700-million runway expansion and renovation that often renders it just as maddening as any other major metropolitan airport. Completion is expected in 2015. In 2009, Sir Richard Branson introduced his **Virgin America** (www.virgin america.com; ✆ **877/FLY-VIRGIN** [359-8474]) service from the West Coast to FLL, offering two daily nonstop round-trips from San Francisco International Airport and two daily nonstop round-trips from Los Angeles International Airport. Some two dozen other airlines, large and small, serve the airport, with plenty of connections to and from the U.S., Canada, and the Caribbean.

The airport has wireless Internet access and a fantastic car-rental center where 10 rental companies are under one roof—very convenient. Levels 1 through 4 are home to Alamo, Avis, Budget, Dollar, Enterprise, E-Z, Hertz, National, Royal, and Thrifty. Levels 5 to 9 provide 5,500 spaces for public parking.

Amtrak (www.amtrak.com; ✆ **800/USA-RAIL** [872-7245]) stations are at 200 SW 21st Terrace (Broward Blvd. and I-95), Fort Lauderdale (✆ **954/587-6692**); and 3001 Hollywood Blvd. (northwest corner of Hollywood Blvd. and I-95), Hollywood (✆ **954/921-4517**).

VISITOR INFORMATION   The **Greater Fort Lauderdale Convention & Visitors Bureau,** 1850 Eller Dr., Ste. 303 (off I-95 and I-595 E), Fort Lauderdale, FL 33316 (www.sunny.org; ✆ **800/22-SUNNY** [227-8669] or 954/765-4466; fax 954/765-4467), is an excellent resource for area information in English, Spanish, and French. Call in advance to request a free comprehensive guide covering events, accommodations, and sightseeing in Broward County. Download the free **iVisitLauderdale** app, featuring all sorts of convenient travel tips; available at **www.sunny. org/iPhone**.

The **Greater Hollywood Chamber of Commerce,** 330 N. Federal Hwy. (at U.S. 1 and Taylor St.), Hollywood, FL 33020 (www.hollywoodchamber.org; ✆ **800/231-5562** or 954/923-4000; fax 954/923-8737), is open Monday through Friday from 9am to 5pm. Here you'll find the lowdown on all of Hollywood's events, attractions, restaurants, hotels, and tours.

Fort Lauderdale

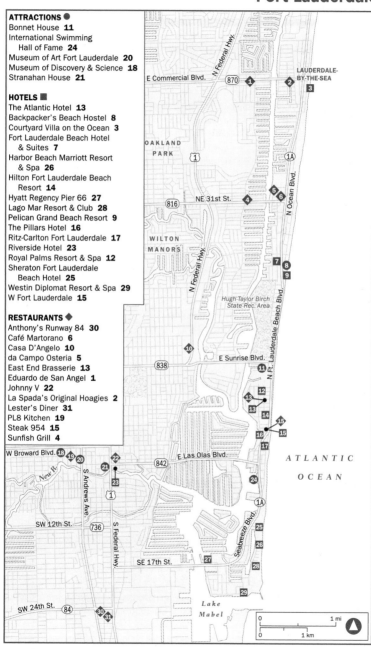

ATTRACTIONS ●
Bonnet House **11**
International Swimming
   Hall of Fame **24**
Museum of Art Fort Lauderdale **20**
Museum of Discovery & Science **18**
Stranahan House **21**

HOTELS ■
The Atlantic Hotel **13**
Backpacker's Beach Hostel **8**
Courtyard Villa on the Ocean **3**
Fort Lauderdale Beach Hotel
   & Suites **7**
Harbor Beach Marriott Resort
   & Spa **26**
Hilton Fort Lauderdale Beach
   Resort **14**
Hyatt Regency Pier 66 **27**
Lago Mar Resort & Club **28**
Pelican Grand Beach Resort **9**
The Pillars Hotel **16**
Ritz-Carlton Fort Lauderdale **17**
Riverside Hotel **23**
Royal Palms Resort & Spa **12**
Sheraton Fort Lauderdale
   Beach Hotel **25**
Westin Diplomat Resort & Spa **29**
W Fort Lauderdale **15**

RESTAURANTS ◆
Anthony's Runway 84 **30**
Café Martorano **6**
Casa D'Angelo **10**
da Campo Osteria **5**
East End Brasserie **13**
Eduardo de San Angel **1**
Johnny V **22**
La Spada's Original Hoagies **2**
Lester's Diner **31**
PL8 Kitchen **19**
Steak 954 **15**
Sunfish Grill **4**

12

THE GOLD COAST: HALLANDALE TO THE PALM BEACHES | Fort Lauderdale

Exploring Fort Lauderdale
HITTING THE BEACH

The southern part of the Gold Coast, Broward County, has the region's most popular and amenities-laden beaches, which stretch for more than 23 miles. Most do not charge for access and all are well maintained. Here's a selection of some of the county's best, from south to north:

Hollywood Beach, stretching from Sheridan Street to Georgia Street, is a major attraction in the city of Hollywood, a virtual carnival of young hipsters, big families, and sunburned French Canadians who dodge bicyclers and skaters along the rows of tacky souvenir shops, T-shirt shops, game rooms, snack bars, beer stands, hotels, and miniature-golf courses. **Hollywood Beach Broadwalk,** modeled after Atlantic City's legendary boardwalk, is the town's popular beachfront pedestrian thoroughfare, a cement promenade that's 30 feet wide and stretches along the shoreline for 3 miles. A recent makeover added, among other things, a concrete bike path, a crushed-shell jogging path, new trash receptacles, and the relocation of beach showers to each street end (all of are them are accessible for people with disabilities). Popular with runners, skaters, and cruisers, the Broadwalk is also renowned as a hangout for thousands of retirement-age snowbirds who get together for frequent dances and shows at a faded outdoor amphitheater. Despite efforts to clear out a seedy element, the area remains a haven for drunks and scammers, so keep alert.

If you tire of the hectic diversity that defines Hollywood's Broadwalk, enjoy the natural beauty of the beach itself, which is wide and clean. There are lifeguards, showers, restroom facilities, and public areas for picnics and parties.

The **Fort Lauderdale Beach Promenade** underwent a $26-million renovation and looks fantastic. It's especially peaceful in the mornings, when there's just a smattering of joggers and walkers; but even at its most crowded on weekends, the expansive promenade provides room for everyone. Note, however, that the beach is hardly pristine; it is across the street from an uninterrupted stretch of hotels, bars, and retail outlets. Also nearby is a retail-and-dining megacomplex, the **Gallery at Beach Place,** that is, more than anything, a drinking complex featuring a Sonic and, if need be, a CVS, on Fla. A1A, midway between Las Olas and Sunrise boulevards.

On the sand just across the road, most days you'll find hard-core volleyball players who always welcome anyone with a good spike, and you'll find an inviting ocean for swimmers of any level. The unusually clear waters are under the careful watch of some of Florida's best-looking lifeguards. Freshen up afterward in the clean showers and restrooms conveniently located along the strip. Pets have been banned from most of the beach in order to maintain the impressive cleanliness; a designated area for pets exists away from the main sunbathing areas.

Especially on weekends, parking at the oceanside meters is nearly impossible. Try biking, skating, or hitching a ride on the water taxi instead. The strip is located on Fla. A1A, between SE 17th Street and Sunrise Boulevard.

Dania Beach's **John U. Lloyd Beach State Park,** 6503 N. Ocean Dr., Dania (www.floridastateparks.org/lloydbeach; ✆ **954/923-2833**), consists of 251 acres of barrier island, situated between the Atlantic Ocean and the Intracoastal Waterway, from Port Everglades on the north to Dania on the south. Its natural setting contrasts sharply with the urban development of Fort Lauderdale. Lloyd Beach, one of Broward County's most important nesting beaches for sea turtles, produces some 10,000 hatchlings a year. The park's broad, flat beach is popular for both swimming and sunning. Self-guided nature trails are great for those too restless to sunbathe. Admission to the park is $6 per vehicle with two to eight people, $4 for a single occupant, and $2 for pedestrians and bicyclists.

SEEING THE SIGHTS

Billie Swamp Safari ★ ADVENTURE TOUR Billie Swamp Safari is an up-close-and-personal view of the Seminole Indians' 2,200-acre Big Cypress Reserva-tion. There are daily tours into reservation wetlands, hardwood hammocks, and areas where wildlife (seemingly strategically placed deer, water buffalo, bison, wild hogs, ornery ostriches, rare birds, and alligators) reside. Tours are provided aboard "swamp buggies," customized motorized vehicles designed to provide visitors with an elevated view of the frontier while they comfortably ride through the wetlands and cypress heads. The more adventurous may want to take a fast-moving airboat ride or trek a nature trail. Airboat rides run about 20 minutes, while swamp-buggy tours last about an hour. A stop at an alligator farm reeks of Disney, but the kids won't care. You can stay overnight in a native Tiki hut for $40 to $60 per night if you're so inclined. Ask about their cool night swamp and VIP swamp packages.

Big Cypress Seminole Reservation, 1½-hr. drive west of Fort Lauderdale. www.billieswamp.com. ☎ **800/949-6101.** Free admission. Swamp-buggy tours $25 adults, $23 seniors 62 and over, $15 children 4–12. Airboat tours $15 for all ages. Swamp Safari Day package including swamp buggy tour, airboat ride, and animal shows $50 adult, $46 seniors, $36 children 4–12. Daily 8:30am–6pm. Airboats depart every 30 min. 9:30am–4:30pm. Swamp-buggy tours leave on the hour 10am–5pm. Reptile and critter shows daily. Day and overnight packages available.

Bonnet House ★★★ HISTORIC HOME This historic 35-acre plantation home and estate, accessible by guided tour only, will provide you with a fantastic glimpse of Old Florida. Built in 1921, the sprawling two-story waterfront home (sur-rounded by formal tropical gardens) is really the backdrop of a love story, which the very chatty volunteer guides will share with you if you ask. Some have actually lunched with the former resident of the house, the late Evelyn Bartlett, wife of world-acclaimed artist Frederic Clay Bartlett. The worthwhile 1¼-hour tour introduces you to quirky people, whimsical artwork, lush grounds, and interesting design.

900 N. Birch Rd. (1 block west of the ocean, south of Sunrise Blvd.), Fort Lauderdale. www.bonnet house.org. ☎ **954/563-5393.** Admission $20 adults, $18 seniors, $16 children 6–12, free for chil-dren 5 and under. Call for hours and tour times.

Butterfly World ★ ☺ NATURE RESERVE After moving to Florida from Illi-nois in 1968, electrical engineer Ronald Boender decided to actively pursue his pas-sion, raising local butterflies at his home and recording data on each. After realizing there was a need for farmed butterflies, Boender set up a company in 1984 and went one step further, building this butterfly house along with the founder of the world-renowned London Butterfly House across the pond. Enter Butterfly World, renowned globally for its butterfly farm and research facility as well as its 10 acres of aviaries and botanical gardens. Kids especially love the "bug museum," which features some of the insect world's biggest celebrities—all of which kids are able to touch, if they dare, with the help of an expert. There's lots to see here in terms of flitting, fluttery things, so set aside at least 2 hours to, uh, flit around yourself.

Tradewinds Park, 3600 W. Sample Rd., Coconut Creek. www.butterflyworld.com. ☎ **954/977-4400.** Admission $25 adults and seniors, $20 children 3–11. Mon–Sat 9am–5pm; Sun 11am–5pm.

Hillsboro Inlet Lighthouse ★ HISTORIC SITE Completed in 1907, the Hillsboro Inlet Lighthouse, which rises 136 feet above water and marks the northern end of the Florida Reef, isn't just any lighthouse. It contains a 5,500,000-candle-power light and is the most powerful light on the East Coast of the United States. And there's more history. This lighthouse was also made famous thanks to one of the "barefoot mailmen," carriers of the first U.S. mail route between Palm Beach and Miami. Because there was no paved road on that route, the mailmen had to get through by boat and by walking the sand along the beach. James Hamilton was the most famous of these after disappearing delivering mail on the route just after October 10, 1887, presumably the victim of drowning or an encounter with a hungry alligator while trying to swim across the Hillsboro inlet to retrieve his boat from the far side. His body was never recovered. A big trial ensued and his death still remains a mystery today. An original stone statue called *The Barefoot Mailman* by Frank Varga is permanently displayed on the shores of the Hillsboro inlet next to the Hillsboro lighthouse with an inscription dedicated to Hamilton.

Hillsboro Inlet, off A1A, Pompano Beach. www.hillsborolighthouse.org. ✆ **954/942-2102.** Tours $15. Call for hours and tour times. Take I-95 to Atlantic Blvd. Go east across the Intracoastal and left at A1A for 2 miles to Pompano Beach City Park. Stop at the SE corner of the Hillsboro Inlet bridge where there is an excellent view of the Hillsboro Lighthouse. Tours meet on the dock across from Riverside Dr. To get there, go east, cross the Intracoastal and make an immediate left on North Riverside Dr. Go 1 block to the parking lot. Park and head west to the dock across Riverside Dr.

International Swimming Hall of Fame (ISHOF) ★★★ MUSEUM Any

aspiring Michael Phelps or those who appreciate the sport will love this splashy homage to the best backstrokers, front crawlers, and divers in the world. The museum houses the world's largest collection of aquatic memorabilia and is the single largest source of aquatic books, manuscripts, and literature. Among the highlights are Johnny Weissmuller's Olympic medals, Mark Spitz's starting block used to win six of his seven 1972 Olympic gold medals, and more than 60 Olympic, national, and club uniforms, warm-ups, and swimsuits. For those who don't mind getting their feet wet, the ISHOF Aquatic Complex is the only one of its kind in the world with two 50m pools, a diving well, and a swimming flume.

1 Hall of Fame Dr., Fort Lauderdale. www.ishof.org. ✆ **954/462-6536.** Admission $8 adults, $6 seniors, $4 children 12 and over. Call for hours and tour times.

Museum of Art Fort Lauderdale ★ 🏛ART MUSEUM A fantastic modern-

art facility, the Museum of Art Fort Lauderdale has permanent collections, including those from William Glackens; the CoBrA Movement in Copenhagen, Brussels, and Amsterdam, with more than 200 paintings; 50 sculptures; 1,200 works on paper from 1948 to 1951, including the largest repository of Asger Jorn graphics outside the Silkeborg Kunstmuseum in Denmark; stunning Picasso ceramics; and contemporary works from more than 90 Cuban artists in exile around the world. Traveling exhibits and continuing art classes make the museum a great place to spend a rainy day, or night—on Thursdays, the cafe and wine bar have happy hour from 5 to 7pm. On the third Thursday of every month, the museum offers free admission from 5 to 8pm.

1 E. Las Olas Blvd., Fort Lauderdale. www.moafl.org. ✆ **954/525-5500.** Admission $10 adults, $7 seniors and children 6–17, free for children 5 and under. Oct–May Fri–Wed 11am–5pm, Thurs 11am–8pm; June–Sept Mon and Wed–Sun 11am–5pm.

Museum of Discovery & Science ★★★ ☺ MUSEUM This museum's high-

tech, interactive approach to education proves that science can equal fun. Adults won't feel as if they're in a kiddie museum, either. Kids ages 7 and under enjoy

In June and July, the John U. Lloyd Beach is crawling with nature lovers who come for the spectacular **Sea Turtle Awareness Program.** Park rangers begin the evening with a lecture and slide show, while scouts search the beach for nesting loggerhead sea turtles. If a turtle is located—plenty of them usually are—a beach walk allows participants to see the turtles nest and, sometimes, their eggs hatch. The program begins at 9pm on Fridays in June and July. Call ℂ **954/923-2833** for reservations. Walks last between 1 and 3 hours. Comfortable walking shoes and insect repellent are necessary. The park entrance fee of $4 to $6 per carload applies.

navigating their way through the excellent explorations in the Discovery Center. Florida Ecoscapes is particularly interesting, with a living coral reef, bees, bats, frogs, turtles, and alligators. Most weekend nights, you'll find a diverse crowd ranging from hip high-school kids to 30-somethings enjoying a rock film in the IMAX theater, which also shows short science-related films daily. Out front in the atrium, see the 52-foot-tall *Great Gravity Clock*, the largest kinetic-energy sculpture in the state. New at the museum in 2012 is the Eco-Discovery Center, in which visitors can hop on an Everglades airboat ride simulator, witness the ferocity of hurricane force winds in the storm center, dig for fossils, and more.

401 SW 2nd St., Fort Lauderdale. www.mods.org. ℂ **954/467-6637.** Admission (includes IMAX film) $18 adults, $17 seniors, $14 children 2–12; without IMAX film $13 adults, $12 seniors, $11 children 2–12. Mon–Sat 10am–5pm; Sun noon–6pm. Movie theater closes later. From I-95, exit on Broward Blvd. E. Continue to SW 5th Ave., turn right; garage is on the right.

Stranahan House ★★★ HISTORIC HOME   In a town where nothing appears to date back earlier than 1940, visitors may want to take a minute to see Fort Lauderdale's very oldest standing structure and a prime example of classic "Florida Frontier" architecture. Built in 1901 by the "father of Fort Lauderdale," Frank Stranahan, this house once served as a trading post for Seminole trappers who came here to sell pelts. It's been a post office, town hall, and general store, and now serves as a worthwhile little museum of South Florida pioneer life, containing turn-of-the-20th-century furnishings and historical photos of the area. It is also the site of occasional concerts and social functions; call for details. *Note:* Self-guided tours are not allowed, so make sure to arrive on time for the 1, 2, or 3pm tours or else you're shut out.

335 SE 6th Ave. (Las Olas Blvd. at the New River Tunnel), Fort Lauderdale. www.stranahanhouse. org. ℂ **954/524-4736.** Admission $12 adults, $11 seniors, $7 students and children. Daily 1–3pm. Tours are on the hour; last tour at 3pm. Accessible by water taxi.

OUTDOOR ACTIVITIES & SPECTATOR SPORTS

BOATING   Often called the "yachting capital of the world," Fort Lauderdale provides ample opportunity for visitors to get out on the water, either along the Intracoastal Waterway or on the open ocean. If your hotel doesn't rent boats, try **Aloha Watersports,** Marriott's Harbor Beach Resort, 3030 Holiday Dr., Fort Lauderdale (www.alohawatersports.com; ℂ **954/462-7245**). It can outfit you with a variety of craft, including jet skis, WaveRunners, and catamarans. Rates start at $65 per half-hour for WaveRunners ($15 each additional rider; doubles and triples available), $70 to $125 for catamarans, $25 an hour for paddleboards or $100 for a 1-hour lesson, and $75 per person for a 15-minute parasailing ride. Aloha also offers a thrilling speedboat ride for $50 for a half-hour or $100 for a 90-minute excursion, a surfing school ($50—though the waves are hardly rippin' here!), and a Coast Guard class (9am daily), through which adults can obtain their Florida boaters license for $3. Treasure hunters can rent a metal detector here for $20 per hour.

FISHING   The **IGFA (International Game Fish Association) World Fishing Center,** 300 Gulf Stream Way, Dania Beach (www.igfa.org; ✆ **954/922-4212**), is an angler's paradise. One of the highlights of this museum, library, and park is the virtual reality fishing simulator that allows visitors to actually reel in their own computer-generated catch. Also included in the 3-acre park are displays of antique fishing gear, record catches, famous anglers, various vessels, and a wetlands lab. To get a list of local captains and guides, call **IGFA headquarters** (✆ **954/927-2628**) and ask for the librarian. Admission is $8 for adults, $5 for seniors and children 3 to 16. The museum and library are open daily from 10am to 6pm. On the grounds is also **Bass Pro Shops Outdoor World,** a huge retail complex set on a 3-acre lake.

GOLF   More than 50 golf courses in all price ranges compete for players. Among the best is **Emerald Hills,** 4100 N. Hills Dr., Hollywood (www.theclubatemerald hills.com; ✆ **954/961-4000**), just west of I-95 between Sterling Road and Sheridan Street. This beauty consistently lands on the "best of" lists of golf writers nationwide. The 18th hole, on a two-tier green, is the course's signature; it's surrounded by water and is more than a bit rough. Greens fees range from $80 to $125. Rates depend on day and time and are cheaper during the brutally hot summers.

Another great course is the Howard Watson–designed 18-hole Pembroke Lakes course at the **Pembroke Lakes Golf Club,** 10500 Taft St., Pembroke Pines (www. pcmgolf.com; ✆ **954/431-4144**), run by the same management company that runs the Miami Beach Golf Club; it was also the recipient of a $7-million renovation that saw the addition of Paspalum Supreme Grass. Best of all, greens fees are almost rock-bottom, ranging from $30 to $60 depending on the time and season.

The **Westin Diplomat Resort & Spa,** 501 Diplomat Pkwy., Hallandale Beach (www.diplomatresort.com; ✆ **954/602-6000**), is across the Intracoastal from the Westin Diplomat Resort. It has fabulous golf facilities, with 8 acres of lakes and 7,000 yards of rolling fairways, plus a fantastic delivery service that brings lunch and drinks to your cart. You pay for the services, however, with greens fees of $139 to $179 during high season and $89 to $99 off season. Twilight fees at 2pm cost from $39 to $89.

For one of Broward's best municipal challenges, try the 18-holer at the **Orange-brook Golf & Country Club,** 400 Entrada Dr., Hollywood (www.orangebrook.com; ✆ **954/967-GOLF** [4653]). Built in 1937, this is one of the state's oldest courses and one of the area's best bargains. Morning and noon rates are around $17 to $23. After 3pm, you can play for about $13, including a cart. Men must wear collared shirts to play here, and no spikes are allowed.

SCUBA DIVING   In Broward County, the best dive wreck is the *Mercedes I,* a 197-foot freighter that washed up in the backyard of a Palm Beach socialite in 1984 and was sunk for divers the following year off Pompano Beach. The artificial reef, filled with colorful sponges, spiny lobsters, and barracudas, is 97 feet below the surface, a mile offshore between Oakland Park and Sunrise boulevards. Dozens of reputable dive shops line the beach. Ask at your hotel for a nearby recommendation, or contact **Neil Watson's Undersea Adventures,** 1525 S. Andrews Ave., Fort Lauderdale (www.nealwatson.com; ✆ **954/462-3400**).

SPECTATOR SPORTS In 2012, the Miami Marlins moved into its $500+ million home, **Marlins Park,** a swell 37,000 seat MLB ballpark complete with retractable roof for those oppressively hot or rainy game days/nights. Tickets go on sale in January for $4 to $100; call **Ticketmaster** (www.ticketmaster.com; ✆ **305/358-5885**) to purchase them.

Pompano Park Racing, 1800 SW 3rd St., Pompano Beach (✆ **954/972-2000**), has parimutuel harness racing from October to early August. Admission is free to both grandstand and clubhouse.

Wrapped around an artificial lake, **Gulfstream Park Racing and Casino,** at U.S. 1 and Hallandale Beach Boulevard, Hallandale (www.gulfstreampark.com; ✆ **954/454-7000**), is pretty and popular, especially after its multimillion-dollar renovation, with a spanking-new casino and restaurants. Large purses and important horse races are commonplace at this recently refurbished suburban course, and the track is often crowded. The most recent renovation has transformed it into a world-class, state-of-the-art facility with shops, bars, higher-end restaurants, 20 luxury suites, private accommodations for top players, and more. It hosts the Florida Derby each March. Call for schedules. Admission and parking are free. From January to April, post times are 1:15pm Wednesday through Sunday, and the doors open at 11:30am.

Broward's only fronton, **Dania Jai Alai,** 301 E. Dania Beach Blvd., at Fla. A1A and U.S. 1 (✆ **954/920-1511**), is a great place to spend an afternoon or evening.

In the sport of ice hockey, the NHL's **Florida Panthers** (http://panthers.nhl.com; ✆ **954/835-7000**) play at the **BankAtlantic Center,** 2555 NW 137th Way, Sunrise (✆ **954/835-8000**). Tickets range from $15 to $100. Call for directions and ticket information.

ONE IF BY LAND, taxi IF BY SEA

Plan to spend at least an afternoon or evening cruising Fort Lauderdale's 300 miles of waterways the only way you can: by boat. The **Water Taxi of Fort Lauderdale** (www.watertaxi.com; ✆ **954/467-6677**) is one of the greatest innovations for water lovers since those cool Velcro sandals. A trusty fleet of older port boats serves the dual purpose of transporting and entertaining visitors as they cruise through the "Venice of America." Because of its popularity, the water taxi fleet has welcomed several sleek, 70-passenger "water buses" (featuring indoor and outdoor seating with an atrium-like roof).

Taxis operate on demand and also along a fairly regular route, carrying up to 48 passengers to 20 stops. If you're staying at a hotel on the route, you can be picked up there, usually within 15 minutes of calling, and then be shuttled to any of the dozens of restaurants, bars, and attractions on or near the waterfront. If you aren't sure where you want to go, ask one of the personable captains, who can point out historic and fun spots along the way.

Starting daily at 8am, boats run until midnight 7 days a week, depending on the weather. Check the website for exact times of pickup. The cost is $20 for an all-day pass with unlimited stops on and off, $17 for seniors and children 4 to 11, and $13 if you board after 7pm. If you want to go to South Beach (Fri–Tues Dec–Apr), it's $33 adults, $30 seniors, and $16 for children 4 to 11. Tickets are available onboard; no credit cards are accepted.

TENNIS There are hundreds of courts in Broward County, and plenty are accessible to the public. Many are at resorts and hotels. If yours has none, try the **Jimmy Evert Tennis Center,** 701 NE 12th Ave. (off Sunrise Blvd.), Fort Lauderdale (✆ **954/828-5378**), famous as the spot where Chris Evert trained. There are 18 lighted clay courts and 3 hard courts here. Nonresidents of Fort Lauderdale pay $9 per hour before 5pm and $11 after. Or, play all day for $18.

Where to Eat

Fort Lauderdale—and, to some extent, Hollywood—finally has several fine restaurants. **Las Olas Boulevard** has so many eateries that the city has put a moratorium on the opening of new restaurants on the 2-mile street. And despite the so-called recession, a slew of high-end restaurants staked their culinary claims to Fort Lauderdale, including Morimoto restaurateur Stephen Starr's **Steak 954** (p. 306), kicking off a trend of big-name, high-end restaurants bypassing Miami for Fort Lauderdale for a change.

VERY EXPENSIVE

Anthony's Runway 84 ★★★ ITALIAN   Meet Anthony, the gregarious owner of this Fort Lauderdale restaurant with an interior all about jet-setting—albeit in the mid- to late '70s—and a bar crafted out of a plane fuselage. Once you meet him, he will introduce your server, whose name is likely to be Tony. Same goes for the bartender. The quintessential, convivial Italian vibe in here (think Travolta in *Saturday Night Fever*) is conducive to one of the most enjoyable meals you'll ever have. The best way to go is—what else?—family-style, in which you'll be able to share lots of dishes such as mussels marinara, fried clams, roasted red peppers in garlic, shrimp *parmigiana,* an out-of-this-world rigatoni with cauliflower, and stellar meat and poultry dishes that frequent fliers to Anthony's rave about each time, as if it were their last meal.

330 S.R. 84, Fort Lauderdale. http://runway-84.com. ✆ **954/467-8484.** Reservations strongly recommended. Main courses $21–$55. AE, DC, DISC, MC, V. Tues–Thurs and Sun noon–10pm; Fri–Sat 5–11pm.

Café Martorano ★★★ ITALIAN   This small storefront eatery doesn't win any awards for decor or location, but when it comes to food that's good enough for an entire Italian family, Café Martorano, which also opened to rave reviews in Las Vegas, is one of the best. People wait for a table for upwards of 2 hours because the restaurant accepts no reservations and can get away with it. An almost-offensive sound system (playing disco tunes and Sinatra) has a tendency to turn off many a diner, but you don't come here for an intimate dinner. Dining here is like being at a big, fat, Italian wedding, where eating, drinking, and dancing are paramount. The menu changes daily, but regulars can request special off-the-menu items. Keep your eyes open for such celebrities as Liza Minnelli, James Gandolfini, and Steven Van Zandt, among others, who make it a point to stop here for a meal while in town.

3343 E. Oakland Park Blvd., Fort Lauderdale. www.cafemartorano.com. ✆ **954/561-2554.** Reservations not accepted. Main courses $13–$34. MC, V. Daily 5–11pm.

Casa D'Angelo ★★★ ITALIAN   Although Fort Lauderdale may be transforming into a thoroughly modern 21st-century beach city, Casa D'Angelo remains steeped in old-school, Old World style and service with an impeccable reputation for some of the best Tuscan-style Italian food in South Florida. Don't be intimidated by the 40-plus-page wine list of regional Italian varietals. The waiters here are friendly and knowledgeable and will help guide you through it if need be. As for chef/owner Angelo Elio's cuisine, insert superlatives here, but you won't truly understand until you taste some of the handmade pastas—handmade ravioli filled with spinach and ricotta, homemade fettuccine with roasted veal ragout, pappardelle with porcini mushrooms. After a while, saying the word *homemade* becomes redundant because, well, it's the standard here. In addition to pastas, there are expertly grilled chops and fresh and simply prepared seafood such as the superb snapper *oreganatta* with sun-dried tomatoes or jumbo prawns sautéed in white wine, garlic, fresh tomato, and imported Ligurian olives, which make the word *flavorful* seem like an understatement.

1201 N. Federal Hwy., Fort Lauderdale. www.casa-d-angelo.com. *©* **954/564-1234.** Reservations recommended. Main courses $14–$34. AE, DC, DISC, MC, V. Sun–Thurs 5:30–10pm; Fri–Sat 5:30–11pm.

da Campo Osteria ★ ITALIAN

da Campo Osteria ★ ITALIAN   Why anyone chose to open a restaurant in a condo hotel off the beaten track is beyond us, but fans of gourmet Northern Italian fare, however, would go through an *Amazing Race*–type challenge to find it. You'll stop wondering about the bizarre location as soon as a server arrives to prepare mozzarella tableside. Skip the simple spaghetti and meatballs—as good as it is, there's better in the form of the ricotta ravioli, prepared old-school Bolognese-style, or the pork Milanese on the bone with olive caper relish. Some people wonder whether to choose da Campo over the neighborhood's reigning Italian royalty, Café Martorano. We say you can't choose between the two—da Campo is a refined, gourmet dining experience, while Martorano is like eating your Italian grandma's cooking—in a disco. Depends on your mood, we guess.

In Il Lugano Suite Hotel, 3333 NE 32nd Ave. (btw. Oakland Park Blvd. and NE 34th Ave.). www. dacampofl.com. *©* **954/226-5002.** Reservations recommended. Main courses $15–$45. AE, DC, DISC, MC, V. Mon–Sat 7am–11pm; Sun 8am–9pm. From I-95, exit at Oakland Park Blvd. Cross the bridge and make a left on NE 32nd Ave. The hotel is straight ahead on the water.

Darrel & Oliver's Cafe Maxx ★★ FLORIBBEAN   Despite its bleak location in an unassuming storefront, Darrel & Oliver's Cafe Maxx is one of the best restaurants in Broward County. When it opened in 1984, it was the first restaurant to have an open kitchen, and what a stir that caused! Now, instead of the kitchen, the marvel is what comes out of it. Consider jumbo lump crab–crusted pompano with Mediterranean cous cous timbale, Pepadew pepper-and-tomato salad and red-pepper coulis; honey-barbecue grilled braised beef short ribs with corn and baco risotto, grilled zucchini and yellow squash with crispy onion rings. Yum. But save room for dessert— the vanilla-bean crème brûlée in an almond lace cup with pineapple-rum-caramel sauce and cookies or the Hawaiian vintage chocolate soufflé are just two of many diet- and mind-blowing options.

2601 E. Atlantic Blvd., Pompano Beach. www.cafemaxx.com. *©* **954/782-0606.** Fax 954/782-0648. Reservations recommended. Main courses $20–$49. AE, DC, DISC, MC, V. Mon–Thurs 5:30–10:30pm; Fri–Sat 5:30–11pm; Sun 5:30–10pm. From I-95, exit at Atlantic Blvd. E. The restaurant is 3 lights east of Federal Hwy.

East End Brasserie ★★★ FRENCH   Imagine Paris with an ocean view and you've got East End Brasserie. Chef Steve Zobel's unfussy cuisine evokes Paris sans attitude. Among our faves: traditional French onion soup, pan-roasted chicken breast and thigh with artichokes, jalapeño, bacon, garlic, and tomato cream, and a coriander-crusted rack of lamb with foie gras–stuffed prunes and served in a port-wine reduction with spinach. The Brasserie is also a fantastic spot for oysters, mussels, or a cheese plate with a glass of wine. They also serve breakfast, lunch, and brunch.

The Atlantic Hotel. 601 N. Fort Lauderdale Beach Blvd., Fort Lauderdale. ⓒ **954/567-8070.** www.atlantichotelfl.com. Reservations recommended. Main courses $20–$42. AE, DC, DISC, MC, V. Mon–Thurs 7am–3pm and 6–10pm; Fri 7am–3pm and 6–11pm; Sat 11am–3pm and 6–11pm; Sun 11am–3pm and 6–10pm.

Steak 954 ★ STEAKHOUSE   Housed in the W Fort Lauderdale, this playful creation of restaurant mogul Stephen Starr, of Morimoto fame, puts the emphasis on the simple flavors of dry-aged meats, but the taste and the scene are anything but simple. While the menu may be steakhouse simple, with steaks, chops, seafood, sandwiches, raw bar, and sides, this is Fort Lauderdale's newest "it" girl, a virtual meat market of seeing and being seen in between stabs at beautiful hunks of steak. For a great alternative to meat, try the miso-glazed black cod. The restaurant is tops for ambience, too—dark woods and bold floral silk wall panels, with the restaurant's centerpiece being a 15-foot-long reef aquarium home to hypnotic jellyfish. Also be sure to check out the restaurant's popular Saturday and Sunday brunch.

W Fort Lauderdale, 401 N. Fort Lauderdale Beach Blvd., Fort Lauderdale. www.steak954.com. ⓒ **954/414-8333.** Reservations recommended. Main courses $26–$65. AE, DC, DISC, MC, V. Sun–Thurs 7am–10pm; Fri–Sat 7am–11pm.

EXPENSIVE

Eduardo de San Angel ★★★ MEXICAN   Gourmet Mexican is *not* an oxymoron, and for those who don't believe that, take one meal at the sublime Eduardo de San Angel and you'll see how true it is. Chef Eduardo Pria has a masterful way with food, as seen in dishes such as sautéed Florida blue crab and yellow corncakes with smoked chipotle-chili sauce and Puebla-style mole, or the ancho chili–flavored crepe filled with *cuitlacoche,* serrano chiles, and onions with melted Asadero cheese laced with a squash blossom sauce. Fresh flowers and candlelight, not to mention the fact that the restaurant resembles an intimate hacienda, add to the ambience. Beer and wine only.

2822 E. Commercial Blvd., Fort Lauderdale. www.eduardodesanangel.com. ⓒ **954/772-4731.** Reservations essential. Main courses $24–$36. AE, DC, DISC, MC, V. Mon–Sat 5:30–10pm.

Johnny V ★★★ FLORIBBEAN   South Florida's favorite so-called Caribbean Cowboy, Chef Johnny Vinczencz, has moved around quite a bit—from South Beach's Hotel Astor (twice!) to Delray Beach's Sundy House. But this Las Olas hot spot looks to be his final stop, and that's good news to all Johnny V's faithful foodies who will travel to the end of the earth to sample some of his barbecue and Caribbean-inspired contemporary cuisine. The menu pops with dishes like sage-grilled Florida dolphin with rock shrimp–plantain stuffing, lobster pan gravy, cranberry-mango chutney, baby green beans, and carrots, plus a slew of other dishes you've likely never seen before.

625 E. Las Olas Blvd. www.johnnyvlasolas.com. ⓒ **954/761-7920.** Reservations suggested. Main courses $25–$42. AE, DC, MC, V. Daily 11:30am–3pm; Sun–Thurs 5–11pm; Fri–Sat 5pm–midnight.

PL8 Kitchen ★ TAPAS   Located on a popular street of bars frequented by Fort Lauderdale's young professionals, PL8 is known for its scene and cuisine. A mezzanine bar upstairs is ideal for people-watching; outdoor tables are tight, but strategically situated in front of all the street's action. On weekend nights, in particular, it's difficult to get a table. However, if you can deal with cramming into the bar, it's worth the wait of a cocktail or two. A menu of all small plates, hence the name, feature such standouts as grilled Korean short ribs, fried chicken breast sliders, and duck fat–roasted marble potatoes. The wine list is impressive. Check out **Side Bar,** the restaurant's very ski-lodgey bar next door featuring live music and a bustling crowd of young hipsters.

210 SW 2nd St. (south of Broward Blvd., west of U.S. 1), Fort Lauderdale. www.pl8kitchen.com. ✆ **954/524-1818.** Reservations recommended. Small plates $6–$12. AE, MC, V. Mon–Thurs 11:30am–2:30pm and 6–10:30pm; Fri 11:30am–2:30pm and 6–11:30pm; Sat 6–11:30pm; Sun 6–10:30pm.

Sage French Café and Oyster Bar ★★ FRENCH/SEAFOOD   A cozy, modern, cacophonous Francophile's dream come true, Sage's Hollywood locale is less bawdy than its Fort Lauderdale counterpart, which comes complete with a Moulin Rouge–meets–Fort Lauderdale Strip burlesque show. We prefer this less flashy location, because it lets us concentrate more on the food, which is the true star of the show. A far cry from a brassy brasserie, this Sage features a backlit bar, an open grill, a shellfish bar, a see-through wine cellar, and a Chihuly-esque chandelier straight out of an animated Disney flick. Chef Laurent Tasic has his shellfish flown in daily from Canada, California, or the Chesapeake Bay. The menu isn't all seafood, though. There's a long list of crepes and French classics such as grilled artichoke, chicken liver pâté, escargot, and a hearty French-onion soup. Entrees include a fabulous cassoulet, a superb plate of steak frites, coq au vin, short ribs Parisienne, and Chef Laurent's meatloaf—ground veal and filet mignon with fresh herbs in a savory mushroom-garlic-merlot sauce. For those who want a side of bawdy with their bourguignon, Sage's Fort Lauderdale location, 2378 N. Federal Hwy. (✆ **954/565-2299**), features Moulin Rouge can can shows from October through May.

2000 Harrison St., Hollywood. www.sagecafe.net. ✆ **954/391-9466.** Reservations recommended. Main courses $18–$30. AE, MC, V. Sun–Thurs 11am–10pm; Fri–Sat 11am–11pm.

Sunfish Grill ★★★ SEAFOOD   Unlike its fellow contemporary seafood restaurants, the Sunfish Grill chooses to focus on fish, not fusion. Chef Bill Bruening is content to leave the spotlight on his fantastic fish dishes, which are possibly the freshest in town, because he buys it at local markets and often from well-known fishermen who appear at his back door with their catches of the day. But this isn't your grandfather's seafooder. Specializing in contemporary American cuisine with a focus on seafood, Sunfish Grill's oft-changing menu offers dishes including pan-seared diver scallops with lobster spaetzle; English peas and lemon-thyme beurre blanc; and prosciutto-wrapped seared rare tuna with parsnip whipped potatoes, with grilled zucchini in a mushroom–red wine glace. Leave room for dessert, too, because pastry chef Erika DiBattista's Symphony of Chocolate is not to be missed.

2775 E. Oakland Park Blvd., Fort Lauderdale. www.sunfishgrill.com. ✆ **954/561-2004.** Reservations recommended. Main courses $22–$39. AE, MC, V. Tues–Sat 5–10pm.

MODERATE

Cap's Place Island Restaurant ★ 📖 SEAFOOD   Opened in 1928 by a bootlegger who ran in the same circles as gangster Meyer Lansky, this barge-turned-restaurant is one of the area's best-kept secrets. Although it's no longer a rum-running restaurant and casino, its illustrious past (FDR and Winston Churchill dined here together) landed it a spot on the National Register of Historic Places. To get here, you have to take a ferryboat, provided by the restaurant. The short ride across the Intracoastal definitely adds to the Cap's Place experience. The food is good, not great. Traditional seafood dishes such as Florida or Maine lobster, clams casino, and oysters Rockefeller will take you back to the days when a soprano was just an opera singer.

2765 NE 28th Court, Lighthouse Point. www.capsplace.com. © **954/941-0418.** Reservations recommended. Main courses $14–$34. MC, V. Daily 5:30pm–midnight. Motor-launch from I-95, exit at Copan's Rd., and go east to U.S. 1 (Federal Hwy.). At NE 24th St., turn right and follow the double lines and signs to the Lighthouse Point Yacht Basin and Marina (8 miles north of Fort Lauderdale). From here, follow the CAP'S PLACE sign pointing you to the shuttle.

Rustic Inn Crabhouse ★ SEAFOOD A Fort Lauderdale rough-and-tumble landmark for more than 50 years, Rustic Inn isn't the place for a romantic, intimate, quiet dinner. The minute you walk into this inn that's more reminiscent of a trailer, you're assaulted by fluorescent interrogation-style lighting and cacophonous banging—a symphony from a packed house of happy diners cracking their crabs with wooden mallets. Although you don't *have* to crack your own crabs, it's all part of the experience. The restaurant is known for its "world-famous garlic crabs" (and we think they are totally deserving of that lofty tag line), but you can also order lobster, pasta, and all sorts of fried fish—even fried alligator (it's chewier than chicken!). The fried clams are especially good, but if you want to gorge yourself, try the Reef Raft, a basket of fried oysters, scallops, and fish. Dress very casually and prepare to wait awhile for a table; but trust us, it's worth it.

4331 Ravenswood Rd., Fort Lauderdale. www.rusticinn.com. © **954/584-1637.** Reservations not accepted. Main courses $14–$44; crabs market price. AE, DC, DISC, MC, V. Mon–Sat 11:30am–10:45pm; Sun 2–9:45pm.

Sugar Reef ★★ FRENCH CARIBBEAN We could go on about this restaurant's priceless ocean view, but the menu of Mediterranean, Caribbean, and French dishes is just as outstanding. A funky fish-shack vibe is bolstered by fresh air wafting in from the Atlantic. Seafood bouillabaisse in coconut milk and green curry and Sugar Reef *pho*—a Vietnamese noodle dish with chicken, shrimp, ginger, and spices—are among the restaurant's most popular dishes. The kitchen puts a savory spin on duck, roasted and topped with mango salsa. This is not a place you'd expect to find on a beach boardwalk, which makes it all the more delightful.

600 N. Surf Rd. (on the Broadwalk, just north of Hollywood Blvd.), Hollywood. www.sugarreefgrill. com. © **954/922-1119.** Reservations accepted for parties of 6 or more. Main courses $12–$33. AE, DISC, MC, V. Mon 4–10:30pm; Tues–Thurs 11am–10:30pm; Fri–Sun 11am–11pm (sometimes later in winter).

INEXPENSIVE

Jaxson's ★ ☺ ICE CREAM South Florida's best and only authentic old-fashioned ice-cream parlor and country store attracts those with a sweet tooth from all over the area. Their cravings are satisfied with an unabridged assortment of homemade ice cream served any which way, from shakes and sundaes to ice-cream sodas and parfaits. Kids love the candy store in the front of the restaurant, and adults love the pre–Ben & Jerry's authenticity. For the calorie conscious, the sugar-free and fat-free versions are pretty good. Jaxson's most famous $12.75 everything-but-the-kitchen-sink sundae in a punch bowl has countless scoops and endless toppings. The ice cream is the reason to come here, but Jaxson's also serves hot dogs, hamburgers, sandwiches, and salads.

128 S. Federal Hwy., Dania Beach. www.jaxsonsicecream.com. © **954/923-4445.** Main courses $8–$20; sundaes $6.75–$14. AE, DISC, MC, V. Mon–Thurs 11:30am–11pm; Fri–Sat 11:30am–midnight; Sun noon–11pm.

La Spada's Original Hoagies ★★ SANDWICHES An institution since 1973, La Spada's is a hero to every sandwich fan, whether you call it a sub or a hoagie. The artful arranging of layers of fresh meats piled into a chewy roll with lettuce, tomato, onion, pickles, and their own blend of marinated sweet peppers make us rethink the whole sandwich-artist moniker. Here, they're sandwich scientists. There are several locations throughout South Florida, including a second in Fort Lauderdale at 1495 SE 17th St. (© **954/522-3483**) and one in Boca Raton at 2240 NW 19th St. (© **561/393-1434**).

4346 Seagrape Dr., Lauderdale-by-the-Sea. www.laspadashoagies.com. © **954/776-7893.** Sandwiches $6–$11. AE, MC, V. Mon–Sat 10am–8pm; Sun 11am–8pm (open at 10am on NFL game days).

Lester's Diner ★ AMERICAN Since 1968, Lester's Diner has been serving swarms of South Floridians large portions of great greasy-spoon fare until the wee hours. Try the eggs Benedict and the 14-ounce "cup" of classic coffee, or sample one of Lester's many homemade desserts. The place serves breakfast 24 hours a day and is a Fort Lauderdale institution that attracts locals, club crowds, city officials, and a generally motley crew of hungry people craving no-nonsense food served by seasoned waitresses with beehive hairdos that contribute to the campy atmosphere. Lester's is also in Sunrise, at 1399 NW 136th Ave. (© **954/838-7473**), and Coconut Creek near a casino at 4701 Coconut Creek Parkway (© **954/979-4722**).

250 S.R. 84, Fort Lauderdale. http://lestersdiner.com. © **954/525-5641.** Main courses $4.50–$19. AE, MC, V. Daily 24 hr.

Le Tub ★★ 🎀 AMERICAN Hands down, this is one of the coolest, most unpretentious, quintessential pre–swanky So Flo restaurants, if not one of the coolest restaurants, period. Established in 1959 as a Sunoco gas station, Le Tub was purchased in 1974 by a man who personally transformed the place into this waterfront restaurant, made out of flotsam, jetsam, and ocean-borne treasures gathered over 4 years of jogging on Hollywood Beach. But the waterfront location and unique building aren't the only things to marvel at. As you walk in, take note of the hand-painted bathtubs and toilet bowls (they're used as planters) lining the walkway. Inside is a divey bar complete with pool table and jukebox; but outside seating on the deck is the real gem. Le Tub is famous for its burgers (which *Esquire* magazine and Oprah have declared the country's best), chili, and seafood, but more appealing than the food is the peaceful, easy feeling exuded by the place.

1100 N. Ocean Dr., Hollywood. www.theletub.com. © **954/931-9425.** Main courses $9–$21. No credit cards. Daily noon–4am.

Shopping

It's all about malls in Broward County and, while most of the best shopping is within Fort Lauderdale proper, other areas are also worth browsing.

Malls here include the upscale **Galleria,** at Sunrise Boulevard near the Fort Lauderdale Beach, and the **Westfield Broward Mall,** west of I-95 on Broward Boulevard, in Plantation.

If you're looking for unusual boutiques, especially art galleries, head to quaint **Las Olas Boulevard** ★, located west of A1A and a block east of Federal Highway/U.S. 1, off SE 8th Street, where there are hundreds of shops with alluring window decorations (like kitchen utensils posing as modern-art sculptures) and intriguing merchandise (such as mural-size oil paintings). For bargains, there's no better place than **Sawgrass Mills,** 12801 W. Sunrise Blvd. (© **954/846-0179**), featuring more than

350 name-brand outlets such as Off Fifth and Nordstrom Rack. Nearby is Florida's first-ever **IKEA,** 151 NW 136th Ave. (www.ikea.com; ✆ **954/838-9292**), purveyor of all things sleek and Swedish—from furniture to meatballs.

Where to Stay

The Fort Lauderdale beach has a hotel or motel on nearly every block, ranging from run-down to luxurious. **Fort Lauderdale Beach Resort Hotel & Suites,** 4221 N. Ocean Blvd. (www.ftlbeachresort.com; ✆ **800/329-7466** or 954/563-2521), has clean, oceanside rooms starting at about $65.

The landmark Sheraton Yankee Clipper received a $30-million makeover and debuted in 2010 as the **Sheraton Fort Lauderdale Beach Hotel** (p. 315). In 2011, **B Ocean Fort Lauderdale,** 999 N. Ft. Lauderdale Beach Blvd. (www.bhotels andresorts.com; ✆ **888/66-BHOTEL** [662-4683]), the flagship property of the W-like B Hotels & Resorts, rose from the ashes of an old Holiday Inn, featuring 240 high-tech, chic rooms; a spa; infinity pool; lounge; bistro; and a sushi restaurant. Rates range from $189 to $499 in winter and start at $129 in summer.

In Hollywood, where prices are generally cheaper, the **Hollywood Beach Resort,** 101 N. Ocean Dr. (www.hollywoodbeach-resort.com; ✆ **954/921-0990**), operates a full-service hotel right on the ocean. With prices starting at around $149 in season, it's a great deal. **Hollywood Beach Marriott,** 2501 N. Ocean Dr. (I-95 to Sheridan St. E. to A1A S.; www.hollywoodbeachmarriott.com; ✆ **866/306-5453** or 954/924-2202), is a recently renovated beach resort with a fantastic location right on the Hollywood Beach Broadwalk. Breaking ground in late 2011 with an anticipated late 2012 debut is **Margaritaville Resort Hotel,** Jimmy Buffett's 17-story, $130-million hotel and entertainment complex.

For those looking to stay near some of the area's best shopping (Sawgrass Mills, mainly), consider the **Hyatt Regency Bonaventure Conference Center and Spa,** 250 Racquet Club Rd., Weston, Florida (http://bonaventure.hyatt.com; ✆ **954/616-1234**), Broward County's first Certified Green Lodging hotel located in suburban Weston. It features 501 luxurious rooms, catering to both business and leisure travelers; rates start at $159 in high season and $109 in the off season.

For rentals for a few weeks or months, check the annual list of small lodgings compiled by the **Greater Fort Lauderdale Convention & Visitors Bureau** (✆ **954/765-4466**); they're especially helpful if you're looking for privately owned, charming, affordable lodgings.

VERY EXPENSIVE

The Atlantic Hotel ★★★   Overlooking 23 miles of white sand, the Atlantic is a 16-story study in minimal modernity—soothing colors and comfortable, stylish decor. Besides the usual high-tech amenities found in all rooms of this category—flatscreen TVs, Wi-Fi—each room has a fully equipped granite kitchen or kitchenette. The Atlantic also has a fantastic French bistro, **East End Brasserie** (p. 305), and a spectacular 10,000-square-foot spa. On the hotel's fifth-floor ocean terrace you'll find a heated pool, casual bar, and restaurant. It's an ideal spot for a frozen drink paired with a sensational view. For those looking to stay here in rock-star style, the Penthouse Collection includes two- and three-bedroom suites, some with private elevators. Service is usually stellar, though we've had some complaints of a bit of attitude.

601 N. Fort Lauderdale Beach Blvd., Fort Lauderdale, FL 33304. www.atlantichotelfl.com. ✆ **866/ 318-1101** or 954/567-8020. Fax 954/567-8040. 124 units. Winter $299–$619 double, $399–$999 suite; off season $199–$329 double, $499 suite. AE, DC, DISC, MC, V. Valet parking $28. **Amenities:**

2 restaurants; bar; bike rentals; concierge; outdoor heated pool; room service; spa; watersports equipment/rentals; free Wi-Fi in lobby. *In room:* A/C, TV, hair dryer, minibar, Wi-Fi.

Harbor Beach Marriott Resort & Spa ★★ ☺   Harbor Beach is loaded with the same amenities as Pier 66 (see below), but has a blissfully more secluded setting on 16 oceanfront acres just south of Fort Lauderdale's "strip." Everything in this place is huge—from the quarter-mile private beach to the 8,000-square-foot lagoon pool and the 22,000-square-foot European-style Spa at Harbor Beach. As huge as it is, however, it doesn't feel like your typical, soulless resort. Accommodations feature pillow-top bedding, marble flooring, designer lighting, and wraparound mirrors. Most units open onto private balconies overlooking the pool, the city, the ocean, or the Intracoastal Waterway. The hotel's **3030 Ocean** is an excellent seafood restaurant and raw bar helmed by executive chef Dean James Max; **Riva**, a Mediterranean-style oceanfront eatery, is also top-notch. **Sea Level Restaurant and Ocean Bar,** the resort's beachfront venue, is a scenic destination that offers regional cuisine, hand-crafted cocktails, and unobstructed views of the Atlantic Ocean. The hotel's complimentary Surf Club for kids ages 5 to 12 provides arts and crafts, video games, a surf simulator, and other activities to keep the young ones happily occupied. This resort also offers on-site water sports, from surfing to parasailing.

3030 Holiday Dr., Fort Lauderdale, FL 33316. www.marriottharborbeach.com. ✆ **800/222-6543** or 954/525-4000. Fax 954/766-6152. 650 units. Winter $345–$659 double, off season $298–$401 double; year-round from $630 suites. AE, DC, DISC, MC, V. Valet parking $30; self-parking $25. From I-95, exit on I-595 E. to U.S. 1 N.; proceed to SE 17th St.; make a right and go over the Intracoastal Bridge past 3 traffic lights to Holiday Dr.; turn right. **Amenities:** 4 restaurants; 3 bars; babysitting; bike rentals; children's programs; concierge; health club; outdoor heated pool; room service; European-style spa; 4 clay tennis courts; extensive watersports equipment/rentals. *In room:* A/C, TV, hair dryer, high-speed Internet, minibar.

Hyatt Regency Pier 66 ★★   Set on 22 tropical acres on the Intracoastal Waterway, this landmark hotel is best known for its world-class marina and a rooftop ballroom and brunch spot that spins a complete 360 degrees every 66 minutes. If you experience vertigo after sitting in the revolving ballroom, an invigorating treatment at the hotel's exquisite **Spa 66** will help relocate your sense of balance. Equally invigorating are the recreational amenities, which include a three-pool complex with a 40-person hydrotherapy pool, tennis courts, and an aquatic center with watersports. **Grille 66 & Bar,** a classy, upscale steakhouse, is a welcome addition. A $40-million refurbishment has transformed the lobby, lawn, and remaining guest rooms with a retro modern decor. New lanai guest rooms have cherrywood furnishings and bathrooms with marble floors and granite vanities. All units have flatscreen televisions, wireless Internet access, and balconies with views of the Intracoastal Waterway and the hotel's lushly landscaped gardens.

2301 SE 17th St. Causeway, Fort Lauderdale, FL 33316. www.pier66.com. ✆ **800/233-1234** or 954/525-6666. Fax 954/728-3541. 384 units. Winter $249–$309 double, off season $119–$200 double; year-round from $899 suite. Rates are cheaper on the hotel's website. AE, DC, DISC, MC, V. Valet parking $23; self-parking $19. **Amenities:** 5 restaurants; 3 bars; bike rentals; concierge; 3 pools; room service; spa; 2 lighted clay Har-Tru tennis courts; watersports equipment/rentals. *In room:* A/C, TV, hair dryer, Wi-Fi.

Ritz-Carlton Fort Lauderdale ★★★   The first and only AAA Five Diamond hotel in Fort Lauderdale, this $160-million property has elevated the strip to an entirely new level of luxury. All rooms feature views of the Atlantic or the Intracoastal Waterway, and have all the high-tech and luxury amenities you'd expect from a hotel of this caliber. Exclusive to guests in Residential Suites and a limited number of oceanfront rooms is the Club Lounge, which features a variety of food and beverage servings throughout the day. We particularly like chef Christian Claire's stellar oceanfront Italian grill, **Via Luna,** and the 5,000-bottle wine vault with nightly wine tastings upon request. The seventh-floor oceanfront pool is nice yet understated, with a private VIP cabana level; and, in true South Florida fashion, the Ritz boasts the only luxury spa in the area to introduce "Chiral" anti-aging treatments and the NûFACE toning device, dubbed "Pilates for the face." Some people have complained that service is snooty, while others deem it refined and top-notch. *Reservation tip:* All rooms ending in "10" offer floor-to-ceiling windows and spectacular views!·

1 N. Fort Lauderdale Beach Blvd., Fort Lauderdale, FL 33304. www.ritzcarlton.com. ℂ **800/241-3333** or 954/465-2300. Fax 954/465-2340. 192 units. Winter from $429 double, off season from $219 double; year-round from $600 suite. AE, DC, DISC, MC, V. Valet parking $32. From I-95, exit on I-595 E. to U.S. 1 N.; proceed to SE 17th St.; make a right and go over the Intracoastal Bridge past 6 traffic lights to Castillo St.; turn left. **Amenities:** 2 restaurants; 3 bars; concierge; fitness center; outdoor heated pool; room service; European-style spa. *In room:* A/C, TV/DVD, hair dryer, minibar, Wi-Fi.

Westin Diplomat Resort & Spa ★★ The Diplomat is a 1,058-room, full-service beach resort loaded with amenities—the only one of its kind in the somewhat desolate, residential area. The main building is a 39-story oceanfront tower. A gorgeous bridged, glass-bottom pool with waterfalls, private cabanas, and a slew of watersports adds a tropical touch. Rooms are a cross between those in a subtle boutique hotel and in an Art Deco throwback, with dark woods, hand-cut marble, and the 10-layer Heavenly Bed, a Westin trademark. Dining options are aplenty, from the fine-dining steakhouse to several more casual places. **Diplomat Landing,** the hotel's shopping-and-entertainment complex across the street, features shops and a waterfront sports bar. The resort's golf resort and spa is located across the Intracoastal, featuring 60 luxurious guest rooms, yacht slips, a 155-acre golf course, and a world-class spa and tennis club.

3555 S. Ocean Dr. (A1A), Hollywood, FL 33019. www.diplomatresort.com. ℂ **888/627-9057** or 954/602-6000. Fax 954/602-7000. 998 units. Winter $305–$515 double, $675–$875 suite; off season $220–$340 double, $475–$675 suite. AE, DC, DISC, MC, V. Valet parking $22. **Amenities:** 9 restaurants; 3 lounges; golf course; health club; 2 pools; room service; spa; 10 clay tennis courts; watersports equipment/rentals. *In room:* A/C, TV, fax, hair dryer, high-speed Internet access, minibar.

W Fort Lauderdale ★★★ Wow. Until this W opened, we thought that if you'd seen one W hotel you'd seen 'em all. Not anymore. Designed to resemble a sailboat, this W comprises two 24-story towers of hotel rooms and condos. Inspired by the sand and sea, the hotel's *pièce de résistance* is the stunning oceanfront pool deck with a glass-enclosed stairway that provides splashy, up-close-and-personal views of the pool from the lobby. Rooms exude a beach-house vibe with neutral colors and gorgeous bathrooms that open into the main living area. There's also a Bliss Spa, and hipster-heavy Whiskey Blue bar/lounge. Unique to this W is **Steak 954** (p. 306), a sexy, see-and-be-sceney steakhouse. *Note:* If the W is too sceney for you, consider its more laid-back sister hotel up the block, the **Westin Beach Resort, Fort Lauderdale,** 321 N. Fort Lauderdale Beach Blvd. (www.starwoodhotels.com; ℂ **954/467-1111**), the recipient of a multimillion-dollar face-lift.

401 N. Fort Lauderdale Beach Blvd., Fort Lauderdale, FL 33304. www.wfortlauderdalehotel.com. ℂ **866/837-4203** or 954/414-8200. Fax 954/414-8250. 517 units. Winter $305–$515 double, $675–$875 suite; off season $220–$340 double, $475–$675 suite. AE, DC, DISC, MC, V. Valet parking $30. **Amenities:** 2 restaurants; 2 lounges; fitness center; 2 pools; room service; spa. *In room:* A/C, TV, hair dryer, minibar, Wi-Fi.

EXPENSIVE

Lago Mar Resort & Club ★★ ☺ A charming lobby with a rock fireplace and saltwater aquarium sets the tone of this utterly inviting resort, a casually elegant piece of Old Florida that occupies its own, 10-acre, lush little island between Lake Mayan and the Atlantic. Guests have access to the broadest and best strip of 500 feet of private beach in the entire city, not to mention two wonderful pools—one large enough for lap swimming and the other a 9,000-square-foot swimming pool lagoon edged with tropical plants and bougainvillea. Lago Mar is very family oriented, with many facilities and supervised activities for children. Service is spectacular. The plush rooms and suites have Mediterranean or Key West influences. A full-service spa offers a wide array of treatments, while the 1,000-square-foot exercise facility may come in handy after you indulge in the hotel's modern American bistro restaurant, **Acquario,** which is worth a visit even if you don't stay here. The six-story wing of oceanfront suites with individual balconies and luxurious bathrooms includes a deck of native tropical landscaping and a 5,000-square-foot saltwater lagoon.

1700 S. Ocean Lane, Fort Lauderdale, FL 33316. www.lagomar.com. ☎ **800/524-6627** or 954/523-6511. Fax 954/524-6627. 204 units. Winter from $315 double; off season from $155 double. AE, DC, MC, V. Free valet parking. From Federal Hwy. (U.S. 1), turn east onto SE 17th St. Causeway; turn right onto Mayan Dr.; turn right again onto S. Ocean Dr.; turn left onto Grace Dr.; then turn left again onto S. Ocean Lane to the hotel. **Amenities:** 4 restaurants; bar; wine room; children's programs during holiday periods; concierge; exercise room; minigolf course; outdoor pool and lagoon; room service; 4 tennis courts; watersports equipment/rentals. In room: A/C, TV, fridge, hair dryer, complimentary high-speed Internet.

The Pillars Hotel ★ ▮▮ One of Fort Lauderdale's best-kept secrets, the Pillars transports you from the neon-hued flash and splash of Fort Lauderdale's strip and takes you to a two-story British colonial, Caribbean-style retreat tucked away on the bustling Intracoastal Waterway. Because it has just 22 rooms, you'll feel as if you have the grand house all to yourself—albeit a house with white-tablecloth room service, an Edenistic courtyard with a free-form pool, lush landscaping, and a private chef. Rooms are luxurious and loaded with amenities such as flatscreen TVs, DVD players, ultraplush bedding, and, if you're so inclined, a private masseuse to iron out your personal kinks. The hotel's restaurant, the **Secret Garden,** open only to hotel guests and members of its Secret Garden Society, provides gourmet dinner served under the stars and overlooking the Intracoastal. A library area (with more than 500 books) is at your disposal, as is pretty much anything else you request here.

111 N. Birch Rd., Fort Lauderdale, FL 33304. www.pillarshotel.com. ☎ **954/467-9639.** Fax 954/763-2845. 22 units. Winter $285–$355 double, $399–$575 suite; off season $195–$235 double, $275–$469 suite. AE, DC, DISC, MC, V. Free off-street parking. **Amenities:** Restaurant; concierge; pool; room service; free Wi-Fi. In room: A/C, TV/DVD, hair dryer, high-speed Internet, minibar.

Riverside Hotel ★★ A touch of New Orleans hits Fort Lauderdale's popular Las Olas Boulevard in the form of this charming, six-story 1936 hotel. There's no beach here, but the hotel is set on the sleepy and scenic New River, capturing the essence of that ever-elusive Old Florida. Rooms and suites are done up in Tommy Bahama-styled design elements and vintage decor, with sweeping views overlooking the city skyline, Atlantic Ocean, and New River. All units have wet bars and French doors that lead to private balconies. The best units face the river, but it's hard to see the water past the parking lot and trees. Twelve rooms offer king-size beds with mirrored canopies and flowing drapes. There are also seven elegantly decorated suites with French doors that lead to private balconies. The hotel restaurant, **Indigo,** is a fantastic seafood spot.

620 E. Las Olas Blvd., Fort Lauderdale, FL 33301. www.riversidehotel.com. $℃$ **800/325-3280** or 954/467-0671. Fax 954/462-2148. 217 units. Winter $399–$660 suite; off season $299–$500 suite. Online discounts available. Special packages available. AE, DC, MC, V. Valet parking $23, self-parking $17. From I-95, exit onto Broward Blvd.; turn right onto Federal Hwy. (U.S. 1); turn left onto Las Olas Blvd. **Amenities:** 2 restaurants; 2 bars; concierge; outdoor pool; limited room service. *In room:* A/C, TV, fridge, hair dryer, high-speed Internet access, minibar.

MODERATE

Courtyard Villa on the Ocean ★   Nestled between a bunch of larger hotels, this small historic hotel is a romantic getaway right on the beach. Courtyard Villa offers spacious oceanfront efficiencies with private balconies; larger suites overlook the pool. Accommodations are plush, with chenille bedspreads and carved four-poster beds; fully equipped kitchenettes are an added convenience. The tiled bathrooms have strong, hot showers to wash off the beach sand. Room nos. 7 and 8 are especially nice, with French doors that open to a private balcony overlooking the ocean. Relax in the hotel's unique heated pool/spa or on the second-floor sun deck. You can also swim from the beach to a living reef just 50 feet offshore. Located on the same street is Courtyard Villa's sister property, **Buena Vista Hotel and Beach Club,** 4225 El Mar Dr. ($℃$ **800/291-3560**), where in-season rates range from $179 to $279 and off-season rates are $99 to $169.

4312 El Mar Dr., Lauderdale-by-the-Sea, FL 33308. www.buenavistacorp.com. $℃$ **800/291-3560** or 954/776-1164. Fax 954/491-0768. 10 units. Winter $159–$359 unit; off season $109–$225. Rates include full breakfast. AE, MC, V. Pets less than 35 lb. accepted with $200 deposit; must be caged while outside; no pit bulls, Dobermans, or Rottweilers. **Amenities:** Free use of bikes; Internet access; Jacuzzi; outdoor heated pool. *In room:* A/C, TV/VCR, hair dryer, kitchenette.

Hilton Fort Lauderdale Beach Resort ★★   This 25-story landmark property is located on the shoreline of Fort Lauderdale's famous A1A between the palm-shaded boulevards of Sunrise and Las Olas. Guests enter the resort through a gracious porte-cochere into a dramatic two-story lobby. The sixth-floor Sunrise Terrace offers unobstructed views of the Atlantic Ocean and features an infinity pool and private poolside cabanas, and is reminiscent of the deck of a luxury yacht. There's a dedicated beach concierge, kids' poolside program, accommodating staff, and deluxe turndown service. Each of the 374 studios and suites is outfitted with a separate shower and soaking tub, high-definition flatscreen TV, kitchen or kitchenette, and private oceanview balcony with expansive views of the Atlantic. The resort features the Spa Q and two distinct dining options, including **ilios**—an upscale signature restaurant of contemporary Mediterranean cuisine—and **Le Marche Gourmet Market & Bakery,** featuring Starbucks drinks, pizzas, panini, gelato, and more.

505 N. Fort Lauderdale Beach Blvd., Fort Lauderdale, FL 33404. www.fortlauderdalebeachresort. hilton.com. ℭ **800/HILTONS** (445-8667) or 954/414-2222. Fax 954/414-2612. 374 units. Seasonal from $159 double. AE, DISC, MC, V. Valet parking $31. **Amenities:** 2 restaurants; concierge; high-speed Internet access; pool; room service; spa. *In room:* A/C, TV, fridge.

Pelican Grand Beach Resort ★ ☺   The Pelican Beach Resort sits on a 500-foot private beach, with 159 oversize accommodations, oceanfront suites with balconies, and a sublimely relaxing, wraparound oceanfront veranda and sun deck with rocking chairs. What also rocks about this place are the zero-entry pool and the lazy river tubing ride. But if you prefer to feel sand between your toes, the private beach is the best thing about this resort, an amenity not too common in this area, where hotels are generally located across the street from the beach instead of being directly on it. This is a great, low-key luxury resort, especially for families looking for a relaxing vacation, as it has all the amenities of a more harried chain resort overwrought with a slew of people. A popu-lar spot here is the **Emporium,** an old-fashioned ice-cream parlor that's command central for your sweet tooth. The resort is also completely smoke-free.

2000 N. Ocean Blvd., Fort Lauderdale, FL 33305. www.pelicanbeach.com. ℭ **800/525-OCEAN** (6232) or 954/568-9431. Fax 954/565-2662. 159 units. Winter $299–$349 double, $520 suite; off season $220–$270 double, $420 suite. AE, DC, MC, V. Parking $24. **Amenities:** Restaurant; ice-cream parlor; bar; fitness center; pool. *In room:* A/C, TV, fridge, hair dryer, high-speed Internet.

Seminole Hard Rock Hotel & Casino ★★★   The Seminole Tribe of Florida has created a miniature Vegas within Hollywood, Florida, and it's doing a booming business, especially after the massive, 130,000-square-foot **casino** added blackjack in addition to thousands of Vegas-style slot machines, baccarat, and all kinds of poker tables that are always packed. The main draw here is the casino, but the guest rooms are surprisingly cushy and swank, with flatscreen TVs, Egyptian-cotton linens, and big bathrooms; the suites are hyperluxurious. Equally impressive is the 4½-acre lagoon-style pool area with waterfalls, hot tubs, and, of course, a bar. Actually, there are lots of bars here, especially at the attached entertainment complex, with two clubs open 24/7, as well as restaurants and stores. There's also a food court, or you can choose from several on-site, full-service restaurants, including **Council Oak,** a swanky steakhouse, Gloria and Emilio Estefan's **Bongo's Cuban Café,** and a branch of Fort Lauderdale's disco-licious Italian hot spot, **Café Martorano** (p. 304). If all this action has you feeling wiped out, there's always the **Body Rock Spa,** which, in Seminole Hard Rock fashion, is also pretty sizable.

1 Seminole Way, Hollywood, FL 33314. www.seminolehardrockhollywood.com. ℭ **800/937-0010** or 954/327-7625. Fax 954/327-7655. 500 units. Year-round $189–$259 double; $279 luxury room; $650–$2,000 suite. AE, DC, DISC, MC, V. **Amenities:** 17 restaurants; 13 nightclubs and lounges; Jacuzzi; pool; room service; spa. *In room:* A/C, TV, CD player, hair dryer, Wi-Fi.

Sheraton Fort Lauderdale Beach Hotel ★★   A dramatic change has taken place at the former Sheraton Yankee Clipper to the tune of $30 million, and it's all for the better. The iconic beachfront property now features a refreshed, playful design throughout its inviting guest rooms and suites, most with views of the Atlantic Ocean or the Intracoastal. The better-than-ever Sheraton features great dining and enter-tainment enticements, including the poolside **Baja Beach Bar and Grill,** the **Link@Sheraton** Internet cafe, and the famed **Wreck Bar** where guests of all ages come to catch a glimpse of mermaids swimming from porthole to porthole. There's also a branch of haute NYC Mexican restaurant **Dos Caminos,** a chic lobby area (aka Living Room), an expanded pool deck and infinity pool as well as a new fitness center, a kids' club, restaurants, and bars.

1140 Seabreeze Blvd., Fort Lauderdale, FL 33305. www.sheraton.com/fortlauderdalebeach. ℰ **954/524-5551.** Fax 954/523-5376. 486 units. Winter $159–$189 studio, $229–$449 suite; off season $159–$189 studio, $269–$319 suite. AE, DC, MC, V. Free valet parking. **Amenities:** Restaurant; bar; kids' programs; fitness center; Jacuzzi; 2 pools; room service; watersports. *In room:* A/C, TV, hair dryer, free Wi-Fi.

INEXPENSIVE

Backpacker's Beach Hostel   For the young, or for backpackers on a budget, this hostel is a great option, with both dorm beds and private rooms at bargain-basement prices. Clean and conveniently located, the hostel is just 654 feet from the ocean. It features free parking, free phones, free food for self-cooking, free breakfast buffet, and, if you're lucky, free use of the surfboards or in-line skates lying around.

2115 N. Ocean Blvd., Fort Lauderdale, FL 33305. www.fortlauderdalehostel.com. ℰ **954/567-7275.** 12 units. Dorm beds $20 per night, $145 per week; private rooms $55 double. Rates include breakfast buffet. MC, V. **Amenities:** Free Internet access. *In room:* A/C, TV.

Hollywood Beach Suites, Hostel + Hotel ★ 🛏   From the owners of Miami's hotelier to the hipster on a budget (South Beach Group) comes this beachy, kitschy hotel and hostel that pays homage to nomadic surfer culture. Rooms—shared female, male, mixed sex, and private rooms and suites—are Key West style, decorated in blues and yellows and featuring bunk beds, queen beds, security lockers, and mini-kitchenettes with microwave, refrigerator, and sink. The main house is where the action is, with a full kitchen, living room, outdoor lounge area, deck, Mexican outdoor restaurant, and bar. It's steps from Hollywood Beach and Broadwalk. Amenities here are exceptional, from free Wi-Fi to free use of surfboards, bikes, and pool tables. Beach access and parking are also free. There's also the **Taco Beach Shack,** a large hip outdoor taco joint.

334 Arizona Ave., Hollywood Beach, FL 33109. www.southbeachgroup.com. ℰ **877/762-3477** or 954/391-9448. 24 units. Dorm beds from $22 per night; private rooms from $79 double. Parking $10. MC, V. **Amenities:** Free use of bikes; free Wi-Fi. *In room:* A/C, TV.

Sea Downs (and the Bougainvillea) ★★   This reasonably priced lodging is often booked months in advance by return guests who want to be directly on the beach and Broadwalk without paying a fortune. The hosts, Claudia and Karl Herzog, live on the premises and keep things running smoothly. This superclean 1950s property has all the modern amenities—flatscreen TVs, free Wi-Fi—with plenty of Old Florida charm. This great location (without being secluded) is an easy stroll to the restaurants, bars and shops of the central beach area. All units have fully equipped kitchens here and at the Herzogs' other, even less expensive 14-unit Bougainvillea, which is next door and has a small tropical garden. Guests at both hotels share the Sea Downs pool (heated in the winter). All rooms are smoke-free.

2900 N. Surf Rd., Hollywood, FL 33019. www.seadowns.com or www.bougainvilleahollywood.com. ℰ **954/923-4968.** Fax 954/923-8747. 12 units. Winter $125–$155 studio, $149–$210 1-bedroom apt; off season $85–$116 studio, $109–$155 1-bedroom apt. Weekly discounted rates available. No credit cards. From I-95, exit Sheridan St. E. to A1A and go south; drive ½ mile to Coolidge St.; turn left. **Amenities:** Concierge; freshwater outdoor pool; free Wi-Fi. *In room:* A/C, TV, Internet access, fully equipped kitchen.

BOCA RATON ★★ & DELRAY BEACH ★

26 miles S of Palm Beach; 40 miles N of Miami; 21 miles N of Fort Lauderdale

Boca Raton is one of South Florida's most expensive, well-maintained cities—home to ladies who lunch and SUV-driving yuppies. The city's name literally translates as "rat's mouth," but you'd be hard-pressed to find rodents in this area's fancy digs.

If you're looking for funky, wacky, and eclectic, look elsewhere. Boca is a luxurious resort community and, for some, the only place worth staying in South Florida. With minimal nightlife, entertainment in Boca is restricted to leisure sports, excellent dining, and upscale shopping. The city's residents and vacationers happily comply.

Delray Beach, named after a suburb of Detroit, is a sleepy-yet-starting-to-awaken beachfront community that grew up completely separate from its southern neighbor. Because of their proximity, Boca and Delray can easily be explored together. Budget-conscious travelers would do well to eat and sleep in Delray and dip into Boca for sightseeing and beaching only. The 2-mile stretch of beach here is well maintained and crowded, though not mobbed. Delray's "downtown" area is confined to Atlantic Avenue, which is known for restaurants from casual to chic, quaint shops, and art galleries. During the day, Delray is slumbering, but thanks to the recent addition of trendy restaurants and bars, nighttime is a much more animated hotbed of hipster activity. Still, compared to Boca, Delray is much more laid back; it's trendy, but hardly as chichi, and definitely more cute little beach town than sprawling, swanky, suburban Boca.

Essentials

GETTING THERE   Like the rest of the cities on the Gold Coast, Boca Raton and Delray are easily reached from I-95 or the Florida Turnpike. Both the Fort Lauderdale Hollywood International Airport and the Palm Beach International Airport are about 20 minutes away. **Amtrak** (www.amtrak.com; ✆ **800/USA-RAIL** [872-7245]) trains make stops in Delray Beach at an unattended station at 345 S. Congress Ave.

VISITOR INFORMATION   Contact or stop by the **Palm Beach County Convention and Visitors Bureau,** 1555 Palm Beach Lakes Blvd., Ste. 800, West Palm Beach, FL 33401 (www.palmbeachfl.com; ✆ **800/554-PALM** [7256] or 561/233-3000; fax 561/471-3990). It's open Monday through Friday from 8:30am to 5:30pm and has excellent coupons and discounts. Monday through Friday from 8:30am to at least 4pm, stop by the **Greater Boca Raton Chamber of Commerce,** 1800 N. Dixie Hwy., 4 blocks north of Glades Road, Boca Raton, FL 33432 (www.bocaraton chamber.com; ✆ **561/395-4433;** fax 561/392-3780), for information on attractions, accommodations, and events in the area. You can also try the **Greater Delray Beach Chamber of Commerce,** 64 SE 5th Ave., half a block south of Atlantic Avenue on U.S. 1, Delray Beach, FL 33483 (www.delraybeach.com; ✆ **561/278-0424;** fax 561/278-0555), but we recommend the Palm Beach County Convention and Visitors Bureau as it has information on the entire county.

Exploring Boca Raton & Delray Beach

HITTING THE BEACH

Thankfully, Florida had the foresight to set aside some of its most beautiful coastal areas for the public's enjoyment. Many of the area's best beaches are located in state parks and are free to pedestrians and bikers, though most do charge for parking. Among the beaches we recommend are Delray Beach's **Atlantic Dunes Beach,** 1600 S. Ocean Blvd., which charges no admission to access a 7-acre developed beach with lifeguards, restrooms, changing rooms, and a family park area; and Boca Raton's **South Beach Park,** 400 N. Ocean Blvd., with 1,670 feet of beach, 25 acres, lifeguards, picnic areas, restrooms, showers, and 955 feet of developed beach south of the Boca Inlet, accessible for an admission charge of $15 Monday through Friday, and $17 Saturday, Sunday and holidays. The two beaches below are also very popular.

Delray Beach, on Ocean Boulevard at the east end of Atlantic Avenue, is one of the area's most popular hangouts. Weekends especially attract a young and good-looking crowd of active locals and tourists. Refreshments, snack shops, bars, and restaurants are just across the street. Families enjoy the protection of lifeguards on the clean, wide strip. Gentle waters make it a good swimming beach, too. Restrooms and showers are available, and there's limited parking at meters along Ocean Boulevard.

Spanish River Park Beach, on North Ocean Boulevard (A1A), 2 miles north of Palmetto Park Road in Boca Raton, is a huge 95-acre oceanfront park with a half-mile-long beach with lifeguards as well as a large grassy area, making it one of the best choices for picnicking. Facilities include picnic tables, grills, restrooms, showers, and a 40-foot observation tower. You can walk through tunnels under the highway to access nature trails that wind through fertile grasslands. Volleyball nets always have at least one game going on. The park is open from 8am to 8pm. Admission is $16 for vehicles Monday through Friday, and $18 on Saturday, Sunday, and major holidays.

Also see the description of **Red Reef Park** under "Scuba Diving & Snorkeling," below.

SEEING THE SIGHTS

Boca Raton Museum of Art ★★ ART MUSEUM   In addition to a relatively small but well-chosen permanent collection that's strongest in 19th-century European oils (Degas, Klee, Matisse, Picasso, Seurat), the museum stages a wide variety of excellent temporary exhibitions by local and international artists. Lectures and films are offered on a fairly regular basis, so call ahead, or check the website, for details.

Mizner Park, 501 Plaza Real, Boca Raton. www.bocamuseum.org. © **561/392-2500.** Admission $14 adults, $12 seniors, $6 students, free for children 12 and under. Additional fees may apply for special exhibits and performances. Free on Wed except during special exhibitions. Tues, Thurs, and Sat 10am–5pm; Wed and Fri 10am–9pm; Sun noon–5pm.

Daggerwing Nature Center ★ NATURE RESERVE   Seen enough snowbirds? Head over to this 39-acre swampy splendor where birds of another feather reside, including herons, egrets, woodpeckers, and warblers. The trails come complete with a soundtrack provided by songbirds hovering above (watch your head). The park's night hikes ($3 per person) will take you on a nocturnal wake-up call for owls at 6pm. Bring a flashlight. A $2-million expansion added a 3,000-square-foot exhibit

Boca Raton

ATTRACTIONS ●
Boca Raton Municipal Golf
Course **17**
Boca Raton Museum
of Art **21**
Daggerwing Nature
Center **16**
Delray Beach Tennis
Center **1**
Gumbo Limbo Environmental
Complex **20**
Mizner Park **22**
Morikami Museum and
Japanese Gardens **11**
Patch Reef Park **14**
Town Center Mall **18**

HOTELS ■
Boca Raton Resort & Club **25**
Crane's Beach House **8**
The Seagate Hotel & Spa **10**
Sundy House **7**

RESTAURANTS ◆
Baja Cafe **23**
English Tap & Beer Garden **19**
Kathy's Gazebo Cafe **15**
Ke'e Grill **13**
Morimoto Sushi Bar **25**
The Office **5**
Sundy House Restaurant **7**
32 East **4**
Tin Muffin Café **24**

ENTERTAINMENT
& NIGHTLIFE ●
Boston's
on the Beach **9**
Caldwell Theatre **12**
Dada **2**
Delux **3**
Falcon House **6**

0	1 mi
0	1 km

Lake Ida Rd.

Lake Ida

NE 2nd Ave.

Swinton Ave.

5th Ave.

6th Ave.

Ocean Blvd.

W. Atlantic Ave.

DELRAY BEACH

NE

Lowson Blvd.

SW 10th St.

Delray
Beach
Public
Beach

A1A

Linton Blvd.

Atlantic
Dunes
Beach

Old Dixie Hwy.

N. Federal Hwy.

Intracoastal Waterway

Clint Moore Rd.

Congress Ave.

NW 51st St.

NW Spanish River Blvd.

Spanish
River
Park
Beach

**Boca Raton
Airport**

**BOCA
RATON**

Ocean Blvd

St. Andrews Blvd.

Military Trail

Powerline Rd.

Glades Rd.

**FLORIDA
ATLANTIC
UNIVERSITY**

NW 20th St.

Federal Hwy.

NE 5th Ave.

South
Beach
Park

W. Palmetto Park Rd.

W. Camino Real

Lake
Boca
Raton

ATLANTIC OCEAN

Barwick Rd.

Military Trail

FLORIDA
Delray Beach
Boca Raton
Fort Lauderdale
Miami

319

hall, a laboratory classroom, and exciting wet forest and conservation exhibits. Best part about the addition is the elevated boardwalk over a swamp featuring two trails and an observation tower from which a keen eye can view the abundant plant and animal life, including osprey, woodpeckers, butterflies (including the park's namesake S. Ruddy Daggerwing), endangered wood storks, alligators, and a wide variety of bromeliads. Gator fans won't want to miss the alligator feedings every Wednesday and Saturday at 3:15 p.m.

South County Regional Park, 11200 Park Access Rd., Boca Raton. © **561/488-9953.** Free admission. Wed–Fri 1–4:30pm; Sat 10am–4:30pm. Call for tour and activity schedule.

Gumbo Limbo Environmental Complex ★★★ If manicured lawns and golf courses aren't your idea of communing with nature, then head to Gumbo Limbo. Named for an indigenous hardwood tree, the 20-acre complex protects one of the few surviving coastal hammocks, or forest islands, in South Florida. Walk through the hammock on a half-mile-long boardwalk that ends at a 40-foot observation tower, from which you can see the Atlantic Ocean, the Intracoastal Waterway, and much of Boca Raton. From mid-April to September, sea turtles come ashore here to lay eggs.

1801 N. Ocean Blvd. (on A1A btw. Spanish River Blvd. and Palmetto Park Rd.), Boca Raton. www.gumbolimbo.org. © **561/338-1473.** Free admission ($5 donation suggested). Mon–Sat 9am–4pm; Sun noon–4pm.

Morikami Museum and Japanese Gardens ★★★ PARK/GARDEN Slip off your shoes and enter a serene Japanese garden that dates from 1905, when an entrepreneurial farmer, Jo Sakai, came to Boca Raton to build a tropical agricultural community. The Yamato Colony, as it was known, was short-lived; by the 1920s, only one tenacious colonist remained: George Sukeji Morikami. But Morikami was quite successful, eventually running one of the largest pineapple plantations in the area. The 200-acre Morikami Museum and Japanese Gardens, which opened to the public in 1977, was Morikami's gift to Palm Beach County and the state of Florida. A stroll through the garden is almost a mile long. An artificial waterfall that cascades into a koi- and carp-filled moat; a small rock garden for meditation; and a large bonsai collection with miniature maple, buttonwood, juniper, and Australian pine trees are all worth contemplation. There's also a cafe with an Asian-inspired menu if you want to stay for lunch.

4000 Morikami Park Rd., Delray Beach. www.morikami.org. © **561/495-0233.** Museum $13 adults, $12 seniors, $8 children 6–17. Museum and gardens Tues–Sun 10am–5pm. Closed major holidays.

OUTDOOR ACTIVITIES

GOLF This area has plenty of good courses. The best ones that are not in a gated community are **Boca Raton Resort & Club** (p. 326) and the **Inn at Ocean Breeze Golf and Country Club,** formerly known as the Inn at Boca Teeca. Another great place to swing clubs is at the **Deer Creek Golf Club,** 2801 Country Club Blvd., Deerfield Beach (www.deercreekflorida.com; © **954/421-5550**), which also features a 300-plus-yard driving range and practice facility. Rates at the Deer Creek Golf Club are seasonal and range from $35 to $95. However, from May to October or November, about a dozen private courses open their greens to visitors staying in Palm Beach County hotels. This "Golf-A-Round" program is free or severely discounted (carts are additional), and reservations can be made through most major hotels. Ask at your hotel or contact the **Palm Beach County Convention and Visitors Bureau** (© **561/471-3395**) for information on which clubs are available for play.

The **Boca Raton Municipal Golf Course,** 8111 Golf Course Rd. (✆ **561/483-6100**), is the area's best public golf course. Renovated in 2010, there's an 18-hole, par-72 course covering approximately 6,200 yards, as well as a 9-hole, par-30 course. Facilities include a snack bar and a pro shop where clubs can be rented. Greens, tees, bunkers, landscaping, bathrooms, and locker rooms have been freshly renovated. Greens fees range from $15 to $60. Ask about special summer discounts.

SCUBA DIVING & SNORKELING **Moray Bend,** a 58-foot dive spot about ¾ mile off Boca Inlet, is the area's most popular. It's home to three moray eels that are used to being fed by scuba divers. The reef is accessible by boat from **Force E Dive Center,** 877 E. Palmetto Park Rd., Boca Raton (www.force-e.com; ✆ **561/368-0555**). Phone for dive times. Dives cost $55 to $70 per person.

Red Reef Park, 1400 N. Ocean Park Blvd. (✆ **561-393-7974**), a 67-acre oceanfront park in Boca Raton, has good swimming and year-round lifeguard protection. There's snorkeling around the shallow rocks and reefs that lie just off the beach. The park has restrooms and a picnic area with grills. Located a half-mile north of Palmetto Park Road, it's open daily from 8am to 10pm. The cost is $16 per car Monday through Friday, $18 on Saturday and Sunday; walkers and bikers get in free.

TENNIS The snazzy **Delray Beach Tennis Center,** 201 W. Atlantic Ave. (www.delraytennis.com; ✆ **561/243-7360**), has 14 lighted clay courts and 5 hard courts available by the hour. Phone for rates and reservations.

The 17 public lighted hard courts at **Patch Reef Park,** 2000 NW 51st St. (www.patchreefpark.org; ✆ **561/367-7090**), are available by reservation. The fee for nonresident adults is $5.75 per person per 1½ hours in winter and $4.50 in summer, and for nonresident juniors 17 and under it's $4.50 in winter and $3.25 in the summer. Courts are available Monday through Saturday from 7:30am to 10pm, and Sunday from 7:30am to dusk; call ahead to see if a court is available. To reach the park from I-95, exit at Yamato Road West and continue past Military Trail to the park.

Where to Eat

Nightlife in Boca means going out to a restaurant. But who cares? This is some of the best dining in South Florida. Delray Beach, on the other hand, has an excellent cuisine and nightlife scene. Best of both worlds.

VERY EXPENSIVE

Kathy's Gazebo Cafe ★★★ CONTINENTAL An elegant, old-school (with an equally old—er, seasoned—crowd) Continental restaurant with chandeliers and white linen tablecloths, Kathy's white-glove restaurant is an ideal spot for special occasions or culinary nostalgia. The food is superb—the Dover sole is flown in from Holland and prepared with nothing fancier than an almandine or meunière sauce; chateaubriand is also spectacular and, in a city smitten by plain ol' steak and sushi, it's a perfect throwback to simpler, delicious days. Fresh homemade pastries and peach Melba are among the desserts. While jackets aren't commonly required at restaurants in South Florida, you'll want to wear one here just to fit in with the dapper moneyed types who frequent the place.

4199 N. Federal Hwy., Boca Raton. www.kathysgazebo.com. ✆ **561/395-6033.** Reservations required. Main courses $20–$45. AE, MC, V. Daily 5:30–10pm.

Morimoto Sushi Bar ★★★ SUSHI A tiny outpost of Iron Chef Masaharu Morimoto's original Philly sushi spot, Morimoto is one of the hottest tickets in Boca, and South Florida in general. Thing is, they say it's only open to guests staying at the resort. We have heard otherwise. So, if you can snag a reservation at this tiny, ultra-modern eatery, take it, even if it's at the unfashionably early hour of, say, 5pm. Don't come expecting a huge selection of dishes, either. It's all about the sushi and sashimi, and if you're a true fan of both, you won't hesitate to order the Omakase Tasting Menu in which the skilled sushi chef trained by the Iron Chef himself will choose for you. Fans of tuna will be thrilled to indulge in a variety of grades of tuna, many rare in South Florida, including *otoro, maguro,* and *chutoro.* In addition to the sushi, there's also excellent rock shrimp tempura, which many say is better than Nobu's, and a sensational seared Kobe beef with abalone mushrooms.

501 E. Camino Real (in the Boca Raton Resort), Boca Raton. www.bocaresort.com. ✆ **561/447-3640.** Sushi/sashimi $3–$9 per piece; *maki* $6–$14; Omakase Tasting Menu $50 and $75 per person. AE, MC, V. Daily noon–3pm and 5–10pm.

EXPENSIVE

Ke'e Grill ★★ SEAFOOD Owners Jim and Debbie Taube respect the seafood they serve, some of the freshest in all of South Florida, by leaving off the bells, whistles, and soppy sauces found on so many fish dishes these days. The beautiful, bustling dining room overlooks a tropical garden. Appetizers include a sensational blue crab cake or perfectly crispy, fried calamari with dipping sauce that's delicious but not even necessary. For entrees, choose from a papaya, roasted garlic, and sweet chili–glazed Chilean sea bass, which makes for a flawless union. Sautéed yellowtail snapper, sautéed yellowfin tuna, or crab cakes all come with two sides: a choice of pasta, rice, veggies, or potato. The house specialty, the Ke'e Grill Cioppino, is a study in fresh seafood—specifically shrimp, scallops, grouper, clams, mussels, and lobster—with pearl pasta in a spicy seafood broth, kind of an all-in-one explanation of why this is one of South Florida's finest seafood spots. It is also one of Boca's most bustling early-bird spots, so from 5 until 6pm go at your own risk.

17940 N. Military Trail, Boca Raton. ✆ **561/995-5044.** Reservations strongly suggested. Main courses $20–$28. AE, DC, DISC, MC, V. Daily 5–9:30pm.

Sundy House Restaurant ★★ FLORIBBEAN This restaurant is a stunning place that combines elegant indoor dining and lush tropical outdoor settings with a gastronomic wizardry of fresh fruits, vegetables, and spices grown on the Sundy House's 5-acre farm. Each dish is prepared with palpable precision. Consider the following: pan-roasted Chilean sea bass with garlic broccolini, balsamic marinated plum tomatoes, and truffled sweet pea and lobster risotto, or the mojo-seared salmon with Manchego cheese corn *arepa,* sweet bell peppers, hearts of palm, watercress salad, and papaya-chili vinaigrette. For a heartier, not quintessentially South Floridian dish, try the wild-boar tenderloin with parsnip purée, pickled apple jam, pine nuts, grain mustard gastrique, and brussel sprout sauté. Save room for dessert, including a decadent vanilla-bean crème brûlée and mandarin-orange chocolate torte. A decadent Sunday-brunch buffet makes the day before you return to work infinitely more bearable. On the negative side, the service here can be surly and spotty.

In the Sundy House, 106 S. Swinton Ave., Delray Beach. www.sundyhouse.com. ✆ **561/272-5678.** Reservations essential. Main courses $26–$38. AE, DC, DISC, MC, V. Tues–Thurs 6–9pm; Fri–Sat 6–10pm; Sun brunch 10:30am–2:30pm. Also Nov–May daily 11:30am–2:30pm.

32 East ★★ NEW AMERICAN The menu changes daily at this popular people-watching outpost of tasty, contemporary American food with a focus on local, seasonal ingredients. Standouts include the sauté of Gulf Coast grouper with Yukon gold potatoes on creamed butternut squash and bacon; brine-cured pork chop with pancetta-braised escarole and cinnamon-spiced mashed yams with autumn fruits brown butter; and local mahimahi on potato purée with sweet corn and green beans in a sherry-mushroom sauce. The buzzing scene makes 32 East a popular hangout for the cocktail set, and while the menu may be sophisticated, the vibe is pure neighborhood bistro, casual and comfortable with two levels of seating—the upper dining room provides better views, while the lower one is obviously in the middle of the action. But we prefer the outdoor seating, a prime vantage point for catching the action on Atlantic Avenue.

32 E. Atlantic Ave., Delray Beach. www.32east.com. ℂ **561/276-7868.** Reservations recommended. Main courses $21–$38. AE, DC, MC, V. Sun–Thurs 5:30–10pm; Fri–Sat 5:30–11pm. Bar until 2am.

MODERATE

English Tap & Beer Garden ★ GASTROPUB   Tucked away in one of Boca's signature, lushly landscaped shopping plazas, celebrity chef Todd English's casual restaurant and bar (it's not really a beer garden unless you consider a few outdoor tables surrounded by trees), is great for, well, beer, and a quick, uncomplicated meal to go with that beer. Among other things on the menu, shepherd's pie, "Bangers and Mashed," sandwiches, flatbreads, pastas, steaks, and, our guilty pleasure, a pricey ($11) but really good gourmet 2-foot-long hot dog. A daily happy hour from 4 to 7pm attracts a lively bar crowd.

5050 Town Center Circle, Boca Raton. www.theenglishtap.com. ℂ **561/544-8000.** Reservations not required. Entrees $9–$28. AE, DC, MC, V. Mon–Sun 11:30am–4:30pm and 5:30pm–2am.

The Office ★ AMERICAN   A gastropub whose cuisine is described as "modern American casual fare with style," the Office is one of those places in which you don't mind doing overtime. Cuisine features an emphasis on local growers, products, and seafood. Think grass-fed pork honey-braised ribs with fennel pollen and celery-root apple slaw; burgers like the Florida Blue Crab Burger; salads; sandwiches; and bar snacks. If you're not in the mood for a full-blown entree, I highly recommend the Office Supplies, a fantastic menu of small plates including truffled deviled eggs, red chile–braised pork soft tacos, and, if you can justify spending $9 for it, heirloom black-kernel popcorn sprinkled with black truffle and Black Sea salt. Decor is reminiscent of an industrial chic, yet cozy, library. Oh, and there's a selection of 35 to 40 beers.

210 E. Atlantic Ave., Delray Beach. www.theofficedelray.com. ℂ **561/276-3600.** Reservations recommended. Entrees $14–$28. AE, DC, MC, V. Daily 11am–11pm.

INEXPENSIVE

Baja Cafe ★ MEXICAN   A jeans-and-T-shirt kind of place with wooden tables, Baja Cafe serves fantastic Mexican food at even better prices. Although the salsa borders on somewhat sweet, they do have the hottest sauces; if you like spicy, they will be happy to slap plenty on your meal if you request it. Dishes have kitschy names like Hellfire and Damnation Enchiladas and Chimichanga Cha Cha Cha, but when it comes to flavor, they aren't kidding. This place is located right by the Florida East Coast Railway tracks, so don't be surprised if you feel a little rattling. Live music and entertainment make this place a hot spot for an unpretentious crowd. A second location is at 1310 S. Federal Hwy. in Deerfield Beach (ℂ **954/596-1305**).

201 NW 1st Ave., Boca Raton. www.bajacafeboca.com. ℂ **561/394-5449.** Reservations not accepted. Main courses $10–$16. No credit cards. Mon–Thurs 11:30am–10pm; Fri–Sat 11:30am–11pm; Sun 5–10pm.

The Tin Muffin Cafe ★ BAKERY/SANDWICH SHOP   Popular with the downtown lunch crowd, this excellent storefront bakery keeps folks lining up for big sandwiches on fresh bread, plus muffins, quiches, and good homemade soups such as split pea or lentil. The curried-chicken sandwich is stuffed with chunks of white meat doused in a creamy curry dressing and fruit. There are a few cafe tables inside and even one outside on a tiny patio. Be warned, however, that service is (forgivably) slow and parking is a nightmare. Try looking for a spot a few blocks away at a meter.

364 E. Palmetto Park Rd. (btw. Federal Hwy. and the Intracoastal Bridge), Boca Raton. ✆ **561/392-9446.** Sandwiches and salads $7–$14. No credit cards. Mon–Fri 11am–5pm; Sat 11am–4pm.

Tom's Place for Ribs ★★ 🍖 BARBECUE   There are two important factors in a successful barbecue: the cooking and the sauce. Tom and Helen Wright's no-nonsense shack wins on both counts, offering flawlessly grilled meats paired with well-spiced sauces. Beef, chicken, pork, and fish are served soul food style, with corn bread and your choice of sides such as rice with gravy, collard greens, black-eyed peas, coleslaw, or mashed potatoes.

400 E. Boynton Beach Blvd., Boynton Beach. www.tomsplaceforribs.com. ✆ **561/843-7487.** Reservations not accepted. Main courses $8.25–$23; sandwiches $9–$10. AE, MC, V. Tues–Thurs 11:30am–10:30pm; Fri 11:30am–10pm; Sat noon–10pm.

Shopping

Even if you don't plan to buy anything, a trip to Boca Raton's **Mizner Park** is essential for capturing the essence of the city. Mizner is the place to see and be seen, where Rolls-Royces, Maseratis, and Ferraris are parked curbside, freshly coiffed women sit amid shopping bags at outdoor cafes, and young movers and shakers chat on their constantly buzzing cellphones. Beyond the human scenery, however, Mizner Park is scenic in its own right, with beautiful landscaping. It's really an outdoor mall, with 45 specialty shops, seven good restaurants, and a multiplex. Each shop front faces a grassy island with gazebos, potted plants, and garden benches. Mizner Park is on Federal Highway, between Palmetto Park and Glades roads (✆ **561/362-0606**).

Boca's **Town Center Mall,** on the south side of Glades Road, just west of I-95, has several major department stores, including Nordstrom, Neiman Marcus, Bloomingdale's, Macy's, and Saks Fifth Avenue. Add hundreds of specialty shops, an extensive food court, and a range of other restaurants, and you have the area's most comprehensive shopping center.

On Delray Beach's Atlantic Avenue, especially east of Swinton Avenue, you'll find a few antiques shops, clothing stores, and galleries shaded by palm trees and colorful awnings. Pick up the *Downtown Delray Beach* map and guide at almost any store on this strip, or call ✆ **561/278-0424** for information.

Entertainment & Nightlife

THE BAR, CLUB & MUSIC SCENE

Atlantic Avenue in Delray Beach has finally gotten quite hip to nightlife and is now lined with sleek and chic restaurants, lounges, and bars that attract the Palm Beach County "in crowd," along with a few random patrons such as New Age musician Yanni, who has a house nearby. Although it's hardly South Beach or Fort Lauderdale's Las Olas and Riverfront (which, for those who frequent here, is a good thing), Atlantic Avenue holds its own as far as a vibrant nightlife is concerned. In Boca Raton, **Mizner Park** is the nucleus of nightlife, with restaurants masking themselves as nightclubs or, at the very least, sceney bars.

Boston's on the Beach This is a family restaurant with a somewhat lively bar scene. It's a good choice for post-sunbathing, with supercasual happy hours Monday through Friday from 4 to 8pm and live reggae on Monday. With two decks overlooking the ocean, Boston's is an ideal place to mellow out and take in the scenery. It also happens to be South Florida's unofficial New England professional sports team hot spot, from Celtics to Bruins and everything in between. Fans of all teams, however, are welcome even if they may be outnumbered. It's open daily from 7am to 2am. 40 S. Ocean Blvd., Delray Beach. www.bostonsonthebeach.com. ✆ **561/278-3364.**

Dada Dada is a nocturnal outpost of food, drink, music, art, culture, and history. In other words, here you can expect to find neobohemian, arty types lingering in their dark glasses and berets on one of the living room's cozy couches, listening to music, poetry, or dissertations on life. Live music, great food, a bar, an outdoor patio area, and a very eclectic crowd make Dada the coolest hangout in Delray. It's open daily from 5:30pm to 2am. 52 N. Swinton Ave., Delray Beach. www.sub-culture.org/dada/home-dada. ✆ **561/330-DADA (3232).**

Delux Believe it or not, this red-hued dance club on Atlantic Avenue is cooler than some of South Beach's big-shot clubs, thanks to a soundtrack of sexy house music, bedlike seating, and a beautiful crowd in which someone as striking as past patron Gwen Stefani can actually blend in without being noticed. It's open Wednesday through Sunday from 7pm to 2am. 16 E. Atlantic Ave., Delray Beach. www.sub-culture.org/delux/home-delux. ✆ **561/279-4792.**

Dubliner A bustling, authentic Irish pub that's popular with the young professional set, Mizner Park's Dubliner features traditional pub fare; pints and pints of Guinness; an impressive selection of beers on tap; assorted spirits; flatscreen TVs for soccer, rugby, and American sporting events; and live music and DJs. It's open 4pm to 2am daily. 435 Plaza Real, Boca Raton. www.dublinerboca.com. ✆ **561/620-2540.**

Falcon House A cozy wine and tapas bar also known as 888 Lounge on a side street off the Atlantic Avenue bustle, Falcon House is reminiscent of a bar you'd find in Napa Valley, with an impressive selection of wine and a hip, well-heeled crowd. It's a haven for those who are over the whole hip-hop scene on Atlantic Avenue. It's open Monday through Saturday from 5pm to 2am. 116 NE 6th Ave., Delray Beach. www.the falconhouse.com. ✆ **561/243-9499.**

THE PERFORMING ARTS

For details on upcoming events, check the *Boca News* or the *Sun-Sentinel,* or call the **Palm Beach County Cultural Council** information line at ✆ **800/882-ARTS** (2787). During business hours, a staffer can give details on current performances. After hours, a recorded message describes the week's events.

For live concerts, featuring everyone from Dolly Parton and Kelly Clarkson to Weird Al Yankovic, the **Count de Hoernle Amphitheater at the Schmidt Family Centre for the Arts** in Mizner Park (✆ **866/571-ARTS** [2787]) is the place to see them in an open-air format, under the stars and, at times, rain. If you're not that big a fan, you'll still hear the concerts from Mizner Park!

Boca's best theater company is the **Caldwell Theatre,** and it's worth checking out. Located in a strip shopping center at 7873 N. Federal Hwy., this Equity showcase does well-known dramas, comedies, classics, off-Broadway hits, and new works throughout the year. Ticket prices are reasonable—usually $38 to $45. Full-time students with ID will be especially interested in the little-advertised student rush:

When available, tickets are sold for $5 if you arrive at least an hour early. Go to www.caldwelltheatre.com or call ℂ **561/241-7432** for details.

Where to Stay

A number of national chain hotels worth considering include the moderately priced **Holiday Inn Highland Beach Oceanside,** 2809 S. Ocean Blvd., on A1A, southeast of Linton Boulevard (www.highlandbeachholidayinn.com; ℂ **800/234-6835** or 561/278-6241). Although you won't find rows of cheap hotels as in Fort Lauderdale and Hollywood, a handful of mom-and-pop motels have survived along A1A between the towering condominiums of Delray Beach. Look along the beach just south of Atlantic Boulevard. The **Delray Beach Marriott,** 10 N. Ocean Blvd. (www.marriott delraybeach.com; ℂ **561/274-3200**), is a popular but expensive stay, directly across from the beach with pool and spa. Rates range from $399 during high season to a lot lower in the summer.

Even more economical options can be found in Deerfield Beach, Boca's neighbor, south of the county line. A number of beachfront efficiencies offer great deals, even in the winter months. Try the **Panther Motel and Apartments,** 715 S. A1A (http://panthermotel.com; ℂ **954/427-0700**), a clean and convenient motel with rates starting as low as $49 (in season, you may have to book for a week at a time; rates then run $465–$650).

VERY EXPENSIVE

Boca Raton Resort & Club ★★ ☺   This landmark resort owned by Waldorf Astoria is a sprawling 350-acre collection of oddly matched buildings: the original Cloister (which is undergoing a long, drawn-out renovation); the drab pink 27-story Tower; the renovated and fantastically modern Beach Club and Pool Oasis, accessible by water shuttle or bus and featuring three redesigned pools, oceanfront bar, beach access, cabana, modern rooms, and sunning terraces; and Yacht Club, a Venetian-style wing of 112 luxury rooms and suites. Fans of the old-school resort should feel right at home as Old World blends beautifully with New World, modern twists. Everything at this resort, which straddles the Intracoastal, is at your fingertips, but may sometimes require some effort to reach. Thankfully, the resort provides transportation shuttles every 10 minutes. Amenities include the grand Spa Palazzo, two 18-hole championship golf courses, a $10-million tennis and fitness center, a 32-slip marina, and a private beach with watersports equipment. The resort's also foodie heaven, with a choice of 12 places to dine, including **Morimoto Sushi Bar** (p. 321), **Cielo, 501 East,** and a bustling branch of NYC's venerable **Serendipity** ice-cream parlor.

501 E. Camino Real (P.O. Box 5025), Boca Raton, FL 33432. www.bocaresort.com. ℂ **888/495-BOCA** (2622) or 561/447-3000. Fax 561/447-3183. 1,047 units. Winter $259–$760 double; off season $169–$329 double. Seasonal packages available. AE, DC, DISC, MC, V. From I-95 N., exit onto Palmetto Park Rd. E. Turn right onto Federal Hwy. (U.S. 1), then left onto Camino Real. **Amenities:** 12 restaurants; 5 bars; extensive children's programs; concierge; 3 fitness centers; 2 18-hole championship golf courses; 7 pools; room service; spa; 30 hydrogrid tennis courts; watersports equipment/rentals. *In room:* A/C, TV, hair dryer, minibar.

The Seagate Hotel & Spa ★★★   Located just 1 block from the beach on Delray's bustling East Atlantic Avenue, the Seagate Hotel & Spa offers you the best of the beach and the city. The best part about the hotel besides its location is the nearby Seagate Beach Club, located less than a mile from the hotel and offering casual and fine dining with gorgeous coastal views, access to watersports equipment rentals, an outdoor swimming pool, and free transportation to and from the hotel. Decor is beachy chic, featuring a 2,500-gallon aquarium in the main lobby and rooms boasting upscale designer furnishings with Egyptian-cotton linens and all the stylish, tranquil, neutral tones you'd find in, say, Martha Stewart's beach house. The pool on the actual hotel property is pretty large and tropically landscaped. An on-site restaurant, the **Atlantic Grille,** offers indoor and terrace seating and seafood, pasta, and steak dishes. The world-class 8,000-square-foot spa has seven treatment rooms and signature treatments, including the Hot Shell Massage.

1000 E. Atlantic Ave., Delray Beach, FL 33483. www.theseagatehotel.com. ⓒ **877/57-SEAGATE** (577-3242) or 561/665-4800. Fax 561/665-4801. 154 units. Winter $339–$419 double, suites $599– $2,500; off season $159–$239 double; suites $329–$850. AE, DC, MC, V. **Amenities:** Restaurant; bar; pool; room service; watersports; free Wi-Fi in public areas. *In room:* A/C, TV/DVD, hair dryer, high-speed Internet, MP3 docking station.

Sundy House ★★★   The oldest residence in Delray Beach, Sundy House is a bona fide 1902 Revival-style home that has been restored to its Victorian glory—on the outside, at least. Inside, the four one- and two-bedroom apartments are in a style best described as Caribbean funky or tropical chic, adorned in brilliant colors and outfitted with state-of-the-art electronics, full modern kitchens, and laundry facilities. Six guest rooms known as the Stables are equestrian chic, with rustic appointments in dark woods. While the rooms here are outstanding, it's the surrounding property that garners the most oohs and aahs. Set on an acre of lush gardens, the Sundy House is surrounded by more than 500 species of exotic plants, streams, and parrots, making an escape here seem more Hawaii than Florida. You can even swim with fish in the hotel's swimming pond! The on-site restaurant features exquisite New Florida cuisine, often using fresh fruits and herbs straight from Sundy House's botanical Taru Gardens.

106 S. Swinton Ave., Delray Beach, FL 33444. www.sundyhouse.com. ⓒ **877/439-9601** or 561/272-5678. Fax 561/272-1115. 11 units. Winter $219–$549 1- or 2-bedroom or cottage; off season $169–$499 1- or 2-bedroom or cottage. AE, DC, DISC, MC, V. **Amenities:** Restaurant; bar; swimming pond; limited room service. *In room:* A/C, TV/DVD, CD player, hair dryer, kitchen.

EXPENSIVE

Crane's BeachHouse ★★   If you can't afford your own South Florida beach house—and why bother with all the maintenance, anyway?—Crane's BeachHouse, meticulously run and maintained by husband and wife Michael and Cheryl Crane, is a haven away from home, located just 1 block from the beach and right in the middle of historic Delray Beach. The main draws here are the whimsical, tropical suites, in which every piece of furniture and bric-a-brac is completely original and often crafted by local artists. Although each unit has its own theme—Hawaii, Amazon, Anacapri, and Capetown, for instance—the beds are all the same, in that they are downright heavenly. Lush gardens, a Tiki bar, and a pool leave you with little reason to flee the premises, but when you do, you'll want to return as quickly as possible.

82 Gleason St., Delray Beach, FL 33483. www.cranesbeachhouse.com. ⓒ **866/372-7263** or 561/278-1700. Fax 561/278-7826. 27 units. Winter $189–$239 double, $289–$499 suite; off season $139–$169 double, $199–$299 suite. AE, DC, DISC, MC, V. Free parking. **Amenities:** 2 small outdoor pools. *In room:* A/C, TV/VCR, hair dryer, Internet access, full kitchen, minibar.

PALM BEACH ★★ & WEST PALM BEACH ★

65 miles N of Miami; 193 miles E of Tampa; 45 miles N of Fort Lauderdale

For generations, Palm Beach has been the traditional winter home of American aristocracy—the Kennedys, Rockefellers, and Trumps, among others, have all fled northern climes for this slice of paradise. Beyond the upscale resorts that cater to such a crowd, Palm Beach holds some surprises, including the world-class Norton Museum of Art, top-notch birding, and the sparkling Intracoastal Waterway.

Beaches   Public beaches are a rare commodity in Palm Beach. **Midtown Beach** is a notable exception, a golden island of undeveloped strand in a sea of glitz and glamour. Groomed beach sand, picnic facilities, and outdoor recreation dominate at **Phipps Ocean Park,** another public beach especially popular with families.

Things to Do   Wherever there is an abundance of sun, sand, and sightseers, there is **golf,** and Palm Beach is no exception. Downtown, the **Norton Museum of Art** displays works by the world's most recognizable names: O'Keeffe, Pollock, Monet, Renoir, and Picasso.

Eating & Drinking   Leave the Bermuda shorts behind in favor of crisply ironed linen for swanky, oceanfront dining in Palm Beach. Overlook the surf dining on platters of freshly caught **seafood,** from Florida lobster to snapper, at beachside dining rooms. **Southern barbecue** reminds visitors that Florida *is* part of the South.

Nightlife & Entertainment   Artists' lofts, sidewalk cafes, bars, restaurants, and galleries dot **Clematis Street,** the pumping heart of Palm Beach nightlife. On weekends, yuppies mingle with stylish Europeans and disheveled artists **sipping tropical cocktails** at sidewalk tables or **dancing** to electronic mixes at youthful bars. The moneyed set in Palm Beach is most likely found sipping high-end ports and brandies at **oceanfront hotel bars.**

Essentials

GETTING THERE   If you're driving up or down the Florida coast, you'll probably reach the Palm Beach area by way of I-95. Exit at Belvedere Road or Okeechobee Boulevard, and head east to reach the most central part of Palm Beach.

Visitors on their way to or from Orlando or Miami should take the Florida Turnpike, a toll road with a speed limit of 65 mph. Tolls are pricey, though; you may pay upwards of $9 from Orlando and $4 from Miami. Those without a Florida Sunpass will pay 25 cents more at each toll. If you're coming from Florida's west coast, you can take either S.R. 70, which runs north of Lake Okeechobee to Fort Pierce, or S.R. 80, which runs south of the lake to Palm Beach.

All major airlines fly to the **Palm Beach International Airport,** at Congress Avenue and Belvedere Road (© **561/471-7400**). **Amtrak** (www.amtrak.com; © **800/USA-RAIL** [872-7245]) has a terminal in West Palm Beach, at 201 S. Tamarind Ave. (© **561/832-6169**).

GETTING AROUND   Although a car is almost a necessity in this area, a recently revamped public transportation system is extremely convenient for getting to some attractions in both West Palm and Palm Beach. **Palm Tran** (www.palmtran.org) covers 32 routes with more than 140 buses. The fare is $1.50 for adults, and 75¢ for

Palm Beach & West Palm Beach

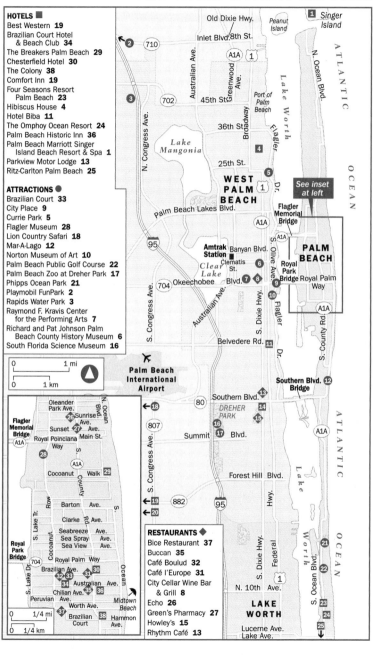

children 3 to 18, seniors, and riders with disabilities. Free route maps are available by calling ✆ **561/233-4BUS** (4287). Information operators are available Monday through Saturday from 6am to 7pm.

In downtown West Palm, free shuttles from City Place to Clematis Street operate Sunday through Wednesday from 11am until 9pm, and Thursday through Saturday 11am until 11pm. Allegedly, the shuttles come every 5 minutes, but count on them taking longer. Look for the bubble gum–pink minibuses throughout downtown. Call ✆ **561/833-8873** for details.

VISITOR INFORMATION The **Palm Beach County Convention and Visitors Bureau,** 1555 Palm Beach Lakes Blvd., Ste. 204, West Palm Beach, FL 33401 (www.palmbeachfl.com; ✆ **800/554-PALM** [7256] or 561/471-3995), distributes an informative brochure and answers questions about visiting the Palm Beaches. Ask for a map as well as a copy of the *Arts and Attractions Calendar,* a day-to-day guide to art, music, stage, and other events in the county.

Exploring Palm Beach & West Palm Beach
HITTING THE BEACH

Public beaches are a rare commodity in Palm Beach. Most of the island's best beaches are fronted by private estates and inaccessible to the general public. However, there are a few notable exceptions, including **Midtown Beach,** east of Worth Avenue, on Ocean Boulevard between Royal Palm Way and Gulfstream Road, which boasts more than 100 feet of undeveloped sand. This newly widened coast is now a centerpiece and a natural oasis in a town dominated by commercial glitz. There are no restrooms or concessions here, though a lifeguard is on duty until sundown. A popular hangout for locals lies about 1½ miles north of here, near Dunbar Street; they prefer it to Midtown Beach because of the relaxed atmosphere. Parking is available at meters along A1A. At the south end of Palm Beach, there's a less popular but better-equipped beach at **Phipps Ocean Park.** On Ocean Boulevard, between the Southern Boulevard and Lake Avenue causeways, there's a lively public beach encompassing more than 1,300 feet of groomed oceanfront. With picnic and recreation areas and plenty of parking, the area is especially good for families.

The only state park in Palm Beach County, **MacArthur Beach** (www.macarthur beach.org; ✆ **561/624-6950**) is as pristine as it gets, with two miles of magnificent beach as well as a nature center, nature trails, kayak rentals, and more.

SEEING THE SIGHTS

Flagler Museum ★★★ HISTORIC HOME The Gilded Age is preserved in this luxurious mansion commissioned by Standard Oil tycoon Henry Flagler as a wedding present to his third wife. Whitehall, also known as the Taj Mahal of North America, is a classic Edwardian-style mansion containing 55 rooms, including a Louis XIV music room and art gallery, a Louis XV ballroom, and 14 guest suites outfitted with original antique European furnishings. Out back, you can climb aboard the *Rambler,* Mr. Flagler's private restored railroad car. Allow at least 1½ hours to tour the stunning grounds and interior. Group tours are available, but for the most part, this is a self-guided museum.

1 Whitehall Way (at Cocoanut Row and Whitehall Way), Palm Beach. www.flaglermuseum.us. ✆ **561/655-2833.** Admission $18 adults, $10 youth 13–18, $3 children 6–12. Tues–Sat 10am–5pm; Sun noon–5pm.

Lion Country Safari ★★ ☺ SAFARI   More than 1,300 animals on this 500-acre preserve (the nation's first cageless drive-through safari) are divided into their indigenous regions, from the East African preserve of the Serengeti to the American West. Elephants, lions, wildebeest, ostriches, American bison, buffalo, watusi, pink flamingos, and many other unusual species roam the preserve. When we visited, most of the lions were asleep; when awake, they travel freely throughout the cageless grassy landscape. In fact, you're the one who's confined in your own car without an escort (no convertibles allowed). You're given a detailed pamphlet with photos and descriptions, and are instructed to obey the 15 mph speed limit—unless you see the rhinos charge (a rare occasion), in which case you're encouraged to floor it. Driving the loop takes slightly more than an hour, though you could make a day of just watching the chimpanzees play on their secluded islands. Included in the admission is Safari World, an amusement park with paddleboats, a carousel, miniature golf, and a baby animal nursery. Picnics are encouraged, and camping is available. The best time to go is late afternoon, right before the park closes; it's much cooler then, so the lions are more active.

Southern Blvd. W. at S.R. 80, West Palm Beach. www.lioncountrysafari.com. © **561/793-1084**, or 561/793-9797 for camping reservations. Admission $28 adults, $25 seniors, $21 children 3–9. Van rental $10–$18 per 90 min. Parking $6. Daily 9:30am–5:30pm (last vehicle admitted at 4:30pm). From I-95, exit on Southern Blvd. Go west for about 18 miles.

Norton Museum of Art ★★★ ART MUSEUM   The Norton is world famous for its prestigious permanent collection and top temporary exhibitions. The museum's major collections are divided geographically. The American galleries contain major works by Hopper, O'Keeffe, and Pollock. The French collection contains Impressionist and post-Impressionist paintings by Cézanne, Degas, Gauguin, Matisse, Monet, Picasso, Pissarro, and Renoir. The Chinese collection contains more than 200 bronzes, jades, and ceramics, as well as monumental Buddhist sculptures. Allow about 2 hours to see this museum, depending on your level of interest. On the second Thursday of every month from 5 to 9pm, it's Art After Dark, featuring music, film, special tours with curators and docents, hands-on art activities, a cash bar, and menu options from Café 1451 at the Norton. General admission applies, but it's worth it.

Unreal Estate

No trip to Palm Beach is complete without at least a glimpse of **Mar-A-Lago,** the stately residence of Donald Trump, the 21st century's answer to Jay Gatsby. In 1985, Trump purchased the estate of cereal heiress Marjorie Merriweather Post for a meager $8 million (for a fully furnished beachfront property of this stature, it was a relative bargain), to the great consternation of locals, who feared that he would turn the place into a casino. Instead, Trump, who sometimes resides in a portion of the palace, opened the house to the public—for a price, of course—as a tony country club (membership fee: $100,000). A long-running, unconfirmed rumor has it that Trump is selling the place. In the meantime, he continues to make his presence loudly known in Palm Beach.

While there are currently no tours open to the public, you can glimpse the gorgeous manse as you cross the bridge from West Palm Beach into Palm Beach. It's located at 1100 S. Ocean Blvd., Palm Beach.

1451 S. Olive Ave., West Palm Beach. www.norton.org. ℂ **561/832-5196.** Fax 561/659-4689. Admission $12 adults, $5 ages 13–21. Tues–Wed and Fri 10am–5pm; Thurs 10am–9pm; Sun 11am–5pm. Take I-95 to exit 52 (Okeechobee Blvd. E.). Travel east on Okeechobee to Dixie Hwy., then south ½ mile to the Norton. Access parking through entrances on Dixie Hwy. and S. Olive Ave.

Palm Beach Zoo at Dreher Park ★ ZOO

If you want animals, go to Lion Country Safari (above). Unlike big-city zoos, this intimate 23-acre attraction is more like a stroll in the park than an all-day excursion. It features more than 1,400 animals representing more than 100 different species. The zoo also features a colorful wildlife carousel, an interactive water-play fountain, a full-service restaurant, and daily performances of the "Wings Over Water" bird show and the "Wild Things" stage show. The zoo also offers guests the opportunity to view more than 50 animal encounters, keeper talks, or training sessions per week. The Cornell Tropics of the Americas exhibit showcases both the animals and the native culture found in the Central and South American regions. Jaguars, bush dogs, Baird's tapirs, and giant anteaters are just a few of the animals that make their home in this 3-acre re-creation of a Central and South American rain forest. Other animal highlights include Malayan tiger, Florida panther, Queensland koala, Komodo dragon, black bear, river otter, and the Florida Reptile House. Allow at least 2 hours to see all of the sights here. New residents at the zoo: three male Malayan tiger cubs, a very significant birth for the zoo as well as for the entire population of this endangered subspecies.

1301 Summit Blvd. (east of I-95 btw. Southern and Forest Hill boulevards). www.palmbeachzoo.org. ℂ **561/547-WILD** (9453). Admission $19 adults, $17 seniors, $13 children 3–12. Daily 9am–5pm. Closed Thanksgiving and Christmas.

Playmobil FunPark ★★ ☺ THEME PARK

For a child, it doesn't get any better than this. The 17,000-square-foot Playmobil FunPark is housed in a replica castle and loaded with themed areas for imaginative play: a medieval village, a Western town, a fantasy dollhouse, and more. Kids can play with the Playmobil boats on two water-filled tables. Tech-minded youths may get bored, but tots up to age 5 or so will love this place. You *could* spend hours here and not spend a penny, but parents, beware: Everything is available for purchase. There's another Playmobil park in Orlando.

8031 N. Military Trail, Palm Beach Gardens. www.playmobil.com. ℂ **800/351-8697** or 561/691-9880. Fax 561/691-9517. Admission $1. Mon–Sat 10am–6pm; Sun noon–5pm. From I-95, go north to Palm Beach Lakes Blvd., then west to Military Trail. Turn left; the park is about a mile down on the right.

Rapids Water Park ★ ☺ WATER PARK

It may not be on the same grand scale as the theme parks in Orlando, but Rapids is a great way to cool off on a hot day. There are 12 acres of water rides (including an aquatic obstacle course), a children's area, and a miniature-golf course. Check out the Superbowl, a tubeless water ride that spins and swirls before dumping you into the pool below, and the Big Thunder, a giant funnel that plunges you down 50 feet in a four-person tube. Claustrophobia, anyone?

6566 N. Military Trail, West Palm Beach (1 mile west of I-95 on Military, btw. 45th St./exit 54 and Blue Heron Blvd./exit 55). www.rapidswaterpark.com. ℂ **561/842-8756.** Admission $37 Mon–Fri ($18 4pm–close), $41 Sat–Sun ($20 4pm–close); free for children 2 and under. Parking $10. Mid-Mar to Sept Mon–Fri 10am–5pm; Sat–Sun 10am–6pm.

Richard and Pat Johnson Palm Beach County History Museum ★

MUSEUM There's more to Palm Beach history than Donald Trump and well-preserved octogenarians. Opened to the public in 2008 within the historic 1916 Courthouse in downtown West Palm Beach, the museum has two permanent exhibits—the People Gallery, a tribute to approximately 100 individuals and families who have contributed to the growth of Palm Beach County, and the Place Gallery, featuring models and photographs exploring Palm Beach county's natural environment and the animals and ecology that make it unique—that are worth a spin through.

300 N. Dixie Hwy., West Palm Beach. Entrance on 2nd floor of courthouse. www.historicalsociety pbc.org. ✆ **561/832-4164.** Free admission. Tues–Sat 10am–5pm.

South Florida Science Museum ★ ☺ MUSEUM/PLANETARIUM   It's hands-on at this veteran West Palm science museum, featuring over 50 interactive exhibits including the newest exhibit, "Bugz!", fresh- and saltwater aquariums, a newly renovated observatory with extended hours of exploration and star gazing for families, an amateur radio center for "ear-to-ear" contact to far-off places, as well as blockbuster traveling exhibitions that are changed every 3 months. The museum received a big boost in 2009 when its Marvin Dekelboum Planetarium became one of only a handful of planetariums in the country to showcase state-of-the-art, full-dome digital projection capability that allows visitors to take a virtual space walk or to explore the realms of the sea. Upgrades also include a new, programmable laser system to continue the popular laser concerts, LED lighting, and Blu-ray high-definition video technology.

4801 Dreher Trail N., West Palm Beach (at the north end of Dreher Park). www.sfsm.org. ✆ **561/832-1988.** Admission $12 adults, $10 seniors, $8.95 children. Planetarium shows $4 adults, $2 children in addition to museum admission. Laser shows $10 per person. Mon–Fri 10am–5pm; Sat 10am–6pm; Sun noon–6pm.

OUTDOOR ACTIVITIES

BIKING   Rent anything from an English single-speed to a full-tilt mountain bike at the **Palm Beach Bicycle Trail Shop,** 223 Sunrise Ave. (www.palmbeachbicycle. com; ✆ **561/659-4583**). Rates are $15 per hour, $29 per half-day (9am–5pm), and $39 for 24 hours, and include a basket and lock (not that a lock is necessary in this fortress of a town). The most scenic route is called the Lake Trail, running the length of the island along the Intracoastal Waterway. On it, you'll see some of the most magnificent mansions and grounds, and enjoy the views of downtown West Palm Beach as well as some great wildlife.

GOLF   There's good golfing in the Palm Beaches, but many private-club courses are maintained exclusively for members' use. Ask at your hotel or contact the **Palm Beach County Convention and Visitors Bureau** (✆ **561/471-3995**) for information on which clubs are available for play. In the off season, some private courses open to visitors staying in Palm Beach County hotels. This "Golf-A-Round" program boasts no greens fees; reservations can be made through most major hotels.

The best hotel for golf in the area is the **PGA National Resort & Spa** (p. 341; ✆ **800/633-9150**), which features a whopping 90 holes of golf.

The **Palm Beach Public Golf Course,** 2345 S. Ocean Blvd. (www.golfonthe ocean.com; ✆ **561/547-0598**), a popular public 18-hole course, is a par-3 that was redesigned in 2009 by Raymond Floyd and includes a new layout, more holes by the ocean, and, down the road, a state-of-the-art clubhouse. The course opens at 8am on a first-come, first-served basis. Club rentals are available. Greens fees are $24 to $38 per person depending on the time, season, and number of holes played. Cart fees are an extra $14.

SCUBA DIVING Year-round warm waters, barrier reefs, and plenty of wrecks make South Florida one of the world's most popular places for diving. One of the best-known artificial reefs in this area is a vintage Rolls-Royce Silver Shadow, which was sunk offshore in 1985. Nature has taken its toll, however, and divers can no longer sit in the car, which has been ravaged by time and saltwater. For gear and excursions, call the **Scuba Club,** 4708 N. Flagler Dr., West Palm Beach (www. thescubaclub.com; ℭ **561/844-2466**).

TENNIS There are hundreds of tennis courts in Palm Beach County. Wherever you are staying, you're bound to be within walking distance of one. In addition to the many hotel tennis courts (see "Where to Stay," p. 339), you can play at **Currie Park,** 2400 N. Flagler Dr., West Palm Beach (ℭ **561/835-7025**), a public park with three lighted hard courts. They're free and available on a first-come, first-served basis.

WATERSPORTS Call the **Blue Water Boat Rental,** 200 E. 13th St., Riviera Beach (www.bluewaterboatrental.com; ℭ **561/840-7470**), to arrange sailboat, jet ski, bicycle, kayak, water ski, and parasail rentals.

Where to Eat

Palm Beach has some of the area's swankiest restaurants. Thanks to the development of downtown West Palm Beach, however, there is also a great selection of trendier, less expensive spots. Dress here is slightly more formal than in most other areas of Florida: Men wear blazers, and women generally put on modest dresses or chic suits when they dine out, even on the oppressively hot days of summer.

VERY EXPENSIVE

Café Boulud ★★★ FRENCH Snowbird socialites and foodies rejoiced over the opening of star chef Daniel Boulud's eponymous restaurant in the Brazilian Court hotel. If you're out to splurge, Boulud is ideal, with an exquisite menu divided into four sections—*La Tradition* (French and American classics), *La Saison* (seasonal dishes), *Le Potager* (dishes inspired by the vegetable market), and *Le Voyage* (world cuisine). The grilled mahimahi with white-bean cassoulet, garlic confit chorizo, and baby squid in a spicy paprika oil is superb. There's also a light and somewhat reasonably priced menu offering salads, sandwiches—including possibly the best we've ever had (though it's not always on the menu), the BLT with smoked beef brisket, lettuce slaw, Creole mustard, fried green tomatoes, and homemade pickles—and even a cheeseburger if you prefer; try the chickpea fries with *piquillo*-pepper ketchup. There are also some excellent prix-fixe deals to be had during lunch and Saturday and Sunday brunch. A late-night menu is also a great option if you happen to be here for the hotel's swingin' Saturday night soirees.

In the Brazilian Court, 301 Australian Ave., Palm Beach. www.danielnyc.com. ℭ **561/655-6060.** Reservations essential. Main courses $17–$40. AE, DC, MC, V. Mon–Fri 7–11am, noon–2:30pm, and 5:30–10pm; Sat–Sun 7am–2:30pm and 5:30–10pm.

Cafe l'Europe ★★★ INTERNATIONAL One of Palm Beach's finest and most popular spots, this 3-decades-plus-old, award-winning, romantic, and formal restaurant gives you a good reason to get dressed up. The enticing appetizers served by a superb staff might include crispy veal sweetbreads, wild mushroom and asparagus, or lobster bisque. Main courses run the gamut from Wiener schnitzel with herbed spaetzle to sautéed potato-crusted Florida snapper to Dover sole in an anchovy tomato sauce. Seafood dishes and steaks in sumptuous but light sauces are always exceptional. For those looking to indulge, the menu offers a caviar collection that may set you back a few hundred bucks. Caviar, we get, but the cheapest pasta dish here is around $42 for a seafood linguine. And as much as this is a haven for Palm Beach see-and-be-scenesters, Café l'Europe, run by husband-and-wife team chef Norbert and Lidia Goldner, is still a mom-and-pop shop, albeit one with French doors, mirrored surfaces, piano bar, and $40-plus pasta.

331 S. County Rd. (at Brazilian Ave.), Palm Beach. www.cafeleurope.com. © **561/655-4020.** Reservations recommended. Main courses $34–$47. AE, DC, DISC, MC, V. Tues–Sat noon–3pm and 6–10pm; Sun 6–10pm.

Echo ★★ ASIAN   This hyperstylish, sleek eatery is the Breakers hotel's homage to young and hip. The hotel runs the restaurant, even though it's off premises, and it's worth leaving the comfy, upper-crust confines of the Breakers for this resounding Echo. The menu is broken down into categories: earth, wind, fire, water, and flavor, which doesn't do the food any real justice. Sushi bar specialties, such as the spicy yellowtail sashimi with jalapeño, shiso emulsion, and garlic soy, and the outstanding echo roll with shrimp tempura, cucumber, avocado, and *tobiko* in a sesame soy sheet with superspicy *sriracha* sauce, are two of our favorites. But it's not all sushi. There are Chinese dim sum specialties, too. The dim sum sampler, at $29, feeds two and is an ideal starter or full-blown meal. Then there's the Thai roast duck and the open-flame wok specialties. There's too much to choose from, but it's all good. Be sure to check out the restaurant's **Dragonfly Lounge** after dinner. It's a hopping scene, especially by Palm Beach standards.

230 Sunrise Ave., Palm Beach. www.echopalmbeach.com. © **561/802-4222.** Reservations essential. Sushi $4–$23; main courses $18–$63. AE, DC, MC, V. Tues–Sun 5:30–9:30pm.

EXPENSIVE

Bice Restaurant ★ NORTHERN ITALIAN   Bice's Milanese cuisine is excellent, but as far as atmosphere, the air in here is a bit haughty and stuffy, bordering on rude. Servers and diners alike have attitudes, but you should forget all that with one bite of the juicy veal cutlet with tomato salad or the *pasta e fagioli* (pasta with beans). Another standout is the grilled swordfish with sautéed escarole and polenta. Ladies who lunch love the chopped salad. As outdated as the interior may seem, wait until you see some of the octogenarians sporting painted-on jeans and makeup. This is the upper crust's bingo hall, for sure, where servers and managers seem to know everyone's names from their first marriage all the way to their last. And for great people-watching and actually nice service, consider the bar, where you can linger over a glass of wine and, if the bartender likes you, free pizza, for hours.

313½ Worth Ave., Palm Beach. http://palmbeach.bicegroup.com. © **561/835-1600.** Reservations essential. Main courses $24–$46. AE, DC, MC, V. Daily noon–10pm.

MODERATE

Buccan ★★ CONTEMPORARY AMERICAN   When Clay Conley packed his knives and left Miami's lauded Azul, foodies were beside themselves. Then they just gassed up the car and made the trip to Palm Beach for Buccan, his progressive American grill with a tinge of an Asian accent. Among the menu highlights: Thai-style rare beef salad with cucumber, jalapeño, mint, and cilantro; a mushroom pizza with Gruyere, green onions, and black-truffle vinaigrette; and barbecued quail with cheddar biscuits, creamed corn, and bacon. Named after the traditional Caribbean wooden framework or spit on which meat was fire-roasted or smoked, Buccan is definitely a bit of a welcome culture shock for stuffy Palm Beach, where food tends to be on the simpler, plainer side. A living room–style lounge also gives way to Palm Beach's younger, hipper scene as the night grows older than the customers—if you can believe that one.

350 S. County Rd., Palm Beach. www.buccanpalmbeach.com. ℂ **561/833-3450.** Reservations suggested. Main courses $13–$30. AE, MC, DC, V. Mon–Thurs 4–11pm; Fri 4pm–midnight; Sat 5pm–midnight; Sun 5–10pm.

City Cellar Wine Bar & Grill ★★ AMERICAN   If the Palm Beach–proper dining scene is too stuffy, head over to City Place to find this yuppie brick-and–pressed tin enclave where people-watching is at a premium. Despite its all-American appearance, City Cellar offers a varied menu, from pizzas and pastas to steak and sea bass. We love the onion-and-mushroom soup with pinot grigio, and the twin 7-ounce pork chops with potato purée, sweet-and-sour shallots, and sherry mustard butter. The place is mobbed on weekends, so plan for a long wait that's best spent at the action-packed bar.

700 S. Rosemary Ave., West Palm Beach. ℂ **561/659-1853.** Reservations suggested. Main courses $22–$37; pizzas $13–$15; sandwiches and salads $13–$17. AE, MC, V. Sun–Wed 11:30am–10:30pm; Thurs–Sat 11:30am–11pm. Bar Sun–Wed 11:30am–1am; Thurs–Sat 11:30am–2am.

Rhythm Café ★ 🍴 ECLECTIC AMERICAN   This funky hole in the wall is where those in the know come to eat some of West Palm Beach's most laid-back gourmet food. On the handwritten, photocopied menu (which changes daily), you'll always find a fish specialty accompanied by a hefty dose of greens and garnishes. Reliably outstanding is the pork tenderloin with mango chutney. Salads and soups are a great bargain, as portions are relatively large, but there's an extensive menu of appetizers and tapas which can be ordered in small or entree form. The kitschy decor of this tiny cafe comes complete with vinyl tablecloths and a changing display of paintings by local amateurs. Young, handsome waiters are attentive, but not solicitous. The old drugstore where the restaurant now resides features an original 1950s lunch counter and stools.

3800 S. Dixie Hwy., West Palm Beach. www.rhythmcafe.cc. ℂ **561/833-3406.** Reservations recommended Sat–Sun. Main courses $17–$31; tapas $4–$13. AE, DISC, MC, V. Tues–Sat 6–10pm; Sun (Dec–Mar) 5:30–9pm. Closed in early Sept. From I-95, exit east on Southern Blvd. Go 1 block north of Southern Blvd.; restaurant is on the right.

INEXPENSIVE

Green's Pharmacy ★ 🍴 AMERICAN   This neighborhood pharmacy offers one of the best meal deals in Palm Beach. Both breakfast and lunch are served coffee shop style, either at a Formica bar or at tables on a black-and-white checkerboard floor. Breakfast specials include eggs and omelets served with home fries and bacon, sausage, or corned-beef hash. The grill serves burgers and sandwiches, as well as ice-cream sodas and milkshakes, to a loyal crowd of pastel-clad Palm Beachers old and young.

151 N. County Rd., Palm Beach. ℂ **561/832-0304.** Fax 561/832-6502. Breakfast $2–$7; burgers and sandwiches $3–$9; soups and salads $2–$9. AE, DISC, MC, V. Mon–Sat 7am–2pm; Sun 7am–3pm.

Howley's ★ 🍴 AMERICAN   An old-school classic American diner founded in 1950, Howley's is a definite throwback to the good ol' days with its Formica tables, fountain with swivel stools, and hula-dancer lamps that were there back during those "Happy Days." Its current owner owns 14 nightclubs and restaurants in Palm Beach county, which could explain the hipster contingency of late. Diner serves booze—check out the craft beer selection, and food is above-average diner fare—try the classic meatloaf or the mac and cheese.

4700 S. Dixie Hwy., West Palm Beach. ☎ **561/833-5691.** Main courses $8–$23. AE, DISC, MC, V. Sun–Thurs 7am–2am; Fri–Sat 7am–5am.

Shopping

No matter what your budget, be sure to take a stroll down Worth Avenue, the "Rodeo Drive of the South" and a window-shopper's dream. Between South Ocean Boulevard and Cocoanut Row, there are more than 200 boutiques, shops, art galleries, and restaurants. If you want to fit in, dress as if you are going to an elegant luncheon, not the mall down the street.

You'd never know there was ever a recession based on the swarms of shoppers armed with bags from **Gucci, Chanel, Armani, Hermès,** and **Louis Vuitton,** among others. And besides the boldface collection of couturiers, there are also a good number of unique, independent boutiques. For privileged feet, **Stubbs & Wooton,** 4 Via Parigi (www.stubbsandwooton.com; ☎ **561/655-4105**), sells velvet slippers that are a favorite of the loofahed locals. For rare and estate jewelry, **Richter's of Palm Beach,** 224 Worth Ave. (☎ **561/655-0774**), has been specializing in priceless gems since 1893. Just off Worth Avenue is the **Church Mouse,** 378 S. County Rd. (☎ **561/659-2154**), a great consignment/thrift shop with antique furnishings and tableware, as well as lots of good castoff clothing and shoes from socialites who've moved on to the next designers or, worse than that, to the big gala in the sky. Best of all, after expenses and salaries, all funds raised go to over 50 area charities. This shop usually closes for 2 months during the summer; call to be sure. Oh, and if you plan

---

PALM BEACH nightlife IS NOT AN OXYMORON

Clematis Street, West Palm Beach's hub of nightlife, also known as the Clematis District, has celebrated an immense resurgence, with a slew of new dining destinations, retailers, and nightspots. Among them are celebrity-driven restaurants and nightlife destinations, including **Feelgood's Rock Bar,** 219 Clematis St. (www.feelgoodswestpalm.com; ☎ **561/ 833-6500**), co-owned by Mötley Crüe's Vince Neil, and **World of Beer,** 101 N. Clematis St. (http://clematis.wobusa. com; ☎ **561/833-3375**), a hip, hops-happy spot featuring an unabridged selection of, you guessed it, beer. Then there's **E.R. Bradley's Saloon,** 104 S. Clematis St. (www.erbradleys.com; ☎ **561/833-3520**), a former Palm Beach landmark that crossed over the bridge and is now a West Palm watering hole and landmark for locals, including Palm

Beachers whose chauffeurs know to take them over the bridge to Bradley's without saying a word, celebrities and bar-flies alike. Back on "the island," in addition to the stalwarts **Leopard Lounge** (in the Chesterfield Hotel, p. 342) and **Colony Bar** (in the Colony, p. 342), there's a big late-night (meaning it goes at least until past 11pm) scene at Italian restaurant **Cucina Dell'Arte,** 257 Royal Poinciana Way (www.cucinadell arte.com; ☎ **561/655-0770**), catering to a motley mixture of young and old locals. It's a scene that may have been stolen from Worth Avenue mainstay **Ta'boo,** 221 Worth Ave. (www.taboo restaurant.com; ☎ **561/835-3500**), which also has somewhat of a nightlife with DJs and live music, but is not nearly as bustling and late night as at Cucina.

to put something up for consignment, make sure to use the special "donor's door" (a nice way of saying "service entrance") on the south side of the building.

City Place, Okeechobee Road (at I-95), West Palm Beach (www.cityplace.com; ✆ **561/820-9716**), is a $550-million, Mediterranean-style shopping, dining, and entertainment complex that's responsible for revitalizing what was once a lifeless downtown West Palm Beach. Among the 78 mostly chain stores are **Macy's, Barnes & Noble, Banana Republic, Armani Exchange, Pottery Barn, Sephora, Lucky Brand,** and **SEE** eyewear. Restaurants include McCormick & Schmick's, Cheesecake Factory, Fort Lauderdale and Hollywood's Taverna Opa, City Cellar Wine Bar and Grill, Brewzzi, BB King's Blues Club, Blue Martini, and Improv Comedy Club and Dinner Theater. Best of all is the Muvico IMAX, a 20-screen movie theater where you can wine and dine while watching a feature.

Entertainment & Nightlife

THE PERFORMING ARTS

With a number of dedicated patrons and enthusiastic supporters of the arts, this area happily boasts many good venues for those craving culture. Check the *Palm Beach Post* or the *Palm Beach Daily News* for up-to-date listings and reviews.

The **Raymond F. Kravis Center for the Performing Arts,** 701 Okeechobee Blvd., West Palm Beach (www.kravis.org; ✆ **561/832-7469**), is the area's largest and most active performance space. With a huge curved-glass facade and more than 2,500 seats in two lushly decorated indoor spaces, plus a new outdoor amphitheater,

THE sport OF KINGS

The posh **Palm Beach Polo and Country Club** and the **International Polo Club** are two of the world's premier polo grounds and host some of the sport's top-rated players. Even if you're not a sports fan, you must attend a match at one of these fields, which are on the mainland in a rural area called Wellington. Rest assured, however, that the spectators, and many of the players, are pure Palm Beach. After all, a day at the pony grounds is one of the only good reasons to leave Palm Beach proper. You need not be a Vanderbilt or a Kennedy to attend—matches are open to the public and are surprisingly affordable.

Even if you haven't a clue how the game is played, you can spend your time people-watching. In recent years, stargazers have spotted Prince Charles, Sylvester Stallone, Tommy Lee Jones, Bo Derek, and Ivana Trump, among others.

Dozens of lesser-known royalty keep box seats right on the grounds.

Dress is casual; a navy or tweed blazer over jeans or khakis is the standard for men, while neat-looking jeans or a pantsuit is the norm for women. On warmer days, shorts and, of course, polo shirts are fine, too.

General admission is $15 to $45; box seats cost $75 to $100 but are usually for members only. Call for more information. Special polo brunches are often available, too, at $85 per person. Matches are held throughout the week. Schedules vary, but the big names usually compete on Sunday at 3:30pm from January to April.

The fields are located at 11809 Polo Club Rd. and 3667 120th Ave., South Wellington, 10 miles west of the Forest Hill Boulevard exit off I-95. Visit www.internationalpoloclub.com or call ✆ **561/793-1440** or 204-5687 for tickets and a detailed schedule of events.

the Kravis stages more than 300 performances each year. Phone or check the website for a current schedule of Palm Beach's best music, dance, and theater.

Where to Stay

The island of Palm Beach is the epitome of *Lifestyles of the Rich and Famous*. Royalty and celebrities come to winter here, and there are plenty of lavishly priced options to accommodate them. Happily, there are also a few special inns that offer reasonably priced rooms in elegant settings. But most of the more modest places to lay your straw hat surround the island.

A few of the larger hotel chains operating in Palm Beach include the **Fairfield Inn and Suites Palm Beach,** 2870 S. Ocean Blvd. (📞 **800/228-2800** or 561/582-2581), across the street from the beach. In West Palm Beach, chain hotels are mostly on the main arteries close to the highways and a short drive from downtown. They include **Best Western,** 1800 Palm Beach Lakes Blvd. (📞 **800/331-9569** or 561/683-8810), and, just down the road, **Comfort Inn,** 1901 Palm Beach Lakes Blvd. (📞 **800/221-2222** or 561/689-6100). Farther south is **Parkview Motor Lodge,** 4710 S. Dixie Hwy., just south of Southern Boulevard (http://parkviewmotor lodge.magnusonhotels.com; 📞 **561/833-4644**). This 28-room motel is the best of many along Dixie Highway (U.S. 1). With rates starting at about $65 for a room with TV, air-conditioning, and free WiFi, you can't ask for more.

For other options, contact **Palm Beach Accommodations** (📞 800/543-SWIM [7946]).

VERY EXPENSIVE

Brazilian Court Hotel & Beach Club ★★★   This elegant, Old World, Mediterranean-style hotel dates from the 1920s and almost looks like a Beverly Hills bungalow. The 80 custom-designed rooms and suites all feature mahogany case goods and crown molding, Provence-style wood shutters, and queen- or king-size beds topped with imported linens. A large hotel by Palm Beach standards (the Breakers notwithstanding), Brazilian Court sprawls over half a block and features a fountain and private courtyards. The only downside? A tiny yet intimate pool where you feel you have to whisper. To counter the size is stellar poolside service—order drinks or food and *voilà!* For those who prefer sand in their feet, let the hotel's driver take you to their private beach club just minutes away on the Atlantic. It's stellar and very VIP. With the addition of renowned Chef Daniel Boulud's hauter-than-thou **Café Boulud** (p. 334), which provides a great bar scene with live music, Brazilian Court is Palm Beach's number-one place to see and be seen. Pets under 20 pounds receive gift bags full of treats for a (required) one-time $100 pet fee.

301 Australian Ave., Palm Beach, FL 33480. www.thebraziliancourt.com. 📞 **800/552-0335** or 561/655-7740. Fax 561/655-0801. 80 units. Winter from $550 studio, from $950 1-bedroom suite, from $1,145 2-bedroom suite; summer from $279 studio, from $429 1-bedroom suite, from $679 2-bedroom suite. Special packages available. AE, DC, DISC, MC, V. Pampered pet fee $100. **Amenities:** Restaurant; concierge; exercise room; heated outdoor pool; beach club; room service; spa treatments. *In room:* A/C, TV, hair dryer, minibar, Wi-Fi.

The Breakers Palm Beach ★★★ ☺   This 140-acre beachfront hotel is quintessential Palm Beach, where old money mixes with new money. After an almost $350 million renovation that stretched over 15 years, the seven-story building is a marvel, with a frescoed lobby and long, palatial hallways. Plush rooms feature marble bathrooms and views of the ocean or the magnificently manicured grounds. The Mediterranean-style

Beach Club offers outstanding vistas of the ocean and is reminiscent of a panoramic island escape. This oceanfront oasis features five pools, four whirlpool spas, expansive pool decks, lush tropical landscaping, and lawn space; a 6,000-square-foot rooftop terrace, 20 private, luxury beach bungalows and pool cabanas; and two casual oceanside restaurants. The hotel's available spa treatments can be performed indoors or out. There are two championship golf courses here: the Ocean Course with a 6,100-yard, championship-level par-70, and the Breakers Rees Jones Course. Kids aren't neglected either at the impressive Family Entertainment Center, which includes an arcade, a toddler's playroom, an arts-and-crafts area, a children's movie theater, and a video game room.

1 S. County Rd., Palm Beach, FL 33480. www.thebreakers.com. © **1-888-BREAKERS** (273-2537) or 561/655-6611. Fax 561/659-8403. 540 units. Winter $539–$1,620 double, $1,240–$5,950 suite; summer $279–$580 double, $420–$2,750 suite. AE, DC, DISC, MC, V. Valet parking $20. From I-95, exit Okeechobee Blvd. E., head east to S. County Rd., and turn left. **Amenities:** 9 restaurants; 5 bars; babysitting; bike rentals; children's programs; concierge; 2 championship golf courses; 2 fitness centers; 5 outdoor pools; room service; indoor/outdoor spa; 10 Har-Tru tennis courts; watersports equipment/rentals. *In room:* A/C, TV/DVD, CD player, hair dryer, minibar, MP3 docking station, Wi-Fi.

Four Seasons Resort Palm Beach ★★ ☺ Situated on the pristine Palm Beach oceanfront, Four Seasons is a quiet retreat from Worth Avenue. The spacious guest rooms, renovated in the summer of 2010, evoke a chic beach-house vibe, with private balconies and lavish new bathrooms. The full-service spa is excellent and also new; at 10,000 square feet, it features 11 treatment rooms including a "Man Room," wet room, spa suite, and full-service salon. **The Restaurant** is a casual seafood-oriented eatery with lovely lounge seating on the outdoor terrace where you can have a cocktail (try their "organic" drinks) and a small plate from the restaurant's raw bar. Two other restaurants, the **Ocean Bistro**—which is subpar for this kind of hotel— and the **Atlantic Bar & Grill,** round out the dining options. The resort offers a complimentary kids' program, and teens will enjoy the game room with Xbox, a pool table, and a large-screen TV. Meanwhile, parents can entertain themselves in the Living Room, a swank lounge, or at the Restaurant's outdoor lounge.

2800 S. Ocean Blvd., Palm Beach, FL 33480. www.fourseasons.com/palmbeach. © **800/432-2335** or 561/582-2800. Fax 561/547-1557. 210 units. Winter $649–$969 double, from $2,200 1-bedroom suite, from $3,970 2-bedroom suite; off season $195–$665 double, $1,100 1-bedroom suite, $2,600 2-bedroom suite. AE, DC, DISC, MC, V. Valet parking $25. From I-95, take the 6th Ave. exit east and turn left onto Dixie Hwy. Turn east onto Lake Ave. and north onto A1A (S. Ocean Blvd.); the resort is just ahead on your right. Pets less than 20 lb. accepted. **Amenities:** 3 restaurants; lounge/ outdoor patio; babysitting; children's programs; concierge; fitness center; outdoor heated pool; spa; 2 tennis courts; watersports equipment/rentals. *In room:* A/C, TV/DVD/VCR, CD player, fridge, hair dryer, high-speed Internet access, minibar, MP3 docking station.

The Omphoy Ocean Resort When it opened in 2009, this 134-room waterfront boutique hotel was the first new resort to open in Palm Beach in nearly 20 years. The stylish Omphoy features an open lobby and a minimalist South Beach modern vibe, and it may be the island's hippest hotel, catering to a younger clientele than many of the area hotels. Rooms feature sleek, high-end furnishings and plush linens and offer panoramic ocean or Intracoastal views. The resort also features New York–based **exhale spa,** with 5,000 square feet of dedicated spa space, featuring both indoor and outdoor treatments that combine fitness and movement with spa and healing.

2842 S. Ocean Blvd., Palm Beach, FL 33480. www.omphoy.com. © **561/540-6440.** 130 units. Winter $450–$700 suite; off season $279–$450 suite. AE, DC, DISC, MC, V. **Amenities:** 2 restaurants; bar; pool; spa; watersports equipment/rentals; free Wi-Fi. *In room:* A/C, TV/DVD.

Palm Beach Marriott Singer Island Beach Resort & Spa ★ ☺ Part of Riviera Beach and located on the water in eastern Palm Beach County is Singer Island, sort of like Marco Island, with condos dotting the shore. Rebranded by Marriott in 2010, this all-suite Singer Island resort offers a condolike experience with luxurious one- and two-bedroom all-suite accommodations ranging from 800 to 2,100 square feet and featuring high-tech kitchens and spectacular views of either the ocean or the Intracoastal. Ideal for big families or extended stays, the rooms also feature washers and dryers so you don't have to schlep your dirty laundry back home. Resort amenities include a spa—the only full-service spa on Singer Island—two pools, beach and pool cabanas, a fantastic kids' club, and a restaurant. If you want to stay in Palm Beach and feel like you live there, this is the place to do it. The hotel is completely smoke-free.

3800 N. Ocean Dr., Singer Island, FL 33404. www.marriottpalmbeach.com. © **561/340-1700.** Fax 561/340-1705. 222 units. Winter $224–$489 suite; off season $199–$489 suite. AE, DC, DISC, MC, V. **Amenities:** 3 restaurants and lounges; babysitting; concierge; fitness center; 2 pools; room service; spa; watersports equipment/rentals; Wi-Fi. *In room:* A/C, TV, hair dryer, minibar, Wi-Fi.

PGA National Resort & Spa ★★★ This expansive Northern Palm Beach resort is a premier golf-vacation spot, but its top-rated 40,000-square-foot European spa could be a destination in itself. With five 18-hole championship courses on more than 2,300 acres, the PGA National Golf Academy complete with Leadbetter and Pelz golf schools, and tour-level club fitting, golfers and other sports-minded travelers will find plenty to keep them occupied. In addition to golf, there's croquet, tennis, swimming, a complete health and fitness center, and a sublime spa. Guest rooms are spacious and comfortable, bordering on residential, with immense bathrooms and private terrace or patio. Club cottages are especially convenient, offering great privacy and serenity. This is not a beach resort, but multiple pools, including a lap pool, main pool, soothing whirlpools, and a collection of outdoor therapy pools, create a true oasis.

400 Ave. of the Champions, Palm Beach Gardens, FL 33418. www.pgaresort.com. © **800/533-9391** or 561/627-2000. Fax 561/225-2595. 339 guest rooms and suites, 40 cottages. Winter $299–$339 double, $369–$829 suite; off season $144–$169 double, $174–$659 suite. Children 16 and under stay free in parent's room. Special packages available. AE, DC, DISC, MC, V. From I-95, take exit 57B (PGA Blvd.) going west and continue for approx. 2 miles to the resort entrance on the left. **Amenities:** 9 restaurants and lounges; babysitting; concierge; 5 18-hole tournament-ready golf courses; 8 pools; room service; European spa; 19 Har-Tru clay tennis courts; Wi-Fi. *In room:* A/C, TV, hair dryer, Internet access, minibar.

Ritz-Carlton Palm Beach ★★★ ☺ If the Breakers is too mammoth for your taste, consider the Ritz. A lot warmer than the Four Seasons, the Ritz, located on a beautiful beach in a tiny town about 8 miles from Worth Avenue, lacks pretension and feels more like a boutique hotel. Guest rooms have flatscreen HDTVs, bedside electronic control "pamper panels," and Italian custom mahogany furniture. Oceanfront suites have oceanview stone soaking tubs, a sofa sleeper, two-line phones, and two HDTVs. Two pools are perfect for families and/or ideal for relaxation. The 42,000-square-foot Eau Spa debuted in 2009, complete with a custom Scrub and Polish Bar, Bath Lounge, Spa Villas with outdoor verdant gardens, and the Self-Centered Garden featuring swings, dipping pools, and water-massage benches. The new Eric Villency–designed Club Lounge has a midcentury Palm Beach theme, with custom Wook Kim–designed wall coverings. There are several dining options, including **Temple Orange,** a casual oceanfront restaurant; **Angle,** an American supper club–style restaurant with local and seasonal fish, all-natural beef, craft beers, and an award-winning wine wall; and **Breeze,** the "gourmet" burger patio and bar.

100 S. Ocean Blvd., Manalapan, FL 33462. www.ritzcarlton.com. (✆) **800/241-3333** or 561/533-6000. Fax 561/588-4202. 309 units. Winter $479–$849 double, $849–$1,599 suite, $6,000 presidential suite; off season $279–$619 double, $639–$969 suite, $2,999 presidential suite. AE, DISC, MC, V. Valet parking $28. From I-95, take exit for Lantana Rd., heading east. After 1 mile, turn right onto Federal Hwy. (U.S. 1/Dixie). Continue south to the next light and turn left onto Ocean Ave. Cross the Intracoastal Waterway and turn right onto A1A. **Amenities:** 2 restaurants; bar; bike rental; children's programs; concierge; fitness center; Jacuzzi; 2 outdoor pools; room service; spa; watersports equipment/rentals. *In room:* A/C, HDTV/DVD, hair dryer, minibar, Wi-Fi.

EXPENSIVE

Chesterfield Hotel ★★★ Reminiscent of an English country manor, the Chesterfield in all its flowery, Laura Ashley–inspired glory is a magnificent, charming hotel with exceptional service. Warm and inviting, the Chesterfield is one of the only places in South Florida where the idea of a fireplace (there's one in the hotel's library) doesn't seem ridiculous. Traditional English tea is served every afternoon, including fresh-baked scones, petits fours, and sandwiches. Rooms are decorated with antiques and with bright fabrics and wallpaper. In 2010, the Chesterfield refurbished 16 rooms and suites to feature new carpeting, draperies, upholstery, and headboards. The roomy marble bathrooms are stocked with an array of luxurious toiletries. A small heated pool and courtyard are nice, and the beach is only 3 blocks away, but the real action is inside: The hotel's retro-elegant **Leopard Lounge,** also refurbished in 2010, serves decent Continental cuisine, but is better as a late-night hangout for live music, schmoozing, and eyeing the local cognoscenti.

363 Cocoanut Row, Palm Beach, FL 33480. www.chesterfieldpb.com. (✆) **800/243-7871** or 561/659-5800. Fax 561/659-6707. 52 units. Winter $395–$465 queen, $495–$570 king, $675–$1,585 suite; off season $175–$249 queen, $259–$319 king, $339–$719 suite. Rollaway bed $15. Packages available. AE, DC, DISC, MC, V. Free valet parking. From I-95, exit onto Okeechobee Blvd. E., cross the Intracoastal Waterway, and turn right onto Cocoanut Row. **Amenities:** Restaurant; lounge; concierge; access to nearby health club; hot tub and heated pool; room service; Wi-Fi. *In room:* A/C, TV, DVD/CD player (in kings/suites only), fridge (in kings/suites only), hair dryer, high-speed Internet access.

MODERATE

The Colony ★ For years, the Colony has been a favorite hangout—hide-out, perhaps—for old-timers, socialites, and mysterious luminaries. The very old-school Polo Lounge features an eclectic mix of local lounge and A-list cabaret singers and entertainers, but the people-watching there is priceless as octogenarian sugar daddies proudly and boldly sashay by with bedecked, bejeweled arm candy at least half their age. The hotel's **Royal Room Cabaret** is also a nocturnal fave, saturated with cocktails, song, and an occasional cameo appearance by the likes of Connie Francis, Jack Jones, and Steve Tyrell. Rooms at the Georgian-style hotel have been totally renovated with a dark-wood British West Indies theme featuring comfy feather duvets, lots of pillows, pale yellow and gold walls, and fabrics in distinctive palm-tree motif. There are also seven two-bedroom villas and three recently renovated penthouses, including the Presidential Penthouse (presidents Bush, Clinton, Carter, and Ford have all stayed there) and the Duke of Windsor Penthouse, where the duke and duchess of Windsor spent part of their time in exile.

155 Hammon Ave., Palm Beach, FL 33480. www.thecolonypalmbeach.com. (✆) **800/521-5525** or 561/655-5430. Fax 561/659-8104. 90 units. Winter $400 double, $500 1-bedroom suite; off season $175 double, $250 1-bedroom suite. AE, DC, MC, V. From I-95, exit onto Okeechobee Blvd. E. and

cross the Intracoastal Waterway. Turn right on S. County Rd. and then left onto Hammon Ave. **Amenities:** Restaurant; bar; concierge; heated pool; limited seasonal room service; spa. *In room:* A/C, TV, hair dryer, Internet access.

Palm Beach Historic Inn ★★   Built in 1923, the Palm Beach Historic Inn is an area landmark within a block's walking distance of the beach (chairs and towels are provided for guests of the hotel), Worth Avenue, and about 10 of Palm Beach's best restaurants. The small lobby is filled with antiques, books, magazines, and a player piano, all of which add to the homey feel of this intimate B&B. In-room snacks, tea, and cookies ensure that you won't go hungry—never mind the excellent continental breakfast that is brought to you daily. All bedrooms are uniquely decorated and have hardwood floors, down comforters, Egyptian-cotton linens, fluffy bathrobes, and plenty of good-smelling toiletries. Here you'll find a casual elegance that's comfortable for everyone. *Note:* Smoking is not permitted.

365 S. County Rd., Palm Beach, FL 33480. www.palmbeachhistoricinn.com. ⓒ **561/832-4009.** Fax 561/832-6255. 13 units. Winter $149–$199 double, $219–$349 suite; off season $79–$149 double, $199–$239 suite. Rates include continental breakfast. Children stay free in parent's room. AE, MC, V. Small pets accepted. *In room:* A/C, TV/VCR, fridge, hair dryer.

INEXPENSIVE

Hibiscus House ★★ 👯   Inexpensive bed-and-breakfasts are a rarity in Southeast Florida, making the Hibiscus House, one of the area's first, a true find. Located a few miles from the coast in a quiet residential neighborhood, this 1920s-era B&B is filled with handsome antiques and tapestries. Every room has a private terrace or balcony. The Red Room has a fabulous bathroom with Jacuzzi. The peaceful backyard retreat has been transformed into a tropical garden, with a heated pool and lounge chairs. There are pretty indoor areas for guests to enjoy; one little sitting room is wrapped in glass and is stocked with playing cards and board games. Huge gourmet breakfast portions are as filling as they are beautiful. Make any special requests in advance; owners Raleigh Hill and Colin Rayer will be happy to oblige.

501 30th St., West Palm Beach, FL 33407. www.hibiscushouse.com. ⓒ **800/203-4927** or ⓒ/fax 561/863-5633. 8 units. Winter $125–$210 double; off season $100–$150 double. Rates include breakfast. AE, DC, DISC, MC, V. From I-95, exit onto Palm Beach Lakes Blvd. E. and continue 4 miles. Turn left onto Flagler Dr. and continue for about ½ mile; then turn left onto 30th St. Pets accepted. **Amenities:** Concierge; heated pool. *In room:* A/C, TV, hair dryer.

Hotel Biba ★ 👯   Located in the historic El Cid neighborhood, just 1 mile from City Place and Clematis Street, the very cool Biba answers the call for an inexpensive, chic hotel that young hipsters can call their own. Housed in a renovated Colonial-style 1940s motor lodge, Biba has been remarkably updated by de rigueur designer Barbara Hulanicki and features a sleek lobby to complement a hip hotel bar, and a gorgeously landscaped outdoor pool area with Asian-inspired gardens. Guest rooms are shabby chic, with private patios, mosaic-tile floors, custom mahogany furniture, Egyptian-cotton linens, down pillows, and flatscreen TVs. The bold color schemes mix nicely with the high-fashion crowd that convenes here. *A word of advice:* This place is not exactly soundproof. Rooms may be cloistered by fence and gardens, but they're still extremely close to a major thoroughfare. Ask for a room that's on the quieter Belvedere Road, as opposed to those facing South Olive Avenue.

320 Belvedere Rd., West Palm Beach, FL 33405. www.hotelbiba.com. ⓒ **561/832-0094.** Fax 561/833-7848. 41 units. Year-round $110–$215 double; $200–$300 suite. Rates include breakfast. Online discounts available. AE, MC, V. **Amenities:** Lounge; concierge; outdoor pool. *In room:* A/C, TV, CD player, hair dryer, free Wi-Fi.

PLANNING YOUR TRIP TO SOUTH FLORIDA

13

Whether you plan to spend a day, a week, 2 weeks, or longer in the southern end of the Sunshine State, you'll need to make many "where," "when," and "how" choices before leaving your home. With a multitude of affordable flights to the region, a balmy climate year-round, a vibrant cultural scene in Miami, and beautiful beaches within city limits and without, there's a good vacation to be had here by everyone, no matter how you choose to answer these questions. What's not a question is whether or not to visit in general. You bought the book, so what are you waiting for?

As South Florida shifts from a seasonal to a more year-round destination, there's always a good time to visit. Really. Even during hurricane season (Jun–Nov), when prices are lower and crowds are thinner, hurricanes are (knock on wood) often elusive. When temperatures freeze elsewhere, crowds flock to the state to thaw and things get a bit more lively, albeit also more crowded. For those who love heat, humidity, and sweating, summertime is the ideal time to visit and saves you a trip to the sauna.

For additional help planning your trip and for further on-the-ground resources, please turn to "Fast Facts: South Florida," on p. 347.

GETTING THERE

By Plane

Most major domestic airlines fly to and from many Florida cities. Choose from **American, Delta, United,** and **US Airways.** Of these, Delta and US Airways have the most extensive network of commuter connections within Florida (see "Getting Around," below).

Several so-called no-frills airlines—with low fares but few, if any, amenities—also fly to Florida. The biggest and best is **Southwest Airlines,** which has flights from many U.S. cities to Fort Lauderdale, Jacksonville, Orlando, Tampa, and Panama City. Others flying to Florida include **AirTran, JetBlue, Virgin America, Frontier Airlines,** and **Spirit.**

The major airports in South Florida are **Miami International Airport (MIA), Fort Lauderdale Hollywood International Airport (FLL),** and **Palm Beach International Airport (PBI).**

Tip: When booking airfare to Miami, consider flying into the Fort Lauderdale Hollywood International Airport for considerably cheaper fares. The airport is only a half-hour from downtown Miami.

Price comparison and booking websites such as **Travelocity** (www.travelocity.com) and **Expedia** (www.expedia.com) make it easy to compare prices and purchase tickets.

By Car

Although four major roads run to and through Miami—I-95, S.R. 826, S.R. 836, and U.S. 1—chances are you'll reach Miami and the rest of South Florida by way of I-95. This north-south interstate is South Florida's lifeline and an integral part of the region. The highway connects all of Miami's different neighborhoods, the airport, the beaches, and all of South Florida to the rest of the country. Miami's road signs are notoriously confusing and notably absent when you most need them. Think twice before you exit from the highway if you aren't sure where you're going; some exits lead to unsavory neighborhoods.

Other highways that will get you to Florida include I-10, which originates in Los Angeles and terminates at the tip of Florida in Jacksonville, and I-75, which begins in north Michigan and runs through the center of the state to Florida's west coast.

Florida law allows drivers to make a right turn on a red light after a complete stop, unless otherwise indicated. In addition, all passengers are required to wear seat belts, and children 3 and under must be securely fastened in government-approved car seats.

See "Getting Around" (below) for more information about driving in Florida and the car-rental firms that operate here.

International visitors should note that insurance and taxes are almost never included in quoted rental car rates in the U.S. Be sure to ask your rental agency about these fees. They can add a significant cost to your car rental.

Most car-rental companies in Florida require that you be 25, and even when they don't, there's a hefty surcharge applied to renters 21 to 24 years old.

By Train

Amtrak (www.amtrak.com; ☎ **800/USA-RAIL** [872-7245]) offers train service to Florida from both the East and West coasts. It takes some 26 hours to reach Miami from New York, and 68 hours from Los Angeles. Amtrak's fares aren't much less—if not more—than many of the airlines' lowest fares.

Amtrak's *Silver Meteor* and *Silver Star* both run twice daily between New York and either Miami or Tampa, with intermediate stops along the East Coast and in Florida. Amtrak's Thruway Bus Connections are available from the Fort Lauderdale Amtrak station and Miami International Airport to Key West; from Tampa to St. Petersburg, Treasure Island, Clearwater, Sarasota, Bradenton, and Fort Myers; and from Deland to Daytona Beach. From the West Coast, the *Sunset Limited* runs three times weekly between Los Angeles and Orlando. It stops in Pensacola, Crestview (north of Fort Walton Beach and Destin), Chipley (north of Panama City Beach), and Tallahassee. Sleeping accommodations are available for an extra charge.

If you intend to stop along the way, you can save money with Amtrak's **Explore America** (or All Aboard America) fares, which are based on three regions of the country.

Amtrak's **Auto Train** runs daily from Lorton, Virginia (12 miles south of Washington, D.C.), to Sanford, Florida (just northeast of Orlando). You ride in a coach while your car is secured in an enclosed vehicle carrier. Make your train reservations as far in advance as possible.

By Bus

Greyhound (www.greyhound.com; ✆ **800/231-2222**) has over 50 stops within the state of Florida and over 2,400 service locations in North America. While buses aren't the fastest way to get to Florida, they can be the most economical.

GETTING AROUND

The best and easiest way to see South Florida's sights or to get to and from the beach is by car. Public transportation is available only in the cities and larger towns, and even there, it may provide infrequent or inadequate service. When it comes to getting from one city to another, cars and planes are the ways to go.

By Plane

The commuter arms of **Delta** and **US Airways** provide extensive service between Florida's major cities and towns. Fares for these short hops tend to be reasonable.

Cape Air flies between Key West and Naples, which means you can avoid backtracking to Miami from Key West if you're touring the region. (You can also take a 3-hour boat ride between Key West and Fort Myers Beach or Naples.) **Collins Aviation** connects Fort Lauderdale with Marathon.

Some large airlines offer transatlantic or transpacific passengers special discount tickets under the name **Visit USA,** which allows mostly one-way travel from one U.S. destination to another at very low prices. Unavailable in the U.S., these discount tickets must be purchased abroad in conjunction with your international fare. This system is the easiest, fastest, cheapest way to see the country.

By Car

If you're visiting from abroad and plan to rent a car in Florida, keep in mind that foreign driver's licenses are usually recognized in the U.S., but you should get an international one if your home license is not in English.

Jacksonville is about 350 miles north of Miami and 500 miles north of Key West, so if you're traveling to South Florida from a northern city, don't underestimate how long it will take you to drive all the way down the state. The speed limit is either 65 mph or 70 mph on the rural interstate highways, so you can, however, make good time between cities. Not so on U.S. 1, U.S. 17, U.S. 19, U.S. 41, and U.S. 301; although most have four lanes, these older highways tend to be heavily congested, especially in built-up areas.

Every major car-rental company is represented here, including **Alamo, Avis, Budget, Dollar, Enterprise, Hertz, National,** and **Thrifty.**

State and local **taxes** will add as much as 20% to your final bill. You'll pay an additional $2.05 per day in statewide use tax, and local sales taxes will tack on at least 6% to the total, including the statewide use tax. Some airports add another 35¢ per day and as much as 10% in "recovery" fees. You can avoid the recovery fee by picking up your car in town rather than at the airport. Budget and Enterprise both have numerous rental locations away from the airports. But be sure to weigh the cost of transportation to and from your hotel against the amount of the fee.

Competition is so fierce among Florida rental agencies that most have now stopped charging **drop-off fees** if you pick up a car at one place and leave it at another. Be sure to ask in advance if there's a drop-off fee.

To rent a car, you must have a valid **credit card** (not a debit or check card) in your name, and most companies require you to be at least 25 years old. Some also set maximum ages and may deny cars to anyone with a bad driving record. Ask about requirements and restrictions when you book, in order to avoid problems once you arrive.

By Train

International visitors can buy a **USA Rail Pass,** good for 15, 30, or 45 days of unlimited travel on **Amtrak** (www.amtrak.com; ✆ **800/USA-RAIL** [872-7245]). The pass is available online or through many overseas travel agents. See Amtrak's website for the cost of travel within the western, eastern, or northwestern United States. Reservations are generally required and should be made as early as possible. Regional rail passes are also available.

By Bus

Greyhound (www.greyhound.com; ✆ **800/231-2222**) is the sole nationwide bus line. International visitors can obtain information about the **Greyhound North American Discovery Pass.** The pass, which offers unlimited travel and stopovers in the U.S. and Canada, can be obtained from foreign travel agents or through www. discoverypass.com.

TIPS ON ACCOMMODATIONS

South Florida accommodations are as varied in personality as the weather in mid-July. All sorts of stays line the Sunshine State, ranging from swanky, five-star luxury hotels and beach resorts to cozy one-room cottages, posh penthouses, B&Bs, and beachfront high-rise condominiums to back-to-nature-style Everglades cabins and campsites. For sports or nature lovers, there are hotels and motels located on golf courses, marinas, or surrounded by nature preserves and hiking trails. For families and admirers of kitsch, there are themed hotels that transport you from Florida to, say, Colorado, or even the Cartoon Network. For the hip, there's the requisite boutique hotel with mandatory celebrity sightings. And for those who just want to get away from it all, there are countless hidden hotels, motels, and cottages—even a few on private islands.

[Fast FACTS] SOUTH FLORIDA

Area Codes   305: All of Miami-Dade County and the Florida Keys of Monroe County: Miami, Homestead, Coral Gables, Key West. **786:** A newer area code covering those Miami-Dade numbers not covered by 305. **954:** All of Broward County: Fort Lauderdale, Hollywood, Coral Springs. **561:** All of Palm Beach County. **772:** Treasure Coast: Vero Beach, Port Saint Lucie, Fort Pierce, Sebastian, Stuart, and central-eastern Florida.

Business Hours "Normal" business hours are 9am to 5pm, but in certain parts of the state—Miami, especially—hours range from "whenever" to "whenever." Always call ahead and ask for hours, as, like the weather, they can change in an instant.

Customs Every visitor 21 or older may bring in, free of duty, the following: (1) 1 U.S. quart of alcohol; (2) 200 cigarettes, 50 cigars (but not from Cuba), or 3 pounds of smoking tobacco; and (3) $100 worth of gifts. These exemptions are offered to travelers who spend at least 72 hours in the United States and who have not claimed them within the preceding 6 months. It is forbidden to bring into the country almost any meat products (including canned, fresh, and dried meat products such as bouillon, soup mixes, and the like). Generally, condiments including vinegars, oils, pickled goods, spices, coffee, tea, and some cheeses and baked goods are permitted. Avoid bringing rice products, as rice can often harbor insects. Bringing fruits and vegetables is prohibited since these may also harbor pests or disease. International visitors may carry in or out up to $10,000 in U.S. or foreign currency with no formalities; larger sums must be declared to U.S. Customs on entering or leaving, and visitors must file form CM 4790. For details regarding U.S. Customs and Border Protection, consult your nearest U.S. embassy or consulate, or **U.S. Customs** (www.customs.gov).

Disabled Travelers Florida is exceptionally accommodating to those with special needs. In addition to special parking set aside at every establishment, out-of-state vehicles with disability parking permits from other states can park in these spots. Florida state law and the Americans with Disabilities Act (ADA) require that guide dogs be permitted in all establishments and attractions, although some ride restrictions do apply. Those with hearing impairments can dial ✆ **711** for **TDD service** via the Florida Relay Service. There are several resources for people with disabilities who are traveling within Florida, including special wheelchairs with balloon tires provided free of charge at many Florida beaches. For the best information on traveling with disabilities, go to www.visitflorida.com/disabilities_travel.

Drinking Laws The legal age for purchase and consumption of alcoholic beverages is 21, though, strangely and somewhat hypocritically, a person serving or selling alcohol can be 18; proof of age is required and often requested at bars, nightclubs, and restaurants, so it's always a good idea to bring ID when you go out. Do not carry open containers of alcohol in your car or any public area that isn't zoned for alcohol consumption. The police can fine you on the spot. Don't even think about driving while intoxicated. Florida state law prohibits the sale of alcohol between 3am and 7am, unless the county chooses to change the operating hours later. For instance, Miami–Dade County liquor stores may operate 24 hours. Alcohol sales on Sundays vary by county; some, such as Palm Beach and Miami–Dade County, can start serving booze as early as 7am, while other counties such as Monroe don't start popping corks until noon. Check with the specific county you're visiting to see what time spirits start being served. Supermarkets and other licensed business establishments can sell only beer, low-alcohol liquors, and wine. The hard stuff must be sold in dedicated liquor stores, which may be in a separate part of a grocery or a drugstore. Beer must be sold in quantities of 32 ounces or less or greater than 1 gallon. Forty- and 64-ounce alcoholic beverages are illegal.

As for open container laws: Having open alcoholic containers on public property, including streets, sidewalks, or inside a vehicle, is prohibited, though open bottles of liquor are allowed inside a car trunk. Drivers suspected to be under the influence of alcohol or drugs must agree to breath, blood, or urine testing under "implied consent laws." Penalties for refusing testing can mean suspension of the driver's license for up to 1 year. In Florida, the first conviction carries a mandatory suspension of the driver's license for 6 months; for the second offense, 1 year; for the third offense, 2 years. Underage drivers (20 or younger) have a maximum legal blood-alcohol content percentage of .02%.

Above this amount, they are subject to DUI penalties. At .20% above the legal limit of .08%, a driver faces much harsher repercussions. This also applies to drivers refusing chemical testing for intoxication.

Electricity Like Canada, the United States uses 110 to 120 volts AC (60 cycles), compared to 220 to 240 volts AC (50 cycles) in most of Europe, Australia, and New Zealand. Downward converters that change 220–240 volts to 110–120 volts are difficult to find in the United States, so bring one with you.

Embassies & Consulates All embassies are in the nation's capital, Washington, D.C. Some consulates are in major U.S. cities, and most nations have a mission to the United Nations in New York City. If your country isn't listed below, call for directory information in Washington, D.C. (*☏* **202/555-1212**) or check **www.embassy.org/embassies**.

The embassy of **Australia** is at 1601 Massachusetts Ave. NW, Washington, DC 20036 (www.usa.embassy.gov.au; *☏* **202/797-3000**). Consulates are in New York, Honolulu, Houston, Los Angeles, and San Francisco.

The embassy of **Canada** is at 501 Pennsylvania Ave. NW, Washington, DC 20001 (www.canadainternational.gc.ca/washington; *☏* **202/682-1740**). Other Canadian consulates are in Buffalo (New York), Detroit, Los Angeles, New York, and Seattle.

The embassy of **Ireland** is at 2234 Massachusetts Ave. NW, Washington, DC 20008 (www.embassyofireland.org; *☏* **202/462-3939**). Irish consulates are in Boston, Chicago, New York, San Francisco, and other cities. See website for complete listing.

The embassy of **New Zealand** is at 37 Observatory Circle NW, Washington, DC 20008 (www.nzembassy.com; *☏* **202/328-4800**). New Zealand consulates are in Los Angeles, Salt Lake City, San Francisco, and Seattle.

The embassy of the **United Kingdom** is at 3100 Massachusetts Ave. NW, Washington, DC 20008 (http://ukinusa.fco.gov.uk; *☏* **202/588-6500**). Other British consulates are in Atlanta, Boston, Chicago, Cleveland, Houston, Los Angeles, New York, San Francisco, and Seattle.

Emergencies To reach the police, ambulance, or fire department, dial *☏* **911** from any phone. No coins are needed.

Family Travel The state of Florida is a favorite destination among families, with Walt Disney World leading the list of theme parks geared to young and old alike. Consequently, most hotels and restaurants throughout the state are willing, if not eager, to cater to families traveling with children. Many hotels and motels let children age 17 and younger stay free in a parent's room (be sure to ask when you reserve). To locate accommodations, restaurants, and attractions that are particularly kid-friendly, look for the "Kids" icon throughout this guide.

At beaches, it's the exception rather than the rule for a resort not to have a children's activities program (some will even mind the youngsters while the parents enjoy a night off!). Even if they don't have a children's program of their own, most will arrange babysitting services.

Recommended family-travel websites include **Family Travel Forum** (www.familytravel forum.com), a site that offers customized trip planning; **Family Travel Network** (www.familytravelnetwork.com), an online magazine providing travel tips; and **TravelWith YourKids.com** (www.travelwithyourkids.com), a comprehensive site written by parents for parents, offering sound advice for long-distance and international travel with children.

Health Florida doesn't present any unusual health hazards for most people. Folks with certain medical conditions, such as liver disease, diabetes, and stomach ailments, should avoid eating raw **oysters.** Cooking kills the bacteria, so if in doubt, order your oysters steamed, broiled, or fried.

Florida has millions of **mosquitoes** and invisible biting **sand flies** (known as no-see-ums), especially in the coastal and marshy areas. Fortunately, neither insect carries malaria or other diseases. (Although there were a few cases of mosquitoes carrying West Nile virus in the Panhandle, this isn't generally a problem in Florida.) Keep these pests at bay with a good insect repellent.

It's especially important to protect yourself against **sunburn.** Don't underestimate the strength of the sun's rays down here, even in the middle of winter. Use a sunscreen with a high protection factor and apply it liberally.

Insurance   Hurricane season (June–Nov) is a time when travel insurance may come in handy.

For information on traveler's insurance, trip-cancellation insurance, and medical insurance while traveling, visit www.frommers.com/planning.

Internet & Wi-Fi   When it comes to Internet and Wi-Fi, South Florida is pretty connected. Most major cities offer free Wi-Fi hot spots. To find cybercafes in your destination, check **www.cybercaptive.com** and **www.cybercafe.com**. Also, most public libraries throughout the state offer free Internet access/Wi-Fi.

Language   Miami owes a lot of its rich culture to the diversity of its inhabitants, over half of whom were born outside of the U.S. This diversity exhibits itself linguistically: Miami is the second-largest U.S. city (after El Paso) with a Spanish-speaking majority. While by no means necessary, knowing a bit of Spanish can help you get around and enrich your experience here.

Legal Aid   While driving, if you are pulled over for a minor infraction (such as speeding), never attempt to pay the fine to a police officer; this could be construed as attempted bribery, a much more serious crime. Pay fines by mail, or directly into the hands of the clerk of the court. If you are accused of a more serious offense, say and do nothing before consulting a lawyer. In the U.S., the burden is on the state to prove a person's guilt beyond a reasonable doubt, and everyone has the right to remain silent. Once arrested, a person can make one telephone call to a party of his or her choice. The international visitor should call his or her embassy or consulate.

LGBT Travelers   The editors of *Out and About*, a gay and lesbian newsletter, have described Miami's **South Beach** as the "hippest, hottest, most happening gay travel destination in the world." Today, however, **Fort Lauderdale**—where gays own more than 20 motels, 40 bars, and numerous other businesses—steals its rainbow-colored crown. For many years, that could also be said of **Key West,** which still is one of the country's most popular destinations for gays.

You can contact the **Gay, Lesbian & Bisexual Community Services of Central Florida,** 946 N. Mills Ave., Orlando, FL 32803 (www.glbcc.org; ✆ **407/228-8272**), whose welcome packets usually include the latest issue of the *Triangle*, a quarterly newsletter, and a calendar of events pertaining to the gay and lesbian community. Although not a tourist-specific packet, it includes information and ads for the area's gay and lesbian clubs.

Watermark, P.O. Box 533655, Orlando, FL 32853 (www.watermarkonline.com; ✆ **407/481-2243;** fax 407/481-2246), is a biweekly tabloid newspaper covering the gay and lesbian scene, including dining and entertainment options, in Orlando, the Tampa Bay area, and Daytona Beach.

The **International Gay and Lesbian Travel Association (IGLTA;** www.iglta.org; ✆ **800/448-8550** or 954/776-2626) is the trade association for the gay and lesbian travel industry, and offers an online directory of gay- and lesbian-friendly travel businesses and tour operators.

Mail   At press time, domestic postage rates were 28¢ for a postcard and 44¢ for a letter. For international mail, a first-class letter of up to 1 ounce costs 98¢ (75¢ to Canada and

79¢ to Mexico); a first-class postcard costs the same as a letter. For more information go to **www.usps.com**.

If you aren't sure what your address will be in the United States, mail can be sent to you, in your name, c/o General Delivery at the main post office of the city or region where you expect to be. (Call ✆ **800/275-8777** for information on the nearest post office.) The addressee must pick up mail in person and must produce proof of identity (driver's license, passport, and so forth). Most post offices will hold mail for up to 1 month, and are open Monday to Friday from 8am to 6pm, and Saturday from 9am to 3pm.

Always include zip codes when mailing items in the U.S. If you don't know your zip code, visit **www.usps.com/zip4**.

Medical Requirements Unless you're arriving from an area known to be suffering from an epidemic (particularly cholera or yellow fever), inoculations or vaccinations are not required for entry into the United States.

Mobile Phones A Florida resident without a cellphone is as rare as an albino crocodile. But a few do exist. Reception varies from excellent to spotty, depending on where you are. The Everglades used to have abysmal cell phone reception, but thanks to new telephone towers, reliable service is almost as guaranteed as a gator sighting. Typically, the more remote the area you are visiting, the smaller the chance is that your phone will work—but reception everywhere is constantly improving.

If you need to stay in touch at a destination where you know your phone won't work, **rent** a phone from **InTouch USA** (www.intouchglobal.com; ✆ **800/872-7626**) or a rental-car location. You'll pay $1 a minute or more for airtime. Or you can purchase an inexpensive pay-as-you-go mobile phone—they're all but ubiquitous at convenience stores and other retail outlets.

If you're not from the U.S., you'll be appalled at the poor reach of our **GSM (Global System for Mobile Communications) wireless network,** which is used by much of the rest of the world. Your phone will probably work in most major U.S. cities; it definitely won't work in many rural areas. To see where GSM phones work in the U.S., check out www.t-mobile.com/coverage/national_popup.asp. And you may or may not be able to send SMS (text messaging) home.

THE VALUE OF THE U.S. DOLLAR VS. OTHER POPULAR CURRENCIES

US$	Aus$	Can$	Euro (€)	NZ$	UK£
1	A$.93	C$.95	€.68	NZ$1.24	£.63

WHAT THINGS COST IN SOUTH FLORIDA

	$
Taxi from the airport to major destination	$18–$25
Double room, moderate	$189
Double room, inexpensive	$150
Three-course dinner for one without wine, moderate	$25–$50
Bottle of beer	$3–$6
Cup of coffee	$2–$6
1 gallon of gas	$3.45–$3.69
Admission to most museums	Free–$20
Admission to most national parks	$2–$8

Money & Costs Frommer's lists exact prices in the local currency. The currency conversions quoted above were correct at press time. However, rates fluctuate, so before you depart, consult a currency-exchange website such as **www.oanda.com/currency/ converter** to check up-to-the-minute rates.

Beware of hidden credit card fees while traveling. Check with your credit or debit card issuer to see what fees, if any, will be charged for overseas transactions. Recent reform legislation in the U.S., for example, has curbed some exploitative lending practices. But many banks have responded by increasing fees in other areas, including fees for customers who use credit and debit cards while out of the country—even if those charges were made in U.S. dollars. Check with your bank before departing to avoid any surprise charges on your statement.

For help with currency conversions, tip calculations, and more, download Frommer's convenient Travel Tools app for your mobile device. Go to **www.frommers.com/go/ mobile** and click on the Travel Tools icon.

Newspapers & Magazines The *Miami Herald* is Miami's only English-language daily. It is especially known for its extensive Latin American coverage and has a decent Friday "Weekend" entertainment guide. The most respected alternative weekly is the giveaway tabloid *New Times,* which contains up-to-date listings and reviews of food, films, theater, music, and whatever else is happening in town. Also free, if you can find it, is *Ocean Drive,* an oversize glossy magazine that's limited on text (no literary value) and heavy on ads and society photos. It's what you should read, er, browse, if you want to know who's who and where to go for fun; it's available at a number of chic South Beach boutiques and restaurants. It is also available at newsstands. In the same vein: *Miami Magazine* has a bit more literary value in addition to the gloss and is free and available throughout the city. The *Sun-Sentinel* covers Fort Lauderdale and Palm Beach counties and *Palm Beach Post* covers Palm Beach. The *New Times* also has a Broward/Palm Beach edition that has excellent nightlife and dining coverage. For the best Florida Keys news not found in either newspaper, check out *The Key West Citizen.*

Packing Florida is typically a warm-weather state, but not always. Be sure to pack a sweater, long sleeves, and pants in case the weather cools or, more likely, you go into a place where the A/C plunges to arctic temperatures. Long sleeves and pants also come in handy during pesky mosquito season. For more helpful information on packing for your trip, download our convenient Travel Tools app for your mobile device. Go to www. frommers.com/go/mobile and click on the Travel Tools icon.

Passports All persons, including U.S. citizens, traveling by air between the United States and Canada, Mexico, Central and South America, the Caribbean, and Bermuda are required to present a valid passport. **Note:** U.S. and Canadian citizens entering the U.S. at land and sea ports of entry from within the Western Hemisphere must now also present a passport or other documents compliant with the Western Hemisphere Travel Initiative (WHTI; see www.getyouhome.gov for details). Children 15 and under may continue entering with only a U.S. birth certificate, or other proof of U.S. citizenship. If you do not have a passport, contact the appropriate agency in your country of citizenship:

Australia Australian Passport Information Service (visit www.passports.gov.au; © **131-232**).

Canada Passport Office, Department of Foreign Affairs and International Trade, Ottawa, ON K1A 0G3 (www.ppt.gc.ca; © **800/567-6868**).

Ireland Passport Office, Setanta Centre, Molesworth Street, Dublin 2 (www.foreign affairs.gov.ie; © **01/671-1633**).

New Zealand Passports Office, Department of Internal Affairs, 47 Boulcott St., Wellington, 6011 (www.passports.govt.nz; © **0800/225-050** in New Zealand or 04/474-8100).

United Kingdom   Visit your nearest passport office, major post office, or travel agency, or contact the Identity and Passport Service (IPS), 89 Eccleston Sq., London, SW1V 1PN (www.ips.gov.uk; © **0300/222-0000**).

United States   To find your regional passport office, check the U.S. State Department website (http://travel.state.gov/passport) or call the **National Passport Information Center** (© **877/487-2778**) for automated information.

Police   To reach the police, dial © **911** from any phone. No coins are needed.

Safety   While crime should not be a matter of extreme concern for travelers to Florida, it pays to use common sense when traveling throughout the state. On the beach, keep close watch on your personal items; when in South Beach, Key West, Fort Lauderdale, and pretty much any other Sunshine State hot spot, watch your drinks and never leave them unattended. And while I generally encourage exploration, there are neighborhoods of Miami you'll want to avoid, such as Liberty City and Overtown, both of which are plagued by high rates of violent crime, as well as desolate parts of downtown. My biggest safety tip, however: sunscreen. Use it generously. You'll still get a tan. Trust me.

Senior Travel   With one of the largest retired populations of any state, Florida offers a wide array of activities and benefits for seniors. Don't be shy about asking for discounts, but always carry some kind of identification, such as a driver's license, that shows your date of birth. Mention the fact that you're a senior when you make your travel reservations. In most cities, people 60 and older qualify for reduced admission to theaters, museums, and other attractions, as well as discounted fares on public transportation.

Members of **AARP**, 601 E St. NW, Washington, DC 20049 (www.aarp.org; © **888/687-2277**), get discounts on hotels, airfares, and car rentals. Anyone 50 or older can join.

The U.S. National Park Service offers an **America the Beautiful—National Park and Federal Recreational Lands Pass—Senior Pass** (formerly the **Golden Age Passport**), which gives seniors 62 years or older lifetime entrance to all properties administered by the National Park Service—national parks, monuments, historic sites, recreation areas, and national wildlife refuges—for a one-time processing fee of $10. The pass must be purchased in person at any NPS facility that charges an entrance fee. Besides free entry, the America the Beautiful Senior Pass also offers a 50% discount on some federal-use fees charged for camping, swimming, parking, boat launching, and tours. For more information, go to www.nps.gov/fees_passes.htm or call © **888/467-2757.**

Many agencies and organizations target the 50-plus market. **Road Scholar** (www.road scholar.org; © **800/454-5768**) arranges worldwide study programs for those age 55 and older. **ElderTreks** (www.eldertreks.com; © **800/741-7956** or 416/558-5000 outside North America) offers small-group tours to off-the-beaten-path or adventure-travel locations, for travelers 50 and older.

Smoking   In November 2002, 71% of Florida's citizens voted for a constitutional amendment to prohibit smoking in all enclosed indoor workplaces. The smoke-free law became effective July 1, 2003. All establishments making more profit from food than from beverages are also smoke-free, though some renegade bars and restaurants defy the law despite the hefty fees and allow smoking indoors.

Taxes   The Florida state sales tax is 6%. Many municipalities add 1% or more to that, and most levy a special tax on hotel and restaurant bills. In general, expect at least 9% to be added to your final hotel bill. The United States has no value-added tax (VAT) or other indirect tax at the national level. Every state, county, and city may levy its own local tax on all purchases, including hotel and restaurant checks and airline tickets. These taxes will not appear on price tags.

Telephones Many convenience stores sell **prepaid calling cards** in denominations up to $50, as well as inexpensive cellphones for which you pay as you go. Many public pay phones at airports now accept American Express, MasterCard, and Visa. **Local calls** made from most pay phones (if you can find one) cost either 25¢ or 35¢. Most long-distance and international calls can be dialed directly from any phone. **To make calls within the United States and to Canada,** dial 1 followed by the area code and the seven-digit number. **For other international calls,** dial 011 followed by the country code, the city code, and the number you are calling.

Calls to area codes **800, 888, 877,** and **866** are toll-free. However, calls to area codes **700** and **900** can be expensive—charges of 95¢ to $3 or more per minute. Some numbers have minimum charges that can run $15 or more.

For **reversed-charge or collect calls,** and for person-to-person calls, dial the number 0 and then the area code and number; an operator will come on the line, and you should specify whether you are calling collect, person-to-person, or both. If your operator-assisted call is international, ask for the overseas operator.

For **directory assistance** ("Information"), dial $\textit{C}$ **411** for local numbers and national numbers in the U.S. and Canada. For dedicated long-distance information, dial 1, then the appropriate area code plus 555-1212.

Time The area covered in this book—in fact, the entirety of the Florida peninsula—observes **Eastern Standard Time.** (Most of the Panhandle, west of the Apalachicola River, is on **Central Standard Time,** 1 hour behind the rest of the state.)

Daylight saving time is in effect from 1am on the second Sunday in March to 1am on the first Sunday in November, except in Arizona, Hawaii, the U.S. Virgin Islands, and Puerto Rico. Daylight saving time moves the clock 1 hour ahead of standard time.

The continental United States is divided into **four time zones:** Eastern Standard Time (EST), Central Standard Time (CST), Mountain Standard Time (MST), and Pacific Standard Time (PST). Alaska and Hawaii have their own zones. For example, when it's 9am in Los Angeles (PST), it's 7am in Honolulu (HST), 10am in Denver (MST), 11am in Chicago (CST), noon in New York City (EST), 5pm in London (GMT), and 2am the next day in Sydney.

For help with time translations and more, download our convenient Travel Tools app for your mobile device. Go to **www.frommers.com/go/mobile** and click on the Travel Tools icon.

Tipping In hotels, tip **bellhops** at least $1 per bag ($2–$3 if you have a lot of luggage), and tip the **chamber staff** $1 to $2 per day (more if you've left a big mess for him or her to clean up). Tip the **doorman** or **concierge** only if he or she has provided you with some specific service (for example, calling a cab for you or obtaining difficult-to-get theater tickets). Tip the **valet-parking attendant** $1 every time you get your car.

In restaurants, bars, and nightclubs, tip **service staff** and **bartenders** 15% to 20% of the check, tip **checkroom attendants** $1 per garment, and tip **valet-parking attendants** $2 per vehicle.

Keep an eye on your bill in tourist hot spots such as South Beach, where as much as a 20% auto gratuity could be already added to the total check.

As for other service personnel, tip **cab drivers** 15% of the fare; tip **skycaps** at airports at least $1 per bag ($2–$3 if you have a lot of luggage); and tip **hairdressers** and **barbers** 15% to 20%.

For help with tip calculations, currency conversions, and more, download our convenient Travel Tools app for your mobile device. Go to **www.frommers.com/go/mobile** and click on the Travel Tools icon.

Toilets   You won't find public toilets or "restrooms" on the streets in most U.S. cities, but they can be found in hotel lobbies, bars, restaurants, museums, department stores, railway and bus stations, and service stations. Large hotels and fast-food restaurants are often the best bet for clean facilities. Restaurants and bars in resorts or heavily visited areas may reserve their restrooms for patrons.

Visas   The U.S. State Department has a **Visa Waiver Program (VWP)** allowing citizens of the following countries to enter the United States without a visa for stays of up to 90 days: Andorra, Australia, Austria, Belgium, Brunei, Czech Republic, Denmark, Estonia, Finland, France, Germany, Greece, Hungary, Iceland, Ireland, Italy, Japan, Latvia, Liechtenstein, Lithuania, Luxembourg, Malta, Monaco, the Netherlands, New Zealand, Norway, Portugal, San Marino, Singapore, Slovakia, Slovenia, South Korea, Spain, Sweden, Switzerland, and the United Kingdom. (**Note:** This list was accurate at press time; for the most up-to-date list of countries in the VWP, consult http://travel.state.gov/visa.) Even though a visa isn't necessary, in an effort to help U.S. officials check travelers against terror watch lists before they arrive at U.S. borders, visitors from VWP countries must register online through the Electronic System for Travel Authorization (ESTA) before boarding a plane or a boat to the U.S. Travelers must complete an electronic application providing basic personal and travel-eligibility information. The Department of Homeland Security recommends filling out the form at least 3 days before traveling. Authorizations will be valid for up to 2 years or until the traveler's passport expires, whichever comes first. Currently, there is a US$14 fee for the online application. Existing ESTA registrations remain valid through their expiration dates. **Note:** Any passport issued on or after October 26, 2006, by a VWP country must be an **e-Passport** for VWP travelers to be eligible to enter the U.S. without a visa. Citizens of these nations also need to present a round-trip air or cruise ticket upon arrival. E-Passports contain computer chips capable of storing biometric information, such as the required digital photograph of the holder. If your passport doesn't have this feature, you can still travel without a visa if the valid passport was issued before October 26, 2005, and includes a machine-readable zone; or if the valid passport was issued between October 26, 2005, and October 25, 2006, and includes a digital photograph. For more information, go to **http://travel.state.gov/visa**. Canadian citizens may enter the United States without visas, but will need to show passports and proof of residence.

Citizens of all other countries must have (1) a valid passport that expires at least 6 months later than the scheduled end of their visit to the U.S., and (2) a tourist visa. For information about U.S. visas go to **http://travel.state.gov** and click on "Visas." Or go to one of the following websites:

Australian citizens can obtain up-to-date visa information from the **U.S. Embassy Canberra,** Moonah Place, Yarralumla, ACT 2600 (☎ **02/6214-5600**), or by checking the U.S. Diplomatic Mission's website at **http://canberra.usembassy.gov/visas.html**.

British subjects can obtain up-to-date visa information by calling the **U.S. Embassy Visa Information Line** (☎ **09042-450-100** from within the U.K. at £1.20 per minute; or ☎ **866/382-3589** from within the U.S. at a flat rate of $16; payable by credit card only) or by visiting the "Visas to the U.S." section of the American Embassy London's website at **http://london.usembassy.gov/visas.html**.

Irish citizens can obtain up-to-date visa information through the **U.S. Embassy Dublin,** 42 Elgin Rd., Ballsbridge, Dublin 4 (☎ **1580-47-VISA** [8472] from within the Republic of Ireland at €2.40 per minute; **http://dublin.usembassy.gov**).

Citizens of **New Zealand** can obtain up-to-date visa information by contacting the **U.S. Embassy New Zealand,** 29 Fitzherbert Terrace, Thorndon, Wellington (**http://newzealand.usembassy.gov;** ☎ **644/462-6000**).

Visitor Information   For the most comprehensive visitor information in the state, check out Visit Florida (www.visitflorida.com), a comprehensive site featuring deals, maps, and all sorts of excellent information on the state's beaten- and off-the-beaten-path hot spots. You can also find a list of Frommer's travel apps at www.frommers.com/go/mobile.

Index

Restaurants